CLEP®
The College-Level Examination Program®
Fourth Edition

CLEP®

The College-Level Examination Program®

Fourth Edition

PUBLISHING

New York

© 2011 by Kaplan, Inc.

Published by Kaplan Publishing, a division of Kaplan, Inc.
395 Hudson Street
New York, NY 10014

Notre Dame Cathedral, Steve Vidler. Digital image courtesy of SuperStock–RGB Ventures.

The Birth of Venus, Sandro Botticelli; Galleria degli Uffizi, Florence, Italy. Digital image courtesy of SuperStock–RGB Ventures.

The Holy Family with Saints Elizabeth and John the Baptist, Peter Paul Rubens; Wallace Collection, London. Digital image courtesy of SuperStock–RGB Ventures.

David, Michelangelo Buonarroti; Galleria Dell Academia, Florence, Italy. Digital image courtesy of SuperStock–RGB Ventures.

Guernica, Pablo Picasso; copyright 2007 Estate of Pablo Picasso/Artists Rights Society (ARS), New York. Digital image courtesy of SuperStock–RGB Ventures.

Casa Mila, copyright 2007 Howard Davis/Artifice Images. Digital image courtesy of Artifice, Inc.

Starry Night, Vincent van Gogh; The Museum of Modern Art, New York. Digital image courtesy of SuperStock–RGB Ventures.

Bathers at Asniers, Georges Pierre Seurat; The National Gallery, London. Digital image courtesy of SuperStock–RGB Ventures.

Eiffel Tower, Dean Fox. Digital image courtesy of SuperStock–RGB Ventures.

Christina's World, Andrew Wyeth digital image, copyright 2007, The Museum of Modern Art, 1948, tempera on panel copyright licensed by SCALA/Art Resource, New York.

Girl with a Pearl Earring, Jan Vermeer; Mauritshuis, The Hague, the Netherlands. Digital image courtesy of SuperStock–RGB Ventures.

Self-Portait with Grey Felt Hat, Vincent van Gogh; Van Gogh Museum, Amsterdam, the Netherlands. Digital image courtesy of SuperStock–RGB Ventures.

Nighthawks, Edward Hopper; copyright 2007 Art Institute of Chicago. Digital image courtesy of SuperStock–RGB Ventures.

Lavendar Mist, Jackson Pollock; copyright 2007 The Pollock-Krasner Foundation/Artists Rights Society (ARS), New York. Digital image courtesy of the National Gallery of Art; Washington, DC.

Printed in the United States of America

March 2011
10 9 8 7 6 5 4 3 2 1

ISBN-13: 978-1-41955-025-6

Kaplan Publishing books are available at special quantity discounts to use for sales promotions, employee premiums, or educational purposes. For more information or to purchase books, please call the Simon & Schuster special sales department at 866-506-1949.

Table of Contents

Contributors xi

How to Use This Book xiii

Section One: Introduction to the CLEP
Chapter One: Introduction. 3

    Which CLEP Exam Should I Take? 3

    Registering for the Exams 4

    Your CLEP Score 4

    CLEP and the Military 6

    How This Book Can Help You 7

Chapter Two: The CLEP Computer Interface 9

    Call It the CCLEP 9

    Should You Take the Computer-Based Test? 9

    The Basics of the Computer CLEP Exam Format 10

    Final Thoughts 16

Chapter Three: Specific CLEP Exam Strategies 17

    Specific Strategies for Specific Tests. 17

    General Test-Taking Strategies. 18

    CLEP College Composition Strategies 19

    CLEP College Mathematics Strategies 26

    CLEP Humanities Strategies 31

    CLEP Social Sciences and History Strategies 35

    CLEP Natural Sciences Strategies 39

    Final Thoughts 42

Section Two: The CLEP College Composition Exam

Chapter Four: Practice Test 1: Diagnostic (College Composition Modular)................. 45

Practice Test 1: Diagnostic Answers and Explanations 73

Chapter Five: CLEP College Composition Review 83

The Big Picture: CLEP College Composition 83

The Big Picture: CLEP College Composition Modular............................. 84

Nuts and Bolts... 84

Conventions of Standard Written English...................................... 85

Revisions Skills and Rhetorical Analysis 95

Ability to Use Source Materials.. 100

The Essays 102

Final Thoughts 106

Chapter Six: Practice Test 2 (College Composition Modular)......................... 107

Practice Test 2 Answers and Explanations.................................... 135

Chapter Seven: Practice Test 3 (College Composition) 145

Practice Test 3 Answers and Explanations.................................... 169

Section Three: The CLEP College Mathematics Exam

Chapter Eight: Practice Test 1: Diagnostic 183

Practice Test 1: Diagnostic Answers and Explanations 195

Chapter Nine: CLEP College Mathematics Review 201

The Big Picture: CLEP College Mathematics 201

Nuts and Bolts.. 202

CLEP College Mathematics Strategy Checklist.................................. 203

Sets... 204

Logic.. 206

Real Number System 208

Functions and Graphs... 210

Probability and Statistics 213

Additional Topics from Algebra and Geometry 216

College Mathematics Resources.. 221

Final Thoughts 221

Chapter Ten: Practice Test 2 223

    Practice Test 2 Answers and Explanations 233

Chapter Eleven: Practice Test 3 241

    Practice Test 3 Answers and Explanations 251

Section Four: The CLEP Humanities Exam

Chapter Twelve: Practice Test 1: Diagnostic 259

    Practice Test 1: Diagnostic Answers and Explanations 281

Chapter Thirteen: CLEP Humanities Review 293

    The Big Picture: CLEP Humanities 293

    Nuts and Bolts 293

    How to Score at Scoring 294

    The Arts 295

    Literature 304

    Final Thoughts 311

Chapter Fourteen: Practice Test 2 313

    Practice Test 2 Answers and Explanations 335

Chapter Fifteen: Practice Test 3 345

    Practice Test 3 Answers and Explanations 365

Section Five: The CLEP Social Sciences and History Exam

Chapter Sixteen: Practice Test 1: Diagnostic 377

    Practice Test 1: Diagnostic Answers and Explanations 399

Chapter Seventeen: CLEP Social Sciences and History Review 409

    The Big Picture: CLEP Social Sciences and History 409

    Nuts and Bolts 409

    History 410

    The Social Sciences 414

    Final Thoughts 420

Chapter Eighteen: Practice Test 2 421

    Practice Test 2 Answers and Explanations 443

Chapter Nineteen: Practice Test 3 453

    Practice Test 3 Answers and Explanations 477

Section Six: The CLEP Natural Sciences Exam

Chapter Twenty: Practice Test 1: Diagnostic 489

    Practice Test 1: Diagnostic Answers and Explanations 511

Chapter Twenty-One: CLEP Natural Sciences Review 521

    The Big Picture: CLEP Natural Sciences 521

    Nuts and Bolts 522

    Biological Sciences 522

    Physical Sciences 536

    Natural Sciences Resources 550

    Final Thoughts 551

Chapter Twenty-Two: Practice Test 2 553

    Practice Test 2 Answers and Explanations 577

Chapter Twenty-Three: Practice Test 3 587

    Practice Test 3 Answers and Explanations 609

Section Seven: Computing Your Practice Test Score

Chapter Twenty-Four: Scoring Your Test 621

Section Eight: CLEP Resources

    Word Roots 625

    Vocabulary Word List 633

    Math in a Nutshell 699

    Math Glossary 717

KAPLAN PUBLISHING

FOR ANY TEST CHANGES OR LATE-BREAKING DEVELOPMENTS

kaptest.com/publishing

The material in this book is up-to-date at the time of publication. However, the College Board may have instituted changes in the tests after this book was published. Be sure to carefully read the materials you receive when you register for your test. If there are any important late-breaking developments—or any changes or corrections to the Kaplan test preparation materials in this book—we will post that information online at **kaptest.com/publishing**.

FEEDBACK AND COMMENTS

kaplansurveys.com/books

We'd love to hear your comments and suggestions about this book. We invite you to fill out our online survey form at **kaplansurveys.com/books**. Your feedback is extremely helpful as we continue to develop high-quality resources to meet your needs.

Contributors

Bay Anapol

Ron Davis

Jeremiah A. Gilbert

Elizabeth Haserick Jackson

Drew Johnson

Mark Metz

Stephanie Reents

Amy Shoultz

Linda Brooke Stabler

How to Use This Book

The following chapters contain strategies, review information, and practice tests covering the topics on the CLEP exams in College Composition, College Mathematics, Humanities, Social Sciences and History, and Natural Sciences.

Step 1

First, read Section One: Introduction to the CLEP, for basic information. Chapter One gives a general introduction to the exams, while Chapters Two and Three offer vital strategies for the computer interface and each of the five subject tests.

Step 2

Once you've gotten familiar with the tests and strategies, turn to the section that addresses the test you plan to take. To ensure that you get the most out of your review time, take a moment for the appropriate full-length diagnostic test. After you take it, you can use the results to give yourself a broad idea of what topics you are strong in and what topics you need to review more.

Step 3

You can use your diagnostic test results to tailor your approach to the following review chapter. Hopefully you'll have time to read the entire chapter, but if pressed, you can start with the subjects you know you need to work on.

Step 4

You can then take the two practice tests, giving yourself practice at taking a test similar to the actual CLEP exam. By the time the real test comes around, you will be highly familiar with this CLEP test and its format. If you're short on time, take the diagnostic test and review the subjects that need the most work. When taking practice tests, time yourself and take the entire test without interruption—you can always call your friend back after you finish.

Step 5

Be sure to read the answer explanations for all questions, even those you answered correctly. Even if you got the problem right, reading another person's answer can give you insights that will prove helpful on the real exam.

Step 6

Finally, to see how your practice test score stacks up, turn to Section Seven: Computing Your Score. You'll be able to see if you're ready to take the actual CLEP exam.

Be sure to take some time to relax before test day, and best of luck!

Introduction to the CLEP

Chapter One: **Introduction**

- **Which CLEP Exam Should I Take?**
- **Registering for the Exams**
- **Your CLEP Score**
- **CLEP and the Military**
- **How This Book Can Help You**

Many students go to college to learn, while others seem to go simply to party. A select few valiantly attempt to do as much of both as humanly possible. Yet regardless of your intentions, college is expensive, and some parts aren't worth your time or money. For instance, taking introductory classes with two hundred other students isn't very educational or interesting, especially if you're already familiar with the material.

This is where the CLEP® comes in. Taking an exam through the College Level Examination Program (CLEP) can help you leapfrog over some basic college coursework—provided, of course, that you score well enough. Overall, it's a good exchange: roughly two hours of testing can get you credit that allows you to bypass entire semesters of college courses.

The decision to take a CLEP test and get college credit doesn't rest entirely in your hands, however. Every university in the United States has its own ideas about whether or not to accept CLEP scores for credit. Some schools don't accept them at all. Others schools give you college credit, but only if you exceed a certain score on the scale of 20–80. Every school has its own take on the test, so make sure you do some homework on the schools you are thinking about applying to before forking over the $77 CLEP fee.

WHICH CLEP EXAM SHOULD I TAKE?

There are over thirty different CLEP exams. You can find a complete list of the test titles, as well as other basic information, at collegeboard.com/student/testing/clep/about.html. This is the official CLEP website, and it contains all of the general facts about the CLEP program.

Some exams are part of the core subjects required by most schools.

English Composition

College Mathematics

Humanities

Social Sciences and History

Natural Sciences

If you're thinking about taking any of these exams, this book can help. If you have your heart set on acing the German Level 2 CLEP exam, then all we can say is, *"Viel glück!"*

As for which CLEP test (or tests) you should take, try to balance the advantage gained by earning a good score with the extra studying you will have to do for each exam. Perhaps you think you won't need any additional studying, since you're already an expert in a particular subject. That may be true (and you can take one of the practice tests in this book to find out if you're right or wrong). Most students however, expert or not, will need to put in some preparation for any new exam.

REGISTERING FOR THE EXAMS

You can register for any of the CLEP exams by contacting a CLEP test center. To find a center in your area, visit collegeboard.com/student/testing/clep/reg.html. After you learn about the center's procedures and schedule your test, you'll fill out a registration form that you can download from the CLEP website. Mail it along with your payment to the test center. The fee for each test is $77, and the average test center registration fee is around $15—be sure to ask your center of choice about its policy. There may be an additional $10 fee for tests with optional essays. If you want to take the CLEP exam the old-fashioned way, on paper instead of on the computer, be prepared to pay $120. Members of the U.S. Armed Forces should refer to the section in this chapter called "CLEP and the Military" for registration information.

YOUR CLEP SCORE

Scores on the CLEP exams range from 20 to 80. The number of questions you get correct is called your *raw score*. Each *correct* answer receives one point, while each *wrong* or *skipped* answer does not receive any points. There are no points subtracted for incorrect answers, so it is in your best interest to answer all questions on the exam. The raw score is not reported; it is adjusted according to a formula specified by the College Board to compensate for differences in question difficulty on various forms of the test. The final score that is reported, called the scaled score, is computed based on this formula.

While most of the CLEP exams are scored by computer, the College Composition essay is graded by two college English professors who are specially trained in the scoring guidelines set forth by the College Board.

Receiving Your Score

With the exception of the College Composition/College Composition Modular exams, you will receive your score on the computer screen right after you have completed the test. Since the CLEP exam is completed through computer-based testing (CBT), it is possible to designate through test software the schools, certifying agency, or employer that you would like to receive your CLEP test score right away. You cannot recall your score once you have viewed it, however. Only after you designate institutions to receive your score can you view your scores.

If you have any questions about the test or your score report that cannot be answered at the testing center, write to

CLEP

P.O. Box 6600

Princeton, NJ 08541-6600

clep@info.collegeboard.org

Canceling Your Score

You can only cancel your score before you view it. Once you have viewed your CLEP test score, the score has been recorded, and you cannot recall it. If you feel that you have done very poorly on the exam and you wish to cancel your score, do so, but realize that no record will be kept of how you did on the test. If you cancel your score, the computer will prompt you to confirm that you really want to cancel your score before the score is nullified.

Obtaining Additional Score Reports

To send a CLEP score report/transcript to additional schools or institutions after you have viewed your score, fill out a transcript request form on the College Board's website at collegeboard. com/student/testing/clep/scores.html or call (800) 257-9558 to order one. Your CLEP transcript will include scores on any CLEP exam that you have taken in the last 20 years. Each transcript request costs $20.

A Passing Score

For the CLEP exams, a passing score is a score that you can either get college credit for or use to skip a course. The following table shows the minimum scores recommended by the American Council on Education (ACE) to receive college credit for each exam. The minimum exam scores that are recommended are equivalent to an average class grade of a C. Each school can have its own credit-granting policies, so check with the school about what scores are acceptable to it before taking the exam.

Minimum Credit-Granting Scores
The American Council on Education (ACE)

Subject	Minimum Recommended Score	Semester Hours
College Mathematics	50	6
College Compostion	50	6
College Composition Modular	50	3/6*
Humanities	50	6
Natural Sciences	50	6
Social Sciences and History	50	6

*If the school does not require an essay for College Composition Modular, the suggestion is three semester hours. If the school does require an essay, the suggestion is six semester hours.

Tests in This Book

While your estimated score on any of the sample full-length tests in this book cannot determine the exact score you will receive on the actual CLEP test, they can help you determine what areas to work on before taking the test, as well as whether or not you are ready to take the test in general.

The College Board has not released the exact scoring guidelines for each test, but you can estimate whether or not you have achieved a passing grade on the sample tests in this book. In general, if you score over 70 percent (a grade of C) on a given test, you probably are well prepared for that CLEP exam. See chapter 24: Scoring Your Test for more information.

CLEP AND THE MILITARY

The CLEP exams offer an especially good opportunity for American servicemen and women. Most members of the U.S. Armed Services (and some civilian employees) can take the CLEP exams for free. Go to collegeboard.com/students/testing/clep/military.html to find a list of eligible personnel. In addition, CLEP exams are offered at College Test Centers on many military bases, on college campuses, and at DANTES Education centers. DANTES stands for Defense Activity for Non-Traditional Education Support, and this organization offers a variety of opportunities, including distance learning and tuition assistance. In addition to the CLEP, it administers a number of other standardized tests. See dantes.doded.mil for information. The difference between taking a CLEP exam on a military base or college campus and at a DANTES Education center is that DANTES only offers the paper-and-pencil tests, while most bases and campuses only offer the computer-based test. To register for a CLEP exam in either location or for information, visit DANTES online at www.dantes.doded.mil.

HOW THIS BOOK CAN HELP YOU

If you are taking any of the five CLEP exams discussed in this chapter, Kaplan's *CLEP: The College-Level Examination Program* can help you focus your studying and maximize your results. This book covers the following key points.

1. **Test strategies geared specifically to the computer-based CLEP exam in general and additional strategies for each subject test.** Many books give the same talk about strategies like Pacing and the Process of Elimination that have been used for every standardized test given in the past twenty years. By now, most of this stuff is common knowledge (although we'll review it again for you, just in case you haven't had enough of it). Since most CLEP exams are given only on the computer, knowledge of specific techniques to navigate this computer interface is something every student should have. These strategies are covered in the next chapter, and they are very useful regardless of what subject test you are taking. Before you read anything else in this book, thoroughly review the contents of the next chapter.

   In addition to the strategies designed to help you attack the computer-based CLEP exams, we have also developed techniques geared specifically for each of the five tests covered in this book. These subject-specific strategies—combined with the computer-specific CLEP strategies—are powerful tools to have at your disposal.

2. **A well-crafted review of all the relevant subjects.** The best test-taking strategies alone won't help you take the CLEP College Mathematics test if you don't know a square from a triangle. Every CLEP exam covers a broad range of topics, and a basic familiarity with these topics is necessary if you want to score well. Obviously, you wouldn't even be trying to take a CLEP test in a particular subject if you didn't feel pretty confident about your mastery of that subject. That's why we won't waste your time with an exhaustive subject review. Instead, we've tailored our review section to focus on how the CLEP tests present information and what you need to know in order to answer the questions correctly.

3. **Three full-length practice tests for each subject.** There's no substitute for experience when it comes to standardized testing. Taking a practice CLEP exam gives you an idea of what it's like to answer questions on a particular topic for 90 minutes. That's not a fun experience, granted, but it is helpful. Practice exams give you the opportunity to find out what areas are your strongest and what topics you should spend some additional time studying. And the best part is . . . it doesn't count! Mistakes you make on our practice exams are mistakes you won't make on the real test.

   At the end of each practice test you will find Quick Reference Tables. The first table shows the topics and/or subtopics of each test and which of the test questions apply to that subject. The second table shows the topics and/or subtopics and how many questions on the test apply to each. The third column is left blank so you can fill in how many of the questions you got correct. Together, these two tables provide you with a quick way to see which topics you need to review more and which topics you might have mastered.

   In the section devoted to each CLEP exam covered in this book, we've placed one diagnostic test at the very beginning of the section. Think of this exam as a "here's what you would score if you took that CLEP exam without much studying" test. You can use the results of this exam (using the Quick Reference tables) to tailor your approach to the review section,

KAPLAN

which follows the diagnostic. Note the topics or categories where you missed the most questions and then concentrate on the section of the review that covers the categories. You may also want to create an additional study plan to shore up these weaker areas. For this, use the relevant sections of the review as your starting point.

Once you've had a chance to work on your weak areas, you have two more full-length tests to take as practice. Also, each test has detailed explanations for each question, so you can learn from all your mistakes. You may even learn from some problems you got right in the first place, so don't neglect to read through the explanations section thoroughly.

Those three points describe the general outline of this book: Strategies, Review, and Practice Exams. Check out the next chapter to learn some specific skills you can use on the five CLEP subject tests covered in this book.

Chapter Two: **The CLEP Computer Interface**

- Call It the CCLEP
- Should You Take the Computer-Based Test?
- The Basics of the Computer CLEP Exam Format
- Final Thoughts

CALL IT THE CCLEP

That first *C* stands for "Computer-based," since most of you reading this book will take your CLEP exam or exams on a computer. There are pencil-and-paper versions of the five CLEP tests covered in this book, but they cost almost twice as much as the computer-based version. For reasons of cost and availability, many of you won't be able to choose between a computer version and a pencil-and-paper version. If you do have a choice, though, consider the pros and cons of the computer test before making your decision.

SHOULD YOU TAKE THE COMPUTER-BASED TEST?

Pro: No Waiting for Results

Once you finish answering all the questions on a computer-based CLEP exam, you get to see your score. (The only time this isn't true is when you take a CLEP test that has an essay portion to it.) Waiting for results from a pencil-and-paper test can take anywhere from two to six weeks. With the computer version, you get your results back after two to six *seconds*. It's quite a difference, one that will save you weeks of anxiety about your scores.

Con: No Experience with the Format

You probably know or remember from your high school days so-called "good test takers," people with average grades who always seem to do very well on exams. What makes them "good" test takers? There are many factors, but confidence and a positive attitude are two attributes most good test takers have. This mindset allows them to avoid anxiety, take educated guesses, and not get bogged down on one or two questions. In general, a positive attitude leads to positive results.

Now here's the question to consider: How confident can you be taking a test in a format you've never experienced before? Most people haven't taken 90-minute multiple-choice tests on a computer, so the experience is something new. This acclimation process adds another layer of difficulty to the test. Not only do you have to take a CLEP exam, but you have to put time into learning the format needed to take a CLEP exam. For some people, this is a nuisance, and for others, it's a bigger problem. Either way, though, having to learn the computer format doesn't make your life any easier.

Pro: The Computer Commands Are Easy to Learn

Although you do have to take the time to learn the computer format, the instructions are fairly simple. There are several buttons on the screen that have self-explanatory labels: if you see a button called "time," you can make a fairly confident guess about what it's for. How to use buttons like "review" and "mark" may be less apparent initially, but they're still easy to learn about. You'll want to get familiar ahead of time with all of the buttons, because some of them can really help you in your test-taking strategy.

Con: The Best Strategies Are Not Always Obvious

When you get to the end of your exam, should you review from the back to the front? When you finish a section, should you immediately exit and go on to the next one? The computer format gives you a lot of options, but not all of them will help you. Going back through your exam question by question using the "previous" button may seem like a good idea, but it would be a very inefficient (not to mention potentially confusing) approach to reviewing your exam.

The best way to use the commands is not always clear, and without some preparation, you can waste precious time and brain power on the day of the exam. This chapter will help you learn how to use the test format to your advantage.

THE BASICS OF THE COMPUTER CLEP EXAM FORMAT

Now that we've convinced you that you need to prepare not only for the subject matter of the CLEP exam you're taking but also for taking it on the computer, where do you begin? This section will take you through everything you'll need to know to navigate the screens you'll actually see in front of you when you take the CLEP exam. After you get familiar with the commands and strategies, we'll tell you how to get some hands-on practice before you take the exam.

Basic Computer Skills for the CLEP Exams

While some computer experience is important if you're taking a CLEP exam, the test won't require any computer skills more advanced than you would use for browsing the Internet or using a word-processing program. You should be sure that you know how to do the following:

- Type on a computer keyboard.
- Identify a computer icon.
- Use a mouse to navigate a computer screen.
- Scroll through a document.

Basically, you need to be able to get around on a computer and be comfortable doing it. If any of the aforementioned concepts make you nervous, find some help learning the basics of computer usage. If they are familiar, you'll be fine using the exam software.

A Quick Review of the Question Screen

The question screen has three basic parts: the title bar at the top, the test question in the center, and the icons at the bottom of the screen. Before we look at each part in depth, take a moment to familiarize yourself with what the CLEP will look like.

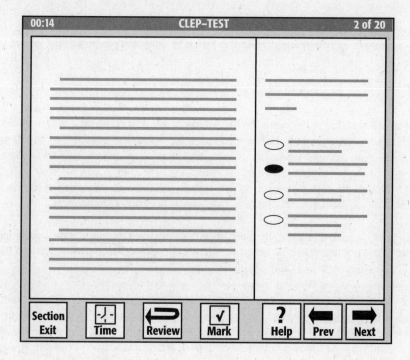

It looks pretty simple, doesn't it? Let's look more closely.

The Title Bar

Across the top of the question screen is the title bar. It's the simplest part of the question screen and is fairly self-explanatory.

1. On the left of the title bar is the time remaining for the section of the exam that you are taking. It is not the time remaining in the exam as a whole (unless you're taking the final section). Checking your time remaining is a good way of keeping track of your progress on the exam. However, if always having the time in front of you makes you nervous, you can hide it. We'll explain how when we go over the icons.

2. In the center of the title bar is the test or section title. It may be useful to be reminded of what section of the exam you are taking, and if the title at the top isn't for the test you planned on taking, you'll want to see a test administrator immediately.

3. On the right of the title bar is the number of the question you are on and the total number of questions in the section. This is helpful for keeping track of where you are. If you're on question 10 out of 20, you know you're halfway through. But remember that some types of questions will take longer than others, so don't use question number alone to gauge your progress.

The Test Questions

You'll always find the test questions in the center of the screen. They will appear one at a time, and you can answer each question (or skip it to return to later) and proceed to the next at your own pace.

One of the great things about taking your CLEP exam on the computer is that you don't need to spend your time making sure that the little oval on the paper is filled in thoroughly. You don't have to worry about filling in the wrong oval and throwing off your numbering system. And if you want to change your answer, you don't have to spend time erasing to get the lead off the paper.

On a computer-based CLEP exam, it's easy to answer a question. For a multiple-choice question, simply click on the answer that you think is correct, and the oval will darken. If you want to change your answer, click on a different oval. Your original selection will disappear.

Some exams will require that you enter a response in an answer box. In this case, you simply put your cursor in the box and type your answer. If you want to change your answer, you can delete your answer by using backspace and type a new one.

Recording your answer is easier on the CCLEP than when you're working with a paper exam, but sometimes getting through the question itself is harder. The test question section is sometimes too small to contain the entire question, especially when the question has a long passage associated with it. When this happens, a scroll bar will appear, and you will have to use it to navigate through the question. This may be frustrating. You won't have all of the information for the question in front of you at one time. It's a limitation of the computer format, and there's not much to do about it but be prepared for it.

The Icons

The icons are the tools that will enable you to take the test. Using them correctly and effectively can make or break your score, so take time to get to know them well.

The icons you see may vary depending on what test you're taking, though the basic ones will stay consistent. However, if you are taking a math exam, you may find a calculator icon available On other tests, an icon may appear gray. That means it's disabled and not needed (or allowed) on this exam.

Moving from the right to the left, here are the icons you'll encounter on the CLEP exam along with some strategies to use them most effectively.

1.   **Next**. To move through the test, you will use the "next" icon. When you answer a question, you will not proceed to the next question until you hit "next." You can also skip a question by hitting "next." This one is pretty obvious.

2.   **Previous**. The "prev" icon is also designed to help you move through the test, but in this case it takes you backward through the questions. You're most likely to use the "prev" icon if you suddenly change your mind about a question you just answered or for a multipart question where you might want to move back and forth between questions.

     It is not a good use of your time to scan through earlier parts of the exam using the "prev" button. The "review" button is a much better option, as we'll explain later on.

3.   **Help**. Help? Didn't you think that you couldn't get additional help on this exam?

     Clicking on the "help" icon opens the help window. There you will find directions for the section of the test that you are taking, which can be very useful if you don't remember some specifics when you get to a new question.

     The "help" icon can also give you other useful information, such as how to answer a question in general or a review of the tools available for the question. You'll find the available help categories as icons along the right side of the help screen. At the bottom you'll find the "return to where I was" icon, which will take you back to the question you were working on.

     You may never need to use the "help" icon, especially if you take time to prepare for the computer functions up front. The exam will be set up so that it isn't essential that you turn to the help window. However, know that it's there if you need it.

4.   **Mark**. Pay attention here: the "mark" icon can be one of the most important tools for taking the exam if you use it effectively. Paired with the "review" icon, it can give you a terrific strategy for dealing with questions whose answers you're not absolutely sure about.

     The "mark" icon allows you to mark a question so that you can return to it easily. It's kind of like adding something to your "favorites" list on your Web browser, except often the questions you will choose to mark won't be your favorites. They'll be the ones you aren't sure you answered correctly.

     To mark a question, just hit the "mark" icon while you're still on that question. A check mark will appear in the "mark" box. If you click on "mark" again, the check mark will be erased. "Mark" is meant to be used in conjunction with the following icon on the list.

5. **Review**. Clicking on the "review" icon opens the review window. In this window you will find a list of all of the questions in the current section of the exam. For each question, you can see its status:

    •   Answered

    •   Not answered

    •   Not seen

Any question you have marked will have a check mark next to it.

You can choose between two ways of sorting the list in the review window. You can sort it by question, which keeps it in the numerical order from the beginning of the section. You can also choose to sort it by status, which will group together all the questions that have been answered, not answered, or not seen. To sort the list, simply click on the "question" or "status" headings at the top of the questions list.

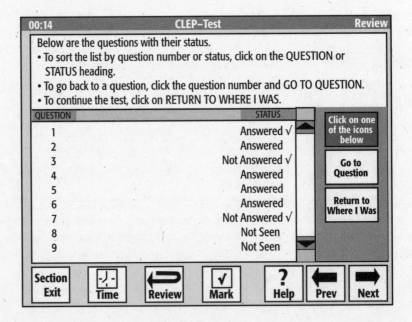

The review window also allows you to return to any question in the section or to go back to where you were in the section. Therefore, if you know that you want to return to question 15, you can sort by question number and simply click on number 15. Then click on the "Go to Question" icon on the right of the screen. You'll return directly to that question.

You may also want to go back to all of the questions that you didn't answer or, alternately, all of the questions that you marked. To do this, sort the questions by status. Now you can click on any question that says "Not Answered" or that has a check mark next to it.

Using the review window can give you a quick snapshot of where you are on the section. You can click on "review," glance at how many questions you've answered, not answered, and not seen, then click on the "Return to Where I Was" icon and go directly back to the question you were working on. It can also be used more comprehensively, however. Here's how.

Strategies for Using Mark and Review

You always want to make at least two passes through any section of the CLEP exam. Mark and Review will make your second pass much more efficient by giving you a simple way to find the questions you want to return to. On your first pass through the exam, answer the questions if you are sure about the answer, but if you don't know the answer to a question, don't waste time trying to decipher it. Move on and return to it later. But what about when you have an idea about a question but just aren't sure?

One strategy is to make your best guess about an answer but then mark the question to return to later. You will have to choose for yourself under what parameters you answer and mark versus leaving a question blank. Perhaps for a multiple-choice question you answer and then mark the question when you can eliminate one choice. Perhaps when you can eliminate two. Remember, there is no penalty for guessing on the CLEP exams. You're better off answering a question than leaving it blank. Before you leave a section, you'll want to have answered all of the questions.

When you make your second pass through an exam, begin at the review window. How much time you spend on the remaining questions will depend on your approach and how much time you have left. Ideally, when you are done with the section, you'll have reviewed all the questions you either didn't answer or you marked, and each question will have an answer.

Using mark and review will save you time on your exam. It will also save you the stress of trying to figure out which questions to go back to.

6. **Time**. Clicking on the "time" icon will hide or show the time remaining for the section you are working on. You can use this button to get rid of the potentially stressful countdown happening on the far left of the title bar. You cannot, unfortunately, use it to buy more time on your exam.

7. **Section Exit**. The "section exit" icon allows you to leave a section and move on to the next. You won't be able to return to a section once you exit it. We don't recommend that you use the "section exit" icon. Here's why.

    Each section of the exam is allotted a specific amount of time. Leaving a section early will not afford you any more time on subsequent sections of the exam. You will simply lose the time you didn't use. So leaving a section early may get you out of the exam earlier, but what are you in such a rush for anyway? Instead of clicking on "section exit," click on "review." Go through the questions again. Check your answers.

8. **Calculator**. On some exams, a "calculator" icon will appear. If it is shaded gray, it is not available for use, but if it is dark, you can use it on the exam questions. You'll find there's not much that's surprising about the calculator. It has the same basic functions as your typical handheld scientific calculator; you'll just be using it on the computer instead of in your palm.

There are just a few things to know about the calculator function. You can use either your mouse or the numbers of your keyboard to enter figures into the calculator. You can choose to display your calculations using either a floating decimal or by scientific notation by clicking your mouse on either "flo" or "sci," respectively. There is also one available memory location. You can access it by using the ">>M" or "M>>" buttons.

The coolest thing about the calculator is that for some questions, you can transfer your answer directly from the calculator to the answer box without having to retype it. There's no chance of entering misplaced decimals or inadvertent typos. To use this feature, hit "transfer display" on the bottom left of the calculator. You'll see your figure appear in the answer box of the question.

Don't Take Our Word for It

This is a lot of information to take in, we realize, and learning computer commands by reading about them is kind of like learning to play tennis by poring through a tennis manual. You need to try it out yourself on the court, in the sun, with a little yellow ball coming straight at you. Or, in this case, you'll want to do so with a mouse and a computer screen before your eyes.

Fortunately, you have the opportunity to do just that before taking the CLEP exam. The College Board offers a free demo to allow you to practice taking a CLEP exam on the computer. It won't help you with the material you'll be tested on, but it will help you get used to what the material will look like when you actually sit down for the exam.

So try it yourself. You'll need to go to the College Board's CLEP website and download the CLEP Sampler. You can do so at collegeboard.com/student/testing/clep/prep.html.

Once you have it, the sampler will take you step by step through all of the windows and all of the commands you'll see when taking the exam. We strongly recommend you take the time to run through the sampler a few times before you set foot in the testing center. Get familiar with seeing the questions on the computer. Picture yourself answering them like an expert.

FINAL THOUGHTS

Mastering a subject is hard work. Before you decided to take a CLEP exam, you probably put in a significant amount of time and effort learning the materials you'll be tested on. This was a good investment, and part of the return on it will be going on to more interesting and challenging subjects and not having to learn the material again. You can also save a lot of money by finishing college earlier. It would be a shame to blow that opportunity because you weren't prepared for the format of the exam.

Taking a computer-based CLEP exam can have many benefits over the pencil-and-paper version, but only if you are prepared for it. Get familiar with the screens. Learn the commands. Go through the demos. Then turn your attention to proving just how well you know your stuff. We're ready to share more strategies for helping you do just that.

Chapter Three: **Specific CLEP Exam Strategies**

- Specific Strategies for Specific Tests
- General Test-Taking Strategies
- CLEP College Composition Strategies
- CLEP College Mathematics Strategies
- CLEP Humanities Strategies
- CLEP Social Sciences and History Strategies
- CLEP Natural Sciences Strategies
- Final Thoughts

SPECIFIC STRATEGIES FOR SPECIFIC TESTS

Now that you have an idea of how to navigate the CLEP computer format, it's time to talk about formulating the right approach to each of the five CLEP tests covered in this book. Every standardized test requires a combination of skills (facts) and strategy in order to get a good score. Think about it: If you've read over a thousand books but are a lousy test taker, your CLEP Humanities exam score will suffer. On the other hand, if you have no problem working fast and guessing aggressively, that will help, but it won't help much if you think Beethoven is a large dog you saw in a movie once.

Before we talk about specific strategies, a quick review of general strategies is in order. Most of these ideas will not be new to you, although one or two might be. Either way, review them, because you need to do more than just be aware of these ideas. You need to understand and feel comfortable using them. Most students know what the process of elimination is, but sadly, too few actually use the process of elimination when taking a test. Don't let this happen to you.

GENERAL TEST-TAKING STRATEGIES

1. **Pacing**. Since many tests are timed, proper pacing allows you to attempt every question in the time allotted. Poor pacing causes students to spend too much time on some questions and then run out of time before getting a chance to answer every problem.

2. **Two-Pass System**. Using the two-pass system is one way to pace yourself on a test. The key idea is that you don't simply start with question 1 and trudge onward from there. Instead, you start at the beginning, but take a first pass through the test answering all the questions that are easy for you. If you encounter a tough problem, you spend only a small amount of time on it and then move on in search of easier questions. This way, you don't get bogged down on a tough problem when you could be earning points answering later problems that you do know. On your second pass, you go back through the section and attempt all the tougher problems that you passed over the first time. You should be able to spend a little more time on them, and this extra time might help you answer the problem. Even if you don't reach an answer, you might be able to employ techniques like process of elimination to cross out some answer choices and then take a guess.

3. **Process of Elimination**. On every multiple-choice test you ever take, the answer is given to you. The only difficulty resides in the fact that the correct answer is hidden among incorrect choices. Even so, the multiple-choice format means you don't have to pluck the answer out of the air. Instead, if you can eliminate answer choices you know are incorrect and only one choice remains, then that must be the correct answer.

4. **Patterns and Trends**. The key word here is the *standardized* in "standardized testing." Being standardized means that tests don't change greatly from year to year. Sure, each question won't be the same, and different topics will be covered from one administration to the next, but there will also be a lot of overlap from one year to the next. That's the nature of *standardized* testing: if the test changed wildly each time it came out, it would be useless as a tool for comparison. Because of this, certain patterns can be uncovered about any standardized test. Learning about these trends and patterns can help students taking the test for the first time.

5. **The Right Approach**. Having the right mindset plays a large part in how well people do on a test. Those who are nervous about the exam and hesitant to make guesses often fare much worse than students with an aggressive, confident attitude. Students who start with question 1 and go on from there don't score as well as students who pick and choose the easy questions first before tackling the harder ones. People who take a test cold have more problems than those who take the time to learn about the test beforehand. In the end, factors like these determine who is a good test taker and who struggles despite knowing the material.

Those are the basics. On to the next level.

CLEP COLLEGE COMPOSITION STRATEGIES

In July 2010, CLEP College Composition replaced English Composition with Essay, and CLEP
College Composition Modular replaced English Composition. It's important for you to learn about
the differences between these exams so you know what to expect and how to prepare.

College Composition versus College Composition Modular

Exam	Major topics (and their percentages) covered in multiple-choice questions	Number of multiple-choice questions	Time allotted for multiple-choice questions	Number of essay(s)	About the essay(s)	Time allotted for essay(s)
College Composition	Conventions of Standard Written English: 10% Revisions Skills: 40% Ability to Use Source Materials: 25% Rhetorical Analysis: 25%	50	50 mins	2	The first essay is based on something you've read, observed, or experienced. The second essay requires you to read, synthesize information, and write (including citations) an essay based on two excerpts provided.	70 mins TOTAL for both mandatory essays: Essay 1: 30 mins Essay 2: 40 mins
College Composition Modular	Conventions of Standard Written English: 10% Revisions Skills, Including Sentence-Level Skills:* 40% Ability to Use Source Materials: 25% Rhetorical Analysis: 25% * Includes a question type called "Improving Sentences."	90	90 mins	0–2	Schools can choose any of these three options: (1) the same two mandatory essays found on the CLEP College Composition exam; (2) a writing assessment that the school develops, administers, and scores; or (3) any other assessment that the college wants to associate with the College Composition Modular exam score.	The time allotted depends on what kind of essay assessment your school uses. If your school uses the two CLEP essays from College Composition, it will be 70 mins TOTAL: Essay 1: 30 mins Essay 2: 40 mins

In this section, we'll cover all the different multiple-choice question types and strategies that you
need to use for each one. For the essay, check out the College Composition review in chapter 5
of this book.

CLEP College Composition Modular features 90 questions to be completed in 90 minutes, and CLEP College Composition features 50 questions to be completed in 50 minutes. This makes it easy to figure out that you should spend about a minute on each question, regardless of which exam you take.

The rest of this strategy section covers the four question types you will encounter on the College Composition and the fifth question type you will encounter on the College Composition Modular exam.

Conventions of Standard Written English
(Appears on College Composition and College Composition Modular)

Let's begin by looking at questions like those you'll find on the Conventions of Standard Written English (CSWE) section of the CLEP College Composition and CLEP College Composition Modular exams.

16. When some Chinese <u>first came to America</u>, many did
                                    A

 dangerous <u>work of blasting</u> and <u>lay railroad ties</u> over the
                          B   C

 <u>treacherous terrain</u> of the high Sierra Mountains. <u>No error</u>
          D   E

Four sections of a sentence are underlined, and if there's a mistake under one of the underlined portions, you are to pick that answer choice. If there is no error under (A), (B), (C), or (D), then pick answer (E).

The College Composition Review in chapter 5 covers the common grammar errors that appear in the CSWE questions and elsewhere. This section is about using the best strategy for CSWE questions, so remember that context is key.

The regular (nonunderlined) portions of the sentence are just as important as the underlined ones. Since they can't be changed, they often have the clue to which underlined portion needs to be changed.

The sample question is a straightforward example of parallelism. With parallelism, each item in a series appears in the same grammatical form. Parallelism is a common grammatical error that appears on the CLEP College Composition (and Modular) exam. For the sample question, the underlined portion (C) has to agree with "blasting." "Blasting" is a gerund, a present tense verb form, so (C) has to be in the same form. Each underlined answer choice has to be grammatically accurate and agree with the rest of the sentence, so (C) has to be "laying" rather than "lay." Since the first two underlined items are correct and the third underlined item has to agree with (B), choice (C) is the correct answer for this question. The verb form in the regular portion of the sentence led you to the underlined portion that was the correct answer.

The regular sentence portions won't always provide the clue. Sometime you just have to listen to your inner ear and trust your grammar instincts. You know more grammar than you think, so if you feel that something is wrong but don't know the exact terminology to explain why it is wrong, trust your instincts. They will lead you in the right direction more often than not.

Revision Skills
(Appears on College Composition and College Composition Modular)

Few early drafts of writing are ready for publication. Revision Skills (RS) questions present you with a "draft" of an essay and then ask you approximately four to six questions about it. All sentences in the draft are numbered so that they can easily be referred to. Let's look at a small version of an RS essay and question.

(1) Ahmed and I attended camp together last summer. (2) We decided a play would be fun. (3) We didn't know what the play would be about, but we wanted it to be fun. (4) Everyone is always saying that Ahmed is creative. (5) He wrote the play for us.

40.   Which of the following is the best way to revise and combine sentences 4 and 5 (reproduced below)?
Everyone is always saying that Ahmed is creative. He wrote the play for us.

(A) Ahmed is creative, so he wrote the play for us.

(B) Ahmed is creative, and everyone is always saying that he is creative, so he wrote the play.

(C) Everyone is always talking about how creative Ahmed is, and he wrote the play.

(D) The play was written by Ahmed who is so creative that everyone always talks about him.

(E) Talking about the creativeness of Ahmed, he decided to write.

Use the following 5 techniques to help you handle RS questions:

1.   **Read the passage quickly for the general idea and nothing else.** Look, the passage has problems—that's the whole point. Spending time trying to understand what those problems are is a waste of your time. You don't get points for reading the passage; you get points for answering questions, so make that your goal. You need to know what each sentence says and have a general idea of what the passage is about, but any deeper understanding is pointless. Get to the questions as soon as you can. Then you can work on fixing some of the problems in the passage … if that's what the question asks you to do.

2.   **Problems are more structural/organizational than grammatical.** Proper grammar is not stressed as much in the RS section, although grammatical errors will appear occasionally. Instead, the focus here is on sentence structure and organization, with questions like "Where could sentence 7 best be placed?" or "Which of the following sentences would work best after sentence 5?" To answer the latter question, you have to read sentence 5 and get an idea of where the paragraph is heading in terms of content. What is being discussed in sentence 5? A good sentence 6 will continue that train of thought or move on to a related point.

3. **Other repeating questions deal with the problem of redundant, repeating sentences that repeat sentences redundantly and say same thing over and over again, repeatedly.** Do you get the feeling the above sentence could be restated with fewer words? You'll get that feeling again and again on this section of the CLEP College Composition and CLEP College Composition Modular exam. Two related sentences will need to be stitched together, or a long sentence like the one above will have to be left out. When you do this, keep in mind that "more words ≠ better grammar" and that keeping it simple and clear is often the hallmark of good writing. The initial sentence could read, "Other questions deal with redundant sentences," or "Other questions deal with sentences that repeat themselves." Both of these are clear, simple alternatives to the initial mess.

4. **Other question types may appear on the exam.** Suppose you have an RS question that looks like this:

> 54. Which is the best version of the underlined portion of sentence 1 (reproduced below)?
>
> Sometimes people like to go to the theater, and sometimes <u>they like to watch *Masterpiece Theater* on TV at home</u>.
>
> (A) No change
> (B) they watch TV at home
> (C) a house is a place to watch TV in
> (D) they thus like to watch plays at a house
> (E) watching TV at home can be a sometimes theatrical experience

This is exactly like an Improving Sentences question (found on College Composition Modular only), even down to the fact that choice (A) states that things are correct the way they are. You might want to study that section of the review even if you are not taking the Modular exam.

Remember the following 4 tips during study sessions and while taking the exam:

1. **Verbs are powerful.** Check subject/verb agreement. During practice, underline verbs; draw an arrow from verb to subject. Check verb tense: Do the tenses match? Or are the verbs in the correct sequence to indicate the times of the actions being described?

2. **Agreement is important.** Check mood: Is one verb in the subjunctive case—that is, expressing a wish, emotion, possibility, judgment, opinion, necessity, or action that has not yet occurred? If so, find the option that also includes the subjunctive case. Also, check noun/pronoun agreement: Circle the nouns. Underline the pronouns. Draw an arrow from a pronoun to the noun it replaces. Do they agree in number, gender, or case? If it is not clear to which noun the pronoun refers, you've probably found the problem to be solved. Choose the option that clarifies the relationship.

3. **Simplicity matters.** Check extraneous wording. If the same idea is expressed in fewer words, choose that option. Can two sentences be combined effectively? Choose the option that does that smoothly.

4. **Order is important.** Check chronology. Check logic. Does one idea lead logically to the next?

Improving Sentences
(Appears on College Composition Modular Only)

Now, let's move on to Improving Sentences questions, which appear on the CLEP College Composition Modular exam only.

These questions begin with a single sentence, and a portion of that sentence—sometimes only a single word, other times every word—is underlined. You are then given four different ways to rewrite the underlined portion of the sentence.

> 20. During the 1920s, legislators were <u>convinced that prohibition would make</u> people stop drinking and would cut down on crime.
>
>   (A) convinced that prohibition would make
>   (B) convincing that prohibition could make
>   (C) and it was convinced that prohibition could make
>   (D) convinced of prohibition's making
>   (E) as they convinced themselves that prohibition would make

The first choice, (A), always repeats the underlined portion exactly as it appears in the question. In this sense, choice (A) on Improving Sentences is like choice (E), "No Error," on a CSWE or an RS question that begins with "No change."

Improving Sentences questions are very similar to RS questions, and your approach will reflect this similarity. Pay attention to context—the nonunderlined portion of the sentence has an important role. If the subject is not underlined but the verb is, check for subject/verb agreement. If there are two items in a list in the regular portion of the sentence, take a very close look at the third parallel item that is underlined.

If you're not quite sure what the right answer is, a good fallback strategy is to remind yourself that

More words ≠ better grammar

Think about this: Grammar is neither horribly complex nor difficult to understand. There are a few rules that many people break, and these cloud communication. For this reason, the CLEP exam repeatedly tests your understanding of a few basic rules so you will recognize and avoid these problems in your own writing. Excess verbiage is one kind of problem. Test takers often get psyched out on Improving Sentences questions and pick choices with long strings of words like *will might could have been searching* when a simple *will search* is correct. If you're ever in doubt, avoid the longer convoluted choices and try to keep things simple.

Now, back to the prohibition question. Choices (C) and (E) contain excess verbiage—phrases that seem to go on forever. Neither one of them is correct, however, since all those extra words are unnecessary. Choices (C) and (E) are there to trap students who think more words equal better grammar. You, however, know better, so you should be leery of picking (C) and (E). They might be right, but probably not.

Look over the underlined portion and compare the text there with context, the regular portion. Use your mental voice and "speak" the sentence out loud in your head. Does it seem right? Is *convinced* (past tense) the right verb form, or is something more involved needed?

In fact, the simple past tense is all that's needed for the verb *convince,* and everything else is fine with the sentence as it stands. (A) is the answer. Don't be afraid to pick (A), since about 20 percent of the Improving Sentences questions will need no improvement.

Ability to Use Source Materials
(Appears on College Composition and College Composition Modular)
This section of the CLEP College Composition and College Composition Modular assesses your ability to use source materials as a writer and a reader. Can you determine what a dictionary entry means? Can you summarize information from another source, punctuate it, cite the source, know where to cite the source, and format a bibliography? Can you determine what information an endnote/footnote should include?

Smith, Benjamin, and Terrence Graft. "Public Polls as Political Weapons." *Journal of Media & Politics* 11.3 (1995): 497–511. Print.

> In the above citation, what does "11.3" stand for?
>
> (A) Year and month of publication
> (B) Chapter and page number
> (C) Edition and page number
> (D) Volume and issue
> (E) Section and subsection

If you don't know this one right off the bat, then you can figure it out by examining and comparing all of the parts of the citation and using the process of elimination. In this case, we know the citation is for a journal because, luckily, the word *journal* is part of the italicized title. But that won't always be the case, so it's important to recognize the formats of different types of citations. **Remember that the purpose of a citation is to help the reader locate the cited material.**

Now let's review the answer choices. Looking at choice (A), we can determine that "11" isn't specific enough to signify which year the journal was published—maybe it was 1911, maybe 1811—so (A) is not a strong choice. Plus, part of the citation is "(1995)," which is more likely to be a year than "11." Choice (B) makes sense until you notice the number range "497–511." When you see a number range in a citation, it's almost always a page range. Therefore "11.3" probably doesn't refer to chapter and page number, making choice (B) incorrect. Choice (C) also includes page number, so we can eliminate it for the same reason as choice (B). Choice (D) and choice (E) are both strong possibilities because they would help the reader to locate the cited material. But choice (E) is redundant because the page numbers have already been listed in the citation, so a section and subsection of the journal aren't necessary for the reader to find the cited material. The key to this question is in knowing that a journal is a type of periodical, meaning that it is published at regular intervals with the same title. The volume and issue number help the reader to know which specific issue contains the cited material. Therefore, choice (D) is the correct answer.

Here are 6 strategies for decoding a citation:

1. Italicized words = titles of books, periodicals, foreign words, part of speech (as in a dictionary entry).
2. Numbers (including roman numerals) = page numbers, years, volume numbers, issue numbers.
3. Names = authors, editors.
4. City names = location where the material was published.
5. Items in quotes = titles of articles, titles of poems.
6. URLs = online address where material is published.

Rhetorical Analysis
(Appears on College Composition and College Composition Modular)

First, remember that rhetoric is the art of persuasion. The speaker or writer is trying to get the audience or reader to believe one thing or another. This part of the exam measures how critically you think about what you read. What about the style and purpose for writing? To whom and for what purpose is the writing intended? Does the writer appeal to the head, the heart, or the pocket of the reader? Is she using empirical data, emotional stories, and financial statistics? Is the writing organized logically for the intended purpose?

In Rhetorical Analysis (RA) questions, you will need to read carefully, paying attention to the way the argument is built. As in a reading comprehension test, you answer questions about the passage. However, in RA, the questions will test not what the sentence says but how it is used. You will see questions such as this one:

> Which of the following best describes the relationship of sentence 2 to the rest of the paragraph?
>
> Which of the following best describes the function of sentence 3?
>
> In sentence 4, the effect of using "whereas" is to...

Rhetorical Analysis questions want you to view a piece of writing as a finely structured building. RA questions then ask you questions about the quality of building blocks and how they fit into the overall architecture of the edifice. It doesn't matter so much what sentence 2 says; what's important is how it fits in with the other sentences in that paragraph or passage.

Next, note that in RA, what is being discussed is not as critical as *how* it is being discussed. Does the writer build the argument logically, concisely, and interestingly? What about tone? Does the author's attitude about the topic come through in the selection of vocabulary and details? Reading a passage this way takes time, but you definitely can't cut corners too much or you won't really understand how the sentences build on one another.

Finally, keep in mind that standardized tests do all they can to be as uncontroversial as possible. *Bland is good!* is the motto for most answers. Correct answers are often statements that are positive in a general way, while wrong answer choices are often filled with extreme wording or controversial statements. So if you have a choice between "Creativity is often a matter of luck or chance," and "Artists feel more intensely than other people," ask yourself, "Which answer is more friendly and digestible? The second sentence makes a point that can't really be proven and could be dead wrong, while the first statement contains the qualifying word "often" to lessen any controversy the statement might create. The first statement is definitely the better guess. Still, watch out for faulty logic and general and unsupported claims.

Those are the five question types (remember that Improving Sentences only appears on College Composition Modular). Regardless of whether you take College Composition or College Composition Modular, you should complete all the practice tests in this book.

CLEP COLLEGE MATHEMATICS STRATEGIES

The CLEP College Mathematics exam consists of 60 questions that you have 90 minutes to answer. Most of the questions are multiple-choice questions with four answer choices, but scattered throughout are 5–10 problems that are more like open-ended short answer problems. For these problems, you will usually be asked to type in the correct numerical value—like 5.3 or –2.

You are also likely to see about 5 questions on the CLEP College Mathematics exam that require you to "click" the correct answer. Look at the following example. Indicate which figure has the largest area.

You don't get answer choices. You get a command to move the mouse to the figure with the largest area and click once. Here's another example.

The number x is an even integer. For each of the following numbers, indicate whether the number is odd or even.

Number	Odd	Even
x^2		
$x + 1$		
$x + 2$		

Again, you're not given answer choices. You have to click on the box (odd or even) that is the answer for each. Here's what the end result will look like.

Number	Odd	Even
x^2		√
$x + 1$	√	
$x + 2$		√

It's a change from just picking an answer, but there's actually nothing more difficult about the questions. If you don't let the odd format bother you, you won't have any trouble with these kinds of problems.

Speaking of odd….

The Odds and the Straightforwards

Imagine two groups of opposing math teachers seated in a room. Someone asks, "What defines a good math student?" One group—call them the Straightforwards—believes that a deep understanding of all the basic principles of math is the defining characteristic of a good math student. They argue that a student must be able to understand a fundamental concept like algebra so well that he or she can use algebra in a variety of situations and in many different ways.

The other group disagrees. This group—let's call them the Odds—feels that knowing the basic concepts is not enough and that what separates a good math student from everyone else is his or her knowledge of a great range of math subjects, including those that are not as common. The Odds believe that everyone knows a bit about geometry, algebra, and number sense but that only a good math student can discuss and use topics like set theory and irrational numbers.

If these two groups got together and wrote a math exam, the result would look a lot like the CLEP College Mathematics exam. Half of the questions cover basic topics in a variety of situations, while the other half covers "nonroutine problems," including topics that are not standard. The CLEP College Mathematics exam ends up looking like two different tests jammed together: one test covers the basics, and the other hits on all sorts of math topics.

Understanding the dual nature of the test is important, because each kind of question requires a different approach. If you see a problem that has variables in it, you can say, "Ah! A problem written by the Straightforwards. I need to apply a basic idea to solve this problem." If you encounter a problem that starts talking about *truth tables*, you can say, "Here's one by the Odds. What do I remember about this topic from my review? If I can remember the topic, chances are good that I can get this problem correct."

These are two different approaches, and neither one works on the other kind of question. If you have the idea of the Odds versus the Straightforwards in your head, you can navigate the CLEP College Mathematics exam much more easily.

Vectoring Through the Test

For a simple paper-and-pencil test, using a two-pass system is a matter of using your eyes to scan and your hands to turn the page. Since the CLEP exam is computerized and you see only one question at a time, this version of the two-pass system doesn't quite work, does it?

Here's how to modify the two-pass system to fit the CLEP College Mathematics exam. With any question on the CLEP, you have four choices. You can answer it and move on, answer it and "mark" it, skip it and move on, or skip it and "mark" it. For the two-pass system, we're suggesting an even simpler method.

For each question, you should do one of three things:

1) Answer the question and move on.

2) "Mark" the question but don't answer it.

3) Don't answer the question and move on.

Even if you could answer every question that shows up, that doesn't mean you want to. For instance, say you encounter a problem that has Roman numerals in it, like this one:

3. Which of the following is NOT true of a rational number?

     I. A rational number can be equal to 0.
     II. A rational number can be the ratio of two nonzero whole numbers.
     III. A rational number cannot be expressed as a fraction.

  (A) I and II

  (B) III only

  (C) II and III

  (D) II only

To answer Roman numeral problems, you often have to address each Roman numeral. This means you have to work three problems to get credit for one. It's not a good use of your time, so you should skip this question for now. Move past it and search for problems that are solvable with less time and effort.

In general, Straightforward problems are going to require more time. If you feel you could answer a problem but that it would take some time, "mark" it on your first pass through a section. There might be easier, simpler problems after it, and you want to try to find all of those on your first pass. On this first run-through, you should "mark" questions that you feel you can answer with a bit of time.

In general, Odd problems are going to require you to have the right facts. Spending a lot of time on these problems might not make a big difference if you don't know the concepts being tested. Leave these problems unanswered during your first pass. You will answer them eventually, even if you don't even attempt them.

After your first pass, you should have answered all the easy questions that you encountered. You can now go click the Review button and sort the remaining problems by Status. Marked problems will be all those problems you thought you could answer with some more work. Well, you've answered all the easier problems, so the time is now to start in on the marked questions. Many of these marked problems will probably be Straightforwards.

When the marked problems are completed, it's time to tackle the unanswered problems. Give these the best shot that you can, but remember the following fact: **if time is running out, make sure you answer every problem**. If the timer shows one minute remaining and there are four problems left, pick (D) (or one of the letters) for every answer and don't worry about it. There's no guessing penalty on the CLEP exam, and the law of averages states that you should get one of those problems right. It's all about getting points wherever, and however, you can.

Here's a recap of an optimal plan of attack.

Problems to Answer on the First Pass:
   Straightforward problems that don't take much time
   Odd problems you know the concept for

Problems to Mark on the First Pass:
   Straightforward problems that might take two minutes
   Odd problems on concepts you remember, but not perfectly
   Open-ended questions (because of the open-ended format, it's best to save these for the second pass to avoid getting bogged down)

Problems to Leave Unanswered (until Time Is Running Out):
   Odd problems on topics you don't know much about
   Roman numeral questions

Make It Real

Many problems on the exam will include variables, either in the answer choices or as part of the question stem. Although variables are an important abstract math concept, working in abstractions on a test is not the best way to get a problem right. **If possible, always replace the variables in a question with actual numbers**. The goal when taking the CLEP College Mathematics exam is to get the highest score possible, not to show off your knowledge of variables. Consider a question like the next example.

13. The width of a farmer's rectangular cornfield is *y* feet. If he needs 1,000 feet of fencing to enclose the field, which of the following represents the length of the field, in feet?

(A) $1,000 - y$

(B) $1,000 - 2y$

(C) $500 - y$

(D) $500 - 2y$

For the love of Pythagoras, give the variable *y* a value and then solve the problem. Look at the answer choices: there's one right answer and three traps designed to catch people who do the algebra incorrectly. If you just decide that $y = 20$ ft, though, then the problem leaves the abstract realm of algebra and becomes an easily workable problem with real-world numbers. Take the formula for the perimeter of a rectangle and plug in the values that you know (or just made up).

$$P = 2(l + w)$$
$$1,000 = 2(l + 20)$$
$$1,000 = 2l + 40$$
$$960 = 2l$$
$$480 = l$$

The length is 480, and that works out to be choice (C), $500 - y$.

Whenever there are variables, remember to try to take the variables out of the equation by making it real.

Work It Out on Paper, Not in Your Head

Since you're staring at a computer screen with a mouse in one hand, there is a great tendency to try to answer questions in your head. It's faster (supposedly), and you've already got one hand tied up using the mouse. The only problem with doing CLEP College Mathematics work in your head is that you almost guarantee yourself a lower score than you need to get.

People—when rushed and under pressure—make mental mistakes. Taking an important exam like this timed CLEP test is almost a textbook definition of a rushed and pressure-filled situation. To avoid the careless errors, make sure to write something down on every problem. Every one. If you make it an automatic habit, you'll find that it doesn't take too long to jot down your thoughts. Writing something down also has a bonus effect on multistep problems. Quite often, students trying to figure out a knotty problem in their heads get lost somewhere along the way, or they are unable to visualize how to take the initial facts and reach the required information that the question wants. If you write your work down, you often find yourself staring down at the intermediate steps needed to determine the right answer. You might be able to get there in your head, but what's the point? You want to answer CLEP questions accurately in a fairly brief amount of time, and writing your work down is the best way to accomplish that.

CLEP HUMANITIES STRATEGIES

This test has 140 questions, and even if you're speedy, answering 140 questions in 90 minutes is going to be a rushed affair. When you combine this with the fact that these questions come from a diverse range of topics, the end result is that you are not going to have time to reflect on every question and come up with an answer. Instead, questions will fall into one of three categories:

Category 1: You know the answer right away.

Category 2: You can answer the question with a bit of work.

Category 3: You have little or no chance of answering this question correctly.

Your goal is to expand categories 1 and 2 and not spend too much time on problems in that last category. You expand category 1 by reviewing, while category 2 questions can be overcome with a mixture of review, strategy, and (a pinch of) luck. Everyone has some category 3 problems; the key is to accept this fact and not let it bother you. Missing one question won't kill your CLEP Humanities exam score, but spending too much time on a problem you have little chance of answering correctly can harm your overall performance.

Word Lover or Art Lover?

Half of the CLEP Humanities test covers literature, and the other 50 percent covers the arts. Ask yourself honestly, Which topic do you know more about? You might have an idea by now. If you don't, take the first test in this book and see what problems you find easier to answer.

It doesn't matter if you're a Word Lover (better at literature) or an Art Lover. All that matters is that you have a clear idea which topic you are better at. Once you know, you can take this knowledge and use the computer format of the CLEP exam to craft a killer plan of attack.

Let's say you are a Word Lover. You're not ignorant of art, but you definitely have a better chance on literature questions than art questions. If this is the case, then refine your two-pass system in the following way.

Word Lover Plan of Attack

1. **On the first pass, look for all Word Lover questions**. Your goal on the first pass is to find all the category 1 (you get them right away) questions you can. Since you're better at litera-ture, look for these problems. If you see italics in a question, that's an immediate indicator that it's probably about a book or play. (Art Lover problems can be spotted very easily too; many have an image—like a painting or sculpture—in them. We doubt you'll be confused.)

   Give yourself a moment to answer every Word Lover question. Even if you are strong in this subject, there will be some questions that you don't know the answer to immediately. That's fine. If you feel you know something about the subject of the question, hit the "mark" button and move on.

2. **If you encounter an Art Lover question that you immediately know the answer to, answer it**. You should be able to hit some art questions out of the park right away. If that's the case, do it and move on. However, don't spend time figuring out an Art Lover question when there are potentially easier literature problems waiting.

3. **If you hit a question you think you know something about but can't answer immediately, "mark" it and move on**. Here is where you can take advantage of the computer format. On your first pass through the CLEP Humanities exam, you can answer all category 1 questions, "mark" all category 2 questions, and leave unanswered (for now) all problems that you don't have a strong chance at.

4. **Once you finish your first pass through the test, hit the Review button and sort by status**. You should have three groups, which just so happen to correspond with the three categories we discussed earlier.

   "Answered"—These will be the category 1 questions.

   "Marked"—These are your category 2 questions. Start going back through these problems, taking some additional time to work out the right answers (or at least give yourself a good guess). Note that the marked problems won't be sorted into a bunch together, but they will clearly have a check mark next to them.

   "Not answered"—Here are the category 3 problems. As time is running out, leave about three minutes to go through and answer every one of these problems. That doesn't mean you have to look at them. If there's no time, just put an answer and move on. There's no guessing penalty on the CLEP exam, so you should pick up some points even by answering blindly.

Now that is a plan of attack. (If you're an Art Lover, simply switch the two terms and proceed the same way.) While other test takers are floundering through the section, you will be using your knowledge of the computer format and your understanding of the test structure to maximize your ability to see all the questions. This gives you the best possible chance of answering them correctly.

Cluster Questions

Cluster Questions are like the game show *Jeopardy!* because the answers come *before* the question. Cluster Questions start off with (A)–(E), and each answer choice has an initial piece of information next to it. One to three questions follow, and each question describes one of the choices (A)–(E) in the initial information. You pick the right letter choice for each problem.

Here's an example of a Cluster Question.

> **Questions 6–8** refer to the following texts.
>
> (A) *The Great Gatsby*
> (B) *Sons and Lovers*
> (C) *Beloved*
> (D) *The Grapes of Wrath*
> (E) *The Cider House Rules*
>
> 6. Which novel was written by Toni Morrison?
>
> 7. Which novel discusses, in part, the immorality and organized crime of the 1920s?
>
> 8. Which novel involves love and loss as experienced through the eyes of an orphan named Homer?

Cluster Questions can be answered quickly, so that's good. But a common mistake is to spend time reading over all the answer choices first. Don't. The whole point is to answer questions, not read answer choices. **Once you encounter a Cluster Question set, read the question and then go back and look at the answer choices**. In the previous example, you should drop down to question 6, read the question, and then look for an answer. Once you have it, move on to questions 7 and 8.

Sometimes the Cluster Question answer choices are very short, so this approach doesn't save you a lot of time. Other times the Cluster Questions answer choices are lengthier. They might even use a format popular on the CLEP Humanities exam that we call the Lineup.

Unusual Suspects: Lineups on the CLEP Humanities Exam

Sometimes one name just isn't good enough for this test. The CLEP Humanities exam likes to place three names together and then ask you how they are related. Consider the following Cluster Question with Lineup format.

> **Question 10** refers to the following people.
>
> (A) Andy Warhol, Maya Angelou, Jack Kerouac
> (B) Michelangelo, Da Vinci, Rousseau
> (C) Socrates, Aristotle, Plato
> (D) Claude Monet, Auguste Rodin, Edouard Manet
> (E) Charlotte Perkins Gilman, Emily Bronte, Charlotte Bronte
>
> 10. Which group is from the twentieth century?

The point to remember about Lineup problems is that because all three names are related in the same way, **you only need to know one of the names**. Sure, there are fifteen names listed, but it's really more like five groups of three. If you know Michelangelo is not from the twentieth century, then it no longer matters who da Vinci and Rousseau are. Similarly, if the Art Lover in you knows that Andy Warhol was a modern artist, the identities of author Maya Angelou and poet Jack Kerouac are irrelevant. The answer has to be (A), because all members of the Lineup are related. You needed to know only one name (Andy Warhol) out of fifteen to get this question right.

Lineup problems can look intimidating at first, since there are a lot of proper names. Students often get worried because they don't recognize all the names. That's the wrong mindset to have, so don't fall prey to it. Instead, when you encounter a Lineup problem in some form or another, tell yourself, "I only need to know one of the names to get the answer right." This can be demonstrated in the following question, which won't be on the CLEP Humanities exam but does show how to attack Lineup questions.

56.   Fennis Dembo, Yinka Dare, and Michael Jordan were all

(A) composers of opera.

(B) professional basketball players.

(C) math professors.

(D) poets.

(E) playwrights.

You don't really need to know the first two names to get this problem right, do you? All you need is one name.

Uh, I'm Guessing . . .

Whenever you can't find the right answer to a problem, switch gears and start looking for wrong answers to eliminate. The CLEP Humanities exam usually does not have one right answer and four very close wrong answers, which is good news for you. Look back at the sample problems we've gone over so far, and you can see that there are one or two choices that are unlikely. Even if you're not a big fan of art, you probably have heard of Michelangelo as a famous *historic* painter. He wasn't painting the Sistine Chapel between World War I and World War II, even if you're not quite sure when he was alive. Using just a smidgeon of factual knowledge can often help you cross out a choice here and there.

Common sense and gut instinct also work well. Look at the following problem.

(A) Salman Rushdie's *The Satanic Verses*

(B) Homer's *The Iliad*

(C) Oscar Wilde's *The Importance of Being Earnest*

(D) William Carlos Williams' *Paterson*

(E) Emily Dickinson's "Nature, the gentlest mother"

6.   Which takes place in and around London?

Does it seem likely that a book called *The Satanic Verses* takes place in London? If it does, you have a low opinion of London. For that matter, does *Salman Rushdie* sound like an English name to you? There's always a chance that answer (A) is correct, but if you're guessing, it's not a good guess. Since the work takes place in London, pick one of the British-sounding names like answer (C) or (D). You might be wrong, because there's no law that states that people's names automatically show where they are from. That's not the point. The point is that if you have to guess, don't overthink things too much. Use common sense, since it will give you a good shot at eliminating some unlikely choices and picking the right one.

When you take the practice tests in this book, go back through after the test is over and look at all the answer choices. On the questions you answered immediately, look at the other answer choices and spot the one or two choices that you would have known were wrong, even if you didn't know the right answer. If you get accustomed to looking at answer choices and eliminating the ones that are highly unlikely to be the answer, you should be in good practice when you come to a question and actually have to use this technique.

CLEP SOCIAL SCIENCES AND HISTORY STRATEGIES

When the College Board states that the CLEP Social Sciences and History (SS&H) exam "covers a wide range of topics," it is not kidding. This 120-question test, which you have 90 minutes to complete, throws everything but the kitchen sink at you. A complete breakdown of the topics covered on the CLEP SS&H exam can be found in chapter 17, but here's a brief rundown.

U.S. History

History of Western Civilization

World History

Government/Political Science

Geography

Economics

Psychology

Sociology

Anthropology

The College Board could have said, "Everything but math, English, and science is on this test," and they wouldn't have been far off.

When you combine a large number of questions (120) with a massive array of topics, you get a situation where getting every question right is almost an impossibility. The truth is that at least one out of every ten CLEP SS&H questions you face will seem completely alien to you. You might not even know what the question is asking for, much less what the answer is. If this happens only 10 percent of the time, consider yourself fortunate.

A perfect score is impossible, but so what? The goal is to get a good score, one that gets you college credit. This goal is still easily within range. However, you have to make good use of your 90 minutes of testing, and to do that you must accept the fact that there will be some questions that you just won't stand much of a chance on. That doesn't mean you won't answer them—there's no guessing penalty, so you should answer every question. It just means that you shouldn't let it bother you when you encounter a problem that you don't have a clue about. That's simply the nature of this exam.

Eating at the Question Smorgasbord

You have less than a minute per question for the CLEP SS&H exam, so managing your time is important. You'll want to use a two-pass system to give yourself a chance to answer every question that you know the answer to. Since the test is on a computer, though, you need to modify the two-pass concept to fit this electronic format. With any question on the CLEP, you have four choices. You can answer it and move on, answer it and "mark" it, skip it and move on, or skip it and "mark" it. For the modified two-pass system, we're suggestion an even simpler method.

For each question, you should do one of three things:

1) Answer the question and move on.
2) "Mark" the question but don't answer it.
3) Don't answer the question and move on.

Those are your three options. Unlike a math test—where computations often have to be done to find an answer—you are going to know the answer to many of the questions on the CLEP SS&H exam immediately. For example, let's say you know what the Fifth Amendment of the U.S. Constitution is. You get a question that asks, "The Fifth Amendment of the U.S. Constitution declares which of the following?" There's one question you can hit out of the ballpark quickly.

Other questions will be solvable but not as rapidly. For instance, you might encounter an economics problem that you feel you could answer if you spent just a bit of time thinking about the answer choices. You could spend the time then, but you would be better off using the "mark" function on the computer and marking that question for later. This would allow you to seek out easier, faster questions.

Still other questions will fall into the third category of "Whhaaaat? I have little or no idea." Leave these questions unanswered and look for easier prey in the rest of the exam.

After your first pass, you should now have answered all the easy questions that you encountered. **You can now go click the Review button and sort the remaining problems by Status.** It's a great way to make the computer format work to your advantage.

Marked problems will be all those problems you thought you could answer with some more work. Well, you've answered all the easier problems, so now is the time to start in on the marked questions. When the marked problems are completed, it's time to tackle the unanswered problems. Give these the best shot that you can, but remember the following tip: **if time is running out, make sure you answer every problem.** If the timer shows two minutes remaining and there are ten unanswered problems left, pick (B) (or one of the letters) for every answer and don't worry about it. There's no guessing penalty on the CLEP exam, and the law of averages states that you should get two of those problems right (since you have a one-in-five chance when guessing randomly). Two out of ten might not seem like a lot, but it's good when you consider you didn't stand a chance on any of those questions, and you didn't waste any precious time trying to work them futilely. Shoot for a good score, not a perfect score.

You Can Be Bland

Standardized testing might be a controversial subject to some, but actual standardized tests are *not* controversial. Every standardized test goes to enormous lengths not to offend anyone, and the CLEP tests—not just the Social Sciences and History exam, but all CLEP exams—are no exception.

You can use this fact about the CLEP exams to your advantage when answering a SS&H question you don't know anything about. If you have to guess, steer clear of answer choices that are extreme and controversial and pick one of the blander, safer answer choices. Here's a sample question. To illustrate our point, we've crossed out the name of the person.

> XXXXXXX XXXX was a military leader during the
> American Revolution and
>
> (A) often was disciplined for fighting with fellow
>   soldiers.
> (B) was known for defecting to Britain.
> (C) lived in Maryland.
> (D) gained power through unscrupulous business dealings
>   in Massachusetts.
> (E) founded a movement in the Methodist Church.

Since we don't even have the name, this question should be very difficult. However, look at the answer choices and cull out those answers that are negative or controversial. Choice (A) gets the axe, and choice (D) should also go. Choice (E) might seem OK, but it refers to religion, and standardized tests do their utmost to steer clear of religious topics if possible.

That leaves only two choices, (B) and (C). Since the word *Britain* is associated with the American Revolution, you might lean toward (B) as the correct answer. It makes sense that a question on the Social Sciences and History test would refer to a specific place in history. Pick (B) and move on. As it turns out, it is the correct answer for this question.

Looking for the bland is a very effective guessing technique, but it doesn't work all the time. On some questions, the answer will be one of the choices that seems a little more unlikely or extreme. The Mystery Person in the question might have "gained power through unscrupulous business dealings," for example. Even so, slicing away the extreme while looking for the bland will work more often than not, and on questions that you don't know the answer to, it's one of your best chances to get the problem correct.

Buy a World Map

This technique pretty much explains itself. Ten percent of the CLEP SS&H exam covers geography, and there may even be a map or two on your test.

Gazing at a nice world map is a great way to learn geography almost without trying to. If you have a place where you regularly do your homework or study, the ideal scenario is to place the world map there where it is easily visible. If you're studying and need a break, look up and stare at a continent for a moment or two. You don't have to strain yourself to memorize every capital: just let your mind relax and soak in the pretty colors. Stare at a different part of the map every time, and you'll find that as weeks go by you actually will be able to recall the location of countries, cities, and other geographic landmarks better than you used to.

There aren't many geography questions on the CLEP SS&H exam, but since this is such an easy way to increase your knowledge of geography, you should do it if possible. It will also aid you after the CLEP SS&H exam, since needing to know where countries are is something that tends to crop up from time to time in college and in the rest of life.

The Test Is All Over the Place. So Are the Answer Choices.

Question: What does famous nineteenth-century Dutch painter Vincent van Gogh have to do with contemporary political cartoons?

If you answered "Nothing," you would be correct. However, that wouldn't stop Vincent from appearing as an answer choice on a CLEP SS&H exam question about contemporary political cartoons. You see, the test doesn't have one correct answer and four really close incorrect choices. Instead, there are often one or two answer choices that just cannot be the answer. The catch is that you have to know who Vincent van Gogh is before you can cross him out as a political cartoonist. If you don't know who he is at all, you can't eliminate him as an answer choice.

> 33. Which of the following was the first major land battle of the Union and Confederate armies in Virginia?
>
>   (A) Battle of Little Big Horn
>   (B) Battle of Bull Run
>   (C) Battle of Gettysburg
>   (D) Battle of Pearl Harbor
>   (E) Battle of Hastings

Even if you don't know the exact answer, you might know one or two of the answer choices are definitely wrong. If you've ever seen the movie *Pearl Harbor* or paid close attention in history class, you'd know that battle was between the United States and Japan in World War II. That's all you need to cross out choice (D): a vague memory of a movie you saw once or a recollection of class. Similarly, if you know that Little Big Horn involved Native Americans, you can cross out choice (A) as well. That gives you a one-in-three chance on this problem.

Sometimes just a minuscule amount of knowledge is all you need to eliminate an answer choice and give yourself a better chance of determining the right answer.

CLEP NATURAL SCIENCES STRATEGIES

The CLEP Natural Sciences exam shares some basic similarities with the CLEP Humanities exam. Both tests contain a large number of questions and both are split into two major categories. Similar tests require similar strategies, so if you are taking the CLEP Humanities and Natural Sciences tests, you will find that the basic approach to both tests is the same. The strategies that follow have been modified to reflect the CLEP Natural Sciences exam, but they are identical in essence with those to use on the CLEP Humanities exam. You might think it's strange that two tests covering greatly different subjects (humanities and natural sciences) would have identical strategies, but it's not the subject matter that's important, only the design of the tests.

The CLEP Natural Sciences exam has 120 questions. Since you only have 90 minutes, you can see that there's not much time on average for each question. These questions come from a wide spectrum of biological science and physical science topics, so you are probably not going to have time to reflect on every question and come up with an answer. Instead, questions will fall into one of three categories:

Category 1: You know the answer right away.

Category 2: You can answer the question with a bit of work.

Category 3: You have little or no chance of answering these questions correctly.

Your goal is to expand Categories 1 and 2, and not spend too much time on problems in that last category. You expand Category 1 by reviewing, while Category 2 questions can be overcome with a mixture of review, strategy, and some luck. Everyone has some Category 3 problems; the key is to accept this fact and not let it bother you. Missing one question won't kill your CLEP Natural Sciences exam score, but spending too much time on a problem you have little chance of ever answering correctly can harm your overall performance.

Are You Bio or Phys?

Half of the CLEP Natural Sciences test covers biology, and the other 50 percent covers the physical sciences. Ask yourself honestly, which topic do you know more about? You might have an idea by now. If you don't, take the first test in this book and see what problems you find easier to answer.

It doesn't matter if you're better at Bio or excel at Phys. All that matters is that you have a clear idea of which topic you are better at. Once you know, you can take this knowledge and use the computer format of the CLEP to craft an excellent plan of attack.

Let's say you are better at biology. You're not ignorant of physics, but you definitely have a better chance at cell questions than atom questions. If this is the case, then refine your two-pass system in the following way.

Bio Plan of Attack

1. **On the first pass, look for all biology questions**. Your goal on the first run-through is to find all the category 1 (you get them right away) questions you can. Since you're better at biology, look for these problems. There's very little overlap between the biology and physical sciences topics, so you probably won't be confused about which question is which. Questions about organisms and heredity fall pretty obviously under the biology umbrella. If you see chemical symbols in the answer choices, you can guess what kind of problem that is.

    Give yourself a moment to answer every Bio question. Even if you are strong in this subject, there will be some questions that you won't know the answer to immediately. That's fine. If you feel you know something about the subject, hit the "mark" button and move on.

2. **If you encounter a Phys question that you immediately know the answer to, answer it**. You should be able to hit some of these questions out of the park right away. If that's the case, do it and move on. However, don't spend time figuring out a physical science question when there are potentially easier biology problems waiting.

3. **If you hit a question you think you know something about but can't answer immediately, "mark" it and move on**. Here is where you can take advantage of the computer format. On your first pass through the CLEP Natural Sciences exam, you can answer all category 1 questions, "mark" all category 2 questions, and leave unanswered (for now) all problems that you don't have a strong chance at.

4. **Once you finish your first pass through the test, hit the Review button and sort by status**. You should have three groups, which just so happen to correspond with the three categories we discussed earlier.

    "Answered"—These will be the category 1 questions.

    "Marked"—These are your category 2 questions. Start going back through these problems, taking some additional time to work out the right answer (or at least give yourself a good guess). Note that the marked problems won't be sorted into a bunch together, but they will clearly have a check mark next to them.

    "Not answered"—Here are the category 3 problems. As time is running out, leave about three minutes to go through and answer every one of these problems. That doesn't mean you have to look at them. If there's no time, just put an answer and move on. There's no guessing penalty on the CLEP eaxm, so you should pick up some points even by answering blindly.

Now that is a plan of attack. (If you're better at physical sciences, simply switch the two terms and proceed the same way.) While others students are floundering through the section, you will be using your knowledge of the computer format and your understanding of the test structure to maximize your ability to see all questions. This gives you the best possible chance of answering them correctly.

Cluster Questions

Cluster Questions are like the game show *Jeopardy!* because the answers come *before* the question. Cluster Questions start off with (A)–(E), and each answer choice has an initial piece of information next to it. One to three questions follow, and each question describes one of the choices (A)–(E) in the initial information. You pick the right letter choice for each problem. Here's an example.

(A) Golgi apparatus

(B) Nucleus

(C) Cell membrane

(D) Chloroplast

(E) mRNA

1. Site of protein synthesis

2. Not found in an animal cell

3. Site of photosynthesis

Cluster Questions can be answered quickly, so that's good. But a common mistake is to spend time reading over all the answer choices first. Don't. The whole point is to answer questions, not read answer choices. **Once you encounter a Cluster Question set, read the question and then go back and look at the answer choices**. In this example, you should drop down to question 1, read the question, and then look for an answer. Once you have it, move on to questions 2 and 3.

The CLEP Natural Sciences exam often starts out with Cluster Questions. This lets you answer a bunch of questions in a short period of time. This helps you in terms of overall time, but there aren't enough Cluster Questions to make a huge impact on the overall pacing.

The Long and the Short of It

You can further refine your two-pass system by skipping long or involved questions on the first pass. For example, some questions will contain Roman numerals (usually I, II, and III). To answer these questions, you often have to address each Roman numeral. This means you have to work three questions to get credit for one. It's not a good use of your time, so you should leave these questions blank during the first pass. Move past them and search for questions that are solvable with less time and effort.

Other questions begin with a brief passage and/or illustrations describing an experiment. This might interest you, but why spend all this time reading an experiment when you only get credit for one question? You can "mark" it if you like and come back to it if there's time, but since there are so many short, simple problems, don't spend too much time on a long problem that is worth the same.

A Little Bit of Knowledge Can Go a Long Way

The CLEP Natural Sciences test rewards students who know biology and physical science. What the test doesn't reward is bad science. It doesn't want answers that are factually incorrect, too extreme to be true, or irrelevant to the topic at hand.

Yet these bad science answers invariably appear, because hey! It's a multiple-choice test, and you have to have four incorrect answer choices around the one right answer. So if you don't know how to answer a problem, look at the answer choices and think "Good Science." This may lead you to find some poor answer choices that can be eliminated.

30. Which gland(s) in the human body secrete(s) steroid hormones and is/are located above the kidneys?

   (A) Pituitary

   (B) Kidney

   (C) Pancreas

   (D) Adrenal

   (E) Heart

Let's say you know about the production of steroid hormones, but during the test your mind draws a blank as to exactly which gland produces them. Even though you don't know the right answer, you still know enough "good science" to eliminate some incorrect answers. This leads you to whack choices (B), (C), and (E), since they are all organs, not glands. That leaves only two answers. At this point, trust your instincts and take a guess. You have a one-in-two chance of getting the right answer, and over the course of the test, these chances will add up and help your final score.

FINAL THOUGHTS

You now have three levels of strategies to approach every CLEP exam: computer strategies, general strategies, and specific strategies. Be sure to employ all relevant techniques when you take the practice tests in this book and the real tests as well.

The CLEP College Composition Exam

Chapter Four: **Practice Test 1: Diagnostic (College Composition Modular)**

Time—90 minutes
90 Questions

> **Directions:** Each sentence tests your knowledge of choice of words (diction), idiom, grammar, and usage. Some sentences are correct, and each sentence can contain no more than one error.
>
> Elements of the sentence that are underlined and lettered may be incorrect. Parts of the sentence that are not underlined can be assumed to be correct. When choosing an answer, follow the conventions of standard written English.
>
> If a sentence contains an error, select the <u>one underlined portion</u> that must be changed to form a correct sentence. For sentences with no error, choose answer (E).

1. The button, <u>which is</u> commonly used to fasten
         A
    two pieces of cloth together, <u>and was</u>
                                      B
    <u>originally viewed</u> as an ornament and <u>worn</u>
         C   D
    like jewelry. <u>No error</u>
                      E

2. If <u>you are</u> preparing to take a standardized test,
       A
    <u>it's important</u> that the person familiarize him-
        B
    or herself with the test, <u>work</u> on areas of weakness,
                                  C
    and <u>get</u> a good night's sleep the night before.
        D
    <u>No error</u>
       E

3. <u>According</u> to experts, playing video games is no
        A
    better than <u>television</u> because it is a passive activity
                    B
    that <u>draws children</u> away from reading or
             C
    <u>participating</u> in physical activities. <u>No error</u>
        D   E

4. The author of nine detective <u>mysteries, Linda Kong,</u>
                                           A
    <u>frequented</u> the police headquarters because
        B
    <u>they</u> provided her with inspiration for her work,
       C
    <u>especially</u> when she was beginning a new novel.
        D
    <u>No error</u>
       E

GO ON TO THE NEXT PAGE >

KAPLAN)

5. Mrs. Aljriha <u>has been teaching</u> third grade for
               A

   twenty years, and <u>though</u> she <u>has found</u> the work
              B   C

   rewarding, she <u>has been deciding</u> to apply for a
                 D

   job as a school administrator this year. <u>No error</u>
                                E

6. <u>In the eyes</u> of some social critics, the quality of life
     A

   in the United States <u>is poorer</u> than <u>that</u> in England
                    B   C

   and other European countries because

   <u>many Americans</u> do not have access to adequate
         D

   healthcare. <u>No error</u>
             E

7. <u>The adventurous spirit</u> of the men and women
            A

   <u>who settled</u> the frontier <u>have all</u> but disappeared,
     B   C

   <u>except</u> in the state of Alaska where adventure and
     D

   hardship still characterize everyday life. <u>No error</u>
                                  E

8. Diving, <u>which began</u> in the latter half of the
           A

   nineteenth century <u>when gymnasts</u> performed in
                   B

   swimming areas, <u>is now</u> an Olympic sport
                C

   <u>and it takes</u> finely tuned coordination and
           D

   strength. <u>No error</u>
            E

9. My professor <u>was</u> surprised that, of my <u>whole</u>
            A   B

   class, scarcely <u>any students</u> had ever <u>written</u> a
                C   D

   research paper. <u>No error</u>
                 E

GO ON TO THE NEXT PAGE

Directions: The passages below are first drafts of student work. The sentences in each passage have been numbered. Parts of the essays require revision.

After reading each passage, answer the questions that follow. Some questions require you to improve sentences by changing word choice (diction) and sentence structure. Other questions ask you to review the whole essay or a part of the essay and evaluate its organization, development, and the suitability of its language for the intended audience and purpose. Follow the rules of standard written English in your answer choices.

Questions 10–15 are based on the following passage.

Dear Mr. Simms,

(1) *Because I feel so strongly about this issue, I decided to write you a letter.* (2) *The food in the cafeteria stinks!* (3) *The cafeteria features three food groups: starch, fat, and meat.* (4) *If you are a vegetarian, you might as well give up your beliefs.* (5) *If you want to be healthy, you better plan to skip a meal.* (6) *If you dislike fried food and fatty sauces, you better look elsewhere.* (7) *Shredded iceberg lettuce and bits of carrot don't really make a salad.* (8) *Ketchup is not a vegetable.* (9) *Hot dogs can barely be included in the category of meat.* (10) *Rather than face another soggy sloppy joe or glob of starchy spaghetti, students avoid the cafeteria.* (11) *Students bring brown-bag lunches from home, or they go out to lunch.*

(12) *Who is forced to eat in the cafeteria?* (13) *Students who qualify for free or reduced-price lunches; students who can't, for whatever reason, bring a lunch from home; students who don't have the cash for a $3 lunch at the local drive-in.* (14) *Is this fair?* (15) *No!* (16) *Why should the poor kids in our school be forced to eat disgusting food?* (17) *They shouldn't be.*

(18) *Obviously, it would be terrific if all students could eat where they pleased, and since this is impossible, I have a simple suggestion: improve the food in the cafeteria.* (19) *Get a salad bar.* (20) *Plan vegetarian options.* (21) *Stop frying everything.* (22) *If this happened, more kids would choose the cafeteria, and that will ultimately built more community in our school.*

10. Which of the following is the best way to revise the underlined portions of sentences 10 and 11 (reproduced below) so that the two sentences are combined into one?

    Rather than face another soggy sloppy joe or glob of starchy spaghetti, <u>students avoid the cafeteria.</u> <u>Students</u> bring brown-bag lunches from home, or they go out to lunch.

    (A) students avoid the cafeteria, but
    (B) students avoid the cafeteria and
    (C) avoiding the cafeteria, students
    (D) students avoid the cafeteria, so they
    (E) students avoided the cafeteria and

11. Which of the following sentences, if added after sentence 11, would best link the first paragraph with the rest of the letter?

    (A) This is what students face in the cafeteria.
    (B) The mediocre quality of the food drives students away and penalizes students who have no other lunch alternatives.
    (C) The quality of the food has declined since my sophomore year.
    (D) Surely, you've noticed that hot dogs aren't as popular as they used to be.
    (E) Every time I eat in the cafeteria I feel sick and wish I hadn't.

GO ON TO THE NEXT PAGE ⟩

KAPLAN

12. Which of the following revisions to sentence 2 (reproduced below) would most help more effectively communicate to the school principal?

    The food in the cafeteria stinks!

    (A) The quality of the food in the cafeteria is mediocre.
    (B) The food in the cafeteria should be tossed.
    (C) The food in the cafeteria is absolutely disgusting!
    (D) The cafeteria food is gross beyond belief.
    (E) The food in the cafeteria is pure garbage.

13. If the writer of this letter were to turn it into an opinion article for the school newspaper, which of the following would make the most logical title for the article?

    (A) The Limited Benefits of Ketchup
    (B) Recent Nutritional Issues
    (C) Tips for Better Eating
    (D) The Food We Are Forced to Eat
    (E) Problems with the Cafeteria Food

14. Which is the best version of the underlined version of sentence 18 (reproduced below)?

    Obviously, it would be terrific if all students could eat where they pleased, and since this is impossible, I have a simple suggestion: improve the food in the cafeteria.

    (A) however in light of the possibility
    (B) but barring the impossibility of this
    (C) and because of the impossibility of this
    (D) but because this is impossible
    (E) and yet this is impossible

15. In the context of the third paragraph, which of the following is the best version of the underlined portion of sentence 22 (reproduced below)?

    If this happened, more kids would choose the cafeteria, and that will have ultimately built more community in our school.

    (A) No change
    (B) that will ultimately build more community
    (C) ultimately building more community
    (D) that would be ultimately building more community
    (E) that would ultimately build more community

GO ON TO THE NEXT PAGE ⇒

Questions 16–21 are based on the following passage.

(1) *Last summer, I had a very unique experience.* (2) *My brother and I decided that we wanted to do something positive in our community.* (3) *We didn't know exactly what, but we knew we wanted to do something to make a difference.* (4) *Everyone is always talking about how our generation is selfish.* (5) *Everyone focuses on the bad things that happen instead of the good things that happen.*

(6) *My brother and I both are good basketball players.* (7) *We decided to start basketball camp for kids in our neighborhood.* (8) *It wasn't anything fancy.* (9) *We divided the kids into two groups: beginning and experienced.* (10) *There are so many ways to divide people into groups.*

(11) *The beginning kids came in the morning for two hours of drills.* (12) *They were mainly younger so we didn't want to work them too hard.* (13) *We mainly wanted to teach them the fundamentals: ball handling, shooting, and the rules of the game.* (14) *The experienced kids were a blast.* (15) *We could play real games with them and run real plays.* (16) *Some of them really improved.* (17) *Nevertheless, we're going to tell the high school coach to look out for them.*

(18) *The kids who came to our camp really enjoyed it, now everyone in the neighborhood knows each other.* (19) *They've kept playing basketball on their own.* (20) *I think the key to making a difference is doing something you enjoy.*

16. Which of the following is the best way to revise and combine sentences 4 and 5 (reproduced below)?

    Everyone is always talking about how our generation is selfish. Everyone focuses on the bad things that happen instead of the good things that happen.

    (A) Everyone is always talking about how our generation is selfish, and everyone focuses on the bad things that happen instead of the good things that happen.

    (B) Focusing on the bad, instead of the good, things that happen, everyone is always talking about how our generation is selfish.

    (C) Everyone is always talking about the selfishness of our generation, focusing on the bad instead of the good.

    (D) Everyone is always talking about how our generation is selfish and focuses on the bad things that happen instead of the good things that happen.

    (E) Talking about the selfishness of our generation, the focus is on the bad things instead of the good things.

17. Which of the following sentences should be deleted to most improve the coherence of the passage?

    (A) Sentence 2
    (B) Sentence 3
    (C) Sentence 8
    (D) Sentence 10
    (E) Sentence 21

18. In context, which is the best alternative for "fundamentals" in sentence 13?

    (A) traditions
    (B) actions
    (C) basics
    (D) strategies
    (E) drills

19. Which of the following would best replace "Nevertheless" at the beginning of sentence 17?

    (A) And
    (B) Instead
    (C) As a result
    (D) However
    (E) Perhaps

GO ON TO THE NEXT PAGE

KAPLAN

20. Which of the following would be the best sentence with which to end the passage?

    (A) Basketball is definitely the best sport.

    (B) It's ten times better than doing chores.

    (C) Basketball camp is, after all, a great way for people to get to know one another.

    (D) At least that's what my brother and I learned.

    (E) I'll always remember working with the kids in the beginning group.

21. Which of the following versions of the underlined portion of sentence 18 (reproduced below) is best?

    The kids who came to our camp really <u>*enjoyed it,*</u> <u>*now*</u> *everyone in the neighborhood knows each other.*

    (A) enjoyed themselves, now

    (B) enjoyed themselves, but now

    (C) had been enjoying it, therefore now

    (D) enjoying it, now

    (E) enjoyed it, and now

Questions 22–27 are based on the following passage.

(1) *Did President Washington really chop down the cherry tree?* (2) *Did President Jackson carry around two bullets in his body while he was president?* (3) *President Carter can read 2,000 words per minute with 95 percent comprehension.*

(4) *If you're dying to know the answer to these and other questions, then you're the perfect person to join the history club.* (5) *History club, you may think, is only for nerds.* (6) *And that's completely wrong.* (7) *History club is for students with inquiring minds.* (8) *It's for students who think understanding the past will make it easier to understand the present.* (9) *Weekly trivia competitions give you an opportunity to flex your mind (and to study for the Advanced Placement American and European history tests).* (10) *Researching the history of our school will let you see whether you have what it takes to be a historian.* (11) *Finally, there's an annual banquet honoring a local historian at the end of the school year that gives students the responsibility of picking.*

(12) *Convinced?* (13) *If you still have doubts, at least come by our meeting in Room 201 next Wednesday at lunch.* (14) *We'll have pizza, and while we can't promise that it will be gourmet, at least it won't be old.* (15) *Do you need another reason?* (16) *Lots of history club members have been accepted at their first-choice college.*

22. In context, which is the best way to revise sentence 3 (reproduced here)?

    President Carter can read 2,000 words per minute with 95 percent comprehension.

    (A) Introduce the sentence with "Amazingly."

    (B) Rephrase it as a question.

    (C) Replace "comprehension" with "understanding."

    (D) Include the president's first name.

    (E) Include a full citation.

GO ON TO THE NEXT PAGE ▷

23. Which of the following would best replace "and" at the beginning of sentence 6?

    (A) Excepting this
    (B) Still
    (C) Therefore
    (D) But
    (E) As a result

24. Which of the following is the best way to revise and combine sentences 7 and 8 (reproduced below)?

    History club is for students with inquiring minds. It's for students who think understanding the past will make it easier to understand the present.

    (A) Inquiring mind students who think understanding the past will make it easier to understand the present are for history club.
    (B) History club is for students who, with inquiring minds, want to understand the past to understand the present.
    (C) History club is for students with inquiring minds who think understanding the past will make it easier to understand the present.
    (D) For students with inquiring minds, history club will make understanding the past easier to understand the present.
    (E) Understanding the past to understand the present, this is the inquiring that students of history club will do.

25. In context, the best phrase to replace "gives students the responsibility of picking" in sentence 11 is

    (A) allows students to explore and evaluate the contributions of contemporary historians.
    (B) allows students to have a lot of fun.
    (C) introduces students to different professionals working in the community.
    (D) helps students explore different historical theories about contemporary life.
    (E) makes it possible for students to share a meal with a real historian.

26. Which of the following is the best way to revise and combine sentences 12 and 13 (reproduced below)?

    Convinced? If you still have doubts, at least come by our meeting in Room 201 next Wednesday at lunch.

    (A) Convinced but still have doubts, at least come by our meeting in Room 201 next Wednesday at lunch.
    (B) Even if you are convinced, at least come by our meeting in Room 201 next Wednesday at lunch.
    (C) Even if you still have doubts about your convictions, at least come by our meeting in Room 201 next Wednesday at lunch.
    (D) Even if you still aren't convinced, at least come by our meeting in Room 201 next Wednesday at lunch.
    (E) Convinced and doubting, at least come by our meeting in Room 201 next Wednesday at lunch.

27. In context, which of the following revisions must be made to sentence 16 (reproduced here)?

    Lots of history club members have been accepted at their first-choice college.

    (A) Change "lots" to "many."
    (B) Make "college" plural.
    (C) Change "have been" to "were."
    (D) Remove the hyphen in "first-choice."
    (E) Change "accepted" to "excepted."

GO ON TO THE NEXT PAGE ⇒

KAPLAN

Questions 28–33 are based on the following passage.

(1) *I am writing to protest the zoo's decision to build Maggie, the elephant, a treadmill so that she will still be able to exercise during the long winter in Alaska.* (2) *This is a good plot for a surreal short story, while it is definitely not a good plan of action for an elephant.* (3) *Elephants are native to regions with warm temperatures.* (4) *They do not thrive in cold places.* (5) *Many zoos are beginning to recognize this fact.* (6) *The Baltimore Zoo, for example, is moving its elephants to a place where the temperature does not dip below 50 degrees.* (7) *Zookeepers recognize that elephants have particular needs.* (8) *Just as it would be unkind to expect polar bears to be happy spending summers in Florida, it's cruel to expect Asian elephants to weather cold winters.* (9) *In contrast, experts note that female elephants are social animals, and they need the company of other elephants.* (10) *Officials are not keeping Maggie's needs in mind by keeping her in a cage all by herself.* (11) *Maggie should be moved to a warm place where she can roam vast tracts of land with other elephants like her.* (12) *If you truly love animals, you should put their needs first.* (13) *I hope the zoo will take this into consideration.*

28. Which is the best version of the underlined portion of sentence 2 (reproduced below)?

    This is a good plot for a surreal short story, <u>while it is definitely not a good plan</u> of action for an elephant.

    (A) No change.
    (B) definitely not a good plan
    (C) and it is definitely not a good plan
    (D) but it is definitely not a good plan
    (E) being definitely not a good plan

29. Which of the following is the best way to revise and combine sentences 3 and 4 (reproduced below)?

    Elephants are native to regions with warm temperatures. They do not thrive in cold places.

    (A) Elephants are native to regions with warm temperatures, but they do not thrive in cold places.
    (B) Though they are native to regions with warm temperatures, elephants do not thrive in cold places.
    (C) Native to regions with warm temperatures, elephants do not thrive in cold places.
    (D) Elephants are native to regions with warm temperatures, not thriving in cold places.
    (E) Cold places do not thrive elephants because they are native to regions with warm temperatures.

30. Which of the following sentences could be deleted without affecting the clarity of the second paragraph?

    (A) Sentence 3
    (B) Sentence 4
    (C) Sentence 6
    (D) Sentence 7
    (E) Sentence 8

31. If added to sentence 6, which of the following pieces of information would clarify and strengthen the writer's argument?

    (A) The impact of temperatures lower than 50 degrees on elephants' health
    (B) The name of the new elephant exhibit
    (C) The number of elephants to be moved
    (D) The position of the new habitat within the zoo
    (E) The type of heating devices present in the new exhibit

GO ON TO THE NEXT PAGE ▷

32. How could the transition between the second and third paragraph be improved?

    (A) By discussing why elephants are social creatures

    (B) By providing a physical description of Maggie

    (C) By explaining what happened to the other elephants in the zoo

    (D) By specifying the size of Maggie's cage

    (E) By clarifying the impact of the zoo's plans on Maggie's physical well-being

33. Which of the following choices would best replace the underlined word in sentence 9? (reproduced below)

    In contrast, experts note that female elephants are social animals, and they need the company of other elephants.

    (A) Furthermore,

    (B) According to them,

    (C) Therefore,

    (D) Whereas,

    (E) Consequently,

Questions 34–39 refer to the following passage.

(1) _The American educator Horace Mann once said, "As an apple is not in any proper sense an apple until it is ripe, so a human being is not in any proper sense a human being until he is educated." (2) This may be true, but there are different ideas about what it means to be educated._

(3) _In prehistoric times, education revolved around learning practical skills. (4) Children are taught to farm, hunt, fish, and make tools by following the examples set for them by their elders. (5) They didn't have formal schooling, except before undergoing puberty rites when they needed to learn about tribal customs._

(6) _Education was rectifying morally and practical in colonial America. (7) If you were wealthy enough to attend elementary school, you could. (8) In school, you would learn reading, writing, and arithmetic alongside religion. (9) Although most poor children didn't attend school, the New England colonies tried to change this by passing a law in 1642 that said all children had to be taught to read, though the underlying reason for the_ decision was not purely altruistic. (10) _Public officials wanted to ensure that citizens developed good morals by reading the Scriptures._

(11) _Afterward, the emphasis of education changed again. (12) Science and commerce made learning more practical skills important. (13) People started academies that offered classes in history, geography, math, languages, and navigation. (14) This trend continued into the nineteenth century with growing public support for free education for students._

34. Which of the following sentences, if added after sentence 2, would best link the first paragraph with the rest of the essay?

    (A) No one can agree upon what it means to be educated.

    (B) How has education been viewed at different times in history?

    (C) What is the connection between apples and human minds?

    (D) Horace Mann was very influential in establishing public schools in the United States.

    (E) Education plays an important role in helping people develop their potential.

35. In the context of the second paragraph, which of the following is the best version of the underlined portion of sentence 4?

    Children are taught to farm, hunt, fish, and make tools by following the examples set for them by their elders.

    (A) No change.

    (B) Taught to farm, hunt, fish, and make tools, children

    (C) Farming, hunting, fishing, and making tools are taught to children

    (D) Children are taught farming, hunting, fishing, and making tools

    (E) Children were taught to farm, hunt, fish, and make tools

GO ON TO THE NEXT PAGE ⇨

KAPLAN

36. Which is the best version of the underlined portion of sentence 9 (reproduced below)?

    Although most poor children didn't attend school, the New England colonies tried to change this by passing a law in 1642 that said all children had to be taught to read, though the underlying reason for the decision was not purely altruistic.

    (A) No change.
    (B) the underlying reason for the decision not being purely altruistic
    (C) and the underlying reason for the decision was not purely altruistic
    (D) based upon not purely altruistic, underlying reasons for the decision
    (E) though the underlying reason and the decision were not purely altruistic

37. Which of the following is the best way to revise the underlined portions of sentences 7 and 8 (reproduced below) so that the two sentences are combined into one?

    If you were wealthy enough to attend elementary school, you could. In school, you would learn reading, writing, and arithmetic alongside religion.

    (A) could, but in school you would learn
    (B) could, and in school you would learn
    (C) would learn
    (D) learn
    (E) learning

38. In context, which is the best phrase to replace "afterward" in sentence 11?

    (A) Thereafter
    (B) Shortly later
    (C) By the middle of the next century
    (D) Sometime in the future
    (E) When the time was right

39. Which of the following is the best way to revise the underlined portion of sentence 6 (reproduced below)?

    Education was rectifying morally and practical in colonial America.

    (A) Rectifying morally, education was practical in colonial America.
    (B) In colonial America, education was both practical and morally rectifying.
    (C) Education was rectifying morally and, in colonial America, practical.
    (D) Practical and morally, education was rectifying in colonial America.
    (E) In colonial America, morally rectifying was practical education.

GO ON TO THE NEXT PAGE

Directions: The following sentences test your knowledge of effective and correct expression. Use the conventions of written English to choose your answer: pay attention to choice of words (diction), punctuation, sentence structure, and grammar.

In each of the following sentences, either the entire sentence or part of the sentence is underlined. There are five versions of the underlined portion below the sentence. Choice (A) is the same as the original sentence, and choices (B)–(E) are different.

Choose the answer that produces the best sentence with the same meaning as the original sentence. If none of the alternatives is as effective as the original sentence, choose (A). The final sentence should be precise and unambiguous.

40. Even though people know it can be extremely dangerous to talk on the phone while they drive, but many refuse to give up the habit.

    (A) Even though people know
    (B) While people know
    (C) People know
    (D) It is known to most people that
    (E) Knowing that

41. Some people claim the hamburger was invented in New Haven, Connecticut, in 1903 when the owner of a local lunch counter ground lean beef, broils it, and presented it between two slices of bread.

    (A) ground lean beef, broils it, and presented it
    (B) grinds lean beef, broils it, and presents it
    (C) ground lean beef, broiled it, and presented it
    (D) ground lean beef, broiled it, presenting it
    (E) grinds and broils lean beef, presenting it

42. The stories told about the role of Sacagawea in the Lewis and Clark expedition are most certainly exaggerated, though it is true that her presence as a woman and a mother signals that the group was on a peaceful mission.

    (A) her presence as a woman and a mother signals that the group was on a peaceful mission
    (B) her presence as a woman and a mother signals that the group is on a peaceful mission
    (C) her presence as a woman and a mother signaled that the group was on a peaceful mission
    (D) her presence as a woman and a mother, signaling that the group was on a peaceful mission
    (E) her presence as a woman and a mother was the signal that the group is on a peaceful mission

GO ON TO THE NEXT PAGE ▷

KAPLAN

43. The movie examines the antislavery movement and the fight for women's suffrage, <u>and it shows how the</u> first gave rise to the second and eventually helped the United States live up to the promises of the Constitution.

   (A) and it shows how the
   (B) and it showed how the
   (C) thus by showing how the
   (D) nevertheless showing how the
   (E) showing how the

44. "Art for art's sake" was the slogan of the late nineteenth-century Aesthetic Movement, <u>which placed their emphasis</u> on beauty and art's potential to please.

   (A) which placed their emphasis
   (B) which emphasized
   (C) placing their emphasis
   (D) and it placed their emphasis
   (E) the placing of their emphasis

45. <u>The pilot announced to them that he would be collecting them, and it would help the flight attendant if the passengers passed the headphones towards the aisle.</u>

   (A) The pilot announced to them that he would be collecting them, and it would help the flight attendant if the passengers passed the headphones towards the aisle.
   (B) The pilot announced to the passengers that the flight attendant would be collecting the headphones, and it would help the flight attendant if they passed them towards the aisle.
   (C) The pilot announced to headphones that he would be collecting the passengers, and it would help the flight attendant if the passengers passed the headphones towards the aisle.
   (D) The pilot announced to the flight attendant that he would be collecting the headphones, and it would help the passengers if they passed the headphones towards the aisle.
   (E) Announcing to them that he would be collecting the headphones, the pilot said it would help the flight attendant if they passed them towards the aisle.

GO ON TO THE NEXT PAGE

Directions: The following questions test your knowledge and use of research source materials. Some of the questions are based on single entries; others refer to passages provided. In the passage-based sets, Revision Skills and Rhetorical Analysis Skills may also be tested.

46. To what kind of resource does this citation refer?

    "For I must love because I live/And life in me is what you give." (Brennan, lines 15–16)

    (A) Poem

    (B) Speech

    (C) Newspaper

    (D) Magazine

    (E) Website

47. The following citation ends with a raised number. What does that kind of citation mean?

    "The five stages of grief are denial, anger, bargaining, depression, and acceptance."[1]

    (A) This citation is the first quotation in the document.

    (B) This citation will appear first in the writer's bibliography.

    (C) This citation appears on page one of the original publication.

    (D) The source of the quotation will be cited in a footnote or endnote.

    (E) The line earned first place in a contest of quotations.

48. What about the format of this entry indicates it is a footnote or endnote?

    1. Elisabeth Kübler-Ross, *On Death and Dying* (New York: Macmillan, 1969) 45–60.

    (A) The author's name is hyphenated.

    (B) The entry begins with a number.

    (C) The title of the book is in italics.

    (D) The city where the book was published is included.

    (E) The entry ends with a period.

49. The number 59 in this bibliographic entry indicates which piece of information listed below?

    Van Heuvelen, A., *American Journal of Physics* 59, 891 (1991).

    (A) The source has several publication dates.

    (B) This is the page number for a quotation.

    (C) The citation is from paragraph 59 of a source by Van Heuvelen.

    (D) The *American Journal of Physics* was first produced in 1959.

    (E) The citation comes from volume 59 of the journal.

GO ON TO THE NEXT PAGE

50. What type of document or presentation is cited below?

E. F. Redish, in *The Proceedings of the Enrico Fermi Summer School in Physics, Course CLVI*, edited by E. Redish, C. Tarsitani, and M. Vicentini (Italian Physical Society, 42 Via Antolini, Florence, Italy, 2004).

(A) Speech
(B) Book chapter
(C) Journal introduction
(D) Newspaper
(E) Poem

51. The citations for the three endnotes/footnotes below should be organized in what order?

A. Collins, J. S. Brown, and S. E. Newman, in *Knowing, Learning, and Instruction.*

Essays in Honor of Robert Glaser, edited by L. B. Resnick (Lawrence Erlbaum Associates, Hillsdale, New Jersey, 1989), pp. 453–494.

N. Nersessian, in *Reading Natural Philosophy: Essays in the History and Philosophy of Science and Mathematics*, edited by D. B. Malament (Open Court, Chicago and La Salle, Illinois, 2002), pp. 129–166.

M. B. Hesse, *Models and Analogies in Science* (University of Notre Dame Press, Notre Dame, Indiana, 1966).

(A) Alphabetically by first word in the entry
(B) Chronologically by date of publication
(C) Alphabetically of type of publication
(D) Numbered in order of their use in the writing
(E) Chronologically in order of the time the writer accessed the resources

Questions 52–59 refer to the following passage.

Noise More Than a Nuisance

(1) *All told, more than 100 million Americans are regularly exposed to noise levels in excess of the 55 decibels that federal agencies have recommended as the reasonable background intensity (Weiss 2007). (2) It is well documented that those who work in noisy environments—avionics mechanics, for example—are many times more likely to suffer hearing loss than those who work in quiet areas (Suter 1991). (3) Studies have also shown that children tend to be more irritable when in noisy environments, as well as more prone to developing nervous disorders when subjected to high levels of noise for extended periods. (4) Noise is more than a nuisance because it can cause health issues and emotional unrest, but you can reduce these detrimental effects with knowledge and action.*

(5) *Noise at high decibels can damage one's hearing. (6) Sound, which is measured on a logarithmic scale in units called* decibels, *travels through the air in what are referred to as longitudinal waves, which compress the air in the direction the wave is traveling (Candler 2007). (7) These waves enter the ear and cause vibrations in tiny, delicate bones, membranes, and hairs within the ear. (8) The waves are then converted into electrical signals that are transmitted to the brain. (9) Exposure to sound waves of a high intensity for an extended duration can cause irregularities in the tiny hairs located within the inner ear. (10) If these hairs become damaged, then hearing will become mildly impaired (Timar 2007), and if the hairs begin to detach from their follicles, then severe hearing loss will occur.*

(11) *So what is a safe level of noise? (12) The truth is that noise at any level can have an impact on one's emotions, even if it is not loud enough to induce hearing loss. (13) Continued exposure to certain sounds may cause nervousness, which can have substantial health effects over the long term. (14) In one study, two groups of participants—one consisting of people living near airports and the other consisting of those who live away from aircraft noise—responded differently to a questionnaire relating to quality-of-life issues. (15) "Aircraft noise, in contrast to other bothersome noises, interfered more*

GO ON TO THE NEXT PAGE ⇒

frequently with daily activities. (16) Subjects who were bothered by aircraft noise were more likely to complain of sleep difficulties and more likely to perceive themselves to be in poorer health" (Bronzaft 1998). (17) Persistent noise can cause various forms of irritation, such as upset stomach and chronic stress, both of which reduce one's ability to concentrate, decrease performance levels at work, and contribute to long-term nervous disorders.

(18) One can do many things to reduce the harmful effects of noise. (19) Dr. Marion Hilnick insists, "Simple avoidance is one key method of prevention." (20) The less often a person is exposed to intense noise, the better off she will be. (21) If one must enter a noisy area, then it is advisable to limit the amount of time spent there. (22) If one must remain in such an area for an extended time, then the best way to prevent health problems is to wear earplugs or protective muffs. (23) Those who fear they have already experienced some hearing loss should visit a hearing specialist and take a diagnostic test to determine the extent of the damage. (24) Consult your doctor for further ways to mitigate hearing loss and other negative consequences of noise. (25) With the proper precautions, you can begin to protect yourself today.

Sources Consulted

Bronzaft, PhD, Arline L., K. D. Ahern, R. McGinn, and B. Savino. "Aircraft Noise: A Potential Health Hazard." Environment and Behavior. Jan. 1998: 101–13. 20 Oct. 2007 http://areco.org/noise.htm.

Candler, Rob. "Introduction to Sensors." Stanford University. May 2007. Mechanical Engineering Department. 20 Oct. 2007 http://www.stanford.edu/class/me220/data/lectures/lect01/lect_1.html.

"noise." The Free Dictionary. Farlex, 2007. 20 Oct. 2007 http://www.thefreedictionary.com/noise.

Suter, PhD, Alice H. "Noise and Its Effects." Noise Pollution Clearing House. Nov. 1991. 20 Oct. 2007 http://www.nonoise.org/library/suter/suter.htm#numbers.

Timar, Gabriel S. "Effects of Noise." 20 Oct. 2007 http://www.areco.org/EFFECTS%20OF%20NOISE.doc.

Weiss, Rick. "Noise Pollution Takes Toll on Health and Happiness." Washington Post Online 5 June 2007: HE05. 20 Oct. 2007 http://www.washingtonpost.com/wp-dyn/content/article/2007/06/04/AR2007060401430_pf.html.

52. What does the underlined part of the following citation refer to?

Bronzaft, Ph.D, Arline L., K. D. Ahern, R. McGinn, and B. Savino. "Aircraft Noise: A Potential Health Hazard." Environment and Behavior. Jan. 1998: 101–13. 20 Oct. 2007 http://areco.org/noise.htm.

(A) Journal title

(B) Article title

(C) Name of website

(D) Article topic

(E) Newspaper title

53. The information in parentheses in sentence 10 informs the reader that

(A) the sentence is a direct quote from a source written by Timar.

(B) Timar conducted research on the general effects of noise.

(C) Timar has published a work discussing different levels of hearing loss.

(D) Timar has published a work discussing mild hearing impairment.

(E) *Timar* is another word for mild hearing impairment.

GO ON TO THE NEXT PAGE

KAPLAN

54. In the citation reproduced below, what do the two dates indicate?

Weiss, Rick. "Noise Pollution Takes Toll on Health and Happiness." <u>Washington Post Online.</u> 5 June 2007: HE05. 20 Oct. 2007 http://www.washingtonpost.com/wp-dyn/content/article/2007/06/04/AR2007060401430_pf.html.

(A) The first date is the first printing; the second is the second printing.

(B) The first date is when the article was published in print; the second is when it was published to the Web.

(C) The first date is when the writer of this article accessed the article; the second is when the article was chosen for this list of sources.

(D) The first date is when the article was written; the second is when it was published by the newspaper.

(E) The first date is when the article was published; the second is when the writer of this article accessed it.

55. Which of the writers named in the Sources Consulted list most likely wrote about how to measure noise levels?

(A) Arline L. Bronzaft, PhD

(B) Alice H. Suter, PhD

(C) Gabriel S. Timar

(D) Rick Weiss

(E) Rob Candler

56. The author of the passage quotes the text by Bronzaft, Ahern, McGinn, and Savino in sentences 15 and 16 most likely in order to

(A) provide evidential support for the claim made earlier in the paragraph.

(B) suggest that it is unfair that some people must live near the airport.

(C) point out that environmental noise is extremely dangerous.

(D) promote further study of the effects of noise.

(E) illustrate the need for public awareness of noise damage.

57. Which is best to do with sentence 19 (reproduced here)?

Dr. Marion Hilnick insists, "Simple avoidance is one key method of prevention."

(A) Leave it as it is.

(B) Paraphrase Dr. Hilnick's statement instead of quoting it directly.

(C) Add information in parentheses that elaborates on Dr. Hilnick's claim.

(D) Provide Dr. Hilnick's credentials as a doctor.

(E) Add a citation indicating the source of the quotation from Dr. Hilnick.

58. What is the purpose of the last paragraph (sentences 18–25)?

(A) It provides a contrast to the other information given in the essay.

(B) It expands on the thesis.

(C) It refutes an earlier assumption.

(D) It serves as a transition to another discussion.

(E) It provides evidence in support of the previous paragraph.

59. What is the correct way to organize the bibliography using the resources listed in "Sources Consulted"?

(A) In order by type of resource materials

(B) Alphabetically by title of book

(C) From oldest to newest publication date

(D) Chronologically by the date the resource was viewed

(E) The present order is correct.

GO ON TO THE NEXT PAGE ⇒

Questions 60–63 refer to the following passage.

(1) *Although it comprises only 2 percent of the human body's average weight, the billions of neurons and trillions of synaptic connections that are the human brain constitute a truly impressive organ.* (2) *In terms of what it can do, the human brain is in some ways unable to match the brain functioning of "lower" animals; in other ways, its capabilities are quite unrivaled.* (3) *Salmon, caribou, and migrating birds, for example, have navigational abilities unparalleled in our own species, and even dogs and cats have senses of hearing and smell known only, in human form, to comic book superheroes.* (4) *Yet no other animal on the planet can communicate, solve problems, or think abstractly about itself and the future as we do.* (5) *While these relative strengths and weaknesses can be attributed to the unique and complex structure of the human brain, neuroscientists also have traced these characteristics to the human brain's remarkable flexibility, or what researchers call plasticity (Rogers 2003).*

(6) *Encased in a hard, protective skull that by the age of two is already 80 percent of its eventual adult size, the human brain has little room for size expansion even while the rest of the body, especially during adolescence, is experiencing significant changes in physical appearance.* (7) *Nevertheless, the human brain's plasticity allows for marked capacity changes because of usage, practice, and experience throughout one's entire life.* (8) *The human brain continues to develop and, some might say, improve over the course of one's life.* (9) *According to researcher Jessica McGovern, "Those who experience a wider range of stimulus develop heavier, thicker brains with more complex neural circuitry and more synaptic connections.* (10) *One's life experiences and environment not only mold the brain's particular architecture but also can continue to spark the expansion of its capacity to function."*

References

McGovern, J. 2005. The Most Powerful Computer. *Neurology Monthly* 119 (3): 189–192.

Rogers, M. 2003. *The Structure and Plasticity of the Human Brain.* New Brunswick, NJ: Rutgers University Press.

60. Which of the following is cited in sentence 5?

    (A) Book
    (B) Journal
    (C) Academic essay
    (D) Newspaper article
    (E) Lecture

61. A citation is missing from sentence 10. What is the proper format for the citation?

    (A) (The Most Powerful Computer 2005)
    (B) (McGovern, J.)
    (C) (McGovern 2005)
    (D) (*Neurology Monthly*, vol. 113)
    (E) (2005, 164–172)

62. The first item in the References section indicates all of the following EXCEPT that

    (A) "The Most Powerful Computer" is an article in a periodical.
    (B) *Neurology Monthly* is published more than once per year.
    (C) "The Most Powerful Computer" appears on page 119 of *Neurology Monthly*.
    (D) "The Most Powerful Computer" is around four pages long.
    (E) "The Most Powerful Computer" was written by J. McGovern.

63. The writer could best increase the reader's understanding of this passage by

    (A) giving examples of the brain sizes of different species.
    (B) clarifying the terms *neural circuitry* and *synaptic connections.*
    (C) providing a list of games for improving brain function.
    (D) giving the exact dimensions of the brain at age two.
    (E) providing the researchers' credentials.

GO ON TO THE NEXT PAGE ⟩

KAPLAN

Questions 64–68 are based on the following passage.

(1) *While Venus is commonly called Earth's sister planet, its proximity to the Sun causes surface temperatures of 900 degrees Fahrenheit, too hot to support life.*[1] *(2) Alternately, due to distance from the Sun, every planet past Mars is too cold. (3) Thus, Mars is the only planet in our solar system, other than Earth, that might be able to support life. (4) While many scientists believe that life may have existed on Mars in the past, some are now beginning to believe that human life may be able to exist there in the future, but not without earthly intervention.*[2] *(5) Scientists have long envisioned human colonization of Mars in space station–like enclosed structures, but some are now beginning to believe in the possibility of altering the Martian climate and atmosphere to create an Earth-like world where humans can live unencumbered by pressurized suits or structures. (6) These scientists point out that before it supported life, Earth was, like Mars, a desolate, uninhabitable planet devoid of oxygen. (7) This situation changed only with the evolution of photosynthetic bacteria that absorb carbon dioxide from the atmosphere and release oxygen back into it. (8) These scientists postulate that a similar catalyst could be used to transform the Martian atmosphere into one inhabitable by humans.*[3]

Notes

[1] "Mars: Our Next Home?" *Journal of Astronomy* 68.2 (2006): 22.

[2] Ibid., 28

[3] Terraforming could take decades, if not centuries or even millennia, and involve technology not yet developed.

64. In the Notes section, what does "Ibid." mean?

(A) There is no source for the citation.

(B) Ibid is the name of the author of the source cited.

(C) The citation comes from the same source as mentioned in the previous note.

(D) The author is known, but not the publication.

(E) The source is a Latin text.

65. How could sentence 2 best be expanded?

(A) Include specific temperature data for Mars.

(B) Give the distance between Earth and Mars.

(C) List the other planets in the solar system.

(D) Describe the landscape on Mars.

(E) Discuss the composition of the atmosphere on Mars.

66. What is missing from note 1?

(A) Page number

(B) Year of publication

(C) Author name

(D) Journal editor name

(E) Journal volume number

67. Which of the following best describes the purpose of sentence 6 (reproduced here)?

These scientists point out that before it supported life, Earth was, like Mars, a desolate, uninhabitable planet devoid of oxygen.

(A) To point out the difference between the two planets

(B) To predict what Earth will be like in the future

(C) To give background information about Mars

(D) To give evidence of the possibility of cultivating life on Mars

(E) To explain why Mars is unlikely to support life

68. Note 3 could be clarified by

(A) adding a source citation.

(B) defining *terraforming*.

(C) describing the technology used for terraforming.

(D) discussing the climatic effects of terraforming.

(E) noting the cost of terraforming.

GO ON TO THE NEXT PAGE

Directions: The passages below consist of numbered sentences. Read each passage and answer the questions below it. These questions test how effectively you can analyze a piece of writing.

Questions 69–73 are based on the following passage.

(1) *These passages raise the issue of "travel class consciousness," a phrase coined by Mark Cocker.* (2) *Travel class consciousness, according to Cocker, refers to travel writers' concern with differentiating themselves from other travelers and tourists whose presence threatens their sense of originality and pluckiness; this consciousness is expressed both intratextually and intertextually, for travel writers are equally concerned with their position with regard to other authors.* (3) *The reason is quite simple: the genre of the travel narrative can't appear too formulaic.* (4) *Whereas tourists can relax and follow the routes plotted for them in their guidebooks, travelers, especially travel writers, eschew guides and are driven, instead, by a need to discover wonders and exotica in places far off the well-trodden path.* (5) *Women travelers are no exception.* (6) *In her tale of bicycling from Kenya to Zimbabwe,* The Ukimwi Road, *Dervla Murphy cites and dismisses all other female-authored accounts of life in East Africa.* (7) *In her account of visiting China, Julia Kristeva wonders, at one point, whether tourists know the schedule of the train passing by and who is riding on it.* (8) *Finally, Robyn Davidson, author of* Tracks, *constantly worries about whether the Aborigines whom she meets on her journey by camel through the desert heart of Australia consider her a traveler or a tourist.*

69. This paragraph is most likely written for

    (A) women who are interested in exploring East Africa, China, and Australia.

    (B) the authors of travel narratives who want to make their stories more engaging.

    (C) experts on world politics who are gathering information on the economies of foreign countries.

    (D) literary theorists who study and explore issues of representation in different types of writing.

    (E) tourists who want to explore areas off the well-trodden path.

70. Which of the following best describes the relationship of sentence 2 to the rest of the paragraph?

    (A) It describes the author's personal experience, which the paragraph will further explore.

    (B) It offers an idea that will be refuted in the rest of the paragraph.

    (C) It establishes the organization for the paragraph as a whole.

    (D) It presents an idea that the rest of the paragraph will explore.

    (E) It describes how all travel writers feel.

71. Which of the following best describes the function of sentence 3?

    (A) It explains why travel writers demonstrate "travel class consciousness."

    (B) It suggests the difference between travelers and tourists.

    (C) It alludes to the difficulty of writing a travel narrative.

    (D) It asks readers to evaluate the travel narratives they have read.

    (E) It provides an example of "travel class consciousness" in a travel narrative.

72. In sentence 4, the effect of using "Whereas" is to

    (A) explain further the idea of travel class consciousness by referring back to it.

    (B) differentiate between the goals of tourists and travel writers.

    (C) prepare the reader for examples of how travel writers express their individuality.

    (D) reveal the author's disdain for tourists who depend on guidebooks.

    (E) emphasize the differences between guidebooks, which point people toward known sites, and travel narratives, which describe unfamiliar places.

GO ON TO THE NEXT PAGE ⟩

73. The function of sentence 6 is primarily to

    (A) introduce the evidence of "travel class consciousness" that follows in sentences 7 and 8.

    (B) present a specific example of a travel writer's attempt to distinguish herself from other tourists.

    (C) provide an example of a travel writer's concern for her originality relative to that of other travel writers.

    (D) show why Dervla Murphy's account of her travels in East Africa is superior to other written accounts.

    (E) illustrate the concept of "travel class consciousness" by interviewing a travel writer.

Questions 74–79 are based on the following passage.

(1) *There is one fact about the origin of life that is reasonably certain.* (2) *Whenever and wherever it happened, it started a very long time ago, so long ago that it is extremely difficult to form any realistic idea of such vast stretches of time.* (3) *The shortness of human life necessarily limits the span of direct personal recollection.*

(4) *Human culture has given us the illusion that our memories go further back than that.* (5) *Before writing was invented, the experience of earlier generations, embodied in stories, myths, and moral precepts to guide behavior, was passed down verbally or, to a lesser extent, in pictures, carvings, and statues.* (6) *Writing has made more precise and more extensive the transmission of such information and, in recent times, photography has sharpened our images of the immediate past.* (7) *Even so, we have difficulty in contemplating the steady march of history, from the beginnings of civilization to the present day, in such a way that we can truly experience the slow passage of time.* (8) *Our minds are not built to deal comfortably with periods as long as hundreds or thousands of years.*

(9) *When we come to consider the origin of life, the time scales we must deal with make the whole span of human history seem but the blink of an eyelid.* (10) *There is no simple way to adjust one's thinking to such vast stretches of time.* (11) *The immensity of time passed is beyond our ready comprehension.* (12) *One can only construct an impression of it from indirect and incomplete descriptions, just as a blind man laboriously builds up, by touch and sound, a picture of his immediate surroundings.*

(13) *One customary way to provide a convenient framework for one's thoughts is to equate the age of our earth with a single week.* (14) *On such a scale the age of the universe, since the Big Bang, would be about two or three weeks.* (15) *The oldest macroscopic fossils (those from the start of the Cambrian Period) would have been alive just one day ago.* (16) *Modern man would have appeared in the last ten seconds and agriculture in the last one or two.* (17) *Odysseus would have lived only half a second before the present time.*

(18) *Even this comparison hardly makes the longer time scale comprehensible to us.* (19) *Another alternative is to compare time to lines of print.* (20) *Let us make a 200-page book equal in length to the time from the start of the Cambrian to the present—that is, about 600 million years.* (21) *Then each full page will represent roughly 3 million years, each line about 90,000 years, and each letter or small space about 1,500 years.* (22) *The origin of the Earth would be about seven books ago and the origin of the universe (which has been dated only approximately) ten or so books before that.* (23) *Almost the whole of recorded human history would be covered by the last two or three letters of the book.*

(24) *If you now turn back the pages of the book, slowly reading one letter at a time—remember, each letter is 1,500 years—then this may convey to you something of the immense stretches of time we shall have to consider.* (25) *On this scale the span of your own life would be less than the width of a comma.*

74. The author most likely describes the impact of writing in sentence 6 in order to

    (A) illustrate an earlier point.

    (B) provide a frame of reference.

    (C) refute an assumption.

    (D) detail the origins of an innovative practice.

    (E) introduce a new topic for discussion.

GO ON TO THE NEXT PAGE ⟩

KAPLAN

75. In context, which of the following transitions would be appropriate at the beginning of sentence 9 (reproduced here)?

    When we come to consider the origin of life, the time scales we must deal with make the whole span of human history seem but the blink of an eyelid.

    (A) Yet
    (B) Consequently
    (C) And
    (D) By extension,
    (E) Therefore

76. In context, the word "ready" in sentence 11 most nearly means

    (A) set.
    (B) agreeable.
    (C) immediate.
    (D) apt.
    (E) willing.

77. Sentence 11 primarily serves to

    (A) restate an earlier point.
    (B) expand on the thesis.
    (C) refute an assumption.
    (D) set up a theme.
    (E) relate the theme to a forthcoming analogy.

78. The author's primary purpose in mentioning the analogy of the "blind man" in sentence 12 is to show that

    (A) humans are unable to comprehend long periods of time.
    (B) myths and legends fail to give an accurate picture of the past.
    (C) human history is only a fraction of the time since life began.
    (D) humans refuse to learn the lessons of the past.
    (E) long periods of time can only be understood indirectly.

79. In sentences 14 and 15, the references to the Big Bang and the Cambrian Period serve to

    (A) illustrate that the age of the Earth can be understood using the time scale of a week.
    (B) suggest that agriculture was a relatively late development in human history.
    (C) argue that no existing fossils predate the Cambrian Period.
    (D) indicate that the Cambrian Period lasted 600 million years.
    (E) argue that the customary framework for thinking about the age of the universe should be discarded permanently.

Questions 80–85 refer to the following passage.

(1) *In the beginning of* Desert Solitaire, *Edward Abbey writes, "This is the most beautiful place on earth.* (2) *There are many such places.* (3) *Every man, every woman, carries in heart and mind the image of the ideal place, the right place, the one true home, known or unknown, actual or visionary."* (4) *To others it may look overgrown, but outside my window is my ideal place.*

(5) *The garden is an oasis in this city, a quiet hidden paradise that seems miles away from the concert of car horns and the clip-clop of passing pedestrians and the hungry yips of dogs returning from their romps.* (6) *There is no order here.* (7) *The aristocratic roses mingle with the common sunflowers, native grasses surround a clump of delicate African violets, the hardy apple tree is weighted down with hanging pots of delicate things.* (8) *What the garden lacks in rhyme or reason, it wholly compensates for with surprise.* (9) *Tucked into the corner is a jar of orange guppies, but you must look carefully to see them through the green seaweed.* (10) *The jay has a twig holder of beautiful blue eggs and fiercely protects them from the prowling cat.* (11) *The hummingbirds torpedo forth from who-knows-where and then defy physics by standing still in the air.* (12) *The squirrels tuck their peanuts into flowerpots, chirping madly when the whereabouts of their next meal slips their small minds.*

(13) *This garden.* (14) *I could spend many afternoons there, and I would still discover something new, a tender green shoot, a flower in its last throes of splendor, a strawberry or a tomato patiently ripening in the sun.*

GO ON TO THE NEXT PAGE

80. Which of the following most accurately describes what happens in the second paragraph?

    (A) The author tries to escape the stress of city life by retreating to the chaos of her garden.
    (B) The author depicts the idiosyncrasies of her garden to show how beauty is relative.
    (C) The author describes her garden in an attempt to convince everyone that it should be his or her ideal place.
    (D) The author conjures up an imaginary garden that she wishes were real.
    (E) The author explains why we must accept chaos and disorder as a necessary part of life.

81. The descriptive details in sentence 5 provide

    (A) an evocation of different senses.
    (B) a description of the neighborhood.
    (C) a sense of the city's noisiness.
    (D) a depiction of urban decay.
    (E) a view from the window of the house.

82. The purpose of sentence 7 is to

    (A) catalog all of the different plants in the garden.
    (B) substantiate the claim made in sentence 6.
    (C) refute the generalization made in sentence 6.
    (D) engage the reader's senses.
    (E) describe the author's one true home.

83. Which of the following best characterizes the author's reaction to her garden?

    (A) Laziness and interest
    (B) Delight and confusion
    (C) Complacency and wonder
    (D) Wonder and curiosity
    (E) Interest and fatigue

84. According to the passage, what is the relationship among the creatures, plants, and objects in the garden?

    (A) They are isolated from one another.
    (B) The plants are the most social elements.
    (C) The creatures help each other to find food.
    (D) There are various interactions among them.
    (E) They are mostly dormant at night.

85. Which of the following is the best description of the overall organization of this passage?

    (A) The second paragraph offers a personal example to support the idea described in the first.
    (B) The second paragraph actively refutes the idea offered in the first.
    (C) The second paragraph continues generalizing about the idea described in the first.
    (D) The second paragraph offers an analysis of the idea put forth in the first.
    (E) The second paragraph goes off on a tangent, offering little that is related to the first.

GO ON TO THE NEXT PAGE

KAPLAN

Question 86–90 refer to the following excerpt.

(1) *Reading, I have found, is a superb way to learn to do things in new and different ways.* (2) *This has been my way of learning about life in other times and in other places.* (3) *In fact, for years I was a historical fiction buff.* (4) *I'd read romance stories set in Regency England—the early 1800s.* (5) *In the mid-1970s, I lived in the northernmost tip of Maine where it is cold and snowy for much of the winter—usually from early October to mid-April or May.* (6) *We had a fireplace in which we kept a fire burning most evenings.* (7) *My husband and I generally liked to sleep in a cool house, but I frequently complained that my feet were too cold.*

(8) *Fine, you say, but what's the connection between my reading historical fiction, fireplaces, and cold feet?* (9) *Keep listening to my story.* (10) *During the 1800s there was no central heating, even in the castles and inns frequented by the wealthy.* (11) *However, few suffered from cold feet when they went to bed.* (12) *You see, the kindly host or hostess would keep warming stones in the fireplaces; the chambermaids would wrap these heated stones in flannel cloths and put them at the foot of the beds of those respected guests.* (13) *Sometimes the maids would use metal warming pans; they would slide the warmed pans up and down the sheets to warm them before the nobles retired for the night.*

(14) *Warming pans.* (15) *Rocks warmed in the fireplace.* (16) *"A-ha!" I thought.* (17) *I have cold feet.* (18) *I have a fireplace and plenty of rocks in my garden.* (19) *I'll do what I've learned in my reading.* (20) *So, for several cold nights, I warmed the rocks in the fireplace while the fire burned between dinner and bedtime.* (21) *I'd carefully remove the rocks, wrap them in a flannel baby blanket and use the rock to warm my own cold feet.* (22) *When I would get into bed, I would flip the rocks over and over to keep my feet warm until I went to sleep.* (23) *It was great and it was inexpensive.* (24) *That is, until one particular night.*

86. Which of the following transition words or phrases, if inserted at the beginning of sentence 5 (reproduced below), would be most logical in the context of the passage?

In the mid-1970s, I lived in the northernmost tip of Maine where it is cold and snowy for much of the winter—usually from early October to mid-April or May.

(A) Furthermore,

(B) In retrospect,

(C) Now,

(D) Consequently,

(E) Therefore,

87. Which of the following is the best description of the overall organization of this passage?

(A) A method for solving a problem is described, and an anecdote is given that refutes it.

(B) A theme is established, and an anecdote is begun in order to illustrate that theme.

(C) A problem is introduced, and a solution is considered.

(D) A historical period is described and contrasted with the present day.

(E) A question is raised and then answered.

88. Which of the following best describes the purpose of sentences 8 and 9?

(A) To summarize key ideas already mentioned

(B) To introduce ideas the speech will address later

(C) To recap the ideas mentioned in the first paragraph

(D) To draw the audience members into the speech and keep them listening for the answer to the question

(E) To provide historical evidence

GO ON TO THE NEXT PAGE

KAPLAN)

89. In context, sentences 10–13 serve to

    (A) justify actions the speaker describes in the next paragraph.

    (B) describe the home in which speaker lives.

    (C) narrate how the speaker's grandparents warmed their home.

    (D) convince the speaker's audience to imitate her speaker.

    (E) discuss the value of hospitality in the 1800s.

90. Sentence 24 (reproduced here) primarily serves to do which of the following?

    That is, until one particular night.

    (A) Change the subject.

    (B) Create suspense.

    (C) Further the speaker's argument.

    (D) Remind the audience of the main idea.

    (E) Evoke doubt.

END OF TEST. STOP

THE ANSWER KEY APPEARS ON THE FOLLOWING PAGE.

ANSWER KEY

1.	B	16.	C	31.	A	46.	A	61.	C
2.	A	17.	D	32.	E	47.	D	62.	C
3.	B	18.	C	33.	A	48.	B	63.	B
4.	C	19.	C	34.	B	49.	E	64.	C
5.	D	20.	D	35.	E	50.	A	65.	A
6.	E	21.	E	36.	A	51.	D	66.	C
7.	C	22.	B	37.	C	52.	A	67.	D
8.	D	23.	D	38.	C	53.	D	68.	B
9.	E	24.	C	39.	B	54.	E	69.	D
10.	B	25.	A	40.	C	55.	E	70.	D
11.	B	26.	D	41.	C	56.	A	71.	A
12.	A	27.	B	42.	C	57.	E	72.	B
13.	E	28.	D	43.	E	58.	B	73.	C
14.	D	29.	C	44.	B	59.	E	74.	B
15.	E	30.	D	45.	B	60.	A	75.	A

76.	C
77.	A
78.	E
79.	A
80.	B
81.	C
82.	B
83.	D
84.	D
85.	A
86.	C
87.	B
88.	D
89.	A
90.	B

DIAGNOSTIC TEST QUICK REFERENCE TABLES

Use the following tables to determine which topics you need to review most.

Topic	Test Question
Conventions of Standard Written English	1–9
Revision Skills	10–39
*Improving Sentences**	40–45
Ability to Use Source Materials**	46–68
Rhetorical Analysis	69–90

* Only found on the College Composition Modular exam

** In Ability to Use Source Materials questions, the elements tested under Revision Skills and Rhetorical Analysis may be tested.

Topic	Number of Questions on Test	Number Correct
Conventions of Standard Written English	9	
Revision Skills	30	
*Improving Sentences**	6	
Ability to Use Source Materials**	23	
Rhetorical Analysis	22	

* Only found on the College Composition Modular exam

** In Ability to Use Source Materials questions, the elements tested under Revision Skills and Rhetorical Analysis may be tested.

KAPLAN

Answers and Explanations

1. (B)

The sentence, as it appears, is incomplete because the verb "is" is part of a subordinate clause modifying "the button." The main clause's verb ("was") is preceded by an unnecessary conjunction ("and"). To correct the mistake, the conjunction "and" should be eliminated. The phrase "was originally viewed" will then serve as the predicate.

2. (A)

All the pronouns in a sentence must agree. Here the pronoun shifts from the second person ("you") to the third person ("the person," "him- or herself").

3. (B)

Comparisons must be written in similar grammatical form. In this sentence, which compares video games to television, the first comparison is written as a phrase ("playing video games") while the second is written as a noun ("television"). To make the comparison parallel, they should be grammatically alike. Therefore, you would write: "playing video games is no better than watching television…."

4. (C)

Pronouns must agree with their antecedents (the nouns that they are replacing). In this sentence, "they" is replacing the noun, "police headquarters." Although "police headquarters" appears to be plural, it is actually singular because it refers to a single place. "They" should be "it."

5. (D)

This sentence refers to two different times: Mrs. Aljriha's teaching over the last twenty years and her recent decision to apply for a job as school administrator. Because Mrs. Aljriha's decision is not ongoing, the verb phrase ("has been deciding") should be written in the present perfect tense ("has decided").

6. (E)

"That" refers to "quality of life" (in the United States). Therefore, the sentence is parallel and there is no error. You may be tempted to choose (B), "is poorer," because you may want to substitute "more poor," but the term "poorer" is correct.

7. (C)

Verbs must always agree with subjects. Intervening words—such as the prepositional phrase "of the men and women who settled the frontier"—should not be confused with the subject. In this case, since the subject is singular ("the adventurous spirit"), the verb should be singular as well ("has" instead of "have").

8. (D)

A compound sentence can often be simplified, especially if the second independent clause in the compound sentence describes some part of the first. In this question, the clause "and it takes finely tuned coordination and strength" describes diving. Therefore, "that" could be used instead of "and" to make it a dependent clause.

9. (E)

This sentence is correct as written. The verb "was" agrees with its subject "professor" and makes sense with the other past tense verb in the sentence. "Whole" correctly modifies "class." "Any students" is idiomatically correct to use with "scarcely." "Written" is the correct form for the past participle.

10. (B)

Since these two sentences share the same subject, "students," it's easy to combine them by eliminating the subject in the second sentence and adding a conjunction ("and"). Choice (A) is incorrect because the two sentences do not contradict each other, and therefore "but" is inappropriate. Choice (C) doesn't make sense, (D) is wordy, and (E) is in the wrong tense.

11. (B)

The final sentence in a paragraph has two purposes: to summarize and serve as a bridge to the next paragraph. Since the second paragraph deals with students who have no other choice but to eat in the cafeteria, (B) is best. Choice (A) isn't a good choice because its scope is too limited. Choices (C), (D), and (E) offer random bits of information that don't add anything to the letter.

12. (A)

Since the audience for this letter is the principal, the writer probably wants to use fairly formal language that will appeal to a person in a position of authority. That means (B), (C), (D), and (E) aren't appropriate since they're emotional, inflammatory, and not objective. In contrast, choice (A) sounds more objective.

13. (E)

The letter mentions ketchup only in passing, so choice (A) fails to convey logically the topic of the letter as a whole. Those nutritional issues (B) the writer mentions are only part of the discussion; economic inequalities are also discussed, as well as the writer's general displeasure at the unappetizing nature of the food. The writer does not provide tips for better eating (C)—this is a discussion of the failings of the cafeteria food. Not all of the students are forced to eat the cafeteria food (D). Many students bring food from home or go out to lunch; only the low-income students are left with no other options besides the cafeteria food. The title "Problems with the Cafeteria Food" (E) efficiently and accurately captures the main idea of the letter.

14. (D)

Choice (D) is correct because the author is making a suggestion that is not possible (and contradicts the first part of the sentence). Although (E)—"and yet this is impossible"—conveys the same idea as choice (D), it's not the correct answer because the phrasing makes it better suited to be placed the end rather than the middle of a sentence.

15. (E)

The first part of the sentence is written using the conditional verb tense. For the sake of consistency, the rest of the sentence should use the same tense, which makes (E) the correct answer. While (D) uses the conditional, it is too wordy.

16. (C)

Since the subject ("everyone") of sentences 4 and 5 is the same, the two sentences can be combined, and (C) is the most effective way to do so. Choice (A) is unnecessarily repetitive (with "everyone" appearing twice), (B) is choppy, (D) is ungrammatical since the two verbs are not in the same form, and (E) is weakened by a dangling modifier since the sentence never says who is doing the talking.

17. (D)

Sentence 10 (D) is the only answer choice that is irrelevant to the development of the passage. Sentences 2 (A) and 3 (B) explain the basis for the writer's decision to start the basketball camp, the whole purpose of the endeavor. Sentence 8 (C) is an attractive choice because removing it wouldn't hinder the reader's understanding of the passage; however, it is useful because it describes the manner in which the writer and his brother conducted the camp. And in comparison with sentence 10 (D), removing sentence 8 is definitely a poorer choice because sentence 10 is off-topic and disruptive. Sentence 21 (E) is vital to the passage because it helps to sum up what the writer learned from his experience

18. (C)

The examples given—dribbling, etc.—are part of the game of basketball; they are the essential elements necessary to play. In that sense, they are not really traditions (A). Actions (B) may cover dribbling, but the term doesn't apply to the rules. In context, the word *fundamentals* most nearly means "basics" (C). Strategies (D) is too advanced to cover fundamental skills like dribbling. Drills (E) can't be used to signify "rules."

19. (C)

"Nevertheless" suggests that the brothers recommended the basketball players even though they weren't good. However, according to the passage, some of the kids were good and improved dramatically. Thus, recommending them is a "result" of the progress they made over the summer, which makes (C) correct.

20. (D)

Choice (A) is attractive at first glance because the writer has implied in the previous sentence that he loves basketball; however, it's a poor conclusion sentence because whether or not basketball is the best sport is irrelevant to the main theme of the passage: doing something positive in the community. Choice (B) is also irrelevant because chores were never mentioned in the passage. Choice (C) is redundant because the writer has already discussed how the camp helped kids in the neighborhood to get to know each other; this doesn't need to be said again. Choice (E) refers to a detail mentioned in the passage but doesn't draw the parts of the passage together as a whole. Choice (D) is the best answer because it neatly ties up the conclusion that the writer reached about how to make a positive difference in the community, relating it back to the experience that made it true for him personally.

21. (E)

The sentence as written is a run-on. Choice (E) corrects the run-on by adding the conjunction "and." Choice (B) adds "but," a conjunction that isn't logical in this sentence. Choice (C) creates a run-on and introduces a verb tense error. Choice (D) creates additional problems with sentence structure.

22. (B)

Rephrasing sentence 3 as a question would create parallelism and improve the flow and rhetorical impact of the paragraph, so choice (B) is the correct answer. None of the other choices would fix the sentence's lack of parallelism with the other sentences in the paragraph. Choice (A) only worsens the lack of parallelism. Choice (C) accomplishes nothing because the two words *comprehension* and *understanding* mean the same thing. Including the president's name (D) wouldn't add or detract from the rhetorical impact of the paragraph. A citation (E) isn't necessary for this type of document—an advertisement flyer.

23. (D)

Choice (D)—"But"—is the correct answer since the speaker is trying to disprove that history club is for nerds. Choice (A) doesn't make sense grammatically, and (B), (C), and (E) suggest that the speaker agrees that history club is for nerds.

24. (C)

The two sentences simply say that history club is for students with inquiring minds who believe in the value of understanding the past. The answer choice that shares this

meaning is (C). The other answers are wordy, grammatically incorrect, or incoherent.

25. (A)

Think about what responsibility students would assume in choosing an honoree for the history club banquet. Choice (A) is the best answer because students would have to evaluate the work and contributions of an historian to decide whom to honor.

26. (D)

The key to answering this question is finding the answer choice that doesn't significantly change the meaning of the original sentences and is grammatically correct. Being "convinced" and having "doubts" are opposing ideas—you can't do both at the same time—so choices (A) and (E) are illogical. Choice (B) doesn't make sense because the writer is addressing readers who *aren't* convinced, and (C) incorporates an idea ("convictions") that wasn't part of the original sentences. Choice (D) effectively uses the negative phrase "aren't convinced" to combine the original sentences while maintaining their meaning.

27. (B)

Choice (A) is ungrammatical without deleting the preposition "of." Making "college" plural (B) is necessary because the different students do not necessarily share the same first-choice college. Changing "have been" to "were" (C) would be the incorrect tense for talking about something that happened at various indefinite times in the past. Removing the hyphen in "first-choice" (D) is incorrect because a compound modifier must be hyphenated when it precedes the noun it modifies. "Accepted" and "excepted" (E) are homophones—they sound the same but have different meanings—but the correct one is already used in the sentence.

28. (D)

The sentence contains two contrasting ideas, but the word "while" de-emphasizes this contrast, therefore muddling the intended meaning of the sentence. The best choice is the one that makes clear the difference between the two ideas in the sentence, and the conjunction "but" is the most appropriate word for doing this.

29. (C)

These sentences don't contradict each other, so choices (A) and (B) can be eliminated. The syntax of choice (D) is confusing, and choice (E) doesn't make sense because the verb "thrive" is intransitive, meaning that it doesn't take an object. Choice (C) combines the sentences succinctly without changing the meaning of the original sentences.

30. (D)

Sentence 7 can be eliminated because sentence 5 ("Many zoos are beginning to recognize this fact.") expresses the same idea at a more optimal moment in the paragraph.

31. (A)

While it would be interesting to include choices (B)–(D) in the sentence, choice (A) is the only one that strengthens the argument that zoos are starting to pay attention to the particular needs of different species. As the sentence is presently written, it's not clear why the Baltimore Zoo chose the specific temperature 50 degrees, as opposed to 40 degrees, 60 degrees, etc.

32. (E)

The first two paragraphs of the letter don't make it clear how Maggie is poorly adapted for cold weather or what effect it will have on her. Therefore, the transition to the third paragraph would be stronger if the writer explained how the zoo's plans would impact Maggie physically before moving on to address how solitude might affect her in other ways.

33. (A)

This question asks for the best transition. Choice (A) provides an appropriate transition because "furthermore" indicates that more information is about to be given to expand on the writer's argument. The phrase "according to them" (B) is confusing because it's not clear whom "them" refers to (and if it refers to "the experts," it's redundant because the experts are already mentioned in the sentence). Choices (C) and (E) are inappropriate because they both signal that the writer is about to state a logical conclusion, whereas in the passage, the writer goes on to present brand-new information. Choice (D) doesn't make sense because the sentence is not presenting a distinction between two things.

34. (B)

Since the essay goes on to discuss different methods of education during different periods, it would be nice to have a transition preparing the reader for this, so choice (B) is the best answer. None of the other choices introduce the discussion to come.

35. (E)

Since the author is discussing the past ("prehistoric times"), the underlined portion of sentence 4 should be revised so that it is in the past tense. While answer (B) is in the past, it doesn't make grammatical sense with the rest of the sentence. Therefore, the best answer is (E).

36. (A)

Although this sentence is long, it is free of grammatical errors, so choice (A) is correct. "Though" sets up the relationship between the two clauses more clearly than "and" (C).

37. (C)

The best way to approach this question is to replace the underlined portion with each answer choice. By doing this, it's clear that answer (C) is the only one that works. The other choices either don't make sense in context or are ungrammatical.

38. (C)

"Afterward" is vague. Far more specific is "by the middle of the next century" (C), and by looking at the dates mentioned in the passage you can determine that this answer is accurate. "Shortly later" (B) should just be "later" or "in a little while"—"shortly" is an unnecessary adjective in the sentence. "Sometime in the future" (D) and "When the time was right" (E) are vague as well.

39. (B)

The syntax of the original sentence is confusing. Choice (A) splits up the two adjectives unnecessarily, which makes the sentence a bit convoluted. Choice (C) is wordy. Choice (D) incorrectly splits the adverb "morally" from the adjective "rectifying," and the sentence doesn't make sense as a result. Choice (E) changes the original meaning of the sentence by creating a new noun phrase, "practical education." The intended meaning of the sentence is captured best by choice (B).

40. (C)

Answer (C) is correct because it eliminates "though," which should not be used here with "but," which appears later in the sentence. Likewise, "while" in (B) should not be used with "but." Answer (D) is incorrect because it is wordy. Answer (E) is wrong because it creates a sentence structure problem.

41. (C)

Answer (C) is correct because all three verbs in the list are in the same tense, the simple past. Answer (B) places all three verbs in the same tense, but the present tense doesn't make sense in context. Answers (A), (D), and (E) are all wrong because they use different tenses for the verbs in the list.

42. (C)

Answer (C) is the best choice because the two verbs ("signaled" and "was") are both in the past tense. The reference to the Lewis and Clark expedition makes it clear that the action happened in the past. Answer (D) is ungrammatical because the form of the verb ("signaling") makes the independent clause incomplete.

43. (E)

Answer (E) is the best way to revise this sentence since the second half of the sentence modifies the first by further describing the movie. While there's nothing grammatically incorrect about writing the sentence as two independent clauses as in (A), choice (E) is better because it's more concise.

44. (B)

Answer (A) is incorrect because there is no plural noun in the sentence for the pronoun "their" to refer to. Answer (B) is correct because it's the only choice that eliminates "their."

45. (B)

In this question, the pronoun references are unclear. The best answer choice is (B) because it clarifies the role of each person and makes reference to the object. The pilot makes an announcement to the passengers; the flight attendant will collect the headphones.

46. (A)

Choice (A) is correct because the citation includes the lines from the source, which is typically done only with poems. Another defining feature of poetry citations is the presence of the "/" symbol, which indicates line breaks—or the way the poet wanted these lines to be separated into different lines on the page. This is the preferred format for poetry in most citation styles. Since most speeches and news and magazine articles are prose, excerpts from them generally are identified by paragraph or sentence, not by line number.

47. (D)

The superscript number indicates that a citation is available for the information included in the preceding sentence. The citation can be found in a note at the bottom of the page or in a list of notes at the end of the document or book. The note will have the same number as the superscript here. Footnotes and endnotes are the only types of citations that use superscript numbers.

48. (B)

This entry begins with a number and the author's first name, then last name. These two features are indicators of footnotes and endnotes in most citation style formats. Hyphenating a name (A) is irrelevant. The title of a book may or may not be italicized, depending on the citation style, so choice (C) is incorrect. Choices (D) and (E), the city of publication and the presence of a period, are not defining features of the format of footnotes and endnotes.

49. (E)

Note "Journal" in the title of this resource, letting you know it's a periodical and probably publishes multiple issues a year. To indicate which issue is being cited, journal citations include the volume of the issue being cited, so (E) is the best answer. If (A) were correct, the entry would have "first published" as part of the entry. This also means (D) is incorrect. The page number "891" follows the volume number "59," so (B) is not correct. Paragraph number (C) may be used for a newspaper article, but this is a journal.

50. (A)

Because the name of an institution is given, along with a detailed address, as well as clues like the words "proceedings" and "summer school," you can deduce that the citation refers to a speech that was given in person. A book citation (B) would include page numbers. Journal (C) and newspaper article (D) citations would include volume and issue numbers. Most importantly, there is no title mentioned, which rules out the work's being a poem (E) or any one of options (B)–(D).

51. (D)

According to the question stem, you're looking for the format for endnotes or footnotes (they're both formatted the same way). You also could have identified these entries as endnotes/footnotes because of the format (first initial, then last name for author's names). As endnotes/footnotes, these would be numbered in the order of their use in the writing (D), corresponding to a superscript number embedded in the text. Choice (A) is the order usually found in a list of references at the end of the paper. Neither (C) nor (E) is a conventional way of ordering notes or references.

52. (A)

The underlined portion is a journal title. The article title (B) is in quotes, directly preceding the underlined portion. If it were a website, it wouldn't have any spaces, and it would have an extension like ".com" or ".org." Citations do not contain article topics (D). This is not a newspaper because the page numbers are in the wrong format.

53. (D)

Because the citation appears in the middle of the sentence, it signifies that only the part of the sentence directly preceding the citation came from that source. Therefore, Timar has written a work that discusses mild hearing impairment but not severe hearing loss.

54. (E)

The first date in the citation is when the *Washington Post* published the article, and the second date is when the writer accessed the article online for use in her paper (E). Newspapers do not release second printings (A). Newspaper articles are published to print and to the Web on the same day, so choice (B) is wrong as well. The date when the author chose the source is never included in a citation (C). The date when an article was written (D) is never included in a citation; the publication date, however, is always included.

55. (E)

Judging by the titles, you can tell that the sources written by the authors in choices (A)–(D) relate to the effects of noise but not necessarily to the measurement of sound levels. Rob Candler (E) wrote a piece about sensors (measuring devices) for a publication related to engineering. This is the most pertinent choice with regard to measuring sound levels.

56. (A)

This quotation is directly connected to the study mentioned in the preceding sentence (A). Choice (B) is a distortion. Choice (C) is too strongly worded; the source does not say that long-term exposure to background noise can be "extremely dangerous." Choices (D) and (E) are both off-topic.

57. (E)

Just as the quote that appears in sentences 15 and 16 includes a citation, sentence 19 needs one as well. The fact that the person quoted is named doesn't mean that the quote doesn't need a citation. Paraphrasing the quote (B) doesn't offer a clear benefit. While choices (C) and (D) could be interesting or useful, they are not strictly necessary, but a citation is.

58. (B)

While the last paragraph seems to go in a slightly different direction from those preceding it, to say that its "purpose" is to create contrast (A) is incorrect. It does not refute any assumptions (C) that are mentioned in the essay; it doesn't serve as a transition (D) because it's the conclusion; and it doesn't support the previous paragraph (E). Look back to the thesis, and you'll see that it clearly says "you can reduce these detrimental effects [of noise] with knowledge and action," which is precisely what the final paragraph discusses.

59. (E)

The current order lists the entries alphabetically by author's last name where there is one and by title where no author is mentioned in the document or resource.

60. (A)

The format of the citation indicates that the source is a book. If it were a journal (B), it would contain an issue number. Academic essays (C) aren't published on their own without taking the format of a book or journal. A lecture title would be in quotation marks; it wouldn't be italicized.

61. (C)

The proper way to format a parenthetical citation is to include the author's name and the year of publication.

62. (C)

Choices (A), (B), (D), and (E) are all indicated by the reference list. But choice (C) contains an error: "119" is not the page number of the citation—it's the volume number of the journal.

63. (B)

While including the brain sizes of different species (A) or brain games for promoting brain health (C) might be interesting additions, they would not clarify any information, provide transitions, or forward the discussion. The same is the case for choice (D)—it's an unnecessary piece of information. Clarifying terms (B), however, is an excellent way to promote understanding, especially for sophisticated science terms that many readers are likely to be unfamiliar with.

64. (C)

The abbreviation "Ibid." is used to indicate that the source of the present note is the same as that of the previous note. It's a way of saving time and space, because often in texts such as this passage, many sequential citations may refer to the same source.

65. (A)

The topic of sentence 2 is the relative temperatures of Mars, Earth, and the other planets in the solar system. Look for an answer that pertains to temperature. There is only one given, choice (A). Distances between planets (B), the names of the planets that are too cold (C), the landscape (D) and atmosphere (E) of Mars—these are all off-topic.

66. (C)

Note 1 is missing the name of the author. All of the other pertinent information is present, and the journal editor's name (D) is never listed in a journal citation.

67. (D)

The writer is actually trying to point out the similarities, not differences, between the two planets, so choice (A) is wrong. The topic of the passage is not what Earth will be like in the future (B) but rather what Mars might be like. Background information on Mars (C) isn't relevant since we're considering Mars's future; background information on Earth, however, is relevant because it may be used to predict possibilities for Mars. Choice (E) contradicts the purpose of the passage.

68. (B)

Terraforming is a sophisticated science term that many readers may not know, so defining it (B) is a good idea. There's no reason to add a source citation to this note (A). The technology used for terraforming (C) cannot be described because, as the note states, this technology hasn't been developed yet. The climatic effects (D) and the cost (E) of terraforming are both off-topic.

69. (D)

Although all of the answer choices relating to travel or international relations may seem correct, it's important to keep in mind that the essay focuses on how travel writers express themselves rather than on travel itself. Therefore, the paragraph would be most interesting to a literary theorist or critic—someone who studies literature.

70. (D)

Choice (D) is the best answer because sentence 2 defines the essay's central idea rather than setting up an idea that will be refuted (B), establishing an organizational strategy (C), or describing how travel writers feel (E).

71. (A)

Sentence 2 asserts that travel writers are concerned with their position vis-à-vis other travel writers, and sentence 3 tries to explain why this is the case. Thus, choice (A) is the best answer.

72. (B)

"Whereas" signals to the reader that the writer is differentiating between two things. In this case, the purpose of "whereas" in sentence 4 is to show how tourists are different from travelers.

73. (C)

The reference to Dervla Murphy serves as an example of how a travel writer strove to prove that her book was more original than others. While choice (D) may seem tempting, it's important to keep in mind that the author of the essay is *not* showing that Dervla Murphy's account is superior. Instead, she is pointing out that Dervla Murphy tried to establish her book as superior.

74. (B)

There's no earlier point (A) to which the mention of writing could reasonably refer. The mention of writing neither confirms nor refutes an assumption, so choice (C) is out. Choice (D) is tempting, but detailing the origins of writing isn't really pertinent to the topic. The advent of writing is instead being used as a sort of signpost in the history of our species—a frame of reference (B).

75. (A)

The transition from the second paragraph to the third hinges on the contrast between the time spans that the human mind is comfortable dealing with and the time spans associated with the development of life on Earth. The transition word must underscore this contrast. The only one of the answer choices that signals contrast is "yet" (A).

76. (C)

The word *ready* can mean several things—choices (A), (C), (D), and (E) are all possible meanings. In this context, however, it most nearly means *immediate*, choice (C). In the sentence before the cited line, the author says *there is no simple way* to understand vast stretches of time. In the sentence following the cited line, the author compares the way we understand time to the way a blind man *laboriously* constructs a picture of his surroundings. This implies that our understanding of time is a difficult and time-consuming task, not something we can do *readily* or *immediately*.

77. (A)

Sentence 11 restates the point (A) made in sentence 10 about how difficult it is for humans to comprehend the vast stretch of time since the origin of life on Earth. Sentence 11 says it in a different way, but the basic idea is the same. This idea is also stated in the thesis (sentence 2). It isn't strictly "expanding" on the thesis (B) because it doesn't add any new ideas.

78. (E)

This question is asking about why the author uses a particular detail. Pay attention to context. Once again, the author is talking about how difficult it is to understand vast stretches of time. The author compares this difficulty to that of a blind man building up a sensory picture of his surroundings. This is an *indirect* process, so choice (E) is right. Choice (C) is dealt with later in paragraph 4, so you can eliminate it right away. (A) is too sweeping; the author never says that human beings are *completely unable to comprehend time*. (B) and (D) have nothing to do with the passage.

79. (A)

Inference skills are required here. What is the author's underlying point in mentioning the Big Bang and the Cambrian Period? In sentence 13, the author introduces the paragraph by saying that *a week* provides a customary analogy for understanding the age of the Earth. The Big Bang and the Cambrian Period are used as examples to support this point. So (A) is right—it's the point about the time scale that the author's trying to demonstrate. Choices (D) and (E) both distort the details in different ways. The development of agriculture, (B), is another supporting example like the Big Bang and the Cambrian Period, but it's not the author's central point here. Choice (C) is wrong because sentence 15 refers only to macroscopic fossils and says nothing about other types of fossils.

80. (B)

In light of the Edward Abbey quote, it's clear that the author is striving to show how her garden is beautiful, even though it may appear overgrown to others. Choice (B) is the most accurate expression of this idea.

81. (C)

All the details that the author focuses on in sentence 5 describe different noises in the city. Therefore, she is trying to convey a sense of the city's noisiness (C) to the reader.

82. (B)

Although the author is describing the different plants that grow in her garden, she does not provide a complete catalog (A). Choice (B) is better because she is focusing on how everything in the garden is mixed together without regard for category or type.

83. (D)

The best way to answer this question is to consider each answer choice in light of the passage. Make sure that you look at both adjectives because while one may be true, the other may not be. While the author is clearly interested in her garden, there is nothing in the passage to indicate that she is lazy (A). Similarly, while she seems delighted, she doesn't appear confused (B). Likewise, while it's true she conveys a sense of wonder, she isn't complacent or self-satisfied (C). Finally, (E) is incorrect because she is interested but she isn't fatigued. The best choice is answer (D).

84. (D)

In the description of the narrator's garden, there are many interactions among the animals, plants, and objects. The other answer choices don't capture this sense of crowded interaction. The inhabitants of the garden are not isolated (A), nothing is said about the plants having more interactions with their surroundings than the animals and objects (B), there are no instances of animals helping each other to find food (C), and there is no mention of what the inhabitants of the garden do at night (E).

85. (A)

The first paragraph in this passage states an idea about the perfect place in the form of a quote from nature writer Edward Abbey. In the second paragraph, the author uses a personal example (her disorderly garden) to explore her idea of what perfect is, thereby supporting the idea described in the first paragraph.

86. (C)

"Furthermore" (A) suggests the speaker is continuing an idea just mentioned. "In retrospect" (B) suggests a look back on something considered earlier. "Consequently" (D) and "therefore" (E) indicate cause and effect, but this is not the relationship between sentences 6 and 7. Choice (C) is the best answer because it fits the context here: the speaker is bringing the listeners along to a specific time not previously mentioned.

87. (B)

Pay close attention to the wording of the question, which asks about the organizational pattern *as a whole*. Choices (A), (C), and (D) focus on parts of the speech but not the overall structure. More specifically, they do not take into account the introduction of the speech, which focuses on reading. Choice (E) is incorrect because there is no "question" that defines the organization of the speech. Choice (B) is the best answer. The speaker introduces the theme of learning from her reading and then begins to tell an anecdote about a time when this practice affected her life.

88. (D)

These two sentences act as a rhetorical tool with a purpose other than providing information or discussing ideas. So choices (A), (B), and (C) are incorrect because they are about the discussion of the essay's ideas. Choice (E) is incorrect because the speech is based on the writer's experience and is not making a historical argument. Choice (D) is the best answer because it acknowledges that the purpose of the pair of sentences is to keep the reader engaged.

89. (A)

Since the speaker has stated in paragraph 1 that the incident she's describing occurred in the 1970s, choices (B) and (C) won't work. The speaker has not presented an argument or call to action, so (D) is wrong. The purpose of the speech is to describe a personal anecdote, not to discuss life in the 1800s, so (E) is wrong. Choice (A) is the best because the speaker uses sentences 10–13 to lay the groundwork, showing how what she has read informs what she chooses to do to keep her feet warm.

90. (B)

While the speaker hints that the story is about to take an unexpected turn, that is not the same thing as changing the subject (A). While sentence 24 furthers the story, to say that it "furthers the speaker's argument" (C) isn't accurate because the speaker isn't making an argument in this piece—it's a personal narrative, not a persuasive or analytical piece. Sentence 24 doesn't remind the audience of the main idea (D). While choice (E) is tempting, it's more accurate to say that the speaker is creating "suspense" (B) rather than "doubt."

Chapter Five: **CLEP College Composition Review**

- The Big Picture: CLEP College Composition
- The Big Picture: CLEP College Composition Modular
- Nuts and Bolts
- Conventions of Standard Written English
- Revisions Skills and Rhetorical Analysis
- Ability to Use Source Materials
- The Essays
- Final Thoughts

Congratulations! You've decided to get a head start on your college education by taking the CLEP College Composition or CLEP College Composition Modular exam. Throughout this chapter, we will refer to it as the CLEP College Composition exam, though if a question type is specific to one or the other of the tests, we will specify which is being referred to.

Remember, CLEP College Composition and CLEP College Composition Modular are two different tests. This chapter covers both, but you should check with the schools of your choice about which exam they require. In this book, Practice Tests 1 and 2 are College Composition Modular exams, and Practice Test 3 is a College Composition exam.

THE BIG PICTURE: CLEP COLLEGE COMPOSITION

The CLEP College Composition exam evaluates test takers' knowledge of the conventions of standard written English, their revision skills, their ability to use source materials, and their ability to analyze writing with 50 multiple-choice questions to be completed in 50 minutes. The exam also tests their ability to write essays that argue a point of view, analyze information, and synthesize two different passages by requiring test takers to write two essays in 70 minutes.

THE BIG PICTURE: CLEP COLLEGE COMPOSITION MODULAR

The CLEP College Composition exam evaluates test takers' knowledge of the conventions of standard written English; their revision skills, including on the sentence level; their ability to use source materials; and their ability to analyze writing with 90 multiple-choice questions to be completed in 90 minutes. With regards to a writing assessment, schools can choose any of these three options:

1. The same two mandatory essays found on the CLEP College Composition exam (This would bring the total testing time to 160 minutes, or 2 hours and 40 minutes.)

2. A writing assessment that the school develops, administers, and scores

3. Any other assessment that the college wants to associate with the College Composition Modular exam score

NUTS AND BOLTS

The following information summarizes the topics and subtopics covered on the multiple-choice questions on the CLEP College Composition exam and the CLEP College Composition Modular exam. Later in the chapter you will find Nuts and Bolts about the essays.

Conventions of Standard Written English (10% of the exam)

Syntax (parallelism, coordination, subordination)

Sentence boundaries (comma splices, run-ons, sentence fragments)

Recognition of correct sentences

Concord/agreement (pronoun reference, case, and number; subject-verb; verb tense)

Diction

Modifiers

Idiom

Active/passive voice

Lack of subject in modifying word group

Logical comparison

Logical agreement

Punctuation

Revisions Skills/Revision Skills Including Sentence-Level Skills* (40% of the exam)

Organization

Evaluation of evidence

Awareness of audience, tone, and purpose

Level of detail

Coherence between sentences and paragraphs

Sentence variety and structure

Main idea, thesis statements, and topic sentences

Rhetorical effects and emphasis

Use of language

Evaluation of author's authority and appeal

Evaluation of reasoning

Consistency of point of view

Transitions

Sentence-level errors primarily relating to the conventions of standard written English

Ability to Use Source Materials** (25% of the exam)

Use of reference materials

Evaluation of sources

Integration of resource material

Documentation of sources (including, but not limited to, MLA, APA, and Chicago manuals of style)

Rhetorical Analysis (25% of the exam)

Appeals

Tone

Organization/structure

Rhetorical effects

Use of language

Evaluation of evidence

* Revision Skills Including Sentence-Level Skills is for College Composition Modular **only** and includes a question type called Improving Sentences.

** Ability to Use Source Materials may test some of the skills from Revision Skills and Rhetorical Analysis:

In the following review, we'll discuss what you need to know to do your best on each part of the CLEP College Composition exam or the CLEP College Composition Modular exam.

CONVENTIONS OF STANDARD WRITTEN ENGLISH

Although this review section is named after the first part of the CLEP College Composition exam, the information in this section also applies to the Improving Sentences section, which is found only on the 90-question College Composition Modular exam. Both the Conventions of Standard

Written English and Improving Sentences sections test your knowledge of grammar, usage, word choice (diction), sentence structure, punctuation, and idiom. This review will cover the following topics:

- Complete Sentences
- Economy and Clarity
- Agreement
- Active versus Passive Voice
- Diction and Idiom
- Syntax and Structure
- Sentence Variation

While the information in this chapter is a good starting point to prepare for the CLEP College Composition exam, you may want to review a more detailed grammar or writing book to supplement your studies.

Complete Sentences

A complete sentence contains a noun and a verb and expresses a complete thought. An incomplete sentence may begin with a capital letter and end with a punctuation mark, but often it will be missing either a subject or a verb or both. In other cases, the sentence will contain a subject and verb but express an incomplete thought, as in this example:

> **INCORRECT:** Because she had an appointment early in the morning.

In a run-on sentence, two complete thoughts, *or independent clauses*, are ungrammatically joined by a comma.

> **INCORRECT:** The school board chair called the meeting into session, the high school principal presented the athletic calendar.

To correct this sentence, a period or semicolon must be added between the two independent clauses. If a period is added, the first word of the second clause must be capitalized—creating two separate sentences.

> **CORRECT:** The school board chair called the meeting into session. The high school principal presented the athletic calendar.

Generally, the best way to handle run-on sentences is to split them into more than one sentence. However, if the two complete thoughts are closely related, a semicolon may be used to separate them. In addition, if the second sentence amplifies an idea expressed in the first sentence, a colon may be used.

Alternatively, you can use a conjunction (i.e., *and*, *but*, *for*, *so*) to join two sentences into one. In this instance, the conjunction indicates the end of one complete thought and the beginning of another. A comma should precede it.

> **CORRECT:** The school board chair called the meeting into session, and the high school principal presented the athletic calendar.

Economy and Clarity

Good writing is clear to the reader and not monotonous or repetitive. Writing well means finding the most efficient and straightforward way to express ideas through words. On the CLEP College Composition exam, some of the questions will ask you to find better ways to write sentences that are grammatically correct but wordy or awkwardly phrased. For example:

> **INCORRECT:** The writer James Baldwin, who was raised in Harlem, moved to France in the middle of his writing career, and this gave him the necessary distance to explore the social problems in the United States.

Although this example is grammatically correct, it can be written more clearly and concisely by combining the two independent clauses (or complete thoughts) as follows.

> **CORRECT:** The writer James Baldwin, who was raised in Harlem, moved to France in the middle of his writing career, gaining the necessary distance to explore the social problems in the United States.

Issues of concision also arise in sentences that only contain one complete thought. These sentences can be redundant or verbose.

> **INCORRECT:** I am capable of speaking the language of France.

The main idea can be stated more simply.

> **CORRECT:** I speak French.

Agreement

Subject-Verb Agreement

The subject and verb of a sentence must agree with each other. *Agreement* means a singular subject is used with a singular verb and a plural subject is used with a plural verb. Sometimes identifying the subject of a sentence can be difficult, especially when a clause or phrase comes between the subject and the verb.

> **INCORRECT:** His understanding of the math concepts always increase after the teacher reviews the homework.

Section Two: The CLEP College Composition Exam
Chapter Five

88

The subject of this sentence, "understanding," is singular. The phrase that follows, "of the math concepts," is a prepositional phrase that further describes "understanding," but "the math concepts" is not the subject of the sentence. Since the subject ("understanding") is singular, the plural verb "increase" must be changed to the singular form, "increases."

> **CORRECT:** His <u>understanding</u> of the math concepts always <u>increases</u> after the teacher reviews the homework.

In other sentences, the verb will come before the subject. In these sentences, the verb must agree with the subject that follows it.

> **CORRECT:** There <u>are</u> many *allusions* in Eliot's poem, *The Waste Land*, which make it extremely difficult to understand without seriously studying it.

In this sentence, the noun ("allusions") is plural, and so is the verb ("are"). The sentence is correct as written.

Let's look at what happens when the subject of a sentence includes more than one person, place, or thing ("Billy and I," "chocolate or vanilla"). In sentences with *compound subjects* (two nouns joined by a conjunction), the verb may be singular or plural. When the conjunction "and" creates the compound subject, the subject is plural.

> **CORRECT:** A dry winter and hot summer increase the likelihood of forest fires.

Since the compound subject ("dry winter and hot summer") is plural, the verb ("increase") is also plural. The sentence is correct as written.

When "or" or "nor" is used to join the subjects, whether the compound subject is plural depends on the subjects themselves. If both are singular, the compound subject is singular and calls for a singular verb.

> **CORRECT:** A dry winter or hot summer increases the likelihood of forest fires.

Since the compound subject ("dry winter or hot summer") is singular, the verb ("increases") is also singular. The sentence is correct as written.

If both subjects are plural, the compound subject is plural and calls for a plural verb. If one is singular and one is plural, the verb should agree with the subject closest to it.

> **CORRECT:** Park rangers believe that either campers or lightning is most likely to cause the next wildfire here.

Since the compound subject ("campers or lightning") contains both a plural and a singular subject, the verb ("is") agrees with the subject closest to it (the singular "lightning"). The sentence is correct as written.

Verb Tense Agreement

Verbs are used to express action (*walk, jump, dive, grin*) or states of being (*are, is*). They appear in six different grammatical *tenses* in the English language.

Present tense:	I study for three hours every evening.
Past tense:	I studied for three hours last night.
Future tense:	I will study for three hours tomorrow afternoon.
Present perfect tense:	I have studied for three hours for three weeks.
Past perfect tense:	I had studied for three hours every evening for a week.
Future perfect tense:	I will have studied for three hours every evening for a month by the time I take the exam.

The *present tense* means that the action is currently taking place. The *present perfect tense* express-es an action that started in the past and may or may not still be continuing ("I have studied").

The *past tense* expresses an action that has already been completed. The *past perfect tense* is used for an action that ended at a particular point in the past: "I had studied for three hours every evening for a week when I passed the test."

The *future tense* indicates that the action has not yet happened. The *future perfect tense* signals that the action will take place in the future after something else happens ("I will have driven fifty miles by the time I get to the mountains.").

On the CLEP College Composition exam, you will need to watch for inconsistencies in verb tense. In some instances, the sentences will contain simple shifts in verb tense.

> **INCORRECT:** *Poets and Writers* contains reviews of recently pub-lished books and offered a list of contests and publishing opportu-nities for writers.

For the sake of consistency, both verbs should be in the present tense ("contains" and "offers") or in the past tense ("contained" and "offered").

Other questions on the exam will be more complicated because all the verbs in a sentence do not always have to be in the same tense. In fact, different verb tenses are used to show when one event happened in relationship to another. For example, the following sentence must be revised.

> **INCORRECT:** Julie will look for a job as a lifeguard after she finished her CPR training.

In this example, the future tense ("will look") is being used. Since the future occurs after the present, the present tense (use of the verb "finishes") is necessary to show when Julie will begin looking for a job.

Here's another sample sentence that needs revision.

> **INCORRECT:** When he has finished his first full-length work, the novelist Caryl Phillips had already graduated from Oxford University.

In this example, the subject is Caryl Phillips, and the verb ("had graduated") is in the past perfect tense. As we've seen, the past perfect indicates that the action of the verb ("graduating") was completed before another action in the *past*. The first verb ("has finished") should appear in the simple *past tense* and not the present perfect, which doesn't necessarily mean that the action is over. Therefore, the sentence should be revised.

> **CORRECT:** When he <u>finished</u> his first full-length work, the novelist Caryl Phillips <u>had already graduated</u> from Oxford University.

Incomplete Verbs

Finally, watch out for incomplete verbs used in sentences. Some verb forms must be used in conjunction with helping verbs (such as *are*, *is*, and *have*). If the helping verb is missing, the sentence will be incomplete or ungrammatical.

> **INCORRECT:** José writing the final paragraph of his essay when the electricity failed and the computer shut down without saving his final changes.

The subject of the sentence is José. The verb ("writing") is missing the helping verb ("was"), making the sentence incomplete. Again, this should sound incorrect to your "mental ear."

Pronoun Reference

Pronouns (*he, she, they, we, it*) must agree with the nouns or antecedents that they replace. The *antecedent* is the word, clause, or phrase that a pronoun replaces. If the noun is singular, then the pronoun must be singular. Similarly, if the noun is plural, then the pronoun must be plural.

> **CORRECT:** <u>Professors Judith Meyers and Tony Abel</u> asked the English department chair for sabbaticals so that <u>they</u> could finish their collaborative project.

"They" agrees with the plural subject "Professors Judith Meyers and Tony Abel," making this sentence grammatically correct.

Shifts in the number of subjects (or pronouns) in a sentence can occur when you aren't sure whether the antecedent is singular or plural. Keep in mind that indefinite subjects, such as *everyone*, *anybody*, and *everything*, are singular even though they sound plural. For example, the following sentence is correct as written.

> **CORRECT:** Everyone who takes my creative writing class must write thirty pages in her journal each week.

Besides watching for agreement in number, you must also make sure that pronouns appear in the same person as the nouns they replace. Pronouns can be categorized by point of view or voice (that is, first, second, or third person). When you read a sentence, note whether the subject is the speaker (first person), someone the speaker is addressing (the second person), or some-one/something not being directly addressed (third person).

First-person pronouns: I, we, me, us, my, mine, our, ours

Second-person pronouns: you, your, yours

Third-person pronouns: she, he, it, one, they, him, her, them, his, her, hers, its, their, theirs, ours

Shifts in point of view can occur when you aren't paying attention to whether the sentence is written in the first, second, or third person. Remember that point of view must stay consistent throughout a sentence. The point of view changes within the next sentence.

> **INCORRECT:** Training for the marathon is tricky: if he logs too many miles, you risk getting an injury, but if you run too few, you may not finish.

The error in this example is that it shifts from the third person ("he") to the second person ("you"). The sentence must be written using either second- or third-person pronouns, but not both.

Active versus Passive Voice

While the passive voice is sometimes acceptable, it's generally preferable to use verbs in the active voice. Sentences that use the active voice more clearly express *who* is performing an action and *what* action is being performed. In *active-voice sentences*, the person or thing that performs the action comes at the beginning of the sentence.

> **CORRECT:** Mrs. Solomon traveled to South America over her vacation and returned with lots of colorful photographs to show the students.

Mrs. Solomon is the one who traveled to South America, returned with photographs, and shared them with her students. It's clear who completed the actions. In contrast, in *passive-voice sentences*, the person or thing performing the actions doesn't appear until the end of the sentence. In some cases, the agent of the action is not mentioned at all. Here is the same sentence written in the passive voice.

> **INCORRECT:** The students were shown many colorful photographs by Mrs. Solomon who traveled to South America over her vacation.

The passive voice can be even more vague. The same sentence would be grammatically correct if it simply stated, "The students were shown many colorful photographs." Here there is no agent at all.

Remember, on the CLEP College Composition exam, you should pick the answer choice that is phrased in the active voice as long as the active voice creates no other grammatical or stylistic errors in the sentence.

Pronoun Case

Pronoun case refers to the correct form of the pronoun as determined by how the pronoun is used in the sentence. To choose the correct pronoun case, ask yourself whether the pronoun is used as a subject or an object.

Subjective case pronouns: I, we, he, she, they, who

Objective case pronouns: me, us, him, her, them, whom

Notice that the pronouns *it* and *you* have only one form in English, so they are not included in the lists above. You'll never find a pronoun case error associated with those two pronouns.

When pronoun case is tested, it's likely to be in a sentence with a compound (phrase with *and* or *or*). Here is a typical error.

INCORRECT: Lucius passed the plate of appetizers to Sally and I.

Because the pronoun "I" is used as the objective of a preposition ("to") here, the objective case pronoun should be used instead.

CORRECT: Lucius passed the plates of appetizers to Sally and me.

Can you tell what is wrong with this sentence?

INCORRECT: Sally and me passed the plates of appetizers to Lucius.

Here, the objective case pronoun "me" is used incorrectly as the subject of the sentence. Here is the correction.

CORRECT: Sally and I passed the plates of appetizers to Lucius.

Diction and Idiom

Diction refers to word choice, and *idiom* refers to phrases that have a meaning different from their literal meaning. On the CLEP College Composition exam, you need to watch for misused words, language that is not appropriate given the context, and idiomatic phrases that are incorrectly used. Often, language is misused when the writer is faced with two words that sound alike or seem to share the same meaning. For example:

Torturous means terrible or painful.
Tortuous means winding or twisting.

Therefore, the following use of *tortuous* would be incorrect:

INCORRECT: Running a mile around the track is tortuous for me because I'm out of shape.

On the CLEP College Composition exam, you will need to identify errors in word choice. A word or phrase may not necessarily be used incorrectly, but its style or tone may be at odds with the rest of the sentence or paragraph.

> Sarah Burnhardt was one of the most famous actresses ever to grace the stage. The people of her day thought she was hot stuff.

Clearly the informal slang expression "hot stuff" doesn't fit the formal style of the rest of the example. Some questions on the CLEP College Composition exam test your ability to distinguish between formal and informal style. Always pay attention to the tone of a passage and select an answer choice that is consistent with the style and purpose of a given selection.

Syntax and Structure

Syntax refers to the order of words in a sentence. In some sentences, the order of words clouds the overall meaning of the sentence. In others, faulty syntax can make the sentence ungrammatical. On the CLEP College Composition exam, you will want to pay close attention to parallel structure, subordination, and misplaced or "dangling" modifiers.

Parallel Structure

Parallel structure means that each item in a series or a comparison appears in the same grammatical form. The next example presents a list that is parallel.

> **CORRECT:** Next summer, I plan to take piano lessons, attend basketball camp, babysit on the weekends, and help my mother with her vegetable garden.

Each of the items in this list is grammatically similar. Each part of the sentence is a simple verbal phrase that begins with a verb in the present tense: *plan, attend, babysit, help*. This sentence would not be parallel if it were written as follows.

> **INCORRECT:** Next summer, I plan to take piano lessons, attend basketball camp, babysit on the weekends, and gardening with my mother.

The last item ("gardening with my mother") is grammatically different from the other items in the series. It should sound wrong or odd to you. The other items are verbs, while the final item is a noun ("gardening," the thing the speaker will be doing).

Parallel structure also applies to items in a comparison. Look at the next example. How would you make it parallel?

> **INCORRECT:** My father believes that eating a home-cooked meal is healthier than what you can get in a restaurant.

Which two things are being compared in the sentence? "Eating a home-cooked meal" and "what you can get in a restaurant" are being compared, but the two phrases are in different grammatical forms. To correct the sentence, put them in the same form.

>**CORRECT:** My father believes that eating a home-cooked meal is healthier than dining at a restaurant.

You should be able to hear that "eating a home-cooked meal" is in the same form as "dining at a restaurant."

Subordination

Subordination refers to how writers show relationships between ideas or emphasize the relative importance of different ideas. Generally, the more important ideas appear in independent clauses, while less important ideas appear in dependent clauses or phrases. *An independent clause* is part of a sentence that expresses a complete idea and could be a grammatically correct sentence on its own.

The CLEP College Composition exam will ask you to correct sentences in which the relationship between ideas is unclear or misstated. Here's a sentence that has an error in subordination.

>**INCORRECT:** Transferring to a large university, Leo was disappointed with his small college's lack of an astronomy department.

The sentence doesn't make sense. It sounds as though Leo transferred before he realized that his college didn't have an astronomy department. There are better ways to write the sentence.

>**CORRECT:** Disappointed with his small college's lack of an astronomy department, Leo transferred to a large university.

In the revision, the relationship between the two ideas is more clearly expressed. Leo transferred because he was disappointed by his college's course offerings. The most important idea—Leo's decision to transfer—appears in the independent clause. The cause of it—his disappointment—appears in the dependent clause. "Leo transferred to a large university" forms a complete sentence, but "Disappointed with his small college's lack of an astronomy department" does not.

Misplaced Modifiers

A *modifier* provides more information about a word or phrase in a sentence. We say that a modifier is "misplaced" when it isn't positioned close enough to the part of the sentence it is describing. As a result, the modifier seems to be modifying something else, making the meaning of the sentence unclear or ridiculous.

>**INCORRECT:** I brought my parrot to the school assembly who speaks only when it rains.

In this sentence, the modifier ("who only speaks when it rains") is too far from the word that it modifies ("parrot"). As a result, the sentence seems nonsensical—does the school assembly only speak when it rains? However, this error is easy to correct.

>**CORRECT:** I brought my parrot, who speaks only when it rains, to the school assembly.

We say that a modifier is "dangling" when the word it is supposed to describe is missing from the sentence, as in the next example.

> **INCORRECT:** Sprinting around the track, Lindsey's shoes came untied, and she tripped and lost the race.

"Sprinting around the track" describes what Lindsey is doing. However, because of how the sentence is constructed, it appears that Lindsey's shoes are sprinting around the track without her. To correct the sentence, either add Lindsey as the subject or rewrite the modifier to include a reference to Lindsey. The second sentence here does this by making the modifier into a dependent clause.

> **CORRECT:** Sprinting around the track, Lindsey tripped and lost the race when her shoes came untied.

OR

> **CORRECT:** While Lindsey was sprinting around the track, her shoes came untied, and she tripped and lost the race.

Sentence Variation

It's important to vary sentence length when you write. Some sentences should be long, others short. Mixing up sentence length keeps the reader engaged in what you have written. It's also important to vary the structure of your sentences. Think about how bored you would be if you read an essay of simple subject-verb-object sentences.

> **INCORRECT:** David went to the store. His mother sent him. She gave him a list. He realized he had lost the list at the store. He couldn't remember the items on the list. He decided to buy his favorite food. He hoped his mother wouldn't be angry.

For some questions on the CLEP exams, the sentences may be perfectly grammatical, but they could be written better so that the text is more interesting for the reader. You should keep sentence variation in mind also when you are writing your own essays on the CLEP College Composition exam.

REVISIONS SKILLS AND RHETORICAL ANALYSIS

Revision Skills and Rhetorical Analysis on the CLEP College Composition exam are related because both test similar topics. Both cover appeals, tone, organization, rhetorical effects, use of language, and evaluation of evidence, but only Revisions Skills additionally test audience, purpose, detail, coherence, sentence variety, consistency, and transitions.

This review section addresses the following topics:

- Central Idea
- Organization
- Evidence (Relevance, Degree of Detail, and Specificity)
- Audience and Purpose
- Logic
- Paragraph Structure and Function
- Rhetorical Emphasis
- Consistency of Tense and Viewpoint
- Combination and Variation of Sentences

Again, while this chapter provides a good starting point to prepare for the CLEP College Composition exam, you may want to review a more detailed writing book to supplement your studies.

Central Idea

The *central idea* is the main point that any piece of writing, whether an essay, letter to the editor, or literary analysis, is attempting to make. The *main idea* is usually introduced in the first paragraph of a piece of writing in the form of a thesis statement. Don't confuse the thesis statement with the subject of the essay. For example, while an essay may be about Emily Dickinson, the thesis will express an opinion about her poetry: "Emily Dickinson's poetry reveals how nineteenth-century women escaped the narrow confines of their domestic responsibilities." In other words, the thesis statement takes a stand on a topic.

Each paragraph in an essay may contain a separate central idea that supports the thesis of the essay. Usually, the writer will state the central idea at the beginning of each paragraph in the form of a topic sentence. On the CLEP College Composition exam, you may be asked to identify the central idea of essays and individual paragraphs.

Organization

There are countless ways to organize essays. Some common ways to structure essays include the following.

- Cause and effect
- Chronological order
- Problem and solution
- Question and answer
- Compare and contrast
- Narrative

Whenever you read a passage, ask yourself how each paragraph relates to the thesis. This will help you determine the passage's structure. Keep in mind that some of the essays on the exam will be deliberately disorganized, especially in the Revision Skills section. You may discover that one sentence or paragraph is totally unrelated to the thesis. If this is the case, you may be asked to identify ways to improve the organization of the essay—perhaps by removing that sentence or paragraph or adding a new one.

In addition, you should be able to identify how ideas are ordered within a paragraph. Generally, a topic sentence will indicate the main point of the paragraph, and the rest of the paragraph will be devoted to providing evidence or making an argument to support the main point. Keep in mind that just as some of the essays will seem disorganized, some of the paragraphs within essays will also seem jumbled or confused. Your job will be to determine which evidence is unnecessary, what missing evidence should be added, and how a paragraph can be restructured so that it makes its main point more effectively.

Evidence (Relevance, Degree of Detail, and Specificity)

The best way to make a point is to provide evidence that is specific and concrete. Evidence can take many forms: it can be based upon experience, analysis, expert opinions, or observation. On the CLEP College Composition exam, you will be asked to do two things: identify the evidence that an author presents to support his or her points and judge the value of the evidence presented.

Some of the writing that appears on the exam will seem vague to you. The author may make a strong claim, such as, "A mandatory community service program for students would be easy to start," but may not provide examples of how she or he would go about launching it. Your job will be to identify the answer choice that offers evidence that is both specific and relevant to the point being made in the passage.

Audience and Purpose

For whom is the essay or letter in the passage being written? This is known as the audience. Why is the passage being written? This is known as the purpose. The audience affects the style, tone, and rhetorical strategies of each piece of writing. If you wrote the editor of your local newspaper, your letter would sound very different from one that you might write to a close friend or relative. You would probably use more formal language in the letter to the editor, whereas in the letter to your friend you would be more casual and perhaps use slang.

The purpose of a piece of writing dictates its tone and structure. There are many reasons for writing. Writers may write to inform, to relate a personal experience, to persuade the reader of something, or to explain how something is done. For example, if your purpose is to explain how to play soccer, you will probably use clear language and relate the rules in a straightforward, methodical way. You may address your readers in the second person (as "you"), since you are telling them what they need to do to play soccer. Your tone and structure would be different if you wanted to write a scary story. In the story, you would use emotional language. You also would present characters and use dialogue to build suspense.

On the CLEP College Composition exam, you will be asked to consider how the writer could more effectively address his or her audience by choosing more appropriate language for a written passage. You will also be asked to analyze written passages to determine their purpose and ideal audience.

Logic

There are two basic types of logical reasoning: inductive and deductive. An inductive argument usually moves from a specific observation to a generalization, while a deductive argument starts with a general statement and ends with specific points.

Inductive: I've noticed that whenever it snows more than six inches, the school district closes the schools for the day. I think that means that the next time it snows six inches, we'll have a snow day.

Deductive: The school district policy states that school must be cancelled if more than six inches of snow fall in twenty-four hours. That means if it snows six inches tonight, we'll have a snow day.

On the CLEP College Composition exam, you won't be asked to determine whether an inductive or deductive argument is being made in a passage; however, you may be asked to explain the role that specific sentences play in how the argument is being made. For example, does the first sentence offer a generalization or a specific detail? How does a sentence in the middle of a passage function? Does it provide a counterexample? Does it serve as a transition to a new idea? Does it provide evidence to support the argument?

Paragraph Structure and Function

In nonfiction writing, a paragraph is like a very short essay. The topic sentence (which is usually the first or second sentence) should announce the main point, and the rest of the paragraph should provide logical support for this point. You should be able to understand how each sentence supports the main idea of the paragraph. Alternatively, you may identify sentences that don't seem related to the main idea and that should be revised or omitted. A paragraph may end with a concluding sentence that returns the reader's attention to the main idea. A concluding sentence also may serve as a transition to the next paragraph.

You should be able to see the connection between all of the different paragraphs in an essay. Sometimes each paragraph will contain transitional sentences that connect it to the previous or subsequent one. At other times, it will be up to you to determine the relationship between paragraphs. The best way to evaluate the excerpt's coherence between paragraphs is to try to summarize the purpose of each paragraph and then explore how the paragraph and passage are interrelated. Consider the following main points of a hypothetical essay:

Paragraph 1: Our town should have a recycling program.

Paragraph 2: Recycling is important because it reduces waste and helps preserve the environment.

Paragraph 3: Because new items can be made from recycled materials, recycling programs are not expensive.

Paragraph 4: By starting a recycling program, we can reduce waste and preserve the environment without spending too much money.

You could say that the essay follows a problem–solution organizational pattern. The first paragraph states the need or problem. The second paragraph explains why this need should be addressed. The third paragraph offers a solution, with the final paragraph serving as a conclusion that sums everything up. Having identified the essay's organization, you can answer almost any question about how the paragraphs relate to one another. Also, if the paragraphs are presented in the wrong order, you can unscramble them once you discover their internal logic.

Rhetorical Emphasis

Rhetorical emphasis simply refers to the way writers use language to create a feeling or effect. Consider the rhetorical device known as personification—giving human qualities to animals or inanimate objects. Read the next example, which makes use of personification, and consider the effect it has on you.

> The house looked blankly at the fields. It seemed to say, "Even though you are in front of me, I refuse to see you." On windy days when the trees shook their branches at the sky, the house held itself very still. Whatever had happened long ago lingered. The house was frozen with grief—or shock.

Personification makes the house seem capable of feeling emotions like grief and shock. Overall, it gives the passage an eerie feeling. Especially in the Rhetorical Analysis section, but in other parts of the exam as well, you will be asked to examine specific details in the passages and determine their effect on the passage. Read carefully, ask yourself what the author is trying to accomplish, and think about how the description makes you feel.

Consistency of Tense and Viewpoint

In each sentence or passage on the exam, you have to be on the lookout for shifts in verb tense. If a passage is mostly written in the past tense, it would be inconsistent if one sentence appeared in the present tense for no particular reason. Likewise, be aware of shifts in point of view (first person, second person, etc.). Most essays are written without reference to a point of view (in other words, they don't refer to "you" or "I" or "she"). Other writing, especially memoir, does have a point of view. If the point of view shifts from the first person to third person, then you know that the point of view has not been sustained throughout the written piece.

Combination and Variation of Sentences

The Revision Skills section puts an emphasis on combining and varying sentences. A paragraph that is composed of many short sentences, all of which contain a single idea, is boring to read. It may also be confusing since it doesn't clearly show the reader how the ideas in the paragraph are related to each other. The CLEP College Composition exam will evaluate your ability to combine sentences by asking you to revise and combine certain sentences from a passage. Look at the next example.

INCORRECT: Derek completed the project two weeks before the deadline. Derek got a raise at work.

To combine these two sentences, you must ask yourself how they are related. Did Derek complete the project before the deadline because he got a raise at work? Or vice versa? Once you understand the connection between the two events, you can revise the sentence accordingly to convey the "missing link."

CORRECT: After Derek completed the project two weeks before the deadline, he got a raise at work.

ABILITY TO USE SOURCE MATERIALS

The CLEP College Composition and College Composition Modular exams each include a section on Ability to Use Source Materials. For this section, you must demonstrate your knowledge of research and references. Some questions are stand-alone, while others associated with a passage. Note that questions associated with a passage may also test some of the skills related to Revision Skills and Rhetorical Analysis. Your primary task in this section, however, is to show you can use reference materials, evaluate source materials, use source materials, and document your sources.

The use of sources and citations is also tested on the College Composition (not College Composition Modular) exam in the second essay. The information that follows here will help you prepare for that essay as well as for the multiple-choice questions about citations and sources.

The following discussion covers source use in general, but if you need more specific details about citations, you should study the MLA (Modern Language Association), APA (American Psychological Association), and Chicago manuals of style.

Use of Reference Materials

In college and in life, you may be required to conduct research and incorporate it into your writing, speeches, or projects using specifically formatted citations to indicate where you found your information. It is a sign of academic honesty to acknowledge and to document the sources of ideas, facts, photos, graphics, and opinions of experts whom you consult and even what you borrow from films, television shows, audio recordings, advertisements, and emails. Be honest and use the preferred format, which may be the APA, MLA, or Chicago style or another.

Evaluation of Sources

You can meet the challenge to choose the best resources yourself and also to recognize them on the CLEP College Composition exam. Pay attention to the intent of the publication or website: to sell; to be a repository of expert research or historical information; to propagate a specific philosophy; to espouse a doctrine; or to house information about an institution. Is the information vetted for accuracy or juried for quality of writing, or can anyone publish without being critiqued?

Do the publications or sites document the sources from which they get *their* information or give the credentials of the author(s)? Is more recent information available on the topic you are researching? Check copyright dates for printed publications. Notice how frequently or recently the website has been updated or when the it was last accessed. How consistent is the information found in different sources?

Each publisher and Internet domain has its special bias. Know what each is, and you'll enhance your ability to recognize and understand source materials and to evaluate the quality of the myriad sources available to you.

Integration of Resource Material

It is academically dishonest to borrow and use information without acknowledgment. Doing so constitutes *plagiarism*. Proper crediting of source materials is the only way to avoid plagiarism. In some cases, you may quote exactly what the original writer has written; in other cases, you may paraphrase, using your own words for the ideas you've borrowed. In both cases, you will be expected to incorporate references or citations for the borrowed information into your writing by indicating explicit details about those resource materials either within the document or at the end.

Along with plagiarism, fabrication is another form of academic dishonesty. *Fabrication* means making up information, data, or evidence and presenting it as factual when it is not.

Documentation of Sources

The format style of the citations may be different, but the content usually is the same. A citation must provide information about the following:

Who?	Author(s)
What?	Complete title (Remember that sources may be published or unpublished, as in lecture notes, handouts, speeches, and personal interviews.)
When?	Date of publication (for electronic sources, date viewed)
Where?	Publisher, city, and state
How?	Was it accessed from a printed hardcopy of book, magazine, or newspaper or from an electronic source, using a search engine or database, or during an interview? Many style formats will cite this information, too. The more specific the entry, the better you can judge the source's value.

When choosing sources, also consider the question **why**? One source may be more credible than another. Check the domain of the website, usually indicated following the period (dot), such as loc.*gov*, c-spanvideo.*org*, hulahoops.*com*, stateuniversity.*edu*, or comcast.*net*.

THE ESSAYS

Nuts and Bolts

Exam	Number of Essays	About the Essay(s)	Time Allotted
College Composition	2	The first essay is based on something you've read, observed, or experienced. The second essay requires you to read, synthesize information, and write (including citations) an essay based on two excerpts provided.	70 mins TOTAL: Essay 1: 30 mins Essay 2: 40 mins
College Composition Modular	0–2	Schools can choose any of these three options: 1. The same two mandatory essays found on the CLEP College Composition exam 2. A writing assessment that the school develops, administers, and scores 3. Any other assessment that the college wants to associate with the College Composition Modular exam score	The time allotted depends on what kind of essay assessment your school uses. If your school uses the two CLEP essays from College Composition, it will be 70 mins TOTAL: Essay 1: 30 mins Essay 2: 40 mins

As of the printing of this book, the CLEP College Composition essays must be typed onto a computer. (CLEP College Composition Modular essays may or may not be handwritten, depending on the school.) The interface resembles a typical word-processing program. Commands that will be available to you include Cut, Paste, and Undo. You will navigate the essay using the mouse and/or the Page Up and Page Down keys on your keyboard. Clicking the Help button will take you to a screen explaining the different commands in the typing program. Download the CLEP Sampler from collegeboard.com/clep to practice using the essay-writing program.

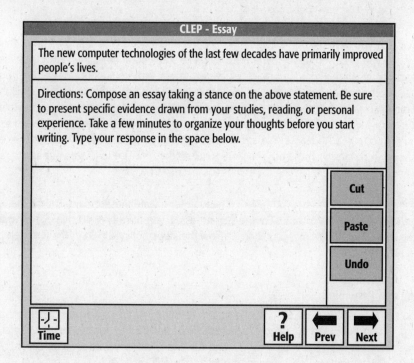

How the College Composition Essays Are Scored

If you are taking College Composition Modular, essays can be scored various ways. Therefore, this section covers only how College Composition essays are scored.

Unlike the rest of the exam, which is scored by computer, the essays are read by two college English teachers. Each teacher gives each essay an independent score between 1 and 6, and then the scores are combined. Your essay score accounts for half of your overall score; your score on multiple-choice questions accounts for the other half of your overall score. Your scores on the multiple-choice questions and essays are combined and ultimately calculated into a scaled score (between 20 and 80) for the entire College Composition exam.

Preparing for the Essays

Since the essays are worth half your score on the College Composition exam, it definitely pays to prepare. Practice planning and writing essays using the following method. Respond to the sample essay prompts in Practice Test 3. It's better to type your practice essays into a computer to simulate the testing experience. You should practice writing on a variety of topics and, if at all possible, have someone else read and grade your essays. You can also practice by reading the work of different authors and trying to identify the rhetorical strategies and organizational patterns they use.

Writing the Essay

Everything that you have learned earlier in this chapter about good writing applies here. That means when you write your essays, you need to make sure you address the topic completely and effectively, organize your ideas, make a clear argument, provide support for each of your points, and demonstrate your mastery of English by writing not only grammatically but also with sophistication and flair appropriate to the task and the audience. In addition, when you write the second essay, you must be able to synthesize information from two sources and be able to cite your sources accurately. To learn more about what is expected of you, you should also review the rubrics found in chapter 7. These are similar to what readers will use to judge your essays, so it is wise to know what they are looking for before you even start writing.

It's important to remember that you have a limited time to write these essays. For the first essay, you have only 30 minutes to write. For the second essay, you have only 40 minutes to write. To make the best use of your time, you should follow the steps outlined below. The first step is to create a plan.

Planning and Prewriting

Give yourself at least five minutes to plan each essay. For Essay 1, examine the statement and directions. For Essay 2, read the directions, introduction, assignment, and passages. Make sure you understand the issue you must address, and don't overlook any part of the directions. An example of a statement and directions for the first essay follows.

> Creative writers and moviemakers do more than simply entertain with their stories and films.

Directions: Write an essay in which you discuss how strongly you agree or disagree with the quotation given. Substantiate your position with facts, details, and illustrations from what you've read, observed, or experienced.

After you read the prompt, brainstorm. Write down lists of ideas you have. If you agree with the statement, perhaps you think that storytellers have inspired technological innovations or social progress. You might list things like space travel, abolition, medical advances, or environmental conservation that emerged after a novel or film sparked people's imaginations. After you have taken a few minutes to generate ideas, look carefully at what you have written down. How can you narrow down the topic? Are some of your ideas or examples related to each other? Circle the ideas that seem connected. Jot down how they are related.

Since the topic is so broad, you need to choose a specific focus for your answer. Perhaps, if you were agreeing with the statement above, you might focus on science fiction. You might think of submarines, cloning, microsurgery, robots, and pacemakers as innovations first described in fiction. You might start by describing the origins of inventions in the writer's imagination. In your next paragraph, you could discuss how these imagined advances became part of our reality. You could finish by looking forward to technology we hope to soon possess because fiction has helped us imagine it. Alternatively, if you disagree with the statement, you might argue that imaginative stories do nothing more than entertain us, providing an escape from daily chores and troubles.

There are no right or wrong answers for the first essay; you must simply take a position and support it fully. Again, it doesn't matter if you agree or disagree as long as you have a narrow focus, a clear position, and examples to support your argument.

Writing and Organization

Given the time limit for each essay, it's best to write a traditionally structured essay that includes an introduction, two or three body paragraphs depending upon the topic, and a conclusion.

In your introduction, you should pique the reader's curiosity and clearly state your thesis; that is, let the reader know your point of view.

Each of the body paragraphs in your essay should address a single idea that reinforces your position. A body paragraph should begin with a topic sentence that tells the reader what you will address in the paragraph. The remainder of the paragraph should support its main idea with examples and specific evidence. By the end of each paragraph, the reader should firmly grasp the main idea of that paragraph.

For the first essay, the content of the body paragraphs is left entirely to your discretion. For the second essay, however, you must remember to incorporate both passages from the essay prompt and include accurate citations for any information you are paraphrasing or quoting.

For both essays, the conclusion gives you a chance to summarize your main points and reiterate your viewpoint on the topic. Given the limited time you have to write each one of the CLEP College Composition essays, don't agonize over the conclusion. It's far more important to have a strong introduction and well-developed body paragraphs. However, try to allow time to wrap up your essay with a concluding paragraph.

Sophistication of Expression

Certainly you should avoid grammatical errors, but sophistication of expression goes beyond grammatical correctness. As you write each essay, focus on writing clearly and choosing words that are appropriate and precise. Use a mix of simple and advanced vocabulary words. Write using the active voice. Include strong verbs in your essay. Vary the length of your sentences to energize the rhythm of the essay. Clarify the relationships between different ideas by using transitional words to help the reader follow the progress of your argument. A few examples of transitional words and phrases are given here.

Cause and effect	Contrast	Continuation
as a result	but	additionally
because	despite	for example
consequently	however	furthermore
so	on the other hand	in fact
therefore	while	indeed
thus	yet	moreover

Proofreading

Be sure to pace yourself and allow three to five minutes to proofread your essay. For the second essay, you should also make sure you have included accurate citations whenever they are required. When writing under time pressure, most people make a few mistakes. Common errors include confused sentences, omitted words, and misspellings. In the time you allot for proofreading, you should reread the essay to ensure that your meaning is clear. Look for spots where adding or deleting a word or two can improve readability. You should also correct any grammatical errors and typos. A few minutes devoted to proofreading will make your final product more polished.

FINAL THOUGHTS

After completing this review and the practice tests in this book, you will be on your way to an excellent score on the CLEP College Composition or CLEP College Composition Modular exam. For further preparation, consult college textbooks or other books on grammar and writing. Keep reading works by many authors on a range of subjects and hone your essay-writing skills by taking a stand on a variety of issues.

Good luck!

Chapter Six: **Practice Test 2 (College Composition Modular)**

Time—90 minutes
90 Questions

Directions: Each sentence tests your knowledge of choice of words (diction), idiom, grammar, and usage. Some sentences are correct, and each sentence can contain no more than one error.

Elements of the sentence that are underlined and lettered may be incorrect. Parts of the sentence that are not underlined can be assumed to be correct. When choosing an answer, follow the conventions of standard written English.

If a sentence contains an error, select the <u>one underlined portion</u> that must be changed to form a correct sentence. For sentences with no error, choose answer (E).

1. Ms. Lane <u>frequently</u> assigns projects <u>where</u> her
         A   B
    students must work <u>in groups</u> and <u>choose</u> their
                                    C   D
    own presentation format. <u>No error</u>
                                         E

2. Dates, which <u>were originally grown</u> in the Middle
                               A
    East, <u>and are now</u> cultivated in regions <u>around</u>
                    B   C
    the world <u>with desert climates</u>. <u>No error</u>
                          D   E

3. After <u>Sarah Clark resigned</u>, word spread quickly
                    A
    among politicians <u>who speculated</u> about the real
                                     B
    reason behind <u>their decision</u> to step down from
                             C
    office <u>so abruptly</u>. <u>No error</u>
                   D   E

4. <u>The members</u> of the Electoral College <u>meets</u> after
          A   B
    the general election and <u>cast</u> their votes <u>to choose</u>
                                          C   D
    the next president of the United States. <u>No error</u>
                                                                E

5. During the Middle Ages, monasteries <u>were centers</u>
                                                               A
    of learning with <u>their own libraries</u> and copying
                                    B
    <u>chambers, here</u> monks <u>copied</u> in beautiful callig
           C   D
    raphy the great works of their age. <u>No error</u>
                                                          E

6. The <u>gray storm clouds</u> <u>that darkened</u> the
              A   B
    afternoon <u>and caused</u> the temperature to
                         C
    plummet gave <u>the allusion</u> of the arrival of
                             D
    autumn although it was only the middle

    of July. <u>No error</u>
                       E

GO ON TO THE NEXT PAGE

KAPLAN

7. Although <u>it was</u> debated for many years and even
           A

   became <u>the subject</u> of a legal case, the difference
          B

   between fruits and vegetables <u>is simple: fruits</u>
                            C

   are usually eaten after a <u>meal, while</u> vegetables
                       D

   are served with a meal. <u>No error</u>
                     E

8. The new student, <u>who our</u> teacher introduced
                A

   <u>to us</u> today in calculus class, has <u>evidently</u>
     B   C

   skipped three <u>grades and</u> is a math and science
              D

   prodigy. <u>No error</u>
          E

9. <u>Although</u> most voters feel that the economy
       A

   <u>being</u> a pressing issue, politicians do not always
      B

   <u>address</u> their economic plans <u>thoroughly</u> during
      C   D

   campaign season. <u>No error</u>
                E

GO ON TO THE NEXT PAGE

KAPLAN

Directions: The passages below are first drafts of student work. The sentences in each passage have been numbered. Parts of the essays require revision.

After reading each passage, answer the questions that follow. Some questions require you to improve sentences by changing word choice (diction) and sentence structure. Other questions ask you to review the whole essay or a part of the essay and evaluate its organization, development, and the suitability of its language for the intended audience and purpose. Follow the rules of standard written English in your answer choices.

Questions 10–15 are based on the following passage.

(1) *I used to hate traveling.* (2) *I didn't see the point of visiting different places when everything and everyone I loved, except for my grandparents, were nearby.* (3) *Last year, however, my mother announced that we were going to spend the next year in Uganda in East Africa.*

(4) *I almost choked.* (5) *My mother, who is a professor, had an opportunity to work at the medical school in Kampala.* (6) *"In light of the growing disparities between industrialized and developing countries, volunteering is an obligation I must fulfill," she said.* (7) *"But what about my friends?" I wailed. "What about school?"* (8) *"It's just for nine months," she told me, "and I think it will be very educational."*

(9) *Even though adjusting to a new culture was difficult, my mother has the right instincts about what I would get out of the experience.* (10) *I attended an international school in Kampala with students hailing from countries located in Africa, Europe, and Asia.* (11) *My new friends introduced me to foreign food (such as ugali, a starch that is a staple in Uganda), new traditions, and even new languages.* (12) *We disagreed about whether American football is more exciting than soccer, but we shared many things, even though we looked different and dressed differently.*

(13) *When we left the United States, I was certain I would be miserable in Uganda.* (14) *When we left Uganda, I vowed to return as soon as I can.* (15) *Traveling truly expands your horizons.*

10. Which of the following is the best way to revise the underlined portions of sentences 1 and 2 (reproduced below) so that the two sentences are combined into one?

    I used to hate traveling. I didn't see the point of visiting different places when everything and everyone I loved, except for my grandparents, were nearby.

    (A) to hate traveling because I didn't see
    (B) to hate traveling, and I didn't see
    (C) to hate traveling, though I didn't see
    (D) to hate traveling because not seeing
    (E) to hate traveling, not seeing the

11. Which of the following sentences, if added after sentence 3, would best link the first paragraph with the rest of the essay?

    (A) I was excited by the opportunity to have an adventure.
    (B) This made me change my opinions completely.
    (C) You can imagine my surprised reaction to the news.
    (D) I have lived in the same town for my whole life.
    (E) My mother had spent several years in East Africa when she was in the Peace Corps.

GO ON TO THE NEXT PAGE ▷

KAPLAN

12. In the context of the third paragraph, which of the following is the best version of the underlined portion of sentence 9 (reproduced below)?

    Even though adjusting to a new culture was difficult, my mother has the right instincts about what I would get out of the experience.

    (A) No change.
    (B) my mother having the right instincts
    (C) my mother had the right instincts
    (D) the right instincts were had by my mother
    (E) my mother, who had the right instincts

13. Which of the following is the best version of the underlined portion of sentence 14 (reproduced here)?

    When we left Uganda, I vowed to return as soon as I can.

    (A) would want to
    (B) would be able to
    (C) were able
    (D) got the money
    (E) could

14. Which of the following is the best version of sentence 12 (reproduced here)?

    We disagreed about whether American football is more exciting than soccer, but we shared many things, even though we looked different and dressed differently.

    (A) No change.
    (B) Even though we all looked different, dressed differently, and disagreed about whether American football is more exciting than soccer, we shared many things.
    (C) We disagreed about whether American football is more exciting than soccer, nevertheless sharing many things, even though looking different and dressing differently.
    (D) We shared many things, but we disagreed about whether American football is more exciting than soccer, and also we looked different and dressed differently.
    (E) Even though looking different and dressing differently and disagreeing about which is better between American football and soccer, we shared many things.

15. In context, which is the best replacement for "hailing from" in sentence 10?

    (A) visiting from
    (B) originating from
    (C) traveling from
    (D) representing
    (E) starting out in

GO ON TO THE NEXT PAGE

Questions 16–21 are based on the following passage.

(1) *Volunteering should be a mandatory part of every student's high school education.* (2) *Doing service for others is a good way to teach teenagers empathy, the value of hard work, respect for diversity, and the meaning of community.* (3) *In contrast, a mandatory service program would help meet nonprofits' needs for more volunteers.*

(4) *A mandatory volunteer program would be easy to run.* (5) *Local service organizations, ranging from food cupboards to soup kitchens to tutoring programs, could put together a menu of volunteer needs.* (6) *Students could choose from the offerings, and schools could support the volunteering by giving students high school credit for their work.* (7) *Teachers could act as liaisons between the students and volunteer organizations; they could also supervise the students' service work.*

(8) *A mandatory volunteer program would address this issue by getting students into "real-world" situations.*

(9) *We need this country's best and brightest young minds to begin thinking about problems like poverty and educational inequity.* (10) *The program I'm proposing will do this.* (11) *And it will go a long way toward instilling tolerance in young people by making them see that the less fortunate have names, faces, and stories.*

(12) *Once they realize this, our young people won't be able to look past those in need.*

(13) *We have an opportunity to meet our community's desperate need for more volunteers and to shape our youth into civic-minded individuals; this is a win-win situation.* (14) *In closing, I hope you will urge the city council to support the mandatory volunteer program and to get our young people out of the classroom, where abstract ideas reign, and into the world, where they can make a difference.*

16. Which of the following would best replace "In contrast" at the beginning of sentence 3?

    (A) At the same time
    (B) And
    (C) Therefore
    (D) Nevertheless
    (E) In short

17. Which of the following versions of sentence 7 (reproduced here) is best?

    Teachers could act as liaisons between the students and volunteer organizations; they could also supervise the students' service work.

    (A) Teachers, while liaising between the students and volunteer organizations, could supervise their service work.
    (B) Teachers could act as liaisons between the students (while supervising their service work) and volunteer organizations.
    (C) Between the students and volunteer organizations, teachers could act as liaisons and supervise the service work of the students.
    (D) Teachers could act as liaisons between the students and volunteer organizations, supervising the students' service work.
    (E) Teachers supervising their service work—the students and volunteer organizations—teachers could act as liaisons between them.

18. Which of the following sentences is best to add before sentence 8?

    (A) The real world is very complicated.
    (B) A mandatory volunteer program would be easy to implement with little cost to the schools.
    (C) Our current education system is inadequate and old-fashioned.
    (D) One oft-repeated criticism of our educational system is students don't learn skills relevant in today's world.
    (E) The gap between the rich and poor is increasing by an alarming rate in this country.

GO ON TO THE NEXT PAGE

19. Which of the following would best replace "And" at the beginning of sentence 11?

    (A) Nevertheless

    (B) Furthermore

    (C) Instead

    (D) But

    (E) In general

20. In context, which is the best replacement for "do this" in sentence 10?

    (A) cause this to happen

    (B) get young people into their communities

    (C) help social service agencies have greater success

    (D) solve these problems immediately

    (E) plant the seeds for a new generation of problem solvers

21. Which is the best version of the underlined portion of sentence 13 (reproduced below)?

    We have an opportunity to meet our community's desperate need for more volunteers and to shape our youth into civic-minded individuals; this is a win-win situation.

    (A) No change.

    (B) individuals, and this will be a win-win situation

    (C) individuals, this being a win-win situation

    (D) individuals, a win-win situation

    (E) individuals, this is a win-win situation

Questions 22–28 are based on the following early draft of a student essay about the Great Pyramid of Egypt.

(1) *The construction of the Great Pyramid in Egypt has been portrayed in many pictures and books.* (2) *These pictures showing Egyptian workers carrying bricks up the side of the pyramid are only legends.* (3) *The feasibility of carrying the rocks up the side has been debated by top experts, who have proven that these pictures are false.* (4) *The idea that one long ramp extending up the side of the large rectangular box would have been sufficient for moving materials is dubious.* (5) *The ramp would have been a struggle to build itself and would have been too steep for workers to move up and down.*

(6) *Even if it had been possible for the workers to carry the stones up the tall ramp, which most experts doubt, building the ramp would have still remained an insurmountable challenge for Egyptian engineers.* (7) *Historians have calculated the amount of materials needed for a single ramp.* (8) *They found that it would have required more materials than were needed to build the entire pyramid.*

(9) *Many myths have surrounded the building of the Great Pyramid.* (10) *Some illustrations picture "teams of laborers hauling stones on sleds up a single giant earth ramp."* (11) *This theory has been rejected by many experts, including Peter Hodges.* (12) *He argued that "a single straight ramp connecting the quarry and the pyramid" would have been insufficient.* (13) *If hauling the stones "up a mile-long ramp had been practical," it would have been ridiculously expensive.* (14) *Not only a "monumental engineering challenge," the ramp would have "required at least three times as much building material as the pyramid."*

GO ON TO THE NEXT PAGE ⟩

22. Which of the following is the best way to revise the underlined portions of sentences 1 and 2 (reproduced below) so that the two sentences are combined into one?

    The construction of the Great Pyramid in Egypt has been portrayed in many pictures and <u>books. These pictures showing</u> *Egyptian workers carrying bricks up the side of the pyramid are only legends.*

    (A) books, but the pictures showing
    (B) books, showing these pictures
    (C) books, and the pictures showing
    (D) books, but having shown
    (E) while these pictures have shown

23. In context, what is the best replacement for "debated" in sentence 3?

    (A) disputed
    (B) discussed
    (C) fought about
    (D) chatted about
    (E) mulled over

24. Which of the following is the best version of the underlined portion of sentence 6 (reproduced below)?

    Even if it had been possible for the workers to carry the stones up the tall ramp, which most experts doubt, building the ramp would have still remained an insurmountable challenge for Egyptian engineers.

    (A) No change.
    (B) Although it had been possible for the workers to carry the stones up the tall ramp, which most experts doubt
    (C) Most experts doubt it had been possible for the workers to carry the stones up the tall ramp
    (D) Given the possibility for the workers to carry the stones up the tall ramp, which most doubt
    (E) Even if it had been possible for the workers to carry the stones up the tall ramp, that most experts doubt

25. Which of the following is the best way to combine sentences 7 and 8?

    (A) Historians have calculated the amount of materials needed for a single ramp and found that it would have required more materials than were needed to built the entire pyramid.
    (B) Building a single ramp would have required more materials than building the entire pyramid, according to historians' calculations.
    (C) Calculating the amount of materials needed for a single ramp, it has been found by historians that it would have required more materials than building the entire pyramid.
    (D) Historians, in calculating the amount of materials for a single ramp, have found that it would have required more materials than building the entire pyramid.
    (E) In terms of the amount of materials needed for a single ramp, the calculations of historians show that it would have required more materials than were needed to build the entire pyramid.

26. In context, all of the following words could replace "picture" in sentence 10 EXCEPT

    (A) portray.
    (B) render.
    (C) design.
    (D) capture.
    (E) depict.

GO ON TO THE NEXT PAGE

27. Which of the following is the best way to combine sentences 11 and 12?

    (A) This theory has been rejected by many experts, including Peter Hodges, and he argued that "a single straight ramp connecting the quarry and the pyramid" would have been insufficient.

    (B) Rejected by many experts, including Peter Hodges, because it would have been insufficient is the theory of a "single straight ramp connecting the quarry and the pyramid."

    (C) The theory of a "single straight ramp connecting the quarry and the pyramid" has been rejected by experts and Peter Hodges because it would have been insufficient.

    (D) Arguing that "a single straight ramp connecting the quarry and the pyramid," experts, including Peter Hodges, reject the theory as insufficient.

    (E) Peter Hodges, along with other experts, rejects this theory, arguing that "a single straight ramp connecting the quarry and the pyramid" would have been insufficient.

28. What is the best word to replace the underlined portion of sentence 13 (reproduced here)?

    If hauling the stones "up a mile-long ramp had been practical," it would have been <u>ridiculously</u> expensive.

    (A) significantly

    (B) profoundly

    (C) prohibitively

    (D) primordially

    (E) sensationally

Questions 29–33 are based on the following passage.

(1) *Although advertisements are designed to be deceptive, advertisers love the audience that doesn't question the message, the viewer who swallows the whole claim.* (2) *What's the claim?* (3) *It is the verbal or print part of the advertisement that makes the assertion that its product is superior.* (4) *You can either believe that the magician can make the elephant disappear—or learn to see through it.*

(5) *Claims run the gamut: a few are patently false, a few undeniably true, but most are worded so that it's hard to distinguish between the true and false.* (6) *Advertisers do this in an attempt to distinguish between products that are almost identical.* (7) *These are called parity products.*

(8) *The first rule in advertisement goes against common sense: "better" actually means "best," and "best" means "equal to."* (9) *That means that if the advertisement says, "Great Grape Soda is the best there is," it actually means "Great Grape Soda is as good as other sodas."* (10) *In contrast, "better" is still used as a comparative.* (11) *If an ad claims, "Great Grape Soda is better than other sodas," then it's saying that Great Grape Soda is indeed superior to other sodas.* (12) *However, since it's impossible to prove that it is better than other sodas, the comparative is only used to compare products with things other than competing brands.* (13) *As an example, it would be perfectly legal to say that "Great Grape Soda is better than fruit."*

(14) *Being bombarded by advertisements with messages aiming to deceive you, it is important that you learn to be a discriminating viewer who can see through the rhetoric.*

29. In context, which is the best replacement for "Although" in sentence 1?

    (A) Because

    (B) Even though

    (C) Surprisingly,

    (D) While

    (E) Today,

GO ON TO THE NEXT PAGE

30. Which is the best revision of "makes the assertion that" in sentence 3?

    (A) pontificates that

    (B) makes the position that

    (C) proposes as an explanation that

    (D) signals

    (E) asserts

31. Which of the following sentences is best to add after sentence 7?

    (A) Disparity products are products that have nothing in common.

    (B) Because the products are so similar, advertisers resort to using misleading language to convince you that one product is better than another.

    (C) Companies spend tens of millions of dollars on advertising.

    (D) The next time you buy something, you should think about what influenced you to buy a particular product.

    (E) Another advertising strategy is to create a catchy jingle that you remember when you walk into a store.

32. Which of the following revisions must be made to sentence 12 (reproduced here)?

    However, since it's impossible to prove that it is better than other sodas, the comparative only is used to compare products with things other than competing brands.

    (A) Change "it" to "Great Grape Soda."

    (B) Transpose "only" and "is."

    (C) Transpose "only" and "is used."

    (D) Change "things other than competing" to "noncompeting."

    (E) Change "than" to "then."

33. Which of the following is the best revision of the underlined portion of sentence 14 (reproduced here)?

    Being bombarded by advertisements with messages aiming to deceive you, it is important that you learn to be a discriminating viewer who can see through the rhetoric.

    (A) Bombarding advertisements with messages aiming to deceive you, you must

    (B) Aiming to deceive you, the messages that bombard you, you need to

    (C) You are bombarded by advertisements with messages aimed to deceive you, it is important that you

    (D) Being bombarded by advertisements with messages aiming to deceive you, the important thing is to

    (E) Bombarded by advertisements with deceptive messages, you need to

GO ON TO THE NEXT PAGE ⟩

Questions 34–39 are based on the following passage.

(1) *As a student having been attending public schools for last twelve years, I've earned the right to call myself an expert on school.* (2) *While it's true that there are many aspects of running schools and teaching that I don't understand, I've observed firsthand the effects of class size, especially the negative consequences of being in large classes.* (3) *For the past year, I was part of a pilot program in which students were broken into pods and taught in small, interdisciplinary classes with no more than fifteen students.* (4) *Now that I have returned to "regular school" and large classes, the advantages of small classes are shockingly clear to me.*

(5) *The learning environment in small classes leads to higher academic achievement.* (6) *Last year, it was the norm, rather than the exception, for all students to participate in class discussions.* (7) *Our teacher got to know each of us individually.* (8) *We developed mutual respect for each other and our teacher.* (9) *Moreover, because we were such a small class, our teacher had time to work with us one-on-one, and as everyone knows, this kind of individual instruction is invaluable.* (10) *Finally, the students in the class dug each other in a really cool way.* (11) *We organized a weekly study group, and the discussions we had in class often continued into the lunch hour.*

(12) *In my regularly sized classes, my passion for learning has disappeared, and I think many of my classmates share my sentiment.* (13) *Only a handful of students contribute their ideas in class discussions; it's impossible to meet one-on-one with our teachers; and it takes ages to get our graded papers returned to us.* (14) *I heard that the current budget squeeze is what has led to larger classes.*

34. Which of the following could best replace the underlined portion of sentence 1 (reproduced here)?

    As a student having been attending public schools for last twelve years, I've earned the right to call myself an expert on school.

    (A) As a student having been attending

    (B) Having attended

    (C) Since I have been attending

    (D) Although I've attended

    (E) Being in attendance at

35. What is the best revision to sentence 3 (reproduced here)?

    For the past year, I was part of a pilot program in which students were broken into pods and taught in small, interdisciplinary classes with no more than fifteen students.

    (A) Begin the sentence with "Although."

    (B) Insert "actually" at the end.

    (C) Change "with no more" to "without more."

    (D) Change "in which" to "where."

    (E) Change "For the past year" to "Last year."

GO ON TO THE NEXT PAGE

36. Which of the following is the best way to rewrite sentence 9 (reproduced here)?

    Moreover, because we were such a small class, our teacher had time to work with us one-on-one, and as everyone knows, this kind of individual instruction is invaluable.

    (A) Moreover, our teacher had time to work with us one-on-one because we were such a small class, and everyone knows this kind of individual instruction is invaluable.

    (B) Moreover, because we were such a small class, our teacher had time to give us invaluable one-on-one instruction.

    (C) Moreover, being such a small class, our teacher gave us what everyone knows is the invaluable time to work one-on-one in this kind of individual instruction.

    (D) With time to work with us one-on-one, moreover, our teacher gave us individual instruction that is invaluable.

    (E) Moreover, our teacher had time to work with us one-on-one and give us invaluable instruction because we were such a small class.

37. In context, the best phrase to replace "dug each other in a really cool way" in sentence 10 is

    (A) became fast and furious friends.

    (B) hung out all the time.

    (C) bonded in a positive way.

    (D) liked each other a lot.

    (E) had a lot of fun.

38. Which is the best version of the underlined portion of sentence 12 (reproduced here)?

    In my <u>regularly sized</u> classes, my passion for learning has disappeared, and I think many of my classmates share my sentiment.

    (A) No change.

    (B) regularly-sized

    (C) regular sized

    (D) regular-size

    (E) regular size

39. Which of the following would be the best sentence with which to end the passage?

    (A) At the end of the day, this budget squeeze will be the undoing of learning.

    (B) Ultimately, however, if the school board really wants to improve education, it should invest in small classes.

    (C) In the end, if we cannot have small classes, then maybe we can have better books.

    (D) Therefore we should all write to our local government representative about how to increase county budget revenue.

    (E) It's really too bad that we can't have small classes, because they're very beneficial as I've shown.

Directions: The following sentences test your knowledge of effective and correct expression. Use the conventions of written English to choose your answer: pay attention to choice of words (diction), punctuation, sentence structure, and grammar.

In each of the following sentences, either the entire sentence or part of the sentence is underlined. There are five versions of the underlined portion below the sentence. Choice (A) is the same as the original sentence, and choices (B)–(E) are different.

Choose the answer that produces the best sentence with the same meaning as the original sentence. If none of the alternatives are as effective as the original sentence, choose (A). The final sentence should be precise and unambiguous.

40. While San Francisco is known for its architectural sights, but many people visit Los Angeles for the beaches.

    (A) While San Francisco is known for its architectural sights, but many people visit Los Angeles for its beaches.

    (B) San Francisco is known for its architectural sights, but visiting Los Angeles is for its beaches.

    (C) The reason people visit San Francisco is for its architectural sights, Los Angeles beaches.

    (D) San Francisco is known for its architectural sights, but Los Angeles is famous for its beaches.

    (E) A city with beaches is Los Angeles, but San Francisco is known for its architectural sights.

41. Theodore Dreiser, an American naturalist novelist who distanced himself from Victorian propriety and realistic fiction, best known for his critiques of the American dream and industrialization.

    (A) best known for his critiques of

    (B) best known for critiquing

    (C) is best known for his critique of

    (D) being best known for his critiques of

    (E) knew his critiques of

42. Microeconomics, a branch of economics that focuses on the interaction of individual economic units, concerning the behavior of consumers, producers, and the markets that bring the two together.

    (A) Microeconomics, a branch of economics that focuses on the interaction of individual economic units, concerning

    (B) It is microeconomics, a branch of economics that focuses on the interaction of individual economic units, concerning

    (C) Concerning microeconomics, a branch of economics that focuses on the interaction of individual economic units, was

    (D) Microeconomics, a branch of economics that focuses on the interaction of individual economic units, is concerned with

    (E) Concerned with microeconomics, a branch of economics that focuses on the interaction of individual economic units, is

GO ON TO THE NEXT PAGE ⇨

43. After fuel and power shortages caused by World War I, a daylight saving time plan was adopted in England.

    (A) a daylight saving time plan was adopted in England

    (B) England adopted a daylight saving time plan

    (C) a daylight saving time was the plan of England

    (D) England's adoption of daylight saving became a plan

    (E) plans for daylight saving became increasingly adopted in England

44. In the early twentieth century, Picasso and others invented a new movement in modern art that immediately has distorted the individual figure and nature and eventually leads to the advent of nonobjective art.

    (A) that immediately has distorted the individual figure and nature and eventually leads to the advent of nonobjective art

    (B) with distorting the individual and nature and eventually leading to the advent of nonobjective art

    (C) that immediately distorts the individual figure and nature and leads to the advent of nonobjective art

    (D) that immediately distorted the individual figure and nature and led to the advent of nonobjective art

    (E) that immediately has distorted the individual figure and nature and has led to the advent of nonobjective art

45. In people with allergies, the body's defense system goes haywire, the antibodies that are produced to combat foreign substances end up attacking the body instead of protecting it.

    (A) system goes haywire, the antibodies

    (B) system goes haywire; the antibodies

    (C) system goes haywire being the antibodies

    (D) system goes haywire with the antibodies

    (E) system goes haywire so the antibodies

GO ON TO THE NEXT PAGE

KAPLAN

Directions: The following questions test your knowledge and use of research source materials. Some of the questions are based on single entries; others refer to passages provided. In the passage-based sets, Revision Skills and Rhetorical Analysis Skills may also be tested.

46. All of the following are true of the below citation EXCEPT

    De Los Santos, Aldana V. *Grilling Secrets of the Argentine Campo.* Ed. Martin B. Ruso and Andrew S. Breeze. Athens, GA: Hill Street Press, 2009. 35–37.

    (A) Aldana V. De Los Santos is the author's full name.

    (B) *Grilling Secrets of the Argentine Campo* was published in the state of Georgia.

    (C) The publication is a book.

    (D) Three pages are cited.

    (E) The publication has one editor.

47. *The following excerpt is taken from a scholarly paper.*

    While poetry has been defined as music made of words because a poem naturally calls upon the reader to speak aloud and hear the linguistic rhythm, several poets have used imagery relating to "unheard music" within their poems. The "unheard" melodies referred to by Keats in "Ode on a Grecian Urn" appear much later in T. S. Eliot's "Burnt Norton." Here, when Eliot refers to "unheard music," he follows Keats in suggesting that that which exists only in the mind is superior to anything that can be apprehended by the senses (Stephenson, 338).

    Which of the following gives the appropriate format to use for the reference above as the work would appear in the "Works Cited" list at the end of the paper?

    A) Stephenson, Martin. *The Irony of Poetry.* Los Angeles: Goodall Press, 2007.

    B) Eliot, T. S., *Burnt Norton.* London: Stephenson Press, 1989.

    C) Parker, John C. and Martin Stephenson. *The Irony of Poetry.* Los Angeles: Goodall Press, 2007.

    D) *Irony of Poetry,* by Stephenson, Martin. Pub. By Goodall Press, Los Angeles, 2007.

    E) Keats, John. "Ode on a Grecian Urn." Quoted in Stephenson.

48. Shannon, Bernie R. "Transitional Moments in Photosynthesis." *Botany Review* 45 (3): 84.

    In the citation, what information is given by "84"?

    (A) Page number

    (B) Issue number

    (C) Volume number

    (D) Chapter number

    (E) Year of first edition

49. Which entry below cites a reference that is part of another publication?

    (A) Alvarez, A. (1970). *The Savage God: A Study of Suicide.* New York: Random House.

    (B) Garner, B. A. (2003). *Garner's Modern American Usage.* New York: Oxford University Press.

    (C) Pepin, R.E. (2003). Introduction. *Selected Poetry of Charles Darling:* 1977–2002 (pp. iv–xxii). Colchester, CT: Colophon Books.

    (D) Stanton, D. C., & Farbman, E. (Eds.). (2003). *The Female Autograph: Theory and Practice of Autobiography.* Middletown, CT: Ibis Bookstore Press.

    (E) Connors, Lucinda (2010). *The Uses of Strategic Incentives.* Denver: Small Business Press.

GO ON TO THE NEXT PAGE

50. In what order should the following news articles be arranged in a bibliography?

    Poirot, C. (2004, March 17). HIV prevention pill goes beyond 'morning after.' *The Hartford Courant*, pp. F1, F6.

    New exam for doctor of future. (1989, March 15). *The New York Times*, p. B10.

    Silverman, P. H. (2004, June). Genetic Engineering. *The Atlantic*, 293, 14.

    Wheatcroft, G. (2004, June). The Tragedy of Tony Blair. *The Atlantic*, 293, 56–72.

    Thomas, E. & Hosenball, M. (2004, May 31). Bush's Mr. Wrong: The rise and fall of Chalabi. *Newsweek, 143*, 22–32.

    (A) Alphabetically by first word in the entry
    (B) Chronologically by date of publication
    (C) Alphabetically of name of publication
    (D) Numbered in order of their use in the writing
    (E) Chronologically in order of the time the writer accessed the resources

51. *The following excerpt is taken from a research paper.*

    In *How to Read a Book,* Adler and Van Doren describe syntopical reading as reading several books on the same topic and comparing them so as to arrive "at a greater understanding of the topic than any of the books alone would provide" (qtd. in Cummings 20).

    The number 20 means that

    A) Adler and Van Doren have jointly written 20 books.
    B) this citation is from a paper whose "Works Cited" list includes 20 sources.
    C) this citation is crediting a direct quotation taken from page 20.
    D) this is the twentieth citation in the paper.
    E) this citation is crediting an indirect quotation taken from page 20.

52. Hillock, S. 2010. Louisiana Delta: Resources at risk. *Environmental Health Perspectives* 113 (2): 164–172.

    The item (reproduced above) in a student's list of references indicates all of the following EXCEPT

    (A) "Louisiana Delta: Resources at risk" is around nine pages long.
    (B) "Louisiana Delta: Resources at risk" was written by S. Hillock.
    (C) "Louisiana Delta: Resources at risk" appears on page 113 of *Environmental Health Perspectives*.
    (D) "Louisiana Delta: Resources at risk" is an article in a periodical.
    (E) *Environmental Health Perspectives* is published more than once a year.

GO ON TO THE NEXT PAGE >

KAPLAN

Questions 53–60 are about the following passage.

(1) *According to a recent tally, in the 17th century, Native Americans in the Lower Amazon were growing at least 138 different crops.*[1] (2) *Then, as now, the staple crop was manioc (or as some call it, cassava), a robust root that people in Brazil roast, chop, fry, ferment, and even grind into an amazing number of different foods.* (3) *Even today, few people who live along the banks of the Amazon set a table without a bowl of* farofa. (4) *Which is a crunchy, toasted meal of manioc that is somewhat the texture of grated Parmesan cheese that they seem to sprinkle on everything they eat.*

(5) *People in the Amazon region have always eaten manioc.*[2] (6) *Even today, it is ever-present in the slash-and-burn farms that encircle one such village along the riverbank.* (7) *It seems to shift from place to place and they look like untouched leftovers from the past.* (8) *As Jacob Karls points out, "For several decades, researchers who wrote regional ecology books seemed to think these village farms were the 'timeless indigenous' adaptation."* (9) *But that's not true at all.* (10) *More recently, professional researchers studying the culture recognize these slash-and-burn agricultural practices as something rather modern and which spread because of technology from Europe.*

(11) *The jungle around the Amazon River is the thickest on earth so the people there had to cut away lots of trees if they wanted to do anything.*[3] (12) *Their basic tool was the stone ax.* (13) *Not surprising, the stone ax is a horrible tool.* (14) *With a stone ax, one does not so much cut down a tree as use the ax to beat a section of the trunk to pulp, weakening the base until the tree can no longer support itself.* (15) *I tried it myself when one of the archeologists at the dig challenged me.* (16) *After walloping it until I was weak as a noodle, I'd only smashed a little tiny dimple in the thick-as-steel coat of the tree.*

Notes

1. Lawrence Johnson, "Amazonian Agriculture," *Agricultural Anthropology* 8, no. 9 (2010): 41.

2. Jacob Karls, *Traditions of Pre-Columbian Latin America* (New York: NYU Press, 1980), 77.

3. Kim, Aleksandr, interview by Richard Roberts, October 19, 2010.

4. Jack Frennish, *Economics of Late 19th-Century North Africa* (London: Beacon Press, 1996), 98.

53. What type of source is cited in sentence 1?

(A) Book

(B) Newspaper

(C) Journal

(D Magazine

(E) Website

54. In note 1, what information is provided by "8"?

(A) Page number

(B) Volume number

(C) Issue number

(D) Title series

(E) Publication month

55. Which of the following sentences, if added after sentence 10, would best relate this paragraph to the one that follows?

(A) Europe was exporting a wide variety of books and products to the colonies at that time.

(B) The Native Americans had hitherto been rather protective of their land's natural beauty.

(C) Performing controlled burns of farmland requires patience and correct technique.

(D) Some of the technology didn't make it, and some of it wasn't accepted.

(E) With the arrival of the stone ax to the New World came significant changes to local methods.

GO ON TO THE NEXT PAGE

56. Which would be the best source to substantiate the claim made in sentence 10 (reproduced here)?

    More recently, professional researchers studying the culture recognize these slash-and-burn agricultural practices as something rather modern and which spread because of technology from Europe.

    (A) Rick Steves, host of television travel show on Brazil

    (B) Glória da Silva Cezar, the writer's classmate from São Paulo, the capital of Brazil

    (C) Dr. Paula Lucia Ferrucio da Rocha, archaeology agronomist, guest lecturer at State University

    (D) Dr. Ludwig Van DeMeer, German history professor from Brazil

    (E) Daniel de Oliveira, Brazilian speaker at the fall meeting of the Archaeology Department

57. What is best to do with note 3?

    (A) Leave it as is.

    (B) Delete it.

    (C) List the interviewer first.

    (D) Switch the order of the interviewee's first name and last name.

    (E) List the location where the interview took place.

58. What is best to do with sentence 8 (reproduced here)?

    As Jacob Karls points out, "For several decades, researchers who wrote regional ecology books seemed to think these village farms were the 'timeless indigenous' adaptation."

    (A) Leave it as it is.

    (B) Add a parenthetical note providing Karls's background.

    (C) Add a superscript number at the end, corresponding to a citation in the Notes section.

    (D) Add a parenthetical note listing the ecology books he's referring to.

    (E) Restate Karls's quote more succinctly.

59. What is the best way to combine sentences 3 and 4?

    (A) To this day, no riverside table is complete without a bowl of *farofa*: crunchy, toasted manioc meal, vaguely resembling grated Parmesan cheese, which Amazonians sprinkle on almost all of their food.

    (B) People today still living along the banks of the Amazon River without a bowl of *farofa* live with the crunchy, toasty manioc that is like grated Parmesan cheese.

    (C) Today people along the Amazon River still are eating *farofa* because it tastes crunchy and toasty almost like the taste of Parmesan cheese every day.

    (D) Few people in Brazil sit down today without getting themselves a bowl of the tasty, crunchy, Parmesan-like *farofa*.

    (E) It would be surprising today to find a family in Brazil who does not like *farofa*.

60. What is best to do with note 4?

    (A) Leave it as is.

    (B) Delete it.

    (C) Include a brief synopsis.

    (D) Switch the order of the author's first name and last name.

    (E) Include a parenthetical at the end of the note, relating it to the topic.

GO ON TO THE NEXT PAGE

KAPLAN

Questions 61–68 are based on the following passage.

(1) *"Beauty in motion," you might think, watching in wonder at the fluid, flowing movements of jellyfish in the Monterrey Aquarium, as classical music streams from hidden speakers as in accompaniment to the ballerina divas gliding through the blue-tinted water.* (2) *So beautiful, but so deadly!* (3) *Ask swimmers who've encountered jellyfish in the ocean.* (4) *Naïve swimmers often are deceived by the delicate transparency of these aquatic hazards.* (5) *In fact, a fairly common hazard of swimming in the ocean is an unexpected meeting with a jellyfish.* (6) *Just contact with the poison in a jellyfish's tentacles can result in sharp, lingering pain, or even death if the person stung is highly allergic.* (7) *While everyone, including the jellyfish, would like to avoid these encounters, they are not uncommon because jellyfish are found in oceans all around the globe (Brison 2008, 12).*

(8) *A news story published in the summer of 2010 reflects this ubiquity.* (9) *The article reported that a dead jellyfish stung about 150 people in the water off the coast of Wallis Sands.* (10) *Even though the 50-pound jellyfish already was dead, the park manager, Kevin Nguyen, told the reporter that stings sent five people to the hospital.* (11) *It turns out that the lifeguard, who had found the large hubcap-sized jellyfish near the shore around 2 p.m., took a pitchfork, snagged and pulled out the gelatinous mass and slapped it into the trashcan.* (12) *However, a quarter of an hour later, mayhem reigned.* (13) *"All of a sudden people just poured out of the water," he said.* (14) *"Crying kids, weeping and wailing all over the place, like a scene from one of the* Jaws *movies" (Dickinson 2010, A1).* (15) *Apparently, the lifeguard had removed only the head of the jellyfish.* (16) *The detached tentacles floated in the water, snagging and stinging the unsuspecting kids as they frolicked at play.* (17) *Even dead, jellyfish are hazardous.*

(18) *Apparently, this incident is a common one.* (19) *This is hardly surprising considering that jellyfish live in every ocean in the world and have done so for more than 650 million years.* (20) *The animals are likely so widespread because of their extreme adaptability—they are quite hardy and can withstand a wide range of temperatures and conditions in their environment.* (21) *In the case of jellyfish, beauty is a beast!*

References

Brison, Joanna. 2008. Jellyfish All Over. *LiveScience*, November, 12–16.

Dickinson, Margaret. 2010. "Detached Jellyfish Tentacles Sting Dozens off Wallis Sands." *New Hampshire Gazette*, July 17, A1.

Okida, Kenzaburo. 2008. Massive Jellyfish Swarms in Hawaii, Gulf of Mexico and Other Locations. *ScienceDaily*, October 14, 29–34.

Oshefsky, Melanie. 2007. Ballerinas of the *Sea*. *National Geographic*, July, 52–59.

61. What is best to do with sentence 9 (reproduced here)?

    The article reported that a dead jellyfish stung about 150 people in the water off the coast of Wallis Sands.

    (A) Leave it as it is.

    (B) Add a parenthetical note telling the area where Wallis Sands is located.

    (C) Give the species of jellyfish.

    (D) Provide a parenthetical citation for the article.

    (E) Name the author of the article.

62. The information in parentheses in sentence 7 informs the reader of all of the following EXCEPT

    (A) Brison wrote a book about marine life.

    (B) The article containing the information in sentence 7 was published in 2008.

    (C) There is a resource in the References section under the name "Brison."

    (D) The relevant information is found on page 12 of the source.

    (E) Brison is the name of the author of a cited source.

GO ON TO THE NEXT PAGE ⟩

63. The author uses the phrase "including the jellyfish" in sentence 7 (reproduced here) for what purpose?

    While everyone, <u>including the jellyfish</u>, would like to avoid these encounters, they are not uncommon because jellyfish are found in oceans all around the globe.

    (A) To introduce humor

    (B) To encourage sympathy

    (C) To ridicule

    (D) To introduce evidence

    (E) To point out a contrast

64. Which of the following, if added to the final paragraph, would most enhance the essay?

    (A) A discussion of ways to protect oneself against jellyfish

    (B) The name of the era that began 650 million years ago

    (C) An explanation of the method of locomotion employed by jellyfish

    (D) Further information about the adaptations that make jellyfish hardy

    (E) Predictions about future population levels of jellyfish

65. The second item in the References list indicates all of the following EXCEPT

    (A) The source is a newspaper.

    (B) Wallis Sands is located in New Hampshire.

    (C) The article is on the front page.

    (D) The article was published on July 17, 2010.

    (E) Margaret Dickinson wrote the article.

66. Which of the following best describes the purpose of the second paragraph?

    (A) It outlines a theme that is continued in the third paragraph.

    (B) It warns of the threats associated with swimming.

    (C) It provides an example of a point made in the first paragraph.

    (D) It casts light on a long-hidden fact.

    (E) It argues for improving conditions.

67. The author of the passage includes a quote from Dickinson's article in sentences 13 and 14 most likely to

    (A) suggest that this type of event could happen anywhere.

    (B) prove that it actually did happen.

    (C) put the discussion of jellyfish into a local context.

    (D) enhance the passage with the commentary of an expert.

    (E) illustrate the atmosphere at the beach when the people were stung.

68. What type of resource is listed last in the References section?

    (A) Journal

    (B) Newspaper

    (C) Magazine

    (D) Book

    (E) Website

GO ON TO THE NEXT PAGE

KAPLAN

Directions: The passages below consist of numbered sentences. Read each passage and answer the questions below it. The questions test how effectively you can analyze a piece of writing.

Questions 69–74 are based on the following passage.

(1) *Recently, laminins, a family of large multidomain glycoproteins, have begun to attract attention.* (2) *Having these proteins in extracellular matrix (ECM) is vital to developing and maintaining the organization of cells.* (3) *Among the cell-level tasks ascribed to laminins are those functions having to do with the way cells grow and differentiate during development, communicate among cells, and also with any projection from the cell body of a neuron.* (4) *This is also called neurite projection.* (5) *In the past, scientists were very interested in knowing more about the function of these laminins they started seeing in their research.* (6) *They are secreted and incorporated into cell-associated extracellular matrices and play an integral part of the structural scaffolding in almost every tissue of an organism.*

(7) *Very early in a gestation, scientists can detect laminins in an embryo.* (8) *They have found these proteins as early as the two-cell stage of fertilized mouse eggs.* (9) *Later, as the embryo develops, and when the tissue matures, the ECM serves as a "ubiquitous and major noncollagenous component of basement membrane," those thin sheets of fibers that underlie the epithelium, tissue composed of cells that line the cavities and surfaces of structures throughout the body.* (10) *Laminins become involved in the assembly of special forms of ECM and serve as a mediator during cell attachment, helping to keep order of the differentiated state of epithelial and endothelial cell layers that are so closely linked to their basement membranes.*

69. In context, sentence 2 serves to

(A) distinguish laminins from other proteins.
(B) define extracellular matrix.
(C) suggest that other functions could be possible.
(D) justify the recent focus on laminins.
(E) introduce the theme of proteins.

70. What is the purpose of the first paragraph?

(A) To define terms
(B) To explain why laminins are creating interest in the scientific community
(C) To show that laminins are the most important proteins
(D) To propose a topic of research study
(E) To demonstrate the value of scientists to academic faculty

71. In context, sentence 6 serves to

(A) show how extracellular matrices get their strength.
(B) clarify the importance of neurite projection.
(C) explain why the writer is so interested in laminins.
(D) explain why laminins caught the attention of past scientists.
(E) describe how laminins are disposed of.

72. In context, "line" (sentence 9) most nearly means

(A) coat.
(B) stripe.
(C) bisect.
(D) mark.
(E) fill.

GO ON TO THE NEXT PAGE ▷

73. How can the organizational pattern of paragraph 2 best be described?

    (A) A substance is described along with its uses and dangers.

    (B) A process is described chronologically.

    (C) A cause-effect relationship is outlined.

    (D) A building process is described in spatial stages.

    (E) A series of terms is listed.

74. In context, "mediator" (sentence 10) most nearly means

    (A) fueler.

    (B) lubricator.

    (C) binding agent.

    (D) protector.

    (E) guide.

Questions 75–80 are based on the following passage.

(1) *Ants take no holidays, use no eight-hour system, and never strike for higher wages.* (2) *They are cheerful little toilers and have neither malice nor back doors to their hearts.* (3) *There are no sedentary loafers among them, and you never see one out of a job.* (4) *They get up early, go to bed late, work all the time, and eat on the run.*

(5) *You never see two ants arguing some foolish question that neither of them understands; they don't care whether the moon is inhabited or not; nor whether a fish weighing two pounds put into a pail of water already full will make the pail slop over or weigh more.* (6) *They ain't hunting after the philosopher's stone or getting crazy over the cause of the sudden earthquake.* (7) *They don't care whether Jupiter is thirty or thirty-one millions of miles up in the air nor whether the earth bobs around on its axis or not, so long as it don't bob over their corncrib and spill their barley.*

(8) *They are simple, little, busy ants, full of faith, working hard, living prudently, praising God by minding their own business, and dying when their time comes, to make room for the next crop of ants.* (9) *They are a reproach to the lazy, an encouragement to the industrious, and a rebuke to the vicious.*

(10) *Ants have bylaws and a constitution and they mean something.* (11) *Their laws ain't like our laws, made with a hole in them so that a man can steal a horse and ride through them on a walk.* (12) *They don't have any legislators that you can buy, nor any judges, lying around on the half-shell, ready to be swallowed.* (13) *I rather like the ants and think now I shall sell out my money and real estate and join them.*

75. The purpose of the phrase "back doors to their hearts" in sentence 2 is to

    (A) suggest that ants, as with any other sentient creatures, can be won over by honest means.

    (B) introduce the concept that people are far superior to ants because people can reason and make conscious decisions.

    (C) conclude that ants are followers, not leaders.

    (D) suggest that ants are straightforward and honest.

    (E) imply that ants cannot be trusted because they work by indirection.

76. According to the first paragraph, ants do all of the following activities and have all the following traits EXCEPT

    (A) assail their enemies through devious means.

    (B) labor in an honest fashion.

    (C) deal openly and honestly with their fellow ants.

    (D) rise early to get a head start on the day.

    (E) work until the job is completed.

GO ON TO THE NEXT PAGE

77. The author's primary purpose for using terms like "ain't" is to

   (A) show that he came from humble beginnings but has worked hard to educate himself.

   (B) reveal himself as a misanthrope who believes that animals and insects are far superior to people.

   (C) appeal to his audience by using vernacular English.

   (D) make it seem as though the passage was written in the early seventeenth century.

   (E) signal to urban intellectuals that the piece is meant for farmers and country people.

78. The primary purpose of sentence 5 is to suggest that

   (A) people do these things.

   (B) ants' priorities are in the wrong place.

   (C) there is a time and a place for certain questions.

   (D) arguing can be productive in the right context.

   (E) ants may one day develop these habits.

79. What is the primary purpose of paragraph 3?

   (A) To list the virtues that humans are unable to demonstrate

   (B) To begin defining a new moral code

   (C) To illustrate how dull ants' lives are

   (D) To outline the virtues to which humans should aspire

   (E) To marvel at the wondrous intelligence of ants

80. The tone of this passage is best characterized as

   (A) bitter.

   (B) satirical.

   (C) serious.

   (D) scathing.

   (E) caustic.

Questions 81–84 are based on the following passage.

   (1) *Fran Claggett, a pioneer in the use of graphics in teaching literature, recommends that professors employ art—either via graphics to help plot out the structure before or after the students read, or in assignments for which students may use art to show what they know.* (2) *Today the word* graphics *seems anachronistic.* (3) *So do the terms* visuals *and* media, *let alone* audiovisual. (4) *In this, the 21st century, students are more versed in digital, computerized media.* (5) *Yet the basics of literature as art and story have not changed.* (6) *There still is skillful use of language and imaginative use of arrangement.* (7) *Therefore, professors should design lessons that incorporate old and new media to show students a work's traditional devices, such as structure and plot lines, images, and symbols.* (8) *With proper guidance, students can use their artistic interests and digital talents to demonstrate their comprehension of works of even the most traditional literature.*

81. The passage is primarily concerned with

   (A) engaging both sides of the brain using interdisciplinary study.

   (B) expanding on the visual potential of written exams.

   (C) blending various forms of media.

   (D) enhancing student comprehension of literature.

   (E) encouraging students to challenge the way professors use technology.

82. In sentence 1, "via" could best be replaced by

   (A) street.

   (B) advanced.

   (C) by means of.

   (D) without.

   (E) digital.

GO ON TO THE NEXT PAGE ⇨

83. In context, "anachronistic" (sentence 2) most nearly means

    (A) not useful.

    (B) high-tech.

    (C) low-tech.

    (D) everyday.

    (E) outdated.

84. Which of the following is implied by sentence 5 (reproduced here)?

    Yet the basics of literature as art and story have not changed.

    (A) The younger generation rejects older art forms.

    (B) Digital media will one day change the basics of art and story.

    (C) Cinema is the meeting ground for all of these media.

    (D) Language skills are atrophying.

    (E) There is something fundamental and timeless about narrative.

Questions 85–90 refer to the following passage.

(1) Suppression is the act of keeping back, restraining, checking. (2) Omission means to leave out or fail to include. (3) Remembering is the process of bringing an event, person, or thing to the mind again. (4) Both remembering and suppressing or omitting, though working in opposite directions, produce accounts that are half true at best. (5) When I moved back to Idaho in my early twenties to work as a reporter, I often told people that I was born and raised there, which was only a small part of the story.

(6) In fact, I had just graduated from Oxford University. (7) I had just flown across the Atlantic and traveled by train across Canada, reading the plays of England's greatest playwright, Shakespeare; the autobiography of a medieval mystic named Margery Kempe who lived in England; and the British magazine Granta's *issue about journeys to far-flung, exotic places. (8) During the train trip, I read through the night, not glancing out the window, until the train climbed through the Rockies and started its slow, rhythmic slide to the Pacific Ocean.*

(9) Then, I started to panic. (10) Moving back to Idaho and taking up work as a reporter was a romantic idea to me. (11) It represented an idea that I possessed about myself as a Westerner, what I remembered about my childhood in Idaho. (12) Whenever the talk at Oxford turned to subjects I didn't understand or didn't care to understand, like the fall of communism or tax cuts or New York private schools or Flemish painting, I withdrew, telling myself that I was a Westerner, and we Westerners were a different breed. (13) "I'm a cross between a barbed-wire fence and a wild coyote," my grandpa was fond of saying. (14) I thought I was, too, but the fact was my time outside of the state had changed me.

GO ON TO THE NEXT PAGE

KAPLAN

85. Which of the following best describes the organization of the first two paragraphs?

    (A) The first paragraph introduces several ideas that the second paragraph explores.

    (B) The first paragraph introduces a thesis that the second paragraph contradicts.

    (C) The first paragraph offers a concrete experience that the second paragraph generalizes about.

    (D) The first paragraph explains the meaning of remembering, while the second paragraph explores the significance of forgetting.

    (E) The first paragraph is completely abstract, while the second paragraph is personal.

86. Which of the following best describes the third paragraph?

    (A) The author emphasizes how adrift she felt during her time at Oxford.

    (B) The author shows that she is relieved to be returning to Idaho.

    (C) The author admits that she is uncertain about her identity.

    (D) The author revels in her feelings about being an outsider.

    (E) The author indicates that reading is her favorite pastime.

87. In context, sentence 4 serves to

    (A) indicate how the process of remembering is always imperfect.

    (B) draw a clear distinction between the acts of suppression or omission and remembering.

    (C) alert the reader to be suspicious of the truthfulness of the writer.

    (D) allude to the similarities between trying to forget something and trying to remember something.

    (E) prove the author is telling the whole story when she says she is an Idaho native.

88. The author's purpose in mentioning the books and magazines she reads on the train is to suggest she

    (A) will not stop reading British literature even though she has left the country.

    (B) is trying to fill the hours of the long train ride across Canada.

    (C) enjoys British literature more than American literature.

    (D) is beginning to prepare for her work in Idaho as a reporter.

    (E) is very connected to England and the world she is leaving behind.

89. Sentence 13 primarily serves to

    (A) show one of the poles of the writer's ambivalence.

    (B) give an image to the basis of the writer's personality.

    (C) paint the West with local color.

    (D) reveal the inferiority of the writer's background.

    (E) endear the writer to the audience.

90. According to the passage, certain conversations in Oxford led to

    (A) boredom and homesickness.

    (B) alienation.

    (C) confusion about identity.

    (D) the desire to return home.

    (E) floods of memories.

END OF TEST STOP

THE ANSWER KEY APPEARS ON THE FOLLOWING PAGE.

ANSWER KEY

1.	B	14.	B	27.	E	40.	D	53.	C	66.	C
2.	B	15.	B	28.	C	41.	C	54.	B	67.	E
3.	C	16.	A	29.	A	42.	D	55.	E	68.	C
4.	B	17.	D	30.	E	43.	B	56.	C	69.	D
5.	C	18.	D	31.	B	44.	D	57.	D	70.	B
6.	D	19.	B	32.	C	45.	B	58.	C	71.	D
7.	E	20.	E	33.	E	46.	E	59.	A	72.	A
8.	A	21.	A	34.	B	47.	A	60.	B	73.	B
9.	B	22.	A	35.	E	48.	A	61.	D	74.	E
10.	A	23.	A	36.	B	49.	C	62.	A	75.	D
11.	C	24.	A	37.	C	50.	A	63.	A	76.	A
12.	C	25.	B	38.	D	51.	E	64.	D	77.	C
13.	E	26.	C	39.	B	52.	C	65.	B	78.	A

79.	D		
80.	B		
81.	D		
82.	C		
83.	E		
84.	E		
85.	A		
86.	C		
87.	D		
88.	E		
89.	A		
90.	B		

PRACTICE TEST 2 QUICK REFERENCE TABLES

Use the following tables to determine which topics you still need to review.

Topic	Test Question
Conventions of Standard Written English	1–9
Revision Skills	10–39
Improving Sentences	40–45
Ability to Use Source Materials**	46–68
Rhetorical Analysis	69–90

* Only found on the College Composition Modular exam.

** In Ability to Use Source Materials questions, the elements tested under Revision Skills and Rhetorical Analysis may be tested.

Topic	Number of Questions on Test	Number Correct
Conventions of Standard Written English	9	
Revision Skills	30	
Improving Sentences	6	
Ability to Use Source Materials**	23	
Rhetorical Analysis	22	

* Only found on the College Composition Modular exam.

** In Ability to Use Source Materials questions, the elements tested under Revision Skills and Rhetorical Analysis may be tested.

Answers and Explanations

1. (B)

This question tests diction. The word "where" is correct only when it refers to a place. In this sentence "where" should be replaced by "for which" or "on which."

2. (B)

The sentence, as it appears, is incomplete because the verb "were" is part of the dependent clause "which were originally grown in the Middle East," and the verb "are" is paired with a conjunction ("and") that separates it from the main clause. To correct the mistake, the conjunction "and" should be eliminated, making "*are* now cultivated" the predicate.

3. (C)

Pronouns must agree in number and person with their antecedents (the words they replace). Since the antecedent is "Sarah Clark," the pronoun should be "her." The way the sentence is currently written, the pronoun "their" refers back to "politicians." The politicians were speculating about Sarah Clark's decision, not their own decision.

4. (B)

Verbs must always agree with their subjects. Here, the subject is "the members." Intervening words such as the prepositional phrase "of the Electoral College" should not be confused with the subject. In this case, since the subject is plural, the verb must take the plural form as well ("meet" instead of "meets").

5. (C)

This sentence is a run-on. "During the Middle Ages, monasteries were centers of learning with their own libraries and copying chambers" is one complete thought, and "here monks copied in beautiful calligraphy the great works of their age" is another. The two independent clauses can be connected (with "where") or separated with a semicolon or a period.

6. (D)

"Allusion" is defined as a reference to something such as a piece of literature, which doesn't make sense in the context of the sentence. The correct answer is "illusion," which means an unreal or misleading image.

7. (E)

This sentence is correctly written. Colons can be used as punctuation between two independent clauses when the second clause clarifies or adds meaning to the first. In this example, the first independent clause establishes a broad concept (the difference between fruits and vegetables), and the second independent clause clarifies the first and makes it more specific. Answer (C) may tempt you if you think that the first letter after the colon should be capitalized. However, the only time that letter should be capitalized is if it is the beginning of a direct quote or if it is a proper noun.

8. (A)

Because the new student is the *object* of the phrase "introduced to us" and not the subject, the subject pronoun "who" should be changed to the object pronoun "whom."

9. (B)

The verb form "being" cannot be used as the main verb in a clause. The error in this sentence can be corrected by replacing "being" with "is."

10. (A)

The second sentence explains the first sentence, which means that there is a causal relationship between them. "Because" is the best word to express this relationship. Choices (B) and (C) do not express the correct relationship between the two ideas. Choice (D) is not grammatical. Choice (E) isn't clear because it can be read to mean something different from the intended meaning of the original two sentences.

11. (C)

The last sentence of a paragraph provides a summary and serves as a transition to the next paragraph. In this case, the best choice is answer (C) because it suggests how the author reacted to his mother's news, preparing the reader for the description in the next paragraph.

12. (C)

Because the author is describing an experience that happened in the past, the past tense (C) should be used throughout the sentence. Answer (B) is incomplete. Answer (D) is incorrect because it uses the passive voice. Answer (E) does use the past tense but creates a fragment rather than a complete sentence.

13. (E)

The best way to answer this question is to use process of elimination. Choice (A) incorrectly uses the conditional verb form "would." Choice (B) also uses a conditional form and is wordy. Choice (C) is written in the wrong tense. Choice (D) introduces a new idea to the sentence, and that's a red flag on these types of questions. The correct answer to a Revisions Skills question shouldn't incorporate new information; it should simply restate the original sentence accurately, correctly, and succinctly. Choice (E) uses the correct verb form and preserves the intended meaning of the original sentence.

14. (B)

The sentence is wordy as written, since it uses both "but" and "even though." Choice (B) eliminates this repetition. Choice (C) doesn't use parallel structure. Choice (D) is wordy. Choice (E) uses parallel verb forms, but the word order is awkward. Choice (B) is a graceful and accurate rewriting of the original, so it's the best answer.

15. (B)

"Hailing from" most nearly means "originating from" (B). The difficult thing about answering this question is that choices (A) and (C) make grammatical sense in the sentence. They don't make *logical* sense, however, when you consider that the speaker is talking about an international school where, presumably, each student is enrolled for at least the length of a school year (as the speaker himself is). A school year is hardly a "visit"—it's quite a bit longer, in fact. "Traveling" (C) implies they're just stopping through. Choices (D) and (E) are awkward.

16. (A)

Because the author is trying to describe how a mandatory volunteer program would meet two different needs simultaneously, the best choice is answer (A). While "And" (B) isn't ungrammatical, it's more precise to say that the two things can happen at the same time.

17. (D)

The key here is to look for simplicity. Choice (D) is grammatically sound and succinct—note how it obviates the need for the word *they* along with *teachers*. When an answer choice can cut down on the number of pronouns used in a sentence, then that's a good clue that it's correct, as long as it's still grammatically sound. The other choices are wordy, awkward, or ungrammatical.

18. (D)

Sentence 8 refers to an issue and says it would be solved by getting students involved in "real-world" situations. Since you know the correct answer is related to the real world, the best choice is answer (D) since it refers to students' need to learn skills that are "relevant in today's world."

19. (B)

The author is discussing the benefits of the program in sentences 8, 9, 10, and 11. That means the ideas are related, and you need a transitional word that shows this. Answers (A), (C), and (D) suggest that the final idea is different from the previous ones, which isn't true. Answer (E) prepares the reader for a generalization that doesn't occur. The best choice, therefore, is answer (B) because it signals that another benefit will be noted.

20. (E)

In sentence 9, the author suggests that a mandatory volunteer program will give young people the opportunity to begin exploring social problems. With this in mind, look at each of the answer choices. Answer (A) is just as vague as the original sentence. Answer (B) is not specific enough. Answer (C) is not related to the young volunteers. Answer (D) is focused on the present, while sentence 9 is focused on the future. Therefore, the best answer is (E). If the country's best and brightest young minds begin thinking about social problems, the seeds will be planted for a new generation of problem solvers.

21. (A)

The sentence, as it is currently written, is correct. A semicolon is correct punctuation for separating two independent but closely related clauses. Answer (B) is unnecessarily set in the future tense. Answer (C) is verbose. In answer (D), the phrase "a win-win situation" mistakenly describes the last noun, "individuals," which is inaccurate. Answer (E) is a run-on.

22. (A)

To combine two independent clauses, ask yourself how they are related. Here, the process of building the Pyramid has been depicted, but part of that process is legend, not fact. There is a contrasting relationship between the two ideas, so a contrast conjunction "but" is appropriate here. Choice (A) is the best answer. Choice (B) is wrong because it uses incorrect word order. Choice (C) is grammatically correct but not as logically precise as (A). Option (D) uses the contrast transition "but," but the answer doesn't sound right when you plug it into the sentence. Likewise, (E) may sound tempting because it uses the contrast transition "while," but it doesn't make sense when you read it into the sentence.

23. (A)

In context, the word *debated* here seems to indicate that the scientists disagree with the prevailing preconception. They contest its validity. Unfortunately, "contested" is not available, so you'll have to look for a word that means the same thing. "Discussed" (B) is tempting, but actually it shares the same problem as choices (D) and (E): they're all a bit inconclusive about the position taken by the scientists. The sentence is quite clear about their rejecting the prevailing view. Choice (C) is adequately conclusive about the scientists' position, but it's much too forceful. The best choice is "disputed" (A), which captures the meaning of the original sentence accurately.

24. (A)

The sentence is correctly written. The clause "which most experts doubt" is correctly placed to qualify the idea of the workers carrying the stones up the ramp. Answer (B) contradicts itself, first saying that it was possible for workers to carry the stones up the ramp and then saying that experts doubt it was possible.

25. (B)

Choice (B) is the only one that effectively condenses the original two sentences into one while retaining their intended meaning. It is the only answer choice to use the word "materials" only once, which demonstrates an economy and succinctness that make it superior to the other, wordier choices, which all use the word "materials" twice.

26. (C)

The word *design* is the only answer choice that cannot serve as a synonym for the verb form of "picture," whose closest meaning is "portray." To portray something is to give a visual form to an idea that already exists, whereas to design something is to create a visual form from scratch.

27. (E)

To pick the answer, read each choice, paying attention to which one expresses the same ideas as the original efficiently and grammatically. The relationship between the two independent clauses is unclear in answer (A). Answers (B) and (C) are awkwardly worded. Answer (D) is incorrect because it is the ramp that is insufficient, not the theory.

28. (C)

The word *significantly* doesn't make sense to modify "expensive," so rule out choice (A). Choice (B) is tempting because it means "very" or "immensely," but it turns out that (C) is better choice in context. The paragraph is about how the costs of creating a ramp would have made it impossible to build. With that in mind, you can see that the word "prohibitively" is definitely the best answer because it expresses the immensity of the cost while also being specific about the cost making the project impossible. Choices (D) and (E) don't make sense in context.

29. (A)

Think through the logical structure of this sentence. There are two ideas that need to be connected: (1) advertising is meant to be deceptive, and (2) advertisers want an audience that will accept the claim without questioning it—an audience that is gullible, or easily deceived. These two ideas are pretty close to one another (they have a causal relationship), yet the word "although" signals a *contrast* between them—that's why "although" is a poor word choice and needs to be changed. Choice (A) is the best option because it demonstrates the causal relationship that is intended in the sentence. Choice (B) is no better than the original because it basically means the same thing. Choice (C) is wrong because there should be no surprise in this very logical, causal relationship. Choice (D), like the original, also signals contrast and therefore destroys the intended meaning of the sentence. Choice (E) is ungrammatical because it makes the sentence a run-on.

30. (E)

As usual, favor simplicity when trying to find a replacement for the wordy phrase "makes the assertion that." For starters, the word *that* isn't even necessary; in fact it's one of the most overused words in the English language. If the phrase "makes the assertion that" were replaced with simply "asserts," then the meaning of the sentence would remain intact, and it would be less wordy. Therefore, choice (E) is the best answer. Don't let the original phrasing fool you into thinking that the sentence *needs* to be wordy. *To make the assertion that X = to assert X.*

31. (B)

The best way to answer this question is to use process of elimination. Eliminate answer (A) because "disparity products" is not related to the article. Eliminate answer (C) because the article is not about the size of different companies' advertising budgets. Eliminate answers (D) and (E) because they would be more relevant if they appeared in paragraph 1. That leaves you with answer (B), which is the best choice because it explains why advertisers use language that goes against common sense.

32. (C)

There's no need to name the brand of soda under discussion (A), as it was named in the previous sentence and, in context, there should be no confusion about what the pronoun "it" refers to. Choice (B) is tempting because moving "only" to another position in the sentence is precisely what is needed, but it doesn't belong after "is." In formal prose, the word "only" should be placed directly before the term it modifies. To put this a different way: its placement in the sentence determines which word it modifies. So the sentence resulting from choice (B) would essentially tell you that the comparative is only "used" (as opposed to being manipulated or polished or celebrated, or any other verb) to compare products. Choice (C) tells you that the use of "the comparative" is only to "compare products" (as opposed to some other use for "the comparative"). Choice

(D) changes the meaning of the sentence drastically. The point is that "the comparative" isn't to be used for any brands at all. Changing "than" to "then" (E) would be to change from the correct to the incorrect one of this pair of often-confused words.

33. (E)

Answer (E) simplifies the descriptive phrases without compromising the meaning of the original sentence. Answers (A), (C), and (D) are grammatically incorrect, and answer (B) is awkwardly worded.

34. (B)

Choice (A) is wordy because it uses "having been" unnecessarily. Choice (B) is the right answer because it is concise. Choice (C) is not grammatically wrong but is less concise than (B). Choice (D) introduces the illogical contrast "although," which doesn't reflect the relationship expressed by the sentence. Choice (E) is wordy.

35. (E)

Choice (A) is wrong because beginning sentence 3 with "although" would create a contrast with sentence 2 that is absolutely inappropriate; the former is meant to build on the latter. Choices (B), (C), and (D) are arbitrary distracters that don't serve a purpose. Choice (E) is the correct answer because it corrects a temporal shift. The phrase "for the past year" means "from one year ago until the present time," but the rest of the sentence indicates that the speaker means to refer to the previous school year ("last year"), from which she has evidently already gained some distance.

36. (B)

The original sentence can be simplified by combining "one-on-one" with "individualized instruction." Since these two phrases refer to the same thing, it's possible to compress the two independent clauses as long you don't lose any meaning. That means you need to make sure you keep the idea that individualized instruction is "invaluable." Answer (B) accomplishes this: it is economical, clear, and grammatically correct.

37. (C)

The tone of this essay is mostly formal and informational. "Dug each other in a really cool way," however, is much more informal. Answers (B), (D), and (E) are also informal ways of describing relationships, and answer (A) makes no sense, as a friendship cannot be "fast and furious." Answer (C) most closely matches the tone of the essay.

38. (D)

The original sentence employs an adverb and a verb, but the intended meaning requires a compound modifier ("regular-size"), so choice (A) is incorrect. When placing a compound modifier before the noun it modifies, you must hyphenate the compound. Therefore choice (E) is incorrect.

39. (B)

Choice (A) is both unconstructive and overblown. Choice (C) introduces a whole new concept, the quality of the books, in the last sentence of the passage. Whenever you see this happen in a CLEP question, you can feel sure that it's wrong; a good conclusion provides insight about what has already been said without making any sharp turns or bringing in new material. Choice (D) does something similar, focusing on civic participation instead of the main theme of the passage, which is the value of small classes. Choice (E) is weak and too informal.

40. (D)

Choice (A) is wrong because it includes two contrast transitions ("while" and "but") when only one is called for. Choice (B) does not use parallel structure. Choice (C) leaves out words, which would be acceptable if the meaning were implied by the rest of the sentence. Since that is not the case here, (C) is wrong. Choice (D) is correct because it uses parallel structure and the appropriate transition "but." Choice (E) uses word order that is not idiomatically correct in English.

41. (C)

The original sentence lacks a verb and is therefore incomplete. Correct the error by adding "is" before "best known" (C). Answers (A) and (B) both lack verbs, answer (D) uses the wrong verb form, and answer (E) makes little sense.

42. (D)

This original sentence is incomplete because "concerning" is not a complete verb. In this sentence, the correct form of the verb is "is concerned with," which makes answer (D) correct. Neither answers (A) nor (B) corrects the problem, and answer (C) implies that microeconomics is an obsolete field of study, which it isn't. Answer (E) is incorrect because the introductory phrase "Concerned with microeconomics" does not logically modify the following noun, "branch."

43. (B)

It's usually better to write sentences in the active voice. This means stating early in the sentence who or what completed the action. In answers (A), (C), and (E), the subject ("England") does not appear until the end of the sentence. Answer (D) is very wordy. Therefore, the best answer is (B), which shows succinctly the relationship between the subject ("England") and the action ("adopted").

44. (D)

The sentence refers to something that happened in the past (as indicated by the verb "invented"). All of the verbs, even those in the dependent clause, must agree. Answer (D) is the only option with all the verbs in the past tense.

45. (B)

The original sentence is a run-on. The two independent clauses ("In people with allergies, the body's defense system goes haywire" and "the antibodies that are produced to combat foreign substances end up attacking the body instead of protecting it") need to be separated by a period or semicolon or joined by a comma and conjunction. Only answer (B) accomplishes this, by supplying the semicolon.

46. (E)

All of the answer choices state true information about the citation except for choice (E). The book has two editors, not one.

47. (A)

Choice (A) is correct because it is the only one that places the cited author's name, Stephenson, first in the entry on the "Works Cited" list.

48. (A)

In a journal citation such as this one, the number after the colon is the page number (A). The number after the title is the volume number (C), and the one in parentheses is the issue number (B). Chapter number (D) and year of first edition (E) are not included in a citation.

49. (C)

Note that (C) gives a citation that is for the Introduction to the book *Selected Poetry of Charles Darling*. If the material cited is from a foreword, preface, introduction, or afterword, list the name of the author of the book element you are citing. Follow the date (which might be different from the actual publication date) with the name of the element, the title of the book, and, in parentheses, the page number or page range on which the element appears (with p. or pp. to indicate page or pages). Choices (A), (B), and (E) have single authors and single publication titles with no mention of a part of a book. Choice (D) lists a book with two editors but does not indicate that a specific part of the book is being cited.

50. (A)

Lists of references, regardless of the name of the list (e.g., Sources Consulted, References, or Bibliography) should be arranged alphabetically by the first word in the entry. In this case, four of these resources include an author, and one has only the title of the article. It is the endnote/footnote entry that is numbered. Neither of these citation elements is organized chronologically by date of publication or day of access, so (B) and (E) are incorrect. Choice (C) would be correct in some cases, but not if there is an author in the entry you're adding to your reference list. A bibliography doesn't list sources according to the time they were accessed, so (D) is wrong.

51. (E)

An indirect quotation is a quotation that a researcher or writer found quoted in a secondary source. In this example, the material in quotation marks, though the words of Adler and Van Doren, was found by the researcher on page 20 of a work by Cummings. Note that the abbreviation "qtd." stands for "quoted."

52. (C)

The 9 pages of the article (164–172) are shown last in the entry, so choice (A) is true. The author's name appears first, so choice (B) is true. Because there is a number following the title of the publication, one can assume it's the volume number, so (D) is true. The number (2) in parentheses following the volume number indicates that this is the second issue published in the year, so (E) is true.

53. (C)

The key to answering this question is to notice the numbers at the end of the citation. When you see numbers arranged like this—"8 (9): 41"—it's an indicator that you're looking at a journal citation. In order, these numbers are the volume number, issue number, and page number of the citation. Magazines (D) include the month of publication, and newspapers (B) include both the month and day.

54. (B)

The number directly following the title of a journal is the volume number.

55. (E)

Since the previous sentence mentions technology imported from Europe and the following paragraph discusses the stone ax, choice (E) is the best sentence to create a logical transition from one paragraph to the next.

56. (C)

Dr. Ferrucio da Rocha has credentials that are specific to this field of study. Steves, in choice (A), may have traveled to Brazil, but the information listed offers no evidence that Steves has expertise in archeology or agronomy. The same is true of (B) and (D). Choice (E) is a tempting answer since Daniel de Oliviera has spoken to the Archaeology Department, but this citation does not give evidence of his speech topic or his area of expertise.

57. (D)

This citation is in the wrong format. Note the other items in the Notes section: they all start with a first name. The best thing to do with note 3 is switch the order of the interviewee's last name and first name so that it reads "Aleksandr Kim."

58. (C)

This quotation needs a citation. The fact that the person who says the quote is named in the sentence doesn't mean a source doesn't need to be cited. Adding a parenthetical note about Karls's background (B) might be interesting, but it is not strictly necessary. Listing the ecology books (D) won't add anything to the discussion, and restating his quote (E) isn't necessary. A citation (C) would be best.

59. (A)

Choice (B) is wordy and doesn't convey the sense of the original sentences, while choice (C) is confusing and suggests people eat *farofa* because of its taste. The original sentences do not suggest this. Choices (D) and (E) leave out the definition of *farofa*, information that helps clarify the term for readers unfamiliar with the word.

60. (B)

This citation lacks a corresponding superscript number embedded in the text. Furthermore, the title indicates that it's unrelated to the topic. Therefore, the best thing to do is to delete it (B), as it's irrelevant to this passage. Choice (E) is wrong because a citation's relation to the topic should be clear through its association with some quote or other piece of information in the text. But in this case, no note 4 is indicated in the body of the passage. Thus, the note 4 listed in the Notes section is extraneous and should be eliminated.

61. (D)

An article is mentioned in the sentence, but we don't know anything about it. There needs to be a citation for it. As it happens, the article appears to be listed in the References section of the passage, so a parenthetical citation referring to that article should appear in the sentence.

62. (A)

The way to attack this question is to check each answer choice to make sure that it checks out against the citation in sentence 7. Information in four of the five choices should be indicated by the parenthetical. Choice (A) is the only one that cannot be verified by looking at sentence 7 alone. There's no way to know what type of publication her work appeared in, much less that it's specifically a book about marine life.

63. (A)

Because the writer does not continue with examples or make further comments eliciting sympathy or ridicule, you should rule out choices (B) and (C). The underlined phrase doesn't qualify as "evidence" (D) because it's unsubstantiated. The word "including" does the opposite of show contrast, so (E) is not the best choice. The main reason for including the underlined phrase is to introduce humor (A).

64. (D)

The last paragraph mentions that jellyfish feature some adaptations that make them "hardy," but they are not discussed. Of the choices listed, elaborating on these adaptations (D) would be the best way to develop the paragraph because it would help the reader to understand vital information about these creatures. Discussing ways to protect oneself against jellyfish (A) is off-topic. Naming the era that began when jellyfish arrived might be interesting, but it's not vital information for understanding the nature of jellyfish. Explaining the method of locomotion employed by jellyfish (C) would be great, but locomotion is only one of several adaptations, so choice (C) is inferior to choice (D). Predicting future populations of jellyfish (E) isn't appropriate for the conclusion. If it were vital information—for example, if a population explosion were on the horizon—then it should have been discussed in the body of the passage.

65. (B)

The source is indeed a newspaper (A), and the article is located on the front page (C), as indicated by the page number "A1" used to indicate the first page of the "A" section. The date (D) and the author (E) are both named in the citation as well. While Wallis Sands is, in fact, located in New Hampshire, that's not indicated by the citation. It could just as easily be running a story on something happening in nearby Maine. The citation doesn't indicate the location of Wallis Sands.

66. (C)

The first sentence of the second paragraph reveals the answer: "A news story published in the summer of 2010 reflects this ubiquity." The sentence is referring to something from the first paragraph and introducing an example to support it. Among the answer choices, (C) best describes this purpose. The theme (A) was already set up in the first paragraph. The passage focuses on jellyfish in particular, not the general threats associated with swimming (B).

67. (E)

Nothing in the quote indicates that this type of event could "happen anywhere" (A). The author doesn't need a direct quote from an eyewitness to prove that the event happened (B). The quote from the lifeguard hardly qualifies as "commentary from an expert" (D), and though it does help to put the discussion into a local context (C), that's not its main purpose, which is to illustrate the atmosphere at the beach at the time of the event.

68. (C)

This source listed last is a magazine (C), as indicated by the month instead of volume and issue numbers, which would be part of a journal citation (A).

69. (D)

The context for sentence 2 is that there has been a recent surge in interest in laminins. Sentence 2 states that laminins are vital to the organization of cells to justify the recent focus on them. Therefore choice (D) is the best answer. Sentence 2 doesn't distinguish laminins from other proteins (A), so that cannot be its purpose. Extracellular matrix is not defined (B). No other functions are suggested (C).

70. (B)

The paragraph does explain terms, but its purpose is not limited to that, so (A) is incorrect. While the paragraph does show that laminins are important, it does not discuss their importance relative to other proteins, so (B) is wrong. Choices (C) and (D) are incorrect because the paragraph does not suggest further study or mention academic faculty members.

71. (D)

To answer this question, you must take it in context. The preceding sentence says that early scientists were very interested in laminins when they noticed them showing up in their experiments, and then sentence 6 points out that laminins are involved in the construction of almost all of our tissues—pretty important! So the purpose of sentence 6, in context, is to explain why laminins caught the eye of early scientists (D).

72. (A)

In context, "line" means to "cover the inside of." The closest answer choice to that is "coat" (A).

73. (B)

Note the transition words: "very early" and "later." They indicate time sequence, so choice (B)—chronological order—is the best answer. No dangers are mentioned (A); neither is a cause-effect relationship (C). Spatial order (D) refers to organization from left to right, near to far, inside/outside, points on the compass, etc. Choice (E) is wrong because the paragraph does more than list terms; it describes the process of embryo development.

74. (E)

The context reveals that laminins help cells to attach to one another by keeping the order of the states of different layers. While binding agent (C) might seem like a good choice because laminins help cells to attach to each other, it's not stated that laminins help them to adhere. Rather, it is stated that laminins help keep cells orderly during attachment. Therefore "guide" (E) is the best choice.

75. (D)

The author uses the phrase "back door to their hearts" to suggest that ants are direct. The overall message of the paragraph helps to support (D) as the correct response. None of the other responses is appropriate. In fact, the description of the ants in paragraph 1 is all positive, so (B) and (C) must be eliminated. Choice (A) is wrong because the paragraph says nothing about how ants can be "won over." Choice (E) is wrong because nothing in the paragraph says ants can't be trusted.

76. (A)

According to the first paragraph, ants do everything *but* "assail their enemies through devious means." The first paragraph clearly describes the ants as hardworking and industrious creatures. Nowhere are negative or critical comments made.

77. (C)

The expression "ain't" has always been considered informal and colloquial. From this expression, as well as other instances of colloquial diction in this passage, you can conclude that the author is using vernacular English to appeal to his audience (C). Choice (A) is incorrect because the author's personal background is not mentioned at all in the passage. The passage gives no evidence that the author is a misanthrope (one who despises humans) (B), even though he does seem to think that as a race we could learn much from the lowly ants. The language of this piece is not consistent with that from the early seventeenth century (D), and while farmers, laborers, and nonintellectuals (E) might be part of the reading audience, they are certainly not all of it. The piece seems directed to more "sophisticated" folk who really need a lesson from the ants.

78. (A)

The paragraph lists several activities that ants never engage in but that people clearly do, so (A) is the right answer. Choice (B) is wrong because the paragraph doesn't mention the ants' priorities. The appropriateness of time and place for asking questions is never mentioned, so (C) is wrong. Choice (D) is wrong because the paragraph is not judging the value of arguing in any context. Clearly the paragraph describes what ants do not do in terms of what people may do, but the author never suggests that ants will become like people, so (E) is wrong.

79. (D)

This piece uses ants as a model for the virtuous and dutiful beings that all humans should aspire to be (D). The writer implies that these virtues are within our power to demonstrate, so choice (A) is wrong. The writer is not defining a new moral code (B), as the precepts he lays out are rather traditional. None of the statements made about ants indicates that their lives are dull, so (C) is incorrect. While the author does use an admiring tone in paragraph 3, it is the ants' apparent respect for laws—not their intelligence—that he speaks highly of, so (E) is wrong.

80. (B)

The tone of this passage is best characterized as *satirical*. The author is writing with a tongue-in-cheek style, gently but successfully pointing out many flaws of mankind that ants seem to have avoided. Nevertheless, the writer is neither *caustic* (E) in his or her remarks nor particularly *bitter* (A) or *scathing* (D). Although the message is a moral one, the overall tone of the passage is far too lighthearted to be considered *serious* (C).

81. (D)

The topic of the passage is using media to enhance student comprehension of literature, so (D) is the right answer. While (C) may be tempting, it is wrong because the passage doesn't talk about blending forms of media in general, only using media in teaching literature. Choice (A) is wrong because the passage doesn't talk about two sides of the brain. Choice (B) is wrong because written exams are not mentioned specifically in the passage. Choice (E) is wrong because the passage doesn't state that students should challenge professors' uses of technology.

82. (C)

"Via" is used as a preposition linking ways of using art to the word "art." Only (C) encompasses the necessary idea of linking.

83. (E)

The word "anachronistic" comes from the root word *chronos*, meaning "time" in Greek. In context of the passage, the word "today" in sentence 2 and the phrase "in this, the 21st century" in sentence 4 suggest that "anachronistic" relates to time. In addition, sentences 2-4 bring up a contrast between the words "graphics," "visuals," "media," and "audiovisual" on the one hand and "digital, computerized media" on the other hand. Because this contrast is related to time, the only choice that relates to time (E) has to be the correct answer.

KAPLAN

84. (E)

This type of question relies heavily on context. The logical flow from one sentence to the next can affect what is implied by either of them. In sentences 4–6, the writer basically says, "Today, students are more familiar with digital media, but the basic elements of literature—language and arrangement—have not changed." Now look at the answer choices and find one that aligns with this idea. Choice (E) is the only answer that aligns with this idea while adding another layer of meaning—narrative has a timeless quality.

85. (A)

In the first paragraph, the author explores the idea of how we remember and forget the past and how this shapes who we are. In the second paragraph, she explores how these ideas are relevant to her life. Therefore, choice (A) is best.

86. (C)

In the third paragraph, the author discusses feeling out of place in Oxford, but she also confesses her anxiety about returning to her home. Taken together, these details indicate that the author feels uncertain about her identity, so (C) is correct.

87. (D)

Sentence 4 indicates that suppressing information and remembering things are similar because neither presents an entirely accurate picture of the situation. The sentence does not refer only to the process of remembering (A) and does not differentiate among suppression, omission, and remembering (B). It certainly doesn't warn the reader to beware of the writer's truthfulness (C). Choice (E) is contradicted by the overall purpose of the passage, which is to describe the author's uncertainty that she truly fits in, either in Idaho or in Oxford.

88. (E)

Since the author is reading books that are all by British authors or related to travel, it suggests that she is still connected to England. Choice (A) simplifies the emotions the writer is feeling toward England and her time spent there. The author does not mention boredom or a need to fill hours (B) and does not downplay the value of American literature (C). There is also no indication that the books she is reading will contribute to her work as a journalist (D).

89. (A)

The writer has suggested that she feels pulled between two places. She is ambivalent, or divided in her loyalties and preferences. One of the poles of her ambivalence (A) is the West, and the other is Oxford. This ambivalence makes (B) incorrect because the "basis of her personality" is a mixture of influences. The writer doesn't seem to feel ashamed of her background, so the suggestion that it is inferior (D) misses the mark. Choice (E) is incorrect because the writer's recollection of her grandfather's remark is to emphasize the idea of ambivalence rather than to affect the audience's attitude toward the writer.

90. (B)

When the author finds herself in an uncomfortable or uninteresting conversation in Oxford, she attributes this to being a Westerner, and she withdraws. This is a way of describing alienation (B). Something happens that makes you feel separate, and you drift away from the social situation. Choices (A) and (D) may be tempting because the passage implies that these uncomfortable conversations in Oxford cause the writer to think immediately of home. But that's really not the same thing as saying she feels homesick (A) or wants to return home (D). Neither do these conversations cause her to feel confused about her identity (C); on the contrary, they make her feel more a Westerner. It appears that the real confusion begins when she sets out to return home. Choice (E) is wrong because the writer never says that conversations in Oxford bring on "floods" of memories.

Chapter Seven: **Practice Test 3 (College Composition)**

PART I
Time—50 minutes
50 Questions

Directions: Each sentence tests your knowledge of choice of words (diction), idiom, grammar, and usage. Some sentences may be correct, and each sentence can contain no more than one error.

Elements of the sentence that are underlined and lettered may be incorrect. Parts of the sentence that are not underlined can be assumed to be correct. When choosing an answer, follow the conventions of standard written English.

If a sentence contains an error, select the <u>one underlined portion</u> that must be changed in order to form a correct sentence. For sentences with no error, choose answer (E).

1. <u>Neither</u> the attorney <u>nor the client</u> <u>were</u>
   A   B   C
   <u>pleased with</u> the outcome of the trial. <u>No error</u>
      D   E

2. <u>At the end</u> of summer vacation, many college
      A
   students <u>are</u> shopping for <u>a new shelving unit</u>
            B   C
   to help them get their rooms <u>organized</u>. <u>No error</u>
                              D   E

3. Margaret <u>told</u> Leticia that <u>she</u> could not
             A   B
   <u>continue in</u> <u>her present</u> job. <u>No error</u>
      C   D   E

4. The group <u>marveled</u> at the <u>tour guide's</u> fluency in
                A   B
   Chinese, <u>her</u> knowledge of history, and
            C
   <u>she managed</u> to keep them on a tight schedule.
      D
   <u>No error</u>
     E

5. <u>A consistent</u> schedule, <u>including</u> predictable
        A   B
   morning and evening routines, <u>have</u> been
                            C
   shown to minimize conflict <u>between</u> parents
                         D
   and their young children. <u>No error</u>
                        E

GO ON TO THE NEXT PAGE ⟶

KAPLAN

Directions: The passages below are first drafts of student work. The sentences in each passage have been numbered. Parts of the essays require revision.

After reading each passage, answer the questions that follow. Some questions require you to improve sentences by changing word choice (diction) and sentence structure. Other questions ask you to review the whole essay or a part of the essay and evaluate its organization, development, and the suitability of its language for the intended audience and purpose. Follow the rules of standard written English in your answer choices.

Questions 6–10 are based on the following early draft of a student essay.

(1) *I used to hate exercise.* (2) *I was the one in gym class who played sick to avoid running the mile.* (3) *Two years ago, my Aunt Sarah got breast cancer.* (4) *It was a real scare for all of us.* (5) *She had surgery then went through chemotherapy.* (6) *Now, she is a survivor.* (7) *To celebrate, last year she decided to participate in a triathlon that benefits breast cancer survivors.* (8) *She asked my cousin Leah, my mother, and I to participate too.*

(9) *I couldn't possibly say no.* (10) *I knew I'd hate it and would probably finish last.* (11) *My mother suggested that we start swimming together—at least it isn't as bad as running.* (12) *We made it a habit to go to the pool every other day to swim half a mile.* (13) *Then, my mother suggested all four of us go on a bike ride together.* (14) *It was actually a lot of fun.* (15) *We started going every week.* (16) *My Aunt Sarah had to force me to go running with her.* (17) *We started with a half a mile.* (18) *I huffed and puffed and was sweating, but I did it.* (19) *By the time the triathlon came around, we were ready for it.* (20) *We all stuck together.* (21) *We took our time and drank lots of water.* (22) *But we finished, and we didn't finish last, either.* (23) *My Aunt Sarah was so thankful, she cried and hugged us all for a long time.*

6. Which of the following sentences, if added after sentence 2, would best connect the first paragraph to the rest of the essay?

(A) But this year, to my surprise, I began to enjoy exercise.

(B) But, changing all that, a strange thing happened.

(C) It seems I hated exercise for as long as I can remember.

(D) Then a terrible thing happened.

(E) For many, exercise is a pleasant experience.

7. Which of the following is the best revision of sentence 8 (reproduced below)?

She asked my cousin Leah, my mother, and I to participate too.

(A) She asked my cousin, Leah, my mother and I to participate, too.

(B) My Aunt Sarah asked my cousin Leah, my mother and I to participate, too.

(C) She asked my cousin Leah, my mother, and me to participate too.

(D) Asking, my cousin Leah, my mother and I participated too.

(E) She had asked my cousin Leah, my mother, and me to participate too.

GO ON TO THE NEXT PAGE ⇒

8. Which of the following is the best way to combine sentences 9 and 10? (reproduced below)

I couldn't possibly say no. I knew I'd hate it and would probably finish last.

(A) I knew I'd hate it and would probably finish last, but still, I couldn't possibly say no.

(B) Being impossible to say no, I knew I'd hate it and would probably finish last.

(C) Despite not being able to say no, I knew I'd hate it and would probably finish last.

(D) Since I couldn't possibly say no, it was then I knew I'd hate it and would probably finish last.

(E) Knowing I'd hate it and would probably finish last, it was impossible to say no.

9. In context, which of the following would be the most logical transition to insert at the beginning of sentence 15 (reproduced below)?

We started going every week.

(A) However,
(B) Even though,
(C) For example,
(D) Rather,
(E) So,

10. Which of the following represents the best revision of sentence 18 (reproduced below)?

I huffed and puffed and was sweating, but I did it.

(A) I was huffing and puffing and getting sweaty, but I did it.

(B) I was huffing and puffing, sweaty, but I did it.

(C) I huffed and puffed and sweated, but I did it.

(D) I huffed and I puffed and I was sweating, but I did it.

(E) I would huff and puff and get sweaty, but I did it.

Questions 11–15 are based on the following passage.

(1) The subways of all major cities ought to run all night. (2) Subways prevent a lot of traffic and provide transportation to people who don't have cars or cannot drive.

(3) It is important to alleviate traffic as much as possible. (4) In most major cities, cars are the biggest factor in air pollution. (5) They contribute to smog, greenhouse gases, and acid rain. (6) Traffic also lessens the quality of life for people who live in a city. (7) Subways that run only during limited hours discourage people from riding them. (8) You never know when you might decide to change your plans and come home later. (9) The other major function of subway systems is to provide transportation for people who cannot drive cars. (10) Some people cannot afford a car, and some are not able to drive one. (11) Many people who cannot afford a car may also have to work night shifts, so they really need one that runs all night. (12) People who cannot drive cars also have the right, like all of us, to go out at night and they can't do that unless the subway runs all night. (13) So all subway systems should run twenty-four hours a day, even if they don't run often during the late-night hours. (14) Some cities in Europe have subways that run regularly 24 hours a day, 365 days per year.

11. Which sentence, if added to the end of paragraph 1, would best connect it to the rest of the essay?

(A) Also, the cities people like the most in the world have all-night subways.

(B) Subways that run all night offer significantly more of both of these important benefits.

(C) But it seems cities are reluctant to operate subway systems all night.

(D) Traffic is one of the most important problems we face.

(E) Reliable subways also encourage tourism.

GO ON TO THE NEXT PAGE

KAPLAN

12. Which of the following is the best way to combine sentences 9 and 10 (reproduced below)?

    The other major function of subway systems is to provide transportation for people who cannot drive cars. Some people cannot afford a car, and some are not able to drive one.

    (A) The other major function of subway systems is to provide transportation for people who cannot drive cars, being either that some people cannot afford a car and some are not able to drive one.

    (B) The other major function of subway systems is to provide transportation for people who cannot drive cars because some people cannot afford a car and some are not able to drive one.

    (C) Some people not affording a car and some not being able to drive one, the other major function of subway systems is to provide transportation for people who cannot drive cars.

    (D) The other major function of subway systems is to provide transportation for people who cannot drive cars, either because they cannot afford one or because they are not able to drive one.

    (E) The other major function of subway systems is to provide transportation for people who cannot drive cars; some people cannot afford cars and some are not able to drive them.

13. Which of the following offers the best version of sentence 11? (reproduced below)

    Many people who cannot afford a car may also have to work night shifts, so they really need one that runs all night.

    (A) No change.
    (B) Really needing one that runs all night, many people who cannot afford a car may also have to work night shifts.
    (C) Needing a subway system that runs all night, many people cannot afford a car and have to work night shifts.
    (D) Because many people who cannot afford a car may also have to work night shifts, they really need one that runs all night.
    (E) Many people who cannot afford a car may also have to work the night shift, so they really need a subway system that runs all night.

14. Which of the following would make the best replacement for sentence 13 (reproduced below)?

    So all subway systems should run twenty-four hours a day, even if they don't run often during the late-night hours.

    (A) Therefore, all subway systems should run twenty-four hours a day, they could run less often at night.
    (B) Therefore, all subway systems in major cities should run twenty-four hours a day, even if late-night hours are limited.
    (C) So, they may not run often during the late-night hours, all subway systems should run twenty-four hours a day.
    (D) Even when not running often during the late night hours, all subway systems should run twenty-four hours a day.
    (E) So all subway systems need not run often during the late-night hours, there must be some service at night, however.

GO ON TO THE NEXT PAGE

15. Which of the following sentences should be deleted to most improve the coherence of the passage?

    (A) Sentence 1

    (B) Sentence 6

    (C) Sentence 8

    (D) Sentence 12

    (E) Sentence 14

Questions 16–20 are based on the following passage.

(1) *There are three basic functions physical education serves in our education.* (2) *First, it gives students a break from schoolwork during the day, allowing them to return refreshed.* (3) *Second, it teaches students an active, healthy lifestyle.* (4) *Third, ideally, it can teach students self-confidence.* (5) *For these reasons, it is very important that school districts should continue to fund physical education programs.* (6) *Students should have physical education every day.* (7) *The activities should be well planned.* (8) *If the teacher just leaves students on their own to play, the students who need physical education the most will be the ones who don't join in.* (9) *They may even be teased by the other students.* (10) *Students cannot teach themselves about the importance of nutrition or stretching in an active lifestyle.* (11) *They need a qualified teacher for their physical education classes.*

16. Which of the following represents the best way to revise sentence 1 (reproduced below)?

    There are three basic functions physical education serves in our education.

    (A) Educationally speaking, there are there ways physical education is important.

    (B) There is physical education in our education, serving three basic functions.

    (C) Physical education serves three basic functions.

    (D) Physical education has served three basic functions in our education.

    (E) Physical education serves three basic functions in our education.

17. Which of the following is the best version of sentence 2 (reproduced below)?

    First, it gives students a break from schoolwork during the day, allowing them to return refreshed.

    (A) No change.

    (B) First, it gives students a break from schoolwork during the day, and it allows them to return refreshed.

    (C) First, allowing them to return refreshed, it gives students a break from schoolwork during the day.

    (D) The first reason is that it gives students a break from schoolwork during the day, allowing them to return refreshed.

    (E) First, because it gives students a break from schoolwork during the day, it has allowed them to return refreshed.

18. In the context of the essay as a whole, which of the following is the best way to revise sentence 5 (reproduced below)?

    For these reasons, it is very important that school districts should continue to fund physical education programs.

    (A) No change.

    (B) Continuing to fund physical education programs for these reasons, it is very important.

    (C) For these reasons being very important, school districts should continue to fund physical education programs.

    (D) For these reasons, it is very important that school districts continue to fund physical education programs.

    (E) That schools are continuing to fund physical education programs being very important for these reasons.

GO ON TO THE NEXT PAGE

KAPLAN

19. Which of the following represents the best way to combine sentences 6 and 7 (reproduced below)?

    Students should have physical education every day. The activities should be well planned.

    (A) Students should have physical education every day and should participate in well-planned activities.

    (B) Students should have physical education every day, being well-planned activities.

    (C) Students should have physical education every day; the activities should be well planned.

    (D) Students should have physical education every day, having the right to participate in well-planned activities.

    (E) Having physical education every day means participating in well-planned activities.

20. Which of the following would be the most appropriate title for the passage?

    (A) Active Lifestyles

    (B) The Importance of Physical Education

    (C) Physical Education Teacher Qualifications

    (D) Promoting a Healthy Lifestyle

    (E) Playground Bullying

Questions 21–25 are based on the following passage.

(1) We should all take a moment to think about how much we will miss Ms. Garcia. (2) Ms. Garcia just retired. (3) A dedicated, passionate teacher, our school counts on teachers like Ms. Garcia. (4) Principal Natto's idea to establish a scholarship in her name is a great one.

(5) It would be impossible to mention everything that Ms. Garcia has meant to us. (6) She began the Student Action Club before any of us were born. (7) It became a very popular extracurricular activity. (8) The Student Action Club has made many important contributions to our school over the years. (9) Recently they got the school district to stop using toxic pesticides at the schools. (10) We also got the school district to commit to green areas at all of the schools. (11) The Student Action Club also raised a lot of money for the Teen Runaway Hotline. (12) Ms. Garcia taught us that we could talk right to

school officials and companies. (13) Even though they didn't always listen, we always felt we had tried.

(14) Ms. Garcia always believed in her students. (15) Ms. Garcia was also nationally known as an excellent teacher. (16) We learned from her both in class, in our after-school activities and out of them. (17) She continues to be an inspiration for all of us. (18) We should remember her inspiration and pass it on to others by developing a scholarship fund in her name.

21. Which of the following is the best way to revise and combine sentences 1 and 2 (reproduced below)?

    We should all take a moment to think about how much we will miss Ms. Garcia. Ms. Garcia just retired.

    (A) We should all take a moment to think about how much we will miss Ms. Garcia, having just retired.

    (B) We should all take a moment to think about how much we will miss Ms. Garcia, and Ms. Garcia just retired.

    (C) We should all take a moment to think about how much we will miss Ms. Garcia, who has just retired.

    (D) Having just retired, we should all take a moment to think about how much we will miss Ms. Garcia.

    (E) We should all take a moment to think about how much we will miss Ms. Garcia—Ms. Garcia just retired.

GO ON TO THE NEXT PAGE ⟩

22. Which of the following is the best, most concise revision of sentence 3 (reproduced below)?

    A dedicated, passionate teacher, our school counts on teachers like Ms. Garcia.

    (A) Our school counts on dedicated, passionate teachers like Ms. Garcia.

    (B) Our school counts on teachers like Ms. Garcia, a dedicated, passionate teacher.

    (C) Like Ms. Garcia, our school counts on dedicated, passionate teachers.

    (D) Like Ms. Garcia, a dedicated, passionate teacher, our school counts on teachers.

    (E) Our school counts on teachers like Ms. Garcia, being a dedicated, passionate teacher.

23. In the context of the second paragraph, which of the following is the clearest way to combine sentences 9 and 10 (reproduced below)?

    Recently they got the school district to stop using toxic pesticides at the schools. We also got the school district to commit to green areas at all of the schools.

    (A) Recently, they got the school district to stop using toxic pesticides at the schools, and we also got the school district to commit to green areas at all of the schools.

    (B) Recently they got the school district to stop using toxic pesticides at the schools, and got them to commit to green areas.

    (C) Recently we got the school district to stop using toxic pesticides and commit to green areas at all of the schools.

    (D) We recently got the school district to stop using toxic pesticides at the schools, committing to green areas at all of them.

    (E) Getting the school district to commit recently to green areas at all of the schools, we got them to stop using toxic pesticides.

24. Which of the following would be the best sentence with which to conclude the passage?

    (A) It might be a lot of work, but Ms. Garcia would tell us not to let that stop us.

    (B) Another great teacher at our school is Dr. Hennesey.

    (C) Scholarship funds always struggle to find contributors, even though no one denies their importance.

    (D) We should also nominate her for a national teaching award.

    (E) You never know where inspiration comes from.

25. Which of the following versions of sentence 16 (reproduced below) is the clearest?

    We learned from her both in class, in our after-school activities and out of them.

    (A) We learned from her both in class and in our after-school activities.

    (B) We learned both in our after-school activities and in class and outside of our after-school activities and classes.

    (C) Whether in class or after-school activities or out of them, we learned from her.

    (D) Whether we were in or out of them, class or after-school activities or both, we learned from her.

    (E) Whether in school hours, in after-school activities or out of, we learned from Ms. Garcia

GO ON TO THE NEXT PAGE

Directions: The following questions test your knowledge and use of research source materials. Some of the questions are based on single entries; others refer to passages provided. In the passage-based sets, Revision Skills and Rhetorical Analysis Skills may also be tested.

26. Profoundly

    See also profound (adj.)

    adverb

    synonyms extremely, very, deeply, exceedingly, greatly, immensely, enormously

    antonyms superficially, weakly, lightly

    All of the following statements are supported by the entry EXCEPT

    (A) This entry comes from a thesaurus.
    (B) This entry comes from a dictionary.
    (C) If something is profound, it is not superficial.
    (D) The adverb "profoundly" is based on an adjective.
    (E) Profound has neutral connotations.

27. Chiang, G., et al. Minot: A History of the North Dakota Town. Seattle: Heathers, 2010.

    In the citation, what does "et al." mean?

    (A) It means the book is not published online.
    (B) It means the book has only one author.
    (C) It means the book has more than three authors.
    (D) It means the full citation is found in the bibliography.
    (E) It means Chiang, G. is the editor.

28. Bell, Albert. The Fixer. Trans. Stuart Davidson. New York: Purveyor, 1999.

    All of the following statements about this entry are true EXCEPT

    (A) Albert Bell wrote The Fixer.
    (B) Purveyor is the publisher.
    (C) Stuart Davidson is the editor.
    (D) The Fixer was published in 1999.
    (E) The Fixer was published in New York City.

29. Hepp, C. Gregorio. Rev. of Second Generation: Children of Immigrants, by Chester Baskin. The Nightingale 81 (2008): 110-11.

    In the citation, the letters "Rev." mean that

    (A) the work was reprinted.
    (B) the work was revised.
    (C) this is a review of another work.
    (D) the author is a reverend.
    (E) the work was reviewed in 2008.

GO ON TO THE NEXT PAGE >

Questions 30–36 are based on the following passage.

(1) *The question of why dinosaurs became extinct has puzzled paleontologists since the first dinosaur fossil was found almost two centuries ago. (2) These great reptiles dominated the Earth for almost 160 million years but mysteriously died out approximately 65 million years ago. (3) Various explanations for this disappearance have been offered, ranging from an epidemic to a sudden, catastrophic drop in temperature, but definitive proof has remained elusive.*

(4) *In 1980, Luis Alvarez, winner of the Nobel Prize in Physics, suggested a novel explanation: cosmic extinction. (5) According to Alvarez and his geologist son Walter, a huge meteor crashed into the earth's surface 65 million years ago, sending up a massive cloud of dust and rock particles. (Sohn 1980, 165) (6) The cloud blocked out sunlight for a period of months or even years, disrupting plant photosynthesis and, by extension, the global food chain. (7) The lack of vegetation, coupled with a significant drop in temperature, resulted in the extinction of the dinosaurs.*

(8) *Alvarez based his theory on a curious piece of evidence: the presence of a thin layer of iridium that had recently been discovered in geologic sediments laid down at approximately the time the dinosaurs died out. (Sherwinter 1979, 3) (9) The metal iridium is rarely found on the earth's surface; Alvarez reasoned that it had either come up from the Earth's core by volcanic action or been deposited from space through the fall of one or more meteorites. (10) He found the latter explanation more likely, given the even distribution of the iridium layer worldwide.*

(11) *But paleontologists scoffed at the Alvarez extinction theory. (12) Neither Luis nor Walter Alvarez was a paleontologist, yet they claimed to have solved a mystery that had defied the efforts of paleontologists for over a century. (13) Professional hostility was also fueled by the somewhat abrasive style of the elder Alvarez. (14) But the most important objection to the Alvarez theory was evidential. (15) In order to create worldwide fallout on the scale suggested by Alvarez, the "doomsday" meteorite would have had to be on the order of five miles in diameter; its impact would have formed a crater perhaps a hundred miles wide. (16) Where was the crater?*

(17) *Finally, a decade after the cosmic extinction theory was first proposed, the crater was found—a discovery that caused noted geologist Minju Patel to say, "It helps solve everything." (18) Lying on the northern edge of Mexico's Yucatan Peninsula, the crater is 110 miles wide. (19) Long buried under sediment, it had actually been discovered in 1981 by oil geologists, but datings of nearby rock samples taken at that time suggested that it was significantly older than 65 million years. (20) New samples of melted rock from the crater itself were recently analyzed by an advanced dating process, however, and were found to be 64.98 million years old. (Diaz 2009, 310) (21) Many scientists now feel that, thanks to the Alvarez theory, the mystery of dinosaur extinction has finally been solved.*

References

Diaz, P. 2009. Rock Sample Dating from the Yucatan Peninsula Crater. *Geology Today* 114 (3): 300–325.

Sherwinter, G. 1979. *Layers in Time*. Chicago: Pressman.

Sohn, H. 1980. *Luis Alverez: Nobel Prize Winner.* New York: Huntington.

30. Which of the following pieces of information, if added to the first paragraph (sentences 1–3), would most effectively introduce the facts of this scientific issue?

    (A) A comparison of the theories listed in sentence 3

    (B) A suggestion that the mystery may have been solved with a discovery in the Yucatan

    (C) Information about recently discovered fossils of dinosaur remains

    (D) A detailed explanation of how the crater was found

    (E) Biographical information about Minju Patel

31. The information in parentheses in sentence 5 tells the reader that

    (A) Sohn wrote a book that detailed Alvarez's findings.

    (B) Sohn completed research that proved a giant meteor struck the Earth 65 million years ago.

    (C) the sentence is a direct quote from a work by Sohn.

    (D) Sohn was born in 1979.

    (E) Sohn wrote a book that was 165 pages long.

32. Which of the following is cited in sentence 8?

    (A) Website

    (B) Newspaper

    (C) Book

    (D) Blog

    (E) Magazine

33. Which of the following statements best explains the purpose of the fourth paragraph (sentences 11–16)?

    (A) It suggests why no one liked Luis Alvarez.

    (B) It explains why paleontologists did not readily accept the extinction theory proposed by Alvarez.

    (C) It explains why a meteor would strike the Earth.

    (D) It gives a detailed definition of a "doomsday" meteorite.

    (E) It shows why a massive crater would never be found.

34. What should the author do with sentence 17?

    (A) Make no change.

    (B) Include a citation for the direct quotation.

    (C) Mention when this quote was made.

    (D) Delete it because it has no relation to the topic.

    (E) Explain why Minju Patel is important to the realm of geology.

35. The first item in the reference list shows that

    (A) the author uses direction quotations from three places in this source.

    (B) Rock Sample Dating from the Yucatan Peninsula Crater is a book.

    (C) *Geology Today* is a website.

    (D) Rock Sample Dating from the Yucatan Peninsula Crater begins on page 300.

    (E) three citations relate to this reference.

36. Which of the following is cited in sentence 20?

    (A) Website

    (B) Anthology

    (C) Article

    (D) Blog

    (E) Encyclopedia

GO ON TO THE NEXT PAGE

KAPLAN

Directions: The passages below consist of numbered sentences. Read each passage and answer the questions below it. The questions for each passage test how effectively you can analyze a piece of writing.

Questions 39–44 refer to the following passage about Leonardo da Vinci.

(1) *What a marvelous and celestial creature was Leonardo da Vinci.* (2) *As a Renaissance scientist and engineer his gifts were unparalleled.* (3) *His accomplishments in these capacities were hindered by the fact that he was, before all else, an artist.* (4) *As one conversant with the perfection of art, and knowing the futility of trying to bring such perfection to the realm of practical application, Leonardo tended toward variability and inconstancy in his endeavors.* (5) *His practice of moving compulsively from one project to the next, never bringing any of them to completion, stood in the way of his making any truly useful technical advances.*

(6) *When Leonardo was asked to create a memorial for one of his patrons, he designed a bronze horse of such vast proportions that it proved utterly impractical—even impossible— to produce.* (7) *Some historians maintain that Leonardo never had any intention of finishing this work in the first place.* (8) *But it is more likely that he simply became so intoxicated by his grand artistic conception that he lost sight of the fact that the monument actually had to be cast.* (9) *Nonetheless, in 1999 Nina Akamu sculpted the horse, and it now stands in the Meijer Gardens and Sculpture Park in Grand Rapids, Michigan.*

(10) *Similarly, in the late 15th century, when Leonardo was commissioned to paint the Last Supper, he left the head of Christ unfinished, feeling incapable of investing it with a sufficiently divine demeanor.* (11) *Yet, as a work of art rather than science or engineering, it is still worthy of our greatest veneration, for Leonardo succeeded brilliantly in capturing the acute anxiety of the Apostles at the most dramatic moment of the Passion narrative.* (12) *Such mental restlessness, however, proved more problematic when applied to scientific matters.* (13) *When he turned his mind to the natural world, Leonardo would begin by inquiring into the properties of herbs and end up observing the motions of the heavens.* (14) *In his technical studies and scientific experiments, he would generate an endless stream of models and drawings, designing complex and unbuildable machines to raise great weights, bore through mountains, or even to empty harbors.* (15) *It is*

this enormous intellectual fertility that has suggested to many that Leonardo can and should be regarded as one of the originators of modern science. (16) *But Leonardo was not himself a true scientist.* (17) *"Science" is not the hundred-odd principles or pensieri that have been pulled out of his Codici.* (18) *Science is comprehensive and methodical thought.*

(19) *Granted, Leonardo always became fascinated by the intricacies of specific technical challenges.* (20) *He possessed the artist's interest in detail, which explains his compulsion toward observation and problem solving.* (21) *But such things alone do not constitute science, which requires the working out of a systematic body of knowledge—something Leonardo displayed little interest in doing.*

39. Which of the following words, if inserted at the beginning of sentence 3 (reproduced below) would best clarify the author's logic?

    His accomplishments in these capacities were hindered by the fact that he was, before all else, an artist.

    (A) Similarly
    (B) Therefore
    (C) Indeed
    (D) Likewise
    (E) However

GO ON TO THE NEXT PAGE

KAPLAN

40. In the context of the second paragraph, what is the function of sentence 7 (reproduced below)?

    Some historians maintain that Leonardo never had any intention of finishing this work in the first place.

    (A) To introduce a statement that the writer will refute

    (B) To offer evidence for a previous statement

    (C) To restate the essay's thesis

    (D) To provide a contrast between Leonardo's sculpture and the one created by Nina Akamu

    (E) To state the writer's opinion

41. In context, sentence 12 (reproduced below) serves to

    Such mental restlessness, however, proved more problematic when applied to scientific matters.

    (A) define the phrase "scientific matters."

    (B) provide a contrast that supports the writer's thesis.

    (C) offer a point of view that differs from the writer's.

    (D) illustrate Leonardo's own opinion of his work.

    (E) prove that Leonardo made no contributions to science.

42. The writer's primary goal in this passage is to

    (A) prove Leonardo was not really a true scientist and engineer.

    (B) show why Leonardo never finished anything.

    (C) portray Leonardo as an artist who dabbled in technology but was not a true scientist.

    (D) question why Leonardo is so admired.

    (E) set forth examples of Leonardo's incomplete projects.

43. What does including the example of Nina Akamu's creation of the *da Vinci Horse* (reproduced here) add to the writer's argument about Leonardo?

    Nonetheless, in 1999 Nina Akamu sculpted the horse, and it now stands in the Meijer Gardens and Sculpture Park in Grand Rapids, Michigan.

    (A) It shows that women are more talented artists than men.

    (B) It suggests that it takes a 20th-century artist to understand the sophistication of Leonardo's drawings.

    (C) It implies that Leonardo's drawings are detailed enough to guide contemporary artists to construct his concept.

    (D) It proves that Leonardo did not have the skill to do in his lifetime what modern artists can do.

    (E) It suggests that Nina Akamu was not held back by restlessness.

44. The author's primary purpose in using the word "science" in sentences 17 and 18 is to

    (A) explain the way in which Leonardo was a scientist.

    (B) contrast the aims of artistic work with those of science.

    (C) define a term that is central to the author's thesis.

    (D) illustrate one of Leonardo's main interests.

    (E) dismiss Leonardo's interest in science.

GO ON TO THE NEXT PAGE ⟶

KAPLAN

Questions 45–50 refer to the following passage.

(1) *I received Everett's* Life of Washington *which you sent me, and enjoyed its perusal.* (2) *How his spirit would be grieved could he see the wreck of his mighty labors!* (3) *I will not, however, permit myself to believe, until all ground of hope is gone, that the fruit of his noble deeds will be destroyed, and that his precious advice and virtuous example will so soon be forgotten by his countrymen.* (4) *As far as I can judge by the papers, we are between a state of anarchy and civil war.* (5) *May God avert both of these evils from us!* (6) *I see that four states had declared themselves out of the Union; four more will apparently follow their example.* (7) *Then, if the Border States are brought into the gulf of revolution, one half of the country will be arrayed against the other.* (8) *I must try and be patient and await the end, for I can do nothing to hasten or retard it.*

(9) *The South, in my opinion, has been aggrieved by the acts of the North, as you say.* (10) *I feel the aggression and am willing to take every proper step for redress.* (11) *It is the principle I contend for, not individual or private benefit.* (12) *As an American citizen, I take great pride in my country, her prosperity and institutions, and would defend any state if her rights were invaded.* (13) *But I can anticipate no greater calamity for the country than dissolution of the Union.* (14) *It would be an accumulation of all the evils we complain of, and I am willing to sacrifice everything but honor for its preservation.* (15) *I hope, therefore, that all constitutional means will be exhausted before there is a resort to force.* (16) *Secession is nothing but revolution.* (17) *The framers of our Constitution never exhausted so much labor, wisdom, and forbearance in its formation, and surrounded it with so many guards and securities, if it was intended to be broken by every member of the Confederacy at will.* (18) *It was intended for "perpetual union," so expressed in the preamble, and for the establishment of a government, not a compact, which can only be dissolved by revolution or the consent of all the people in convention assembled.* (19) *It is idle to talk of secession.* (20) *Anarchy would have been established, and not a government, by Washington, Hamilton, Jefferson, Madison, and the other patriots of the Revolution. . . .* (21) *Still, a Union that can only be maintained by swords and bayonets, and in which strife and civil war are to take the place of brotherly love and kindness, has no charm for me.* (22) *I shall mourn for my country and for the welfare and progress of mankind.* (23) *If the Union is dissolved, I shall return to my native state and share the miseries of my people; and, save in defense, will draw my sword on none.*

45. As used in this context, "perusal" in the first sentence most nearly means

    (A) generosity.
    (B) appearance.
    (C) thoughtfulness.
    (D) examination.
    (E) arrival.

46. The "he" the speaker refers to in the opening paragraph is

    (A) Everett, author of *Life of Washington*.
    (B) George Washington.
    (C) General Robert E. Lee.
    (D) the president in office when the selection was written, Abraham Lincoln.
    (E) the governor of the Border States.

47. What conclusion can you draw about the speaker's character from the final paragraph?

    (A) He is cowardly and faint of heart.
    (B) He is a natural leader who has much experience with public service.
    (C) He is judgmental and rigid.
    (D) He is belligerent and contemptuous of those who hesitate to take up arms for their country.
    (E) He is devoted to his state but abhors war.

GO ON TO THE NEXT PAGE ⇒

KAPLAN

48. In context, what is the function of sentence 16 (reproduced below)?

    Secession is nothing but revolution.

    (A) To define a word that readers might not otherwise understand

    (B) To refute the opinion of the framers of the Constitution

    (C) To indicate a parallel relationship between events the writer considers undesirable

    (D) To prove that secession is the most desirable resolution

    (E) To explain a past event

49. The thesis or main idea of the passage is that

    (A) the Union is being tested by wrongs committed by both the North and the South.

    (B) the Union will always endure, no matter what happens.

    (C) only the speaker is qualified to lead the Union in this time of terrible strife.

    (D) anarchy is a healthy state because it leads to positive change.

    (E) people must take up arms in defense of their country; to do any less is cowardice.

50. The narrator's attitude toward George Washington is that he

    (A) admires Washington for his personal traits but recognizes that his style of leadership would be ill-suited to the present conflict.

    (B) excoriates Washington for his unwillingness to take appropriate action.

    (C) understands that Washington would be aggrieved by the acts of the North.

    (D) praises Washington as a man of great actions, fine advice, and unshakable ethics.

    (E) believes that Washington contributed to the present state of anarchy and civil war.

END OF PART I.   STOP

The next section of the exam is designed to assess your ability to write argumentative essays under time constraints. You will be allotted 30 minutes to write an essay based on what you've read, observed, or experienced.

For the second essay, you will have 40 minutes to read carefully two passages and then to synthesize and cite information from those two sources. As always, take a few moments to preplan your writing or monitor your time so you have plenty of time to revise. Use whatever strategy works best for you.

PART II
Time—30 minutes

Directions: Write an essay in which you discuss how strongly you agree or disagree with the quotation given. Substantiate your position with facts, details, and illustrations from what you've read, observed, or experienced.

"Advertising has done more to cause the social unrest of the twentieth century than any other single factor."

Clare Barnes Jr.

_____

_____

_____

_____

_____

_____

_____

_____

_____

_____

_____

_____

_____

_____

_____

_____

GO ON TO THE NEXT PAGE

KAPLAN

END OF PART II. STOP

PART III
Time—40 minutes

Directions: You must write a well-constructed and fully developed essay in which you make use of the information in the two news articles given. This means you must not only incorporate into your writing those sources to support or refute a clearly stated position, but you must also cite the title or last name of each author within the text of your essay. Carefully read the introduction, the question, and the two articles that follow, and then write an essay that answers the question and uses and cites information from the articles to support or refute your answer to the question.

Introduction

With expanding debate on the health of Americans, various organizations have proposed solutions to improve the overall health of those who live in the United States. One of these solutions is preventative care. Some of the proponents of preventative care argue that people need information in order to make healthy choices when planning what they eat. One of the ways to help consumers to make better choices is to mandate that calorie counts be included on restaurant menus. The mandate became a law in 2010.

Assignment

Read the following carefully. Then write an essay in which you decide your position on whether the mandate to post calorie counts on restaurant menus will solve the problem and significantly improve the health of Americans who have the medical condition called obesity. Use and cite both of the sources as you develop your essay.

Calorie Postings Don't Change Habits, Study Finds
By Anemona Hartocollis, Published: October 6, 2009

A study of New York City's pioneering law on posting calories in restaurant chains suggests that when it comes to deciding what to order, people's stomachs are more powerful than their brains.

April Matos, 24, bought a Happy Meal at a McDonald's for her 3-year-old son, Amari, and a Snack Wrap for herself. "Life is short," she said. "I started eating everything now I'm pregnant."

The study, by several professors at New York University and Yale, tracked customers at four fast-food chains—McDonald's, Wendy's, Burger King, and Kentucky Fried Chicken—in poor neighborhoods of New York City where there are high rates of obesity.

It found that about half the customers noticed the calorie counts, which were prominently posted on menu boards. About 28 percent of those who noticed them said the information had influenced their ordering, and 9 out of 10 of those said they had made healthier choices as a result.

But when the researchers checked receipts afterward, they found that people had, in fact, ordered slightly more calories than the typical customer had before the labeling law went into effect, in July 2008.

GO ON TO THE NEXT PAGE ⟶

"Calorie Count Labels on Restaurant Menus
Are Helping Consumers Make Better Choices"
By Drucilla Dyess, Wednesday, 28 October 2009

Since New York issued a mandate in 2008 requiring fast-food restaurants to post calorie counts on their menus, consumers have become more calorie conscious and are making better meal choices. The city is the first in the U.S. to have issued such a mandate.

Although a recent independent study found that calorie-count labeling had no effect on consumer eating habits, the New York Department of Health and Mental Hygiene has just released initial findings of a recent analysis on the impact of the city's menu-labeling laws. Results indicate that consumers have become more selective in choosing food with fewer calories. In fact, people purchased lower-calorie meals at 9 of 13 fast-food restaurant and coffee chains that were included in the study. The findings were presented at the annual meeting of the Obesity Society in Washington.

To gather their data, researchers began by surveying more than 10,000 customers at a total of 275 locations during the early months of 2007, and then followed up with another survey of 12,000 customers earlier this year.

_____

_____

_____

_____

_____

_____

_____

_____

_____

_____

_____

_____

_____

_____

GO ON TO THE NEXT PAGE >

_____

_____

_____

_____

_____

_____

_____

_____

_____

_____

_____

_____

_____

_____

_____

_____

_____

_____

_____

_____

_____

_____

_____

GO ON TO THE NEXT PAGE ⟩

_____

_____

_____

_____

_____

_____

_____

_____

_____

_____

_____

_____

_____

_____

_____

_____

_____

_____

_____

_____

END OF TEST STOP

KAPLAN

ANSWER KEY

1. B	11. B	21. C	31. A	41. B
2. C	12. D	22. A	32. C	42. C
3. B	13. E	23. C	33. B	43. C
4. D	14. B	24. A	34. B	44. C
5. C	15. E	25. A	35. D	45. D
6. A	16. C	26. B	36. C	46. B
7. C	17. A	27. C	37. B	47. E
8. A	18. D	28. C	38. B	48. C
9. E	19. A	29. C	39. E	49. A
10. C	20. B	30. B	40. A	50. D

PRACTICE TEST 3 QUICK REFERENCE TABLES

Use the following tables to determine which topics you still need to review.

Topic	Test Question
Conventions of Standard Written English	1–5
Revision Skills	6–25
Ability to Use Source Materials*	26–38
Rhetorical Analysis	39–50

* In Ability to Use Source Materials questions, the elements tested under Revision Skills and Rhetorical Analysis may be tested.

Topic	Number of Questions on Test	Number Correct
Conventions of Standard Written English	5	
Revision Skills	20	
Ability to Use Source Materials*	13	
Rhetorical Analysis	12	

* In Ability to Use Source Materials questions, the elements tested under Revision Skills and Rhetorical Analysis may be tested.

Answers and Explanations

PART I

1. (B)

When "neither..nor" is used to combine two singular nouns, the subject is considered singular. Therefore, "were" should be "was."

2. (C)

Related nouns in a sentence should be consistent in number. Since many "students" are not all shopping for the same "shelving unit," the plural is called for. The underlined portion can be corrected by changing it to "new shelving units."

3. (B)

"She" does not have a clear reference, because it could mean either Margaret or Leticia could not continue at her job. For this sentence to be correct, the person's name should appear again.

4. (D)

This sentence exhibits a parallel structure problem. Items in a list must take the same form. Here, the first two items in the list are noun phrases ("*fluency* in Chinese," "*knowledge* of history"), but the third item is an independent clause ("and she managed . . ."). It needs to be changed to match the first two items. One might say, "her *success* in keeping the group on schedule."

5. (C)

The problem here is subject-verb agreement. The subject of "have been" is not "routines" but "schedule." Therefore, "have" should be changed to "has."

6. (A)

Only answers (A) and (D) make any sense at all, but answer (A) covers the whole passage rather than just the second paragraph, so it is the better choice. In answer (C) the verb tenses "seems," "hated," and "can remember" do not fit together.

7. (C)

The problem here is that you can't say "she asked . . . I" because "I" is a subject pronoun, not an object pronoun. Simply change "I" to "me" to get answer (C). Choice (D) makes it sound as though the author, the author's mother, and the author's cousin were "asking."

8. (A)

The two sentences express opposing sentiments, so they are best united by "but," which only appears in answer (A). Answer (E) is not logical: you would not refuse to say no *because* you know you'd hate the race.

9. (E)

There is a cause-and-effect relationship between sentences 14 and 15, so the appropriate transition will reflect that. Only "so," (E), expresses cause and effect.

10. (C)

This question asks about parallel structure. Just think, "I huffed and puffed and blew the house down." Change "blew the house down" to "sweated," and you have answer (C). In answer (B), "puffing" and "sweaty" are not parallel.

11. (B)

Answers (A), (C), and (E) introduce ideas that don't appear anywhere else in the passage. While answer (D) only connects the first paragraph to the second, answer (B) summarizes the central idea of the whole essay.

12. (D)

Answers (A), (B), and (C) add to the complexity of the sentences and are therefore easy to eliminate. While not ungrammatical, the use of a semicolon to join the two sentences in answer (E) does not specify the relationship between them. Answer (D) does this while simplifying the structure of the statement.

13. (E)

"One" does not have a clear reference and needs to be replaced by "a subway system." Only answers (C) and E) do that. Choice (C) puts the ideas of the original sentence into the wrong logical order.

KAPLAN

14. (B)

Choice (B) is correct because all of the other choices create sentence structure problems.

15. (E)

All of the sentences make the passage coherent. The introduction of the topic of subways in European cities (E) does not follow the rest of the passage.

16. (C)

Four of the choices are wordy. Option (C) is best because it's most concise.

17. (A)

Options (B) and (D) are slightly wordier than the original sentence. Choice (C) includes a dangling modifier, and (E) contains a verb-tense error. Therefore (A) is the best choice.

18. (D)

"It is very important that they *should* continue" is awkward. "It is very important that they continue" is the standard usage. "It is very important" in answer (B) is a phrase by itself at the end of the sentence.

19. (A)

It is easy to make both sentences have the same subject ("students"). Doing so makes the connection clearer and uses the active voice.

20. (B)

Only choice (B) gives a title that is broad enough to cover the thesis of the passage. The other choices either relate to details that are too specific or are so broad that they don't relate to the passage directly.

21. (C)

When the object of the first clause is also described in the second clause, use the pronoun "which." However, when the pronoun refers to a person, use "who" (when the pronoun refers to the subject of the second clause) or "whom" (if it refers to the object). The correct answer is also the most straightforward.

22. (A)

This sentence includes a misplaced modifier. "Our school" is not the "dedicated, passionate teacher." "Ms. Garcia" needs to be right next to this description of her. Answers (A) and (B) make this adjustment, but answer (A) is simpler.

23. (C)

The task here is to get rid of the we/they problem. "We" is used most consistently in the passage, so eliminate (A) and (B), which use "they." Then there is no need to repeat "got the school district." Answer (D) has a dangling modifier ("committing . . .") that grammatically describes "we." Answer (E) produces an unnecessarily complicated sentence.

24. (A)

Only (A) follows the ideas presented in the passage and refers to Ms. Garcia. The other examples introduce brand new ideas or ideas that do not logically follow the sentences before it.

25. (A)

Choice (B) is wordy. Choices (C), (D), and (E) are awkward. Using "whether" complicates this sentence unnecessarily.

26. (B)

The correct answer is (B) because this entry does not provide a definition. Instead, it lists synonyms and antonyms the way a thesaurus (A) would. The other statements are true about this entry.

27. (C)

When a book has more than three authors, it is not customary for all the authors to be listed. Instead, one author is listed, and "et al.," which is an abbreviation of the Latin phrase *et alia* meaning "and others," is used.

28. (C)

"Trans.", which appears before the name Stuart Davidson, indicates that he is the translator of the work. The other statements are true.

29. (C)

In citations, the abbreviation "Rev." before the work's title means that the work cited is a review of another work.

30. (B)

The first paragraph introduces the topic. Choice (A) would change the focus of the topic. Choice (C) is unrelated to the main topic. Choices (D) and (E) would be more appropriate in the last paragraph.

31. (A)

This parenthetical citation indicates that the information came from a book written by Sohn about Alvarez's findings. Choice (C) cannot be correct because quotation marks would precede the citation if the material were a direct quote from the source.

32. (C)

If you look at the reference, there is nothing to indicate that the work being referenced is anything but a book. Choices (A) and (D) would have URL addresses, and choices (B) and (E) would have dates, issues, or volume numbers.

33. (B)

Choice (B) is correct because it explains the main idea of the paragraph. Choice (A) is too specific. Choices (C), (D), and (E) relate to topics found in the paragraph, but they are not accurate statements about the purpose of the paragraph.

34. (B)

Direct quotations should have a citation so that the reader knows the source of this quote. The other answer choices are incorrect.

35. (D)

Only choice (D) is supported by the information in the reference. Choice (A), 2009, is the year the book was published. Choice (B) is an article. Choice (C) is incorrect because there is no URL information. Finally, Choice (E) is incorrect because 3 is the volume number.

36. (C)

Because this citation has page numbers and both an article title and a publication title, it is a citation for an article.

37. (B)

Occasionally an author or an editor will invite other people to contribute a chapter to a publication. In that case, the author of the chapter would be first in the entry, then the title of the chapter. Then comes the name of the book and the name of the editor.

38. (B)

In many format style guides, the date a website is viewed is shown with the day, month, and year in parentheses. However, the placement within the entry varies from style to style.

39. (E)

The relationship between sentences 2 and 3 is one of contrast: Leonardo's scientific gifts were "unparalleled" in his time, but his accomplishments were "hindered." Only (E) provides the appropriate transition here.

40. (A)

The word "some" is a clue that sentence 7 gives the opinion of someone other than the author. The word "but" in sentence 8 makes it clear that the author disagrees with the view of "some historians" as described in sentence 7. Therefore, the author brings up this view only to introduce a point he will argue against. Choice (A) is the only one that reflects this purpose.

41. (B)

The word "however" in sentence 12 indicates that it provides contrast. The author suggests that while "mental restlessness" may have enhanced Leonardo's work as an artist, it detracted from his efforts as a scientist. This contrast is, in fact, central to the author's thesis, so (B) is correct.

42. (C)

The author's thesis is expressed in sentences 2 and 3: Leonardo was talented in science and engineering, but those talents were both limited by and overshadowed by the fact that he was primarily an artist. Choice (C) matches this idea. Choice (A) is too limited in scope; the author praises Leonardo as well as showing that he cannot be considered a true scientist. Choice (B) is also too narrow; it focuses on one detail in the passage. Choice (D) is irrelevant to the passage. Choice (E) is wrong because the author only mentions Leonardo's unfinished works to make a larger point.

43. (C)

In the context of this essay, the author claims that Leonardo was a skilled and talented artist who completed a number of art projects and left detailed drawings about others. The fact that he did not complete the project does not mean he could not have; therefore (B) and (D) are not good choices. Choice (A) is wrong because the passage does not address the gender issue. The name of the artist here is incidental. Since (C) is true (E) cannot be.

44. (C)

Read the context. Sentence 16 states that Leonardo "was not a true scientist." Therefore, it makes sense that the next sentence will give information about what the author thinks it means to be a "true" scientist. This idea matches (C). Choice (A) is wrong because it doesn't specifically address the use of the word "science" in sentences 17 and 18. Choice (B) is wrong because "art" isn't mentioned at all in sentences 15–18. Choice (D) may be tempting because the passage states that Leonardo was interested in science; however, in the cited sentences, it is the definition of science that is discussed. Choice (E) is wrong because in sentences 17 and 18 the author is not talking about Leonardo's understanding of science but only about science in general.

45. (D)

As used in this context, *perusal* in the first sentence most nearly means *examination*. To peruse means to examine, to scrutinize, to look over, to inspect. The other choice that might have tempted you is (B) *appearance. Examination* is a closer synonym for this vocabulary word. You might be able to create a scenario for (E) in which the book has recently arrived. However, upon reading the next couple of sentences, we understand that the narrator is actually referring to the reading of the book, not just its arrival. Neither (A) nor (C) would be appropriate synonyms for perusal as it is used in the first sentence of the passage.

46. (B)

The "he" the speaker refers to in the opening paragraph is George Washington. In this paragraph, "he" and "his" refer to the antecedent George Washington, as implied by the title of the book to which the narrator refers. The "wreck of his mighty labors" does not refer to the Everett's labors (the author) (A) but to the efforts of the Founding Father to establish the Union. Similar reference is found in the phrase "his [Washington's] noble deeds will be destroyed" (sentence 3) and that the nation will soon forget all that he worked so hard to establish.

47. (E)

The speaker is devoted to his state but abhors war. Nothing suggests that the speaker is cowardly or faint of heart (A), nor does the passage mention anything about any special leadership abilities (B). Although it is clear he does not want to see any dissolution of the "perpetual Union," there is no indication of his being judgmental and rigid (C) nor belligerent and contemptuous of others (D). He will wait to see what happens to the Union. He has no desire to see a Union that can be held together only through swords and bayonets. Strife and lack of brotherly love have "no charm" for him. If the Union is dissolved, he will return to his "native state" and share the "miseries of [his] people." Obviously, this man does not want to see the Union dissolved, but more importantly, he does not want to see war. He would rather suffer at home and be separated from the Union than live in a state of strife and civil war.

48. (C)

Because the sentence uses the word "is," (A) may be tempting. However, sentence 16 isn't really defining or explaining a term. Choice (C) is correct because the writer is saying that the two things, "secession" and "revolution," are equivalent; thus he is setting up a parallel relationship. Clearly the writer values the maintenance of the union, so he doesn't consider secession or revolution desirable. Choice (D) states the opposite of this view, so it is wrong. Choice (B) is incorrect because the author sets up his view as one that he believes to be consistent with the view of those who wrote the Constitution. Option (E) is wrong because the writer is talking about what could happen in the future, not something that has already happened.

49. (A)

The main idea of this passage is that the Union is being tested by wrongs committed by both the North and the South. It is the very fact that the Union may not endure (B) that has prompted the speaker/narrator to express himself. Again, nowhere does the passage refer to any great leadership prowess (C) on the part of the narrator. He makes it clear that anarchy (D) is not an acceptable situation, and he himself prefers to take up arms only in his own defense (E).

50. (D)

The narrator praises Washington as a man of great actions, fine advice, and unshakable ethics. The narrator's attitude toward Washington is clearly expressed in the first paragraph. He refers to Washington's "noble deeds," his precious advice," and his "virtuous example." The only other response you might be tempted to choose would be (A). However, the narrator believes that Washington's example and advice are relevant to his day. It would be inappropriate for the narrator to "excoriate" Washington (B) for his inaction since he is no longer alive at the beginning of the Civil War. That is also the argument against (C). Far from believing that Washington has contributed to anarchy, (E), the writer praises him for encouraging unity.

PART II

Essay 1

Scoring Guidelines

This essay is read by two college English teachers who each assign it a grade of 1–6, based on the following criteria. Read the scoring guidelines and the sample essay that follows and try to decide what score you would give the sample essay. If possible, ask someone to read your essay and assign a score of 1–6.

Level 6 essays:

- Cover all aspects of the assignment in an insightful manner.
- Contain thoroughly developed ideas supported with specific, relevant evidence.
- Are organized and focused.
- Exhibit superior skill with vocabulary and sentence variation.
- Display grammar mastery only with minor errors, if any.

Level 5 essays:

- Cover the assignment effectively.
- Contain well-developed ideas supported with appropriate evidence.
- Are organized and focused for the most part.
- Exhibit skill with vocabulary and some sentence variation.
- Display a good grasp of grammar with only minor errors.

Level 4 essays:

- Cover the assignment competently.
- Contain adequately developed ideas supported with evidence.
- Are adequately organized and focused.
- Exhibit competence with vocabulary but little sentence variation.
- Display a grasp of grammar for the most part, with some errors apparent.

Note that for categories below Level 4, an essay only has to contain *one* of the specified problems.

Level 3 essays:

- Cover only part of the assignment.
- Contain uneven development and unsupported assertions.
- Are poorly organized and focused.

- Exhibit multiple problems in communicating.
- Display mediocre or inconsistent grammar.

Level 2 essays:

- Cover a small part of the assignment.
- Lack development and contain little evidence.
- Are unfocused and disorganized.
- Display grammar and usage errors that obscure meaning.

Level 1 essays:

- Fail to cover the assignment.
- Are undeveloped.
- Display persistent errors in grammar and usage that significantly obscure meaning.

If your essay is on a different topic than the one given, if it merely restates the topic, or if it can't be understood by the graders, it will receive a score of 0.

Sample Essay 1

Look at the following sample essay and think about how you would grade it. What are its strengths, and how might it be improved?

Advertisements are everywhere. They are in the magazines we read, plastered on the billboards we drive past. They are on the radio waves we listen to and on our television screens. Every single day people are subject to seeing, hearing, and reading hundreds of advertisements. There are ads for everything, for food, for grocery stores that sell food, for fast food chains that sell food, even commercials advertising how we should help create a healthier planet, supporting the people who grow our food; advertisements aren't simply about the products these days; it is much more extensive than that. Being barraged by so many advertisements every single day it brings to mind the question of just how influential these ads are.

Clare Barnes, Jr. is quoted making the statement that "Advertising has done more to cause the social unrest of the twentieth century than any other single factor." I find this statement to be absolutely, 100%, undeniably true.

There is no doubt that advertising has an effect on the people that are subject to it. But is the effect it has on the general population of the people of the twentieth century one of "social unrest?" Let's think about it for a moment.

Why is it that advertising companies are willing to pay small fortunes to have their material put on the television for a mere 30 seconds or less? Why is it that companies fight over that glossy page in a magazine? It is because the methods of advertising are effective. Why is it that they are so effective? It is because they make us as human beings unhappy or unsatisfied or lusting after or dreaming for the things we don't have, the things we are shown to "need." From Big Macs to cell phones, these ads place seeds of want in our brains and any level of such shallow dissatisfaction with the lives we have is not healthy.

Now it could be disputed that it is impossible to live a life without at least a small amount of dissatisfaction in the lack of things we have; everybody wishes they had a more up to date item or find themselves drooling over the newest pizza creation at their nearby carry out pizza joint. It seems impossible to avoid. But why is that? I feel that 99.9% of the time, it is because we have seen these things. Where? In the advertisements all around us.

The want to upgrade, to make better, to expand, to gain items of this world is not inherently evil. To be bombarded constantly with the message that what we *do* have is not enough, will never be enough, needs to be replaced, however, is. We need to be content with what we have. And sure, let's strive to buy that new car as soon as we save up some money. And yes, let's go try that new coffee at our nearest Starbucks. But let us not be consumed with a lust for those items and such a lust is the advertisers main goal.

The people of the twenty-first century are at unrest for many reasons and claiming that advertisements have done more than any other single factor to cause this may seem a harsh accusation. When you think about it though, what else invades our subconscious and conscious mind more often? What invades our minds more persistently? And one may argue that being instilled with a lust for the newest weight machine is frivolous but it goes so much deeper than that. Not only do we become unhappy with what we DO have but with many of the things advertised we are being sold a message that we as people aren't good enough as we are, that we need these new things or diets or datelines or dvd's to become better. Girls need the new makeup. Guys need the Axe body wash to have any hopes of getting any girls, and when you do, when having washed with Axe, they will throw themselves at you. With that message comes the dangerous message that such sexual behavior is not only appropriate but "normal."

Advertisements are all around us. They are nearly impossible to escape. There are some advertisements out there dedicated solely to the promotion of good things such as hospitals but in the end it's all about money. It's all about causing an attitude of unrest and dissatisfaction among the people, the consumer.

PART III

Essay 2

Scoring Guidelines

This essay is read by two college English teachers who each assign it a grade of 1–6, based on the following criteria. Read the scoring guidelines and the sample essay that follows and try to decide what score you would give the sample essay. If possible, ask someone to read your essay and assign a score of 1–6.

Level 6 essays:

- Cite sources correctly.
- Contain thoroughly developed ideas supported with specific, relevant evidence.
- Use both sources effectively, with a strong connection between the sources and the thesis.
- Are organized and focused.

- Exhibit superior skill with vocabulary and sentence variation.
- Display grammar mastery only with minor errors, if any.

Level 5 essays:
- Cite sources correctly.
- Contain well-developed ideas supported with appropriate evidence.
- Use both sources well, with a good connection between the sources and the thesis.
- Are organized and focused for the most part.
- Exhibit skill with vocabulary and some sentence variation.
- Display a good grasp of grammar with only minor errors.

Level 4 essays:
- Cite sources correctly.
- Contain adequately developed ideas supported with evidence.
- Use both sources adequately, with a connection between the sources and the thesis.
- Are adequately organized and focused.
- Exhibit competence with vocabulary but little sentence variation.
- Display a grasp of grammar for the most part, with some errors apparent.

Note that for categories below Level 4, an essay only has to contain *one* of the specified problems.

Level 3 essays:
- Cite sources problematically.
- Contain uneven development and unsupported assertions.
- Use both sources poorly, with a almost nonexistent connections between the sources and the thesis.
- Are poorly organized and focused.
- Exhibit multiple problems in communicating.
- Display mediocre or inconsistent grammar.

Level 2 essays:
- Do not cite sources.
- Lack development and contain little evidence.
- Use only one source poorly, with an almost nonexistent connection between the sources and the thesis.
- Are unfocused and disorganized.
- Display grammar and usage errors that obscure meaning.

Level 1 essays:

- Do not cite sources or do not use the sources.
- Are undeveloped.
- Display persistent errors in grammar and usage that significantly obscure meaning.

If your essay is on a different topic than the one given, if it merely restates the topic, or if it can't be understood by the graders, it will receive a score of 0.

Sample Essay 2

Look at the following sample essay and think about how you would grade it. What are its strengths, and how might it be improved?

You are on your way out to a movie with some of your friends. The four of you waltz into your nearest McDonalds to get some dinner before you hit the cinema. You stand in front of the menu and amid the chatter of your friends you glance over the menu. There are so many choices. Perhaps the first thing that comes to your mind isn't whether or not the meal is healthy for you. You may not find yourself wondering how many calories are in this item or that item. However, seeing the big, fat number of calories slapped next to the item at least keeps it near the front of your mind.

According to the article "Calorie Counts in Calorie Count Labels on Resturant Menus are Helping Consumers Make Better Choices," Drucilla Dyess states that in 2008 New York was the first state to put into effect a calorie counting policy for fast food restaurants. Dyess takes the stand that such methods of plastering the calorie count onto items of ordered food and making available the calorie count near the menus helps people make smarter, healthier choices. I agree with her stance... but I don't see it as the method that will solve the problem.

In Dyess' article she lays out evidence of this calorie posting law being effective on people's food choices, saying that a study by the New York Department of Health and Mental Hygiene found that "people purchased lower calorie meals at 9 of 13 fast-food and restaurant and coffee chains that were included in the study."

This must be encouraging. Here is proof from a study that the posting of calorie counts in restaurants does make a difference in how people order and what they order when going out to eat. But the question is not whether or not the posting of these numbers will help; the question is, will it solve the problem of obesity?

Studies have proven that such calorie postings don't help very much, let alone solve America's obesity problem. Such a study is examined in the article "Calorie Postings Don't Change Habits, Study Finds" by Anemona Hartocollis. According to Hartocollis, a study was done by professors from New York University and Yale on the effect the posting of calorie count has on consumers. It states that "half the customers noticed the calorie counts, which were prominently posted on menu boards. About 28 percent of those who noticed them said the information had influenced their ordering, and 9 out of 10 of those said they had made healthier choices as a result."

It cannot be denied, as it couldn't in Dyess' article, that these numbers in your face when you order food does help influence our decision making. It takes the first step in fighting obesity by making us aware of just what it is we are eating. Yet, as this study proves, it doesn't keep us from eating it. It's the difference between wanting that new bike in the store and stealing it; there is a big difference between simply wishing you had the bike for yourself or taking action on that impulse and actually taking the bike. And both Dyess' article's findings by the New York Department of Health and Mental Hygiene and Hartocollis' article's findings by the professors at NYU and Yale prove that the majority of Americans are still choosing to steal that bike, despite knowing the consequences.

Perhaps that is the problem. I argue that perhaps we should focus less on plastering calorie counts on things and more on getting the word out on just what the consequences are to eating so unhealthily. Take the younger generation of older children and young teens. They don't care about a bunch of numbers. And even if they have been educated on just what those numbers mean, that doesn't mean that they will turn down something that tastes good because a bunch of high numbers are supposed to equate to unhealthiness in their young minds. It is more important to encourage healthy eating habits early and, better yet, illuminate the unhealthy choices.

It is understood that fast food chains are not to be expected to get rid of their menus and replace them with salads with a side of ice water. So let's go back to the concept of giving the calorie count to consumers when they order. Hartocollis states in her article that "about half the customers noticed the calorie count." Half. Only. Half.

I don't feel that the posting of calorie count will solve our obesity problem. But if restaurant chains are going to post those numbers, they somehow need to firstly be paid attention to by the consumers in order to even have a chance to have any effect! What we have in America, what we really need over calorie counts, is a change of attitude. I don't think it is that the numbers were too difficult for the consumers to see. I think it was simply a lack of a drive to actually let those numbers affect their choices. They didn't notice the numbers because they weren't actively looking for them.

In my experience, people are constantly calorie counting. Society has instilled it in us that doing such a thing is the "cool" thing to do. Society must always be striving to lose weight, to keep it off, to look model thin, to keep up appearances and look finicky and healthy when we eat. The trend I notice, looking at it from another angle than the article's studies did, is not that we as American's don't see the numbers but that we don't take the action to avoid the high ones.

American's need more than numbers to save our "round ones." We need a change of taste.

The CLEP College Mathematics Exam

Chapter Eight: **Practice Test 1: Diagnostic**

Time—90 minutes
60 Questions

Directions: For the following questions, either select the BEST answer of the choices given or input your answer.

You can use the computer-based scientific calculator during this exam.

Notes:

(1) Unless otherwise stated, the domain of any function f consists of the set of all real numbers x for which $f(x)$ is a real number.

(2) i represents $\sqrt{-1}$.

(3) Unless otherwise indicated, all geometric figures lie in a plane. The appearance of all figures is accurate UNLESS the question states that the figure is not drawn to scale.

1. If $A = \{x \mid x$ is a whole number$\}$ and $B = \{x \mid x$ is an odd integer less than 10$\}$, which of the following is a subset of $A \cap B$?

    (A) $\{3, 5, 7, 9\}$
    (B) $\{-3, 7, 9\}$
    (C) $\{2, 3, 5, 7\}$
    (D) $\{1, 7, 9, 11\}$

2. What type of transformation flips a graph of a figure on a coordinate plane over a line of symmetry to create a mirror image of the original figure?

    (A) Rotation
    (B) Dilation
    (C) Reflection
    (D) Translation

3. Which of the following is NOT true of a prime number?

    I. A prime number is always divisible by itself.
    II. A prime number is always divisible by 1.
    III. A prime number is always odd.

    (A) I and II only
    (B) III only
    (C) II and III only
    (D) II only

GO ON TO THE NEXT PAGE

KAPLAN

4. Below is a Truth Table:

p	q	r
T	T	T
T	F	T
F	T	T
F	F	F

According to this table, which of the following statements describes r?

(A) $p \wedge q$

(B) $p \rightarrow q$

(C) $p \leftrightarrow q$

(D) $p \vee q$

5. Cherine is on vacation and wants to dine at three different restaurants while in town. How many ways could she choose three restaurants if there are ten restaurants in all to choose from and order doesn't matter?

(A) 100

(B) 120

(C) 140

(D) 160

6. Click on the expression that is equivalent to $\left| \dfrac{5^2 - 45 \times 3}{10} \right|$.

$|-12 + 1|$	$|-10 + 1|$
$|-11 + 1|$	$|10 - 1|$

7. What is the domain of the function $f(x) = \dfrac{x}{x^2 - 4}$?

(A) All real numbers except for 2 and −2

(B) All real numbers except for 4 and −4

(C) All real numbers except for 0

(D) All real numbers

8. Which of the following is a factor of $2x^3 - x^2 + 3x - 4$?

(A) $x + 1$

(B) $x + 2$

(C) $x - 1$

(D) $x - 2$

9. Suppose the mean for a set of numbers is 6. If all the numbers in the set are doubled, what would the mean then be?

(A) 12

(B) 6

(C) 3

(D) 24

10. Which is the converse of "If P, then Q"?

(A) If Q, then P

(B) If not P, then not Q

(C) If not Q, then not P

(D) If P, then not Q

11. Suppose $R = \{u, v\}$ and $S = \{x, y\}$. Which of the following ordered pairs is NOT in the Cartesian product $R \times S$?

(A) (u, x)

(B) (v, x)

(C) (v, y)

(D) (u, v)

12. Values for the functions f and g are given in the following tables:

x	2	3	4
$f(x)$	5	6	7

x	4	5	6
$g(x)$	2	3	4

What is the value of $f(g(4))$?

(A) 7

(B) 5

(C) 4

(D) 2

GO ON TO THE NEXT PAGE

13. The width of a rectangular yard is x feet. If 200 feet of fencing is needed to enclose the yard, which of the following represents the length of the yard, in feet?

    (A) $200 - x$

    (B) $200 - 2x$

    (C) $100 - x$

    (D) $100 - 2x$

14. Click on the expression that is equivalent to $-\left|\dfrac{2^3 \div 2^2 \times 7}{-2}\right|$.

$|-10 - 4|$	$-|-10 + 4|$
$|-10 - 3|$	$-|-10 + 3|$

15. One digit from the number 5,473,343 is written on each of seven cards. What is the probability of drawing a card that shows 4?

    (A) $\dfrac{4}{7}$

    (B) $\dfrac{2}{7}$

    (C) $\dfrac{5}{7}$

    (D) $\dfrac{1}{7}$

16. In a right triangle, what is the sum in degrees of the measures of the two acute angles?

17. Which of the following could be the graph of a function of x?

    (A)

    (B)

    (C)

    (D)

18. If $\dfrac{a}{b}$ and $\dfrac{c}{d}$ are rational numbers, then $\dfrac{a}{b} \div \dfrac{c}{d} =$

    (A) $\dfrac{(a - c)}{(b - d)}$

    (B) $\dfrac{ac}{bd}$

    (C) $\dfrac{ad}{bc}$

    (D) $\dfrac{a \div d}{b \div c}$

GO ON TO THE NEXT PAGE

KAPLAN

19. The following graph shows the bicycle sales for Ben's Bikes. Approximately how many more bikes were sold in 2008 than in 2007?

Bicycle Sales at Ben's Bikes

(A) 50

(B) 75

(C) 100

(D) 150

20. If $P(x) = 2x^4 - 8x^3 - 7x + 1$, use the remainder theorem to find the remainder of $P(x)$ divided by $(x - 5)$.

(A) 205

(B) 215

(C) 216

(D) 275

21. Which of the following choices represents the shaded area of the Venn diagram?

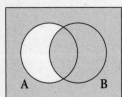

(A) $(A \cup B) \cap A'$

(B) $(A \cup B)'$

(C) $(A \cup B)' \cup B$

(D) $(A \cup B)' \cup A$

22. In five basketball games, Joreon scored 14, 17, 12, 18, and 24 points. What is the difference between his mean and median score?

23. What is the range of the function $f(x) = (x - 2)^2$?

(A) All real numbers greater than or equal to 0

(B) All real numbers except for 2

(C) All real numbers greater than or equal to 2

(D) All real numbers

24. The statement "A is a necessary condition for B," is equivalent to which of the following?

(A) If not A, then B

(B) If not B, then A

(C) If A, then B

(D) If B, then A

25. What is the slope of a line perpendicular to a line with slope $\frac{4}{5}$?

(A) $-\frac{5}{4}$

(B) $-\frac{4}{5}$

(C) $\frac{4}{5}$

(D) $\frac{5}{4}$

26. What is the prime factorization of 60?

(A) 6×10

(B) $2 \times 2 \times 3 \times 5$

(C) $3 \times 4 \times 5$

(D) $2 \times 3 \times 3 \times 5$

GO ON TO THE NEXT PAGE

27. The following chart shows the percentages of students who participate in sports programs at Northern High School. If there are 150 students in the school, how many students participate in football or soccer?

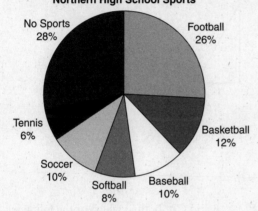

Northern High School Sports

No Sports 28%
Football 26%
Tennis 6%
Soccer 10%
Softball 8%
Baseball 10%
Basketball 12%

(A) 39

(B) 46

(C) 54

(D) 60

28. Kiernan's eight test scores are shown below. What is the range of his scores?

88 80 79 72 90 94 79 83

(A) 22

(B) 26

(C) 72

(D) 83

29. Which of the following is the inverse of the function $f(x) = \frac{x-4}{3}$?

(A) $f^{-1}(x) = 3x + 4$

(B) $f^{-1}(x) = \frac{x+4}{3}$

(C) $f^{-1}(x) = \frac{x-3}{3}$

(D) $f^{-1}(x) = 3x - 4$

30. Which of the following numbers is irrational?

(A) $\sqrt{9}$

(B) $\sqrt{25}$

(C) $\sqrt{49}$

(D) $\sqrt{50}$

31. The volume of a rectangular box is found by multiplying its length, width, and height. If each dimension of a particular box is doubled, then the volume of the new box is how many times the volume of the original box?

(A) 2

(B) 8

(C) 6

(D) 4

32. In a barrel of 25 apples, 5 are green. If you select 2 apples, without replacement, what is the probability they are both green?

(A) $\frac{2}{25}$

(B) $\frac{1}{5}$

(C) $\frac{1}{30}$

(D) $\frac{11}{30}$

33. If $X = \{x \mid x$ is a prime number$\}$ and $Y = \{x \mid x$ is an even integer less than 15$\}$, how many elements are in $X \cap Y$?

(A) 1

(B) 0

(C) 5

(D) 6

34. If a and b are both odd integers, what can be said about $a^2 + 2ab + b^2$?

(A) It is always odd.

(B) It is sometimes odd.

(C) It is always divisible by 3.

(D) It is always even.

GO ON TO THE NEXT PAGE

35. A friend tells you that if n is any number, then $2n + 1$ is always odd. Which of the following values of n provides a counterexample to this?

    (A) 2
    (B) $\frac{1}{2}$
    (C) 3
    (D) −1

36. Suppose $f(x) = 3x + 4$ and $g(x) = x − 2$. For what value of x does $f(x) = g(x)$?

    (A) 3
    (B) 1
    (C) −2
    (D) −3

37. Click on the interval that represents the solution set of the following system of inequalities.

    $$4x − 9 \leq 3$$
    $$x + 1 \geq −20$$

[−21, 3]	(−21, 3)
[−9, 3]	(9, 21)

38. If you roll three standard dice, how many outcomes are possible?

39. If $\log_n x = 4$ and $\log_n y = 6$, then $\log_n\left(\frac{x^2}{y}\right) =$

    (A) 10
    (B) 2
    (C) 14
    (D) $\frac{8}{3}$

40. If $x − 2$ is a factor of $x^4 − 2x^3 + kx − 4$, what is the value of k?

41. What is the value of x in the following figure?

    (A) 12
    (B) 14
    (C) 21
    (D) 23

42. If $A \subset B$ and $C \subset B$, then which of the following is NEVER true?

    (A) $A \subset C$
    (B) $B \subset C$
    (C) $C \subset A$
    (D) $A = \varnothing$

GO ON TO THE NEXT PAGE

43. The graph of $y = f(x)$ is given below:

Which of the following could be the graph of $y = -3f(x)$?

(A)

(B)

(C)

(D)

44. A jar contains 6 red, 5 yellow, and 4 blue jellybeans. If 2 jellybeans are selected one after the other without replacing the first, what is the probability that the first one is red and the second one is yellow?

(A) $\frac{2}{15}$

(B) $\frac{8}{75}$

(C) $\frac{11}{15}$

(D) $\frac{1}{7}$

45. If A → B and B → C, what does ~C imply?

(A) A

(B) B

(C) ~A

(D) It implies a contradiction.

46. If $x^2 + 9 = 0$, then which of the following are the two roots of the equation?

(A) $3i, -3i$

(B) $3i, -3$

(C) $3, -3i$

(D) $3, -3$

47. If x is odd, which of the following expressions must also be odd?

(A) $x + 1$

(B) $2x$

(C) $x + 2$

(D) $2x + 2$

48. Which of the following is the standard deviation for this set of numbers?

$$6, 8, 9, 13, 14$$

(A) 2.46

(B) 3.03

(C) 4.83

(D) 4.59

49. If $f(g(x)) = \frac{1}{x-4}$ and $g(x) = x + 4$, what is $f(x)$?

(A) $\frac{1}{x+4}$

(B) $\frac{x}{x-4}$

(C) $\frac{1}{x-4}$

(D) $\frac{1}{x-8}$

GO ON TO THE NEXT PAGE

KAPLAN

50. Click on the correct representation of the interval $[-1, 9)$.

$-1 < x < 9$	$-1 \leq x < 9$
$0 \leq x \leq 9$	$1 \leq x < 9$

51. Which statement is TRUE regarding the standard deviations of the data in Set A and Set B?

   Set A: 20, 21, 19, 23, 22, 21, 19, 20, 21

   Set B: 8, 31, 20, 11, 7, 42, 28, 30

   (A) The standard deviation of the data in Set A equals the standard deviation of the data in Set B.

   (B) The standard deviation of the data in Set A equals 0.

   (C) The standard deviation of the data in Set A is greater than the standard deviation of the data in Set B.

   (D) The standard deviation of the data in Set B is greater than the standard deviation of the data in Set A.

52. If $g(x) = 2x^3 - 3x^2 + 5x - 4$, then $g(-2) =$

   (A) -10
   (B) 10
   (C) -42
   (D) 12

53. Yoshi is five years older than Sam. Three years ago, Yoshi was twice as old as Sam. How old is Sam now?

54. Which of the following are finite sets?

   I. The set of hours in the day
   II. The set of days in the week
   III. The set of weeks in the year

   (A) I and II only
   (B) II and III only
   (C) I and III only
   (D) I, II, and III

55. Sliding the graph of a triangle on the coordinate plane to the right 3 units and down 2 units is an example of what type of transformation?

   (A) Dilation
   (B) Rotation
   (C) Translation
   (D) Reflection

56. The probability it will snow on Monday is 0.6, while the probability it will snow on Tuesday is 0.3. What is the probability it will snow on Monday but not on Tuesday?

   (A) 0.18
   (B) 0.12
   (C) 0.42
   (D) 0.9

57. Which of the following truth tables shows the conjunction of p and q? Click on the correct representation.

p	q	$\neg q$
T	T	F
T	F	T
F	T	F
F	F	T

p	q	$\neg q$
T	T	F
T	F	F
F	T	T
F	F	T

p	q	$p \wedge q$
T	T	T
T	F	F
F	T	F
F	F	F

p	q	$p \wedge q$
T	T	T
T	F	T
F	T	T
F	F	F

GO ON TO THE NEXT PAGE

KAPLAN

58. Suppose you toss a coin three times. What is the probability of getting at least two heads?

(A) $\frac{1}{4}$

(B) $\frac{1}{2}$

(C) $\frac{3}{4}$

(D) $\frac{3}{8}$

59. Which of the following represents a line of symmetry for the graph below?

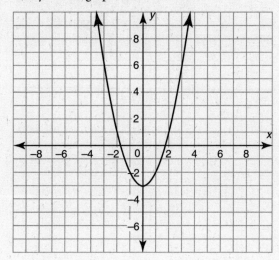

(A) x-axis

(B) y-axis

(C) $y = x$

(D) $x = 3$

60. The following set of data shows rainfall amounts, in inches, for the past nine months. What is the mode of this set of data?

0.8 1.2 0.4 2.8 1.2 0.9 3.2 2.8 1.2

(A) 0.8

(B) 1.2

(C) 2.8

(D) 3.2

END OF TEST. STOP

ANSWER KEY

1.	A	11.	D	21.	C	31.	B	41.	C
2.	C	12.	B	22.	0	32.	C	42.	B
3.	B	13.	C	23.	A	33.	A	43.	A
4.	D	14.	$-\lvert-10+3\rvert$	24.	D	34.	D	44.	D
5.	B	15.	B	25.	A	35.	B	45.	C
6.	$\lvert-12+1\rvert$	16.	90	26.	B	36.	D	46.	A
7.	A	17.	A	27.	C	37.	$[-21, 3]$	47.	C
8.	C	18.	C	28.	A	38.	216	48.	B
9.	A	19.	D	29.	A	39.	B	49.	D
10.	A	20.	C	30.	D	40.	2	50.	$-1 \le x < 9$

51.	D
52.	C
53.	8
54.	D
55.	C
56.	C
57.	lower left table
58.	B
59.	B
60.	B

DIAGNOSTIC TEST QUICK REFERENCE TABLES

Use the following tables to determine which topics you need to review most.

Topic	Test Question
Sets	1, 11, 21, 33, 42, 54
Logic	4, 10, 24, 35, 45, 57
Real Number System	3, 6, 8, 14, 18, 26, 30, 34, 37, 40, 47, 50
Functions and Graphs	2, 7, 12, 17, 23, 29, 36, 43, 49, 52, 55, 59
Probability and Statistics	5, 9, 15, 19, 22, 27, 28, 32, 38, 44, 48, 51, 56, 58, 60
Additional Topics	13, 16, 20, 25, 31, 39, 41, 46, 53

Topic	Number of Questions on Test	Number Correct
Sets	6	
Logic	6	
Real Number System	12	
Functions and Graphs	12	
Probability and Statistics	15	
Additional Topics	9	

Answers and Explanations

1. (A)

$A \cap B$ would be the set of odd whole numbers less than 10, so a subset of this set must also include odd whole numbers that are less than 10. (B) includes a negative number (the whole numbers are positive), (C) includes an even number, and (D) includes a number greater than 10, so none of these are the right answer. (A) is the only set listed that includes only odd whole numbers less than 10.

2. (C)

The transformation that flips a graph over a line to create a mirror image on the opposite side of the line is called a reflection. In this type of transformation, the size and shape of the graph do not change.

3. (B)

A prime number is only divisible by itself and 1, so I and II are true. Since 2 is a prime number, a prime number is not always odd. (B) is the correct answer.

4. (D)

Notice that if p or q is true, then r is true. Therefore, the answer is (D) $p \vee q$.

5. (B)

A subset of restaurants, with no sense of order, is selected in this problem. That means this is a combination problem. The problem can be solved using the combination formula, $C(n, r) = \dfrac{n!}{r!(n-r)!}$. Here $n = 10$ and $r = 3$, so

$$C(10, 3) = \frac{10!}{3!(10-3)!} = \frac{10!}{3!7!} =$$

$$\frac{(10 \times 9 \times 8 \times 7 \times 6 \times 5 \times 4 \times 3 \times 2 \times 1)}{(3 \times 2 \times 1) \times (7 \times 6 \times 5 \times 4 \times 3 \times 2 \times 1)}$$

Canceling and reducing will leave you with 120.

6. $|-12 + 1|$

First simplify the given ab___

$$\left| \frac{5^2 - 45 \times 3}{10} \right|$$

$$= \left| \frac{25 - 135}{10} \right|$$

$$= \left| \frac{-110}{10} \right|$$

$$= |-11|$$

$$= 11$$

Now, simplify each choice until you find one that equals 11. Begin with the upper left: $|-12 + 1| = |-11| = 11$. This is the correct answer.

7. (A)

The domain of a function includes all the values of x for which the function is defined. The given function is defined for all real numbers except for those that make the denominator 0. This happens when $x^2 - 4 = 0$. Solving this equation gives us $x = 2$ or $x = -2$. The domain is therefore all real numbers except for 2 or -2.

8. (C)

If any number c is plugged into a polynomial to get 0, then $x - c$ is a factor of the polynomial. Looking at the possible answers, there are four choices for c: 1, -1, 2, and -2. Plugging 1 into the polynomial gives us

$$2(1)^3 - (1)^2 + 3(1) - 4 = 2 - 1 + 3 - 4 = 0$$

Thus, $x - 1$ is a factor of the polynomial.

9. (A)

The mean (or average) of a set of numbers is found by adding all the numbers then dividing by how many numbers were added. If these numbers are doubled, then the mean should also be doubled. For instance, the mean of the set of numbers 2, 4, 6, 8, 10 is 6 because $\dfrac{2+4+6+8+10}{5} = \dfrac{30}{5} = 6$. If you double each number, you get the set 4, 8, 12, 16, 20, whose mean is 12 because $\dfrac{4+8+12+16+20}{5} = \dfrac{60}{5} = 12$.

10. (A)

To find the converse of a conditional statement, we switch the two statements that make up the conditional. That is, "If P, then Q" becomes "If Q, then P."

11. (D)

Since R and S are small sets, the Cartesian product can quickly be determined: $R \times S = \{(u, x), (u, y), (v, x), (v, y)\}$. The only answer choice that is not in this set is (u, v).

12. (B)

First you need to find $g(4)$. According to the second table, if $x = 4$, then $g(x) = 2$; therefore $g(4) = 2$. Now find $f(2)$. According to the first table, when $x = 2$, $f(x) = 5$, so $f(2) = 5$. Thus $f(g(4)) = f(2) = 5$.

13. (C)

If you add the length and width of a rectangle, you've gone half the distance around the rectangle, in this case 100 feet. So length + width = 100. Since width is x, the equation becomes length + x = 100 or length = 100 − x.

14. −|−10 + 3|

First simplify the given absolute value expression:

$$-\left|\frac{2^3 \div 2^2 \times 7}{-2}\right|$$

$$= -\left|\frac{8 \div 4 \times 7}{-2}\right|$$

$$= -\left|\frac{2 \times 7}{-2}\right|$$

$$= -\left|\frac{14}{-2}\right|$$

$$= -|-7|$$

$$= -7$$

Scan the four choices. The only choice that is equivalent to −7 is (D): −|−10 + 3| = −|−7| = −7. This is the correct answer.

15. (B)

Out of seven cards, two will have 4 written on them, since 4 appears twice in the number 5,473,343. The probability of getting a 4 would therefore be $\frac{2}{7}$.

16. 90

The sum of the three angles of any triangle is 180°. Since we are talking about a right triangle, we know one of the angles must measure 90°. This leaves 90° for the sum of the other two angles.

17. (A)

The graph of a function of x must pass the *vertical line test*, which says that any vertical line drawn on the Cartesian plane should intersect the graph of a function no more than once. (B), (C), and (D) all fail this test.

18. (C)

To divide two fractions, multiply the first by the reciprocal of the second. The reciprocal of $\frac{c}{d}$ is $\frac{d}{c}$, so $\frac{a}{b} \div \frac{c}{d} = \frac{a}{b} \times \frac{d}{c} = \frac{ad}{bc}$.

19. (D)

The number of bicycles sold in 2008 was about 850. The number of bicycles sold in 2007 was 700. There were 850 − 700 = 150 more bicycles sold in 2008 than in 2007.

20. (C)

The remainder theorem states that to find the remainder when dividing a polynomial by $(x − a)$, you only need to substitute a for the variable in the polynomial and then simplify. In this question, the polynomial is $P(x) = 2x^4 − 8x^3 − 7x + 1$, and you are dividing by $(x − 5)$. Therefore, substitute 5 for x and simplify:

$P(5) = 2(5)^4 − 8(5)^3 − 7(5) + 1$
$P(5) = 1{,}250 − 1{,}000 − 35 + 1$
$P(5) = 216$

21. (C)

Notice that the area outside of the two circles is shaded. The shaded area is what is not in A or B, which is $(A \cup B)'$. Also, all of circle B is shaded. So the Venn diagram here represents $(A \cup B)' \cup B$.

22. 0

Joreon's mean score is $\frac{14 + 17 + 12 + 18 + 24}{5} = \frac{85}{5} = 17$. To find his median score, list the numbers from smallest to largest and identify the number in the middle. The middle number of 12, 14, 17, 18, 24 is 17, so his median score is 17. Since the mean and median scores are the same, the difference in scores is 0.

23. (A)

No matter what value we substitute for x, x^2 will always be greater than or equal to 0. Likewise, $(x - 2)^2$ will always be greater than or equal to 0, so the range of the function is all real numbers greater than or equal to 0.

24. (D)

"A is a necessary condition for B" means that whenever B happens, A happens. In other words, if B, then A.

25. (A)

Two lines are perpendicular if their slopes are negative reciprocals of each other. The negative reciprocal of $\frac{4}{5}$ is $-\frac{5}{4}$, so the answer is (A).

26. (B)

We are looking for 60 written as a product of prime numbers. Answer choices (A) and (C) can be discounted because they both include numbers that are not prime. If answer choice (D) is multiplied, we get 90, so this answer can also be discarded. This leaves us with (B).

27. (C)

To find the number of students who play football or soccer, add the percentages from the table to get 26% + 10% = 36%. Multiply 150 by 0.36 to get 54 students. The correct answer is (C), 54 students.

28. (A)

To calculate the range of a set of data, subtract the smallest value from the greatest value. In this case, the lowest test score is 72, and the highest test score is 94. Therefore, the answer is 94 − 72 = 22.

29. (A)

The inverse of a function "undoes" the function. In this problem, the function takes x, subtracts 4, then divides by 3. To undo this, we would need to multiply by 3, then add 4. Answer choice (A) completes this calculation.

30. (D)

If you simplify the first three choices, you get rational numbers: $\sqrt{9} = 3$, $\sqrt{25} = 5$, and $\sqrt{49} = 7$. Choice (D), $\sqrt{50}$, simplifies to $5\sqrt{2}$. Since $\sqrt{2}$ cannot be written as a ratio of two integers, it is not a rational number. Therefore, it is the correct answer.

31. (B)

Suppose the original box had a length of 2, width of 3, and height of 4. The volume of the box would be $2 \times 3 \times 4 = 24$. If each of these dimensions were doubled, the new volume would be $4 \times 6 \times 8 = 192$, which is 8 times the original volume.

32. (C)

When choosing the first apple, 5 out of 25 apples are green, so the probability of getting a green apple would be $\frac{5}{25} = \frac{1}{5}$. Once this apple has been chosen, there are 4 out of 24 remaining apples that are green, so the probability of the second apple being green would be $\frac{4}{24} = \frac{1}{6}$. Thus, the probability of them both being green is $\frac{1}{5} \times \frac{1}{6} = \frac{1}{30}$.

33. (A)

$X \cap Y$ denotes the set of elements that are both prime and even integers less than 15. There is only one even prime number, and that is the number 2. This is the only number that would be in the set $X \cap Y$, so the number of elements in the set is 1.

34. (D)

$a^2 + 2ab + b^2 = (a + b)^2$, so for any odd numbers a and b, $(a + b)$ and $(a + b)^2$ will always be even.

35. (B)

$2n + 1$ is always odd if n is an integer, but plugging $\frac{1}{2}$ into the equation produces $2\left(\frac{1}{2}\right) + 1 = 1 + 1 = 2$, which is not odd.

36. (D)

Set $f(x)$ equal to $g(x)$ and solve:

$$3x + 4 = x - 2$$
$$2x + 4 = -2$$
$$2x = -6$$
$$x = -3$$

37. [–21, 3]

To find the solution set, begin by solving both inequalities for x:

$$4x - 9 \leq 3$$
$$4x \leq 12$$
$$x \leq 3$$

And

$$x + 1 \geq -20$$
$$x \geq -21$$

Putting together these two constraints, x must be greater than or equal to –21 and less than or equal to 3. The only interval that correctly represents these constraints is the closed interval [–21, 3]. The interval is closed because it includes the values –21 and 3.

38. 216

Each time you roll a die, there are 6 possible outcomes, so if you roll three dice, there are $6 \times 6 \times 6 = 216$ possible outcomes.

39. (B)

This problem requires using some properties of logarithms:
$$\log_n\left(\frac{x^2}{y}\right) = \log_n x^2 - \log_n y = 2\log_n x - \log_n y = 2(4) - 6 = 2.$$

40. 2

If $x - 2$ is a factor of $x^4 - 2x^3 + kx - 4$, then plugging 2 into the polynomial would make the polynomial 0. Solve the equation:

$$(2)^4 - 2(2)^3 + k(2) - 4 = 0$$
$$16 - 16 + 2k - 4 = 0$$
$$2k - 4 = 0$$
$$2k = 4$$
$$k = 2$$

41. (C)

To find the length of the leg of the right triangle, use the Pythagorean theorem.

$$35^2 = 28^2 + x^2$$
$$1{,}225 = 784 + x^2$$
$$441 = x^2$$
$$21 = x$$

You may also have noticed that the sides of this right triangle are in the proportion 3-4-5. Each side is multiplied by 7 to arrive at the dimensions of this triangle. Therefore, a 3-4-5 triangle can have sides measuring 21, 28, and 35.

42. (B)

The symbol $\subset$ in the problem states that both A and C are proper subsets of B. While it could be true that $A \subset C$, $C \subset A$, or $A = \emptyset$, it is never true that if $C \subset B$ then $B \subset C$. This is because C must have fewer elements than B, since it is a proper subset of B.

43. (A)

Having –3 before the function will make the graph open down instead of up and will make the graph more narrow.

44. (D)

When you choose the first jellybean, there are 6 red out of 15 total, so the probability of selecting a red jellybean would be $\frac{6}{15} = \frac{2}{5}$. The first jellybean is not replaced, so there are 14 jellybeans left. Five of the 14 remaining jellybeans are yellow, so the probability of choosing a yellow jellybean second would be $\frac{5}{14}$. The probability of choosing a red then a yellow jellybean would be $\frac{2}{5} \times \frac{5}{14} = \frac{1}{7}$.

45. (C)

Since A → B and B → C, it can be concluded that A → C. This is logically equivalent to ~C → ~A, so ~C implies ~A.

46. (A)

Solving the equation produces

$$x^2 + 9 = 0$$
$$x^2 = -9$$
$$x^2 = \pm\sqrt{-9}$$
$$x^2 = \pm 3i$$

47. (C)

If x is odd, then adding 1 will result in an even number. Therefore, answer (A) is incorrect. If x is odd, then multiplying it by 2 or multiplying by 2 and adding 2 will also result in an even number; therefore, answers (B) and (D) are also incorrect. Answer (C) is correct because adding 2 to any odd number will always result in another odd number.

48. (B)

To find the standard deviation, follow these steps:

1. Calculate the mean: 10
2. Find the amount each number deviates from the mean: 4, 2, 1, −3, −4
3. Square those differences: 16, 4, 1, 9, 16
4. Add the squares together: $16 + 4 + 1 + 9 + 16 = 46$
5. Divide by the number of squares: $\frac{46}{5} = 9.2$
6. Take the square root of this number: $\sqrt{9.2} = 3.03$

When calculating the standard deviation with a sample of numbers from a larger population, divide the sum of the squares (in step 5) by the number of items *minus one*. In this case, we would have divided 46 by 4 if this number set were a sampling from a larger population.

49. (D)

Since $f(g(x)) = \frac{1}{(x-4)}$, $x + 4$ needs to be plugged into each choice to see which gives us the desired result. Plugging $x + 4$ into (D) we get $\frac{1}{(x+4)-8} = \frac{1}{x-4}$.

50. $-1 \le x < 9$

The interval notation [−1, 9) means all numbers greater than or equal to −1 and less than but *not* equal to 9. The upper right choice, $-1 \le x < 9$, is the only interval that correctly includes all numbers greater than or equal to −1 and less than 9.

51. (D)

The standard deviation of a set of data describes the average distance from the mean of each number in the set. So you can look at the numbers in both sets to see which set has a larger range of numbers in the set. Set A has a minimum value of 19 and maximum value of 23. The numbers are closely centered on the mean of 20.7 and do not deviate far from the center. Set B has a much larger range of numbers. The minimum value is 8 and the maximum is 42. The numbers stray much farther from the mean of 22.1. Therefore, without calculating the exact standard deviation for each set of data, it is clear that the standard deviation for Set B is greater. The correct answer is (D).

52. (C)

Replacing x with −2 produces

$$g(-2) = 2(-2)^3 - 3(-2)^2 + 5(-2) - 4$$
$$= -16 - 12 - 10 - 4$$
$$= -42$$

53. 8

If we let x represent Sam's current age, Yoshi's age is $x + 5$. Three years ago, Yoshi's age was $(x + 5) - 3$ and Sam's was $(x - 3)$. Yoshi's age was also twice Sam's, or $2(x - 3)$. We now have two equivalent expressions for Yoshi's age three years ago, allowing us to solve the problem:

$$(x + 5) - 3 = 2(x - 3)$$
$$x + 2 = 2x - 6$$
$$2 = x - 6$$
$$8 = x$$

54. (D)

A set is finite if all elements in the set can be listed. The answer is (D), since a list can be made of the elements of all three sets described.

55. (C)

The transformation that simply slides a figure or graph to a new location on the coordinate plane is called a translation. The size and shape of the figure remain the same while it is shifted vertically, horizontally, or both.

56. (C)

The probability it will snow on Tuesday is 0.3, so the probability it will not snow on Tuesday is 0.7. The probability it will snow on Monday but not on Tuesday would be $0.6 \times 0.7 = 0.42$.

KAPLAN

57.

p	q	$p \wedge q$
T	T	T
T	F	F
F	T	F
F	F	F

The conjunction of p and q is represented as "$p \wedge q$" and is read "p and q." The statement "$p \wedge q$" is only true when both p and q are true. Therefore, the table shown is correct. The entries in the third column of this table are true only when the entries in the columns for p and q are both true.

58. (B)

If you flip a coin three times, there are eight possible outcomes: HHH, HHT, HTH, HTT, THH, THT, TTH, and TTT. Of these eight possible outcomes, only four contain at least two heads: HHH, HHT, HTH, and THH. Therefore, the probability of getting at least two heads is $\frac{4}{8}$ or $\frac{1}{2}$.

59. (B)

The figure shows the graph of the function $f(x) = x^2 - 3$. Of the four lines described in the choices, only the y-axis is a line of symmetry for this function. It separates the function into two halves that are mirror images of each other. Therefore, the answer is (B).

60. (B)

The mode of a data set is the number that appears most often. The number that appears most often in this set is 1.2. It appears three times in the set, more times than any other number. Therefore, the correct answer is (B).

Chapter Nine: **CLEP College Mathematics Review**

- **The Big Picture: CLEP College Mathematics**
- **Nuts and Bolts**
- **CLEP College Mathematics Strategy Checklist**
- **Sets**
- **Logic**
- **Real Number System**

- **Functions and Graphs**
- **Probability and Statistics**
- **Additional Topics from Algebra and Geometry**
- **College Mathematics Resources**
- **Final Thoughts**

You've decided to get a head start on higher education by taking the CLEP College Mathematics exam. Many institutions of higher learning will grant six semester hours of credit to high-scoring candidates. (You should check with the schools you are considering to find out their policies.) This guide will help you achieve your goal of a great score.

THE BIG PICTURE: CLEP COLLEGE MATHEMATICS

Let's start with some good news. Since the College Mathematics exam consists of material generally taught in a college course for non–mathematics majors, the material on the test can easily be learned by most students (that includes you). None of the material covered on the exam requires advanced mathematical knowledge. In fact, most of the material on the exam has been taught to students by the tenth grade.

Before you delve into any subject, it is important to know what you are getting into. Understanding the structure of the CLEP College Mathematics exam will help you maximize your score, so let's start talking facts.

This particular exam consists of 60 questions to be completed in 90 minutes. Do some basic math, and you can see that means that you can spend one and a half minutes on each question.

Approximately half of the questions on the exam require you to understand and solve simple, routine problems, which should be as easy to solve as going through your day-to-day activities.

The other half of the exam involves nonroutine problems that require test takers to understand concepts and the application of these concepts. The nonroutine problems require you to call upon your bank of mathematical concepts, your "troops," to carry out your plan. Most of the exam questions are multiple-choice, with four possible answers to choose from. Some problems may require a numerical answer to be calculated and entered into the box provided.

The different areas or topics covered on the exam include sets, logic, the real number system, functions and their graphs, and probability and statistics. There are also additional topics from algebra and geometry, including complex numbers, logarithms, properties of triangles and circles, and application problems. Just as it is important to keep up with current events, you should be familiar with currently taught mathematical notation, symbols, and vocabulary.

The exam does not focus on arithmetic, and a calculator will not be required for any problems. However, a scientific (nongraphing) calculator will be provided for you on the computer as a test-taking tool during the exam.

NUTS AND BOLTS

The key mathematical topics to study, along with how much of the CLEP College Mathematics exam consists of questions on each, can be found in the following list.

10% Sets

Union and intersection

Subsets, disjoint sets, and equivalent sets

Venn diagrams

Cartesian product

10% Logic

Truth tables

Conjunctions, disjunctions, implications, and negations

Conditional statements

Necessary and sufficient conditions

Converse, inverse, and contrapositive

Hypotheses, conclusions, and counter examples

20% Real Number System

Prime and composite numbers

Odd and even numbers

Factors and divisibility

Rational and irrational numbers

Absolute value and order

Open and closed intervals

20% Functions and Graphs

Properties and graphs of functions

Domain and range

Composition of functions and inverse functions

Simple transformations of functions: translations, reflections, and symmetry

25% Probability and Statistics

Counting problems, including permutations and combinations

Computation of probabilities of simple and compound events

Simple conditional probability

Mean, median, mode, and range

Concept of standard deviation

Data interpretation and representation: tables, bar graphs, line graphs, circle graphs, pie charts, scatterplots, and histograms

15% **Additional Topics from Algebra and Geometry**

Complex numbers

Logarithms and exponents

Applications from algebra and geometry

Perimeter and area of plane figures

Properties of triangles, circles, and rectangles

The Pythagorean theorem

Parallel and perpendicular lines

Algebraic equations, systems of linear equations, and inequalities

Fundamental theorem of algebra, remainder theorem, and factor theorem

Percentage of the exam and the number of problems that are from each topic are approximate. There may be more or fewer problems from a particular topic on the actual exam.

While this list may seem intimidating, keep in mind that some of the subtopics listed above will only appear once on the exam, while some may not appear at all. It is best to study all of them, however, just in case you are tested on every topic. It is important to have a solid knowledge base so that few questions are complete surprises when you take the CLEP College Mathematics exam.

CLEP COLLEGE MATHEMATICS STRATEGY CHECKLIST

Preparing for any exam takes time. In order to maximize your study time and be prepared for the fast-paced format of the actual exam, consult the following list:

Be familiar with all the symbols and terms that may appear on the exam. While you may be familiar with symbols such as $\neq$, $\leq$, and $\approx$, more specific symbols may not be as familiar, such as $\cup$, $\subseteq$, and $\in$ from set theory, or $\sim$, $\wedge$, and $\vee$ from logic. Similarly, terms such as *contrapositive* or *permutation* may not immediately be familiar.

Be on the lookout for general keywords such as *all*, *never*, or *always*. While it may sometimes be true that n^2 is greater than n, for example, it is not *always* true. Likewise, adding two odd numbers will *never* produce an odd number.

Be on the lookout for specific keywords such as *positive*, *negative*, *odd*, *even*, or specific types of numbers such as *integers* or *whole numbers*. Knowing that you are dealing with integers in a problem, for instance, indicates that you can have negative numbers but not fractions, which may be important.

Know probability. Approximately a fourth of the exam covers probability and statistics, so be sure to be familiar with the types of problems that may appear here. Also keep in mind that probability is often written as a fraction and this fraction will need to be reduced in your answer.

Backsolve. If you're asked which number solves a particular equation, there's no need to solve the equation if you're provided possible answers. Plug the answer choices into the equation until the right answer is found.

Pace your study schedule. Many test takers stay up late and try to cram a lot of information the night before, which makes them too tired to answer exam questions in the most efficient way possible. When your mind is dragging due to lack of sleep, it is difficult to answer 60 questions in 90 minutes. If you skip breakfast the day of the exam, your mind may be focused on how hungry you are, rather than how to solve the next problem on the test.

SETS

The CLEP College Mathematics exam will cover the general topic of *sets*, which are collections of objects. Sets can be represented by words, letters, or numbers. A comic book collection, for instance, would be a set. The objects that make up a set are called *elements*. For example, if you have 50 comic books in a collection, the set of 50 comic books would be composed of 50 individual elements, each comic book in the collection.

Sets are typically represented by capital letters. Braces, { and }, are often used to enclose the elements of a set. For instance, sets can be written as follows:

$A = \{a, b, c, d, e\}$ or $B = \{1, 3, 5\}$

The order in which the elements are listed is not important. The number of elements in a set is called the *cardinal number* of the set. If a set has 5 elements, then its cardinal number is 5. Sets that have the same cardinality are called *equivalent sets*. For example, the sets $\{1, 2, 3, 4, 5, 6\}$ and $\{7, 8, 9, 10, 11, 12\}$ are equivalent sets because they both contain six elements. A set is considered *well defined* when its component elements are objectively clear. For example, "all the comic books in my collection" is a well-defined set, but "the best television shows on Monday night" is not because that category is definitely subjective!

The symbol $\in$ can be used to indicate that an element belongs to a particular set, and the symbol $\notin$ —which contains the "not" slash you've seen on so many signs—can indicate that an element does not belong to a set. So, if $A = \{1, 3, 5, 7\}$, it can be said that $3 \in A$ and $6 \notin A$. The set that contains no elements is called the *empty set*, or *null set*, and is denoted as either $\emptyset$ or $\{ \}$. A set can contain elements and later become a null set, provided that all elements of the set are no longer available. For example, as a species becomes extinct, the set of individuals of that species gradually dwindles until there are no individuals left in the set. When there are no individuals left to fill the set, the set becomes null. (The dodo set is a null set.)

Listing the elements of a set between braces is called *roster notation*. Another way to write a set is called *set-builder notation*. In this notation, a variable such as x is used to represent an element of the set, and a vertical bar, $|$, stands for the phrase "such that," followed by a brief description of the variable. For example, the set of all integers less than 10 could be written as $\{x \mid x$ is an integer less than 10$\}$.

A set can be broken down into smaller units. A is a *subset* of B, denoted $A \subseteq B$, if every element in A is also in B. For instance, if $A = \{a, b, c\}$ and $B = \{a, b, c, d, e\}$, then $A \subseteq B$. Sets A and B are *equal*, denoted $A = B$, if they contain the exact same elements. If $A \subseteq B$ but $A \neq B$, then we say A is a *proper subset* of B, denoted $A \subset B$. If, for example, $A = \{$peanut butter, jelly, milk, bananas$\}$ and $B = \{$peanut butter, jelly, milk, bananas, butter, raisins, and lettuce$\}$, A is a proper subset of B since A contains some, but not all, of the elements of B.

Now let's look at the big picture. The *universal set*, U, is the set that contains all the possible elements needed for a particular problem. The *complement* of set A, denoted A', is the set of elements that are in U but not in A. For example, suppose U is the set of all integers for a particular problem. If A represents the set of all negative integers, A' represents the set of all nonnegative integers.

The *union* of sets A and B, denoted $A \cup B$, is the set of elements in A or in B. The *intersection* of two sets A and B, denoted $A \cap B$, is the set of elements in A and B. For example, if $A = \{1, 2, 3\}$ and $B = \{2, 3, 4, 5\}$, then $A \cup B = \{1, 2, 3, 4, 5\}$ and $A \cap B = \{2, 3\}$. If $A \cap B = \emptyset$, then A and B are called *disjoint* and do not have any values in common.

A way to visualize sets is to use a *Venn diagram*. Each Venn diagram uses a rectangle to represent the universal set and circles within the rectangle to represent all other sets. Anything that belongs to set A is inside circle A:

Anything not in A is outside of circle A:

The operations of union and intersection are represented in the following Venn diagrams:

$$A \cup B \qquad\qquad A \cap B$$

There is another way to combine two sets beyond union and intersection. Let $A = \{2, 3\}$ and $B = \{5, 6, 7\}$. The set of all possible ordered pairs (a, b), with $a \in A$ and $b \in B$, is called the Cartesian product of A and B, denoted $A \times B$. In this case, $A \times B = \{(2, 5), (2, 6), (2, 7), (3, 5), (3, 6), (3, 7)\}$.

Sets Review Questions

1. If $A = \{1, 3, 5, 7\}$ and $B = \{2, 3, 4, 5\}$, find $A \cup B$ and $A \cap B$.

    Solution: $A \cup B$ is the set of elements that are in A or in B, so $A \cup B = \{1, 2, 3, 4, 5, 7\}$. $A \cap B$ is the set of elements that are in A and in B, so $A \cap B = \{3, 5\}$.

2. If $U = \{2, 4, 6, 8, 10, 12\}$ and $A = \{2, 8, 10\}$, find A'.

    Solution: A' represents the set of elements in U that are not in A, so $A' = \{4, 6, 12\}$.

3. What is the notation for the following Venn diagram?

    Solution: The shaded area of the diagram represents the set of elements that are not in A or in B. Since there are no elements inside circle A or circle B, the notation would be $(A \cap B)'$.

LOGIC

In logic, algebraic techniques are used to determine when statements are true and when they are false. A *statement* conveys one idea and can be labeled either true or false. Examples of statements are "She has green eyes," and "My dog is a beagle." Letters such as p, q, r, and s are used to represent statements. *Compound statements* are formed by connecting two or more statements. An example of a compound statement would be "She has green eyes and my dog is a beagle." Two separate ideas are conveyed in this compound statement.

If two statements are connected using the word *and*, the resulting compound statement is called a *conjunction*. This math term means pretty much the same thing that it does when talking about conjunctions in grammar; it combines two statements. If p and q are statements, then the conjunction "p and q" is written $p \wedge q$. To determine when a compound statement is true, we have to consider when the statements that make up the compound statement are true and when they are false. This can be done by creating a *truth table*. The truth table for the conjunction is this:

p	q	$p \wedge q$
T	T	T
T	F	F
F	T	F
F	F	F

Conjunction

The first row of this table tells us that when p is true and q is true, $p \wedge q$ is true. The second row says that when p is true and q is false, $p \wedge q$ is false. The third and fourth rows also give us results of "false," telling us that the conjunction is only true when both p and q are true.

If two statements are connected using the word *or*, the resulting compound statement is called a *disjunction*. If p and q are statements, then the conjunction "p or q" is written $p \vee q$. The truth table for the disjunction p or q is

p	q	$p \vee q$
T	T	T
T	F	T
F	T	T
F	F	F

Disjunction

The table shows that a disjunction is only false when both p and q are false. Note that in logic, the word *or* is used to mean either or both.

If p is a statement, its *negation* can be found by inserting the word *not* into it. For instance, the negation of "It is raining," is "It is not raining." The negation of statement p is symbolized $\sim p$ and read "not p." The truth table for the negation is this:

p	$\sim p$
T	F
F	T

Negation

So when p is true, $\sim p$ is false; when p is false, $\sim p$ is true. For example, it cannot be raining (p) and not raining ($\sim p$ or not p) at the same time and place.

If p and q are statements, then $p \rightarrow q$ represents the compound statement "if p, then q." A compound statement of this form is called an *implication* or *conditional statement*. Its truth table is this:

p	q	$p \rightarrow q$
T	T	T
T	F	F
F	T	T
F	F	T

Implication/Conditional

The compound statement $p \rightarrow q$ is also read "p implies q" and is only false when p is true and q is false. Another compound statement is the *biconditional*, which is symbolized $p \leftrightarrow q$ and is read "p if and only if q." The biconditional is true only when p and q are both true or both false. The truth table for the biconditional is this:

p	q	$p \leftrightarrow q$
T	T	T
T	F	F
F	T	F
F	F	T

Biconditional

If we start with the conditional statement $p \to q$, then its *converse* is $q \to p$. For example, the converse of "If it is sunny, then it is warm," is "If it is warm, then it is sunny." Similarly, $\sim p \to \sim q$ is the *inverse* of $p \to q$, while $\sim q \to \sim p$ is called the *contrapositive* of $p \to q$.

In logic, necessary and sufficient conditions are discussed. A is *necessary* for B if and only if B cannot occur without A. That is, whenever you have B, you have A. On the other hand, A is *sufficient* for B if and only if A guarantees B. That is, whenever you have A, you have B. For example, getting an 83 on a test is sufficient for passing.

An *argument* is a claim that a series of statements, called *hypotheses* or *premises*, imply a final statement, called the *conclusion*. An argument is called *valid* if its conclusion is true whenever all of its hypotheses are true. An argument that is not valid is called a *fallacy*.

One way to show that an argument or assertion is not valid is to provide a *counterexample*. This is an example that satisfies the hypotheses of the argument but does not agree with the conclusion. For instance, suppose it is asserted that "If m and n are odd numbers, then $m + n$ is an odd number." For a counterexample, choose two odd numbers, say $m = 3$ and $n = 5$. According to the assertion, $m + n$ should also be odd, but $m + n = 3 + 5 = 8$, which is even.

Logic Review Questions

1. Write the converse, inverse, and contrapositive of "If it is milk, then it contains calcium."

    Solution: If we think of this statement as $p \to q$, then the converse is $q \to p$ or "If it contains calcium, then it is milk"; the inverse is $\sim p \to \sim q$ or "If it is not milk, then it does not contain calcium"; and the contrapositive is $\sim q \to \sim p$ or "If it does not contain calcium, then it is not milk."

2. If p represents a true statement and q represents a false statement, determine the truth values of the compound statements $p \wedge \sim q$, $\sim p \vee q$, and $\sim(p \vee q)$.

    Solution: As q is a false statement, $\sim q$ is true, so $p \wedge \sim q$ is the conjunction of two true statements, which is true. Similarly, as p is true, $\sim p$ is false, so $\sim p \vee q$ is the disjunction of two false statements, which is false. Finally, as p is true and q is false, $p \vee q$ is true, so $\sim(p \vee q)$ must be false.

3. Provide a counterexample to the assertion "If n is an integer, then $2n > n$."

    Solution: You need to find an integer that doesn't satisfy $2n > n$. One choice would be $n = -3$, for $2n = -6$ and -6 is not greater than -3.

REAL NUMBER SYSTEM

The real number system is divided into many different types of numbers. The numbers that are used for counting $\{1, 2, 3, 4, 5 \ldots\}$ are called *natural* or *counting numbers*. If we add zero to this set, we get *whole numbers*. If we also include negative versions of the counting numbers we get *integers*.

A real number is rational if it can be written as the ratio of two integers, where the denominator is not 0. For instance, $\frac{2}{3}$, $-\frac{5}{8}$, and $\frac{11}{3}$ are all rational numbers. This set also includes mixed numbers and decimals that stop or repeat, such as 0.25 and 7.6888. Think of a rational number as a bag of apples. Regardless of how many apples are in the bag, you cannot start out with zero apples in the bag and expect five apples to magically appear. On the other hand, if you started out with three apples in the bag and removed one, you would still have a rational number to deal with, since $\frac{2}{3}$ of the apples are left.

Any real number that cannot be written as the ratio of two integers is called *irrational*. These numbers include decimals that do not stop and do not repeat. Examples of irrational numbers are $\sqrt{2}$, $-\sqrt{7}$, and π.

Whole number m is divisible by whole number n if, when m is divided by n, there is no remainder. For example, if you divide 35 by 7, there is no remainder, so we say 35 is divisible by 7. Furthermore, 7 is said to be a factor of 35.

Any integer that is divisible by 2 is called an *even* integer. Any integer that is not divisible by 2 is called an *odd* integer. These definitions include negative integers, so that −4 is even and −5 is odd.

A whole number greater than 1 that is only divisible by itself and 1 is called a *prime number*. Examples of prime numbers are 2, 3, 5, 7, 11, 13, and 17. Note that 2 is the only even prime number. A whole number greater than 1 that is divisible by some number other than itself and 1 is called *composite*. Composite numbers include 4, 6, 8, 9, 10, 12, 14, 15, etc.

Every composite number can be written as a product of prime numbers. For instance, the composite number 20 can be written as $2 \times 2 \times 5$, while the composite number 30 can be written as $2 \times 3 \times 5$. This is known as *prime factorization*.

The *absolute value* of a number is its distance from zero on the number line. If n is a number, its absolute value is indicated by $|n|$. As distance is always positive, absolute value is always positive. The absolute value of a positive number is just the number, while the absolute value of a negative number is that number without the negative sign. For example, $|5| = 5$ and $|−3| = 3$.

Number A is *greater than* number B, written $A > B$, if A is to the right of B on the number line. Number A is *less than B*, written $A < B$, if A is to the left of B on the number line. These definitions can help when ordering negative numbers, for while it may be easy to see that $7 > 5$ without using a number line, it is not always so easy to see that $−7 < −5$.

Greater than and less than signs are also useful to denote ranges of numbers. The notation $4 < x < 10$ represents all numbers greater than 4 but less than 10. This is an example of an *open interval*—one that does not include the endpoints 4 and 10. It can also be written as (4, 10). A *closed interval* does include the endpoints and can be written as $4 \leq x \leq 10$ or [4, 10]. This notation represents all numbers greater than or equal to 4 but less than or equal to 10.

The number system that is used to represent numbers is called a *decimal* system because it represents numbers in terms of powers of 10. Think of the place values of whole numbers: ones

$(10^0 = 1)$, tens $(10^1 = 10)$, hundreds $(10^2 = 100)$, thousands $(10^3 = 1,000)$, and so on. Any number in the decimal system can be broken down using these powers of ten. For example:

$$1,862 = 1,000 + 800 + 60 + 2$$
$$= 1(1,000) + 8(100) + 6(10) + 2(1)$$
$$= 1(10^3) + 8(10^2) + 6(10^1) + 2(10^0)$$

Real Number System Review Questions

1. Determine the rational and irrational numbers in the set of numbers
   $\left\{\frac{5}{4}, 3.7, \sqrt{8}, 9.525, \sqrt{9}, \sqrt[3]{4}, \frac{2}{3}\right\}$.

   Solution: Rational numbers are fractions and decimals that either stop or repeat, so the rational numbers in the set are $\frac{5}{4}$, 3.7, 9.525, $\sqrt{9}$ (= 3), and $\frac{2}{3}$.

   This leaves $\sqrt{8}$ and $\sqrt[3]{4}$ as the irrational numbers (decimals that don't stop and don't repeat).

2. Which one of the numbers 42, 45, 49, 51, and 53 is prime?

   Solution: The only even prime number is 2, so it's not 42. Then 45 is divisible by 5, 49 is divisible by 7, and 51 is divisible by 3. This leaves only 53.

FUNCTIONS AND GRAPHS

Let X and Y be any two sets. A *function* is a rule that assigns to each element $x \in X$ one and only one $y \in Y$. A function is usually notated $f(x)$, which is read "f of x." For example, $f(x) = 2x + 5$ is the function that takes a number x, doubles it, then adds 5. By replacing x with different numbers, we can see each function has a different outcome. For instance, $f(2) = 2(2) + 5 = 9$ while $f(-1) = 2(-1) + 5 = 3$.

The *domain* of a function is the set of numbers that can be plugged into a function so that the function is defined. If $f(x) = x^2$, then the domain is the set of all real numbers, since any real number can be squared. On the other hand, if $f(x) = \sqrt{x}$, the domain is the set of real numbers such that $x \geq 0$, because the square root of a negative number cannot be taken.

The *range* of a function is the set of numbers that the function produces. For example, the range of the function $f(x) = x^2$ is all real numbers such that $y \geq 0$, because if you square a number, you always get a nonnegative result. Similarly, the range of $f(x) = |x|$ is the set of real numbers such that $y \geq 0$, because the absolute value of any number is always nonnegative.

Functions can be added, subtracted, multiplied, and divided. Let $f(x)$ and $g(x)$ be two functions. The following four functions can then be defined:

The *sum* of $f(x)$ and $g(x)$ is given by $(f + g)(x) = f(x) + g(x)$.

The *difference* of $f(x)$ and $g(x)$ is given by $(f - g)(x) = f(x) - g(x)$.

The *product* of $f(x)$ and $g(x)$ is given by $(f \times g)(x) = f(x)g(x)$.

The *quotient* of $f(x)$ and $g(x)$ is given by $\left(\dfrac{f}{g}\right)(x) = \left(\dfrac{f(x)}{g(x)}\right)$, where $g(x) \neq 0$.

For example, suppose $f(x) = 3x - 2$ and $g(x) = x + 5$. Then

$(f + g)(x) = (3x - 2) + (x + 5) = 4x + 3$

$(f - g)(x) = (3x - 2) - (x + 5) = 2x - 7$

$(f \times g)(x) = (3x - 2)(x + 5) = 3x^2 + 13x - 10$

$\left(\dfrac{f}{g}\right)(x) = \dfrac{(3x - 2)}{(x + 5)}$

Note that this last function is not defined when $x = -5$, so its domain is all real numbers except -5.

There is a fifth way of combining two functions f and g, known as a *composition function*. This is written $f \circ g$ and is defined as $(f \circ g)(x) = f(g(x))$. The idea is to substitute whatever the g function is into f and then simplify the result. If $f(x) = 3x - 2$ and $g(x) = x + 5$, then $(f \circ g)(x) = f(g(x)) = 3(x + 5) - 2 = 3x + 13$. Note that $(g \circ f)(x) = g(f(x))$, which is not the same as $(f \circ g)(x)$. In the example, $(g \circ f)(x) = g(f(x)) = (3x - 2) + 5 = 3x + 3$.

The *inverse* of a function, which is written $f^{-1}(x)$, "undoes" the action of a function. That is to say that if the function assigns the domain value of 2 to 5, then the inverse assigns 5 back to 2. An inverse can be obtained by replacing $f(x)$ with y, then interchanging x and y in the resulting equation. Solving this equation for y will result in the inverse of the original function.

For example, to find the inverse of $f(x) = 3x - 2$, we first write $y = 3x - 2$. Now interchange x and y, resulting in $x = 3y - 2$. Solving this equation for y, we get $y = \dfrac{x + 2}{3}$. So $f^{-1}(x) = \dfrac{x + 2}{3}$.

Functions can be graphed on a coordinate system by plotting domain values on the x-axis and their corresponding y values on the y-axis. A function of the form $f(x) = c$, where c is a constant, is called a *constant function*. Its graph is a horizontal line passing through the y-axis at c. A function of the form $f(x) = mx + b$, where m and b are constants, is called a *linear function*. Its graph is a straight line that crosses the y-axis at b and has a slope of m (that is, for every unit the graph moves horizontally, it rises m units vertically). For example, the graph of $f(x) = 3x + 2$ is linear, so we only need to find two values to draw the graph. As $f(0) = 2$ and $f(1) = 5$, we have

A function of the form $f(x) = ax^2 + bx = c$ is called a *quadratic function*, and its graph is always a parabola. For instance, $f(x) = x^2 + 2x - 3$ is a quadratic function. To draw its graph, we need to find several points to plot:

$$f(0) = -3$$
$$f(1) = 0$$
$$f(2) = 5$$
$$f(-1) = -4$$
$$f(-2) = -3$$
$$f(-3) = 0$$
$$f(-4) = 5$$

To determine whether or not a graph is the graph of a function, apply the *vertical line test*, which says that a vertical line will cross the graph of a function at no more than one point. Applying this rule to the previous graphs will show you that they are indeed graphs of functions.

A function or other geometric shape can be *transformed* by reflection or translation. *Reflection* refers to the "flipping" of a shape or graph around a *line of symmetry* to create an identical image. The graph below shows triangle *ABC* reflected around the line $y = x$ to create triangle *A'B'C'*.

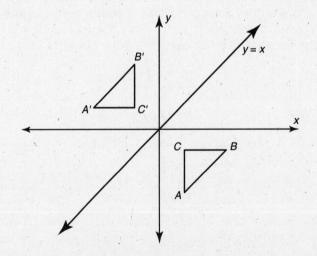

In this example, line $y = x$ is a line of symmetry, a line that divides an image or graph into two identical halves.

When a graph keeps its size and shape but "slides" vertically, horizontally, or both on the coordinate grid, the function is said to be *translated*. In the following example, triangle *ABC* is translated from the fourth quadrant to the second quadrant to form *A'B'C'*.

Functions and Graphs Review Questions

1. If $f(x) = 2x^2 - 3x + 1$, find $f(2)$, $f(3)$ and $f(-1)$.

    Solution: $f(2) = 2(2)^2 - 3(2) + 1 = 8 - 6 + 1 = 3$
    $f(3) = 2(3)^2 - 3(3) + 1 = 18 - 9 + 1 = 10$
    $f(-1) = 2(-1)^2 - 3(-1) + 1 = 2 + 3 + 1 = 6$

2. State the domain and range of the function $f(x) = \frac{1}{x^2}$.

    Solution: This function is defined for all values of x except for $x = 0$ (which would give us division by 0), so the domain is the set of all real numbers except for 0. As for the range, any number we plug into the function will turn out to be positive because of x^2. So the range is the set of all positive real numbers.

PROBABILITY AND STATISTICS

Suppose you have a series of choices to make. You go out to dinner and want to have an appetizer, entree, and dessert. If the restaurant has 5 choices of appetizer, 12 choices of entree, and 3 choices of dessert, how many possible meals could you order? In a problem like this, take the number of ways each choice can be made and multiply:

5 appetizers × 12 entrees × 3 desserts = 5 × 12 × 3 = 180 possible meals.

This principle can be extended to however many choices you have.

A *permutation* is a selection of items where order matters. For instance, suppose you want to arrange three books on a shelf. If we call the books A, B, and C, then there are six possible ways to do this:

ABC, ACB, BAC, BCA, CAB, CBA

To compute the permutation without listing every possible outcome, simply note that for the first book (book A) there are 3 choices. Once the first book has been selected, there are 2 books left to choose from. Once the second book has been selected, there is only 1 left. By multiplying these together, we get the result $3 \times 2 \times 1 = 6$.

The product $3 \times 2 \times 1$ can be written in what is known as *factorial notation* as 3!, which is read "three factorial." Similarly, $5! = 5 \times 4 \times 3 \times 2 \times 1$. In general, $n! = n \times (n-1) \times (n-2) \times \cdots \times 3 \times 2 \times 1$. Therefore, the number of permutations of a set with n items is $n!$.

Things get more involved when we select a subset of items. For example, suppose you want to arrange 3 books on a shelf, but you have 12 books to choose from. In this case you have 12 ways to make your first choice, then 11, then 10, so that there are $12 \times 11 \times 10 = 1,320$ ways to do this. The number of ways the books can be arranged can be computed using the *permutation formula*. The number of permutations of n items taken r at a time is given by $_nP_r = \dfrac{n!}{(n-r)!}$. In this example, $n = 12$ and $r = 3$, so that $_{12}P_3 = \dfrac{12!}{(12-3)!} = \dfrac{12!}{9!} = 12 \times 11 \times 10 = 1,320$.

A *combination* is a selection of items where order does not matter. For example, suppose a department of 10 wants to select 3 members for a selection committee. We can compute how many ways these 3 members can be selected by using the *combination formula*. The number of combinations of n items taken r at a time is given by $_nC_r = \dfrac{n!}{r!(n-r)!}$. For the example, $n = 10$ and $r = 3$, so $_{10}C_3 = \dfrac{10!}{3!(10-3)!} = \dfrac{10!}{3!7!} = \dfrac{10 \times 9 \times 8}{3 \times 2 \times 1} = 120$.

Probability is a measure of the likelihood that some event will occur. The value of probability is always between 0 and 1. The closer the value is to 0, the less likely it is that the event will occur; the closer it is to 1, the more likely the event is to occur. The probability of an event occurring = $\dfrac{\text{The number of favorable outcomes}}{\text{The total number of possible outcomes}}$.

Suppose you roll a die. The total number of possible outcomes is 6 (you could roll 1, 2, 3, 4, 5, or 6). Now say you are interested in rolling an even number. This is what we consider a favorable outcome. In this case there are 3 favorable outcomes: 2, 4, or 6. So the probability of rolling an even number is $\dfrac{3}{6} = \dfrac{1}{2}$.

Two events are *independent* if the occurrence of one does not affect the probability of the occurrence of the other. For instance, if you toss a die then roll a coin, getting a 2 on the die has no effect on getting tails on the coin. When two events are independent, the probability of both happening is the product of their individual probabilities. In the example, the probability of getting a 2 when rolling a die is $\dfrac{1}{6}$, while the probability of getting tails when tossing a coin is $\dfrac{1}{2}$, so the probability of both happening is $\left(\dfrac{1}{6}\right)\left(\dfrac{1}{2}\right) = \dfrac{1}{12}$.

If there are two events and the first event affects the second, be careful when computing the probability of the events occurring. While the probability of both events happening is still the product of their individual probabilities, it is necessary to see how the first event affects the second one. For instance, suppose you choose two cards from a deck of cards by selecting the first card, leaving it out of the deck, then selecting the second card; and you want to find the probability of selecting two aces. The probability of selecting the first ace would be $\frac{4}{52} = \frac{1}{13}$ as there are 4 aces in a deck of 52 cards. Once the first ace has been selected, there are only 3 aces left in a deck of 51 cards, so the probability of getting a second ace is $\frac{3}{51} = \frac{1}{17}$. The probability of getting two aces in this instance would be $\left(\frac{1}{13}\right)\left(\frac{1}{17}\right) = \frac{1}{221}$.

This last example brings up what is known as *conditional probability*. Remember that when you roll a die, there are 6 possible outcomes, so the probability of rolling a 5 is $\frac{1}{6}$. Suppose the number you rolled was odd. There are only three possible odd outcomes (1, 3, and 5), so the probability of rolling a 5 would now be $\frac{1}{3}$. When new information is presented about the experiment you are interested in, the probability of certain events can be affected.

Given a set of numbers, the *mean* (or *average*) can be found by first adding the numbers, then dividing by how many numbers were added. For example, suppose you want to find the mean of the numbers 22, 25, 14, 26, and 18. This can be found by adding the numbers and dividing by 5:

$$\frac{22 + 25 + 14 + 26 + 18}{5} = \frac{105}{5} = 21.$$

Given a set of numbers, the number in the middle if you arrange the values from smallest to largest is called the *median*. In the example, if we arrange the numbers in order from smallest to largest (14, 18, 22, 25, 26), the median is 22. If there is no middle number, the median is the mean of the middle two numbers. For instance, to find the median of 11, 13, 14, 16, 18, and 20, the middle two numbers, 14 and 16, are added and divided by 2: $\frac{14 + 16}{2} = \frac{30}{2} = 15$.

A third measure of center is called the *mode*. It refers to the number that appears most often in a set of data. Given the set of numbers {5, 9, 17, 11, 10, 6, 11}, the mode is 11 because it appears twice in the set. Every other number appears only once. A set of numbers can have no mode if it contains no duplicate elements. An example of a set with no mode is {6, 8, 11, 2, 1}. The *range* of this set is the difference between the smallest and the largest number in the set: $11 - 1 = 10$.

The *standard deviation* of a set is a measure of how widely each number varies from the mean. To calculate the standard deviation of the set {6, 8, 11, 2, 1}, proceed as follows:

1. Calculate the mean: 5.6
2. Subtract each number from the mean: −0.4, −2.4, −5.4, 3.6, 4.6
3. Square those differences: 0.16, 5.76, 29.16, 12.96, 21.16
4. Add the squares together: 69.2
5. Divide by the number of squares: 69.2/5 = 13.84
6. Take the square root: 3.72

The average distance of each number in the set {6, 8, 11, 2, 1} from the mean of 5.6 is 3.72.

Data can be represented using tables, bar graphs, line graphs, circle graphs, scatterplots, or histograms. In particular, a line graph is useful to illustrate a change in data over a period of time. A circle graph, or pie chart, is often used to show the relationship of parts to a whole. A scatterplot shows how closely two variables are correlated; it consists of a collection of points scattered on a coordinate grid. Histograms, which appear much like bar graphs, display frequency distributions.

Probability and Statistics Review Questions

1. A student code requires you to enter a four-digit number. If you can repeat digits, how many codes are possible?

    Solution: For each digit, there are 10 possible choices (0, 1, 2, 3, 4, 5, 6, 7, 8, or 9) and there are four digits, so there are $10 \times 10 \times 10 \times 10 = 10,000$ possible codes.

2. If a jar contains 3 red, 4 yellow, and 5 blue jellybeans, what is the probability of selecting a red or yellow jellybean if you select one jellybean at random?

    Solution: There are 12 jellybeans in all. Three of the jellybeans are red, so the probability of selecting a red jellybean is $\frac{3}{12}$. Four jellybeans are yellow, so the probability of selecting a yellow jellybean is $\frac{4}{12}$. The probability of selecting a red or yellow jellybean is then $\frac{3}{12} + \frac{4}{12} = \frac{7}{12}$.

ADDITIONAL TOPICS FROM ALGEBRA AND GEOMETRY

What follows are many concepts that may crop up on the CLEP College Mathematics exam in some form or another. The test is not going to be full of these ideas, but some of them will definitely make an appearance, so it always helps to be ready.

Complex Numbers

In the real number system, the square root of a negative number cannot be taken. We can get around this in the complex number system by defining $i = \sqrt{-1}$. Then, for any real number n, $\sqrt{-n} = \sqrt{(-1)n} = \sqrt{(-1)} \sqrt{n} = i\sqrt{n}$. For example, $\sqrt{-36} = 6i$.

A number of the form bi, where b is any real number, is called an *imaginary number*. Any number of the form $a + bi$, where a and b are real numbers, is called a *complex number*. For example, $7i$ is an imaginary number, while $2 + 3i$ is a complex number. For any complex number $a + bi$, $a - bi$ is called its *complex conjugate*. The complex conjugate of $2 + 3i$ is $2 - 3i$.

Logarithms and Exponents

An *exponent* indicates repeated multiplication. For instance, $5^3 = 5 \times 5 \times 5 = 125$ and $2^5 = 2 \times 2 \times 2 \times 2 \times 2 = 32$. In the first example, 5 is called the *base* while the exponent is 3. In the second example, 2 is the base while the exponent is 5. Exponents are not just positive integers.

Negative exponents are defined by $a^{-n} = \frac{1}{a^n}$, so that $4^{-3} = \frac{1}{4^3}$. Also, by definition, $a^0 = 1$. There are five basic rules to keep in mind when dealing with exponents. In general, if m and n are integers, and a and b are any numbers:

Rule 1: $\qquad a^m \times a^n = a^{m+n}$

Rule 2: $\qquad (a^m)^n = a^{mn}$

Rule 3: $\qquad (ab)^m = a^m \times b^m$

Rule 4: $\qquad \left(\frac{a}{b}\right)^m = \frac{a^m}{b^m}$

Rule 5: $\qquad \frac{a^m}{a^n} = a^{m-n}$

An *exponential equation* is an equation whose variable appears as an exponent. An equation of this type can be solved algebraically if both sides of the equation can be expressed as powers of the same base. For example, to solve the equation $2^{x+4} = 64$, 64 would be rewritten as 2^6, giving the equation $2^{x+4} = 2^6$. This means that $x + 4 = 6$, so that $x = 2$.

If the bases cannot both be changed to the same number, then the equation can be solved using a logarithm. The *logarithm* of a number is the power to which a given base is raised to in order to produce the number. For example, $\log_3 81 = 4$ because $3^4 = 81$. While logarithms can be written to any base, logarithms to base 10 are used so often that they are referred to as common logarithms, and "log" is often used to stand for "$\log_{10}$." A "log" button can be found on scientific calculators and can be a great shortcut to finding the "log" of a number, provided you know what you're doing and input correct numbers. The calculator available to you as part of the CLEP testing software will have the "log" function.

Note that the logarithm of 0 or of a negative number cannot be found. As with exponents, there are several rules for logarithms. The three most common rules are these:

Rule 1: $\qquad \log_b xy = \log_b x + \log_b y$

Rule 2: $\qquad \log_b \left(\frac{x}{y}\right) = \log_b x - \log_b y$

Rule 3: $\qquad \log_b x^n = n\log_b x$

Perimeter and Area

To find the *perimeter* of a plane figure, simply add the lengths of the sides of the figure. For instance, if a triangle has sides measuring 4 ft, 6 ft, and 10 ft, its perimeter would be $4 + 6 + 10 = 20$ ft.

Area is a measure of the surface covered by a plane figure. There is a formula for finding area depending upon the figure in question. The three most common formulas for different figures are these:

The area A of a rectangle with length l and width w is given by $A = lw$.

The area A of a square with sides measuring s is given by $A = s^2$.

The area A of a triangle with base b and height h is given by $A = \frac{1}{2}bh$.

So if a rectangle has width 5 ft and length 12 ft, its area is (5 ft)(12 ft) = 60 ft^2.

Triangles, Circles, and Rectangles

A *triangle* is a plane figure with three sides and three angles. If all three sides of a triangle have different lengths, the triangle is called *scalene*. If two of the sides have the same length, the triangle is called *isosceles*. If all three sides have the same length, the triangle is called *equilateral*.

The sum of the three interior angles of a triangle is always 180°. If all three angles of a triangle are less than 90°, the triangle is called *acute*. If one of the angles measures 90°, the triangle is called a *right triangle*. If one of the angles is more than 90°, the triangle is called *obtuse*. If all three angles have the same measure, then the triangle is called *equiangular*.

A *circle* is the set of all points a fixed distance from a given point, called the *center*. The distance from the center to the circle is called *radius*, while the distance between two points on the circle described by a line that passes through the center is called *diameter*. The distance around a circle is called *circumference* and is given by the formula $C = 2\pi r$, where r is the radius and $\pi \approx 3.14$. Circumference is also given by the formula $C = \pi d$, where d is the diameter of the circle.

The area of a circle is given by the formula $A = \pi r^2$. So if a circle has a radius of 5 in, then its area would be $(3.14)(5 \text{ in})^2 = (3.14)(25 \text{ in}^2) = 78.5 \text{ in}^2$.

A *rectangle* is a quadrilateral with four right angles. It has a length, l, and a width, w. The perimeter of a rectangle is the distance around the entire figure and is given by the formula $P = 2(l + w)$. The area of a rectangle is given by the formula $A = lw$.

The Pythagorean Theorem

The side opposite the right angle in a right triangle is called the *hypotenuse*, while the other two sides are called *legs*. There is a special relationship between the hypotenuse and legs of a right triangle, which is given by the Pythagorean theorem. If the hypotenuse of a right triangle has length c and the legs have lengths a and b, then $c = \sqrt{a^2 + b^2}$.

For example, if the legs of a right triangle measure 3 cm and 4 cm, then the hypotenuse c would be given by $c = \sqrt{3^2 + 4^2} = \sqrt{25} = 5$ cm.

Applications from Algebra and Geometry

There are two common special triangles: 30-60-90 and 45-45-90. The lengths of the sides of a triangle whose angle measures are 30°, 60°, and 90° are in the proportion $1 : 2 : \sqrt{3}$, as shown in the following diagram.

Example:

If the long leg of a 30-60-90 triangle is $4\sqrt{3}$ units long, what is the perimeter of the triangle?

If the long leg measures $4\sqrt{3}$ units, then the short leg (the side across from the 30° angle) must measure $4\sqrt{3} \div \sqrt{3} = 4$. Since the hypotenuse is twice the length of the short leg, the hypotenuse measures 8 units. Therefore, the perimeter of the triangle is $8 + 4 + 4\sqrt{3} = 12 + 4\sqrt{3}$ units.

The lengths of the sides of a triangle whose angle measures are 45°, 45°, and 90° are in the proportion $1:1:\sqrt{2}$, as shown in the following diagram.

Example:

If the hypotenuse of a 45-45-90 triangle is $10\sqrt{2}$ units long, what is the perimeter of the triangle?

If the hypotenuse measures $10\sqrt{2}$ units, then a leg measures $10\sqrt{2} \div \sqrt{2} = 10$. Since a 45-45-90 triangle is isosceles, the perimeter of the triangle is $10 + 10 + 10\sqrt{2} = 20 + 10\sqrt{2}$ units.

Finding Parallel and Perpendicular Lines

Two lines are *parallel* if they never intersect. This means that they have the same slope. Train tracks are like parallel lines. If the equation of a line is written in the form $y = mx + b$, m indicates the slope of the line. For instance, the line $y = 3x + 5$ has slope 3. To see if two lines are parallel, just check to see if they have the same slope.

For example, to see if $y = 2x - 4$ and $2y - 4x = 6$ are parallel, first write the second equation in the form $y = mx + b$ to solve for y. In doing this we obtain $y = 2x + 3$. The slope of both lines is 2, so they are parallel.

Two lines are *perpendicular* if their intersection forms right angles. If two lines are perpendicular, their slopes are negative reciprocals of each other. For example, if the slope of a line is $\frac{2}{3}$, then the slope of a line perpendicular to it would be $-\frac{3}{2}$. As with parallel lines, putting the equation of both lines in the form $y = mx + b$ and comparing the slopes will quickly tell us if the lines are perpendicular.

Word Problems

A fundamental CLEP College Mathematics requirement is the ability to translate a written problem into math expressions, equations, or inequalities and then solve for a variable. For example, the expression "Girard has three times as many shoes as Pilar," can be written mathematically as $g = 3p$. If Girard has eight more shoes than Pilar, the statement $g = p + 8$ is also true. This *system of linear equations* can be solved using substitution. If $g = 3p$, substitute $3p$ for g into the equation $g = p + 8$:

$$3p = p + 8$$
$$2p = 8$$
$$p = 4$$

Pilar has 4 pairs of shoes, and Girard has $3p$ or 12 pairs.

Given a *system of inequalities*, solve each one individually. The answer will be a range of numbers.

$$3x + 6 < 36 \qquad 8x - 2 > 22$$
$$3x < 30 \qquad\quad 8x > 24$$
$$x < 10 \qquad\quad\ x > 3$$

The solution to the system of inequalities is $3 < x < 10$.

The CLEP College Mathematics exam will also test your knowledge of functions. To find the highest possible number of complex roots of a function, use the *fundamental theorem of algebra*. It states that every polynomial function (of positive degree) with at least one complex coefficient has at least one complex root. It also states that the highest degree of that polynomial is the largest number of possible complex roots. The polynomial function $H(x) = 5ix^4 + 3x^3 - 2x^2 + 1$ is a fourth-degree polynomial, so $H(x)$ has four complex roots.

The remainder theorem and the factor theorem can be used to simplify polynomial division. The *remainder theorem states* that when a polynomial $K(x)$ is divided by $(x - b)$, the remainder is equal to $K(b)$.

Example:

If $K(x) = 2x^3 + 4x^2 - x + 6$, what is the remainder when $K(x)$ is divided by $(x - 3)$?

$$K(3) = 2(3)^3 + 4(3)^2 - 3 + 6$$
$$K(3) = 54 + 36 - 3 + 6$$
$$K(3) = 93$$

The *factor theorem* states that if $K(x)$ is a polynomial, and $K(b) = 0$, then $(x - b)$ is a factor of $K(x)$.

Example:

If $K(x) = 3x^3 - 5x^2 - x - 2$, is $(x - 4)$ a factor of $K(x)$?

$$K(4) = 3(4)^3 - 5(4)^2 - 4 - 2 = 192 - 80 - 4 - 2 = 106 \neq 0$$

Since $K(4) \neq 0$, $(x - 4)$ is not a factor of $K(x)$.

Additional Topics from Algebra and Geometry Review Questions

1. Add $3 + 2i$ and $4 - 5i$.

    Solution: We add complex numbers as we do polynomials, by combining like terms. So $(3 + 2i) + (4 - 5i) = (3 + 4) + (2i - 5i) = 7 - 3i$.

2. Write $5^3 = 125$ as a logarithm.

    Solution: Any exponential expression can be written as a logarithm. Remember that a logarithm is the power to which the base is raised in order to produce a specific number. In this case, base 5 is raised to the power 3 to produce 125, which can be written as $\log_5 125 = 3$.

3. Suppose a triangle has sides of length 3 ft, 5 ft, and 3 ft. What type of triangle is this?

    Solution: Notice that two of the three sides have the same length. When this is the case, the triangle is called *isosceles*.

COLLEGE MATHEMATICS RESOURCES

For an in-depth, detailed review—we've covered the basic points—of the material found on the CLEP College Mathematics exam, consult textbooks that contain explanations and practice problems. Almost any textbook used in college-level mathematics classes covers at least some of the topics you need to study. As textbooks may have differing approaches to solving problems, it's always good to look at two or more different texts to find the approach that makes the most sense to you.

Algebra and geometry topics covered on the exam can usually be found in an elementary algebra text. This text should also include information on the real number system and functions. Sets, logic, and probability can often be found in texts for courses with names like "Finite Mathematics" or "Ideas of Mathematics." These texts typically also have chapters on algebra and geometry. It is, of course, best to obtain the textbooks for free at the library, through teachers at your school if you are a student, or through the local college.

When selecting a text to study from, be sure to compare its table of contents against the outline of topics on the exam so that during your study time you are able to cover every topic that you need to know.

FINAL THOUGHTS

While there are many rules to learn in mathematics, a lot of math just involves common sense and logic. Even if you are not a "logic" person, math can be learned based on the principles reviewed in this chapter. The review section, the diagnostic test, and the two practice tests should prepare you well for the CLEP College Mathematics exam, but there is always more information that can be studied prior to the test. Many of the concepts on the exam are covered in elementary algebra and geometry. If you don't remember much from your algebra and geometry classes, have no fear—with a bit of outside study and the use of this book, you are on your way to a solid base of knowledge to apply to the CLEP College Mathematics exam.

Good luck!

KAPLAN

Chapter Ten: **Practice Test 2**

Time—90 minutes
60 Questions

Directions: For the following questions, either select the BEST answer of the choices given or input your answer into the box provided.

You can use the computer-based scientific calculator during this exam.

Notes:

(1) Unless otherwise stated, the domain of any function f consists of the set of all real numbers x for which $f(x)$ is a real number.

(2) i represents $\sqrt{-1}$.

(3) Unless otherwise indicated, all geometric figures lie in a plane. The appearance of all figures is accurate UNLESS the question states that the figure is not drawn to scale.

1. Which of the following represents an irrational number?

(A) $\dfrac{\sqrt{100}}{5}$

(B) $\dfrac{34}{(15+2)}$

(C) $\dfrac{\sqrt{14}}{\sqrt{7}}$

(D) $\dfrac{\sqrt{72}}{\sqrt{8}}$

2. What is the domain of the function $f(x) = \dfrac{4x}{(x-1)(x+8)}$?

(A) All real numbers

(B) All real numbers except for 1

(C) All real numbers except for −1 and 8

(D) All real numbers except for 1 and −8

3. Suppose A is any event. Which of the following statements about event A are true?

   I. The probability that event A will occur can be greater than 1.

  II. The probability that event A will occur can be equal to 0.

 III. The probability that event A will occur plus the probability that event A will not occur is less than 1.

(A) I and II only

(B) II and III only

(C) II only

(D) III only

GO ON TO THE NEXT PAGE

4. Which of the following is the inverse of "If R, then S"?

   (A) If S, then R
   (B) If not R, then not S
   (C) If not S, then not R
   (D) R and not S

5. If m is an odd integer, which of the following is also odd?

   (A) $m + 1$
   (B) $m - 1$
   (C) $m^2 - m$
   (D) $m^2 + m + 1$

6. If $f(x) = x^3 - 3x + 1$, then $f(-1) =$

   (A) 3
   (B) -3
   (C) -1
   (D) 5

7. If $i = \sqrt{-1}$, then $i + i^2 + i^3 =$

   (A) i
   (B) $-i$
   (C) -1
   (D) 1

8. How many odd prime numbers are there between 1 and 30?

   (A) 9
   (B) 10
   (C) 14
   (D) 28

9. If $f(x) = \{(4, 2), (5, 3), (6, 4)\}$ and $g(x) = \{(3, 4), (4, 6), (5, 8)\}$, what is the value of $f(g(4))$?

   (A) 6
   (B) 4
   (C) 2
   (D) 3

10. Which of the following are infinite sets?

    I. The set of all integers between 0 and 10
    II. The set of all rational numbers between 0 and 10
    III. The set of all real numbers between 0 and 10

    (A) I and II only
    (B) II and III only
    (C) I and III only
    (D) I, II, and III

11. When Tarok goes to lunch, he can choose from 3 kinds of soup, 5 kinds of sandwiches, and 4 kinds of drinks. If he chooses one soup, one sandwich, and one drink, how many different lunches could he choose from?

    (A) 12
    (B) 19
    (C) 32
    (D) 60

12. If x is an odd integer and y is an even integer, which of the following MUST be even?

    (A) $x + y$
    (B) $x - y$
    (C) xy
    (D) $\frac{x}{y}$

13. Given the functions $f(x) = 4x + 3$ and $g(x) = x - 5$, what is the value of $(f + g)(x)$ when $x = 2$?

    (A) {8}
    (B) {11}
    (C) {-3}
    (D) {5}

GO ON TO THE NEXT PAGE

14. If $p \land q$ is true, what statement must also be true?

    (A) $p \land q$

    (B) $\lnot p \land q$

    (C) $\lnot p \land \lnot q$

    (D) $\lnot p \land \lnot q$

15. The sum of five times a number n and the reciprocal of n is equal to 11. Which of the following is an algebraic representation of the statement above?

    (A) $5\left(n + \frac{1}{n}\right) = 11$

    (B) $(5n)\left(\frac{1}{n}\right) = 11$

    (C) $5n + \frac{1}{n} = 11$

    (D) $(5 + n)\left(\frac{1}{n}\right) = 11$

16. Thirty employees took a training course. Afterwards, each took a 5-question multiple choice test. The results are summarized in the table below:

Number Correct:	0	1	2	3	4	5
Frequency:	7	8	6	3	5	1

    If an employee who answered at least 2 questions correctly is selected at random, what is the probability that the employee who answered all 5 questions correctly will be selected?

    (A) $\frac{1}{30}$

    (B) $\frac{1}{15}$

    (C) $\frac{6}{30}$

    (D) $\frac{6}{15}$

17. What is the smallest positive integer that is divisible by both 12 and 15?

18. If $f(x)$ is a linear function such that $f(5) = 7$ and $f(1) = -1$, then $f(x)$ equals

    (A) $x + 2$

    (B) $x^2 - 1$

    (C) $2x - 3$

    (D) $x - 2$

19. If $A = \{x \mid x > 2\}$ and $B = \{x \mid x \le 6\}$, what is the number of integers in $A \cup B$?

    (A) 4

    (B) 3

    (C) 6

    (D) 0

20. The difference between the mean and median of the numbers 16, 18, 17, 27, and 22 is

    (A) 7

    (B) 4

    (C) 3

    (D) 2

21. A fair coin is tossed three times. What is the probability that it will come up tails three times in a row?

    (A) $\frac{3}{8}$

    (B) $\frac{1}{3}$

    (C) $\frac{1}{8}$

    (D) $\frac{1}{2}$

22. The product of all distinct positive factors of which number below is the smallest?

    (A) 7

    (B) 6

    (C) 4

    (D) 8

GO ON TO THE NEXT PAGE

KAPLAN

23. The following shows five triangles on a coordinate plane. If the *y*-axis is used as a line of symmetry, which triangle is a reflection of triangle *LMN*? Click on the correct triangle.

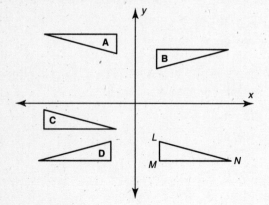

24. If $\log_2 x = 6$, then $\log_4 x =$

    (A) 3

    (B) 2

    (C) 1

    (D) 4

25. If $f(x) = 2x$ and the domain of $f(x)$ is all positive integers less than 50, what is the range of $f(x)$?

    (A) Positive integers less than 100

    (B) Even positive integers less than 50

    (C) Even positive integers less than 100

    (D) Even positive integers less than 200

26. In a group of 51 students, 27 have brown eyes, 13 have blue eyes, 8 have green eyes, and 3 have hazel eyes. The likelihood that a person chosen at random from this group will have either blue or green eyes is

    (A) $\frac{7}{17}$

    (B) $\frac{9}{17}$

    (C) $\frac{13}{51}$

    (D) $\frac{8}{51}$

27. A student claims that n^3 is greater than or equal to n for all real numbers n. Of the following, which is a value of n that provides a counterexample to the student's claim?

    (A) 2

    (B) -1

    (C) $\frac{1}{2}$

    (D) 1

28. What is the measure of angle M?

    (A) 48°

    (B) 42°

    (C) 52°

    (D) 132°

29. If $0 \le x \le 150$, how many values of x are both the square of an integer and the cube of an integer?

    [   ]

30. A collector of vases wants to arrange five different pieces from her collection on a shelf in her home. In how many different ways could she arrange the five vases?

    (A) 120

    (B) 625

    (C) 15

    (D) 1

31. Suppose $A = \{1, 2\}$ and $B = \{2, 3\}$. Which of the following ordered pairs is NOT in the Cartesian product $A \times B$?

    (A) (1, 2)

    (B) (1, 3)

    (C) (2, 2)

    (D) (3, 2)

GO ON TO THE NEXT PAGE ▷

32. Which statement best describes the standard deviations of Sets 1 and 2?

    Set 1 = {34, 32, 28, 39, 37, 40, 35, 36}

    Set 2 = {3, 49, 55, 13, 19, 4, 45, 17}

    (A) The standard deviation of Set 1 is greater than the standard deviation of Set 2.

    (B) The standard deviation of Set 2 is greater than the standard deviation of Set 1.

    (C) The standard deviation of both sets is 0.

    (D) The standard deviation of Set 1 is equal to the standard deviation of Set 2.

33. Which of the following is NOT a prime number?

    (A) 17

    (B) 11

    (C) 23

    (D) 51

34. Your favorite band is coming to town, but you're not sure if you should go to the concert. You reason, "If I go to the concert, I will have to call in sick. If I call in sick, then my boss will get angry. If my boss gets angry, then I'll lose my job." What conclusion can you draw from this?

    (A) If I go to the concert, then I'll lose my job.

    (B) If my boss gets angry, then I called in sick.

    (C) If I lose my job, then I went to the concert.

    (D) If I don't go to the concert, then I won't lose my job.

35. Let $f(x) = \dfrac{x+1}{x(x+2)}$. Which of the following is the domain of $f(x)$?

    (A) All real numbers

    (B) All real numbers except for -1

    (C) All real numbers except for -2

    (D) All real numbers except for 0 and -2

36. Which of the following is a rational number?

    (A) $2\sqrt{2}$

    (B) $\sqrt{3}$

    (C) π

    (D) $\sqrt{9}$

37. If $x = -3$, then $|x - 5| =$

    (A) 2

    (B) -2

    (C) 8

    (D) -8

38. Let $M = \{4, 7, 9, 13, 17\}$. What is the sum of the mean and median of M?

    (A) 10

    (B) 19

    (C) 59

    (D) 90

39. If $K(x) = 4x^3 + x^2 - 3x + 7$, what is the remainder when $K(x)$ is divided by $(x - 2)$?

    _____

40. Which of the following lines has the same slope as $y = -5x + 3$?

    (A) $y = -5x + 9$

    (B) $y = -3x + 5$

    (C) $y = 5x + 4$

    (D) $y = \frac{1}{5}x + 7$

41. If $A \subset C$ and $B \subset C$, which of the following statements is ALWAYS true?

    (A) A is a subset of B.

    (B) B is a subset of A.

    (C) $A \cup B$ is a subset of C.

    (D) $A \cap C = C$.

GO ON TO THE NEXT PAGE

KAPLAN

42. The table shows the sales of Dale's Used Cars for six months. During which month were the sales equal to the average monthly sales? Click on the correct month.

Month	Number of Cars Sold
January	13
February	20
March	23
April	16
May	23
June	25

43. If $x > y > 0$, which of the following is NOT true?

    (A) $|x| > |y|$

    (B) $\frac{1}{x} > \frac{1}{y}$

    (C) $x^2 > y^2$

    (D) $\frac{1}{y} > \frac{1}{x}$

44. Below is a Truth Table:

p	q	r
T	T	T
T	F	F
F	T	F
F	F	F

According to this table, which of the following statements describes r?

    (A) p or q

    (B) If p then q

    (C) p or not q

    (D) p and q

45. If $-3 < x < 4$, which of the following expresses the range of possible values of x^2?

    (A) $0 \le x \le 16$

    (B) $-9 < x < 16$

    (C) $9 < x < 16$

    (D) $-6 < x < 8$

46. What is the standard deviation of the set {6, 15, 9, 10, 18, 7}?

47. What type of figure is the figure below?

    (A) Rectangle

    (B) Trapezoid

    (C) Rhombus

    (D) Quadrilateral

48. Which of the following is a translation of rectangle $WXYZ$? Click on the correct rectangle.

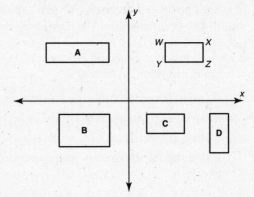

GO ON TO THE NEXT PAGE

49. Which figure has an area of 30 square units? Click on the correct figure.

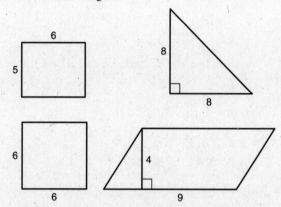

50. The number of absences and their probabilities for any given day in a math class are given in the table below:

Absences:	0	1	2	3	4
Probability:	0.10	0.25	0.30	0.15	0.20

What is the expected number of absences for any given day of the class?

(A) 1

(B) 2.1

(C) 1.9

(D) 3.2

51. Let A represent the statement "x is an even integer," and B represent the statement "x is an integer divisible by 2." What can be said about statements A and B?

(A) A is necessary but not a sufficient condition for B.

(B) A is not necessary but is a sufficient condition for B.

(C) A is a necessary and sufficient condition for B.

(D) A is neither necessary nor sufficient for B.

52. Which of the following represents a line of symmetry of the given figure? Click on the correct line.

53. Which of the following choices represents the Venn diagram?

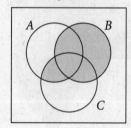

(A) $A \cup B \cup C$

(B) $(A \cup B) \cap C$

(C) $(A \cap C) \cup B$

(D) $(A \cap B) \cup (A \cap C)$

54. Which is the inverse of the function $f(x) = \frac{1}{x}$?

(A) $f^{-1}(x) = x$

(B) $f^{-1}(x) = \frac{1}{x}$

(C) $f^{-1}(x) = \sqrt{x}$

(D) $f^{-1}(x) = \frac{1}{\sqrt{x}}$

GO ON TO THE NEXT PAGE

55. Joe, Michael, Ralph, Terry, and Steve have formed a band. Larry, Joe, Terry, William, and Ralph have formed another band. How many musicians are in both bands?

   (A) 3
   (B) 2
   (C) 1
   (D) 0

56. The graph shows the Morrison's family budget for last month. The total monthly budget is $1,200. In which category did the family spend $204 last month?

Morrison Family Budget

   (A) Food
   (B) Clothing
   (C) Rent
   (D) Entertainment

57. How many different ways can you make up a committee of 3 people from a group of 8 people?

   [   ]

58. Set A contains the numbers {3, 5, 2, 8, 10, 16, 5, 2, 5}. What is the mode of Set A?

   (A) 2
   (B) 5
   (C) 8
   (D) 10

59. Which of the following could be the graph of a function of x?

   (A)

   (B)

   (C)

   (D)

60. A rectangle has a width of 5 cm and a length of 12 cm. What is the measure of a diagonal of the rectangle?

   (A) 17 cm
   (B) 13 cm
   (C) 16.9 cm
   (D) 34 cm

END OF TEST. STOP

THE ANSWER KEY APPEARS ON THE FOLLOWING PAGE.

ANSWER KEY

1. C	11. D	21. C	31. D	41. C	51. C
2. D	12. C	22. A	32. B	42. February	52. line *l*
3. C	13. A	23. Triangle D	33. D	43. B	53. C
4. B	14. A	24. A	34. A	44. D	54. B
5. D	15. C	25. C	35. D	45. A	55. A
6. A	16. B	26. A	36. D	46. 4.3	56. B
7. C	17. 60	27. C	37. C	47. D	57. 56
8. A	18. C	28. B	38. B	48. Rectangle C	58. B
9. B	19. A	29. 3	39. 37	49. 5×6 rectangle	59. A
10. B	20. D	30. A	40. A	50. B	60. B

PRACTICE TEST 2 QUICK REFERENCE TABLES

Use the following tables to determine which topics you still need to review.

Topic	Test Question
Sets	10, 19, 31, 41, 53, 55
Logic	4, 14, 27, 34, 44, 51
Real Number System	1, 5, 8, 12, 17, 22, 29, 33, 36, 37, 43, 45
Functions and Graphs	2, 6, 9, 13, 18, 23, 25, 35, 48, 52, 54, 59
Probability and Statistics	3, 11, 16, 20, 21, 26, 30, 32, 38, 42, 46, 50, 56, 57, 58
Additional Topics	7, 15, 24, 28, 39, 40, 47, 49, 60

Topic	Number of Questions on Test	Number Correct
Sets	6	
Logic	6	
Real Number System	12	
Functions and Graphs	12	
Probability and Statistics	15	
Additional Topics	9	

Answers and Explanations

1. (C)

Simplify each choice.

(A) $\dfrac{\sqrt{100}}{5} = \dfrac{10}{5} = 2$

(B) $\dfrac{34}{(15+2)} = \dfrac{34}{17} = 2$

(C) $\dfrac{\sqrt{14}}{\sqrt{7}} = \sqrt{\dfrac{14}{7}} = \sqrt{2}$

(D) $\dfrac{\sqrt{72}}{\sqrt{8}} = \sqrt{\dfrac{72}{8}} = \sqrt{9} = 3$

The only irrational choice is (C), $\sqrt{2}$.

2. (D)

To find the domain of $f(x)$, focus on the denominator of the fraction. If $x = 1$, the first factor in the denominator would equal 0. If $x = -8$, the second factor in the denominator would equal 0. Therefore, the domain of $f(x)$ is all real numbers except for 1 and -8.

3. (C)

This problem requires being familiar with two basic properties of probability:

1) The probability that event A will occur is always between 0 and 1, including 0 and 1.

2) The probability that event A will occur plus the probability that event A will not occur is always equal to 1.

With these properties in mind, you can quickly see that II is the only choice that is true, which means the solution is (C).

4. (B)

To find the *inverse* of a conditional statement, negate both statements in the conditional. That is, the inverse of "If P, then Q" is "If not P, then not Q." In this case, the inverse of "If R, then S" is "If not R, then not S." Choice (A) represents the converse, while (C) represents the contrapositive.

5. (D)

The easiest way to solve a problem like this is to pick a number for m and plug it into the possible solutions. Since m is an odd integer, 3 would be a good choice for m. Substitute 3 for m in each possible solution:

(A) $m + 1 = 3 + 1 = 4$

(B) $m - 1 = 3 - 1 = 2$

(C) $m^2 - m = 3^2 - 3 = 9 - 3 = 6$

(D) $m^2 + m + 1 = 3^2 + 3 + 1 = 9 + 3 + 1 = 13$

(D) is the only answer that ends up being odd, so it is the solution to the problem.

6. (A)

Substitute -1 for x in the function and simplify: $f(x) = x^3 - 3x + 1$, so $f(-1) = (-1)^3 - 3(-1) + 1 = -1 + 3 + 1 = 3$. A common mistake here is to not change the sign of the second term, which would give you choice (B). Also, remember that $(-1)^3 = -1$, otherwise you could end up with answer choice (C) or (D).

7. (C)

Quickly compute i^2 and i^3, then add these two values to i:

$i^2 = (\sqrt{-1})^2 = -1$

$i^3 = i^2 \times i = -1 \times i = -i$

So $i + i^2 + i^3 = i + (-1) + (-i) = -1$

8. (A)

There are two easy mistakes that could be made in this problem. The first mistake would be to only read "odd" numbers; there are 14 odd numbers between 1 and 30. The second mistake would be to only read "prime" numbers; there are 10 prime numbers between 1 and 30. Notice that the problem is asking for "odd prime" numbers. Make a quick list of odd prime numbers between 1 and 30: {3, 5, 7, 11, 13, 17, 19, 23, 29}. The list shows that there are 9 odd prime numbers between 1 and 30.

9. (B)

The functions here are given as ordered pairs; the first number tells you what number is going into the function and the second part of the pair tells you what number is coming out of the function. With this in mind, to compute $f(g(4))$, you first need to see what the function $g(x)$ does to 4. If you look at the ordered pairs in this function, you'll find (4, 6), which says the function $g(x)$ takes 4 and turns it into 6. Now we need to see what $f(x)$ does to 6. Looking at the ordered pairs listed for $f(x)$, you'll find (6, 4), which means $f(x)$ takes 6 and turns it into 4. Thus, $f(g(4)) = 4$.

10. (B)

An infinite set is a set with an infinite number of elements. In other words, if you were to try to list all of the elements in an infinite set, you could never list them all. You could easily list all of the elements in the set described in I, so this set is not infinite. The sets in II and III are infinite, since you could never list all of the numbers described by either set. This eliminates all the answer choices except (B).

11. (D)

This is a simple counting problem. For a problem like this, you just need to see how many ways you can make a series of choices, then multiply. In this case, a lunch is made up of soup, a sandwich, and a drink. There are 3 soups, 5 sandwiches, and 4 drinks to choose from, so there are $3 \times 5 \times 4 = 60$ different possible lunches. A common mistake is to add the parts of the lunches together, which would give you the incorrect solution (A).

12. (C)

Choose values for x and y, say $x = 5$ and $y = 2$. Then

(A) $x + y = 5 + 2 = 7$

(B) $x - y = 5 - 2 = 3$

(C) $xy = (5)(2) = 10$

(D) $\frac{x}{y} = \frac{5}{2}$

Since only (C) yields an even number, it is the correct answer.

13. (A)

The problem states that $f(x) = 4x + 3$ and $g(x) = x - 5$. The value of $(f + g)(x) = (4x + 3) + (x - 5) = 5x - 2$. So when $x = 2$, $(f + g)(x) = 5(2) - 2 = 8$.

14. (A)

If $p \wedge q$ is true, then *both* p and q must be true. Choice (A) read aloud is "p or q," and this is true because we

know both p and q are true. The other three statements, not p and q, not p and not q, and not p or not q, are all false because both p and q are true.

15. (C)

In a problem like this, keep your eyes open for key words. *Sum* means addition, so expect to see addition in the answer. What is being added? According to the problem, five times (multiplication) a number n and the reciprocal of n, which are $5n$ and $\frac{1}{n}$, are being added. When these two values are added, you get 11, so the answer is $5n + \frac{1}{n} = 11$. Misreading the question could lead you to choose (A), which is 5 times the sum of a number and its reciprocal.

16. (B)

This is a conditional probability problem, meaning that instead of using all of the employees to chose from, we only use those the employees that the problem specifies. In this case, instead of choosing from all 30 employees, we only want those that got at least two problems correct on the test, which means answers (A) and (C) can be eliminated. Only one person got all 5 correct answers, so the answer is (B), $\frac{1}{15}$.

17. 60

If you start to list the multiples of 12 and the multiples of 15, the first number to appear in both lists will be the number we want:

Multiples of 12: 12, 24, 36, 48, 60, 72, ...

Multiples of 15: 15, 30, 45, 60, 75, 90, ...

Since 60 is the first number to appear in both lists, the answer is 60.

18. (C)

First, we can discount (B) because $x^2 - 1$ is not linear. For the other choices, substitute in 5 and 1 to see which one gives you the desired results. (A) isn't the answer because $f(1) = 1 + 2 = 3$, not −1. (D) is not the answer because $f(5) = 5 - 2 = 3$, not 7. But (C) works because $f(5) = 2(5) - 3 = 10 - 3 = 7$ and $f(1) = 2(1) - 3 = 2 - 3 = -1$.

19. (A)

We are looking for integers greater than 2 and less than or equal to 6, which is the set {3, 4, 5, 6}. There are 4 elements in this set.

20. (D)

To find the mean, add the numbers and divide by 5 (how many numbers you've added), which gives you (16 + 18 + 17 + 27 + 22) ÷ 5 = 100 ÷ 5 = 20. The median is the middle number if you list the numbers from smallest to largest: 16, 17, 18, 22, 27. The median is 18, so the difference between the mean and median is 20 − 18 = 2. A common mistake is to find the median without listing the numbers from smallest to largest, which would give you 17 as the median and a difference of 3 instead of 2.

21. (C)

There are two ways to solve this problem. The first is to realize that the probability of a coin coming up tails in one toss is $\frac{1}{2}$, so the probability of it being tails in three tosses is $\frac{1}{2} \times \frac{1}{2} \times \frac{1}{2} = \frac{1}{8}$. The other way to solve the problem is to list all the possible outcomes of tossing a coin three times: HHH, HHT, HTH, HTT, THH, THT, TTH, TTT. Of these 8 outcomes, only one has three tails.

22. (A)

It's easy to think that one of the smallest numbers listed will be the right choice, but this is not the case. The positive factors of 4 are 1, 2, 4 and 1 × 2 × 4 = 8. The positive factors of 6 are 1, 2, 3, 6 and 1 × 2 × 3 × 6 = 36. 7 is prime, so its only factors are 1 and 7, which have a product of 7.

23. Triangle D

A reflection is a mirror image centered on a line of symmetry. If the *y*-axis is used as the line of symmetry, then the correct reflection is triangle D. Be careful. Triangle B is also a reflection, but it uses the *x*-axis as a line of symmetry instead of the *y*-axis.

24. (A)

First we need to find *x*: $\log_2 x = 6$. means that $2^6 = x$, so *x* = 64. Next, find $\log_4 x$. Substituting 64 for *x* gives us $\log_4 64 = ?$ The equation can be verbalized as "4 to what power equals 64?" The answer is 3.

25. (C)

The range of *f*(*x*) is all possible values of 2*x*, where *x* is a positive integer less than 50. This means that whatever value we plug in for *x*, it will be doubled. Not only would 50 become 100, but all the numbers in the range would be even. Thus, the answer is (C).

26. (A)

The problem is asking for the probability of one event *or* another event, so we need to find each probability and then add them. The probability of a student with blue eyes being chosen is $\frac{13}{51}$, while the probability of a student with green eyes being chosen is $\frac{8}{51}$. Their sum is $\frac{21}{51}$, which can be reduced to $\frac{7}{17}$.

27. (C)

The student in the problem claims that $n^3 \geq n$ for all real numbers *n*, which may not sound unreasonable at first. To see which number works as a counterexample, plug each in to see which one is not correct:

$2^3 \geq 2$ is true because $8 \geq 2$.

$(-1)^3 \geq -1$ is true because $-1 \geq -1$.

$\left(\frac{1}{2}\right)^3 \geq \frac{1}{2}$ is not true because $\left(\frac{1}{2}\right)^3 = \frac{1}{8}$ and $\frac{1}{8}$ is less than $\frac{1}{2}$, not greater than it. So the answer is (C).

28. (B)

The sum of the angles of a triangle is always 180°. Here we are given a right triangle, so we know one of the angles is 90°. We're given a second angle that measures 48°, so that leaves 180° − 90° − 48° = 42° for the third angle.

29. (3)

It's easiest to list the cubes from 0 to 150 and see which, if any, are also squares. The cubes are 0, 1, 8, 27, 64, and 125. Only three of these are also squares: 0, 1, and 64. The answer is 3. Be sure to notice that the range given for *x* includes 0, which is both a square and a cube.

30. (A)

If you want to arrange five items, then you have 5 choices for the first item, 4 for the second, 3 for the third, and so on. This is 5!, where $5! = 5 \times 4 \times 3 \times 2 \times 1 = 120$. Keep in mind that you are counting the number of ways to arrange the items, which always involves multiplication.

31. (D)

The Cartesian product of two sets is the set of all ordered pairs whose first entry comes from the first set and whose second entry comes from the second set. Since A and B are small sets, we can easily list the Cartesian product: $A \times B = \{(1, 2), (1, 3), (2, 2), (2, 3)\}$. We can see that $(3, 2)$ is not in this set, so the correct answer is (D). If you don't want to list the elements in $A \times B$, you could also keep in mind that the first number in the ordered pairs comes from A, meaning it has to be 1 or 2. Since (D) begins with 3, it can't be one of the elements.

32. (B)

The standard deviation of a set of numbers is a measure of how widely the numbers in the set vary from the mean. The range of Set 1 is $40 - 28 = 12$. The numbers all fall close to the mean of 35.1. The range of set 2 is $55 - 3 = 52$. The numbers in Set 2 are much farther from the mean of 26.6. Since the numbers in Set 1 vary less from the mean, it can be seen without calculation that the standard deviation of Set 2 is greater than the standard deviation of Set 1.

33. (D)

At first glance the choices may all appear to be prime numbers, but keep in mind that a prime number is only divisible by itself and 1. This is certainly true for the first three choices, but 51 is divisible by 3, so it is not prime.

34. (A)

Following the logic of the problem, you start by going to the concert, which means calling in sick. But if you call in sick, you know your boss will get angry. If your boss gets angry, you know you'll lose your job. Going to the concert ultimately means you will lose your job.

35. (D)

When a function is written as a fraction, you have to be concerned when its denominator is equal to zero, since the function will not be defined there. In this case, the denominator is zero when $x(x + 2) = 0$, which happens when either $x = 0$ or $x = -2$.

36. (D)

Some very common irrational numbers are $\sqrt{2}$, $\sqrt{3}$, and π. Each of these three numbers cannot be written as a ratio of two integers. Therefore, choices (A), (B), and (C) are incorrect. The square root of 9 equals 3, which is rational. The correct answer is (D).

37. (C)

If $x = -3$, then $x - 5 = -3 - 5 = -8$. Therefore, $|x - 5| = |-8| = 8$. Remember that the absolute value of a negative number is its opposite. Be sure to do the subtraction carefully. At a quick glance you may just notice the difference between 3 and 5 and mistakenly end up with an answer of 2 or −2.

38. (B)

To find the mean of the numbers, first add them ($4 + 7 + 9 + 13 + 17 = 50$), then divide by 5 (how many numbers you added). The mean is $50 \div 5 = 10$. To find the median, list the numbers from smallest to largest and find the number in the middle. The middle number, or median, is 9. The sum of the mean and median is $10 + 9 = 19$. Notice that answer choice (A) is just the mean, while choice (D) is the product of the mean and median. You get answer (C) if you forget to divide by 5 to get the mean.

39. 37

To find the remainder when $K(x)$ is divided by $(x - 2)$, use the remainder theorem. It states that to find the remainder when a function is divided by $(x - b)$, substitute the value of b into the function and simplify.

$K(2) = 4(2)^3 + 2^2 - 3(2) + 7 = 32 + 4 - 6 + 7 = 37$

40. (A)

A line written in the form $y = mx + b$ has slope m. All four choices are already written in this form. Only choice (A), $y = -5x + 9$, has the same slope as the given equation $y = -5x + 3$. They both have a slope of -5. The correct answer is (A).

41. (C)

We are told that A is a subset of C and that B is a subset of C. While it may be true that either $A \subset B$ or $B \subset A$, we don't know this for sure (it could be true but is not *always* true), so answer choices (A) and (B) can be discarded. What is true is that $A \subset C$, so if both A and B are subsets of C, then $A \cup B$ is also a subset of C.

42. February

First, calculate the average monthly sales:

$$\frac{(13 + 20 + 23 + 16 + 23 + 25)}{6} = \frac{120}{6} = 20$$

The only month that Dale sold 20 cars was February. The correct answer is February.

43. (B)

Choose values for x and y, such as $x = 5$ and $y = 2$. These values satisfy the conditions of the problem because $5 > 2 > 0$. Plug the values into each possible solution:

(A) $|5| > |2|$ True

(B) $\frac{1}{5} > \frac{1}{2}$ False

(C) $5^2 > 2^2$ True

(D) $\frac{1}{2} > \frac{1}{5}$ True

You can always stop plugging in values when you reach the solution that does not work, in this case (B).

44. (D)

Notice that r is only true when both p and q are true. This is true of the statement "p and q." Process of elimination can also be used to find the solution: The answer is not (A) because "p or q" is only false once, but r is false three times. Answer choices (B) and (C) can be discounted for the same reason.

45. (A)

If you remember that x^2 is always greater than or equal to zero, you can eliminate (B) and (D) from the choices. Also note that 0 is between -3 and 4, and since $0^2 = 0$, it must be included in the range. Answer choice (C) does not include 0, so the answer must be (A).

46. 4.3

To find the standard deviation, follow these steps:

1. Calculate the mean:	10.8
2. Find the amount each number deviates from the mean:	4.8, −4.2, 1.8, 0.8, −7.2, 3.8
3. Square those differences:	23.04, 17.64, 3.24, 0.64, 51.84, 14.44
4. Add the squares together:	110.84
5. Divide by the number of squares:	18.5
6. Take the square root of this number:	4.3

When calculating the standard deviation with a sample of numbers from a larger population, divide the sum of the squares (in step 5) by the number of items *minus one*. In this case, we would have divided 18.5 by 5 instead of 6 if this number set were a sampling from a larger population.

47. (D)

Since no further information is given about this figure, all we can conclude is that it is a quadrilateral, meaning it has four sides. For it to be a rectangle, we'd need to know that the opposite sides were parallel and that the angles measured 90°. To be a rhombus, we'd need to know that the opposite sides were parallel and that all four sides had the same length. A trapezoid could never look like this, so (B) can easily be discarded.

48. Rectangle C

A translation takes a shape or graph and shifts it horizontally, vertically, or both. Rectangle C is the only choice that keeps the size and shape of the rectangle constant and does not rotate the rectangle. Rectangle C has simply been shifted down and to the left of rectangle *WXYZ*.

49.

The rectangle measuring 5 × 6 has an area of 30 square units, so it is the correct choice. The triangle has an area of $\frac{1}{2}$ × 8 × 8 = 32. This is an incorrect answer. The square has an area of 6 × 6 = 36. This is an incorrect answer. The parallelogram has an area of 9 × 4 = 36. This is also an incorrect answer.

50. (B)

This is an *expected value* problem. For a problem like this, we need to find the product of each outcome and its probability, then add the two together. In this case,

(0 × 0.10) + (1 × 0.25) + (2 × 0.30) + (3 × 0.15) + (4 × 0.20)

= 0.25 + 0.60 + 0.45 + 0.80

= 2.1

Notice that the number of absences with the largest probability is 2, so we should expect the result to be around 2. With this in mind, answer choices (A) and (D) can be discounted.

51. (C)

In order for an integer to be even, it must be divisible by 2. Likewise, if an integer is divisible by 2, then we know that it is even. A number must be an even integer for it to be divisible by 2. Therefore, A is both necessary and sufficient for B.

52. line *l*

The only line that divides the pentagon into two identical halves is line *l*. The *y*-axis doesn't pass through the pentagon. If you fold the pentagon along the *x*-axis, the two halves do not match. Similarly, if you fold the pentagon along line *m*, the two halves do not match.

53. (C)

Notice in the diagram that all of *B* is shaded, so we will be looking for a *B* union with another area or areas. The other shaded piece comes from where *A* and *C* intersect. This means the diagram represents $(A \cap C) \cup B$.

54. (B)

To find the inverse of a function, replace $f(x)$ with y, interchange x and y, then solve the equation for y. The result will be $f^{-1}(x)$, the inverse of the function. In this case,

$$f(x) = \frac{1}{x}$$
$$y = \frac{1}{x} \qquad \text{Replace } f(x) \text{ with } y.$$
$$x = \frac{1}{y} \qquad \text{Interchange } x \text{ and } y.$$
$$xy = 1 \qquad \text{Solve for } y.$$
$$f^{-1}(x) = \frac{1}{x} \qquad \text{Replace } y \text{ with } f^{-1}(x).$$

This is sort of a trick question because the function and inverse are the same. A common mistake here is to think that since $f(x)$ is a fraction, the reciprocal is the inverse, which would give you the incorrect answer (A).

55. (A)

Since this is a counting problem, all you need to do is see which names appear in both lists. Looking at the lists, you will find that Joe, Terry, and Ralph are in both bands, answer (A).

56. (B)

Since the total monthly budget is $1,200, the fraction spent on the unknown category is

$$\frac{204}{1,200} = 0.17 = 17\%$$

The correct answer is (B), clothing.

57. 56

Note that we are selecting a subset of people and that there is no sense of order. That means this is a *combination* problem. The problem can be solved using the combination formula, $C(n, r) = \frac{n!}{r!(n-r)!}$. Here $n = 8$ and $r = 3$, so

$$C(8, 3) = \frac{8!}{3!(8-3)!} = \frac{8!}{3!5!} =$$

$$\frac{(8 \times 7 \times 6 \times 5 \times 4 \times 3 \times 2 \times 1)}{(3 \times 2 \times 1)(5 \times 4 \times 3 \times 2 \times 1)}$$

Reducing the fraction will leave you with 56. If you had used the permutation formula (which is used when there is a sense of order) instead of the combination formula, your answer would be 336.

58. (B)

The mode is the number that appears most often in a set of numbers. Although the number 2 appears twice in the set, the number 5 appears three times. Therefore, the correct answer is (B), 5.

59. (A)

The graph of a function of x must pass the *vertical line test*, which says that any vertical line drawn on the Cartesian plane should intersect the graph of a function no more than once. (B), (C), and (D) all fail this test.

60. (B)

The diagonal of a rectangle forms the hypotenuse of a right triangle, with the width and length of the rectangle forming the legs of the triangle. With this in mind, this problem can be solved using the *Pythagorean theorem*, which says that the square of the hypotenuse of a right triangle equals the sum of the squares of the legs. In symbols, if c is the measure of the hypotenuse with a and b as the measures of the legs, then $c^2 = a^2 + b^2$. In this case $a = 5$, $b = 12$, and we want to find c, so

$$c^2 = 5^2 + 12^2$$
$$c^2 = 25 + 144$$
$$c^2 = 169$$
$$c = \sqrt{169}$$
$$c = 13$$

Chapter Eleven: **Practice Test 3**

Time—90 minutes
60 Questions

Directions: For the following questions, either select the BEST answer of the choices given or input your answer into the box provided.

You can use the computer-based scientific calculator during this exam.

Notes:

(1) Unless otherwise stated, the domain of any function f consists of the set of all real numbers x for which $f(x)$ is a real number.

(2) i represents $\sqrt{-1}$.

(3) Unless otherwise indicated, all geometric figures lie in a plane. The appearance of all figures is accurate UNLESS the question states that the figure is not drawn to scale.

1. Which of the following is logically equivalent to "If you are not young, then you are old"?

    (A) If you are young, then you are not old.

    (B) If you are old, then you are not young.

    (C) You are not young or you are old.

    (D) If you are not old, then you are young.

2. If $x = -3$, then $|x| - 3 =$

    (A) 6

    (B) 0

    (C) 9

    (D) −6

3. An athlete wants to arrange four different trophies on a shelf. In how many ways could he arrange the four trophies?

    [   ]

4. Which of the following statements includes a cardinal number?

    (A) Today is my 25th birthday.

    (B) Our class meets in room 409.

    (C) There are 30 volumes in that set of encyclopedias.

    (D) My ID number is 555345.

5. How many prime numbers are there between 1 and 20?

    (A) 19

    (B) 10

    (C) 7

    (D) 8

GO ON TO THE NEXT PAGE

KAPLAN

6. What is the range of the function graphed below?

(A) $-2 \leq x \leq 2$

(B) $0 \leq y \leq 3$

(C) $y \geq 0$

(D) $-2 \leq y \leq 2$

7. The sum of the mean and median of the numbers 22, 41, 13, 17, and 32 is

(A) 147

(B) 47

(C) 550

(D) 38

8. Which of the following is an irrational number?

(A) $\sqrt{49}$

(B) $\sqrt{36}$

(C) $\sqrt{27}$

(D) $\sqrt{9}$

9. Which is the inverse of the function $f(x) = 3x + 4$?

(A) $f^{-1}(x) = 3x - 4$

(B) $f^{-1}(x) = 4x + 3$

(C) $f^{-1}(x) = \frac{x}{3} - 4$

(D) $f^{-1}(x) = \frac{x-4}{3}$

10. Below is a Truth Table:

p	q	r
T	T	T
T	F	F
F	T	F
F	F	T

According to this table, which of the following statements describes r?

(A) $p \leftrightarrow q$

(B) $p \rightarrow q$

(C) $p \vee q$

(D) $p \wedge q$

11. Which of the following lines is perpendicular to the line $2y - 3x = 8$?

(A) $y = 3x - 4$

(B) $y = \frac{2}{3}x + 6$

(C) $y = -\frac{2}{3}x - 4$

(D) $y = \frac{3}{2}x + 4$

12. The probability an event will occur is 0.4. What is the probability the event will not occur?

(A) 0.6

(B) 0.4

(C) 0

(D) 1

13. Which of the following is a factor of $x^4 + 5x^3 - x^2 - 3x - 2$?

(A) $x^2 + 3x + 2$

(B) $x - 1$

(C) $x + 1$

(D) $x - 2$

GO ON TO THE NEXT PAGE ⇨

14. If $A = \{x \mid x$ is a positive integer$\}$ and $B = \{x \mid x$ is an even integer less than 50$\}$, which of the following is a subset of $A \cap B$?

    (A) {12, 15, 16, 18}

    (B) {−4, 6, 8, 10}

    (C) {22, 34, 56}

    (D) {12, 20, 36, 48}

15. Simplify $\sqrt{-49} + \sqrt{-36} - \sqrt{-25}$.

    (A) 8

    (B) 15

    (C) $8i$

    (D) $15i$

16. If $f(x) = 2x - 3$ and $g(x) = x^2 + 1$, then $f(g(-3)) =$

    [   ]

17. If a and b are prime numbers, which of the following is NEVER true?

    I. $a + b$ is a prime number.
    II. $a - b$ is a prime number.
    III. ab is a prime number.

    (A) I only

    (B) II only

    (C) I and II only

    (D) III only

18. At a music store, there are 10 types of guitars, 3 types of cases, and 5 types of amplifiers. If Leo wants to purchase one of each, how many different combinations of guitars, cases, and amplifiers are possible?

    (A) 18

    (B) 150

    (C) 35

    (D) 80

19. What is the domain of the function $f(x) = \{(1, 4), (2, 5), (3, 6)\}$?

    (A) {1, 2, 3}

    (B) {4, 5, 6}

    (C) {1, 4, 2}

    (D) {5, 3, 6}

20. A friend claims that $2n$ is always greater than or equal to n for all integers n. Of the following, which is a value of n that provides a counterexample to your friend's claim?

    (A) 2

    (B) $\frac{1}{2}$

    (C) 0

    (D) −1

21. What type of triangle is given below?

    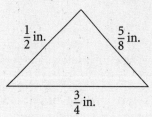

    (A) Isosceles

    (B) Scalene

    (C) Equilateral

    (D) Obtuse

22. Which set of numbers has the smallest standard deviation?

    (A) {1, 2, 3}

    (B) {1, 4, 7}

    (C) {0, 5, 10}

    (D) {2, 8, 14}

GO ON TO THE NEXT PAGE

KAPLAN

23. Suppose $A = \{a, b\}$ and $B = \{c, d\}$. Which of the following ordered pairs is in the Cartesian product $A \times B$?

    (A) (a, b)

    (B) (a, c)

    (C) (c, d)

    (D) (d, a)

24. If $2x < 26$ and $x + 9 \geq 2$, which interval correctly describes all possible values of x?

    (A) $(7, 13)$

    (B) $(-7, 13)$

    (C) $[-7, 13)$

    (D) $[-7, 13]$

25. If $f(x) = 3x^2 - 2x + 5$ and $g(x) = 4x - 5$, then $(f - g)(x) =$

    (A) $3x^2 - 6x + 10$

    (B) $3x^2 - 6x$

    (C) $3x^2 - 2x + 10$

    (D) $3x^2 - 6x - 10$

26. The sum of three consecutive odd integers is 39. What is the value of the largest odd integer?

    ☐

27. Which of the following is an irrational number?

    (A) $\sqrt{9}$

    (B) $\sqrt{16}$

    (C) $\sqrt{20 + 5}$

    (D) $\sqrt{3}$

28. Consider the set of numbers $\{4, 9, 11, 17, 23, 27\}$. If one number is chosen at random from this set, what is the probability the number would be prime?

    (A) $\frac{1}{2}$

    (B) $\frac{2}{3}$

    (C) $\frac{1}{3}$

    (D) $\frac{3}{4}$

29. Consider the set of numbers $\{3, 6, 7, 9, 10\}$. What is the relation between the mean and the median of this set?

    (A) The median is greater than the mean.

    (B) The mean is greater then the median.

    (C) The median and the mean are exactly the same.

    (D) More information is required.

30. Let A represent the statement "You are 18 years old," and B represent the statement "You can register to vote." What can be said about statements A and B?

    (A) A is a sufficient but not a necessary condition for B.

    (B) A is a necessary but not a sufficient condition for B.

    (C) A is a necessary and sufficient condition for B.

    (D) A is neither necessary nor sufficient for B.

GO ON TO THE NEXT PAGE

31. Which of the following choices represents the Venn diagram?

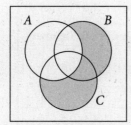

    (A) $(A \cup B) \cap C'$

    (B) $(B \cup C) \cap A'$

    (C) $(B \cap C) \cup A'$

    (D) $A' \cap B \cap C$

32. What is $2^4 = 64$ written as a logarithm?

    (A) $\log_2 64 = 4$

    (B) $\log_2 4 = 64$

    (C) $\log_4 2 = 64$

    (D) $\log_{64} 2 = 4$

33. If $f(x) = x^3 - 2x^2 + 5$, then $f(-2) =$

    (A) 5

    (B) 21

    (C) −2

    (D) −11

34. Which of the following is equivalent to $|90 - 100|$?

    (A) −1

    (B)   1

    (C) −10

    (D)   10

35. In a race with 8 runners, in how many ways could there be prizes given for first, second, and third place, assuming there are no ties?

    [   ]

36. What is the area of the rectangle given below?

    (A) 24 in^2

    (B) 20 in^2

    (C) 576 in^2

    (D) 36 in^2

37. Let $f(x) = \sqrt{x - 3}$. Which of the following is the domain of $f(x)$?

    (A) All real numbers

    (B) All real numbers greater than or equal to 0

    (C) All real numbers greater than or equal to 3

    (D) All real number greater than or equal to −3

38. Which is the prime factorization of 45?

    (A) 9×5

    (B) 1×45

    (C) $3 \times 3 \times 5$

    (D) $2 \times 3 \times 5$

39. The number of absences and their probabilities for any given day in an English class are given in the table below:

Absences:	0	1	2	3	4
Probability:	0.15	0.15	0.30	0.30	0.10

What is the probability that there will be an odd number of absences for any given day of the class?

    (A) 0.45

    (B) 0.55

    (C) 0.50

    (D) 0.30

GO ON TO THE NEXT PAGE

KAPLAN

40. Which of the following is the converse of "If not R, then not S"?

    (A) If R, then S
    (B) If S, then R
    (C) If not S, then not R
    (D) If R, then not S

41. If $2^2 x^{-3} = 32$, then $x =$

    [   ]

42. Which of the following is NOT the graph of a function of x?

    (A)

    (B)

    (C)

    (D)

43. Suppose A and B are distinct sets such that $A \cap B = \varnothing$. What do we know about sets A and B?

    (A) A is a subset of B.
    (B) B is a subset of A.
    (C) A and B are disjoint.
    (D) A and B are both empty.

44. The table shows the number of members who joined a fitness club for six months. How many members joined in January and February?

Month	Number of New Members
January	24
February	28
March	18
April	30
May	19
June	15

    (A) 24
    (B) 52
    (C) 70
    (D) 28

45. If the sum of three consecutive odd numbers is 27, what is the smallest of the three odd numbers?

    (A) 7
    (B) 9
    (C) 11
    (D) 13

46. Suppose A is any event. Which of the following statements about event A are NEVER true?

    I. The probability that event A will occur can be greater than 1.
    II. The probability that event A will occur can be less than 0.
    III. The probability that event A will not occur is less than the probability event A will occur.

    (A) I only
    (B) I and II only
    (C) II and III only
    (D) III only

GO ON TO THE NEXT PAGE

47. The following graph shows an octagon on a coordinate plane. Click on the line that represents the line of symmetry of the figure.

48. What is the length of the unknown side in the figure below?

(A) 12 cm

(B) $\sqrt{35}$ cm

(C) $\sqrt{74}$ cm

(D) 9 cm

49. A number that is the sum of its proper factors is called "perfect." Which of the following numbers is perfect?

(A) 28

(B) 8

(C) 12

(D) 4

50. The circle graph shows the number of fundraising dollars a university receives each year. Which category provides the second highest amount of money for the school? Click on the correct category.

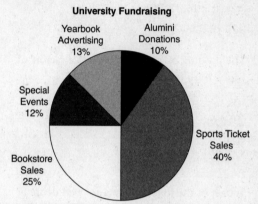

51. All dogs bark. Sparky barks. What can you conclude about Sparky?

(A) Sparky is a dog.

(B) Sparky is not a dog.

(C) Sparky doesn't bark.

(D) None of the above conclusions is warranted.

52. The graph shows four triangles on a coordinate plane. Using the x-axis as a line of symmetry, determine which triangle is a reflection of $\triangle DEF$. Click on the correct triangle.

GO ON TO THE NEXT PAGE

KAPLAN

53. Which of the following sets of data has the largest standard deviation?

    (A) $\{5, 6, 8, 9\}$

    (B) $\{4, 6, 9, 12\}$

    (C) $\{15, 16, 18, 20\}$

    (D) $\{9, 25, 32, 66\}$

54. The product of all distinct positive factors of which number below is the largest?

    (A) 5

    (B) 6

    (C) 8

    (D) 11

55. Which of the following sets are well defined?

    I. $\{x \mid x$ is an even number$\}$
    II. $\{x \mid x$ is a good movie$\}$
    III. $\{x \mid x$ is a difficult instructor$\}$

    (A) I only

    (B) II only

    (C) III only

    (D) II and III only

56. A deck of 52 cards contains 13 cards of each of four suits—clubs, spades, diamonds, and hearts. If you select three cards from a deck without replacement, what is the probability the third card is a spade given that the first two cards were diamonds?

    (A) $\frac{13}{52}$

    (B) $\frac{11}{52}$

    (C) $\frac{11}{50}$

    (D) $\frac{13}{50}$

57. What are the x-intercepts of the function $f(x) = x^2 - x - 12$?

    (A) 1 and 12

    (B) −3 and 4

    (C) 3 and −4

    (D) −3 and −4

58. If $4n \leq 20$ and $n - 1 > -10$, which interval correctly describes all possible values of n?

    (A) $(5, 9)$

    (B) $(-9, 5]$

    (C) $[-9, 5)$

    (D) $[5, 9]$

59. The following list shows Joran's science test grades for this semester. Click on the number that represents the mode of this set of data.

    $$\{91, 75, 89, 85, 88, 89, 92, 91, 89\}$$

60. The figure shows four rectangles on a coordinate plane. Click on the rectangle that is a translation of rectangle $WXYZ$.

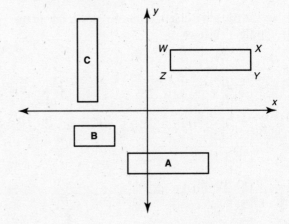

END OF TEST. STOP

KAPLAN

THE ANSWER KEY APPEARS ON THE FOLLOWING PAGE.

ANSWER KEY

1. D	11. C	21. B	31. B	41. 4	51. D
2. B	12. A	22. A	32. A	42. D	52. Triangle X
3. 24	13. B	23. B	33. D	43. C	53. D
4. C	14. D	24. C	34. D	44. B	54. C
5. D	15. C	25. A	35. 336	45. A	55. A
6. B	16. 17	26. 15	36. A	46. B	56. D
7. B	17. D	27. D	37. C	47. line p	57. B
8. C	18. B	28. A	38. C	48. C	58. B
9. D	19. A	29. C	39. A	49. A	59. 89
10. A	20. D	30. A	40. C	50. Bookstore Sales	60. Rectangle A

PRACTICE TEST 2 QUICK REFERENCE TABLES

Use the following tables to determine which topics you still need to review.

Topic	Test Question
Sets	4, 14, 23, 31, 43, 55
Logic	1, 10, 20, 30, 40, 51
Real Number System	2, 5, 8, 17, 24, 26, 27, 34, 38, 45, 49, 58
Functions and Graphs	6, 9, 16, 19, 25, 33, 37, 42, 47, 52, 57, 60
Probability and Statistics	3, 7, 12, 18, 22, 28, 29, 35, 39, 44, 46, 50, 53, 56, 59
Additional Topics	11, 13, 15, 21, 32, 36, 41, 48, 54

Topic	Number of Questions on Test	Number Correct
Sets	6	
Logic	6	
Real Number System	12	
Functions and Graphs	12	
Probability and Statistics	15	
Additional Topics	9	

Answers and Explanations

1. (D)

Given a conditional statement, the contrapositive is always equivalent. To find the contrapositive, switch and negate the statements that make up the original conditional. In this case, "If you are not young, then you are old" is equivalent to "If you are not old, then you are young."

2. (B)

If $x = -3$, then $|x| = 3$. Therefore, $|x| - 3 = |-3| - 3 = 3 - 3 = 0$.

3. 24

If you want to arrange four items, then you have 4 choices for the first item, 3 for the second, 2 for the third, and 1 for the fourth. There are $4 \times 3 \times 2 \times 1 = 24$ total ways to arrange the four items.

4. (C)

A cardinal number indicates the number of elements in a set. Of all the possible answers, only (C) could be thought of as a set (the set of books that make up the encyclopedia).

5. (D)

If you can make a quick list of the prime numbers between 1 and 20 you get the set {2, 3, 5, 7, 11, 13, 17, 19}. This gives you 8 numbers.

6. (B)

The range of a function is always in terms of y or $f(x)$, so we can eliminate (A) as a possible answer. Notice the graph is always above the x-axis, meaning it is always positive, so choice (D) can also be eliminated. In terms of the y-axis, the function never goes above 3 or below 0, so the range is $0 \leq y \leq 3$.

7. (B)

To find the mean, add the numbers and divide by 5. This gives you: $\frac{22 + 41 + 13 + 17 + 32}{5} = \frac{125}{5} = 25$. The median is the middle number if you list the numbers from smallest to largest: 13, 17, 22, 32, 41. The median is 22, so the sum of the mean and median is $25 + 22 = 47$.

8. (C)

Square roots often give us irrational numbers, but three of the square roots here simplify to whole numbers: $\sqrt{49} = 7$, $\sqrt{36} = 6$, and $\sqrt{9} = 3$. This leaves only $\sqrt{27}$, which is irrational.

9. (D)

The inverse of a function "undoes" the function. The function in this problem multiplies x by 3 then adds 4. To undo this, we would need to subtract 4 then divide by 3. Answer (D) completes this process.

10. (A)

Notice that r is true when p and q are both true or both false. Of the four choices, r is only true in the statement $p \leftrightarrow q$.

11. (C)

Two lines are perpendicular if their slopes are negative reciprocals of each other. If we solve the given line for y, we can find its slope:

$$2y - 3x = 8$$
$$2y = 3x + 8$$
$$y = \frac{3}{2}x + 4$$

The slope of this line is $\frac{3}{2}$ (the number in front of x), so the slope of a line perpendicular to it would be $-\frac{2}{3}$. Choice (C) is the only line with this slope.

12. (A)

The probability that an event will occur plus the probability that it will not occur always equals 1. In this case, the probability the event will occur is 0.4, so we need to add 0.6 to get 1. Therefore, the probability that the event will not occur must be 0.6.

13. (B)

If we plug any number c into a polynomial and get 0, then $x - c$ is a factor of the polynomial. Looking at answers (B), (C), and (D), there are three choices for c: 1, –1, and 2. Plugging 1 into the polynomial produces $(1)^4 + 5(1)^3 - (1)^2 - 3(1) - 2 = 1 + 5 - 1 - 3 - 2 = 0$. Thus, $x - 1$ is a factor of the polynomial.

14. (D)

$A \cap B$ denotes the set of positive even integers less than 50. A subset of this set must also include positive integers that are less than 50. (A) includes an odd number, (B) includes a negative number, and (C) includes a number greater than 50, so none of these are the right answer. (D) is the only set listed that includes only positive even integers less than 50.

15. (C)

Keeping in mind that $i = \sqrt{-1}$, we can simplify each square root in the problem as follows: $\sqrt{-49} = \sqrt{49(-1)} = \sqrt{49}$ $\sqrt{-1} = 7i$. Similarly, $\sqrt{-36} = 6i$ and $\sqrt{-25} = 5i$, so $\sqrt{-49} + \sqrt{-36} - \sqrt{-25} = 7i + 6i - 5i = 8i$.

16. 17

First we need to find $g(-3)$. Since $g(x) = x^2 + 1$, $g(-3) = (-3)^2 + 1 = 9 + 1 = 10$. Therefore, $f(g(-3)) = f(10) = 2(10) - 3 = 20 - 3 = 17$.

17. (D)

If a and b are prime numbers, $a + b$ will also be prime sometimes (for instance, 2 + 3 = 5). Likewise, $a - b$ will also be prime sometimes (for example, 7 – 5 = 2). If you multiply two prime numbers, the result will always be a composite number and never a prime number.

18. (B)

For a problem like this you need to see how many ways you can make each choice, then multiply. In this case, there are 10 guitars, 3 cases, and 5 amplifiers, so there are $10 \times 3 \times 5 = 150$ different combinations.

19. (A)

When a function is written as a series of ordered pairs, the first number in each ordered pair comes from the domain. With this in mind, the domain of this function would be the first number in each ordered pair, which is the set {1, 2, 3}.

20. (D)

First, we can exclude (B) because $\frac{1}{2}$ is not an integer. To see which of the remaining numbers works as a counterexample, plug each number in to see which one is not correct:

$2(2) \geq 2$ is true because $4 \geq 2$.

$2(0) \geq 0$ is true because $0 \geq 0$.

$2(-1) \geq -1$ is not true because $-2 < -1$.

The answer is (D).

21. (B)

Notice that all three sides of the triangle have different lengths. When this is the case, the triangle is called scalene.

22. (A)

For this question, you don't need to calculate the standard deviation for each set. You just need to understand what the term means. The standard deviation of a set of numbers is a measure of how widely the numbers in the set vary from the mean. Therefore, look at each set to see how spread out the numbers are from the mean. In the first set, the mean is 2, and the numbers 1 and 3 are each one unit away from the mean. In the second set, the mean is 4, and the numbers 1 and 7 are each three units away from the mean. In the third set, the mean is 5, and the numbers 0 and 10 are each five units away from the mean. In the fourth set, the mean is 8, and the numbers 2 and 14 are each six units away from the mean. Since the first set contains numbers that are closer to the mean, it has the smallest standard deviation.

23. (B)

Since A and B are small sets, we can quickly list the Cartesian product: $A \times B = \{(a, c), (a, d), (b, c), (b, d)\}$. Ordered pair (a, c) is only choice listed that is in this set.

24. (C)

Solve each inequality:

$2x < 26; x < 13$

$x + 9 \geq 2; x \geq -7$

The range of possible values of x is $-7 \leq x < 13$ or $[-7, 13)$. Note that the closed bracket symbol "[" means that -7 is included in the range. The open bracket symbol ")" after 13 means that 13 is *not* included in the range.

25. (A)

To find the answer, use the fact that $(f - g)(x) = f(x) - g(x)$:

$$(f - g)(x) = f(x) - g(x)$$
$$= (3x^2 - 2x + 5) - (4x - 5)$$
$$= 3x^2 - 2x + 5 - 4x + 5$$
$$= 3x^2 - 6x + 10$$

26. 15

The quickest way to do this problem is to divide 39 by 3, which produces 13. This is the middle number we are adding to get 39. The odd number before 13 is 11 and after 13 is 15. You can check to see that $11 + 13 + 15 = 39$ and can see that the largest of these odd numbers is 15.

27. (D)

Choice (A) simplifies to 3, which is rational. Choice (B) simplifies to 4, which is rational. Choice (C) simplifies to 5, which is also rational. The answer is (D), $\sqrt{3}$, which is an irrational number because it cannot be written as a ratio comparing two integers.

28. (A)

Of the six numbers listed, three are prime: 11, 17, and 23. The probability of selecting a prime number would therefore be $\frac{3}{6} = \frac{1}{2}$.

29. (C)

The mean of this set is $\frac{3 + 6 + 7 + 9 + 10}{5} = \frac{35}{5} = 7$.

The median is the middle number when the numbers are put in order from smallest to largest, which they are above, so the median is also 7. The answer is therefore (C).

30. (A)

It is true that if you are 18 years old, you can register to vote. This means that A is sufficient for B. On the other hand, it is not necessarily true that if you can register to vote, then you are 18 years old. You could be older than 18. So A is a sufficient but not necessary condition for B.

31. (B)

None of A is shaded, so we are looking for something with A', which eliminates choice (A). Most of B and C are shaded, except where A is A' can be found in the regions where $B \cup C$. This Venn diagram therefore represents $(B \cup C) \cap A'$.

32. (A)

The base of the exponential expression is 2, so the base of the logarithm also needs to be 2. This narrows our choices down to (A) or (B). The logarithm of a number is the power to which a given base is raised to in order to produce that number. Here the power is 4, so the logarithm must equal 4. The only answer with base 2 that equals 4 is (A).

33. (D)

Substitute -2 for x into the function and simplify:
$f(x) = x^3 - 2x^2 + 5$, so $f(-2) = (-2)^3 - 2(-2)^2 + 5 = -8 - 8 + 5 = -11$.

34. (D)

Simplify the expression: $|90 - 100| = |-10| = 10$. Remember that the absolute value sign removes the negative from the number contained within. So -10 becomes 10.

35. 336

There are 8 possible runners for first place. Once first place has been taken, there are 7 runners left for second place. After that, there are only 6 runners left for third place. In total, there are $8 \times 7 \times 6 = 336$ ways prizes could be given for first, second, and third place.

36. (A)

The area of a rectangle is given by length × width. In this case, the area of the rectangle is 6 in × 4 in = 24 in^2.

37. (C)

The domain of a function includes all the values of x for which the function is defined. The function $f(x) = \sqrt{x}$ is only defined for $x \geq 0$, so the function $f(x) = \sqrt{x-3}$ is only defined for $x - 3 \geq 0$, which means $x \geq 3$.

38. (C)

The prime factorization of a number is the number written as a product of prime numbers. 9 is not prime, so choice (A) is out. Likewise, 45 is not prime, so choice (B) is out. Choice (D) multiplies to 30, not 45, so it's also out. This leaves only choice (C).

39. (A)

The possible numbers of absences listed are 0, 1, 2, 3, and 4. The only odd numbers here are 1 and 3. The probability of 1 person being absent is 0.15, while the probability of 3 people being absent is 0.30. The total probability of 1 or 3 people being absent is therefore $0.15 + 0.30 = 0.45$.

40. (C)

The converse of a conditional statement $p \rightarrow q$ is $q \rightarrow p$. In this case, the converse of "If not R, then not S" would be "If not S, then not R."

41. 4

To solve a problem where the variable is given in the exponent, we first need to make the bases the same. In this case, $32 = 2^5$, so $2^{2x-3} = 2^5$. Once the bases are the same, then the exponents must be equal, so we can solve the resulting equation:

$2^{2x-3} = 2^5$

$2x - 3 = 5$

$2x = 8$

$x = 4$

42. (D)

The graph of a function of x must pass the vertical line test, which says that any vertical line drawn on the Cartesian plane should intersect the graph of a function no more than once. (A), (B), and (C) all pass this test, but (D) fails it.

43. (C)

Since A and B are distinct sets, they cannot both be empty, so choice (D) can be eliminated. By definition, two sets are disjoint if $A \cap B = \varnothing$, so the answer is (C).

44. (B)

To find the number of members who joined in January and February, add the new members listed for each month: $24 + 28 = 52$.

45. (A)

The easiest way to solve this problem is to divide 27 by 3 to get 9. Nine is then the middle number, making the other consecutive odd numbers 7 and 11. Check that the sum is 27: $7 + 9 + 11 = 27$. The smallest of the three is 7.

46. (B)

For any event A, the probability that event A will occur is always between 0 and 1, so I and II are never true. While the probability that event A will not occur can be greater than the probability that event A will occur, it can also be less. Choice (B) is the right answer.

47. line p

A line of symmetry divides a figure or graph into two identical halves. The only line that divides the octagon into two identical halves is line p.

48. (C)

The figure shown is a right triangle and the side marked ? is the hypotenuse. The length of the hypotenuse of a right triangle can be found by using the Pythagorean theorem, which says that if the length of the hypotenuse of a right triangle is given by c and the length of the legs are a and b, then $c = \sqrt{a^2 + b^2}$. In this problem, $a = 5$, $b = 7$, and c is what we want to find. Therefore,

$c = \sqrt{a^2 + b^2}$

$c = \sqrt{5^2 + 7^2}$

$c = \sqrt{25 + 49}$

$c = \sqrt{74}$

49. (A)

The proper factors of a number are factors of the number that are less than the number. The proper factors of 28 are 1, 2, 4, 7, and 14. Adding these factors produces $1 + 2 + 4 + 7 + 14 = 28$. The number 28 is therefore "perfect." A quick check will show you the other choices are not "perfect."

50. Bookstore Sales

By looking at the graph, you should be able to see that the largest amount of money comes from sports ticket sales. Forty percent of the fundraising money comes from this category. The second highest amount of money is represented by the next largest section of the circle graph, bookstore sales. Twenty-five percent of the fundraising money comes from bookstore sales.

51. (D)

Being told "All dogs bark," means that "If it is a dog, then it barks." All we know about Sparky is that he barks. This does not guarantee that he's a dog. For instance, he could be a parrot that's been trained to bark or a child that is imitating the bark of a dog. Consequently, there is no conclusion that can be drawn, so the answer must be (D).

52. Triangle X

Imagine folding the graph along the *x*-axis. If you did, triangle X would be the reflection or mirror image of $\triangle DEF$. Triangle Z is incorrect because it is a reflection around the *y*-axis. Triangle Y is incorrect because it is a reflection around the line $y = -x$.

53. (D)

Standard deviation is a measure of how widely each number in a set varies from the mean. Without calculating the standard deviation for each set, you should be able to see that the numbers in choice (D) vary much more widely than the numbers in any other set. The range of the first set is $9 - 5 = 4$ units. The range of the second set is $12 - 4 = 8$ units. The range of the third set is $20 - 15 = 5$ units. The range of the last set is $66 - 9 = 57$ units. Therefore, (D) has the largest standard deviation.

54. (C)

The distinct positive factors of 11 are only 1 and 11, and $1 \times 11 = 11$. Similarly, the only distinct positive factors of

5 are 1 and 5, whose product is 5. On the other hand, the distinct positive factors of 6 are 1, 2, 3, and 6, and $1 \times 2 \times 3 \times 6 = 36$, which is considerably larger than 5 or 11. The distinct positive factors of 8 are 1, 2, 4, and 8, and $1 \times 2 \times 4 \times 8 = 64$. Hence, (C) is the right answer.

55. (A)

A set is well defined if it is clear what elements make up the set. This is true of the set $\{x \mid x$ is an even number$\}$ because an even number can easily be defined and elements from the set can easily be listed. The choices for II and III are not well defined because they are too subjective.

56. (D)

Knowing the first two cards are diamonds affects the number of cards left (50 instead of 52) but does not affect the number of spades. For the third card, there are 13 spades out of a total of 50 remaining cards, so the probability of the third card being a spade is $\frac{13}{50}$.

57. (B)

The *x*-intercepts of a function are where the function equals zero, so set the function equal to zero and factor to find the answer:

$$f(x) = x^2 - x - 12$$
$$0 = x^2 - x - 12$$
$$0 = (x + 3)(x - 4)$$

This tells us that the function equals zero when either $x + 3 = 0$ or $x - 4 = 0$. Solving these equations produces the values $x = -3$ or $x = 4$.

58. (B)

Solve each inequality:

$4n \leq 20; n \leq 5$

$n - 1 > -10; n > -9$

So the range of possible values of *n* is $-9 < n \leq 5$ or $(-9, 5]$. Note that the closed bracket symbol "]" means that 5 is included in the range. The open bracket symbol "(" before −9 means that −9 is *not* included in the range.

59. 89

The mode of a data set is the number, or response, that appears most often. In this case, it may help to put the numbers in order.

75, 85, 88, 89, 89, 89, 91, 91, 92

It is now clear that the mode is 89. It appears three times in this set, more than any other number.

60. Rectangle A

A translation of a figure on a graph slides the figure horizontally, vertically, or both. It does not rotate or resize figures on a graph. The only rectangle that keeps the size and shape of rectangle *WXYZ* constant and simply moves it down and to the left is rectangle A. Rectangle B is not the same size and shape as rectangle *WXYZ*. Rectangle C is rotated and therefore cannot be a translation of rectangle *WXYZ*.

The CLEP Humanities Exam

Chapter Twelve: **Practice Test 1: Diagnostic**

Time—90 minutes
140 Questions

Directions: For each of the following questions or incomplete statements, select the best answer or completion from the five options given.

1. Doric columns are a characteristic trait of which architectural period?

    (A) Prehistoric
    (B) Gothic
    (C) Postmodern
    (D) Modern
    (E) Classical

2. Which of the following is characteristic of Byzantine architecture?

    (A) Eclecticism of styles
    (B) Simplicity of design
    (C) Ornamention and complexity
    (D) Elimination of unnecessary details
    (E) Emphasis on vertical and horizontal lines

3. Sigmund Freud had a profound impact on which literary movement?

    (A) Modern
    (B) Victorian
    (C) Restoration
    (D) Romantic
    (E) Renaissance

Questions 4–6 refer to the following people.

    (A) Immanuel Kant, David Hume, Voltaire
    (B) Ted Hughes, Robert Browning, Edmund Spenser
    (C) Auguste Rodin, Henri Matisse, Jean-Auguste Dominique Ingres
    (D) Frank Lloyd Wright, Buckminster Fuller, Louis Sullivan
    (E) Paul Verlaine, Paul Valery, Simone de Beauvoir

4. Which group consists of American architects?

5. Which is the only group that does NOT consist of three people from the same country?

GO ON TO THE NEXT PAGE

KAPLAN

6. Which group consists of figures from the eighteenth century?

7. In art, a dark shape outlined against a brighter background is called a(n)

    (A) shadow.

    (B) silhouette.

    (C) underpainting.

    (D) trompe l'oeil.

    (E) watermark.

8. Which type of music contains the descriptive term *bel canto*?

    (A) Chamber music

    (B) Orchestral music

    (C) Opera

    (D) Jazz

    (E) Church music

9. The Romantic composer Frédéric Chopin is best known for composing music to accompany what type of dance?

    (A) Minuet

    (B) Allemande

    (C) Bagatelle

    (D) Cakewalk

    (E) Waltz

10. Which of the following poets is famous for his or her poetic "Essays"?

    (A) Sappho

    (B) Alexander Pope

    (C) Pindar

    (D) Marina Tsvetayeva

    (E) Octavio Paz

11. In musical terminology, a movement means

    (A) a section.

    (B) a tone.

    (C) parallel motion.

    (D) tempo.

    (E) faster motion.

12. Which of the following works was written in Old English?

    (A) *The Winter's Tale*

    (B) "A Valediction Forbidding Mourning"

    (C) *Beowulf*

    (D) *To the Lighthouse*

    (E) *White Teeth*

13. "When the evening is spread out against the sky Like a patient etherised upon a table;" This is an example of which of the following?

    (A) Metaphor

    (B) Synecdoche

    (C) Synesthesia

    (D) Simile

    (E) Couplet

GO ON TO THE NEXT PAGE ▷

Photograph by Steve Vidler. Courtesy of SuperStock, Inc.

14. Based on the picture above, which of the following structures was the chief preoccupation of Gothic architecture?

    (A) Bridge

    (B) Cathedral

    (C) Triumphal arch

    (D) Lighthouse

    (E) Aqueduct

15. Which of the following would best describe the Rococo period?

    (A) Expressionistic, esoteric

    (B) Devotional, sacred

    (C) Somber, stark

    (D) Political, agenda driven

    (E) Voluptuous, lighthearted

16. Illusionism came into prominence in which period?

    (A) Hellenic

    (B) Baroque

    (C) Romantic

    (D) Postmodern

    (E) Modern

17. What do Max Ernst, El Greco, Mary Cassatt, and Marc Chagall all have in common?

    (A) They all started out as architects.

    (B) They all worked in the Impressionist period.

    (C) Their primary medium was watercolor.

    (D) They all made their reputations as expatriates.

    (E) They all based their works on the relationship between mother and child.

18. Which bold experimental film did Alfred Hitchcock create to appear as though it had been shot as a single continuous take?

    (A) *Rope*

    (B) *Rear Window*

    (C) *Vertigo*

    (D) *Shadow of a Doubt*

    (E) *Sabotage*

Questions 19–21 refer to the following people.

    (A) D. H. Lawrence, Thomas Hardy, Rudyard Kipling

    (B) Ezra Pound, Marianne Moore, Emily Dickinson

    (C) Henrik Ibsen, Anton Chekhov, August Strindberg

    (D) Jacques Derrida, Paul de Man, Helen Cixous

    (E) Edward Gibbon, Suetonius, Herodotus

19. Which of these is a group of historians?

20. Which of these is a group of authors who were both poets and novelists?

21. Which of these is a group of dramatists?

GO ON TO THE NEXT PAGE

22. Which of the following philosophers influenced the French Revolutionaries?

    (A) Jean-Paul Sartre and Claude Levi-Strauss
    (B) Henri Bergson and Jan Husserl
    (C) Voltaire and Henri Rousseau
    (D) Marcus Aurelius and Thomas Hobbes
    (E) The Buddha and Bertrand Russell

23. This American journalist was also known as the father of American landscape architecture.

    (A) Frederick Law Olmsted
    (B) Joseph Paxton
    (C) John Dobson
    (D) Welton Becket
    (E) Adolf Behne

24. Which of the following writer's life and work is associated with the painter Pablo Picasso?

    (A) Robert Browning
    (B) Emily Bronte
    (C) Gertrude Stein
    (D) Jane Austen
    (E) Eudora Welty

25. A term used to denote "background" music is

    (A) gala.
    (B) furniture music.
    (C) skating music.
    (D) gamelan.
    (E) fusion.

26. Of the following, which story has NOT been made into a ballet?

    (A) *Carmen*
    (B) *Don Quixote*
    (C) "Sleeping Beauty"
    (D) "Scheherazade"
    (E) "Goldilocks and the Three Bears"

27. *Troy*, Wolfgang Petersen's 2004 film starring Brad Pitt and Orlando Bloom, is based on which work of classical Greek literature?

    (A) *History of the Peloponnesian War*, by Thucydides
    (B) *Iliad*, by Homer
    (C) *The Art of War*, by Sun Tzu
    (D) *Oedipus Rex*, by Sophocles
    (E) *Odyssey*, by Homer

28. Which of the following might be a synonym for *hubris*?

    (A) Intelligence
    (B) Empathy
    (C) Regret
    (D) Pride
    (E) Reticence

29. Which of the following artists was known simply as "M," short for Michelangelo Merisi?

    (A) Dubuffet
    (B) Rivera
    (C) Caravaggio
    (D) Gentileschi
    (E) Picasso

Questions 30–32 refer to the following playwrights.

    (A) August Wilson
    (B) Lope de Vega
    (C) George Bernard Shaw
    (D) Friedrich von Schiller
    (E) John Osborne

30. Which of these playwrights is NOT European?

31. Which of these playwrights was a contemporary of Johann von Goethe?

GO ON TO THE NEXT PAGE ⇒

32. Both the musical and film versions of *My Fair Lady* are based on a work by which of these playwrights?

33. Blanche DuBois is the protagonist of which of the following plays?

    (A) *The Caucasian Chalk Circle*
    (B) *Outward Bound*
    (C) *Six Characters in Search of an Author*
    (D) *Our Town*
    (E) *A Streetcar Named Desire*

34. The term *musique concrète* describes

    (A) a movement away from abstract music.
    (B) a style of composition developed in the Romantic period.
    (C) music using electro-acoustic sounds captured on tape.
    (D) music that is performed before a live audience.
    (E) "furniture music."

35. In music, the term *arco* means that the musicians should

    (A) pluck the strings of their instruments.
    (B) increase the tempo of the music.
    (C) gradually play louder.
    (D) play in unison.
    (E) use their bows in the usual way.

36. John Updike's *Rabbit, Run*, the story of an ordinary man trying to get ahead in his profession, is based upon the similarly themed classic novel *Babbit* written by which writer?

    (A) Theodore Dreiser
    (B) Sinclair Lewis
    (C) Preston Sturges
    (D) Margaret Mitchell
    (E) F. Scott Fitzgerald

37. This memoir, written in a series of volumes, contains many experiences from the narrator's childhood and later life, written with bittersweet regret for time's passing.

    (A) Proust's *Remembrance of Things Past*
    (B) Wolfe's *You Can't Go Home Again*
    (C) Austen's *Northanger Abbey*
    (D) Woolf's *Mrs. Dalloway*
    (E) Didion's *Slouching Towards Bethlehem*

38. Siblings from this Victorian family were noted for their stirring, often socially astute romantic novels set in the secluded English countryside.

    (A) Bronte
    (B) James
    (C) Rossetti
    (D) Austen
    (E) Shelley

39. The play and movie *Amadeus* are based on the life of which noted composer?

    (A) Bach
    (B) Mozart
    (C) Beethoven
    (D) Strauss
    (E) Wagner

40. Which style of dance began in the fifteenth century as an interpretation of fencing?

    (A) Bassadance
    (B) Pavane
    (C) Ballet
    (D) Galliard
    (E) Bagatelle

GO ON TO THE NEXT PAGE

KAPLAN

41. Alexander Pope, Sir Joshua Reynolds, and Johann Sebastian Bach were all considered part of what eighteenth-century movement?

    (A) Restoration

    (B) Enlightenment

    (C) Neoclassical

    (D) Elizabethan

    (E) Renaissance

42. The eighteenth-century philosopher Diderot's *Memoirs of a Nun* famously attacked

    (A) capitalism.

    (B) Martin Luther's 95 Theses.

    (C) atheism.

    (D) religion.

    (E) reason.

43. Which composer was known as the Master of the Symphony?

    (A) Johann Sebastian Bach

    (B) Claude Debussy

    (C) Ludwig van Beethoven

    (D) Béla Bartók

    (E) Antonin Dvořák

44. The poet William Carlos Williams and the playwright Anton Chekhov both learned compassion while working at which profession?

    (A) Law

    (B) Missionary work

    (C) Philanthropy

    (D) Farming

    (E) Medicine

45. Which of the following artists is correctly matched to his or her discipline?

    (A) Berthe Morisot . . . etching

    (B) Phidias . . . oil painting

    (C) Fernand Leger . . . architecture

    (D) Frank Lloyd Wright . . . installation art

    (E) Louise Nevelson . . . sculpture

46. In a novel, "roman à clef" involves characters that are

    (A) based on real historical figures.

    (B) unacquainted with each other.

    (C) Italian.

    (D) of mixed ethnicity.

    (E) predominantly female.

47. *Steppenwolfe* and *Siddhartha* are novels by which of the following authors?

    (A) Thomas Mann

    (B) W. G. Sebald

    (C) Günther Grass

    (D) Vladimir Nabokov

    (E) Herman Hesse

48. Which of the following artists was famous for his or her murals?

    (A) Auguste Rodin

    (B) Jenny Holzer

    (C) Christo

    (D) Theodore Gericault

    (E) Diego Rivera

GO ON TO THE NEXT PAGE

Questions 49–51 refer to the following portion of a poem.

THE KNIGHT'S TALE

WHILOM*, as olde stories tellen us,	*formerly
There was a duke that highte* Theseus.	*was called
Of Athens he was lord and governor,	
And in his time such a conqueror	
That greater was there none under the sun.	
Full many a riche country had he won.	
What with his wisdom and his chivalry,	
He conquer'd all the regne of Feminie,	
That whilom was y-cleped* Scythia;	*called
And weddede the Queen Hippolyta	
And brought her home with him to his country	
With muchel* glory and great solemnity,	*great
And eke her younge sister Emily,	
And thus with vict'ry and with melody	
Let I this worthy Duke to Athens ride,	
And all his host, in armes him beside.	

49. What type of language is the poem written in?

    (A) Gaelic
    (B) Standard English
    (C) Old Earlton
    (D) Middle English
    (E) American

50. Who is the author of this tale?

    (A) Sir Arthur Conan Doyle
    (B) Henrik Ibsen
    (C) Christopher Marlowe
    (D) William Shakespeare
    (E) Geoffrey Chaucer

51. What is the name of another part of *The Canterbury Tales*?

    (A) "The Second Nun's Tale"
    (B) "The Mariner's Tale"
    (C) "The Princess' Tale"
    (D) "The King's Tale"
    (E) "The Midwife's Tale"

52. Which of the following poets did NOT compose his major work in Latin?

    (A) Ovid
    (B) Virgil
    (C) Terence
    (D) Catullus
    (E) Dante

53. Which modern classical composer composed *The Rite of Spring*?

    (A) Ludwig van Beethoven
    (B) Igor Stravinsky
    (C) Franz Schubert
    (D) Leo Delibes
    (E) David Oistrakh

54. A sonata is a

    (A) musical form created by Wolfgang Amadeus Mozart.
    (B) piece that is played prior to the entrance of the principal characters in a play.
    (C) short piece that is played as the melody of an opera.
    (D) composition in three or four different movements, using one or more solo instruments.
    (E) tragic melody sung by the principal actor of a play.

55. The term *mise en scène*, as it applies to theater and film, refers to

    (A) the narrative aspects of a story.
    (B) the dialogue spoken by the actors.
    (C) the preproduction rehearsals of scenes.
    (D) the theme that underlies the action.
    (E) the visual composition of a play or film.

GO ON TO THE NEXT PAGE

KAPLAN

56. Orson Welles made his cinematic masterpiece, *Citizen Kane*, at age 25. For his next film, he adapted Booth Tarkington's 1918 Pulitzer Prize-winning novel. The film and novel are titled

    (A) *The Magnificent Ambersons.*

    (B) *Alice Adams.*

    (C) *Touch of Evil.*

    (D) *The Age of Innocence.*

    (E) *The Hours.*

57. During which holiday does *The Nutcracker* take place?

    (A) Thanksgiving

    (B) Christmas

    (C) Easter

    (D) Bastille Day

    (E) New Year's Eve

58. Which composer, who wrote primarily for the piano, is known for his use of ambiguous chords and unconventional clashes of melody?

    (A) George Gershwin

    (B) Aaron Copland

    (C) Antonio Vivaldi

    (D) Frédéric Chopin

    (E) Wolfgang Amadeus Mozart

59. The Blue Rider and The Bridge were both expressionistic movements in

    (A) Ireland.

    (B) Australia.

    (C) Germany.

    (D) the United States.

    (E) India.

60. Which of the following is NOT associated with the painter Vincent van Gogh?

    (A) Sunflowers

    (B) Paul Gauguin

    (C) Self-portraits

    (D) Madness

    (E) Elongated faces

61. Which of the following painters was a member of the Pre-Raphaelite brotherhood?

    (A) Claude Monet

    (B) Dante Gabriel Rossetti

    (C) Amedeo Modigliani

    (D) Alberto Giacometti

    (E) Damien Hirst

Questions 62–64 refer to the following people.

    (A) Ludwig van Beethoven, William Wordsworth, Eugene Delacroix

    (B) Arnold Schoenberg, Gertrude Stein, Pablo Picasso

    (C) Wolfgang Amadeus Mozart, Samuel Johnson, Sir Joshua Reynolds

    (D) Phillip Glass, Rita Dove, Chuck Close

    (E) Claudio Monteverdi, William Shakespeare, Caravaggio

62. Which is a group of modernists?

63. Which group worked in the eighteenth century?

64. Which group consists of Romantics?

GO ON TO THE NEXT PAGE

65. Max Ernst, Mark Rothko, and Willem De Kooning all emigrated from their native countries to live and work in

    (A) the United States.
    (B) Spain.
    (C) Algeria.
    (D) Australia.
    (E) Tahiti.

66. Which of the following matches the writer to his or her discipline?

    (A) Czeslaw Milosz . . . philosopher
    (B) Rabindranath Tagore . . . novelist
    (C) George Santayana . . . dramatist
    (D) W. H. Auden . . . poet
    (E) Flannery O'Connor . . . journalist

67. Contemporary writers Ann Beattie, Raymond Carver, and Lori Moore are best known for which kind of fiction?

    (A) Essays
    (B) Memoirs
    (C) Novels
    (D) Historical fiction
    (E) Short stories

68. A novel written in the second person addresses the reader with which pronoun?

    (A) We
    (B) I
    (C) You
    (D) Us
    (E) He or she

Questions 69–71 refer to the following terms.

    (A) Aside
    (B) Play within the play
    (C) Soliloquy
    (D) Tableau vivant
    (E) Prologue

69. Which is spoken before the beginning of a play?

70. Which involves an actor, alone on stage, giving a speech to the audience?

71. The players' performing *The Murder of Gonzago* in Shakespeare's *Hamlet* is an example of what?

72. Which of the following artists is a key figure in the photorealism movement?

    (A) Artimesia Gentileschi
    (B) Phillip Guston
    (C) Max Ernst
    (D) Hans Holbein
    (E) Chuck Close

73. Which of the following is a famous tragicomic figure often painted by Rococo artists like Jean-Antoine Watteau?

    (A) Mephistopheles
    (B) Pierrot
    (C) Aphrodite
    (D) Rasputin
    (E) Bismarck

GO ON TO THE NEXT PAGE

KAPLAN

74. A pas de deux is a dance for how many people?

    (A) Two

    (B) Three

    (C) Four

    (D) Five

    (E) One

75. Which of the following people is NOT associated with existentialism?

    (A) Albert Camus

    (B) Jean-Paul Sartre

    (C) Soren Kierkegaard

    (D) Samuel Beckett

    (E) Blaise Pascal

76. Which of the following figures are from the nineteenth century?

    (A) Friedrich Nietzsche, Lord Byron, Richard Wagner

    (B) Plutarch, Marcus Aurelius, Galen

    (C) Rene Descartes, John Milton, Aphra Behn

    (D) Montesquieu, Edward Gibbon, George Handel

    (E) Hannah Arendt, Jhumpa Lahiri, Merce Cunningham

77. Mark Twain's Huckleberry Finn has his adventures on and along which of the following rivers?

    (A) Ohio River

    (B) Snake River

    (C) Mississippi River

    (D) Missouri River

    (E) Po River

Questions 78–80 refer to the following novels.

    (A) *The House of the Seven Gables*

    (B) *Moby-Dick*

    (C) *Beloved*

    (D) *Fathers and Sons*

    (E) *A Connecticut Yankee in King Arthur's Court*

78. Which of these novels was NOT written in the nineteenth century?

79. Which of these novels was NOT written by an American?

80. Which of these novels was written by Nathaniel Hawthorne?

81. The novel *A Day in the Life of Ivan Denisovich* by Aleksandr Solzhenitsyn takes place

    (A) in the Gulag (Russian prison camp).

    (B) in an upscale Moscow neighborhood.

    (C) in a cemetery.

    (D) during the Napoleonic wars.

    (E) in a Cossack village.

82. Thomas Hardy's novels and poems are marked by

    (A) pessimism and resignation.

    (B) joie de vivre and optimism.

    (C) mysticism and imagination.

    (D) technology and futurism.

    (E) indifference and apathy.

GO ON TO THE NEXT PAGE ⇨

Questions 83 and 84 refer to the following.

In classical music, tempo marks are used to indicate a steady rate of speed, an acceleration, or a slackening in speed. Identify the following in relation to these indications.

83. *Largo* means

   (A) increasing rapidity.
   (B) twice as fast.
   (C) a slow, steady tempo.
   (D) a walking tempo.
   (E) a moderate tempo.

84. *Tardando* means to

   (A) speed up quickly.
   (B) gradually grow slower.
   (C) gradually speed up.
   (D) grow slower and softer.
   (E) be slower than the preceding movement.

85. Which Indian filmmaker known for his Apu trilogy brought international attention to Indian cinema for the first time in its history?

   (A) Satyajit Ray
   (B) Raj Kapoor
   (C) Bimal Roy
   (D) Guru Dutt
   (E) Mebeeb Khan

86. *The Persistence of Memory* is all of the following EXCEPT

   (A) a Surrealist work.
   (B) a painting by Salvadore Dali.
   (C) a landscape with timepieces.
   (D) a twentieth-century work.
   (E) a mosaic.

87. The word *Dada*

   (A) refers to a city in Switzerland.
   (B) means "ancient" in Old English.
   (C) has no meaning.
   (D) means "liberty" in French.
   (E) refers to a Norse God.

88. Which of the following books was illustrated by the author?

   (A) William Faulkner's *Absalom, Absalom*
   (B) William Blake's *The Marriage of Heaven and Hell*
   (C) Flannery O'Connor's *The Violent Bear it Away*
   (D) Ludovico Ariosto's *Orlando Furioso*
   (E) Sharon Olds' *The Dead and the Living*

Courtesy of SuperStock, Inc.

89. The *Birth of Venus*, shown here, is a painting by which of the following artists?

   (A) Edvard Munch
   (B) Sandro Botticelli
   (C) Christo
   (D) Edward Hopper
   (E) Sonia Delaunay

GO ON TO THE NEXT PAGE

KAPLAN

90. Wole Soyinka's *The Strong Breed* takes place on which continent?

    (A) Asia
    (B) North America
    (C) Africa
    (D) Australia
    (E) Europe

91. The poems and novels of D. H. Lawrence are most concerned with what subject?

    (A) Children
    (B) Politics
    (C) Injustice
    (D) Sexuality
    (E) Life in the big city

92. *Satyricon* and *La Dolce Vita* are two of the films made by which internationally acclaimed Italian filmmaker?

    (A) Michelangelo Antonioni
    (B) Bernardo Bertolucci
    (C) Sergio Leone
    (D) Roberto Rossellini
    (E) Federico Fellini

93. Which of the following novels begins with a long poem?

    (A) Vladimir Nabokov's *Pale Fire*
    (B) Herman Melville's *Moby-Dick*
    (C) F. Scott Fitzgerald's *The Great Gatsby*
    (D) Aldous Huxley's *Brave New World*
    (E) Emily Bronte's *Wuthering Heights*

94. Lorraine Hansberry's depiction of an African-American family's struggle to survive and flourish in an urban world is entitled

    (A) *for colored girls who have considered suicide/ when the rainbow is enuf.*
    (B) *Broken Glass.*
    (C) *West Side Story.*
    (D) *A Raisin in the Sun.*
    (E) "Sonny's Blues."

95. Jack Kerouac's *On the Road* and Allen Ginsberg's "Howl" are landmark works from

    (A) the Restoration period.
    (B) the Beat generation.
    (C) the Fugitive poets.
    (D) the Imagists.
    (E) the Dadaist Conference in Zurich.

96. Henri Matisse, Vincent van Gogh, and Pablo Picasso are all considered to be

    (A) Cubists.
    (B) Post-Impressionists.
    (C) Impressionists.
    (D) Minimalists.
    (E) Color Field painters.

GO ON TO THE NEXT PAGE

Courtesy of SuperStock, Inc.

97. Which of the following painters is best known for his rotund and rosy nudes, as in his painting shown here?

    (A) Claude Monet
    (B) Jean-Michel Basquiat
    (C) Jacob Lawrence
    (D) Peter Paul Rubens
    (E) Willem de Kooning

98. Robert Frost's poetry can best be described as a blend of

    (A) Surrealism and fascism.
    (B) free verse and Greek drama.
    (C) Romanticism and Rococo hedonism.
    (D) mysticism and colloquial wisdom.
    (E) cosmopolitanism and elitism.

99. Satan is the protagonist of which of the following works?

    (A) *The Canterbury Tales*
    (B) *Paradise Lost*
    (C) *The Alchemist*
    (D) *1984*
    (E) *Love in the Time of Cholera*

100. Thomas Gray's "Elegy Written in a Country Churchyard" sings the praises of

    (A) technology.
    (B) peasant folk.
    (C) royalty.
    (D) continental philosophy.
    (E) priests.

101. Which of the following would be considered a picaresque novel?

    (A) *Pride and Prejudice*
    (B) *The Color Purple*
    (C) *Tom Jones*
    (D) *Diary of a Superfluous Man*
    (E) *The Recognitions*

102. David Hume famously contested standing theories of

    (A) time and space.
    (B) historical materialism.
    (C) cause and effect.
    (D) supply and demand.
    (E) moral relativism.

GO ON TO THE NEXT PAGE

103. Which late Romantic-era composer was a contemporary of the philosopher Friedrich Nietzsche?

    (A) Dmitri Shostakovich (1906–1975)
    (B) Wolfgang Amadeus Mozart (1756–1791)
    (C) Niccolo Paganini (1782–1840)
    (D) Johannes Brahms (1833–1897)
    (E) Robert Fayrfax (1464–1521)

104. "A cappella" is a form used in which type of music?

    (A) Choral
    (B) Orchestral
    (C) Jazz
    (D) Bebop
    (E) Opera

105. Margot Fonteyn, Darci Kissler, and Mikhail Baryshnikov are all best known as

    (A) composers.
    (B) jazz musicians.
    (C) modern dancers.
    (D) ballet dancers.
    (E) novelists.

106. Which of Ludwig van Beethoven's symphonies is often described as "Fate knocking at the door?"

    (A) Ninth
    (B) Fifth
    (C) First
    (D) *Eroica*
    (E) *Pastoral*

107. Which of the following is a novel written by Jane Austen?

    (A) *Daniel Deronda*
    (B) *Wuthering Heights*
    (C) *Frankenstein*
    (D) *The Yellow Wallpaper*
    (E) *Sense and Sensibility*

108. Which of the following novels is recounted by a recluse from his basement apartment?

    (A) *Diary of a Superfluous Man*
    (B) *Invisible Man*
    (C) *Man Walks into a Room*
    (D) *Man's Fate*
    (E) *The Man Without Qualities*

109. Which of the following plays was NOT written by Aristophanes?

    (A) *The Iliad*
    (B) *The Frogs*
    (C) *The Knights*
    (D) *The Clouds*
    (E) *Lysistrata*

110. What is the title of Niccolo Machiavelli's most famous work?

    (A) *Being and Time*
    (B) *The Will as Representation*
    (C) *Civilization and its Discontents*
    (D) *The Prince*
    (E) *The Raw and the Cooked*

GO ON TO THE NEXT PAGE

111. Robert Browning's "My Last Duchess" and "Porphyria's Lover" are

    (A) sonnets.

    (B) romances.

    (C) epics.

    (D) sestinas.

    (E) dramatic monologues.

112. Which of the following lines are taken from Matthew Arnold's "Dover Beach"?

    (A) "Where ignorant armies clash by night"

    (B) "To strive, to seek, to find, and not to yield."

    (C) "How can we know the dancer from the dance?"

    (D) "Because I could not stop for Death—"

    (E) "The old lie: Dulce et decorum est/Pro patria mori."

113. Whose famous maxim was "No ideas but in things"?

    (A) Robert Frost

    (B) Anna Akhmatova

    (C) Gwendolyn Brooks

    (D) William Carlos Williams

    (E) Oscar Wilde

Courtesy of SuperStock, Inc.

Questions 114–116 refer to the sculpture shown here.

114. The sculptor of the piece is

    (A) Donatello.

    (B) Bernini.

    (C) Michelangelo.

    (D) Ghiberti.

    (E) Verrochio.

115. The piece was produced in which of the following periods?

    (A) Renaissance

    (B) Baroque

    (C) Postmodern

    (D) Romantic

    (E) Hellenic

GO ON TO THE NEXT PAGE

116. The sculptor's attitude toward the human form resembles

    (A) Alberto Giacommetti's.
    (B) Jean Arp's.
    (C) Henri Matisse's.
    (D) Fernand Botero's.
    (E) Phidias'.

117. Which of the following is NOT a poem?

    (A) *The Faerie Queene*
    (B) "Song of Myself"
    (C) *As I Lay Dying*
    (D) "Howl"
    (E) "Skunk Hour"

Questions 118–120 refer to the following poem.

Let me not to the marriage of true minds
Admit impediments; love is not love
Which alters when it alteration finds,
Or bends with the remover to remove:
O, no, it is an ever-fixed mark,
That looks on tempests and is never shaken;
It is the star to every wand'ring bark,
Whose worth's unknown, although his highth be taken.
Love's not Time's fool, though rosy lips and cheeks
Within his bending sickle's compass come;
Love alters not with his brief hours and weeks,
But bears it out even to the edge of doom.
If this be error and upon me proved,
I never writ, nor no man ever loved.

118. Who is the author of this work?

    (A) William Shakespeare
    (B) John Milton
    (C) Djuna Barnes
    (D) Boris Pasternak
    (E) Robert Browning

119. What sort of poem is this?

    (A) Villanelle
    (B) Sestina
    (C) Epic
    (D) Sonnet
    (E) Rondeau

120. Which might best paraphrase the lines ". . . love is not love/Which alters when it alteration finds"?

    (A) Love is fickle.
    (B) Infidelity is the inevitable outcome of a romantic relationship.
    (C) Love is constant, come what may.
    (D) Love is like stitching trousers.
    (E) Love changes and changes and changes ad infinitum.

121. Which of the following would be considered an epic poem?

    (A) *The Faerie Queene* by Edmund Spenser
    (B) "In a Station of the Metro" by Ezra Pound
    (C) "The Man-Moth" by Elizabeth Bishop
    (D) "America" by Allen Ginsberg
    (E) "Ulysses" by Alfred Lord Tennyson

122. Samuel Beckett's *Waiting for Godot* is which type of play?

    (A) Realist
    (B) Romantic
    (C) Absurdist
    (D) Anarchist
    (E) Comedy of manners

GO ON TO THE NEXT PAGE

123. In which of the following ballets does the Sugar Plum Fairy appear?

    (A) *Swan Lake*

    (B) *Coppelia*

    (C) *Peter and the Wolf*

    (D) *The Nutcracker*

    (E) *Sleeping Beauty*

124. Goya's later paintings can best be described as

    (A) optimistic and joyful.

    (B) bleak and disturbing.

    (C) diffuse and colorless.

    (D) natural and authentic.

    (E) sane and moralistic.

125. Tony Kushner's *Angels in America* confronts the tragedy of

    (A) poverty.

    (B) AIDS.

    (C) suicide.

    (D) terrorism.

    (E) genocide.

126. *La Giocanda* is another name for which of the following paintings?

    (A) *The Scream*

    (B) *The Blue Boy*

    (C) *Mona Lisa*

    (D) *Self-Portrait in a Convex Mirror*

    (E) *Impression: Sunrise*

Used by permission. See copyright page (iv) for information.

Questions 127–129 refer to the painting shown here.

127. Who is the artist?

    (A) Emily Carr

    (B) Pablo Picasso

    (C) Goya

    (D) Eugene Delacroix

    (E) Paul Klee

128. What is the subject of this painting?

    (A) Religion

    (B) Philanthropy

    (C) War

    (D) Sport

    (E) Democracy

129. In which century was this work produced?

    (A) Fifteenth

    (B) Sixteenth

    (C) Eighteenth

    (D) Nineteenth

    (E) Twentieth

GO ON TO THE NEXT PAGE

KAPLAN

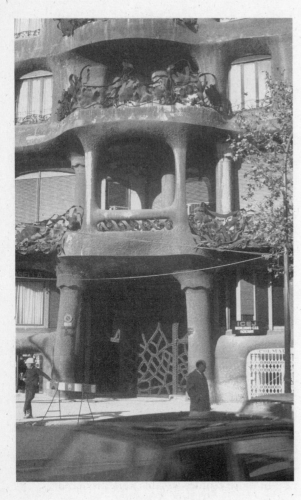

*Casa Mila © 2006
Howard Davis/Great Buildings.com. Used by permission.*

130. The architecture of Antoni Gaudi, as shown here, could best be described as

(A) amorphous.

(B) geometric.

(C) Cubist.

(D) minimalist.

(E) utilitarian.

131. Which of the following novels was NOT written by Henry James?

(A) *The Ambassadors*

(B) *Daisy Miller*

(C) *The Golden Bowl*

(D) *Portrait of a Lady*

(E) *This Side of Paradise*

132. Which of the following novelists is/was most prolific?

(A) Malcolm Lowry

(B) J. D. Salinger

(C) Djuna Barnes

(D) Joyce Carol Oates

(E) Ralph Ellison

133. Which of the following musicians wrote *The Well-Tempered Clavier* in 1722?

(A) Johann Sebastian Bach

(B) Aaron Copland

(C) Antonio Salieri

(D) Emmanuel Ax

(E) Isaac Stern

134. Of the following operas, which were written by Wolfgang Amadeus Mozart?

(A) *La Boheme, Madame Butterfly*

(B) *The Tales of Hoffman, Orpheus in the Underworld*

(C) *Don Giovanni, The Marriage of Figaro*

(D) *William Tell, The Barber of Seville*

(E) *Salome, Elektra*

GO ON TO THE NEXT PAGE

135. Which of the following works does NOT deal with the horrors of war?

    (A) "In Parenthesis"

    (B) *The Red Badge of Courage*

    (C) "Dulce et Decorum est"

    (D) *Apocalypse Now*

    (E) *The Jungle*

136. *Poetics* is a philosophical work written by

    (A) Thales of Miletus.

    (B) Pythagoras.

    (C) Aristotle.

    (D) Ptolemy.

    (E) Anaximander.

137. Which of the following adjectives best describes the poetry of William Blake?

    (A) Understated

    (B) Logical

    (C) Prophetic

    (D) Prosaic

    (E) Inhibited

138. What is the setting of Edgar Lee Masters' *Spoon River Anthology*?

    (A) A graveyard

    (B) The desert

    (C) The sea

    (D) An industrial warehouse

    (E) An anonymous city

139. What do Gerard Manley Hopkins and Emily Dickinson have in common?

    (A) They were both conventional poets.

    (B) They were dramatists of the Romantic period.

    (C) They were both largely unpublished in their lifetimes.

    (D) They both used pen names.

    (E) They were both born in the United States.

140. Which of the following is NOT an aspect of the heroic couplet?

    (A) Iambic

    (B) Rhyming

    (C) Consisting of two lines

    (D) Common in Elizabethan poetry

    (E) Common in short stories

END OF TEST. STOP

ANSWER KEY

1. E	21. C	41. B	61. B	81. A	101. C	121. A
2. C	22. C	42. D	62. B	82. A	102. C	122. C
3. A	23. A	43. C	63. C	83. C	103. D	123. D
4. D	24. C	44. E	64. A	84. B	104. A	124. B
5. A	25. B	45. E	65. A	85. A	105. D	125. B
6. A	26. E	46. A	66. D	86. E	106. B	126. C
7. B	27. B	47. E	67. E	87. C	107. E	127. B
8. C	28. D	48. E	68. C	88. B	108. B	128. C
9. E	29. C	49. D	69. E	89. B	109. A	129. E
10. B	30. A	50. E	70. C	90. C	110. D	130. A
11. A	31. D	51. A	71. B	91. D	111. E	131. E
12. C	32. C	52. E	72. E	92. E	112. A	132. D
13. D	33. E	53. B	73. B	93. A	113. D	133. A
14. B	34. C	54. D	74. A	94. D	114. C	134. C
15. E	35. E	55. E	75. E	95. B	115. A	135. E
16. B	36. B	56. A	76. A	96. B	116. E	136. C
17. D	37. A	57. B	77. C	97. D	117. C	137. C
18. A	38. A	58. D	78. C	98. D	118. A	138. A
19. E	39. B	59. C	79. D	99. B	119. D	139. C
20. A	40. C	60. E	80. A	100. B	120. C	140. E

DIAGNOSTIC TEST QUICK REFERENCE TABLES

Use the following tables to determine which topics you need to review most.

Topic	Test Question
Literature	
Drama	21, 28, 30, 31, 33, 44, 69, 70, 71, 90, 94, 109, 122, 125
Poetry	13, 49, 50, 51, 52, 88, 98, 99, 100, 111, 112, 117, 118, 119, 120, 121, 137, 139, 140
Fiction	12, 20, 36, 38, 46, 47, 67, 68, 77, 78, 79, 80, 81, 82, 91, 93, 95, 101, 107, 108, 131, 132, 138
Nonfiction/Philosophy	3, 10, 19, 22, 37, 42, 66, 75, 76, 87, 102, 110, 113, 136
The Arts	
Visual Arts (painting, sculpture, etc.)	6, 7, 15, 16, 17, 24, 29, 45, 48, 59, 60, 61, 64, 65, 72, 73, 86, 89, 96, 97, 114, 115, 116, 124, 126, 127, 128, 129
Architecture	1, 2, 4, 5, 14, 23, 130
Music	8, 9, 11, 25, 26, 34, 35, 41, 43, 53, 54, 58, 62, 63, 83, 84, 103, 104, 106, 133, 134
Performing Arts (film, dance, etc.)	18, 27, 32, 39, 40, 55, 56, 57, 74, 85, 92, 105, 123, 135

Topic	Number of Questions on Test	Number Correct
Literature	70	
Drama	14	
Poetry	19	
Fiction	23	
Nonfiction/Philosophy	14	
The Arts	70	
Visual Arts (painting, sculpture, etc.)	28	
Architecture	7	
Music	21	
Performing Arts (film, dance, etc.)	14	

Answers and Explanations

1. (E)

Doric columns are characteristic of the classical style of architecture of ancient Greece. One of the most famous examples of a structure that uses these columns is the Parthenon.

2. (C)

Byzantine architecture is best known for its complexity and ornamentation. Eclecticism (B) is a characteristic of Postmodern architecture. The other choices are most often associated with Modern architecture.

3. (A)

Along with Darwin, Nietzsche, and Einstein, Freud (1856–1939) was a key figure in the break with classical ideas. None of the other choices (except for the very late Victorian period) could have been chronologically possible.

4. (D)

Note that Wright, Fuller, and Sullivan are the only Americans listed. Kant, Hume, and Voltaire (A), were philosophers. Hughes, Browning, and Spenser were poets (B). Rodin, Matisse, and Ingres (C), were artists. Verlaine, Valery, and de Beauvoir (E) were writers and poets.

5. (A)

Kant, Hume, and Voltaire were born in Germany, Scotland, and France respectively. All the other choices include people from the same country, namely England (B), the United States (D), and France [(C) and (E)].

6. (A)

Kant, Hume, and Voltaire all lived during the eighteenth century. Hughes and Browning lived during the nineteenth century, while Spenser lived in the sixteenth century (B). Answer (C) is not correct because Ingres was born in the eighteenth century but did most of his work in the nineteenth. The other figures listed all lived in the nineteenth and twentieth centuries.

7. (B)

Do not confuse a silhouette with a shadow. The dark outline of a silhouette is the result of strong backlighting.

8. (C)

Bel canto literally means "beautiful song" in Italian and always refers to operatic singing.

9. (E)

Chopin is well known for his waltzes for solo piano. He did not compose music for any of the other dances mentioned.

10. (B)

Pope's "Essay on Man" is the most notable and representative of the somewhat dry, clinical approach of the Restoration poets. The work of the other poets could not be termed essaylike.

11. (A)

A section of a classical piece is called a movement. A tone (B) is a distinct pitch. While parallel motion (C) is a tempting choice, this refers to the movement of intervals in the same direction. Tempo (D) refers to the speed at which a piece is played, while faster motion (E) refers to a descent of pitch and melodic ascent.

12. (C)

While *The Winter's Tale* by Shakespeare (A) and "A Valediction Forbidding Mourning" by Donne (B) were written in an older version of present-day English, they are not considered Old English. *White Teeth* by Zadie Smith (E) is a recent novel, and *To the Lighthouse* by Virginia Woolf (D) is a modernist novel from 1927.

13. (D)

The sky being "like" (rather than simply being) an etherized patient makes the quote a simile rather than a metaphor (A). A synecdoche (B) is a part is used for a whole part of speech, and vice versa. Synesthesia (C) is the use of words that normally describe one sense impression (such as vision) to describe another (such as hearing). A couplet (E) is a unit of two lines of verse that usually rhyme and express a complete thought.

14. (B)

While Gothic architects did not relegate themselves to the erection of a single type of edifice, their central concern was the glorification of God with grand and imposing cathedrals. None of the other choices were central to Gothic architecture.

15. (E)

The Rococo period was the first flourishing of art for art's sake and was sensual and celebratory. The period was far from stark and somber (C), and it did not express overtones of religion (B) or politics (D). The Rococo period was not esoteric (A): it was not meant to be understood by only a small group of people.

16. (B)

Illusionist painters use foreshortening and perspective to create images that trick the eye. Although most of the periods mentioned make use of certain elements of illusionism, the technique came into prominence during the Baroque period.

17. (D)

All of the people mentioned were painters, but not all of them worked during the Impressionist period (B), primarily used watercolor (C), or based their work on the relationship between mother and child (E). However. they all left the country of their birth, so the correct answer is (D).

18. (A)

The other films listed are also works by Hitchcock but were not created to appear as if they were shot in a single continuous take. *Rope* was Hitchcock's first film as a producer, and it was shot in scenes of ten minutes without cuts in between the scenes.

19. (E)

Some of the literary critics listed in the other answer choices may have done some historical work, and Pound's poetry is steeped in history, but none would be considered historians. Lawrence, Hardy, and Kipling were poets and novelists (A). Pound, Moore, and Dickinson were poets (B). Answer (C), Ibsen, Chekhov, and Strindberg, consists of dramatists. Answer (D), Derrida, de Man, and Cixous, includes literary critics and theorists.

20. (A)

D. H. Lawrence and Rudyard Kipling were prominent novelists who also made a name for themselves as poets. Thomas Hardy was prominent as a novelist and as a poet in the late nineteenth and early twentieth centuries.

21. (C)

Henrik Ibsen, Anton Chekhov, and August Strindberg are three of the most influential playwrights in the modern theater.

22. (C)

Voltaire and Henri Rousseau are representative of the nineteenth century's demand for equality and rights regardless of class or birth. Jean-Paul Sartre was a twentieth-century philosopher, while Claude Levi-Strauss (A) is a modern anthropologist. Both Henri Bergson and Jan Husserl (B) were philosophers of the late nineteenth and early twentieth centuries. Marcus Aurelius was a Roman emperor, while Thomas Hobbes was a seventeenth-century English philosopher (D). The Buddha created the religion of Buddhism in the sixth century B.C.E., and Bertrand Russell was a twentieth-century logician (E).

23. (A)

Frederick Law Olmsted is known as the father of landscape architecture and is famous for designing Central Park in New York City.

24. (C)

A knowledge of life chronologies will help you deduce that there are only two real options. Robert Browning (A), Emily Bronte (B), and Jane Austen (D) did not live at the same time as Picasso. Eudora Welty (E), who was Picasso's contemporary, had no contact or affinity with the artist.

25. (B)

Furniture music is a term created by the composer Erik Satie to denote "background" music. A gala (A) is a festive occasion, skating music (C) is played while a person is skating, and a gamelan (D) is an Indonesian orchestra of primarily percussion instruments. Fusion (E), in reference to music, describes the blending of two or more styles, especially jazz and rock.

26. (E)

"Goldilocks and the Three Bears" is the only story listed that has not been made into a ballet.

27. (B)

Homer's *Iliad* is an epic poem nearly three thousand years old that tells of the legendary war between the Greeks and the people of Troy. *History of the Peloponnesian War* (B) was written by Thucydides in 431 B.C.E. *The Art of War* (C) was written by the Chinese author Sun Tzu. Sophocles' *Oedipus Rex* (D) is a play about Oedipus, the king of Thebes. Homer's *Odyssey* (E) recounts the adventures of King Odysseus on his return home from the Trojan War.

28. (D)

Hubris means pride, particularly in relation to defiance of the gods. The other terms have no relation to *hubris*.

29. (C)

Caravaggio's given name was Michelangelo, shortened to "M" by his compatriots and many art historians.

30. (A)

August Wilson is an African-American playwright of the late twentieth and early twenty-first centuries. Lope de Vega (B) was from Spain, George Bernard Shaw (C) was a native of Ireland, Friedrich von Schiller (D) hailed from Germany, and John Osborne (E) was from England.

31. (D)

Friedrich von Schiller was a close friend of Goethe, and the two of them were largely responsible for the German Romantic movement. None of the other playwrights listed were contemporaries of Goethe.

32. (C)

George Bernard Shaw's *Pygmalion* was the inspiration for the popular musical *My Fair Lady*, which was made into a film in 1964. In *Pygmalion*, Eliza Doolittle is tutored by professor Henry Higgins on the refinement of her speech and manner. Both works comment upon the complexities of human relationships in a social context.

33. (E)

Blanche DuBois, the quintessential faded Southern belle, is the protagonist in *A Streetcar Named Desire* by Tennessee Williams.

34. (C)

Musique concrète is an early- to mid-twentieth century technique that describes the organization of sound using electro-acoustic material that is captured on tape. Knowing the time period relevant to this technique might allow you to make an educated guess based on the technology that it makes use of.

35. (E)

The term *arco* in music lets string players know that they should use their bows in the usual way. The term comes from the shape that the strings make over the sound board of traditional instruments in the string family.

36. (B)

The word *babbit* from the book by Sinclair Lewis came to mean a kind of comic American "go-getter," and it was used in the same satiric fashion by John Updike. While Theodore Dreiser (A) also commented on contemporary values and hypocritical notions in books like *Sister Carrie*, it was Lewis who remained a great influence on writers like Updike. Preston Sturges (C) was a playwright and screen-writer, Margaret Mitchell (D) wrote *Gone With the Wind*, and F. Scott Fitzgerald (E) wrote *The Great Gatsby*.

37. (A)

Proust's *Remembrance of Things Past*, a series of volumes, is justifiably famous for its chronicle of one man's life. Of the other choices, only Didion (E) wrote nonfiction; this contemporary writer is not a memoirist like Proust.

38. (A)

Charlotte, Emily, and Anne Bronte wrote novels and poetry, including Emily's classic novel *Wuthering Heights* and Anne's novel *The Tenant of Wildfell Hall*. The James brothers, Henry and William (B), were American writers not known for the type of novel described. Rossetti (C) was a painter and poet, not a novelist. Jane Austen's many siblings (D) did not leave any writings, and Mary Shelley (E), the author of *Frankenstein*, was the wife of a poet, Percy Shelly, not a novelist.

39. (B)

The play and film *Amadeus* chronicle the supposed rivalry between Wolfgang "Amadeus" Mozart and the less well-known composer, Salieri. It's a good idea to know the full names of artists.

40. (C)

All of the dances except the bagatelle (E) were developed in the fifteenth century, but only ballet was based on the movements in fencing. You might recognize the similarities between the grand gestures in ballet and those in fencing.

41. (B)

The eighteenth century was the ideal host to this movement (the Enlightenment), which gained strength as the power of the aristocracy declined and revolutions did away with the old order. Note the time period. The Renaissance (E), Elizabethan period (D), and Restoration (A) occurred before the eighteenth century. Although the Neoclassical movement lasted from the seventeenth to the nineteenth centuries, the unemotional, severe overtones of the movement were not adopted by Pope, Reynolds, and Bach.

42. (D)

This French philosopher was a leader of the Enlightenment in the 1700s, before the Age of Reason (E), the advent of the Industrial Age, and capitalism (A) as we know it today. The book did not attack Martin Luther (B); rather, it denigrated the idea of the Church deciding how a country should be run. Prior to the Enlightenment, the Church was still heavily linked to many European governments, a situation largely unquestioned by most citizens. The book attacked religion, rather than the lack thereof (C).

43. (C)

Beethoven, having completed nine symphonies, bridged the Classical and Romantic periods in music and was known as the Master of the Symphony. The other composers, while prolific, were not known for their masterful symphonies.

44. (E)

Both writers practiced medicine while finding the time to write distinguished poems, short stories, and plays. The question contains the word *compassion*, so you may be tempted to choose answer (B), missionary work, but that answer is incorrect.

45. (E)

Nevelson was an innovative and prominent sculptor of the twentieth century. While she may not be very well known, the correct answer could be arrived at by eliminating the other, better known options. Berthe Morisot (A) was a French Impressionist who worked with oil on canvas. Phidias (B) was a Greek sculptor, Fernand Leger (C) was a French Cubist painter, and Frank Lloyd Wright (D) was an American architect.

46. (A)

Primary Colors, which satirizes former President Clinton, is a good example of *roman á clef*. Only answer (A), based on real historical figures, defines the term *roman á clef*.

47. (E)

Both *Steppenwolfe* and *Siddhartha* are indicative of Herman Hesse's preoccupation with spiritual angst and isolation. Thomas Mann (A) wrote *The Magic Mountain* among other novels, W. G. Sebald (B) wrote *After Nature*, Günther Grass (C) wrote *The Tin Drum*, and Vladimir Nabokov (D) wrote *Lolita*.

48. (E)

Rivera promoted the shift to larger, more socially conscious artwork executed in the public arena. Rodin (A) was a sculptor, Holzer (B) uses media such as LCD screens for her displays, Christo (C) is an environmental artist who uses fabric and other materials in his pieces, and Gericault (D) was an eighteenth-century Romantic painter.

49. (D)

Gaelic is an Irish language (A). The poem is not written in standard English (B), and Old Earlton (C) is a made-up language. While most Americans speak English, the language used in the poem is in Middle English. Note how the spelling and usage of many words does not follow conventional English-language standards.

50. (E)

Chaucer wrote this tale in the fourteenth century, as part of *The Canterbury Tales*. Sir Arthur Conan Doyle (A) was a nineteenth-century Scottish author and doctor who wrote the Sherlock Holmes detective novels. Henrik Ibsen (B) was a nineteenth-century Norwegian playwright. Christopher Marlowe (C) was a playwright who may actually have written Shakespeare's plays. He did not write in Middle English. Shakespeare (who may have been Marlowe!) did not write in Middle English either.

51. (A)

"The Second Nun's Tale" is the only choice that represents an actual section from *The Canterbury Tales*. All of the other choices are made up.

52. (E)

Dante's *Commedia* was a landmark work both because of its aesthetic innovations and because it was written in Italian and thus accessible to the average reader. All of the other poets wrote in Latin.

53. (B)

Note the use of the word *modern*, which lets you know the time period. Beethoven (A), Schubert (C), and Delibes (D) are earlier composers, while Oistrakh (E) is a violinist.

54. (D)

Mozart (A) did not create the sonata form, but he did compose individual sonatas, as did Bach, Beethoven, and various other classical composers. A sonata is not necessarily played for an opera or play [(B), (C), and (E)]. A sonata can be shortened into a sonatina, which is less complex.

55. (E)

Mise en scène refers to all of the visual components that make up a scene in a play or film: costume, makeup, movement of the actors, scenery, etc.

56. (A)

The Magnificent Ambersons was made by Welles in 1942. *Alice Adams* (B) was Booth Tarkington's second novel to win the Pulitzer Prize, in 1922. Welles directed *Touch of Evil* (C) in 1958, based on a novel by Whit Masterson. Edith Wharton's *The Age of Innocence* (D) won the Pulitzer Prize in 1921 and was adapted to the screen by Martin Scorcese in 1993. Michael Cunningham's *The Hours* (E) won the Pulitzer Prize in 1999 and was adapted to film by Stephan Daldry in 2002.

57. (B)

The ballet *The Nutcracker* takes place on Christmas Eve, unfolding as a fantasy in the mind of the little girl, Clara.

58. (D)

Frédéric Chopin lived and wrote during the 1800s. He is known for composing primarily for the piano and for employing unusual chords and occasionally dissonant melodies. None of the other composers listed have all of these characteristics.

59. (C)

The movements took place in Germany. Both movements were offshoots of German Expressionism.

60. (E)

Elongated faces are associated with Modigliani. Van Gogh was famous for including sunflowers (A) in his work, he knew Paul Gauguin (B), he created many self-portraits (C), and he was known for madness—he chopped off his own ear (D).

61. (B)

Rossetti formed the Pre-Raphaelite brotherhood in response to what he considered to be the contemporary affectation in the arts, which he and his followers traced back to Raphael. None of the other choices were members of the Pre-Raphaelite brotherhood.

62. (B)

In answer (B), each person is exemplary of the modernist movement in their respective disciplines. Schoenberg was a composer, Stein was a writer, and Picasso was a painter. For answer (A), Beethoven was an eighteenth-century Austrian composer, Wordsworth was an English poet, and Delacroix was a French Romantic painter. Answer (C) includes eighteenth-century composer Mozart, eighteenth-century British writer Samuel Johnson, and eighteenth-century English Rococo painter, Sir Joshua Reynolds. Answer (D) is composed of twentieth-century musician Philip Glass, twentieth-century poet Rita Dove, and twentieth-century artist Chuck Close. Answer (E) contains sixteenth/seventeenth-century musician Claudio Monteverdi, sixteenth/seventeenth-century Elizabethan playwright William Shakespeare, and sixteenth-century Italian painter Caravaggio.

63. (C)

Mozart, Johnson, and Reynolds, although from different artistic disciplines, all worked during the eighteenth century.

64. (A)

Beethoven, Wordsworth, and Delacroix were the seminal figures of Romanticism in each of their disciplines. Beethoven was a composer, Wordsworth a poet, and Delacroix a painter. The other choices do not include composers, writers, and artists of the Romantic movement.

65. (A)

The political turmoil of the twentieth century reversed the trend of American artists and writers emigrating to the old country. The United States became the haven of poets, artists, philosophers, and scientists alike.

66. (D)

Although there are philosophical elements in Milosz's work (A) and dramatic elements in Santayana's (C), neither person's vocation matches the one listed. Milosz was a poet born in Poland who emigrated to the United States. Tagore (B) was a poet from India; Santayana was a literary critic, poet, and philosopher; and O'Connor (E) was a Southern writer of stories and novels. Only choice (D), W. H. Auden, matches the discipline given.

67. (E)

While Carver did write essays (A), and Beattie, like Moore, is the author of an accomplished novel (C), the three are best known for their short fiction. The authors are not well known for writing memoirs (B) or historical fiction (D). Memoir is not a form of fiction.

68. (C)

Much less common than third-person or first-person novels, a novel written in second person (like Jay McInerney's *Bright Lights, Big City*) addresses the reader as "you," giving the text a more direct appeal to the reader. First-person voice uses the pronouns "I" (B) and "me." Third-person voice uses "he or she" (E) and "they."

69. (E)

Some plays preface the beginning of the play's dialogue with a brief explanation of the play's point of departure, termed a prologue. An aside (A) is a piece of dialogue intended only for the audience to hear, not the actors on stage. A play within the play (B) is just what it sounds like, for example when *The Murder of Gonzago* is staged in

Shakespeare's *Hamlet* (see explanation for question 71). A soliloquy (C) is when a character reveals thoughts without directly addressing a listener, or talks to him- or herself. A tableau vivant (D) is a scene on stage where actors, in costume, remain motionless and silent.

70. (C)

Hamlet's "To be or not to be" speech is a prominent example of a soliloquy. An aside (A) is also spoken for the benefit of the audience but always involves a second character onstage. A play within a play (B) and a tableau vivant (D) involve more than one actor. A prologue is what the audience learns before the play starts, not necessarily from one actor.

71. (B)

Shakespeare fashioned this particular episode from one by Thomas Kyd in *The Spanish Tragedy*. The murder scene is meant to unnerve the king, who is guilty of a similar murder. None of the other answer choices are correct, since the players murdering Gonzago in *Hamlet* do not all have an aside (A), a soliloquy (C), a tableau vivant (D), or a prologue (E). See definitions in explanation for question 69.

72. (E)

Close is one of America's most prominent living artists; he is famous for his blown-up, detailed portraits of average people. Only two of the other artists listed lived during the twentieth century: Max Ernst (C), who worked in abstract art, and Phillip Guston (B), a muralist, Expressive Realist, and Abstract Expressionist. Artimesia Gentileschi (A) was a Baroque painter. Hans Holbein (D) was a late fifteenth- to early sixteenth-century German Northern Renaissance painter.

73. (B)

Watteau's famous painting of Pierrot in his oversized clown's costume is representative of the Rococo period's lighthearted wit tinged with sadness. None of the other choices were subjects often chosen by Rococo artists.

74. (A)

Deux means two, and therefore a *pas de deux* literally means "step for two" (in French).

75. (E)

Pascal's life's work involved rationalizing the existence of God. Kierkegaard (C) is considered to be the father of existentialism, and the other choices are key figures of the movement in the twentieth century.

76. (A)

Nietzsche, Byron, and Wagner were all working in the spirit of Romanticism. Nietzsche was a philosopher who lived from 1844 to 1900, Byron was a poet who lived from 1788 to 1824, and Wagner was a composer who lived from 1813 to 1883. Answer (B) contains figures from the first and second century, the people in answer (C) lived during the seventeenth century, answer (D) includes individuals from the eighteenth century, and answer (E) contains twentieth-century figures.

77. (C)

The Mississippi River is thought to be allegorical of Odysseus' Aegean in Homer's *Odyssey*. Huckleberry Finn is the main character in Twain's novel *Huckleberry Finn*, but he also appears alongside Tom Sawyer in Twain's *The Adventures of Tom Sawyer*.

78. (C)

Beloved is a novel set in the nineteenth century but was written in the late twentieth century by Toni Morrison. *The House of the Seven Gables* (A) is a Gothic horror novel written by Nathaniel Hawthorne in 1851. *Moby-Dick* (B) was written by Herman Melville in 1851, *Fathers and Sons* (D) was written by Ivan Turgenev in 1861, and *A Connecticut Yankee in King Arthur's Court* (E) was written by Mark Twain in 1889.

79. (D)

Fathers and Sons was written by the Russian novelist Ivan Turgenev. All the other authors were/are Americans.

80. (A)

The House of the Seven Gables is one of Hawthorne's great novels in which "the sins of the father are visited upon the son." The book is the epitome of the Gothic horror novel. None of the other books listed were written by Hawthorne (see explanation of question 78 for authors and their works).

81. (A)

Solzhenitsyn wrote from firsthand experience, having been imprisoned by Stalin in the Gulag for his subversive writings.

82. (A)

Pessimism and resignation are the cornerstones of almost all of Thomas Hardy's work. Hardy was a sad stoic whose books explore the hardships of being human. Answers (B), (C), and (D) are way off, and answer (E) would be too much of a stretch.

83. (C)

Largo means a slow, steady tempo. Largo does not speed up, nor is it a walking or moderate tempo, as suggested by the other answer choices.

84. (B)

Tardando means gradually growing slower or to "retard." None of the other answer choices represent tardando.

85. (A)

The other Indian filmmakers listed were contemporaries of Satyajit Ray's, but none of their works brought as much attention to Indian cinema as Ray's Apu trilogy. Never before had Indian cinema been so widely scrutinized by an international audience.

86. (E)

The Persistence of Memory is Dali's most famous work (B) and perhaps the most prominent painting of the Surrealist period (A). The Surrealist period occurred during the twentieth century (D). *The Persistence of Memory* was a landscape with timepieces (C), not a mosaic.

87. (C)

The Dadaists chose the term *Dada* because they felt a nonsensical utterance would best represent their subversive aesthetic.

88. (B)

William Blake's *The Marriage of Heaven and Hell* was a landmark book for Romantic poetry, and its author was also a prominent artist of the period. None of the other books were illustrated by the author.

89. (B)

This painting is Sandro Botticelli's most famous and one of the most notable works of the Renaissance. Each of the other artists listed has a style that is radically different from Botticelli's.

90. (C)

Nobel Prize winner Soyinka is the foremost African literary artist of his era. His international fame attests to the post-modern goal of globally known literature. His novel, *The Strong Breed*, takes place in Africa.

91. (D)

Lawrence takes a clinical approach to the sexual instincts and involutions of both man and animal. Most of his work is set in the English countryside. The work of Lawrence is not as concerned with children (A), politics (B), injustice (C), or life in the big city (E).

92. (E)

Antonioni (A), a contemporary of Fellini's, made *L'Avventura* and *Blowup*. Bertolucci (B), from the generation after Fellini, is known for his films *The Conformist* and *The Sheltering Sky*. Leone (C) is known for the films *Ben Hur* and *Helen of Troy*, among others. Rossellini (D) is known for *The Messiah*.

93. (A)

The novel *Pale Fire* is a lengthy extension of a poem. *Moby-Dick* (B) and *The Great Gatsby* (C) open with famous lines, not poetry. The other two choices [(D) and (E)] are full works of prose.

94. (D)

A Raisin in the Sun is a powerful homage to the African-American experience. *for colored girls who have. . .* (A) and "Sonny's Blues" (E) are also written by African-American authors (Ntozake Shange and James Baldwin, respectively). *for colored girls who have. . .* is a play, *Broken Glass* (B) is a play by Arthur Miller, and *West Side Story* (C) is a musical by Leonard Bernstein and Stephen Sondheim. "Sonny's Blues" is a short story.

95. (B)

Kerouac and Ginsberg were Beat generation poets, most prominent in the 1950s. Kerouac's novel promotes his maxim "first word, best word" in an organic stream of consciousness prose-poetry, while Ginsberg's poem recalls Whitman's effusive, unfettered verse. The Restoration period (A) occurred between 1660 and 1800, much earlier than the Beat generation. The Fugitive poets (C) wrote during the twentieth century and were Southern classic poets. The Imagists (D) wrote during the twentieth century as well. The Dadaist Conference in Zurich (E) occurred between 1916 and 1924, when a group of European artists (the Dadaists) met.

96. (B)

Each painter came into prominence at the end of the Impressionist period (C). Van Gogh could not be considered a Cubist (A), nor could any of the three be considered Color Field painters (E). The three painters were not Minimalists, which eliminates choice (D).

97. (D)

The term *Rubenesque* now refers to people (especially women) who are curvaceous. The other choices include Claude Monet (A), a French Impressionist; Jean-Michel Basquiat (B), a twentieth-century postcolonialist; Jacob Lawrence (C), a twentieth-century Harlem Renaissance painter; and Willem de Kooning (E), a twentieth-century Abstract Expressionist painter.

98. (D)

Frost presented himself as a kind of homespun rural sage (the opposite of choice (E)), but upon close inspection of his work we find an elusive and somewhat esoteric philosophy. Very little of his work is free verse (B), and while there are Surreal (A) and Romantic elements (C) in his work, neither is predominant.

99. (B)

Satan is the protagonist in *Paradise Lost*. Although there may be evil elements in the other works, Satan himself does not actually appear.

100. (B)

Gray's elegy is a touching ode to the soul and character of the common man and woman. "Priests" (E) is a tempting answer, as it references the church. However, it is incorrect.

101. (C)

A picaresque novel typically is a full-length fictional and usually satirical book, based on the adventures of a social underdog who is the protagonist. The first picaresque novel was Mateo Alemán's *Guzmán de Alfarache*, published in Spain in 1599. Fielding's bawdy, episodic masterpiece was a high point in the genre. Turgenev's *Diary* (D) is episodic but far too sober to be picaresque.

102. (C)

Hume contested theories of cause and effect. He claimed that all we can know (and predict) is that one thing invariably follows another thing; we cannot infer that one thing is the cause of the other.

103. (D)

Johannes Brahms lived from 1833 to 1897. The Romantic era of music spanned from about 1815 to 1910, and Nietzsche lived from 1844 to 1900. Notice the use of dates in this question: none of the other composers lived during a time that was compatible with Nietzsche's.

104. (A)

A cappella means "as in chapel" and refers to singing without instrumental accompaniment.

105. (D)

All three people are noted for their principal performances as ballet dancers. They are not known as musicians [(A) and (B)], modern dancers (C), or writers (E).

106. (B)

This choice is the correct answer due to the dramatic chords opening the work. None of the other choices are associated with the phrase "Fate knocking at the door."

107. (E)

Jane Austen wrote *Sense and Sensibility*. George Eliot is the author of *Daniel Deronda* (A), Emily Bronte composed *Wuthering Heights* (B), Mary Shelley produced *Frankenstein* (C), and Charlotte Perkins Gilman wrote *The Yellow Wallpaper* (D).

108. (B)

Invisible Man (B) is Ellison's outcry against a restrictive, racist society. *Diary of a Superfluous Man* (A), by Ivan

Turgenev, is recounted by a wealthy nobleman from his deathbed. *Man Walks into a Room* (C), by Nicole Krauss, is the story of Samson Greene, a professor of English at Columbia University, who was found walking in the Nevada desert with a brain tumor. *Man's Fate* (D), by Andre Malraux, is a fictional account of the early days of the Chinese Revolution. *The Man Without Qualities* (E), written by Robert Musil, has a main character called Ulrich, the "Man of Qualities."

109. (A)

The *Iliad* is not a play at all. It is an epic poem about the Trojan War that is attributed to the author Homer. The rest of the choices are in fact plays by Aristophanes.

110. (D)

The Prince is Machiavelli's guide to strong-arm government. The other choices are by Heidegger (A), Schopenhauer (B), Freud (C), and Levi-Strauss (E).

111. (E)

Browning was the master of the dramatic monologue. No aspect of either poem could be considered epic (C) or elemental of romance (B). The works are not sonnets (A) or sestinas (D).

112. (A)

"Where ignorant armies clash by night" is taken from "Dover Beach." The other choices are from works by Tennyson (B), Yeats (C), Dickinson (D), and Wilfred Owen (E).

113. (D)

"No ideas but in things" is the famous maxim of William Carlos Williams. Many succeeding poets would try to follow this maxim.

114. (C)

Michelangelo's sculpture *David* may be the most famous sculpture on the planet. Donatello (A) produced a slightly less famous and more diminutive *David*.

115. (A)

The piece is quintessentially high Renaissance style, which bases its principles on the Hellenic period. Michelangelo worked during the Renaissance, not during the other periods listed.

116. (E)

Michelangelo represents the physical form as the Greeks did, glorious and idealized, somewhere between Giacommetti's attenuated figures and Botero's blimp-ish ones. The other choices are not represented by Michelangelo's work.

117. (C)

As I Lay Dying is a modernist novel by William Faulkner. The other choices are all poems.

118. (A)

This is a Shakespearian sonnet. Of the other choices, only Milton (B) worked significantly with the form, and he is better known for his longer works.

119. (D)

A defining feature of sonnets is that they are fourteen lines long. A villanelle (A) is a nineteen-line poem of fixed form, containing five tercets (three-line groups) and a final quatrain (four-line stanza) with two rhymes. A sestina (B) is a verse form composed of six six-line stanzas and a three-line envoy. The sestina reuses the same line-ending words across stanzas in a specific pattern. An epic (C) is an extended narrative poem written in elevated language. The rondeau (E) originated in France and contains ten or thirteen lines, with an opening phrase repeated two times as a refrain. Be sure to review any unfamiliar poetry terms.

120. (C)

The lines mean "Love is constant, come what may." The other options mean the opposite of "love is constant."

121. (A)

The Faerie Queene is an epic poem. Spenser's long magnum opus is the quintessential epic poem, whereas none of the other poems are longer than a page and a half, nor do they have particularly epic themes.

122. (C)

Beckett's play is the high point of the absurdist movement, which included playwrights like Eugene Ionesco and Jean Genet. While facets of the other choices may be included in the play, overall *Waiting for Godot* is not realist (A), romantic (B), anarchist (D), or a comedy of manners (E).

123. (D)

All of the other choices are ballets, but the Sugar Plum Fairy only appears in Act II of *The Nutcracker* (in the Land of Sweets). *The Nutcracker* is performed on stages throughout the world at Christmastime.

124. (B)

Goya's later works are the products of a burgeoning madness married to the atrocities of his time. They may be authentic, but none of the other adjectives would apply.

125. (B)

Angels in America brought awareness of AIDS to its audience and questioned what Kushner considered to be "the implicit lack of compassion in the Reagan era." It is a perfect example of postmodernism's move toward a more socially conscious art form.

126. (C)

La Giocanda is another name for the *Mona Lisa*, Leonardo da Vinci's most famous painting.

127. (B)

Although the painting displays the violence of Delacroix (D) and the horror of Goya (C), it is in fact Picasso's masterpiece, *Guernica*. Picasso was a famous Cubist painter.

128. (C)

Guernica is Picasso's depiction of the atrocities of war.

129. (E)

Produced in the twentieth century, the work is characteristic of the modern movement away from realistic interpretation.

130. (A)

Amorphous refers to a lack of definite form, or shapelessness. Many of Gaudi's buildings seem to be melting like wax and lack a definite form throughout. While Gaudi's buildings may have some elements of the other answer choices, the best answer is (A), amorphous, since the buildings do not express the clear-cut lines of Cubism (C) or geometric shapes (B), and they are not minimalist (D) or utilitarian (E).

131. (E)

F. Scott Fitzgerald is the author of *This Side of Paradise*. All of the other novels were written by Henry James.

132. (D)

Joyce Carol Oates has written over a hundred novels. Lowry (A), Salinger (B), and Barnes (C) published only a handful of books, and Ellison (E) went through thirty years of writer's block after *Invisible Man*.

133. (A)

Johann Sebastian Bach lived from 1685 to 1750. Aaron Copland (B) was a contemporary composer (1900–1990), Antonio Salieri (1750–1825) was an Italian composer who lived too late to write this music (C), and both Emmanuel Ax (D) and Isaac Stern (E) are musicians but not composers.

134. (C)

Don Giovanni and *The Marriage of Figaro* were written by Mozart. The operas in answer (A) were written by Giacomo Puccini, *The Tales of Hoffman* and *Orpheus in the Underworld* were written by Jacques Offenbach (B), *William Tell* and *The Barber of Seville* were written by Gioacchino Rossini (D), and *Salome* and *Elektra* were written by Richard Strauss (E).

135. (E)

The Jungle is Upton Sinclair's socialist indictment of the meatpacking industry and urban squalor of Chicago. All of the other poems and books deal with the horrors of war.

136. (C)

In this work, Aristotle details the criteria for a work of art or literature to be great and refers often to the playwrights Aeschylus, Sophocles, and Euripides.

137. (C)

Blake's poems are unfettered songs of divine inspiration. All the other adjectives are antonyms of *prophetic*.

138. (A)

The *Spoon River Anthology* consists of epitaphs, or poems spoken about deceased individuals. A graveyard is a fit setting for spoken epitaphs.

139. (C)

Gerard Manley Hopkins and Emily Dickinson were both highly unconventional poets, eliminating answer (A). Emily Dickinson was a recluse for most of her life. They did not live during the Romantic period (B), and Hopkins was born in the United Kingdom, so answer (E) is wrong. The authors did not both use pen names (D), but they were both largely unpublished during their lifetimes.

140. (E)

There may be a heroic couplet or two sprinkled in short stories, but they look out of place in most stories. Iambic (A), rhyming (B), consists of two lines (C), and common in Elizabethan poetry (D) all relate to the heroic couplet.

Chapter Thirteen: **CLEP Humanities Review**

- **The Big Picture: CLEP Humanities**
- **Nuts and Bolts**
- **How to Score at Scoring**
- **The Arts**
- **Literature**
- **Final Thoughts**

Congratulations on making the important and exciting decision to challenge yourself by taking the CLEP Humanities exam. The material in this chapter, if studied well, will help you to prepare adequately for the test. While the CLEP Humanities exam may seem daunting at first, don't despair: much of the unfamiliar information on the exam can be acquired with some thought, practice, and study.

THE BIG PICTURE: CLEP HUMANITIES

Before looking at the individual arts sections of the exam, take a look at the big picture. It's important to understand that this test is general in scope and broad in outlook. The CLEP Humanities exam tests for a thorough knowledge of classical to contemporary culture in many different fields: art, architecture, poetry, prose, philosophy, drama, music, dance, and film. You will be asked to demonstrate your understanding of key concepts, to recognize famous works of art and important techniques, and to interpret and recall information from a variety of subject areas. Be prepared to cross-reference categories and interpret dates and eras of work. The reward for studying hard for the exam is definitely worth it: a good score on this exam may get you up to six semester hours of college credit (or fulfillment of a requirement). Some schools may choose to grant credit for a particular course with content that matches the exam.

NUTS AND BOLTS

Brace yourself: it is highly unlikely that you will achieve expert status in every section of the exam. The exam is designed so that you will not know the answer to every question. As mentioned, the test is exceedingly broad in scope, with 90 minutes allotted to answer 140 multiple-choice questions. Questions on the exam often involve information taught to college students in year-long survey courses. While you will most likely achieve a higher score in some sections than others, it is best to keep in mind the percentage of the exam taken up by each topic.

About half of the exam questions will ask you to identify the names and works of various authors, artists, or composers spanning several centuries. Another 30 percent of the questions will test your ability to recognize the style, rhyme scheme, or characteristics of these writers and artists or the time period or movement during which their work was created. Finally, you will need to present clearly an interpretation of literary passages and photographs of artwork that may be unfamiliar to you. This level of question (discussion and interpretation) will make up about 20 percent of the test. These question types and the different topics are mixed together on the exam, rather than sorted into separate sections.

Here is the approximate breakdown of subject areas:

50% The Arts
    20% Visual arts (painting, sculpture, etc.)
    15% Music
    10% Other performing arts (film, dance, etc.)
    5% Architecture

50% Literature
    10% Drama
    10–15% Poetry
    15–20% Fiction
    10% Nonfiction (including Philosophy)

Emphasis is placed on Western culture and art, focusing on the Classical, Medieval, Renaissance, and Romantic periods, as well as the seventeenth, eighteenth, nineteenth, and twentieth centuries. Expect 7–14 questions to touch on Latin American, Russian, African, or Asian studies. Be particularly alert for questions that cross disciplines and/or periods. It's especially important to have a clear understanding of terminology and genre for each topic covered.

HOW TO SCORE AT SCORING

Reading is fundamental to this exam. Read that sentence again! The only way to understand the fine arts is by experiencing them, either through books or firsthand. Learning about the fine arts takes effort on your part—you can't learn everything there is to know about the arts through one book. Visit your library on a regular basis. Read college textbooks for survey courses in drama, literature, and fine arts.

Make a conscious effort to attend fine arts events. Go see independent films rather than mainstream movies at the multiplex. Rent classic movies that transformed cinematic history, such as *Citizen Kane*. Go to museums and jazz or classical concerts. Attend a ballet, play, or gallery event. If you must turn on the TV, turn off MTV and turn on PBS. Go online and find websites that discuss the arts. Look up an author you want to know more about or an art period you would like to study. The broader your range of experience and expertise in the arts, the better you will do on the CLEP Humanities exam.

At the end of each section in this review, there will be suggestions for further reading and study, as well as tips for how to make the most of your prep time. When you're taking the exam, be sure to read each question as quickly and efficiently as you can. If you're familiar with time periods, for example, you'll be able to rule out some multiple-choice answers quickly. Try to remember one important fact about each era. This will help you to remember what occurred during each time period.

Let's examine each category of the arts and discover what you need to know in order to score well—and how to get there.

THE ARTS

VISUAL ARTS AND ARCHITECTURE

What You Need to Know

The visual arts portion of the CLEP Humanities exam will contain approximately 28 questions on a variety of artistic genres, including sculpture and painting. There will be another 7 or so questions about architecture. You will be asked to identify familiar and unfamiliar work by creator, discipline, and style. In addition, you'll be asked to recognize terms related to these fields.

Art Terms to Learn

One of the most important things you can do to prepare for each subject on the exam is to create a glossary of significant terms. Take the time to compile, consider, and understand the terminology, along with the types of art the terms are connected with. Here are some of the terms to learn:

Action painting A style of abstract painting that relies on the physical movement of the artist and vigorous brushwork or pouring on the canvas.

Camera obscura A dark room (or box) with a small hole in one side that external images are projected through. An inverted image of what can be seen through the hole is projected onto an opposing surface, where it can be traced. Vermeer was said to have used this instrument to aid his rendering of light and shadow.

Casting The process that involves pouring liquid material like clay, wax, or plaster into a mold.

Chiaroscuro Describes the effect of light and shade in a painting or drawing, especially where strong contrasts are given.

Collage A technique in which an artist uses materials other than paint, such as glass, paper, or wood.

Fresco A technique in which pigments are dispersed in plain water and applied to a damp plaster wall. The wall becomes both the binder and the support.

Mosaic Small pieces of colored glass or tessera are embedded into plaster or mortar.

Architecture Terms to Learn

Arcade A series of arches supported by columns or piers, or a passageway between two series of arches.

Arch A curved structure designed to span an opening, usually made of stone or other masonry. Roman arches are semicircular; Islamic and Gothic arches come to a point at the top.

Façade The front exterior of a building.

Gothic An architectural style popular from the twelfth through the fifteenth centuries, characterized by pointed arches, flying buttresses, and stone buildings that reached great heights.

Truss A structural framework of wood or metal that reinforces or supports walls, ceilings, piers, or beams.

Since art terms are constantly evolving, look over a recent college art textbook. Put these words on flashcards and practice learning them nightly. Try to find sketches or images to glue to the front of the cards, since you will be asked to identify pictures of various kinds of art. To prepare for the architectural aspect of this exam, find photographs of famous buildings, identifying the trusses, arches, and other components, or look for different styles of architecture as you walk around. Try to remember the time periods associated with each architectural form. Remembering, for example, that pointed arches are connected with Gothic buildings will be of great help to you.

Different Schools of Art

As you learn the previous terms, add the important schools of art to your base of knowledge, along with at least one noted artist in each school. Study the following chart, which lists popular schools of art along with a representative artist for each. Sometimes it is easier to remember a school of art when you are able to connect the works of an artist with it.

School of Art	Description	Artist Associated with School of Art
Abstract art	Art that departs significantly from natural appearances.	Willem de Kooning
Art Nouveau	A style of the late 1880s, based on the curves of plants.	Gustav Klimt
Baroque	Popular in the seventeenth century, this style uses dramatic light and shade, strong composition, and exaggerated emotions.	Peter Paul Rubens
Bauhaus	This German school of art existed from 1919 to prewar 1933 and was interested in mass production along with greatly affected design styles.	Paul Klee
Classical	Greek art and architecture during the fifth century B.C.E. or art that emphasizes balance and proportion.	Myron, Polyclitus, Phidias; the Acropolis at Athens, the Parthenon
Conceptual art	This art believes that ideas and process take precedence over a tangible form. Developed in the late 1960s, Conceptual works include performance art.	Judy Chicago
Cubism	Cubism began in 1907. It is based upon the geometric reconstruction of objects into a surface of shifting planes.	Pablo Picasso
Dada	An early twentieth-century anarchic movement, which ridiculed the accepted standards of conventional art.	Marcel Duchamp
Expressionism or Abstract Expressionism	Used to describe emotional art by featuring distortion and color. It was popular from the late nineteenth to the early twentieth century.	Vassily Kandinsky
Fauvism	A style of painting from the early twentieth century with bright color and simple shapes.	Henri Matisse
Futurism	Originating in Italy around 1910, this school aimed to express the violent, energized, ever-changing quality of modern life; it was an outgrowth of Cubism.	Umberto Boccioni
Hellenistic	Style of the last of three phases of ancient Greek art (300–100 B.C.E.), characterized by emotion, drama, and the interaction of sculptural forms with surrounding space.	
Impressionism	A style of painting that originated in France around 1870 with casual outdoor subjects and divided brush strokes to capture the transitory effects of light and color.	Claude Monet
Minimalism	A late 1960s style of sculpture and painting with simple geometric shapes.	Agnes Martin
Neoclassicism or Romanticism	New Classicism, or the revival of classical Greek and Roman forms in art, music, and literature, particularly during the eighteenth and nineteenth centuries.	Jacques Louis David
Photorealism	A style of painting popular in the 1970s, using photographs as subjects.	Chuck Close

Pointillism	A system of painting using tiny dots or "points" of color; developed in the 1880s.	Georges Seurat
Pop Art	Developed in America and England in the late 1950s and early 1960s, based on the impersonal style of the popular mass media. Think Marilyn Monroe on soup cans.	Andy Warhol
Post-Impressionism	A general term applied to French artists from about 1885 to 1900; concerned with symbols and expressiveness.	Vincent Van Gogh or Paul Cézanne
Postmodernism	A trend of the 1970s, 1980s, and 1990s; characterized by an eclectic acceptance of all periods and styles.	Damian Hirst
Renaissance	The late fourteenth through the sixteenth centuries; characterized by an interest in human subjects and classical art.	Sandro Botticelli
Rococo	Late Baroque style; playful, romantic, pastel, and elaborate.	Jean Antoine Watteau
Surrealism	A term for a type of literature and art from the 1920s to the 1940s concerned with fantastic and dreamlike images.	Salvador Dali

While there are other art movements to keep in mind, this chart is a good start. Taking out a variety of art books from the library will furnish you with the familiarity that cannot come from memorization alone. If you live in a city or have access to museums, visit them. There is no substitute for seeing actual works whether via photo, reproduction, or, with luck, the work itself. Remember the identifying characteristics of the artist and time period. For example, Dali's melting clocks should bring to mind Surrealism.

Creating Timelines and Flashcards

A timeline can be an effective way to learn art movements. Create a simple timeline, adding artists and their schools, styles, and periods. Here is an example of a blank timeline for you to copy and fill in:

1500   1550   1600   1650   1700   1750   1800   1850   1900

The following is a handy website for creating great looking timelines. Bookmark it for use with your study guide: teach-nology.com/web_tools/materials/timelines.

Flashcards can be created for artwork and art movements as well as for art terms. Search the Internet or magazines for pictures of famous works or examples and print and paste the pictures on index cards. Focus on remembering what distinguishes one style of art from another.

Art Resources

Besides museums and galleries, there are many fine books to be found on this subject. Some recommendations are *Architecture: The World's Greatest Buildings Explored and Explained* by Neil Stevenson (Collingdale, PA: DIANE Publishing Company, 2000; hardcover edition from DK

Publishing, 1997), *The Annotated Mona Lisa: A Crash Course in Art History* by John Boswell and Carol Strickland (Kansas City, MO: Andrews McMeel, 1992), and *Learning to Look at Paintings* by Mary Acton (New York: Routledge, 1997). Check out great art websites such as that of the Metropolitan Museum of Art at metmuseum.org (which includes a helpful timeline of art through the ages) or the Art by Period site at teacheroz.com/Art_Periods.htm. For architectural information online, try GreatBuildings.com/gbc.html. This site includes a fine listing of buildings through the ages.

PERFORMING ARTS: MUSIC, DANCE, AND FILM

What You Need to Know

In all these categories, you'll be asked to identify specific works such as symphonies, ballets, operas, or films. You'll also be questioned on important composers, filmmakers, choreographers, and musicians, both classical and jazz. Some questions will ask you to place these artists inside their time period or movement. The largest number of questions will cover music, with a smaller number of questions about dance and film. Plan on being quizzed about the work of such American music greats as Cole Porter, George Gershwin, or Billie Holiday and dance and film luminaries like Margot Fonteyn, George Balanchine, or Charlie Chaplin.

If you aren't a dancer or musician, these areas will take some study to master. If you do have a background in ballet or if you've ever played an instrument, you're in luck. Many of the questions will focus on musical terms such as the difference between a symphony and a sonata or how many notes form a scale. If you've been an avid appreciator of music, you may already be familiar with works and composers on the test. Ballet dancers will be relieved to find they are already familiar with the language of dance (French) and are able to recognize notable dancers and ballets. Questions also will be asked about modern dance and notable dancers, such as Isadora Duncan.

The film section will be a breeze if you have a taste for important films older than the *Star Wars* trilogy. You will probably be asked fewer questions about specific terminology in this area, but you should be familiar with the plot and direction of great movies such as those by filmmaker Preston Sturges.

Music

This subject makes up 15 percent of the exam, or approximately 21 questions, so it's not one you can overlook! Let's start with some common terms.

Music Terms to Learn

A cappella Vocal or choral music performed without accompaniment.

Aria A song for solo voice with instrumental accompaniment.

Articulation The way notes are struck, sustained, and released, including legato, staccato, tenuto, etc.

Atonality A term for twentieth century music where a "key" is avoided.

Bass The lowest male voice.

Bebop A 1940s term for jazz including improvised solos in dissonant patterns.

Cadence A pause or stopping point.

Contralto The lowest female voice.

Counterpoint Music consisting of two lines or melodic lines played simultaneously.

Crescendo Music getting progressively louder.

Diminuendo Music growing progressively softer.

Harmony The simultaneous occurrence of musical tones, as opposed to melody.

Leitmotiv A short musical passage that brings to mind a character or situation in a musical drama.

Libretto The text of an opera.

Plainsong Gregorian chant of the Middle Ages.

Quartet A composition written for four instruments or voices, or the four performers assembled to play such a work.

Quintet A composition for five instruments or voices.

Scat singing A style of jazz singing with nonsense syllables.

Sonata The most important form of instrumental music from the Baroque era to the present. It usually consists of four independent pieces called movements.

Swing A popular style of jazz that originated about 1935.

While memorizing these and many other music terms may be a good beginning, listening to music is an important aspect of learning as well. Check out the classical section of your local music store or library. Shuffle your music collections and see if you can name the type of music you are listening to. Some online sites have audio samples of various symphonies and compositions. This can be an enjoyable study session, if you use your time to become more familiar with great works. Take the opportunity to attend recitals. In addition to listening to music, it's wise to acquire a book on opera and composers and to create a series of flashcards for better recognition of terms.

Music Through the Ages

Once again, we'll take a timeline approach to learning this information. We'll start with the Middle Ages, when most music was religious in nature and connected to the Church. As we did before for well-known artists, we will group musicians with their respective centuries and the musical period in which they composed. That done, consult a musical encyclopedia or an online source to connect at least one piece to each musician listed.

Pre-Medieval and Medieval	Renaissance	Seventeenth Century (Baroque)	Eighteenth Century (Classical)	Nineteenth Century (Romantic)	Twentieth Century (Modern)	Postmodern
Giovanni Gabrieli	Francesco Landini	Arcangelo Corelli	George Frideric Handel	Franz Schubert	Arnold Schoenberg	John Cage
Jan Pieters Sweelinck	John Dunstable	Jean-Baptiste Lully	Wolfgang Amadeus Mozart	Richard Wagner	Claude Debussy	Philip Glass
Thomas Morley	Thomas Tallis	Jean-Baptiste Lully	Franz Joseph Hayden	Gustav Mahler	Igor Stravinsky	Miles Davis
Luca Marenzio		Antonio Vivaldi	Ludwig van Beethoven	Franz Liszt	George Gershwin	
				Frédéric Chopin	Cole Porter	
				Hector Berlioz	Duke Ellington	

You also can use another kind of musical timeline, which incorporates other events:

The Nineteeth Century

Music Resources

While music might seem to be a big topic, source material in this area is especially diverse. Any text on the history of great composers would not be amiss for studying for the exam. To begin, try *The Lives of the Great Composers* (Third Edition) by Harold Schonberg (New York: Norton, 1997). Other helpful texts include *The NPR Guide to Building a Classical CD Collection: The 350 Essential Works* (Second Edition) by Theodore Libbey (New York: Workman, 1999), *The Symphony: A Listener's Guide* by Michael Steinberg (New York: Oxford University Press, 1998), and *Guide to Symphonic Music* by Edward Downes (New York: Walker & Company, 1981).

Any guide to the stories behind great opera can be studied, along with a book on jazz roots in American music, such as *The Oxford Companion to Jazz* by Bill Kirshner (New York: Oxford University Press, 2000). If you feel you require more in-depth study in this area, Geoffrey C. Ward and Ken Burns' *Jazz: A History of America's Music* (New York: Knopf, 2002) is highly recommended. A plethora of websites contain both valuable information about music and timelines. For classical information, classicalworks.com is a very helpful site that is easy to navigate. One of the best sites, HyperMusic, can be found at hypermusic.ca. The site contains information and quizzes on every category of music.

Dance and Film

Together, these categories make up 10 percent of the exam, or approximately 14 questions. The dance section of the CLEP Humanities exam includes references to both ballet and modern dance. Remember that the language of ballet is French, so it is handy to be somewhat familiar with this language. The film section will be more concerned with the films themselves, rather than the terminology of film.

Dance Terms to Learn

Arabesque A pose on one leg with the other leg raised back.

Ballet Classical form of dance characterized by graceful, precise movements of the arms, legs, and rest of the body.

Choreographer The artist who selects or invents the steps, movements, and patterns of a dance.

Coda The last section of a pas de deux or of a full ballet.

Danseur Noble The male classical dancer, counterpart to the classical ballerina.

Five Positions of the Feet Every ballet step or movement must begin with positions one, two, three, four, or five, and return to one of these positions.

Jazz Dance influenced by the rhythm and technique of jazz music, it relies on improvisation and rejects strict constructs of the classical ballet.

Modern Dance that rejects the constructs of classical ballet, allowing for movement derived from inner feeling.

Pas de Deux A dance duet.

Rhythm Variation of movement according to the tempo of music.

Tempo The pace of a dance.

Film Terms to Learn

Aperture Camera lens with a valve to control the amount of light that comes through.

Dissolve A transition between two shots, where one shot fades away and another shot simultaneously fades in.

Dubbing Recording of dialogue in a sound studio after a film has been shot. Actors match the lip movements on the film to dialogue that they speak.

Edit The arrangement of shots.

Frame A single image on film.

Looping Film is on a loop to give an actor several tries to get a line correct.

Negative Original film used in the camera used to make a positive, final print from.

Dance and Film Names to Know

For these subjects, it's more important to remember great works than terminology. Instead of making a timeline, look up information about well-known ballets, dancers, films, and directors. It is important to know the plots of landmark films and ballets. As always, this is not a complete list. It's always important to do your own research.

Ballets	Dancers and Choreographers	Films	Directors
Cinderella	George Balanchine	*8 1/2*	Federico Fellini
Giselle	Mikhail Baryshnikov	*Battleship Potemkin*	Sergei Eisenstein
Manon	Erik Bruhn	*Citizen Kane*	Orson Welles
The Nutcracker	Isadora Duncan	*Metropolis*	Fritz Lang
Romeo and Juliet	Margot Fonteyn	*Modern Times*	Charlie Chaplin
Sleeping Beauty	Martha Graham	*Rashomon*	Akira Kurosawa
Swan Lake	Vaslav Nijinsky	*The Searchers*	John Ford
	Rudolf Nureyev	*Vertigo*	Alfred Hitchcock
	Anna Pavlova		Ingmar Bergman
	Jerome Robbins		Francis Ford Coppola
	Maria Tallchief		Stanley Kubrick
			Jean Renoir
			Billy Wilder

Dance and Film Resources

The most enjoyable way to do research for this section is through your local library or film rental system. Rent DVDs of great ballets and films. Good books on these subjects include *101 Stories of the Great Ballets* by George Balanchine (New York: Anchor Books, 1989), *Technical Manual and Dictionary of Classical Ballet* by Gail Grant (Mineola, NY: Dover Publishing, 1982), *The Classic Ballet: Basic Technique and Terminology* by Lincoln Kirstein (New York: Knopf, 2004), and *Ballet and Modern Dance: A Concise History* by Jack Anderson (Hightstown, NY: Princeton Book Company, 1992). For film, try the book *Film History: An Introduction* by Kristin Thompson (New York: McGraw-Hill, 2002), visit the expansive websites from Sight and Sound and the British Film Institute at bfi.org.uk, or visit the inclusive group of film sites at dmoz.org/Reference/Archives/Arts/Film.

LITERATURE

DRAMA

What You Need to Know

The drama section of the exam will ask you to identify the plots, authors, and themes of theater over the course of several centuries. This section comprises 10 percent of the exam, approximately 14 questions. Expect the exam to focus on important playwrights such as Shakespeare. The exam will cover common theatrical terms, such as *soliloquy*, *epilogue*, or *farce*. Finding examples within plays of terms and constructs is a great way to learn this material.

Drama Terms to Learn

Act Major division of a play; composed of scenes.

Allegory Symbolic representation of abstract ideas or principles through characters or events.

Antagonist A character against which another character struggles.

Aside Lines spoken by an actor directly to the audience that are not "heard" by the other characters.

Catharsis The feelings of pity and fear that, according to Aristotle, occur in the audience of a tragedy.

Climax The turning point in a drama; culmination of a crisis or moment of culminating intensity in a drama.

Denouement The resolution of the plot.

Deus ex machina A god who resolves the entanglements of a play, or the use of artificial means to resolve the plot.

Epilogue Short speech by a character at the conclusion of a play, directed at the audience.

Farce Humorous play with light, dramatic effect and outrageous characters.

Protagonist The main character of a literary work.

Prologue Introduction to a play, a speech providing background information on the scene before the play starts.

Scene Part of an act in a play in which time is continuous and the setting is fixed.

Soliloquy A speech in a play heard by the audience, usually when only one actor is onstage.

Tableau vivant Scene in a play where costumed actors remain motionless and silent.

Tragedy Play that ends in extreme, meaningful sorrow, typically leading to the downfall of the main character due to a moral weakness or tragic flaw.

Drama Through the Centuries

Theater is a good area to study by forming a timeline and timeline study chart. The study chart is ascending, covering great modern playwrights all the way back to playwrights of the Elizabathan era. While the chart in this section is by no means all-inclusive, you may want to begin studying the chart by finding a famous play by each author. For example, Oscar Wilde's *The Importance of Being Earnest* is a classic farce and remains, even today, a popular work. You might also want to connect such later works as *My Fair Lady* to the work it is based on, *Pygmalion*. Set up your flashcards. Put the name of a play on the front of each card and the name of the playwright on the back. Do the same with the time period each playwright worked in. Cluster Shakespeare with Marlowe to remember that they are Elizabethan playwrights. Do the same with plots and titles.

Modern		**Early Modern**		**Restoration (Manners)**	
Albee	1928–	Lady Gregory	1852–1932	Dryden	1631–1700
Anouilh	1910–1987	O'Neill	1888–1953	Marivaux	1688–1763
Beckett	1906–1989	Pirandello	1867–1936	Sheridan	1751–1816
Brecht	1898–1956	Synge	1871–1909	Wilde	1854–1900
Cocteau	1889–1963				
Genet	1910–1986	**Naturalist**		**Post-Shakespeare**	
Ionesco	1909–1994	Chekhov	1860–1904	Corneille	1606–1684
Miller	1915–2005	Ibsen	1828–1906	Moliere	1622–1673
Sartre	1905–1980	Shaw	1856–1950	Racine	1639–1699
Stoppard	1937–	Strindberg	1849–1912		
Wilder	1897–1975			**Elizabethan-Jacobean**	
Williams	1911–1983	**Romantic**		Jonson	1572–1637
		Byron	1788–1824	Marlowe	1564–1593
		Goethe	1749–1832	Shakespeare	1564–1616
		Schiller	1759–1805	Webster	1580–1625

The following is a simple example of a drama timeline. Copy it or create your own version with more dates and authors, along with the movements to which they belonged (i.e. Shakespeare: Elizabethan).

Theater

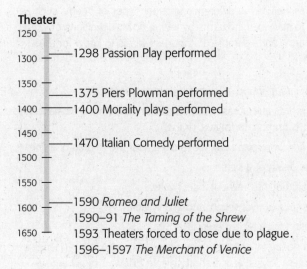

1250
1298 Passion Play performed
1300
1350
1375 Piers Plowman performed
1400 Morality plays performed
1450
1470 Italian Comedy performed
1500
1550
1590 *Romeo and Juliet*
1600
1590–91 *The Taming of the Shrew*
1593 Theaters forced to close due to plague.
1650
1596–1597 *The Merchant of Venice*

Drama Resources

This is a good time to go to the theater. Important plays are performed fairly often in large cities, and seeing these plays performed live will help you remember important concepts and plot-lines. If you cannot attend plays in person, rent DVDs. Keep in mind that movie versions do not always follow the actual text of the play. Try to get a digital recording of the actual play filmed. Books abound on the history of theater as well. A few books to look for include *Masterpieces of the Drama* (6th Edition) by Alexander W. Allison, et al. (New York: Pearson, 1990), *Theories of the Theatre: A Historical and Critical Survey, from the Greeks to the Present* by Marvin Carlson (Ithaca, NY: Cornell University Press, 1994), *The Wadsworth Anthology of Drama* (Fourth Edition) by W. B. Worthen (Boston: Heinle, 2003), and *The Oxford Illustrated History of Theatre* by John Russell Brown (New York: Oxford University Press, 2001). If you'd like to check the Internet for information on particular works, try Open Source Shakespeare at opensourceshakespeare.org. You might also try the Theatre History Online Course at connectedcourseware.com/ccweb/start.htm.

POETRY

What You Need to Know

The poetry section of the CLEP Humanities exam will ask you to identify the name of a poet by his or her genre, identify the work of a particular poet, or correctly note a technique or scheme of a poem. You'll be asked questions about poems and poets from ancient Greece to the twentieth century. This section comprises 10–15 percent of the exam, or approximately 14–21 questions.

Poetry Terms to Learn

If you are unfamiliar with poetry as an art form, now is the time to brush up. It's especially important to know some poetic terminology as well as the difference between types of poems such as free verse and sonnets. You may want to start learning terms by jotting down definitions of words you want to remember. The following terms are a sample of important terms to know for the CLEP Humanities exam.

Alliteration The repetition of the same starting sound in several words of a sentence.

Antithesis A figure of speech in which words and phrases with opposite meanings are balanced against each other. For example, "To err is human, to forgive, divine."

Caesura A natural break or pause in a line of poetry. Look for caesura near the middle of a line.

Elegy Typically a poem that laments the death of a person.

Free verse Uses either rhymed or unrhymed lines without a set meter.

Haiku Japanese poetic form with three lines of five, seven, and five syllables.

Hyperbole The literary use of exaggeration for effect or emphasis.

Iambic pentameter A type of meter in poetry in which there are five iambs to a line. An iamb is an unstressed syllable followed by a stressed syllable or a short syllable followed by a long syllable. For example, "I *know* that *I* will *pass* the *CLEP* exam" is an iambic pentameter line. Say it out loud to get a sense of the rhythm. Keep in mind that most of Shakespeare's plays were written in iambic pentameter—this is a very common type of meter in English poetry.

Metaphor A figure of speech in which a word or phrase that ordinarily represents one thing is used to denote another, creating a comparison without using *like* or *as*.

Onomatopoeia Use of words to represent the sounds of actions or objects they refer to.

Simile A figure of speech used to compare two unlike things joined by the word *like* or *as*.

Sonnet A verse of fourteen lines with a conventional rhyme scheme.

There are many more poetic terms to learn. It's a good idea to get a poetry textbook from the library and create flashcards. Another good study method is to read poems and write down examples of terms you find within their lines. Reading poetry aloud is helpful as well. It is much easier to hear the differences in meter, rather than simply to see them on a page. Check the Internet for glossaries of poetry terms, if you prefer online sources.

Covering Extensive Time Periods

If knowing every poet from every century seems an impossible task, break the task up into segments. One way to study the names of poets is to create a timeline. Your timeline should include the important poets (or poems) of each period along with the type of verse each poet or poem covers. Before you begin, gather the most important figures of each period according to the time period they lived in. A table of poets by century they lived in might look like this.

Century	Sixteenth Century	Seventeenth Century	Eighteenth Century	Nineteenth Century
Well-Known Poets	Edmund Spenser	John Dryden	Thomas Gray	Samuel Coleridge
	Sir Phillip Sidney	John Milton	Alexander Pope	William Wordsworth
	Christopher Marlowe	Andrew Marvell		John Keats
		John Donne		Lord Byron
				Heinrich Heine

Find a famous example of a poem by each poet (Spenser's classic epic poem *The Fairie Queene* is a good bet for study, as is Andrew Marvell's "To His Coy Mistress") and place it next to the century in which that poet wrote. You may also want to note the time periods for different movements. For example, Romanticism was a product of the late 1700s. Put the different movements on your timeline and memorize them along with poets for each time period.

You can use the following type of timeline to put your thoughts together:

Timeline: History of Poetry

15th Century	16th Century	17th Century	18th Century	19th Century	20th Century
John Skelton, John Lydgate	Edmund Spenser, Sir Phillip Sidney, Christopher Marlowe	John Dryden, John Milton, Andrew Marvell, John Donne	Thomas Gray, Alexander Pope	Samuel Coleridge, William Wordsworth, John Keats, Lord Byron, Heinrich Heine	Jack Kerouac, Allen Ginsburg, Rita Dove

Poetry Resources

There is no shortage of books and websites offering information on poetry. The Norton Anthologies are particularly good for studying poetry. Acquire *The Norton Anthology of Poetry* (Fourth Edition), edited by Margaret Ferguson, Mary Jo Salter, and John Stallworthy (New York: Norton, 1996) and *The Norton Anthology of Modern and Contemporary Poetry* (Third Edition), edited by Jahan Ramazani et al (New York: Norton, 2003). Try reading some poems before bed every night. The Anthologies tie in quite well with a copy of a good college poetry textbook of terms. Consult poets.org for an extensive guide to movements in poetry, including the Beats and Surrealists. "Voice of the Shuttle" at vos.ucsb.edu is an easy-access guide to many academic websites.

FICTION, NONFICTION, AND PHILOSOPHY

What You Need to Know

This is a fairly large part of your exam, with 21–28 questions on fiction and 14 questions asking about nonfiction and philosophy. Once again, the content tested spans from the days of the ancient Greeks to recent or contemporary work. The fiction and nonfiction section of the CLEP Humanities exam will ask you to identify the names of writers, the particular work of a particular writer, or to correctly note a theme or plot. There will be some questions testing your general knowledge of philosophy, as well as some comparing plot and theme of several works. The philosophy section covers the Western philosophical tradition, with some attention given to principles and thinkers of Eastern traditions such as Hinduism, Buddhism, Taoism, Confucianism, and Islam.

Fiction, Nonfiction, and Philosophy Terms to Learn

Characterization The way writers reveal character, typically through speech, dress, manner, and actions.

Conflict A struggle between opposing forces in a novel or story.

Epistemology The branch of philosophy that investigates the grounds and limits of human knowledge.

Flashback The presentation of an incident that occurred prior to the main timeframe of the work.

Foreshadowing Hints of things to come in a story or a novel.

Metaphor A comparison between unlike things without the use of *like* or *as*.

Metaphysics The branch of philosophy that seeks to understand the nature of reality and existence.

Plot The structure of incidents or events.

Resolution The end of the plot.

Simile A comparison between unlike things using *like* or *as*.

Style Choice of words and actions, aided by description, imagery, and other techniques.

Theme The central idea put forth in a work.

Tone The attitude of a writer toward his or her subject or characters.

Covering Extensive Time Periods

Your fiction, nonfiction, and philosophy timeline should include the important writers (and their works) of each period with the school of literature that they belong to (if applicable). Before you begin, gather the most important writers of each period by dates. Try to remember one great work by each writer.

Authors to Know
Classics/Ancient

Euripides

Herodotus

Homer

Ovid

Sappho

Sophicles

Suetonius

Thucydides

Virgil

*Aristotle

*Confucius

*Lao Tzu

*Plato

*Socrates

*Sun Tzu

Middle Ages

Margery Kempe

Sir Thomas Malory

Julian of Norwich

Geoffrey Chaucer

*Saint Augustine

*Ibn Khaldun

*Ibn Rushd

*Ibn Sina

Renaissance
(early)

Dante Alighieri

Francesco Petrarch

*Niccolo Machiavelli

(late)

Giovanni Boccaccio

Miguel de Cervantes

Rene Descartes

Michel de Montaigne

*Francis Bacon

*Thomas Hobbes

*Baruch Spinoza

Age of Reason/
Restoration (Eighteenth
Century)

Daniel Defoe

Samuel Richardson

Laurence Sterne

Jonathan Swift

*David Hume

*Immanuel Kant

*Gottfried Wilhelm Leibniz

*John Locke

*Adam Smith

Romantic (Eighteenth/
Nineteenth Century)

Jane Austen

Johann Goethe

Victor Hugo

Sir Walter Scott

Mary Shelley

*G. W. F. Hegel

Victorian (Nineteenth
Century)

Charles Dickens

George Eliot

Gustave Flaubert

Henry James

Herman Melville

Leo Tolstoy

Emile Zola

*Soren Kirkegaard

*Karl Marx

*John Stuart Mill

*Friedrich Nietzsche

Modern (Twentieth
Century)

F. Scott Fitzgerald

Ernest Hemingway

Zora Neale Hurston

James Joyce

Franz Kafka

Marcel Proust

Virginia Woolf

*Bertrand Russell

*Ludwig Wittgenstein

Late Modern (Twentieth
Century)

Ralph Ellison

Andre Gide

Gabriel Garcia Marquez

Flannery O'Connor

Postmodern (Twentieth
Century)

Raymond Carver

Phillip Roth

Salman Rushdie

*Jacques Derrida

* indicates philosopher

Fiction, Nonfiction, and Philosophy Resources

As with poetry, there is no shortage of books and websites offering information on fiction, nonfiction, and philosophy. Since it will not be possible to read dozens of novels prior to taking the CLEP Humanities exam, try to write down plot points for yourself. Reading shorter fiction is helpful. The Norton Anthologies are particularly useful. Acquire *The Norton Anthology of English Literature* (Seventh Edition) edited by M. H. Abrams (New York: Norton, 1999) or *The Norton Anthology of American Literature* (Sixth Edition) edited by Judith Tanka and Nina Baym (New York: Norton, 2003) and *The Norton Anthology of World Masterpieces* (Sixth Edition) edited by Maynard Mack (New York: Norton, 1992) and try to read a bit before bed every night. Any Oxford edition is a very good source of information as well.

Voice of the Shuttle at vos.ucsb.edu, as mentioned in the poetry section, is a great portal to many academic and literary websites.

FINAL THOUGHTS

Now that you're armed with enough information to begin studying, it's time to learn the best way to conquer the CLEP Humanities exam. A formula for success includes the following points.

Study Nightly, Don't Cram

Cramming won't help you pass the exam. There is too much to memorize in such a short amount of time, and cramming won't provide you with all the necessary facts you need to learn for the exam. It's best to spend an hour a day studying, without trying to cover everything at once. Break study time down into categories and schedule your time section by section.

Create a Master Timeline

Since a fair number of questions are cross-referential, it would be helpful to take your individual timelines and put them together into a master timeline reference sheet. A master sheet will clearly show various types of art in different eras. For example, Romantic art, poetry, and literature had to do with the emotions. Pinpoint each period or movement on your master list.

Remember One Painting, Book, or Fact

While there is no certainty it will be asked on the exam, it's helpful to know that Cervantes' most famous work is *Don Quixote*. Add to your list of names in each category the most important work by each writer, artist, or playwright.

Relax!

If you take the time to study hard, you can trust that you know the material. On test day, try to relax. Take deep breaths and focus your thoughts on the task at hand. Gentle stretching such as yoga and meditation can relax your mind before the test. Remember, you are prepared.

Good luck!

Chapter Fourteen: **Practice Test 2**

Time—90 minutes
140 Questions

Directions: For each of the following questions or incomplete statements, select the best answer or completion from the five options given.

Questions 1–2 refer to Marcel Duchamp's *Fountain*.

1. Duchamp's *Fountain* is a urinal placed on the floor of an art gallery. The piece is an example of

   (A) a found object.
   (B) rotogravure.
   (C) novice art.
   (D) Surrealism.
   (E) Neoclassicism.

2. Which of the following would best describe the piece's tone?

   (A) Melodramatic
   (B) Satirical
   (C) Romantic
   (D) Sober
   (E) Celebratory

3. In architecture, an arcade is

   (A) an open space used for recreational activities.
   (B) a row of arches that creates a covered walkway.
   (C) an outdoor, open air structure used for leisure and relaxation.
   (D) an ornate facade.
   (E) a row of benches used for leisure and relaxation.

4. Rene Descartes' "Cogito ergo sum" translates into

   (A) "do unto others."
   (B) "the set of all subsets."
   (C) "being *qua* being."
   (D) "I think therefore I am."
   (E) "all is vanity."

5. Which of the following were the most prominent artists of the Surrealist movement?

   (A) Salvador Dali and René Magritte
   (B) Morris Louis and Yves Klein
   (C) Jan Vermeer and Hans Holbein
   (D) Titian and Tintoretto
   (E) Anthony van Dyck and Albrecht Dürer

6. Designed and built in the mid-twentieth century, the Guggenheim Museum's spiral structure was conceived by the architect

   (A) Gottfried Bohm.
   (B) David Chipperfield.
   (C) Le Corbusier.
   (D) Aldo Van Eyck.
   (E) Frank Lloyd Wright.

GO ON TO THE NEXT PAGE

7. Which fifth-century B.C.E. Athenian philosopher set the standard for Western philosophy?

   (A) Aristotle

   (B) Henry David Thoreau

   (C) Bertrand Russell

   (D) Plato

   (E) Socrates

8. Who is R. Mutt?

   (A) Georgia O'Keefe

   (B) Fra Lippo Lippi

   (C) Robert Indiana

   (D) Marcel Duchamp

   (E) Hieronymus Bosch

9. Thomas Aquinas based his philosophy on the work of which of the following?

   (A) Marcus Aurelius

   (B) Aristotle

   (C) David Hume

   (D) Voltaire

   (E) Erasmus

10. Artist Salvador Dali and this young Spanish filmmaker collaborated on the classic *Un chien andalou.*

    (A) Federico Garcia Lorca

    (B) Diego Rivera

    (C) Luis Buñuel

    (D) Gabriel Garcia Marquez

    (E) Carlos Fuentes

11. Dali's film *Un chien andalou* is a work of

    (A) Super-realism.

    (B) Photorealism.

    (C) Impressionism.

    (D) Surrealism.

    (E) Classical cinema.

12. Which of the following was a contemporary of Franz Schubert?

    (A) Arthur Rubinstein

    (B) Arnold Schoenberg

    (C) Niccolo Paganini

    (D) Igor Stravinsky

    (E) Giuseppi Verdi

13. Which of the following philosophers claimed that all philosophical problems are problems of language and is responsible for the statement "What we cannot speak of, we must pass over in silence"?

    (A) Adam Smith

    (B) Euclid

    (C) Henri Rousseau

    (D) Ludwig Wittgenstein

    (E) John Dewey

14. Which of the following styles traces its roots to the Roman Empire?

    (A) Romantic

    (B) Baroque

    (C) Romanesque

    (D) Rococo

    (E) Postmodern

GO ON TO THE NEXT PAGE

15. The film *Battleship Potemkin*, which contains the Odessa massacre sequence—considered to be the greatest and most influential montage sequence in the history of cinema—is the work of this master Soviet filmmaker.

    (A) Dziga Vertov
    (B) Sergei Eisenstein
    (C) Lev Kuleshov
    (D) Vsevolod Pudovkin
    (E) Alexander Dovzhenko

16. In a symphony, the word *modulation* refers to

    (A) descending tones.
    (B) a change of key.
    (C) diapason.
    (D) "built on a second scale step."
    (E) ascending tones.

17. This comic genius of the silent era is known for risking life and limb in his stunts. He wrote, directed, and starred in films that include *The General*.

    (A) Billy Wilder
    (B) Charlie Chaplin
    (C) Howard Hawks
    (D) Buster Keaton
    (E) Frank Capra

18. Renowned choreographer George Balanchine founded this landmark dance company.

    (A) American Ballet Theater
    (B) Ballet Russe
    (C) Ballet Society
    (D) Miami City Ballet
    (E) Ballet New York

19. Which of the following artists is considered an "Abstract Expressionist"?

    (A) Paul Cézanne
    (B) Piet Mondrian
    (C) Odilon Redon
    (D) Pablo Picasso
    (E) Georges de la Tour

20. The phrase "like boats against the current" is an example of which literary device?

    (A) Simile
    (B) Characterization
    (C) Narrative
    (D) Structure
    (E) Dialogue

21. When the protagonist's voice tells the story of the novel, this is known as

    (A) first-person narration.
    (B) third-person narration.
    (C) second-person narration.
    (D) narrative drive.
    (E) unreliable narrator.

GO ON TO THE NEXT PAGE

KAPLAN

Courtesy of SuperStock, Inc.

22. Who is the painter of the work shown here?

    (A) Jacob Lawrence

    (B) Man Ray

    (C) Kenneth Noland

    (D) Vincent van Gogh

    (E) Mary Cassatt

23. Sinclair Lewis' *Babbit*, Evelyn Waugh's *The Loved One*, and Tom Wolfe's *The Bonfire of the Vanities* are all novels that

    (A) proclaim the rights of women.

    (B) call for the end of government.

    (C) politicize world events.

    (D) plead for a return to small-town values.

    (E) satirize American culture.

24. In Hawthorne's *The Scarlet Letter*, the *A* for adultery sewn to the dress of the protagonist is an example of which literary term?

    (A) Conceit

    (B) Theme

    (C) Point of view

    (D) Symbolism

    (E) Denouement

25. Which of the following is NOT a novel written by Somerset Maugham?

    (A) *Cakes and Ale*

    (B) *The Moon and Sixpence*

    (C) *Tom Jones*

    (D) *The Razor's Edge*

    (E) *Of Human Bondage*

26. N. Scott Momaday, Sherman Alexie, and Louise Erdrich have all written books based on an inside understanding of which culture?

    (A) Eastern European

    (B) Native American

    (C) African American

    (D) Cuban American

    (E) Central Asian

27. *Gigi* tells the story of a young girl groomed to become a courtesan in turn-of-the-century Paris who rebels and marries instead. The film is based on the work of which iconoclastic French writer?

    (A) Colette

    (B) Honore de Balzac

    (C) Jean Cocteau

    (D) Marguerite Duras

    (E) Simone de Beauvoir

GO ON TO THE NEXT PAGE

28. The *Federalist Papers* was originally published as a series of separate articles encouraging

    (A) ratification of the U.S. Constitution.

    (B) war between the colonists and Great Britain.

    (C) the signing of the Articles of Confederation.

    (D) a Constitutional Convention in Philadelphia.

    (E) war between the Northern and Southern states.

29. Which author published *Thus Spoke Zarathustra*, a philosophical treatise written as a series of allegories?

    (A) Soren Kierkegaard

    (B) Jean-Paul Sartre

    (C) Denis Diderot

    (D) Friedrich Nietzsche

    (E) Thomas Aquinas

30. The unfolding of events within a novel or play is known as

    (A) characterization.

    (B) symbolism.

    (C) plot.

    (D) denouement.

    (E) climax.

31. Which of the following writers is correctly matched with his school of literature?

    (A) Robert Frost . . . play

    (B) Christopher Marlowe . . . essay

    (C) Yukio Mishima . . . poetry

    (D) E. M. Forster . . . novel

    (E) Niccolo Machiavelli . . . prose poem

32. Which of the following instruments is the smallest string instrument found in an orchestra?

    (A) Bass

    (B) Violin

    (C) Cello

    (D) Viola

    (E) Double bass

33. *Pamela* by Samuel Richardson and *Lady Susan* by Jane Austen are both examples of which early style of novel?

    (A) Narrative

    (B) Formulaic

    (C) Epistolary

    (D) Serial

    (E) Religious

34. The novel *Grendel*, by John Gardner, is based upon this sixth-century Anglo-Saxon poem but written from the point of view of the monster.

    (A) *Gulliver's Travels*

    (B) *The Inferno*

    (C) *Beowulf*

    (D) *The Seafarer*

    (E) *The Battle of Maldon*

35. In the novel, *Gulliver's Travels*, the Yahoos that Gulliver encounters are meant to be symbolic of

    (A) his English peers.

    (B) early American settlers.

    (C) the Puritans.

    (D) the Shakers.

    (E) mentally ill patients.

GO ON TO THE NEXT PAGE

36. *Bard* is a Middle English word for which type of writer?

    (A) Novelist
    (B) Poet
    (C) Essayist
    (D) Short-story writer
    (E) Journalist

37. In Isabel Allende's *House of the Spirits* and Toni Morrison's *Beloved*, fantastic and inexplicable events take place amid ordinary lives. This style of novel is often referred to as

    (A) epistolary.
    (B) creative nonfiction.
    (C) magical realism.
    (D) reactionary.
    (E) epic.

38. The opera *Eugene Onegin* is based on a work by which of the following authors?

    (A) William Makepeace Thackeray
    (B) Daniel Defoe
    (C) Anna Akhmatova
    (D) Colette
    (E) Aleksandr Pushkin

39. Li Po and So Shu are famous

    (A) Chinese poets.
    (B) Taiwanese composers.
    (C) Japanese philosophers.
    (D) Indian mystics.
    (E) Korean architects.

40. Which of the following instruments is NOT a woodwind?

    (A) Oboe
    (B) Flute
    (C) Bassoon
    (D) Saxophone
    (E) Harp

41. The Pulitzer Prize-winning novel *The Hours* is based upon *Mrs. Dalloway*, the classic novel by which turn-of-the-century writer?

    (A) Jane Austen
    (B) Charlotte Bronte
    (C) Emily Bronte
    (D) Virginia Woolf
    (E) Harriet Beecher Stowe

42. Langston Hughes, Richard Wright, Jean Toomer, and Zora Neale Hurston were collectively known as part of the

    (A) Brotherhood of the Book.
    (B) Harlem Renaissance.
    (C) Narrative Collective.
    (D) New York Experience.
    (E) Brooklyn Book Circle.

43. Which group of writers is considered to be part of the Romantic movement in British literature?

    (A) Edmund Spenser, John Milton, William Shakespeare
    (B) Mary Shelley, Robert Burns, Jane Austen
    (C) Dante, Thomas More, Mary Herbert
    (D) Thomas Wyatt, John Davies, Philip Sidney
    (E) Charles Dickens, Henry James, Edith Wharton

GO ON TO THE NEXT PAGE ▷

44. Which of the following dramatists was a contemporary of William Shakespeare?

(A) Christopher Marlowe

(B) John Dryden

(C) William Wycherley

(D) Thornton Wilder

(E) Harold Pinter

45. Which of the following works is a Renaissance painting?

(A) *The School of Athens*

(B) *Las Meninas*

(C) *Embarkation to the Island of Cythera*

(D) *Guernica*

(E) *The Fountainhead*

46. If a play is called a farce, it might also be called a

(A) tragedy.

(B) comedy.

(C) masterpiece.

(D) drama.

(E) romance.

47. In this play and subsequent film, the restless son and isolated daughter of a fading Southern belle invite an old schoolmate to visit, with the forlorn hope that he will be interested in marrying the shy daughter. When this does not happen, the son abandons his mother and sister to their lonely life and inability to accept reality. What is the play's title?

(A) *Our Town*

(B) *Sweet Bird of Youth*

(C) *A Streetcar Named Desire*

(D) *After the Fall*

(E) *The Glass Menagerie*

48. When a literary work does not follow or dispenses with traditional patterns of plot, characters, or dialogue, it might be called

(A) a narrative.

(B) romantic.

(C) a genre.

(D) experimental.

(E) technical.

49. Which of the following is a group of Cubist painters?

(A) Michelangelo, Leonardo da Vinci, Jan van Eyck

(B) Pablo Picasso, Juan Gris, Georges Braque

(C) Claude Monet, Camille Pissarro, Berthe Morisot

(D) Jean Dubuffet, Alberto Giacometti, Francis Bacon

(E) Ellsworth Kelly, Agnes Martin, Franz Kline

50. Paul Cézanne painted which of the following objects over and over?

(A) A cathedral

(B) A mountain

(C) A haystack

(D) An ox

(E) A boot sole

51. John Constable, Frederic Church, and Claude Lorrain are all famous for painting

(A) self-portraits.

(B) the demise of historical figures.

(C) with sand.

(D) landscapes.

(E) murals.

GO ON TO THE NEXT PAGE

52. John Webster and Ben Johnson are two play-wrights who wrote during the

    (A) Restoration.
    (B) modern era.
    (C) Elizabethan era.
    (D) classical era.
    (E) post–World War II era.

53. The plays of Samuel Beckett, Jean-Paul Sartre, and Harold Pinter are all considered to be

    (A) existential.
    (B) optimistic.
    (C) anticlimactic.
    (D) episodic.
    (E) melodramatic.

54. When a character in a play speaks directly to the audience, this is known as

    (A) "characterization."
    (B) "foreshadowing."
    (C) "peripety."
    (D) "breaking the fourth wall."
    (E) "point of attack."

55. In theater, the Greek term *deus ex machina* refers to

    (A) an implausible ending where everything is resolved.
    (B) a play that ends in death for all the characters.
    (C) a scene leading to another scene.
    (D) a particularly happy ending.
    (E) a character arriving at the last minute.

56. According to Aristotle's *Poetics*, what element is intertwined with plot?

    (A) Structure
    (B) Character
    (C) Setting
    (D) Narration
    (E) Dialogue

57. *Little Dorrit*, *The Pickwick Papers*, and *Bleak House* were all written by this prolific nineteenth-century English novelist.

    (A) Washington Irving
    (B) Charles Dickens
    (C) Victor Hugo
    (D) Leo Tolstoy
    (E) Edith Wharton

58. This film tells the story of a rich but lonely newspaper magnate who alienates everyone around him, including his two wives. He dies alone, remembering his forgotten childhood and uttering the name of his lost sled.

    (A) *The Heart Is a Lonely Hunter*
    (B) *A Clockwork Orange*
    (C) *The Lion in Winter*
    (D) *Citizen Kane*
    (E) *The Last Angry Man*

59. Thornton Wilder won a Pulitzer Prize for the play *Our Town*. He also had won a Pulitzer Prize ten years earlier for this novel.

    (A) *Breakfast at Tiffany's*
    (B) *The Executioner's Song*
    (C) *Red Sky at Morning*
    (D) *The Bridge of San Luis Rey*
    (E) *Goodbye, Columbus*

GO ON TO THE NEXT PAGE

60. The great composer Ludwig van Beethoven and the poet Lord Byron both died in which century?

    (A) Fifteenth

    (B) Sixteenth

    (C) Seventeenth

    (D) Eighteenth

    (E) Nineteenth

61. The late composer George Gershwin is renowned for inspiring the symphony form of what type of music?

    (A) Ballet

    (B) Piano

    (C) Violin

    (D) Jazz

    (E) Chamber

62. The plays *Medea*, *Oedipus Rex*, and *Mourning Becomes Electra* are all considered to be

    (A) romances.

    (B) comedies.

    (C) experimental.

    (D) farces.

    (E) tragedies.

63. The classic operas *The Magic Flute* and *The Marriage of Figaro* were both composed by

    (A) Modest Mussorgsky.

    (B) Giuseppi Verdi.

    (C) Wolfgang Amadeus Mozart.

    (D) Camille Saint-Saens.

    (E) Peter Ilych Tchaikovsky.

64. What time frame spanned the Classical period in music?

    (A) 1600–1750

    (B) 1750–1825

    (C) 1825–1900

    (D) 1850–1920

    (E) 1725–1850

65. *The Nutcracker* ballet is an annual Christmas event that was originally choreographed in 1882. Which of the following composers wrote the score?

    (A) Igor Stravinsky

    (B) Darius Milhaud

    (C) Peter Ilych Tchaikovsky

    (D) Aaron Copland

    (E) Johann Sebastian Bach

66. In which of the following works is the philosopher Gottfried Leibniz satirized as Dr. Pangloss?

    (A) *Light in August* by William Faulkner

    (B) *The Sufferings of Young Werthe*r by Johann von Goethe

    (C) *Thousand Cranes* by Yasunari Kawabata

    (D) *Interpreter of Maladies* by Jhumpa Lahiri

    (E) *Candide* by Voltaire

67. The music of the Middle Ages was almost always inspired by

    (A) weddings.

    (B) religion.

    (C) childbirth.

    (D) funerals.

    (E) good harvests.

GO ON TO THE NEXT PAGE ▷

68. A villanelle is a kind of

 (A) oil painting.

 (B) architectural nuance.

 (C) poem.

 (D) play.

 (E) orchestral movement.

69. Debussy, Ravel, and Monet were members of this school of art and music, which flourished in the late 1800s.

 (A) Romantic

 (B) Renaissance

 (C) Impressionist

 (D) Experimental

 (E) Neoclassical

70. The Romantic Age in music, art, and literature is associated with which attribute?

 (A) Logic

 (B) Delicacy

 (C) Imagination

 (D) Emotion

 (E) Spectacular design

71. Of the following instruments, which one is least likely to be found in a classical orchestra?

 (A) Flute

 (B) Dulcimer

 (C) Piccolo

 (D) Viola

 (E) Cymbals

Questions 72–74 are based on the following people.

 (A) Philip Glass, Johann Strauss, Stephen Sondheim

 (B) Jackson Pollack, Marc Chagall, Henri Matisse

 (C) Jane Austen, Marcel Proust, Tillie Olson

 (D) Martha Graham, George Balanchine, Jerome Robbins

 (E) T.S. Eliot, George Sand, Paul Auster

72. Which are composers?

73. Which are visual artists?

74. Which are choreographers?

75. Benjamin Britten, Felix Mendelsohn, Richard Wagner, and Karl Maria von Weber were all renowned as what type of artists?

 (A) Opera singers

 (B) Poets

 (C) Composers

 (D) Novelists

 (E) Choreographers

76. The figures in Paul Gauguin's most famous paintings are for the most part

 (A) Tahitian.

 (B) Hawaiian.

 (C) Inuit.

 (D) Jamaican.

 (E) Alsatian.

GO ON TO THE NEXT PAGE

Questions 77–78 are based on the following choices.

(A) *La Sylphide, Giselle, Sleeping Beauty*

(B) *Don Giovanni, Tristan and Isolde, Carmen*

(C) *Don Quixote, Madame Bovary, Anna Karenina*

(D) *Sleeping Beauty, Snow White, Little Red Riding Hood*

(E) *La Traviata, The Marriage of Figaro, Faust*

77. Which is a group of ballets?

78. Which is a group of novels?

79. Describing a piece of music or a ballet as being "adagio" means that the work is

(A) jumpy.

(B) slow.

(C) a pas de deux.

(D) climatic.

(E) fast.

80. Jazz singers like Ella Fitzgerald gave life to a unique style of singing that ran up and down the scales instead of hitting certain notes. This type of singing is known as

(A) aria.

(B) recitative.

(C) Beat.

(D) scat.

(E) contained.

81. Futurism was an art movement that emphasized

(A) motion.

(B) line.

(C) primary colors.

(D) cool colors.

(E) juxtaposition of disparate objects.

82. In this film, an ordinary man realizes how much his life has affected others when an angel visits him on Christmas Eve.

(A) *It Happened One Night*

(B) *A Streetcar Named Desire*

(C) *Citizen Kane*

(D) *Gone with the Wind*

(E) *It's a Wonderful Life*

83. What does the poetic term *hyberbole* mean?

(A) The use of exaggeration for effect or emphasis

(B) The use of similar words that have different meanings

(C) The use of *like* or *as* to compare two different things

(D) The use of words to denote the sound objects or actions make

(E) The repetition of predominantly consonant sounds at the beginning of words or syllables

84. Which language is also known as the language of ballet?

(A) Russian

(B) English

(C) French

(D) Romanian

(E) Spanish

85. Which of the following plays has a tragic character lost in the illusion that "personality will win the day?"

(A) Tennessee Williams' *A Streetcar Named Desire*

(B) Arthur Miller's *After the Fall*

(C) William Saroyan's *The Time of Your Life*

(D) Arthur Miller's *Death of a Salesman*

(E) Tennessee Williams' *The Glass Menagerie*

GO ON TO THE NEXT PAGE >

KAPLAN

86. Which of the following did T. S. Eliot NOT write?

    (A) "The Waste Land"
    (B) "Murder in the Cathedral"
    (C) "The Love Song of J. Alfred Prufrock"
    (D) "The Hollow Men"
    (E) "Goblin Market"

87. Which of the following was an ancient Greek poet?

    (A) Horace
    (B) Pericles
    (C) Sappho
    (D) Dante
    (E) Marcus Aurelius

88. William Shakespeare used the work of which of the following as sources for his plays?

    (A) Geoffrey Chaucer, Geoffrey of Monmouth, Plutarch
    (B) David Hume, Baruch Spinoza, Soren Kierkegaard
    (C) Edward Gibbon, Thomas Babington Macauley, Benjamin Disraeli
    (D) John Donne, Aphra Behn, John Dryden
    (E) Arthur Miller, Thornton Wilder, Lillian Hellman

89. Which of the following is NOT a device used in poetry?

    (A) Synecdoche
    (B) Metonymy
    (C) Foreshortening
    (D) Alliteration
    (E) Assonance

90. Which of the following is an example of alliteration?

    (A) "this morning morning's minion"
    (B) "in the room the women come and go"
    (C) "Tell me, Ramon Fernandez, if you know"
    (D) "all seems yellow to the jaundiced eye"
    (E) "All my pretty ones? Did you say all?"

91. Kobo Abe, Yukio Mishima, and Yasunari Kawabata are all

    (A) Chinese artists.
    (B) Japanese novelists.
    (C) Korean poets.
    (D) sculptors.
    (E) installation artists.

Questions 92–94 refer to the following people.

    (A) William Wordsworth, Lord Byron, John Keats
    (B) Rabindranath Tagore, Rumi, Kahlil Gibran
    (C) Horace, Ovid, Virgil
    (D) James Welch, Leslie Marmon Silko, Joy Harjo
    (E) Marianne Moore, H.D., Edna St. Vincent Millay

92. Which group belongs in the Romantic period?

93. Which group is composed of Native Americans?

94. Which group would be considered Modernist poets?

95. Henry Moore was a sculptor from

    (A) England.
    (B) the United States.
    (C) Australia.
    (D) Iceland.
    (E) Canada.

GO ON TO THE NEXT PAGE

Questions 96–98 refer to the following terms.

   (A) Installation art
   (B) Dance
   (C) Music
   (D) Poetry
   (E) Painting

96. Which of these activities would Niccolo Paganini be associated with?

97. Which of these activities would involve a choreographer?

98. Which of these activities first came into prominence in the second half of the twentieth century?

99. Which of the following types of art was brought into prominence in the Byzantine period?

   (A) Watercolor
   (B) Portrait painting
   (C) Landscape painting
   (D) Mosaic
   (E) Statuary

100. Spondee, anapest, and iamb all refer to what aspect of a poem?

   (A) Rhyme scheme
   (B) Theme
   (C) Trope
   (D) Meter
   (E) Stanza

Questions 101–103 refer to the following poem.

LXXXII.

I grant thou wert not married to my Muse
And therefore mayst without attaint o'erlook
The dedicated words which writers use
Of their fair subject, blessing every book
Thou art as fair in knowledge as in hue,
Finding thy worth a limit past my praise,
And therefore art enforced to seek anew
Some fresher stamp of the time-bettering days
And do so, love; yet when they have devised
What strained touches rhetoric can lend,
Thou truly fair wert truly sympathized
In true plain words by thy true-telling friend;
And their gross painting might be better used
Where cheeks need blood; in thee it is abused.

101. This text was written by

   (A) George Herbert.
   (B) William Shakespeare.
   (C) Wallace Stevens.
   (D) Coventry Patmore.
   (E) Gustave Apollinaire.

102. What poetic form does this text use?

   (A) Free verse
   (B) Prose
   (C) Sonnet
   (D) Metaphor
   (E) Simile

GO ON TO THE NEXT PAGE

KAPLAN

103. What is iambic pentameter?

   (A) A series of rhymed lines

   (B) A type of poem in which stressed and unstressed syllables alternate five times per line

   (C) An ironic work in which the author puts a lot of feeling into the text

   (D) A political rebuttal written in Britain during the Enlightenment

   (E) A rhyme scheme in which consonant sounds are repeated throughout each line

104. Gertrude Stein, William Carlos Williams, and Maria Rainer Rilke are all close contemporaries of which of the following?

   (A) I. M. Pei, Isamu Noguchi, Phillip Glass

   (B) Christopher Wren, Rembrandt, Johann Sebastian Bach

   (C) John Ruskin, Richard Wagner, Theodore Gericault

   (D) Frank Lloyd Wright, Paul Gaugain, Claude Debussy

   (E) Filippo Brunelleschi, Titian, Claudio Monteverdi

105. Which of the following figures of the twentieth century is INCORRECTLY matched to his or her art form?

   (A) Le Corbusier . . . architect

   (B) Pablo Neruda . . . conceptual artist

   (C) Moses Isegawa . . . novelist

   (D) Jean Arp . . . sculptor

   (E) Nelly Sachs . . . poet

106. "Adonais" was an elegy for John Keats written by

   (A) William Wordsworth.

   (B) Percy Bysshe Shelley.

   (C) John Donne.

   (D) Dante Alighieri.

   (E) Heinrich Heine.

107. Which of the following musicians is a cellist?

   (A) Yo-Yo Ma

   (B) Jennifer Koh

   (C) Arthur Rubinstein

   (D) Vladmir Feltzman

   (E) Mischa Elman

108. Leopold and Molly Bloom are characters from a novel by which of the following authors?

   (A) Laurence Sterne

   (B) Moses Isegawa

   (C) Chinua Achebe

   (D) Kate Chopin

   (E) James Joyce

109. *Jane Eyre* is a novel written by whom?

   (A) Charlotte Bronte

   (B) Jane Austen

   (C) Aphra Behn

   (D) Anne Bronte

   (E) Emily Bronte

110. Which instruments form a string quartet?

   (A) Two flutes, one piccolo, one trumpet

   (B) One clarinet, two French horns, one bass

   (C) One viola, two violins, one cello

   (D) Two cellos, one saxophone, one double bass

   (E) One drum, one bass, one piano

GO ON TO THE NEXT PAGE

111. Thomas Hobbes' *Leviathan* argues for which kind of political system?

    (A) Democracy

    (B) Socialism

    (C) Autocracy

    (D) Communism

    (E) Plutocracy

112. In the film as well as the novel by William Makepeace Thackeray, the protagonist, Becky Sharp

    (A) is born into a wealthy family.

    (B) is an Olympic swimmer.

    (C) schemes and connives her way into high society.

    (D) is a naive young woman in a wicked world.

    (E) doesn't care for material things.

113. What is the title of the novel referred to in question 112 by Thackeray?

    (A) *Vanity Fair*

    (B) *Look Back in Anger*

    (C) *Death Be Not Proud*

    (D) *The House of Mirth*

    (E) *The Age of Grief*

114. *The Human Comedy* was produced by

    (A) Georges Bizet.

    (B) Hector Berlioz.

    (C) Honore de Balzac.

    (D) Gustave Flaubert.

    (E) Arthur Rimbaud.

115. Photorealism is a movement in

    (A) photography.

    (B) installation art.

    (C) land art.

    (D) painting.

    (E) poetry.

116. In painting, chiaroscuro involves

    (A) light and shadow.

    (B) color.

    (C) theme.

    (D) the vanishing point.

    (E) figures.

117. You would most likely find a bas-relief

    (A) on a canvas.

    (B) in a video installation.

    (C) on the face of a building.

    (D) in an etching.

    (E) in a post-Impressionist painting.

Courtesy of SuperStock, Inc.

118. Pointillism, developed by Georges Seurat, painter of *Bathers at Asniers* above, is a method involving

    (A) straight lines.

    (B) points of color.

    (C) pointed political commentary.

    (D) photorealism.

    (E) multiple vanishing points.

GO ON TO THE NEXT PAGE →

KAPLAN

Used by permission. See copyright page (iv) for information.

119. Who is the painter of this work?

  (A) Jacob Lawrence

  (B) Man Ray

  (C) Kenneth Noland

  (D) Andrew Wyeth

  (E) Mary Cassatt

120. Filippo Brunelleschi is most famous for his work on which of the following structures?

  (A) Column

  (B) Amphitheatre

  (C) Statuary

  (D) Dome

  (E) Arch

121. Which of the following were both artists and poets?

  (A) Dante Gabriel Rossetti, William Blake, Michelangelo

  (B) Edith Wharton, Rene Descartes, Renzo Piano

  (C) Federico Garcia Lorca, Francisco de Zurburan, Gabriela Mistral

  (D) Gail Tsukiyama, Vikram Seth, Margaret Atwood

  (E) Robert Browning, Alfred Lord Tennyson, Charlotte Bronte

122. A novel concerning the moral and psychological development of the protagonist is called a

  (A) roman á clef.

  (B) bildungsroman.

  (C) young-adult literature.

  (D) fairy tale.

  (E) saga.

Questions 123–125 refer to the following artists.

  (A) Auguste Rodin, Michelangelo, Giovanni Bernini

  (B) Frank Gehry, I. M. Pei, Christopher Wren

  (C) Judy Chicago, Jenny Holzer, Barbara Kruger

  (D) Piet Mondrian, Vincent van Gogh, Jan Vermeer

  (E) Andy Warhol, Roy Lichtenstein, Richard Hamilton

123. Which is a group of Dutch-born painters?

124. Which is a group of Pop artists?

125. Which is a group of sculptors?

126. Which of the following novels was NOT written by Ayn Rand?

  (A) *The Fountainhead*

  (B) *Atlas Shrugged*

  (C) *Anthem*

  (D) *We the Living*

  (E) *This Side of Paradise*

GO ON TO THE NEXT PAGE

127. Which of the following is a twenty-first century author?

    (A) Charlotte Perkins Gilman
    (B) Matthew Mauri
    (C) Charles Dickens
    (D) Charlotte Bronte
    (E) Toni Morrison

Questions 128–130 refer to the following people.

    (A) Jacques Lipchitz
    (B) George Eliot
    (C) Federico Garcia Lorca
    (D) I. M. Pei
    (E) Fomich Nijinsky

128. Which is a sculptor?

129. Which is a woman?

130. Which is a poet?

131. The first three books of John Galsworthy's *The Forsythe Saga* revolve around the failed relationship of

    (A) Tristan and Isolde.
    (B) Novalis and Sophie.
    (C) Hero and Leander.
    (D) Soames and Irene.
    (E) Clarissa and Peter.

132. "Naturalist" or "Realist" novels are works in which human beings

    (A) triumph over nature.
    (B) succumb to natural forces.
    (C) come to understand the beauty of nature.
    (D) retreat to idyllic, natural landscapes.
    (E) tamper with nature through medical science.

133. Dadaism was a movement in which

    (A) artists returned to classical techniques.
    (B) artists subverted classical notions of art.
    (C) drawing revolved around new sketching techniques.
    (D) the human figure returned to oil painting.
    (E) sculptors worked exclusively with marble.

Questions 134–136 refer to the following structure.

Photograph by Dean Fox. Courtesy of SuperStock, Inc.

134. The architect of this structure is

    (A) Frank Lloyd Wright.
    (B) Buckminster Fuller.
    (C) Mies van der Rohe.
    (D) Alexandre-Gustave Eiffel.
    (E) Renzo Piano.

GO ON TO THE NEXT PAGE

135. This piece is located in

    (A) Normandy.

    (B) Geneva.

    (C) Chicago.

    (D) Buenos Aires.

    (E) Paris.

136. It is primarily considered

    (A) a place of business.

    (B) a lighthouse.

    (C) a temporary edifice.

    (D) a storage facility.

    (E) a work of art.

137. The sonnets of Shakespeare and most of his plays are written in

    (A) iambic pentameter.

    (B) trochaic hexameter.

    (C) blank verse.

    (D) free verse.

    (E) spondaic tetrameter.

138. Assonance is the repetition of

    (A) vowel sounds.

    (B) interior consonant sounds.

    (C) initial consonant sounds.

    (D) verbs.

    (E) adjectives.

139. *The Laocoon Group* is a(n)

    (A) Hellenic sculpture.

    (B) medieval sculpture.

    (C) Romanesque façade.

    (D) Egyptian sculpture.

    (E) Asian sculpture.

140. Lady Gregory and J. M. Synge were key figures in the dramatic Renaissance of which country?

    (A) England

    (B) Australia

    (C) Poland

    (D) the United States

    (E) Ireland

END OF TEST. STOP

THE ANSWER KEY APPEARS ON THE FOLLOWING PAGE.

ANSWER KEY

1. A	21. A	41. D	61. D	81. A	101. B	121. A
2. B	22. D	42. B	62. E	82. E	102. C	122. B
3. B	23. E	43. B	63. C	83. A	103. B	123. D
4. D	24. D	44. A	64. B	84. C	104. D	124. E
5. A	25. C	45. A	65. C	85. D	105. B	125. A
6. E	26. B	46. B	66. E	86. E	106. B	126. E
7. E	27. A	47. E	67. B	87. C	107. A	127. E
8. C	28. A	48. D	68. C	88. A	108. E	128. A
9. B	29. D	49. B	69. C	89. C	109. A	129. B
10. C	30. C	50. B	70. D	90. A	110. C	130. C
11. D	31. D	51. D	71. B	91. B	111. C	131. D
12. C	32. B	52. C	72. A	92. A	112. C	132. B
13. D	33. C	53. A	73. B	93. D	113. A	133. B
14. C	34. C	54. D	74. D	94. E	114. C	134. D
15. B	35. A	55. A	75. C	95. A	115. D	135. E
16. B	36. B	56. B	76. A	96. C	116. A	136. E
17. D	37. C	57. B	77. A	97. B	117. C	137. A
18. C	38. E	58. D	78. C	98. A	118. B	138. A
19. B	39. A	59. D	79. B	99. D	119. D	139. A
20. A	40. E	60. E	80. D	100. D	120. D	140. E

PRACTICE TEST 2 QUICK REFERENCE TABLES

Use the following tables to determine which topics you still need to review.

Topic	Test Question
Literature	
Drama	30, 44, 46, 48, 50, 52, 54, 55, 59, 62, 85, 88, 137, 140
Poetry	36, 39, 42, 68, 83, 86, 87, 89, 90, 92, 93, 94, 100, 101, 102, 103, 104, 106, 130
Fiction	21, 23, 24, 25, 33, 34, 35, 37, 41, 43, 57, 78, 91, 108, 109, 113, 114, 122, 126, 127, 129, 131, 132
Nonfiction/Philosophy	4, 7, 9, 13, 20, 26, 28, 29, 31, 53, 56, 66, 111, 138
The Arts	
Visual Arts (painting, sculpture, etc.)	1, 2, 5, 8, 14, 19, 22, 45, 49, 51, 73, 76, 81, 95, 98, 99, 115, 116, 117, 118, 119, 121, 123, 124, 125, 128, 133, 139
Architecture	3, 6, 105, 120, 134, 135, 136
Music	12, 16, 32, 38, 40, 60, 61, 63, 64, 65, 67, 69, 70, 71, 72, 75, 79, 80, 96, 107, 110
Performing Arts (film, dance, etc.)	10, 11, 15, 17, 18, 27, 47, 58, 74, 77, 82, 84, 97, 112

Topic	Number of Questions on Test	Number Correct
Literature	70	
Drama	14	
Poetry	19	
Fiction	23	
Nonfiction/Philosophy	14	
The Arts	70	
Visual Arts (painting, sculpture, etc.)	28	
Architecture	7	
Music	21	
Performing Arts (film, dance, etc.)	14	

Answers and Explanations

1. (A)

Fountain is an example of a found object. Not to be confused with novice art (C) or mock-primitive art, the piece is an example of the artist's taking something found in everyday life and attributing artistic value to it. Rotogravure (B) is an Intaglio printing process, Surrealism (D) was a twentieth-century artistic and literary movement, and Neoclassicism (E) is a revival of classical forms and aesthetics.

2. (B)

The piece is satirical. Duchamp was thumbing his nose at the art world and its rigid notions of what constituted "art."

3. (B)

Do not be fooled into believing that an architectural arcade is the same thing as a modern-day arcade with games. In terms of architecture, an arcade is a row of arches that creates a covered walkway. Note how the root *arc* in *arcade* looks like *arch*.

4. (D)

"I think therefore I am," is Descartes' statement of the only irrefutable fact of existence. "Cogito ergo sum," is Latin for "I think therefore I am."

5. (A)

Salvador Dali and René Magritte were the most prominent artists of the Surrealist movement. Louis and Klein (B) were predominantly color field painters, and the rest were long dead by the advent of Surrealism.

6. (E)

Frank Lloyd Wright designed the Guggenheim Museum. Wright is the only American architect listed as an answer choice. Since the Guggenheim is located in New York, an educated guess could have led you to the correct answer.

7. (E)

Socrates is considered to have set the standard for Western philosophy. Plato (D) was a student of Socrates and an important philosopher who wrote down Socrates' ideas. Aristotle (A) lived in the fourth century and was an important philosopher as well. Henry David Thoreau (B) was an American writer and philosopher who lived during the nineteenth century. Bertrand Russell (C) was a twentieth-century British philosopher and essayist.

8. (C)

All of these authors are African-American writers. Zora Neale Hurston died in 1960 and wrote during the Harlem Renaissance; her most notable work is *Their Eyes Were Watching God*. Toni Morrison is still alive and writing. Her first novel, *The Bluest Eye*, is taught in many classrooms and is considered a modern classic. Rita Dove is a Pulitzer Prize-winning poet.

9. (B)

Aquinas' system was a reaction to St. Augustine's Platonic-based philosophy. Except for Marcus Aurelius, the other choices were born long after Aquinas.

10. (C)

Luis Buñuel lived from 1900–1983. The other individuals are known for their achievements in literature and the visual arts.

11. (D)

Even if you are unfamiliar with the plot of *Un chien andalou*, remember that Salvador Dali is a Surrealist and is connected with Surrealist work. Super-realism (A) occurred between 1965 and 1975 and exemplified true-to-form sculpture. Photorealism (B) occurred during the later 1960s and exhibited realistic paintings. Impressionism (C) occurred between the years 1860–1900 and was another form of painting. Classical cinema lasted through 1928 and emphasized important narrative information. *Un chien andalou* was filmed during the Surrealist movement, which lasted from 1924 until the 1950s.

12. (C)

Paganini lived 1782–1840, in the same era as Schubert. Answers (A), (B), and (D) are all twentieth-century composers. Verdi (E), a tempting answer, lived in the late 1800s.

13. (D)

Wittgenstein was the most prominent and influential philosopher of the twentieth century and was single-handedly responsible for philosophy's current preoccupation with language. While some of the other choices such as Rousseau (C) were philosophers, only Wittgenstein emphasized language's importance to philosophy.

14. (C)

While Baroque style (B) has a peripheral relationship to classical art, Romanesque style is named for its Roman lineage. The Romantic era (A), Rococo (D), and postmodern (C) do not date back to the Roman Empire.

15. (B)

Eisenstein was, with American D. W. Griffith, one of the two pioneering geniuses of the modern cinema. The other filmmakers listed all made important contributions to Soviet cinema and the theory of montage.

16. (B)

"A change of key" is the definition of *modulation*. While notes ascend and descend on a scale [(E) and (A)], they do not necessarily modulate. A diapason (C) is an outpouring of sound, utilizing the whole range of a person's voice or an instrument. A modulation is not built on a second scale step (D).

17. (D)

Buster Keaton's influence on comic filmmaking continues to this day. Chaplin (B) was a contemporary of Keaton's. Wilder (A), Hawks (C), and Capra (E) worked after Keaton in the sound era.

18. (C)

The twentieth-century dancer and choreographer George Balanchine's first ballet company was called Ballet Society. It later became New York City Ballet. The other choices are also ballet companies.

19. (B)

Mondrian's work used simple colors and geometric shapes in a spare yet mesmerizing form. Georges de la Tour (E) predated Mondrian's work by several centuries, and while some of the other painters worked at roughly the same time as Mondrian, they all had greatly different styles.

20. (A)

These words from *The Great Gatsby* compare one thing or experience to another using *like* or *as*, the definition of "simile."

21. (A)

A story told in third person (B) removes the narrator's voice from the tale. Second person (C), which is rarely used, uses the pronoun *you*.

22. (D)

Starry Night is a painting created by Vincent van Gogh. It is currently held in the Museum of Modern Art in New York.

23. (E)

While these writers are not contemporaries of each other, all three of these novels poke fun at American culture and society. Instead of pleading for a return to small-town values (D), the novels suggest that these values have led to conformity and hypocrisy in American life. The novels did not all proclaim the rights of women (A), call for the end of government (B), or politicize world events (C).

24. (D)

"Conceit" (A) is a literary comparison, but the letter is not compared to any other item or person in the text. "Point of view" (C) refers to the method of narration used in the book, and "denouement" (E) refers to the end of a literary work. While *The Scarlet Letter* asks the reader to reconsider the morality of the time period, the scarlet letter itself serves as a *symbol* of this theme, not the theme itself (B).

25. (C)

Tom Jones is a novel written by Henry Fielding. The other novels were all written by Somerset Maugham.

26. (B)

All three of these writers are members of Native American tribes. Their books focus on daily life in modern Native American culture.

27. (A)

The film *Gigi* is based on Colette's short stories about life in Paris. While Simone de Beauvoir (E) is renowned as a feminist writer, she wrote in a later time period, as did Marguerite Duras (D).

28. (A)

The *Federalist Papers* were originally published between 1787 and 1788 and were intended to persuade the public to ratify the new Constitution.

29. (D)

Friedrich Nietzsche wrote *Thus Spoke Zarathustra*, a philosophical book in the form of allegories about a hermit named Zarathustra, between the years 1883 and 1885.

30. (C)

The unfolding and often linked events within a traditional novel or play form the plot. Characterization (A) involves representing a character by presenting mannerisms and movement. Symbolism (B) involves attributing symbolic meaning to objects, events, and people. Denouement (D) is the winding down of the play, while the climax (E) is the culmination of a crisis or period of intensity.

31. (D)

E. M. Forster is renowned for such novels as *A Room with a View*. Robert Frost (A) wrote poetry, Yukio Mishima (C) wrote novels, and Marlowe (B) wrote Elizabethan-era plays. Machiavelli's fourteenth-century nonfiction book about leadership (E), *The Prince*, is still often read today.

32. (B)

A violin is the smallest string instrument in an orchestra. While viola (D) is a tempting answer, it resembles a large violin, not a smaller one. A cello (C) is a large instrument, sometimes requiring a musician to stand up while playing. Bass (A) and double bass (E) are the largest string instruments in an orchestra.

33. (C)

The novels are epistolary. Like many early novels, both of these texts are written in the form of letters to other characters. While other early writers concentrated on religious themes, neither *Pamela* nor *Lady Susan* is concerned with religious topics (E), nor were they written to formula (B).

34. (C)

This award-winning novel chronicles the famous epic poem of *Beowulf*, but it is written in the sympathetic point of view of the monster, Grendel. While "The Seafarer"

(D) and "The Battle of Maldon" (E) are also early English works, they are incorrect choices.

35. (A)

A social satire, *Gulliver's Travels* pokes fun at the mores of author Jonathan Swift's contemporaries. To drive home the link between the brutish, humanlike Yahoos and Englishmen, the protagonist Gulliver begins to confuse the two cultures within the novel. Answers (B), (C), and (D) all involve Americans, while choice (E) is meant to distract test takers.

36. (B)

Bard is a Middle English word for "poet." The word *bard* can also refer to playwrights who wrote in verse like Shakespeare, but never to the other choices listed.

37. (C)

Magical realism is a school of writing that introduces magical elements to ordinary lives, often without explanation. Epistolary (A) refers to a novel written in letters or missives, and an epic novel (E) often spans many generations of lives. Do not be led astray by the term *creative nonfiction* (B). While it may contain some fictional elements, creative nonfiction refers to actual events.

38. (E)

The opera *Eugene Onegin* is based on a work by Aleksandr Pushkin, a prose poem written in the heart of the Romantic era. The poem has the same title as the opera.

39. (A)

Li Po and So Shu are famous Chinese poets. Both are notable poets of the Tang Dynasty (618–907). The other choices involve different nationalities and professions.

40. (E)

The harp is a string instrument, not a wind instrument. Wind instruments compress air to create sounds, or they create sounds when the musician blows through their mouthpiece. Woodwinds are characterized by their tubular shape and typically have keys or holes allowing the musician to produce different notes. Oboe (A), flute (B), bassoon (C), and saxophone (D) are all woodwinds.

41. (D)

Virginia Woolf wrote *Mrs. Dalloway* at the turn of the century. Note that the other writers did not write at the turn of the century.

42. (B)

Hughes, Wright, Toomer, and Hurston were all part of the Harlem Renaissance in the twentieth century. None of the other answers are art movements like the Harlem Renaissance, which was a flowering of African-American literature and art in the 1920s.

43. (B)

The Romantic movement flourished from the late 1700s through the early 1800s in Britain, giving voice to novels like Mary Shelley's *Frankenstein*. The other choices include writers from the Renaissance and nineteenth-century England.

44. (A)

Sometimes rumored to be the true author of Shakespeare's plays—a theory often disputed—Marlowe was born the same year as Shakespeare (1564) and also wrote in the Elizabethan era. Dryden (B) wrote after Shakespeare's death in the Restoration era, as did Wycherley (C). Thornton Wilder (an American) (D) and Harold Pinter (E) are both modern writers.

45. (A)

This painting by Raphael is representative of the Renaissance's fascination with classical Greek culture. *Las Meninas* (B) was painted by Diego Velázquez in 1656. *Embarkation to the Island of Cythera* (C) is a French Rococo painting by Jean-Antione Watteau. *Guernica* (D) is a modern painting by Pablo Picasso. *The Fountainhead* (E) is a novel by Ayn Rand.

46. (B)

Farce refers to broad comedy, often involving mistaken identity. A farce is too lighthearted and nonsensical to be a tragedy (A), masterpiece (C), drama (D), or romance (E).

47. (E)

A Streetcar Named Desire (C) and *Sweet Bird of Youth* (B) are also by Tennessee Williams and may be tempting answers, since they are also about fading Southern

women. Look for the hint of "isolated"; during *The Glass Menagerie*, Laura liked to be alone to stare at her glass animals. *Our Town* (A) and *After the Fall* (D) do not involve aging Southern belles.

48. (D)

Sometimes known as postmodern, experimental fiction pushes the boundaries of traditional writing. Test out each word in your mind: an experiment often results in "new" findings. None of the other terms work.

49. (B)

Picasso, Gris, and Braque all worked to bring Cubism into prominence. Other artists listed who followed the Cubists may have been influenced by Cubist techniques, but they would not be considered strictly Cubists.

50. (B)

Cézanne painted a local mountain from several different perspectives at different times of day. Monet had worked with haystacks (A) earlier on and worked with the Rouen Cathedral (A) in a similar way. Phillip Guston used the boot sole (E) as the central symbol of his work.

51. (D)

Each person was a prominent landscape painter in England, the United States, and France, respectively. None of the other choices reflect the painters' work.

52. (C)

Webster and Johnson wrote during the Elizabethan era. This era spanned the many years of Queen Elizabeth's rule and spawned great playwrights, due to the queen's continuing interest and financial investment in the theater.

53. (A)

The three playwrights listed are concerned with the meaningless nature of life and are considered to be part of the philosophical movement of existentialism. If you have seen any plays by these writers, you probably would never consider them optimistic (B).

54. (D)

In a realistic play, the audience is contained by a "fourth wall" and should not be addressed. Shakespeare had his characters address the audience at times, and Bertolt Brecht's plays are particularly renowned for this effect.

55. (A)

The term *deus ex machina* literally means "god in the machine," referring to the practice in Greek plays of a god figure descending and solving all the problems of the play. While answer (E), a character arriving at the last minute, could occur at this time, answer (A), an implausible ending where everything is resolved, is the better choice. The term does not refer to a play ending in death of all the characters (B), a scene leading to another scene (C), or a particularly happy ending (D).

56. (B)

Aristotle wrote in his classic text, *Poetics*, that without character there is no plot to set in motion and vice versa. The two are always, according to his ideas, dramatically linked. The other terms are not linked to *Poetics*.

57. (B)

Look for key words like "English" and "nineteenth-century." Edith Wharton (E) was American, Victor Hugo (C) was French, and Tolstoy (D) was Russian. Washington Irving (A), an American, wrote in the eighteenth century.

58. (D)

Kane famously intones the name "Rosebud" as he dies, which no one around him understands but which was actually the name of his childhood sled. The word symbolizes Kane's lost innocence.

59. (D)

Wilder is the rare artist who conquered two mediums with utter success—he was a master playwright and novelist.

60. (E)

Beethoven died in 1827, and Lord Byron died in 1824. Remember that the nineteenth century refers to the 1800s.

61. (D)

George Gershwin's *Rhapsody in Blue*, often called the first jazz symphony, uses elements of jazz never before entwined with classical forms. Gershwin did not inspire

ballet (A), piano (B), violin (C), or chamber (E) symphonic music.

62. (E)

As the characters in the plays listed meet their sad fate of death or, in the case of Oedipus, blindness, their downfalls are seen as great and unavoidable tragedies. None of the other choices are correct, especially choices (B) and (D). The tragic stories are far from being comedic, nor are they experimental (C) or quintessential romance (A).

63. (C)

Verdi (B) also wrote many famous operas, but Mozart's comic touch infuses the two operas listed. The other composers were not known for their operas.

64. (B)

The Baroque period spanned 1600–1750 (A). The Classical period spanned 1750–1825 (B); the Romantic era was 1825–1900 (C).

65. (C)

Igor Stravinsky (A) composed many ballet scores; however, he was born in 1882 and lived until 1971, much later than the era of *The Nutcracker*. Aaron Copland (D) was also a twentieth-century composer. Clearly, Bach (E) lived long before *The Nutcracker* was written, and Milhaud (B) never composed for the ballet.

66. (E)

Gottfried Leibniz is satirized in *Candide*. The work ridicules Leibniz's optimistic outlook by having Pangloss repeatedly utter the philosopher's maxim, "This is the best of all possible worlds," in the face of atrocities and disasters.

67. (B)

The music of the Middle Ages, both intensely superstitious and religious, sprang from the church and monasteries. The other choices did not have as much of an influence on music of the Middle Ages.

68. (C)

A villanelle is an elaborately structured poem, a literary structure often employed by Edna St. Vincent Millay.

69. (C)

This new way of looking at art and the world often depicted a pastoral setting. Debussy's "Afternoon of a Faun" is one of the most famous pieces from the Impressionist era.

70. (D)

Read the words carefully. "Romantic" refers not only to love but to the sentimental as well. This period was associated with the emotions.

71. (B)

A dulcimer is a simple, three-stringed instrument used for centuries to accompany ballads. All the other instruments would be used in an orchestral piece, including cymbals, used at intervals.

72. (A)

Glass, Strauss, and Sondheim are all composers. Glass and Sondheim are modern composers, while Strauss worked during the late Romantic period.

73. (B)

Pollack, Chagall, and Matisse were all visual artists. The other choices contain artists, dancers and choreographers, composers, and authors.

74. (D)

Graham, Balanchine, and Robbins were all choreographers. Graham is known for her work in the modern dance movement, while Balanchine worked in classical ballet.

75. (C)

Be careful to read the entire list of names before deciding on an answer. All of the choices listed are composers.

76. (A)

Gauguin's greatest work was produced during his exile in Tahiti. Paul Gauguin lived from 1848–1903 and was a Post-Impressionist artist.

77. (A)

La Sylphide, *Giselle*, and *Sleeping Beauty* are all ballets. The other choices contain a mixture of operas, novels, and ballets. Note that while answer (D) contains *Sleeping*

Beauty, which is a famous ballet, the other works are operas.

78. (C)

Don Quixote, *Madame Bovary*, and *Anna Karenina* are all novels. *Madame Bovary* and *Anna Karenina* both end tragically.

79. (B)

Adagio is a slow movement in music as well as in ballet. The movement is not jumpy (A), a pas de deux (C), climatic (D), or fast (E).

80. (D)

While Beat (C) may look right, remember that the Beat era popularized writing styles, not singing styles. Ella Fitzgerald practiced the scat style of singing.

81. (A)

The Futurists were concerned with the dynamism of motion as it pertained to the technological advancements of the time. Each of the other options was emphasized by different movements.

82. (E)

This classic Jimmy Stewart movie has often been copied but never duplicated as it follows an ordinary life and the reverberations every person has on others. It airs frequently on television between Thanksgiving and Christmas.

83. (A)

Choice (B) defines *homonyms*, choice (C) defines *simile*, choice (D) defines *onomatopoeia*, and choice (E) defines *alliteration*.

84. (C)

Since ballet originated in France, ballet terms such as *pas de deux* and *bras* (referring to the position of the arms) still exist in the French language today. While Russian (A) is a tempting answer since so many dancers are Russian, recalling balletic terms will help you to find the correct answer.

85. (D)

Often considered to have elements of Greek tragedy, Arthur Miller's *Death of a Salesman* features a protagonist who cannot accept the reality that he is no longer useful. While some of the other plays have tragic characters, none of them have the type of character that Willy Loman, the protagonist of *Death of a Salesman*, represents.

86. (E)

The noted and prolific poet T. S. Eliot composed many poems in his lifetime, including the other choices listed. "Goblin Market," however, is by Christina Rossetti.

87. (C)

Sappho's fragments compose one of the earliest bodies of verse known to us today. Pericles (B) was a famous Greek, but he was a statesman, not a poet. The remaining choices are Roman or Italian.

88. (A)

Only a select few of Shakespeare's plays have an original point of departure. It was important that the audience know the basic storyline of any play, so Shakespeare used preexisting tales by the three authors listed to formulate his own plays. The other answer choices feature authors who lived after Shakespeare.

89. (C)

Foreshortening is a technique used by painters. The other choices are all devices used in poetry.

90. (A)

This fragment from Gerard Manley Hopkins' poem "The Windhover" contains the repetition of initial consonant sounds that defines alliteration.

91. (B)

The trio are considered to be the greatest Japanese novelists of the twentieth century. Since the three writers are not from China or Korea and are not artists, the other answers cannot be correct.

92. (A)

Wordsworth, Byron, and Keats were English poets who wrote during the Romantic era. Poets in all of the other groups lived outside of the Romantic period.

93. (D)

Welch, Silko, and Harjo are all Native Americans. Each name under choice (D) is a poet of the latter half of the twentieth century. None of the other groups is composed of Native Americans.

94. (E)

Each woman in choice (E) wrote in the golden age of modern poetry. The Native American poets would be considered postmodern (or not attributable to any particular epoch). While the Romantics (as well as Tagore and Gibran) wrote in the modern era, they would not be considered Modernist, which is a distinct movement in the arts and philosophy.

95. (A)

Moore was England's most prominent sculptor (if not its most prominent artist) of the twentieth century. He lived 1898–1986. The sculptor Henry Moore is not to be confused with the English painter of the same name, who lived 1831–1895.

96. (C)

Paganini was a virtuoso violinist and composer during the Romantic period. The composer is not associated with installation art (A), dance (B), poetry (D), or painting (E).

97. (B)

A choreographer is primarily associated with dance. There may be some choreography involved in installation art (A), but the artist would not be considered a choreographer.

98. (A)

There may have been quasi-installation pieces from as early as the Byzantine period, but the art form didn't come into prominence until the past few decades. All of the other answer choices include art forms developed prior to the twentieth century.

99. (D)

Although not an exclusive mode for the Byzantine artist, mosaic became the popular medium of the Eastern portion of the Roman Empire. The other forms of art became prominent during different time periods.

100. (D)

Each term in the question refers to a system of stressed and unstressed syllables, which comprises a poem's meter. Although *iamb* can refer to a rhyme scheme (A), *spondee*, *anapest*, and *iamb* all refer to meter.

101. (B)

Note the focus on love, the iambic pentameter, and the fact that the poem is a sonnet. Shakespeare utilized all these devices/forms. George Herbert (A) was a seventeenth-century British poet who wrote about the metaphysical, which is not discussed in the poem. Wallace Stevens (C) was a twentieth-century modern American poet, who would not use words such as *thou* in his work. Coventry Patmore (D) was a British poet of the Victorian era (nineteeth century), so his works would not contain the same language as Shakespeare's either. Gustave Apollinaire (E) lived in France during the nineteenth and twentieth centuries.

102. (C)

Shakespeare was famous for his sonnets—this piece of work is his eighty-second sonnet. Free verse (A) is poetry written without rhythm, form, meter, or rhyme, some of which the poem employs. Prose (B) is matter-of-fact and unmetered, which does not constitute the work in question. Metaphor (D) and simile (E) are literary devices, not forms.

103. (B)

Iambic pentameter is a poetic device in which stressed and unstressed syllables alternate five times (*penta* refers to "five"). Lines in iambic pentameter do not have to rhyme (A). Iambic pentameter has nothing to do with irony (C), and it is not a political rebuttal (D). Consonant sounds may be repeated throughout each line (E), but they have nothing to do with a rhyme scheme or the poetic device of iambic pentameter.

104. (D)

While Victorian critic Ruskin (C) died in 1900, he is of a different era than writers Gertrude Stein or Rilke and far distant from the prime of Williams. Wright, Gaugain, and Debussy are all close contemporaries of Stein, Williams, and Rilke.

105. (B)

Pablo Neruda was a great Chilean poet, known for his touching love poems among other work. He was not known as a conceptual artist. All of the other figures are correctly matched to their discipline and art form.

106. (B)

The poem was written by Shelley shortly after Keats' death. Two of the options are chronologically impossible—John Donne (C) and Dante Alighieri (D). Both lived well before John Keats.

107. (A)

Jennifer Koh (B) is a violinist, while Arthur Rubinstein (C) and Vladmir Feltzman (D) are pianists. Mischa Elman (E) is also a violinist.

108. (E)

Leopold and Molly Bloom are a husband and wife who represent Ulysses and Penelope in Joyce's novel, *Ulysses*.

109. (A)

Charlotte Bronte's *Jane Eyre* bridges the Romantic and Victorian eras. Her sisters Anne (D) and Emily (E) were also writers, so those choices may confuse you. Anne wrote *The Tenant of Wildfell Hall*, while Emily wrote *Wuthering Heights*.

110. (C)

While a trio or a piano quartet can include different instruments, a string quartet always consists of four instruments: two violins (first and second), a viola, and a cello. Drums, flutes, French horns, saxophones, and other instruments are not included in a string quartet.

111. (C)

Hobbes was suspicious of the masses (especially the undereducated, landless peasants) and felt that if they were given power, the state would decline into anarchy.

112. (C)

Becky Sharp is a sympathetic character because Thackeray illustrates, through her, the difficulties and prejudices young women had to face in a male-dominated, materialistic society. Through scheming and conniving, Becky could make her way into high society.

113. (A)

Becky Sharp is a character in Thackeray's *Vanity Fair*. *The House of Mirth* (D), a tempting answer, is by Edith Wharton.

114. (C)

The Human Comedy refers to the group of novels in which Balzac, a French realist, attempts to depict life in Paris as accurately as possible.

115. (D)

Artists like Close and Estes have used painting techniques to render photographic images. Photography (A) may be a tempting answer, since the paintings of photorealism are supposed to look so much like actual photos, but that choice is incorrect.

116. (A)

While color (B) may be an element in chiaroscuro, by definition this term refers to the manipulation of light and shadow. Theme (C), the vanishing point (D), and figures (E) are not central to chiaroscuro.

117. (C)

Bas-relief refers to a surface sculpture raised from a wall or door. None of the other choices could contain this feature.

118. (B)

Seurat's close study of the juxtaposition of colors enabled him to enhance certain colors, while producing novel effects of shadow and light. Pointillism is the use of points of color. The full effect of a Pointillist painting is often best when viewed from across a room.

119. (D)

The painting *Christina's World* is indicative of Wyeth's examination of perspective in American landscapes.

120. (D)

Brunelleschi's dome in Florence is a landmark in Renaissance art and architecture. While Brunelleschi worked with different architectural forms, he is most famous for his work on domes.

121. (A)

While some of the other people may have dabbled in one medium or the other, the only group that fits the question's criteria is answer choice (A). Michelangelo was a poet, but he was not famous for his poetry.

122. (B)

Hesse's *Siddhartha* is a perfect example of a bildungsroman type of novel. Siddhartha, the main character in the book, finds himself through a journey of internal and external reflection.

123. (D)

Though they painted in different styles, each artist in answer (D) was born in the Netherlands. The artists in the other choices were born in different places, including Italy, Austria, and America.

124. (E)

While there are elements of Pop Art in the work of the feminist artists listed (C), they are not considered to be Pop Artists. Warhol is famous for his use of Campbell's soup cans and other everyday cultural objects in his work.

125. (A)

While Judy Chicago (C) might be considered a sculptor, both Kruger and Holzer focus on installation art. Only group (A)—Rodin, Michelangelo, and Bernini—contains all sculptors.

126. (E)

This Side of Paradise was written by F. Scott Fitzgerald. All of the other choices were written by Ayn Rand.

127. (E)

Charlotte Perkins Gilman (A) wrote during the Victorian era, Matthew Mauri (B) is a made-up name, Charles Dickens (C) wrote in the 1800s in England, and Charlotte Bronte (D) also wrote during the 1800s. Toni Morrison, author of *Beloved* among other works, is the only twenty-first-century author.

128. (A)

Jacques Lipchitz was a sculptor. Lipchitz was a seminal figure in the modern art movement. None of the other choices are sculptors.

129. (B)

Born Mary Ann Evans, George Eliot took a man's name to gain credibility and went on to become the most prominent novelist of the Victorian period.

130. (C)

Federico Garcia Lorca was a prominent Spanish dramatist and poet mysteriously murdered by Franco's fascists early in the twentieth century. None of the other choices are poets.

131. (D)

Galsworthy uses the relationship of Soames and Irene to expose the overly materialistic transaction of marriage in the late Victorian period. Answers (A) and (C) refer to mythological or legendary figures, answer (B) refers to an actual relationship, and answer (E) refers to Virginia Woolf's novel *Mrs. Dalloway*.

132. (B)

This turn-of-the-(twentieth)-century movement was inspired by Darwin and the new view of the natural world as hostile and indifferent.

133. (B)

There were no specific media or techniques attributable to Dadaism; rather it was a philosophical (or non-philosophical) examination of the deeply entrenched principles of art. The Dadaists named themselves based on the word *Dada*, which has no meaning.

134. (D)

Alexandre-Gustave Eiffel constructed the Eiffel Tower. The French architect received the commission for this work amid much controversy.

135. (E)

After initial ambivalence from residents, the Eiffel Tower has come to symbolize the city of Paris. The Eiffel Tower is now a major tourist attraction for France, along with its wineries, metropolitan areas, and countryside villas.

136. (E)

The Eiffel Tower was erected for art's sake rather than from any utilitarian motivation. It was built in 1889 to commemorate the French Revolution.

137. (A)

While the sonnets occasionally and the plays often depart from this meter, it is the prominent mode in Shakespeare's work. There is some blank verse (C), though rarely any free verse (D), in his plays.

138. (A)

Assonance is a device used throughout lines of text to create a mood or atmosphere. No particular part of speech (such as verb, adjective, or noun) is preferred in the use of this literary device.

139. (A)

The sculpture depicts the torture of Laocoon and his sons for trying to warn the Trojans about the Trojan horse. The artist is unknown.

140. (E)

At the turn of the century, Ireland experienced a flourishing in the literary arts in general and the theater specifically, due in large part to the efforts of Lady Gregory and J. M. Synge.

Chapter Fifteen: **Practice Test 3**

Time—90 minutes
140 Questions

Directions: For each of the following questions or incomplete statements, select the best answer or completion from the five options given.

1. John Ashberry, W. S. Merwin, Adrienne Rich, Louise Gluck, and Yousef Komunyaka were all poets of

   (A) the first half of the twentieth century.

   (B) the early Renaissance.

   (C) the second half of the twentieth century.

   (D) the late Victorian period.

   (E) the Imagist movement.

2. Which modern classical composer pioneered twelve-tone composition?

   (A) Gustav Mahler

   (B) Arnold Schoenberg

   (C) Frederic Chopin

   (D) Claude Debussy

   (E) Yo-Yo Ma

3. Which of the following would best describe the central concern of Wallace Stevens in his poetry?

   (A) Imagination

   (B) Socialism

   (C) Poverty

   (D) Women's issues

   (E) Science

4. The opening movement of an opera is called

   (A) a prelude.

   (B) an epilogue.

   (C) a prologue.

   (D) an overture.

   (E) an overtone.

5. Which of the following poets has a type of sonnet named after him or her?

   (A) Walt Whitman

   (B) Petrarch

   (C) Anna Swir

   (D) Cathy Song

   (E) Samuel Taylor Coleridge

GO ON TO THE NEXT PAGE

KAPLAN

Questions 6–8 refer to the following authors and texts.

   (A) James Joyce's *Ulysses*

   (B) Virginia Woolf's *Orlando*

   (C) Ezra Pound's *Cantos*

   (D) Salman Rushdie's *The Satanic Verses*

   (E) William Carlos Williams' *Paterson*

6. Which takes place in Dublin?

7. Which takes place in New Jersey?

8. Which is patterned after a work by Dante?

9. Which of the following matches the poet to his/her epoch?

   (A) Elizabeth Barrett Browning . . . Age of Reason

   (B) Johann Wolfgang von Goethe . . . Romantic

   (C) John Dryden . . . Hellenic

   (D) Imamu Baraka . . . medieval

   (E) Emily Dickinson . . . postmodern

Questions 10–12 refer to the following people.

   (A) David Smith, Jean Arp, Louise Nevelson

   (B) Praxiteles, Phidias, *The Laocoon Group* sculptor

   (C) Michelangelo, Donatello, Lorenzo Ghiberti

   (D) Auguste Rodin, Antonio Canova, Honore Daumier

   (E) Gianlorenzo Bernini, Antoine Coysevox, Gregorio Fernandez

10. Which group is from the twentieth century?

11. Which group is from the fifteenth century?

12. Which group is from the nineteenth century?

Questions 13–15 refer to the following.

Used by permission. See copyright page (iv) for information.

13. Who is the MOST likely painter of this work?

   (A) Paul Cezanne

   (B) Agnes Martin

   (C) Jackson Pollock

   (D) Honore Daumier

   (E) Leonora Carrington

14. Which term describes the artist's method?

   (A) Minimalism

   (B) Action painting

   (C) Happening

   (D) Jugendstil

   (E) Cubism

GO ON TO THE NEXT PAGE

15. In which century was this work first shown?

    (A) Seventeenth
    (B) Eighteenth
    (C) Nineteenth
    (D) Twentieth
    (E) Twenty-first

16. In this Dickens novel, Pip and Estella are manipulated by a jilted bride grown old.

    (A) *A Tale of Two Cities*
    (B) *Oliver Twist*
    (C) *Great Expectations*
    (D) *Our Mutual Friend*
    (E) *Hard Times*

17. Cassio, Iago, and Desdemona can all be associated with which Shakespearean protagonist?

    (A) Hamlet
    (B) King Lear
    (C) Troilus
    (D) Timon of Athens
    (E) Othello

Questions 18–19 refer to the following poets.

    (A) William Butler Yeats
    (B) Walt Whitman
    (C) Hart Crane
    (D) Sylvia Plath
    (E) Marianne Moore

18. Which of these poets did not produce work in the twentieth century?

19. This poet examined small subjects such as strange animals, steeplejacks, and baseball fans. Rather than quoting Dante or Shakespeare, he or she used encyclopedia snippets and newspaper blurbs to compose poems.

20. "The Miller's Tale," "The Franklin's Tale," and "The Wife of Bath's Prologue" are all parts of which literary work?

    (A) *Moll Flanders*
    (B) *The Flowers of Evil*
    (C) *The Sorrows of Young Werther*
    (D) *One Hundred Years of Solitude*
    (E) *The Canterbury Tales*

21. Which of the following figures would you be LEAST likely to find in a painting by Edgar Degas?

    (A) A ballerina
    (B) A choreographer
    (C) A horse
    (D) A Greek god
    (E) A jockey

22. The Fugitive Poets like Allen Tate, John Crowe Ransom, and Robert Penn Warren were working in

    (A) the American South.
    (B) Wales.
    (C) Canada.
    (D) the Balkans.
    (E) New York.

23. Sophocles's *Oedipus Rex* presents a hero with

    (A) a tragic flaw.
    (B) humility.
    (C) good fortune.
    (D) brains, but no physical strength.
    (E) a comical sidekick.

GO ON TO THE NEXT PAGE

KAPLAN

24. "The Second Coming," "Sailing To Byzantium," "The Lake Isle of Innisfree," and "Under Ben Bulben" are all poems by

    (A) William Butler Yeats.
    (B) Walt Whitman.
    (C) Gwendolyn Brooks.
    (D) e. e. cummings.
    (E) Emily Dickinson.

25. *The Four Seasons* is a piece in four movements: "Spring," "Summer," Autumn," and "Winter." Which of the following composers produced this famous work?

    (A) Richard Strauss
    (B) Johann Sebastian Bach
    (C) Antonio Vivaldi
    (D) Arcangelo Corelli
    (E) Alfredo Casella

26. In musical terminology, what does the term *counterpoint* refer to?

    (A) A male singer
    (B) A sequence of single tones
    (C) A composition with two or more simultaneous melodies
    (D) A composition with two or more simultaneous tones
    (E) Ascending notes

27. Which of the following authors wrote *One Hundred Years of Solitude*?

    (A) Isabel Allende
    (B) Gunter Grasse
    (C) Gabriel Garcia Marquez
    (D) Joyce Carol Oates
    (E) Charlotte Bronte

28. A full-length ballet consists of how many acts?

    (A) Six
    (B) Two
    (C) Four, plus two intermissions
    (D) One, plus a finale
    (E) Three

29. Which of the following were contemporaries of Jacques Louis David and Eugene Delacroix?

    (A) Napoleon, Goethe, Hegel
    (B) Margaret Thatcher, Gabriel Garcia Marquez, Jacques Derrida
    (C) Mohandas Gandhi, Gabriela Mistral, Simone de Beauvoir
    (D) Pericles, Sappho, Plato
    (E) Peter the Great, Alexander Pope, Gottfried Wilhelm Leibniz

30. *A Christmas Carol* by Charles Dickens has seen many film adaptations, including the comic movie, *Scrooged*. It was originally published as a

    (A) short novel.
    (B) narrative poem.
    (C) collection of essays.
    (D) short story.
    (E) chapter of a longer novel.

31. Which of the following is NOT a play written by Eugene O'Neill?

    (A) *Moon for the Misbegotten*
    (B) *The Ice Man Cometh*
    (C) *Mourning Becomes Electra*
    (D) *The Cherry Orchard*
    (E) *Long Day's Journey into Night*

GO ON TO THE NEXT PAGE

KAPLAN

32. How many acts would a full-length play most likely include?

    (A) Five
    (B) Eight
    (C) Ten
    (D) Twelve
    (E) One

33. The Baroque period in music spanned the years 1600–1750. Which composers are associated with this period?

    (A) Frédéric Chopin and Richard Strauss
    (B) Ludwig van Beethoven and John Cage
    (C) Wolfgang Amadeus Mozart and Richard Strauss
    (D) George Frideric Handel and Johann Sebastian Bach
    (E) Gustav Mahler and Glenn Miller

34. Which of the following terms refers to a stage actor?

    (A) Cooper
    (B) Thespian
    (C) Aesthete
    (D) Angler
    (E) Chandler

35. Which of the following playwrights is correctly matched with his or her own play?

    (A) Lillian Hellman . . . *Accidental Death of an Anarchist*
    (B) August Strindberg . . . *Twelfth Night*
    (C) Moliere . . . *The Misanthrope*
    (D) Henrik Ibsen . . . *The Infernal Machine*
    (E) Christopher Marlowe . . . *Tiger at the Gates*

36. Which classical composer wrote the ballet music *Bolero*?

    (A) Vittorio Rieti
    (B) Maurice Ravel
    (C) Igor Stravinsky
    (D) Arnold Schoenberg
    (E) Werner Egk

37. In architecture, a "spire" is

    (A) an arched entryway.
    (B) a decorated facade.
    (C) a column used for support.
    (D) a tapered conical or pyramidal structure.
    (E) a bell tower.

38. Pragmatism is a philosophy in which the validity of a proposition is considered true if

    (A) the consequences of accepting it as true are positive.
    (B) it can be proven by logical argument.
    (C) it is not contradicted by empirical data.
    (D) the reasons for accepting it as true are sound.
    (E) it has been traditionally accepted as truth.

39. Jean-Paul Sartre is most closely associated with which philosophical movement?

    (A) Positivism
    (B) Phenomenology
    (C) Idealism
    (D) Existentialism
    (E) Transcendentalism

GO ON TO THE NEXT PAGE

KAPLAN

40. Praxiteles and Phidias were close contemporaries of

   (A) Marcel Proust and Claude Debussy
   (B) Boccaccio and Petrarch
   (C) Jonathan Swift and Thomas Gainsborough
   (D) Euripides and Aeschylus
   (E) Horace and Ovid

41. The nonprofit organization Boston Women's Health Book Collective formed in 1973 to publish this book, which reflects the goals and values of the feminist movement of the time.

   (A) *The Second Sex*
   (B) *The Feminine Mystique*
   (C) *Our Bodies, Ourselves*
   (D) *The Woman's Bible*
   (E) *A Room of One's Own*

42. Jean Genet, Eugene Ionesco, and Arthur Adamov are all playwrights of which movement in theater?

   (A) Neorealism
   (B) Commedia dell'arte
   (C) Theatre of the Absurd
   (D) Theatre of the Oppressed
   (E) Postmodernism

43. Bauhaus was an institution famous for producing

   (A) poets.
   (B) composers.
   (C) architects.
   (D) musicians.
   (E) literary critics.

44. Which of the following artists is NOT a famous portrait painter?

   (A) Thomas Gainsborough
   (B) Franz Hals
   (C) Chuck Close
   (D) Amedeo Modigliani
   (E) Wassily Kandinsky

45. Which of the following were close contemporaries of Georges Seurat and Henri Toulouse-Latrec?

   (A) Claude Debussy and Thomas Hardy
   (B) Ludwig van Beethoven and Lord Byron
   (C) Jonathan Swift and George Handel
   (D) Duke Ellington and Sylvia Plath
   (E) John Cage and Toni Morrison

Questions 46–48 refer to the following portion of a poem.

Hail to the virtues which that perilous life
Extracts from Nature's elemental strife;
And welcome glory won in battles fought
As bravely as the foe was keenly sought.
But to each gallant Captain and his crew
A less imperious sympathy is due,
Such as my verse now yields, while moonbeams play
On the mute sea in this unruffled bay;
Such as will promptly flow from every breast,
Where good men, disappointed in the quest
Of wealth and power and honours, long for rest;
Or, having known the splendours of success,
Sigh for the obscurities of happiness.

46. Who is the British poet who ushered in the Romantic era and wrote this poem?

   (A) Sylvia Plath
   (B) Henry David Thoreau
   (C) William Wordsworth
   (D) Virginia Woolf
   (E) William Shakespeare

GO ON TO THE NEXT PAGE ⟩

47. What defining subject of Romantic poetry is found in this poem?

    (A) The evils of war
    (B) Nature
    (C) Relationships
    (D) Taxation without representation
    (E) Britain's relationship with America during the nineteenth century

48. Where did the poet write this poem?

    (A) In the middle of the woods
    (B) By the sea
    (C) Beside a stream
    (D) In his house
    (E) In India

49. Tom Stoppard's *Rosencrantz and Guildenstern Are Dead* is based on a play by which playwright?

    (A) John Webster
    (B) Jean Racine
    (C) Antonin Artaud
    (D) Lady Gregory
    (E) William Shakespeare

50. Walt Whitman's *Leaves of Grass* can best be described as

    (A) an esoteric take on capitalism.
    (B) a return to classicism.
    (C) a concise, compact masterwork.
    (D) an overflowing celebration of humanity.
    (E) a dark, Kafkaesque appraisal of the new America.

51. Russian artist Kasimir Malevich was the progenitor of which of the following movements?

    (A) Impressionism
    (B) Vorticism
    (C) Fauvism
    (D) Suprematism
    (E) Pointillism

52. Akira Kurosawa's epic masterpiece *Ran*, in which an old Japanese warlord divides his land between his three children, is an adaptation of which play by Shakespeare?

    (A) *King Lear*
    (B) *Measure for Measure*
    (C) *Henry IV*
    (D) *Titus Andronicus*
    (E) *As You Like It*

53. Which of the following poets' work could be described as evocative nonsense?

    (A) Sir Philip Sidney
    (B) Thomas Hardy
    (C) Edith Sitwell
    (D) Lewis Carroll
    (E) Juana Ines de la Cruz

54. John Milton's *Paradise Lost* is written in

    (A) blank verse.
    (B) trochaic hexameter.
    (C) heroic couplets.
    (D) free verse.
    (E) spondaic tetrameter.

GO ON TO THE NEXT PAGE ▷

Questions 55–56 refer to the following centuries.

    (A) Sixteenth

    (B) Seventeenth

    (C) Eighteenth

    (D) Nineteenth

    (E) Twentieth

55. Which century is known primarily as an era of science and logic?

56. Which century is the Victorian period predominantly situated in?

57. Which of the following women is renowned for her role in popularizing modern dance?

    (A) Hilary Hahn

    (B) Suzanne Farrell

    (C) Billie Holiday

    (D) Jane Austen

    (E) Isadora Duncan

58. In which century did Rainer Maria Rilke publish *The Duino Elegies*?

    (A) Sixteenth

    (B) Seventeenth

    (C) Eighteenth

    (D) Nineteenth

    (E) Twentieth

59. Which of the following poets is matched with his or her own work?

    (A) Robert Lowell . . . "The Quaker Graveyard in Nantucket"

    (B) A.E. Housman . . . "The Marriage of Heaven and Hell"

    (C) Pablo Neruda . . . *The White Goddess*

    (D) Derek Walcott . . . "The Idea of Order at Key West"

    (E) Amy Lowell . . . "The Drunken Boat"

60. This experimental filmmaker scripted, directed, edited, and performed in the central role of *Meshes of the Afternoon*.

    (A) Stan Brakhage

    (B) Kenneth Anger

    (C) Godfrey Reggio

    (D) Bruce Connor

    (E) Maya Deran

61. Roy Lichtenstein's paintings resemble

    (A) Rembrandt's portraits.

    (B) John Constable's landscapes.

    (C) comic strips.

    (D) photographs.

    (E) collages.

62. John Locke is responsible for which of the following philosophical theories?

    (A) Tabula rasa

    (B) The categorical imperative

    (C) Communism

    (D) Language games

    (E) Idealism

GO ON TO THE NEXT PAGE

Courtesy of SuperStock, Inc.

63. Which of the following is most closely associated with the artist of the painting shown here?

    (A) Bas-relief

    (B) Manipulation of light and shadow

    (C) Etching

    (D) Allegory

    (E) Religious sentiment

64. Which of the following philosophers was a student of Socrates?

    (A) Xenophanes

    (B) Archimedes

    (C) Thales of Miletus

    (D) Plato

    (E) Hippocrates

65. "Lord, what fools these mortals be!" is uttered by Puck in this comedy by Shakespeare.

    (A) *As You Like It*

    (B) *A Midsummer Night's Dream*

    (C) *All's Well That Ends Well*

    (D) *The Tempest*

    (E) *The Comedy of Errors*

66. Which of the following are literary critics?

    (A) Helen Vendler, Jacques Derrida, Harold Bloom, Julia Kristeva

    (B) Joseph Haydn, Giacomo Puccini, Phillip Glass, Edvard Grieg

    (C) Charlotte Corday, Guy Fawkes, John Wilkes Booth, Aaron Burr

    (D) Anthony van Dyck, Hans Holbein, Frans Hals, Sir Joshua Reynolds

    (E) Auguste Rodin, Alberto Giacometti, Maya Lin, Jean Arp

67. Which country was the birthplace of modern dance?

    (A) Russia

    (B) United States

    (C) England

    (D) France

    (E) Sweden

68. Which American dancer was known for his collaborations with composer John Cage?

    (A) Alvin Ailey

    (B) Merce Cunningham

    (C) Michael Kidd

    (D) Donald McKayle

    (E) Marc Platt

GO ON TO THE NEXT PAGE

KAPLAN

69. Jasper Johns is most famous for painting

    (A) nudes and landscapes.

    (B) portraits and battle scenes.

    (C) flags and targets.

    (D) political figures and ballet dancers.

    (E) dogs and birds.

70. The protagonist of Malcolm Lowry's *Under the Volcano* is

    (A) a bullfighter.

    (B) an alcoholic.

    (C) a princess.

    (D) a firefighter.

    (E) a cancer patient.

71. A term often applied in the seventeenth century to ensemble music for voices and instruments is

    (A) "concerto."

    (B) "symphony."

    (C) "movement."

    (D) "chorus."

    (E) "harmony."

Questions 72–74 refer to the following choices.

    (A) Idealism

    (B) Continental philosophy

    (C) Empiricism

    (D) Logical positivism

    (E) Utilitarianism

72. This philosophy is concerned with constructive theories that are applicable to the functioning of daily life.

73. Bishop Berkeley is this philosophical school's most notable adherent.

74. This school is distinguished from Anglo-American philosophy.

75. A prose work consisting of around 120 pages would be considered

    (A) an epic.

    (B) a saga.

    (C) a novella.

    (D) a ballad.

    (E) a sestina.

76. An extended work for orchestra, usually in three or four movements, is called a

    (A) scherzo.

    (B) symphony.

    (C) trio.

    (D) concerto.

    (E) quartet.

77. In Toni Morrison's *Beloved*, the title refers to

    (A) an old woman.

    (B) a dead child.

    (C) a young boy.

    (D) a telepathic teenager.

    (E) an animal.

78. Which of the following is the highest voice in a polyphonic texture?

    (A) Alto

    (B) Tenor

    (C) Bass

    (D) Virtuoso

    (E) Soprano

79. "Fallingwater" is a famous

    (A) painting.

    (B) opera.

    (C) ballet.

    (D) edifice.

    (E) tone poem.

GO ON TO THE NEXT PAGE

80. In musical notation, how many lines are used to write music?

    (A) Four
    (B) Three
    (C) Five
    (D) One
    (E) Two

81. Which of the following works were published in 1922?

    (A) *Tristram Shandy* and "Essay on Man"
    (B) "The Waste Land" and *Ulysses*
    (C) *One Hundred Years of Solitude* and *Men of Maize*
    (D) *Hamlet* and *The Alchemist*
    (E) *My Last Duchess* and *In Memorium*

82. What is the name used to describe big-band jazz music from the 1930s and 1940s?

    (A) Swing
    (B) Tap
    (C) Dixieland
    (D) Ballroom
    (E) Bebop

83. Which of the following was NOT a Romantic composer?

    (A) Frédéric Chopin
    (B) Niccolo Paganini
    (C) Felix Mendelssohn
    (D) Franz Liszt
    (E) George Frideric Handel

84. Gregg Toland, esteemed for his deep-focus cinematography on *Citizen Kane*, also shot this classic 1940 film directed by John Ford and adapted from a John Steinbeck novel.

    (A) *Stagecoach*
    (B) *The Long Voyage Home*
    (C) *Tobacco Road*
    (D) *The Grapes of Wrath*
    (E) *How Green Was My Valley*

85. Which of the words below is the definition of a composition, or compositional technique, in which a theme (or themes) is extended and developed mainly by imitative counterpoint?

    (A) Chorus
    (B) Fugue
    (C) Stanza
    (D) Madrigal
    (E) Fandango

86. This major figure of the French New Wave made the films *The 400 Blows*, *Jules and Jim*, and *The Last Metro*.

    (A) Alain Resnais
    (B) Jean-Luc Godard
    (C) Claude Chabrol
    (D) François Truffaut
    (E) Louis Malle

87. Which of the following novels was written by Emile Zola?

    (A) *The Mill on the Floss*
    (B) *Germinal*
    (C) *Hard Times*
    (D) *Madame Bovary*
    (E) *La Bas*

GO ON TO THE NEXT PAGE

KAPLAN

88. In which century was the sonata form of classical music invented?

    (A) Eighteenth
    (B) Nineteenth
    (C) Twentieth
    (D) Seventeenth
    (E) Sixteenth

89. Film noir, a genre of American filmmaking so labeled by the French because of its cynicism, darkness, and despair, emerged during which period of American history?

    (A) The Depression
    (B) Post-World War II
    (C) The McCarthy/blacklist era of the 1950s
    (D) The Vietnam War
    (E) The Watergate era

90. In Dostoyevsky's *Crime and Punishment*, where does Raskolnikov end up at the novel's conclusion?

    (A) Moscow
    (B) Paris
    (C) Siberia
    (D) Berlin
    (E) Australia

91. Who was considered by Dostoyevsky, Tolstoy, Turgenev, and others to be the "father" of Russian literature?

    (A) Mikhail Lermontov
    (B) Vladimir Nabokov
    (C) Victor Pelevin
    (D) Nikolai Gogol
    (E) Aleksandr Solzhenitsyn

Questions 92–94 refer to the following disciplines.

    (A) Drama
    (B) Poetry
    (C) Ballet
    (D) Architecture
    (E) Philosophy

92. Which of these disciplines are Frank Gehry, Mies van der Rohe, and Le Corbusier associated with?

93. In which of these disciplines would the term *aside* be used?

94. In which of these disciplines would the terms *architrave* and *flying buttress* be used?

95. In Arthur Koestler's *Darkness at Noon*, the main character is awaiting

    (A) a thunderstorm.
    (B) an execution.
    (C) the birth of his first daughter.
    (D) the arrival of his beloved.
    (E) the coronation of his queen.

96. Oscar Wilde's *The Picture of Dorian Gray* tells the story of a man who

    (A) never looks any older.
    (B) is sent to prison for ten years of hard labor.
    (C) paints landscapes in the open air.
    (D) turns into a cockroach.
    (E) travels to the North Pole.

GO ON TO THE NEXT PAGE ⟩

97. Which of the following correctly matches the artist to his or her country of birth?

    (A) Francis Bacon . . . France

    (B) Berthe Morisot . . . Holland

    (C) El Greco . . . Spain

    (D) Titian . . . Ireland

    (E) Edward Hopper . . . the United States

98. All of the following are novels by Fyodor Dostoyevsky EXCEPT

    (A) *The Brothers Karamazov.*

    (B) *The Possessed.*

    (C) *The Idiot.*

    (D) *House of the Dead.*

    (E) *Doctor Zhivago.*

99. During the Baroque era, which composer worked as a church organist?

    (A) Johann Sebastian Bach

    (B) Franz Haydn

    (C) Wolfgang Amadeus Mozart

    (D) Richard Wagner

    (E) Johannes Brahms

100. Fauvism was a movement in which art form?

    (A) Painting

    (B) Music

    (C) Ballet

    (D) Drama

    (E) Opera

101. Which of the following did Robert Frost describe as "playing tennis without the net"?

    (A) Vorticism

    (B) Free verse

    (C) Writing plays

    (D) Automatic writing

    (E) Imagism

102. Of the following composers, which one is known as the *enfant terrible* of avant garde music?

    (A) Richard Wagner

    (B) Samuel Barber

    (C) Ralph Vaughn Williams

    (D) John Cage

    (E) Willem de Kooning

103. The author Dorothy Parker was renowned for her

    (A) wit.

    (B) epic novels.

    (C) prolific output.

    (D) dramatic depth.

    (E) kind-hearted protagonists.

104. Which of the following is a noted photographer?

    (A) Dorothea Lange

    (B) Andrea del Sarto

    (C) Buckminster Fuller

    (D) Isadora Duncan

    (E) Djuna Barnes

105. What does the musical term *lieder* mean?

    (A) A symphony

    (B) An operetta

    (C) A song

    (D) A violin solo

    (E) A cello solo

106. Which of the following was famous for his or her Civil War photographs?

    (A) Alfred Stieglitz

    (B) Ansel Adams

    (C) Matthew Brady

    (D) Edouard Vuillard

    (E) Edith Wharton

GO ON TO THE NEXT PAGE ⇨

KAPLAN

107. The film *The Third Man* was based on a novel by which author?

(A) Lope de Vega

(B) Mark Twain

(C) Colette

(D) Graham Greene

(E) Laurence Sterne

Questions 108–110 refer to the following painting.

Courtesy of SuperStock, Inc.

108. Who is the man pictured?

(A) Paul Gauguin

(B) Fernand Leger

(C) Roberto Matta

(D) John Constable

(E) Vincent van Gogh

109. What type of painting is this?

(A) Still life

(B) Landscape

(C) Fresco

(D) Self-portrait

(E) Portrait

110. What period is this painting associated with?

(A) Baroque

(B) Postmodern

(C) Post-Impressionist

(D) Pre-Raphaelite

(E) Neoclassical

111. Which of the following Shakespearean characters does NOT serve as comic relief?

(A) Prospero

(B) Falstaff

(C) Feste

(D) Touchstone

(E) Puck

112. The main character in M. Scott Momaday's *House Made of Dawn* is

(A) a Native American.

(B) a gypsy.

(C) a fireman.

(D) an African-American.

(E) an Irish immigrant.

113. The Hellenistic sculptor's approach to the human form can be described as

(A) idealistic.

(B) understated.

(C) ambivalent.

(D) ironic.

(E) modest.

114. Many of the "Seven Wonders of the Ancient World" come from which period?

(A) Baroque

(B) Byzantine

(C) Medieval

(D) Romantic

(E) Hellenistic

GO ON TO THE NEXT PAGE ⟩

Questions 115–117 refer to the following choices.

(A) Charlotte Bronte's *Jane Eyre*

(B) Marcel Duchamp's *Nude Descending a Staircase*

(C) Georges Bizet's *Carmen*

(D) Carolyn Forche's "The Colonel"

(E) Ludwig van Beethoven's *Eroica*

115. Which is a symphony?

116. Which is a painting?

117. Which is a poem?

118. A libretto is a manuscript used in which genre?

(A) Novel

(B) Opera

(C) Ballet

(D) Epic ballad

(E) Symphony

119. In which of the following novels does the main character die?

(A) George Eliot's *Middlemarch*

(B) Mark Twain's *The Adventures of Huckleberry Finn*

(C) Fyodor Dostoyevsky's *Crime and Punishment*

(D) Charles Dickens' *The Old Curiosity Shop*

(E) Edith Wharton's *Ethan Frome*

120. Ray Bradbury and Isaac Asimov are both authors associated with

(A) the Romantic movement.

(B) Naturalism.

(C) science fiction.

(D) Robert Browning.

(E) absurdist drama.

121. Which of the following would you most likely find in an Andy Warhol work?

(A) Soup cans and Marilyn Monroe

(B) Trees and peasants

(C) Rocks and hawks

(D) Horses and Napoleon

(E) Sides of beef and Pope Urban II

Questions 122–124 refer to the following picture.

Used by permission. See copyright page (iv) for information.

122. What country is this scene taken from?

(A) Belgium

(B) France

(C) England

(D) United States

(E) Mexico

123. The mood of this painting can best be described as

(A) tense.

(B) stark.

(C) light-hearted.

(D) violent.

(E) comical.

GO ON TO THE NEXT PAGE

KAPLAN

124. Who is the painter?

    (A) Jackson Pollock
    (B) Arthur Dove
    (C) Georgia O'Keefe
    (D) Edward Hopper
    (E) Andrew Wyeth

125. The novels of Joseph Conrad are chiefly concerned with

    (A) power, corruption, and evil.
    (B) the Black Death.
    (C) the passage of time.
    (D) love.
    (E) art and music.

126. Which of the following is another term for the main character of a novel?

    (A) Deus ex machina
    (B) Thespian
    (C) Protagonist
    (D) Comic relief
    (E) Bridge

127. Which of the following artists wrote a famous autobiography?

    (A) Praxiteles
    (B) Vincent van Gogh
    (C) Benvenuto Cellini
    (D) Giotto
    (E) Lorenzo Lotto

128. Where would a J. M. W. Turner painting most likely be set?

    (A) The sea
    (B) The desert
    (C) A nursery
    (D) Ancient Egypt
    (E) Sub-Saharan Africa

129. "Mrs. Dalloway would buy the flowers herself," is the first line of a novel by

    (A) James Joyce.
    (B) H. D.
    (C) Virginia Woolf.
    (D) L. F. Celine.
    (E) M. A. Marcom.

130. Gioacchio Rossini composed which opera?

    (A) *Don Giovanni*
    (B) *The Barber of Seville*
    (C) *Orfeo*
    (D) *Die Freischutz*
    (E) *Aida*

131. *A Bend in the River* and *Half a Life* are novels by

    (A) V. S. Naipaul.
    (B) Selma Lagerlof.
    (C) Thomas Hardy.
    (D) Kate Chopin.
    (E) Gail Tsukiyama.

GO ON TO THE NEXT PAGE ▷

132. The narrative structure of Faulkner's *The Sound and the Fury* can best be described as

    (A) third-person omniscient.
    (B) multiple first-person points of view.
    (C) second-person direct address.
    (D) first-person singular.
    (E) third-person limited.

Questions 133–135 refer to the following authors.

    (A) Michael Ondaatje
    (B) Oliver Goldsmith
    (C) Milan Kundera
    (D) Gore Vidal
    (E) Italo Calvino

133. Which of these authors was born in the United States?

134. Which of these authors did NOT publish a work in the twentieth century?

135. The film *The English Patient* was based on a novel by which of these authors?

136. The stories of James Thurber can best be described as

    (A) language based.
    (B) melodramatic.
    (C) mysterious.
    (D) dark.
    (E) comic.

137. Salman Rushdie's *The Satanic Verses* was controversial in its satire of which of the following religions?

    (A) Christianity
    (B) Islam
    (C) Buddhism
    (D) Hinduism
    (E) Zoroastrianism

Questions 138–139 refer to the following continents and countries.

    (A) Ireland
    (B) United States
    (C) Australia
    (D) Africa
    (E) Soviet Union

138. From which country/continent did Mark Rothko and Marc Chagall emigrate?

139. Where were William Butler Yeats and George Bernard Shaw born?

140. Where are J. M. Coetzee's *Disgrace*, Barbara Kingsolver's *The Poisonwood Bible*, Norman Rush's *Mating*, and Chinua Achebe's *Things Fall Apart* all set?

END OF TEST. STOP

ANSWER KEY

1. C	21. D	41. C	61. C	81. B	101. B	121. A
2. B	22. A	42. C	62. A	82. A	102. D	122. D
3. A	23. A	43. C	63. B	83. E	103. A	123. B
4. D	24. A	44. E	64. D	84. D	104. A	124. D
5. B	25. C	45. A	65. B	85. B	105. C	125. A
6. A	26. C	46. C	66. A	86. D	106. C	126. C
7. E	27. C	47. B	67. B	87. B	107. D	127. C
8. C	28. E	48. B	68. B	88. A	108. E	128. A
9. B	29. A	49. E	69. C	89. B	109. D	129. C
10. A	30. A	50. D	70. B	90. C	110. C	130. B
11. C	31. D	51. D	71. A	91. D	111. A	131. A
12. D	32. A	52. A	72. E	92. D	112. A	132. B
13. C	33. D	53. D	73. C	93. A	113. A	133. D
14. B	34. B	54. A	74. B	94. D	114. E	134. B
15. D	35. C	55. C	75. C	95. B	115. E	135. A
16. C	36. B	56. D	76. B	96. A	116. B	136. E
17. E	37. D	57. E	77. B	97. E	117. D	137. B
18. B	38. A	58. E	78. E	98. E	118. B	138. E
19. E	39. D	59. A	79. D	99. A	119. D	139. A
20. E	40. D	60. E	80. C	100. A	120. C	140. D

PRACTICE TEST 3 QUICK REFERENCE TABLES

Use the following tables to determine which topics you still need to review.

Topic	Test Question
Literature	
Drama	17, 23, 31, 32, 34, 35, 42, 49, 54, 65, 67, 93, 111, 139
Poetry	1, 3, 5, 9, 18, 19, 20, 22, 24, 46, 47, 48, 50, 53, 58, 59, 101, 117
Fiction	6, 7, 8, 16, 27, 70, 77, 81, 87, 90, 91, 103, 106, 112, 119, 120, 126, 129, 131, 132, 134, 136, 137, 140
Nonfiction/Philosophy	38, 39, 41, 55, 56, 62, 64, 66, 72, 73, 74, 75, 127, 133
The Arts	
Visual Arts (painting, sculpture, etc.)	10, 11, 12, 13, 14, 15, 21, 44, 51, 61, 63, 95, 96, 97, 100, 104, 105, 108, 109, 110, 113, 116, 121, 122, 123, 124, 128, 138
Architecture	37, 40, 43, 69, 79, 92, 114
Music	2, 4, 25, 26, 33, 36, 45, 68, 71, 76, 78, 80, 82, 83, 85, 88, 99, 102, 115, 118, 130
Performing Arts (film, dance, etc.)	28, 29, 30, 52, 57, 60, 84, 86, 89, 94, 98, 107, 125, 135

Topic	Number of Questions on Test	Number Correct
Literature	70	
Drama	14	
Poetry	18	
Fiction	24	
Nonfiction/Philosophy	14	
The Arts	70	
Visual Arts (painting, sculpture, etc.)	28	
Architecture	7	
Music	21	
Performing Arts (film, dance, etc.)	14	

Answers and Explanations

1. (C)

All of these poets would probably be categorized as post-modernists. All the poets listed are from the second half of the twentieth century.

2. (B)

Schoenberg invented twelve-tone composition, an approach that rejected conventional tonality and harmony. Note the use of the word *modern*, a hint toward the time period the composer lived in. Choices (A), (C), and (D) are earlier composers, while (E) is a cellist.

3. (A)

Stevens was never particularly concerned with society in general, only with ideas and the nexus of reality and the imagination. Issues of socialism (B), poverty (C), women's issues (D), and science (E) were not important to him. Stevens lived 1879–1955 and produced such works as "Sea Surface Full of Clouds."

4. (D)

A prelude (A) is a musical introduction to a drama or composition, while an epilogue (B) is a concluding part of a literary work. A prologue (C) occurs at the beginning of a literary work, and an overtone (E) is a harmonic tone.

5. (B)

The Petrarchan (or Italian) sonnet is slightly different than a Shakespearean (or English) sonnet. An Italian sonnet contains fourteen lines and two stanzas. The first stanza is composed of eight lines and the second stanza is composed of six lines. None of the other poets listed are noted for writing sonnets.

6. (A)

In Joyce's *Ulysses*, the character Leopold Bloom wanders the streets of Dublin for an entire day before returning to his wife Molly. None of the other stories takes place in Dublin.

7. (E)

Paterson is a town in New Jersey by the Passaic Falls and is the name of a main character in the work. None of the other answer choices takes place in New Jersey.

8. (C)

Pound's *Cantos* is an homage to the Italian Bard (poet). It is patterned after a work by Dante, who lived in the thirteenth century.

9. (B)

Goethe was the quintessential Romantic poet. The rest are all far distant from their corresponding time periods.

10. (A)

Smith, Arp, and Nevelson are from the twentieth century. Praxiteles, Phidias, and the sculptor of *The Laocoon Group* are ancient Greek artists (B), while the group of Bernini, Coysevox, and Fernandez (E) worked in the seventeenth century. See explanations for questions 11 and 12 for the periods of other artists mentioned.

11. (C)

Michelangelo, Donatello, and Ghiberti (C) are from the fifteenth century. See explanations for questions 10 and 12 for the periods of other artists mentioned.

12. (D)

Rodin, Canova, and Daumier are from the nineteenth century. See explanations for questions 10 and 11 for the periods of other artists mentioned.

13. (C)

Jackson Pollock is most famous for his "drip" paintings. Pollock was the first "all-over" painter, forgoing the use of a palette and brushes, using his hands and movement to create works of art.

14. (B)

Pollock was revolutionary in his consideration of process, placing as much emphasis on "how" the work was produced as on the final product. The entire process of creating a work involved action on the part of Pollock as he poured, dripped, and splashed paint over canvasses.

15. (D)

The "action painting" movement got underway in the 1950s. Never before had action painting been practiced and viewed as a form of acceptable art.

16. (C)

Miss Havisham, Pip, and Estella are three of the most notable characters in all of Dickens' work. The other novels do not contain a jilted bride grown old, nor do they contain characters with these names.

17. (E)

In *Othello*, Iago is the ultimate villain who entangles Cassio, Desdemona, and Othello in a purported love triangle, which brings about the demise of all but Cassio. The other choices appear in *Hamlet* (A), *King Lear* (B), *Troilus and Cressida* (C), and *Timon of Athens* (D).

18. (B)

Walt Whitman lived 1819–1892, prior to the twentieth century. Although Yeats (A) had a career that straddled two centuries, and he can be considered both a Victorian and a modern poet, the bulk of his most famous work was created after the turn of the century. Crane (C), Plath (D), and Moore (E) all created work during the twentieth century.

19. (E)

Like Williams' *Paterson* and Pound's *Cantos*, Whitman's *Leaves of Grass* (B) and Crane's *The Bridge* (C) are indicative of the epic or lofty ambitions of modern poets. In contrast, Moore (E) traces her lineage back to Emily Dickinson. While Plath's (D) poems are similarly thoughtful, they are self-reflexive.

20. (E)

The Canterbury Tales is a collection of medieval tales by author Geoffrey Chaucer. The *Tales* are written in Middle English verse. *Moll Flanders* (A) is a novel by Daniel Defoe, *The Flowers of Evil* (B) is a book of poems by Baudelaire, *The Sorrows of Young Werther* (C) is a novel by Johann Wolfgang Goethe, and *One Hundred Years of Solitude* is a novel by Gabriel Garcia Marquez.

21. (D)

Degas' chief preoccupations were horse racing and the ballet. You would be least likely to find a Greek god in one of Degas' paintings, since a choreographer (B) and a jockey (E) have to do with ballet and horse racing, respectively.

22. (A)

The "Fugitives" were in favor of a more colloquial, idyllic verse. They were poets of the American South.

23. (A)

Aristotle suggested that for a successful tragedy, the protagonist must have a tragic flaw that causes his downfall. For many centuries in the arts, the term *tragic flaw* has been applied to figures from Othello to Jay Gatsby. While some classic heroes may have humility (B), good fortune, (C) brains but no physical strength (D), or a comical sidekick (E), these qualities and instances are not found in *Oedipus Rex*.

24. (A)

These poems are Yeats' most notable works. Yeats lived 1865–1939 and was an Irish dramatist and prose writer, as well as poet.

25. (C)

Antonio Vivaldi composed *The Four Seasons*. Each choice is a musical composer. Note that three of the options are Italian composers: Vivaldi, Corelli, and Casella. This suggests that one of them is correct.

26. (C)

A male singer has many different names depending on the range of his voice. A sequence of single tones (B) is called a progression. Counterpoint is two or more simultaneous melodies, not tones (D). Ascending notes (E) move up the musical scale and do not define counterpoint.

27. (C)

This book is one of the first novels to come under the rubric "magical realism." Marquez was Colombia's most famous writer and was granted a Nobel Prize in Literature.

28. (E)

"Full length" always means an evening-long piece with at least one pause and one intermission. There are three acts in a full-length ballet.

29. (A)

David and Delacroix are seminal artistic figures in the Romantic period while the contemporaries listed are historical, literary, and philosophical figures. The other choices listed lived and worked during different time periods.

30. (A)

While Dickens did write many long novels and often published them as serial chapters in magazines, his lean masterpiece, "A Christmas Carol," is now considered a novella or short novel. The story is retold on stage every year at Christmas.

31. (D)

Though *The Cherry Orchard's* bleak outlook on life is characteristic of O'Neill, it is the most famous work of the Russian playwright Anton Chekhov. All of the other choices are plays written by O'Neill. Eugene O'Neill was the winner of the 1936 Nobel Prize in Literature and lived 1888–1953.

32. (A)

A standard full-length play usually contains five (though occasionally four or three) acts. If a play had only one act (E), by definition it would be considered a one-act play rather than a full-length play.

33. (D)

The Baroque era spans 1600 to 1750. Bach lived from 1735 to 1782, and Handel's life spanned 1685 to 1759, putting both solidly in the Baroque period. Richard Strauss (1864–1949) and Frédéric Chopin (1810–1849) were Romantic composers (A). Ludwig van Beethoven lived from 1770 to 1827, while John Cage is a twentieth-century composer (B). Mozart lived during the eighteenth century in the Classical era (C). Mahler lived during the nineteenth century, and Glenn Miller was a modern musician.

34. (B)

The title of "thespian" is usually reserved for serious stage actors but is occasionally used for actors in general. A cooper (A) is a person who makes wooden barrels, an aesthete (C) is a person who highly admires beauty, an angler (D) is someone who is scheming or who fishes with a hook, and a chandler (E) is a person who sells or makes candles.

35. (C)

Only Moliere is matched with the correct play—he wrote *The Misanthrope*. Dario Fo is the author of *Accidental Death of an Anarchist* (A), Shakespeare wrote *Twelfth Night* (B), *The Infernal Machine* is by Jean Cocteau (D), and Jean Giaudoux wrote *Tiger at the Gates* (E).

36. (B)

French composer Maurice Ravel (1875–1937) wrote *Bolero*. *Bolero* later became famous when it was used as the theme music for the movie *10* in 1979.

37. (D)

The word *spire* shares the same etymology as the word *spear*. Looking at a spire, it is obvious why. They are imposing structures, topping off buildings with their high, sharp points.

38. (A)

Pragmatism, developed by William James in the late nineteenth century, posits that an idea is true if it is practical or useful to think it so.

39. (D)

Jean-Paul Sartre was a French philosopher who lived through World War II. Perhaps his best-known work is *Being and Nothingness*, a cornerstone of existential philosophy.

40. (D)

Praxiteles and Phidias were ancient Greek sculptors while Euripides and Aeschylus were ancient Greek dramatists. None of the others were close contemporaries of Praxiteles and Phidias.

41. (C)

Although all of the books listed are important feminist books, only one was co-authored by a group of professionals from a variety of fields. These women got together in 1973 to publish *Our Bodies, Ourselves*.

42. (C)

All three playwrights were part of the Theatre of the Absurd movement, which broke with many of the conventions of realistic drama.

43. (C)

Although there were many artists and artisans involved in programs at Bauhaus, the architectural school was the most famous. Poets (A), composers (B), musicians (D), and literary critics (E) came out of Bauhaus, but the school was predominantly known for architecture.

44. (E)

While he may have painted a portrait or two in his younger years, Kandinsky is known for his work in Abstract Expressionism. The first three options are almost exclusively portrait artists, while Modigliani's most famous pieces are his portraits with elongated faces.

45. (A)

Seurat and Toulouse-Latrec were working at the cusp of modernism. Debussy was perhaps the first great modern composer, and Hardy had one career as a Victorian novelist and a second as a quasi-modern poet.

46. (C)

William Wordsworth was considered to have initiated English Romantic poetry, along with Samuel Coleridge. Sylvia Plath (A) was an American poet who lived during the twentieth century. Thoreau (B) was American as well, and although he lived during the Romantic era, he was a Transcendentalist. Virginia Woolf (D) was British but was a novelist who lived during the twentieth century. Shakespeare (E) was British also but lived during the sixteenth century.

47. (B)

Nature was at the center of Romantic poetry. Romantic poetry did not focus on war (A), taxation without representation (D), or Britain's relationship with America (E). Although relationships (C) can sometimes be found in Romantic poetry, nature is the main focus of Wordsworth's poetry, as shown at the beginning of the excerpt.

48. (B)

William Wordsworth wrote this poem in 1833 on an excursion to his son's house by the sea at Moresby. The poem is called "Composed by the Seashore" and can be found in Wordsworth's "Evening Voluntaries."

49. (E)

Rosencrantz and Guildenstern Are Dead is basically Shakespeare's *Hamlet* viewed from the perspective of Rosencrantz and Guildenstern (two minor characters who get caught up in the tragic twists of plot). The play is not as famous or acclaimed as *Hamlet*, as it was written in the twentieth century.

50. (D)

Whitman's work is neither esoteric (A) nor classical (B), nor compact (C). Whitman also does not express a dark, Kafkaesque appraisal of the new America in his poems (E).

51. (D)

Malevich was the progenitor of Suprematism. He employed single or dual colors to put forth simplistic paintings that tried to convey a sense of perfection and completion. Minimalists trace their roots to his work. Malevich was not part of any of the other artistic movements.

52. (A)

In Kurosawa's screenplay, Shakespeare's three daughters become three sons. Other characters such as the Fool also occupy central roles, aiding our understanding of the protagonist's descent into madness. *Ran* literally means "chaos."

53. (D)

The other answer choices are all particularly coherent poets.

54. (A)

Milton's *Paradise Lost* is written in blank verse: unrhymed iambic pentameter. While heroic couplets (C) are another form of iambic pentameter, they consist of sets of two rhyming lines. Alexander Pope frequently used this form. Free verse (D) has no rhyme or meter, while answers (B) and (E) represent different metrical patterns.

55. (C)

The eighteenth century was the age of Newton, the era of science and logic (also known as the Age of Reason). Traditional religious and aesthetic ideas were turned upside down, provoking a reaction in the nineteenth century. Galileo and Copernicus were key advocates of science in previous centuries, but they did not so thoroughly affect the ethos of their eras.

56. (D)

Queen Victoria ruled for over half a century, dying in 1901. There were some novelists (though few poets) still writing in the Victorian mode in the twentieth century, but the period is considered to last only as long as Victoria's reign.

57. (E)

Isadora Duncan virtually created the free-flowing movements that we know as modern dance. While Suzanne Farrell (B) is a tempting choice, she was a great ballerina, not a modern dancer.

58. (E)

Rilke was born in the nineteenth century but published the bulk of his work in the twentieth. *The Duino Elegies* strive to determine the meaning of humanity in the modern world.

59. (A)

Robert Lowell wrote "The Quaker Graveyard in Nantucket." (B), (C), (D), and (E) were respectively written by Blake, Bridges, Stevens, and Rimbaud.

60. (E)

Maya Deran performed every major production task on *Meshes of the Afternoon*. The film established the independent avant-garde film movement in the United States. All the other experimental filmmakers listed came after Deran.

61. (C)

Lichtenstein was a Pop Artist who tested the boundaries of artistic material by blowing up images from comic strips. The American artist lived from 1923–1997.

62. (A)

Tabula rasa roughly translates as "blank tablet" and characterizes Locke's theory that the human mind begins in a

pristine state and is the complete product of its environment. John Locke is not responsible for any of the other philosophical theories listed.

63. (B)

Vermeer's paintings are most concerned with the effects of shadow and light. The other options are not associated at all with this great artist.

64. (D)

There are no primary texts of Socrates. All of his work was passed on through his student, Plato. Archimedes was a student of Plato at the Academy in Greece.

65. (B)

Only two of the plays mentioned feature supernatural elements. *The Tempest* (D) is a rational answer since it features magical elements, but Puck is the catalyst for the events in *A Midsummer Night's Dream*.

66. (A)

Vendler, Derrida, Bloom, and Kristeva are all literary critics. Answer (B) is a group of composers, answer (C) is a group of assassins, answer (D) includes portrait painters, and answer (E) is a group of sculptors.

67. (B)

Modern dance is now popular in many countries, but it originated in the United States, spurred on by the great Isadora Duncan. Duncan is considered to be the founder of modern dance.

68. (B)

John Cage was known for his avant garde music. Although all of the dancers listed are American, only Merce Cunningham (B) is known for his work in avant garde dance and his work with Cage.

69. (C)

Johns was one of many experimental American artists trying to present new perspectives on old symbols. Flags and targets had been subjects of art for a long time, but Johns tried to paint them differently. None of the other choices concerned Jasper Johns.

70. (B)

The protagonist of this novel is an alcoholic. The story revolves around the protagonist's drunken reveries and waking delusions, which eventually degrade into a desperate situation. The main character is not a bullfighter (A), a princess (C), a firefighter (D), or a cancer patient (E).

71. (A)

Ensemble music for voices and instruments is called a concerto. While the other choices are musical terms, only *concerto* refers to ensemble music for both voices and musical instruments.

72. (E)

Expounded by John Stuart Mill and later picked up by John Dewey and William James, this philosophical approach wanted to do away with the fruitless questions philosophers had been asking for millennia and address practical questions about life. Utilitarianism involved asking questions that mattered to everyday functioning.

73. (C)

Berkeley was a prominent empiricist who believed that only perceptions are experienced and experience is the source of most knowledge. His ideas are often compared to those of fellow empiricist John Locke.

74. (B)

Continental philosophy refers to European (especially German) philosophy's tendency toward involved, complex, and cerebral theories in contrast to those of Anglo-Americans' pragmatic, logical empiricism. This is a distinction of predominance rather than an absolute classification.

75. (C)

A novella is a relatively new distinction given to what used to be called a short novel or long short story. An epic (A) and a saga (B) are often much longer than 120 pages. A ballad (D) and a sestina (E) are poetic forms much shorter than 120 pages. A sestina contains six stanzas of six lines and one envoy of three lines.

76. (B)

An extended work for an orchestra is known as a symphony. Beethoven was considered to be the "Master of the Symphony."

77. (B)

In the novel, the dead child comes back as a ghost and torments the house's inhabitants. The child was the "beloved" person in the house; hence the name of the novel.

78. (E)

Soprano is the highest female voice and the highest voice in a polyphonic texture. Alto (A) is a lower female voice. Bass (C) is the lowest male voice, while tenor (B) is the highest male voice. A virtuoso (D) is a person highly skilled in the arts.

79. (D)

"Fallingwater" is the name of a home built by Frank Lloyd Wright. The building is masterfully integrated with its landscape. None of the other choices refer to "Fallingwater."

80. (C)

Five lines are used to write music on a staff. On the treble staff, the lines in ascending order correspond to the musical notes E, G, B, D, and F, with F being the highest.

81. (B)

1922 is considered by most critics to have been the advent of modernism in literature, which "The Waste Land" and *Ulysses* exemplify.

82. (A)

"Swing" is a name for big-band jazz music from the 1930s and 1940s. The name is derived from the "swinging" rhythms of the band.

83. (E)

George Frideric Handel lived 1685–1759, in the Baroque period. All the other composers are from the Romantic era.

84. (D)

The Grapes of Wrath was published in 1939. The book and film concern a family of dispossessed farmers migrating to California across the Dust Bowl of the Southwest during the Depression. The other choices listed are other films directed by John Ford.

85. (B)

A fugue is a composition in which the theme is developed mainly by an imitative counterpoint. *Stanza* (C) is a poetic term. A madrigal (D) is a work for several voices featuring a poetic text. The form dates from the Middle Ages and Renaissance. Fandango (E) is music accompanying a Spanish-American triple-time dance.

86. (D)

Francois Truffaut made the films *The 400 Blows*, *Jules and Jim*, and *The Last Metro*. The other filmmakers listed were also important directors of the French New Wave.

87. (B)

Emile Zola wrote *Germinal*. The other novels were written by George Eliot (A), Charles Dickens (C), Gustave Flaubert (D), and J. K. Huysmans (E).

88. (A)

One of Johann Sebastian Bach's sons, Karl Philipp Emanuel Bach, helped create the piano sonata in 1744. Wolfgang Amadeus Mozart gave us the violin sonata as we know it today.

89. (B)

These films, characterized by a downbeat atmosphere and graphic violence, carried postwar American pessimism to the point of nihilism by assuming the absolute irredeemable corruption of society and everyone in it. Billy Wilder's corrosive *Double Indemnity* may be regarded as the prototypical film noir. The other time periods did not involve film noir.

90. (C)

Raskolnikov is sent to a prison camp in Siberia where he must begin to redeem himself. Dostoyevsky based the novel on his own experiences of serving time at a Russian prison camp.

91. (D)

Nikolai Gogol's *Dead Souls* was a landmark work and led the great Russian novelists of the nineteenth century to describe him as "the father of us all." Great Russian novelists at the time included Dostoyevsky, Tolstoy, Turgenev, etc.

92. (D)

All three were architects. Mies van der Rohe was closely associated with the minimalist Bauhaus school. Gehry and Le Corbusier were known for their highly original, stylistic structures.

93. (A)

An "aside" is a line spoken for the benefit of the audience, understood to be unheard by the other characters onstage. The term is not used in poetry (B), ballet (C), architecture (D), or philosophy (E).

94. (D)

Both terms are used in architecture. An architrave is the lowest division of an entablature, and a flying buttress is a kind of support.

95. (B)

Koestler's narrative described the real-life terrors of communism. In the book, the narrator is awaiting an execution, a common occurrence during Communist Party rule.

96. (A)

The "picture" or portrait of Dorian Gray ages and grows more and more grotesque with every sin he commits, while Dorian's youthful good looks remain untouched by time. None of the other choices apply. In *The Metamorphosis* by Franz Kafka, the main character turns into a cockroach (D).

97. (E)

Edward Hopper was born in the United States. Francis Bacon (A) was born in England, Berthe Morisot (B) was born in France. El Greco (C) spent most of his career in Spain but was born in Greece; hence the nickname "El Greco." Titian (D) was born in Italy.

98. (E)

Doctor Zhivago was written by Russian poet Boris Pasternak. All of the other novels were written by Fyodor Dostoyevsky.

99. (A)

Bach is the only one of the choices who lived and worked during the Baroque era. Haydn (B) and Mozart (C) are from the Classical era, while Wagner (D) and Brahms (E) are from the Romantic era. Bach is also the only one who worked as an organist.

100. (A)

Henri Matisse was the most notable member of the Fauvist movement, which advocated bright colors and (to the critic's eye) savage imagery. The impact of Fauvism on other disciplines was minimal.

101. (B)

While most subsequent poets have at least acknowledged the validity of free verse (poetry without fixed rhyme or meter), Frost saw it as an excuse for sloppiness. He preferred more structured forms of poetry.

102. (D)

John Cage was a twentieth-century composer who began the avant-garde music movement. Barber (B), Williams (C), and Wagner (A) were all composers but did not participate in this movement. Willem de Kooning (E) was a twentieth-century painter.

103. (A)

Parker's stories are exercises in irony and sardonic humor. Dorothy Parker, an American poet and writer of short stories, was born in 1893 and died in 1967. Her poetic volumes include *Enough Rope* and *Sunset Gun*.

104. (A)

Dorothea made a name for herself in the Depression years by capturing the despair and resilience of Americans in their darkest age. Del Sarto (B) was an artist, Fuller (C) was an architect, Duncan (D) was a dancer, and Barnes (E) was an author.

105. (C)

Lieder literally means "song" in German. It was a popular form in the nineteenth century.

106. (C)

Matthew Brady's war-camp photographs compose the earliest body of work in what was then a new medium. Stieglitz (A) and Adams (B) were twentieth-century photographers. Edith Wharton (E) was a novelist, and Edouard Vuillard (D) was a French Post-Impressionist/Nabi painter.

107. (D)

The film *The Third Man* was based on a novel by Graham Greene. Greene was a British author of the twentieth century whose novels involve mysterious plot twists and penetrate the psychological crises of the protagonist.

108. (E)

Gauguin (A) was a contemporary and for a short time a close friend of Vincent van Gogh, but he is not in the portrait. Van Gogh created many self-portraits over the course of his career.

109. (D)

This self-portrait is one of many Van Gogh painted over the course of his tortured life. A portrait (E) could be a painting of anyone and is not as specific as answer (D). A still life (A) is a painting of inanimate objects, such as fruit and a vase of flowers. A landscape (B) is a painting of the countryside, and a fresco (C) is a painting on plaster created with dissolved pigments.

110. (C)

Van Gogh was the foremost artist (retrospectively) in the move away from Impressionism toward more Expressionist art. He was a member of the Post-Impressionist movement but not any of the other movements listed.

111. (A)

Prospero is the wizard banished to an island with his daughter Miranda in *The Tempest*. He is a more serious character, not a comic figure such as Puck (E) in *A Midsummer Night's Dream*.

112. (A)

Momaday's novel is one of the first award-winning novels written by a Native American. The main character does not represent any of the other choices.

113. (A)

The sculptures from this age all display the human form as athletic, muscular, and in perfect proportion. The sculptures of humans are idealistic but not understated (B), ambivalent (C), ironic (D), or modest (E).

114. (E)

The key word in this question is *ancient*. All the other periods occurred long after what is considered ancient.

115. (E)

Eroica was written in honor of Napoleon, but Beethoven removed Napoleon's name from the composition in disgust after Napoleon declared himself emperor.

116. (B)

Nude Descending a Staircase was the most notable painting displayed at the famous Armory show just prior to World War I.

117. (D)

"The Colonel" is a poem that relates an incident with a particularly brutal Colonel in El Salvador. Forche is a prominent late twentieth-century poet who, like many of her fellow postmodernists, is most concerned with sociopolitical realities.

118. (B)

A libretto is the script that goes along with the music in opera.

119. (D)

Little Nell's death at the conclusion of *The Old Curiosity Shop* is one of the most pathos-evoking scenes in all of literature. In the Dostoyevsky (C) and Wharton (E) novels, the main characters meet bad endings but survive.

120. (C)

Along with Kurt Vonnegut, these two authors are the most notable writers in the genre of science fiction. They are not associated with the Romantic movement (A) (which occured well before the twentieth century), the painting style of Naturalism (B), author Robert Browning (D), or absurdist drama (E).

121. (A)

Warhol's paintings of soup cans, movie stars, and political figures reproduced with slight modifications took the art world in a new direction in the middle of the twentieth century. Since Warhol did not focus on nature, you are not likely to find trees and peasants (B), or rocks and hawks (C), in his work. Warhol did not include horses and Napoleon (D) or sides of beef and Pope Urban II (E) in his work.

122. (D)

The painting is *Nighthawks* by Edward Hopper. Hopper's main concern was with a distinctly American loneliness. He painted scenes in desolate, depressed areas to show the futility and emptiness of the American Dream.

123. (B)

Hopper chose particularly barren, soulless scenes to portray the emptiness in the American Dream. His work was not tense (A), light-hearted (C), violent (D), or comical (E).

124. (D)

Among the work of American artists, Edward Hopper's paintings are perhaps the most easily identifiable due to the uniformity of his subject matter. Hopper chiefly uses American scenes of desolation in his work. In contrast, Georgia O'Keefe (C) primarily painted flowers.

125. (A)

Conrad's work delves into the machinations of colonial tyrants and corrupted natives. He studies the facets of power, corruption, and evil in novels such as *Heart of Darkness*. None of the other choices apply to Conrad's work.

126. (C)

Main character and *protagonist* are two terms that are generally interchangeable. *Deus ex machina* (A) refers to an unexpected character or plot device to solve a situation in a drama or fiction. A thespian (B) is a person who acts in plays, comic relief (D) presents a light-hearted moment, scene, or character for the audience of a play, and a bridge (E) is found in some string instruments as a thin, upright piece of wood.

127. (C)

Benvenuto Cellini's autobiography is read both as a great work in the genre as well as a means of examining the Renaissance through the eyes of one of its most prominent sculptors.

128. (A)

Turner's depictions of storms and sunsets at sea were a prelude to the Impressionist movement. Rarely will you find a Turner painting set elsewhere.

129. (C)

The line of text contains the name of the novel's title character, "Mrs. Dalloway." The novel was written by English writer Virginia Woolf in 1925 and covers the thoughts of several people during a single day.

130. (B)

The Barber of Seville (B) was written in 1816. *Don Giovanni* (A) was written by Wolfgang Amadeus Mozart, *Orfeo* (C) was composed by Claudio Monteverdi, *Die Freischutz* (D) was written by Carl Maria von Weber, and *Aida* (E) was written by Guiseppi Verdi.

131. (A)

V. S. Naipaul's books are mostly set in Africa and describe the relationship between natives and immigrants. Naipaul won the Nobel Prize in Literature in 2001, and he is considered the leading novelist of the Caribbean today.

132. (B)

Multiple first-person points of view are given in this novel. The story is told from one perspective and then retold from the point of view of other characters.

133. (D)

Gore Vidal is a noted novelist, critic, and historian and considered by many to be the foremost "man of letters" in the United States. None of the other authors was born in the United States.

134. (B)

Oliver Goldsmith was a British author of humorous novels in the eighteenth century. All the other authors published work in the twentieth century.

135. (A)

The film *The English Patient* (1996) was based on the novel by Michael Ondaatje. The Sri Lankan-born author's novel *The English Patient* magnifies the personal to coexist with the historical.

136. (E)

Thurber's modus operandi is satirizing certain kinds of people and social (or political) situations. His tone is light-hearted in works such as *My Life and Hard Times*. James Thurber is a twentieth-century author.

137. (B)

The Ayatollah Khomeini of Iran called for Rushdie's death in response to what he felt was the author's disrespectful treatment of the prophet Muhammad. *The Satanic Verses* was published in 1988.

138. (E)

Both Rothko and Chagall were persecuted by the Stalinist regime and exiled to the United States and France respectively. Rothko was an Abstract Expressionist, while Chagall was a stained-glass artist and painter.

139. (A)

Although Shaw spent most of his adult life in England, he was born in Ireland. Yeats traveled widely, but he was always associated with the Irish landscape and political strife.

140. (D)

All three novels are set in Africa. Rushd, Coetzee, and Achebe all live in Africa. Kingsolver, while an American writer, set *The Poisonwood Bible*, a novel about a family of missionaries, in Africa.

The CLEP Social Sciences and History Exam

Chapter Sixteen: **Practice Test 1: Diagnostic**

Time—90 minutes
120 Questions

Directions: For each of the following questions or incomplete statements, select the best answer or completion from the five options given.

1. The part of the brain associated with balance, smooth movement, and posture is

    (A) the hypothalamus.
    (B) the temporal lobe.
    (C) the cerebral hemisphere.
    (D) the cerebellum.
    (E) more highly developed in older adults than in adolescents.

2. *The Gift*, a pioneering book first published in 1923–1924 about the importance of exchanging objects, was written by

    (A) Jacques Derrida.
    (B) Claude Lévi-Strauss.
    (C) Marcel Mauss.
    (D) Jacques Marie Émile Lacan.
    (E) Michel Foucault.

3. Which world leaders are most closely linked with bringing about the end of Soviet domination in Eastern Europe?

    (A) Ronald Reagan, Margaret Thatcher, Pope John Paul II
    (B) Jimmy Carter, Margaret Thatcher, Pope John Paul II
    (C) Ronald Reagan, Leonid Brezhnev, Pope John Paul II
    (D) Jimmy Carter, Anwar Sadat, Menachim Begin
    (E) George H. W. Bush, Margaret Thatcher, Tony Blair

4. The Egyptian president assassinated by radicals in his own country for making peace overtures toward Israel was

    (A) Menachim Begin.
    (B) Hosni Muborak.
    (C) Gamal Nasser.
    (D) Hafez al Asad.
    (E) Anwar Sadat.

GO ON TO THE NEXT PAGE

KAPLAN

5. Supply-side economics holds that lowering taxes

    (A) causes higher interest rates because of excess consumption.

    (B) leads to recession because the government will have less money to spend.

    (C) increases unemployment because of lowered demand for goods and services.

    (D) causes the economy to expand because consumers have more money to spend.

    (E) causes the Federal Reserve to lower the money supply.

6. Which of these statements would the Luddites have agreed with?

    (A) Advances in technology are always good for society.

    (B) It is more important to preserve jobs than to produce lower-priced goods.

    (C) Taxation without representation is tyranny.

    (D) Trade with all other nations benefits all parties.

    (E) Mass-produced goods are preferable to individually created goods.

7. What is the deepest lake in the world?

    (A) Great Salt Lake

    (B) Lake Biwa

    (C) Lake Superior

    (D) Lake Victoria

    (E) Lake Baikal

8. The names "Johanson" and "Lucy" will forever be associated. What is their relationship?

    (A) Johanson discovered Lucy, the oldest known human ancestor.

    (B) Johanson cloned a sheep he nicknamed Lucy.

    (C) Lucy was Johanson's first wife and the author of *Coming of Age in Samoa*.

    (D) They were husband-wife paleontologists.

    (E) They were father-daughter archaeologists.

9. What are subduction zones?

    (A) Areas where the temperature is lower than freezing for the majority of the year

    (B) Regions with less than 10" of rain each year

    (C) Areas where tectonic plates collide and slide under one another

    (D) Areas where the ice caps are melting, causing the flooding of nearby lands

    (E) Places where there is abnormal electromagnetic activity, possibly due to sunspots

10. The term *Gilded Age* refers to what era of American history?

    (A) It comes from a Mark Twain novel and alludes to the outwardly showy but inwardly corrupt nature of American society in the late 1800s.

    (B) It was coined by F. Scott Fitzgerald to describe the decadent days of the "flappers" and "bootleggers."

    (C) It is an ironic term referring to the dark days after the stock market crash on Black Monday in 1987.

    (D) The Beat Generation used the name to describe what they perceived to be the empty consumer culture of the 1950s.

    (E) It was another name for Reconstruction, when carpetbaggers from the North poured into the South to take advantage of government programs and make fortunes for themselves.

11. Which of the following are methodologies used to study social groups?

    I. Experiments
    II. Surveys
    III. Cross-cultural comparison

    (A) I only

    (B) II only

    (C) III only

    (D) I and II only

    (E) I, II, and III

GO ON TO THE NEXT PAGE ⟩

12. In which of the following geographic features is a canal likely to be found?

(A) Archipelago

(B) Isthmus

(C) Cape

(D) Island

(E) Valley

13. Tornadoes are thought to occur when

(A) there is lightning in the area.

(B) cool and warm air collide, forcing the warm air to rise rapidly.

(C) earthquakes on the ocean floor cause huge tidal waves.

(D) warm air blows debris over a wide area.

(E) barometric pressure rises from 900 to 1,000 millibars.

14. Which country is composed of the most islands?

(A) Indonesia

(B) Fiji

(C) Japan

(D) Maldives

(E) Philippines

15. The Great Wall of China was built

(A) to repel potential invaders from the north.

(B) to prevent Chinese citizens from escaping.

(C) in the mistaken belief that it would keep out the plague.

(D) to prevent traders from bringing in goods without paying tariffs.

(E) to keep prisoners busy so they would not rebel.

16. According to this map of Africa, which of these countries is NOT labeled correctly?

(A) Democratic Republic of the Congo

(B) Egypt

(C) Saudi Arabia

(D) South Africa

(E) Algeria

17. What was the name of Leningrad prior to 1924?

(A) Moscow

(B) Warsaw

(C) St. Petersburg

(D) Minsk

(E) Kiev

GO ON TO THE NEXT PAGE

KAPLAN

18. What were the precipitating causes of the Great Depression?

    (A) World War II and a hard winter
    (B) An uneven distribution of wealth and stock market speculation
    (C) Crop failures and excessive foreign debt
    (D) High interest rates and low unemployment
    (E) Disruption of global trade based on political tensions in Europe

19. The following anthropological method would reveal if an early ape, man, or woman walked upright.

    (A) Carbon-14 dating
    (B) An examination of fossilized footprints
    (C) Uranium-235 dating
    (D) Discovery of sticks near humanoid skeletons
    (E) Process of elimination

20. In his Social Conflict theory, Karl Marx

    (A) proposed that the struggle between the "working class" and the "owner class" would result in a classless society.
    (B) observed that class struggle inevitably leads to democracy.
    (C) advocated suppression of the working class.
    (D) anticipated the Solidarity movement.
    (E) suggested that class struggle could be prevented.

21. Chimpanzees are descended from an ancestor shared with the only hominid remaining today. What is the name of this contemporary hominid?

    (A) *Australopithecus robustus*
    (B) gorilla
    (C) *Homo sapiens sapiens*
    (D) orangutan
    (E) *Homo sapiens robustus*

22. Margaret Mead is best known for her work

    (A) focusing on adolescent boys in American Samoa.
    (B) focusing on adolescent girls in British Samoa.
    (C) with the elderly in New Guinea.
    (D) on death and dying.
    (E) focusing on adolescent girls in American Samoa.

23. While aboard the HMS *Beagle*, Charles Darwin developed his theory of

    (A) the origin of the cosmos.
    (B) plate tectonics.
    (C) evolution.
    (D) natural rights.
    (E) artificial selection.

24. Which of the following statements about Ferdinand Magellan is TRUE?

    (A) He discovered a land route to China.
    (B) He was commissioned by the Pope to prove that the Earth was flat.
    (C) He sailed with the *Niña*, *Pinta*, and *Santa Maria*.
    (D) He sailed under the flag of England.
    (E) He was the first explorer to circumnavigate the globe.

25. Richard Milhous Nixon was associated with what infamous organization that orchestrated the Watergate break-in?

    (A) The Quakers
    (B) The Labor Party
    (C) The Committee to Re-Elect the President
    (D) Whitewater
    (E) The Freemasons

GO ON TO THE NEXT PAGE

26. An earthquake would be LEAST likely to occur in which geographic area?

    (A) Sahara desert

    (B) California

    (C) France

    (D) Antarctica

    (E) Japan

27. What was the reason for the Twenty-sixth Amendment?

    (A) To abolish slavery

    (B) To limit the President to no more than two elected terms of office

    (C) To lower the voting age from twenty-one to eighteen

    (D) To repeal Prohibition

    (E) To prevent senators and representatives from voting for an immediate pay increase for themselves

28. Why do some economists prefer monetary policy over fiscal policy?

    (A) They believe monetary policy is less political and faster to implement.

    (B) They believe fiscal policy is less political.

    (C) They believe Congress is best suited to manage the economy.

    (D) Monetary policy is less likely to be overturned by the Supreme Court.

    (E) Monetary policy produces more concrete results.

29. Considered one of the "fathers of modern sociology," Emile Durkheim conceptualized

    (A) behaviorism.

    (B) utilitarianism.

    (C) the Oedipus complex.

    (D) functionalism.

    (E) survival of the fittest.

30. Art, science, and philosophy flourished in Europe in the time following the Middle Ages. The name for this period, "Renaissance," is a French word that means

    (A) reason.

    (B) related to the arts.

    (C) relapse.

    (D) reformation.

    (E) rebirth.

31. Which of the following statements is TRUE about "socialization"?

    (A) Socialization is a static process.

    (B) Socialization begins at the close of enculturation.

    (C) Socialization is a lifelong process that begins at birth.

    (D) Those who are closest to us have the least effect on the socialization process.

    (E) Mass media is to blame for most alienation.

32. According to Max Weber,

    (A) division of labor is not necessary in a bureaucracy.

    (B) society is characterized by status-quo maintenance.

    (C) class struggle always leads to social harmony.

    (D) social stratification is based solely on personal wealth.

    (E) bureaucracies represent the ideal organization of large-scale modern societies.

GO ON TO THE NEXT PAGE

KAPLAN

33. What is the difference between an archipelago and an atoll?

   (A) An archipelago is found in the Northern Hemisphere and an atoll in the Southern Hemisphere.

   (B) An archipelago is a chain of islands and an atoll is a ring of islands or one ring-shaped island.

   (C) An archipelago is able to support only plant life, while an atoll can support plant and animal life.

   (D) An archipelago is natural and an atoll is manmade.

   (E) There is no difference.

34. Which of the following are symbolic components of culture?

   (A) Values and norms

   (B) Cultures and subcultures

   (C) Folkways and mores

   (D) Taboos and sanctions

   (E) Language and gestures

35. Which of the following is TRUE about deviance?

   (A) It always performs a negative function in society.

   (B) It sometimes performs a positive function in society.

   (C) It should never be encouraged or discouraged.

   (D) It is always a sign of societal dysfunction.

   (E) It operates independently of the wider society.

36. Which of the following explains the significance of Gresham's law as it applied during the Great Depression?

   (A) During the Great Depression, people hoarded their money at home because they did not trust banks.

   (B) People were eager to trade their dollars for foreign currency because they thought it would hold its value better.

   (C) Congressman Gresham ordered the banks to remain open five days a week.

   (D) People held on to gold and spent paper money, causing the amount of gold in circulation to decline.

   (E) Simple bartering systems emerged to replace cash in day-to-day transactions.

37. The psychologist Erik Erikson is best known for his writings on

   (A) psychosocial development.

   (B) class warfare.

   (C) chaos theory.

   (D) survival of the fittest.

   (E) naval strategy.

38. In her book *On Death and Dying*,

   (A) Elizabeth Cady Stanton chronicles her husband's slow death from Alzheimer's.

   (B) reincarnation and the afterlife are explored.

   (C) Elizabeth Kübler-Ross introduces her theory about the stages of grief.

   (D) Elizabeth Kübler-Ross debunks the stage theory of grief.

   (E) Elizabeth Cady Stanton discusses the depression associated with dying.

GO ON TO THE NEXT PAGE

39. Assuming that when we grow older we become less productive and examine our options for retired life, upon reaching this age

    (A) most people sink into irreversible depressions.

    (B) our lives become increasingly less productive, therefore lacking in satisfaction.

    (C) we long for social acceptance.

    (D) we are able to develop integrity if we see ourselves as having led a successful life.

    (E) despair and alienation are the most common experience.

40. What was the significance of Richard Nixon's 1972 trip to China?

    (A) It was his first overseas trip.

    (B) He signed a peace treaty with Chairman Mao Tse-tung.

    (C) China agreed to withdraw from Hong Kong.

    (D) No American president had ever visited China before.

    (E) His cultural insensitivity increased tensions with China.

41. Whose victory at the Battle of Hastings in 1066 changed the culture of Great Britain?

    (A) Saladin

    (B) William of Normandy

    (C) Frederick the Great

    (D) Charlemagne

    (E) Attila the Hun

42. A country where all economic decisions are made by the government is best described as

    (A) socialist.

    (B) capitalist.

    (C) anarchist.

    (D) fascist.

    (E) totalitarian.

43. The U.S. government is best described as a

    (A) monarchy.

    (B) representative democracy.

    (C) pure democracy.

    (D) aristocracy.

    (E) dictatorship.

44. What was the argument against the creation of the Federal Reserve Bank?

    (A) It would give Congress too much power over monetary policy.

    (B) It would be harder to open new banks.

    (C) It would make it more difficult to implement fiscal policy.

    (D) It would violate the system of checks and balances.

    (E) It would concentrate power in the hands of Eastern bankers.

45. *The Federalist Papers* are significant because

    (A) they contain the personal thoughts of George Washington, the nation's first president.

    (B) they outline the manner in which our federal government should function.

    (C) they outline basic rights and liberties reserved for the citizens of the United States.

    (D) they provide the best insight into the framers' purposes in creating the Constitution.

    (E) they lay out the civil liberties that members of a democracy enjoy.

46. Which two adversaries did NOT sign a peace treaty at the end of World War II?

    (A) Japan and Italy

    (B) Japan and China

    (C) Russia and Japan

    (D) Germany and Italy

    (E) Canada and the United States

GO ON TO THE NEXT PAGE

47. Who created the American monetary system?

    (A) Aaron Burr

    (B) John Jay

    (C) James Madison

    (D) Alexander Hamilton

    (E) Thomas Jefferson

48. One purpose of the Electoral College is

    (A) to lengthen the election process, giving people longer to make up their minds.

    (B) to involve additional parties in the electoral process, to prevent the likelihood of fraud.

    (C) to give larger states more representation in the Electoral College.

    (D) to give smaller states equal representation in the electoral process.

    (E) to make sure every citizen's vote is counted.

49. Which of the following is NOT a potential effect of global warming on worldwide food production?

    (A) Cold climates would be able to grow more food.

    (B) Hot climates would be able to grow less food.

    (C) Higher amounts of carbon dioxide in the atmosphere would have a fertilizing effect, aiding in agricultural production.

    (D) Weather prediction would be more difficult.

    (E) Demand for exotic ingredients would increase.

50. What did Andrew Carnegie, Cornelius Vanderbilt, and John D. Rockefeller have in common?

    (A) They opposed monopolies.

    (B) They married wealthy widows.

    (C) They were pro-Union.

    (D) They were known as "Robber Barons."

    (E) They were originally European royalty.

51. The Fall of Constantinople at the hands of the Turks resulted in

    (A) the defeat of Islam in the West.

    (B) the rise of the Ottoman empire.

    (C) the opening up of trade routes to the New World.

    (D) the capture of Jerusalem.

    (E) the conversion of millions of Muslims to Christianity.

52. Lengthening the period of time a worker can collect unemployment benefits tends to

    (A) encourage job seekers to look harder for new jobs.

    (B) make it harder for job seekers to find work.

    (C) encourage illegal immigration.

    (D) raise the unemployment rate.

    (E) have no effect on the unemployment rate.

53. Where in the U.S. Constitution does the phrase "separation of church and state" appear?

    (A) Article II, Section 1

    (B) The Bill of Rights

    (C) The Fifth Amendment

    (D) The First Amendment

    (E) These words do not appear in the Constitution

54. What is the "collective unconscious"?

    (A) Jung's name for knowledge passed automatically through generations

    (B) Freud's theory of human desires employed in dream analysis

    (C) A psychosocial memory that is encoded in DNA

    (D) An example of the negative effect of groupthink

    (E) An idea Freud introduced in opposition to Jung's theory of uniformity

GO ON TO THE NEXT PAGE ⇨

55. Which U.S. president said, "The only thing we have to fear is fear itself"?

    (A) Jimmy Carter

    (B) George W. Bush

    (C) Gerald Ford

    (D) Franklin D. Roosevelt

    (E) Ronald Reagan

56. The political party MOST likely to support lower taxes and less government spending is

    (A) the Democratic Party.

    (B) the Green Party.

    (C) the Republican Party.

    (D) the Socialist Party.

    (E) the Liberal Party.

57. Presidents John F. Kennedy and Dwight D. Eisenhower are often held up as symbols of two radically different eras; which of the following is TRUE?

    (A) Kennedy represents the prosperous, tranquil 1950s.

    (B) Kennedy himself was a product of the Eisenhower era and his policies are not necessarily as progressive as the Kennedy Myth maintains.

    (C) Eisenhower represents the turbulent, socially progressive 1950s.

    (D) Kennedy represents the socially and sexually repressive 1960s.

    (E) Eisenhower's policies are deceptively socialist in nature, advocating communal labor practices.

58. The Crusades were a series of wars

    (A) declared by Protestants on Catholics and Papal authority.

    (B) initiated by Christians to win back their Holy Land from the Muslims.

    (C) fought by the French and British for nearly one hundred years.

    (D) fought between Jews and Palestinians over the Gaza Strip.

    (E) initiated by Muslims to win back their Holy Land from the Christians.

59. The term *aboriginal* *typically* applies to persons living in the

    (A) Gobi desert.

    (B) south seas.

    (C) western part of Africa.

    (D) Australian outback.

    (E) Amazon rainforest.

60. Which country is the world's most populous democracy?

    (A) China

    (B) United States

    (C) Russia

    (D) India

    (E) Japan

61. An example of a stateless people would be the

    (A) Kurds.

    (B) Cambodians.

    (C) Ethiopians.

    (D) Panamanians.

    (E) Irish.

GO ON TO THE NEXT PAGE ▷

62. The Europeans were first interested in exploring Africa

    (A) because they wanted slaves to work in their colonies.

    (B) because there were great sources of gold and diamonds.

    (C) because Europe was becoming overpopulated and they needed new land to explore.

    (D) to convert Africans to Christianity.

    (E) because they were seeking a water route to India.

63. In the stage of precontact,

    (A) societies are characterized by an openness to change.

    (B) a primeval society has never encountered outsiders.

    (C) an industrialized nation practices isolation.

    (D) a primeval society aggressively pursues dominance.

    (E) a society aspires to be a part of the global technological revolution.

64. What is the final stage of Freud's theory of psychosocial development?

    (A) Anural stage

    (B) Genital stage

    (C) Electra stage

    (D) Oral stage

    (E) Latency stage

65. Who is second in succession to the U.S. presidency?

    (A) The secretary of state

    (B) The president pro tempore of the Senate

    (C) The vice president

    (D) The attorney general

    (E) The speaker of the House

66. The Fertile Crescent is known as

    (A) the cotton capital of the South.

    (B) the breadbasket of Egypt.

    (C) the cradle of civilization.

    (D) the temple of the gods.

    (E) the gateway to the east.

67. World War I coincided with what other pivotal event in Russian history?

    (A) The breakup of the Balkan states

    (B) A return to feudalism and an agrarian lifestyle

    (C) The Russian potato famine

    (D) The Russian revolution, which ended the monarchy and brought Lenin to power

    (E) Stalin's rise to power and the beginning of a nascent democracy

68. Sir Isaac Newton's experiments and discoveries

    (A) led to a smallpox vaccination.

    (B) allowed ships to sail around the world.

    (C) led to today's scientists being able to design rockets.

    (D) led to the discovery of microorganisms.

    (E) allowed mapmakers to draw more accurate maps.

69. Which skirmish was the final imperial struggle between the United States and Britain, leaving the Americans with undisputed control over their own destiny?

    (A) Battle of Little Big Horn

    (B) War of 1812

    (C) Battle of Midway

    (D) Attack on Harpers Ferry

    (E) Battle of Gettysburg

GO ON TO THE NEXT PAGE ⟹

70. Why do diamonds cost more than salt?

    (A) There is more salt available on the Earth than there are diamonds.

    (B) Salt is necessary for human life, and diamonds are not.

    (C) Salt is harder to mine than diamonds.

    (D) The price of salt is kept low by the government.

    (E) Some countries export more diamonds than salt.

71. The two variables represented by the Phillips curve are

    (A) interest rates and inflation.

    (B) inflation and unemployment.

    (C) aggregate supply and aggregate demand.

    (D) price and quantity.

    (E) money supply and money demand.

72. What is the relationship between interest rates and inflation?

    (A) There is no relationship between interest rates and inflation.

    (B) When interest rates fall, inflation rises.

    (C) Interest rates and inflation move in the same direction.

    (D) When inflation falls, interest rates rise.

    (E) There is not enough information given to answer.

73. The Supreme Court decision *Brown v. Topeka Board of Education*

    (A) outlawed prayer in public schools.

    (B) outlawed the practice of "separate but equal" education for minority children.

    (C) forced public schools to stop saying the Pledge of Allegiance because of the words "under God."

    (D) forced public schools to offer equal athletics programs for girls.

    (E) permitted the posting of the Ten Commandments in public schools.

74. The social definition of a people based on cultural ties (such as language, dress, customs, and beliefs) is called

    (A) race.

    (B) regionalism.

    (C) social stratification.

    (D) ethnicity.

    (E) assimilation.

75. Changing one's attitudes, beliefs, ways of thinking, or behavior in order to be more consistent with others is an example of

    (A) peer pressure.

    (B) mimesis.

    (C) disorientation.

    (D) conditioning.

    (E) conformity.

76. Fiscal policy is implemented by

    (A) the Federal Reserve System.

    (B) the Supreme Court.

    (C) Congress.

    (D) the Surgeon General.

    (E) the FBI.

77. The approach to researching societies known as cultural relativism

    (A) always involves an ethnocentric stance.

    (B) is in stark contrast to ethnocentrism.

    (C) views other cultures from the point of view of an individual's own values.

    (D) never necessitates a suspension of judgment.

    (E) involves family dynamics.

GO ON TO THE NEXT PAGE

KAPLAN

78. Which of the following is NOT a duty of the Federal Reserve System?

    (A) Raising and lowering reserve requirements for member banks

    (B) Examination and regulation of national banks

    (C) Printing currency

    (D) Setting the discount rate

    (E) Keeping track of economic statistics

79. Which group of Americans was largely Republican in the years following the Civil War but votes mostly Democratic today?

    (A) White men

    (B) Women

    (C) African Americans

    (D) Hispanics

    (E) Young adults

80. What was Winston Churchill referring to when he coined the phrase "the iron curtain"?

    (A) The rise of the communist party in China

    (B) Ever-increasing government spending and the resulting budget deficit

    (C) The increasing industrialization of rural England

    (D) The military threat posed by a newly re-armed Germany

    (E) Domination of Eastern Europe by the Soviet Union

81. Milton Friedman is the leading proponent of what school of economic thought?

    (A) Supply-side economics

    (B) Monetarism

    (C) Keynesianism

    (D) Socialism

    (E) Fiscal policy

82. Which of the following statements is TRUE in regards to the American construct of "Manifest Destiny"?

    (A) It was a phrase used by leaders and politicians to explain northward expansion.

    (B) It expressed a sense of mission for many Americans to extend the boundaries of freedom and democracy.

    (C) As the birth rate and immigration declined in the original thirteen colonies in the 1840s, continental expansion was not only desired but necessary.

    (D) Frontier land was typically expensive but the overcrowding and disease of urban centers were bigger problems.

    (E) Liberal racial policy offered uncommon opportunities for freed slaves.

83. The suffrage movement resulted in

    (A) divorce rights for women.

    (B) property rights for slaves.

    (C) enfranchisement for women.

    (D) voting rights for former slaves.

    (E) the end of Prohibition.

84. Which is TRUE of crystallized intelligence?

    (A) It represents our acquired knowledge.

    (B) It is fluid in nature.

    (C) It refers to our ability to utilize acquired knowledge.

    (D) It is determined according to the Rorschach scale.

    (E) It represents our innate intelligence.

GO ON TO THE NEXT PAGE ⇨

85. Which is TRUE of the New Deal?

    (A) It was Teddy Roosevelt's plan to put people back to work following the Great Depression.

    (B) It refers to the Pop Art movement popularized by Andy Warhol and Roy Lichtenstein.

    (C) It was a failed social program meant to force integration between whites and African Americans in the rural South.

    (D) It opened up trade routes and reduced tariffs throughout North America in order to encourage free trade among Mexico, the United States, and Canada.

    (E) It included Franklin Delano Roosevelt's WPA projects, which put American artists to work on public arts projects.

86. Who was largely responsible for the Second Red Scare?

    (A) Joseph McCarthy

    (B) Vladimir Lenin

    (C) Benito Mussolini

    (D) Mikhail Gorbachev

    (E) Chairman Mao

87. The term *détente*

    (A) refers to the thawing out of international tension at the start of the Cold War.

    (B) applies to the growing fear of nuclear holocaust after the Cold War.

    (C) is a French term now typically used in reference to mounting Franco-American tension.

    (D) refers to an accord established at the Geneva Convention.

    (E) is usually associated with China, the Soviet Union, and the United States and refers to the relaxation of international tension.

88. Which is TRUE of *Uncle Tom's Cabin*?

    (A) It was heralded in the South and denounced in the North.

    (B) It was written by Catherine Beecher and advocated abolitionism.

    (C) It was a stop on the Underground Railroad.

    (D) It was not a cabin at all, but a mansion in Newport.

    (E) It was a bestselling book advocating emancipation.

89. The phenomenon in medicine where the subject's beliefs about a treatment can significantly affect the cure is known as

    (A) selection bias.

    (B) the Moro reflex.

    (C) the placebo effect.

    (D) the Paracea effect.

    (E) sample standard deviation.

90. The Vikings were fierce warriors and skilled sailors who hailed from

    (A) Norway, Sweden, and Nova Scotia.

    (B) Nova Scotia, the Ottoman empire, and Denmark.

    (C) Norway, Sweden, and Denmark.

    (D) Valhalla and Iceland.

    (E) Greenland, Sweden, and Holland.

91. The term *indentured servitude* refers to

    (A) a system of apprenticeship.

    (B) written contracts between African immigrants and landholders.

    (C) a common labor practice throughout the South today.

    (D) an opportunity for refugees seeking political asylum.

    (E) a system of importing servants to the New World.

GO ON TO THE NEXT PAGE

KAPLAN

92. One reason cartels can become unstable over time is that

    (A) countries will go to war over economic issues.

    (B) buyers will stop buying if the prices are too high.

    (C) when the goods are homogenous, the price will fall.

    (D) people stop using drugs because they want to be healthier.

    (E) a member will break with the cartel for individual gain.

93. William Byrd was a gentleman planter who was educated in England and

    (A) whose sharp tongue landed him in jail after an argument with a colonial governor.

    (B) whose detailed diaries are a valuable record of Southern colonial life.

    (C) who founded a Utopian community in Virginia.

    (D) who gained infamy after a scandalous affair with his slave Sally Hemings.

    (E) who conducted tent-style revivals on his plantation.

94. Which of these countries did Napoleon Bonaparte NOT attempt to conquer or control?

    (A) Italy

    (B) Russia

    (C) Germany

    (D) Switzerland

    (E) England

95. Nat Turner's Rebellion resulted in

    (A) the lynchings of more than twenty plantation owners in South Carolina.

    (B) the "separate but equal" approach to segregation.

    (C) the bloodiest insurrection by the Whigs against the Tories.

    (D) the deaths of 60 white Virginians.

    (E) the Fugitive Slave Act of 1866.

96. The 1912 "discovery" of this inauthentic human ancestor was a hoax that set back the study of human evolution for at least 40 years. What was its name?

    (A) Java Man

    (B) Neanderthal Man

    (C) Cro-Magnon Man

    (D) Lucy

    (E) Piltdown Man

97. What was significant about the Missouri Compromise?

    (A) It marked the beginning of sectional reunification between the North and the South.

    (B) It allowed Missouri to enter the Union as a free state.

    (C) It permitted South Carolina to secede from the Union.

    (D) It granted fugitive slaves amnesty within the Missouri border.

    (E) It prohibited slavery above the 36°30' latitude line.

GO ON TO THE NEXT PAGE

98. The Greek mathematician and inventor Archimedes is best known for

    (A) discovering that the Earth revolves around the sun.

    (B) proving that the Earth is round.

    (C) inventing calculus.

    (D) discovering that mass can be measured by displaced water.

    (E) inventing the telescope.

99. Which statement does NOT explain why some countries such as Japan, which lack nearly all natural resources, are still relatively wealthy?

    (A) They have a highly educated, industrious workforce.

    (B) They have a high level of technology.

    (C) Their governments implement policies friendly to business and investment.

    (D) They have a financial system capable of supporting economic development.

    (E) They maintain colonial empires elsewhere in the world.

100. Which of these hypothetical individuals could not be elected president of the United States?

    (A) Bob, a 50-year-old man born in Ohio

    (B) Sally, a 36-year-old woman born in Florida

    (C) Howard, a 45-year-old man born in England

    (D) Ellen, a 60-year-old woman born in Montana

    (E) Antoine, a 40-year-old man born in Alaska

101. Considered the father of behavioral therapy, B. F. Skinner once stated that

    (A) with hard work and psychoanalysis a dysfunctional person may be reintegrated.

    (B) personality is entirely genetically predetermined.

    (C) our cognitions or thoughts control a large portion of our behavior.

    (D) negative reinforcement and aversion therapy should never be used on children.

    (E) with control of a child's environment, he could raise a child to become anything.

102. The Spanish founded the first European colony in North America in 1565 and named it

    (A) St. Augustine.

    (B) Plymouth.

    (C) San Antonio.

    (D) San Francisco.

    (E) Acadia.

103. In which way or ways was ancient Greek democracy, known as direct democracy, different from contemporary democracy?

    I. It did not presuppose equality of individuals.
    II. It limited democracy to natural-born citizens.
    III. It withheld political rights from women.

    (A) I only

    (B) II only

    (C) III only

    (D) I and III only

    (E) I, II, and III

GO ON TO THE NEXT PAGE

KAPLAN

104. The Magna Carta was the first attempt to

   (A) codify British common law.
   (B) limit the power of a monarch.
   (C) create a uniform tax code.
   (D) impose taxation without representation.
   (E) express individual civil liberties.

105. The country once known as Ceylon is now called

   (A) Rhodesia.
   (B) Indonesia.
   (C) Ulan Bator.
   (D) Sri Lanka.
   (E) Myanmar.

106. Abraham Lincoln was a member of which political party?

   (A) Republican
   (B) Federalist
   (C) Independent
   (D) Whig
   (E) Democratic-Republican

107. The origins of Rome are steeped in myth and legend. Many ancient Romans believed that

   (A) Zeus created Rome to house his oracle.
   (B) Rome was built for the goddess Aphrodite.
   (C) Rome was built in a day.
   (D) the god Remus created the city.
   (E) the city was founded by twin boys named Romulus and Remus.

108. The three branches of the U.S. government are

   (A) the House of Representatives, the Senate, and the Congress.
   (B) legislative, executive, and judicial.
   (C) the Federal Reserve, the Supreme Court, and the FBI.
   (D) Democrats, Republicans, and Independents.
   (E) the president, the vice president, and the speaker of the House.

109. What war did the Treaty of Versailles end?

   (A) World War I
   (B) World War II
   (C) The Hundred Years' War
   (D) The French and Indian War
   (E) The French Revolution

110. Which is TRUE of sensory memory?

   (A) It is very brief, lasting only a few seconds.
   (B) It differs depending upon the cognitive dissonance of the subject.
   (C) It takes over when our short-term memory expires.
   (D) It is possible only where displacement of old information occurs.
   (E) It is the opposite of semantic memory.

111. In 1940, four teenagers made what discovery in a cave at Lascaux, France?

   (A) Paintings of bison and engravings of animals
   (B) Evidence of the nomadic lifestyle of prehistoric humans
   (C) Evidence of the gender-oriented division of labor in the Paleolithic Period
   (D) Remains of the first tools
   (E) Evidence of a mythological king

GO ON TO THE NEXT PAGE

KAPLAN

112. Why is Virginia Dare notable?

    (A) She was the first English child born in North America.

    (B) She was the last woman to be burned at the stake for practicing witchcraft in Salem, Massachusetts.

    (C) She was the designer of the first American flag.

    (D) She was the first settler to be held captive by Native American chief Powhatan.

    (E) She was the first woman to vote in America.

113. Why did Martin Luther nail his 95 Theses to the door of the Castle Church?

    (A) To protest against corruption in the Catholic Church, initiating the Reformation

    (B) In an effort to buy indulgences for his salvation from the Archbishop of Castlebury

    (C) As a written confession of his sins, ushering in the Reconstruction

    (D) To assert the authority of the Augustinian works over the Dominican self

    (E) In an effort to promote the Anglican movement in Germany

114. Aggressive behavior is an interpersonal style

    (A) where the long-term goals of an individual determine behavior.

    (B) typically characteristic of passive personality types.

    (C) where the needs of the self are considered rather than the needs of others.

    (D) similar to assertive behavior, only with more anger involved.

    (E) possessed only by those in leadership roles.

115. What is the strong bond that a child forms with his or her primary caregiver called?

    (A) Pair-bonding

    (B) Attachment

    (C) Association

    (D) Fraternal attachment

    (E) Oedipus complex

116. Reconstruction refers to the period

    (A) of community rebuilding after a natural disaster.

    (B) after the American Civil War when the country attempted to reunite physically, legally, and spiritually.

    (C) after the Protestant Reformation when the Catholic Church tried to reconstitute its power.

    (D) of security and border reinforcement after the September 11, 2001, attacks.

    (E) of economic prosperity as a result of the New Deal.

117. What does a double-blind study mean?

    (A) Random assignment will counteract the experimenter bias.

    (B) Only the subjects are blind to the purpose of the study.

    (C) The researcher is blind to the purpose of the study, but the subjects are not.

    (D) Both the experimenter and the subjects are unaware of the purpose of the study.

    (E) The researcher and subject will never have a face-to-face meeting.

GO ON TO THE NEXT PAGE

118. What occurred as a result of the law of primogeniture?

    (A) Eldest sons joined the Church.

    (B) Families tended to be smaller.

    (C) Younger sons tended to join the military or explore new frontiers.

    (D) Sons had more value than daughters.

    (E) Daughters tended to marry late in life.

119. In 1630, what charismatic preacher led a Puritan migration of 900 colonists to Massachusetts Bay?

    (A) William Penn

    (B) Roger Williams

    (C) John Winthrop

    (D) Winthrop Fry

    (E) Brigham Young

120. What European explorer is credited with being the first to set foot on North America?

    (A) Ponce de Leon

    (B) Leif Erikson

    (C) Christopher Columbus

    (D) Amerigo Vespucci

    (E) Hernando Cortes

END OF TEST. STOP

THE ANSWER KEY APPEARS ON THE FOLLOWING PAGE.

ANSWER KEY

1.	D	21.	C	41.	B	61.	A	81.	B
2.	C	22.	E	42.	A	62.	E	82.	B
3.	A	23.	C	43.	B	63.	B	83.	C
4.	E	24.	E	44.	E	64.	B	84.	A
5.	D	25.	C	45.	D	65.	E	85.	E
6.	B	26.	D	46.	C	66.	C	86.	A
7.	E	27.	C	47.	D	67.	D	87.	E
8.	A	28.	A	48.	D	68.	C	88.	E
9.	C	29.	D	49.	E	69.	B	89.	C
10.	A	30.	E	50.	D	70.	A	90.	C
11.	E	31.	C	51.	B	71.	B	91.	E
12.	B	32.	E	52.	D	72.	C	92.	E
13.	B	33.	B	53.	E	73.	B	93.	B
14.	A	34.	E	54.	A	74.	D	94.	D
15.	A	35.	B	55.	D	75.	E	95.	D
16.	E	36.	D	56.	C	76.	C	96.	E
17.	C	37.	A	57.	B	77.	B	97.	E
18.	B	38.	C	58.	B	78.	C	98.	D
19.	B	39.	D	59.	D	79.	C	99.	E
20.	A	40.	D	60.	D	80.	E	100.	C

101.	E
102.	A
103.	E
104.	B
105.	D
106.	A
107.	E
108.	B
109.	A
110.	A
111.	A
112.	A
113.	A
114.	C
115.	B
116.	B
117.	D
118.	C
119.	C
120.	B

DIAGNOSTIC TEST QUICK REFERENCE TABLES

Use the following tables to determine which topics you need to review most.

Topic	Test Question
History	
United States History	10, 25, 40, 50, 55, 57, 69, 82, 83, 85, 86, 88, 91, 93, 95, 97, 112, 116, 119, 120
Western Civilization	6, 30, 41, 51, 62, 68, 80, 90, 94, 98, 102, 103, 104, 107, 109, 111, 113, 118
World History	4, 15, 24, 46, 58, 59, 60, 66, 67, 87
Social Sciences	
Government/Political Science	3, 27, 42, 43, 44, 45, 47, 48, 53, 56, 65, 73, 79, 100, 106, 108
Geography	2, 7, 9, 12, 13, 14, 16, 17, 26, 33, 49, 61, 105
Economics	5, 18, 28, 36, 52, 70, 71, 72, 78, 81, 92, 99
Psychology	1, 37, 54, 64, 75, 84, 89, 101, 110, 114, 115, 117
Sociology	11, 20, 29, 31, 32, 34, 35, 38, 39, 74, 75, 77
Anthropology	8, 19, 21, 22, 23, 63, 96

Topic	Number of Questions on Test	Number Correct
History	48	
United States History	20	
Western Civilization	18	
World History	10	
Social Sciences	72	
Government/Political Science	16	
Geography	13	
Economics	12	
Psychology	12	
Sociology	12	
Anthropology	7	

Answers and Explanations

1. (D)

The cerebellum is located at the bottom rear of the head directly above the brainstem and is important for a number of motor functions including skilled, voluntary, and precise movements. The temporal lobe plays a role in language, memory and emotion, so answer (B) is incorrect. The hypothalamus (A) sits at the top of the brain stem and regulates hunger, thirst, sexual behavior, and aggression. The cerebral hemisphere (C) is a distracter since there are two hemispheres, the left and the right, which house all brain functions. Answer (E) is a distracter: an answer choice intended to draw attention away from the correct answer.

2. (C)

In *The Gift*, sociologist and anthropologist Marcel Mauss argued that across cultures, a person who gives a gift obliges the receiver to give something back, thereby creating an exchange and an interdependent social bond. It has had a large influence on the field of anthropology. Even if you didn't know Mauss, you may have known that the other four scholars were all active after *The Gift* was published. Try to narrow your choices any way you can.

3. (A)

Common beliefs about the evils of repression and totalitarianism forged a bond between Reagan, Thatcher, and the Pope, emboldening countries in the Soviet bloc to break away and establish independent governments.

4. (E)

The Egyptian president Sadat and Israeli prime minister Begin (A) met at Camp David in 1978, pledging to work toward peace between the two nations. Muborak (B) followed Sadat as president of Egypt and Nasser (C) preceded Sadat as president, so both choices are incorrect. Al Asad (D) was the president of Syria.

5. (D)

Supply-side economics calls for lowering taxes to increase economic output because consumer spending accounts for two-thirds of economic activity. If consumers have additional disposable income they will spend it, causing business to increase output. This in turn will mean higher demand for the inputs involved in the production of goods, such as labor and raw materials.

6. (B)

The Luddites were radicals who roamed the early nineteenth-century English countryside smashing machinery, vandalizing factories, and even murdering the owners of factories that had begun to use emerging labor-saving technology. They believed that any innovation that resulted in jobs being lost was a threat, and resolved to stop such progress. Answer (E) directly contradicts the Luddite philosophy. In answer (A) the term "always" should indicate an incorrect answer choice; absolutes almost *always* appear *only* in wrong answers.

7. (E)

Lake Baikal, located in Siberia, in eastern Russia, is the world's deepest lake at 1,700 meters, over one mile deep. It accounts for 20 percent of the Earth's fresh water.

8. (A)

In 1974, the anthropologist Donald Johanson was in Ethiopia on a research expedition when he uncovered a dramatic discovery—the skeleton of a hominid he named "Lucy." The most amazing revelation came in the analysis of her leg bones, which indicated that she walked upright, making her, at 3.2 million years old, the oldest human ancestor ever discovered—at least at that time. In late 2009, scientists revealed that another, older hominid, dating back 4.4 million years, had been discovered in another area of Ethiopia. "Ardi" didn't get the press that Lucy did, but no doubt more details will be forthcoming as tests are completed.

9. (C)

Subduction zones are areas of geological activity, where the Earth's tectonic plates collide with and slide under one another. The energy released can result in the formation of new volcanoes and undersea mountain ranges.

10. (A)

The term comes from a Twain novel of the same name, and *Gilded Age* has come to represent American life in the late nineteenth century. This was a time when entrepreneurs with names like Carnegie and Vanderbilt celebrated their wealth with unprecedented lavish lifestyles. Though bohemian writers like Allen Ginsberg and Jack Kerouac (D) did reject the materialism of the 1950s, they didn't coin a name for the age but instead called themselves the Beats. In the 1980s (C), Tom Wolfe called the era's Wall Street power brokers "Masters of the Universe" in his novel *Bonfire of the Vanities*. Reconstruction (E) was a deflationary era; there was nothing "gilded" about it.

11. (E)

This is a fairly straightforward sociology question about methods of study. Answer choices (A), (B), and (C) all refer to correct methodologies, but since there is only one answer to the question, (E) is the best answer. Pay careful attention to the word *only* when it appears in answer choices.

12. (B)

A canal is likely to be found crossing an isthmus—a narrow strip of land between bodies of water, as in Panama or Suez. A canal greatly benefits the inhabitants on either side by facilitating the transport of people and goods from one body of water to another.

13. (B)

Tornadoes generally occur when atmospheric conditions force warm and cool air to collide, forming a column of air that reaches from the ground to a cloud. Since warm air rises and cool air falls, a swirling motion results from this contact. Answer (D) describes one aspect of a tornado but is not the best answer.

14. (A)

Indonesia is made up of over 17,500 islands, of which about 6,000 are inhabited. In contrast, the Philippines (E) has 7,107 islands, Japan (C) has 3,000 islands, the Maldives (D) consist of 1,192 tiny islets, and Fiji (B) has a mere 322.

15. (A)

No one knows precisely when the building of the Great Wall began, but it is popularly believed that the Wall origi-nated as a military fortification against invasions from Huns of the north.

16. (E)

The nation labeled as Algeria is actually Nigeria.

17. (C)

The city of St. Petersburg, once Russia's capital, has expe-rienced a tumultuous history. The Soviet government renamed the city Leningrad in 1924 after the leader of the Bolshevik Revolution, V. I. Lenin. In 1991, with the col-lapse of the Soviet Union, the city of Leningrad regained its original name.

18. (B)

Two causes of the Great Depression were wild speculation in the stock market by investors using borrowed money and a trade war capped by the enactment by Congress of the Smoot-Hawley Tariff Act, which levied tariffs on imported goods. Other nations promptly enacted tariffs of their own, which reduced the sale of American-made goods abroad at a time when domestic demand was weak.

19. (B)

An analysis of ancient footprint impressions can reveal if primates walked upright in two-footed strides. Footprints also can help to establish weight transference and size. Carbon-14 (A) and uranium-235 (C) dating are used to determine the age of a fossil or artifact. Sticks (D) have been used as tools by apes regardless of their posture, so their presence does not indicate walking upright.

20. (A)

Marx was communism's primary proponent but was not directly related to Poland's Solidarity movement; answer (D) can be eliminated. Answer (C) is in direct opposition to Marxist theory, which champions the working class, and (E) is incorrect because Marx believed that class struggle was inevitable. He also believed that democracy (B) would lead inevitably to socialism.

21. (C)

Hominid is a taxonomic term referring to humans and our ancestors. The hominids evolved and branched into at least twelve distinct species—humans *(Homo sapiens*

sapiens) are the sole surviving hominids. *Australopithecus robustus* was a hominid but died out millions of years ago, so (A) is incorrect. Answer (E) is a scientific-sounding made-up name.

22. (E)

Margaret Mead published *Coming of Age in Samoa*; it became a bestseller and popularized cultural anthropology. This work advanced the idea that an individual's experience of developmental stages could be shaped by cultural expectations. Mead conducted her research with adolescent girls, not boys, so (A) is incorrect; she was studying in American Samoa, not British Samoa, so (B) is also incorrect.

23. (C)

In 1859 Darwin published his theory of evolution in the book *On the Origin of Species,* igniting a controversy that continues today. Darwin formulated the idea of natural selection, not "artificial selection" (E). *Natural rights* (D) is a political term and does not relate to Darwin.

24. (E)

Magellan sailed under the flag of Spain, and it took him fourteen months to find the southern opening to the Pacific Ocean. The unsuspecting navigator expected Asia to be only a few hundred miles past the coast of South America. Instead, the expedition traveled 12,600 miles before reaching the island of Guam. Only one of Magellan's five ships found its way back to Spain. Magellan himself died in the Philippines.

25. (C)

The Committee to Re-Elect the President—or CREEP as it was nicknamed—was an association working to help Nixon's second bid for the White House. The group was involved in the infamous Watergate cover-up scandal. President Nixon was a Quaker but Quakers are hardly an "infamous" group, so answer (A) is incorrect. Answer (D) uses the term "Whitewater," which refers to a different presidential scandal.

26. (D)

Earthquakes are least likely to occur in Antarctica, as it is relatively free of the major fault lines that trigger this sudden movement of the Earth. Both California (B) and Japan (E) have well-known earthquakes in their history.

27. (C)

Passed during the Vietnam War, the Twenty-sixth Amendment lowered the voting age to eighteen. Because eighteen-year-olds were old enough to fight, and conceivably die, for their country, most Americans felt they had earned the right to vote for the elected officials who would make decisions on their behalf. Slavery was abolished with the Thirteenth Amendment, Prohibition was repealed by the Twenty-first Amendment, and presidential terms were limited with the Twenty-second Amendment.

28. (A)

Monetary policy, which controls interest rates and money supply, is controlled by the Federal Reserve System. Fiscal policy involves changing federal taxes and spending and is controlled by Congress. Some economists advocate monetary policy over fiscal policy because they believe the Federal Reserve makes its decisions in a less political manner than Congress and, because of this, is able to act more quickly.

29. (D)

The starting point of functionalism is that all societies have certain basic needs or *functional* requirements that must be met if a society is to survive. The Oedipus complex (C) is a Freudian construct. The "survival of the fittest" concept (E) originated with Charles Darwin.

30. (E)

This question contains plenty of clues that point to the correct answer. Answers (A) and (B) are too narrow, and both answers (C) and (D) can be eliminated since neither "relapse" nor "reformation" makes sense in the context of flourishing creativity.

31. (C)

Answer (A) expresses the opposite of (C). When there are two answer choices that are direct opposites, there is a good chance that one of them is the correct answer. Answers (D) and (E) are both nonsensical distracters.

32. (E)

German sociologist Max Weber was the first to observe and write about bureaucracies that developed in Germany during the nineteenth century. Weber saw bureaucracies as a big improvement over the haphazard style of government they replaced; he found bureaucracies to be rational, efficient, and honest.

33. (B)

Archipelagos and atolls are both island groups, differing only in shape. An archipelago is a chain of islands, while an atoll is a low-lying coral reef surrounding a lagoon that can consist of either one ring-shaped island or several islets in the shape of a ring. This is a fairly straightforward geography question. Answer (D) is suspicious because there are few if any "man-made" islands.

34. (E)

The correct answer can be found by eliminating any choices that are not representative or "symbolic" in nature—only "language" and "gestures" fit this description. All words are really stand-ins for ideas; they represent or symbolize something else. Each of the other four answers refers to an "actual" cultural component.

35. (B)

Even if you know nothing about deviance, the answer choices contain information that can help you find the correct answer. Words like *never*, *always*, and *should* usually indicate potential wrong answers. In psychology and sociology, deviant actions are those that go against accepted cultural norms of behavior. Sometimes deviant actions—civil disobedience, for example—can change and improve society.

36. (D)

Gresham's law states, "Bad money drives out good money." During the Great Depression, people believed that gold was more valuable than paper money, so they spent paper money and hoarded their gold money. This had the effect of reducing spending by consumers, making the Depression worse. In 1933, President Franklin D. Roosevelt made it illegal for Americans to own more than $100 in gold, other than in the form of jewelry and minor industrials.

37. (A)

The question lets you know that Erikson is a psychologist. Armed only with this knowledge, you can eliminate answer choices. *Class warfare* is a topic generally associated with sociology or political science, so (B) is incorrect.

Chaos theory (C) is a term from physics, so it must be incorrect. Similarly, (D) and (E) refer to evolution and the military, so they are also both incorrect.

38. (C)

Sociologist Elizabeth Kübler-Ross published *On Death and Dying* in 1969. She was a pioneer for the advancement of research into the psychosocial aspects of the dying process, particularly from the perspective of the dying individual.

39. (D)

When you encounter a question that asks you to assume a statement is true, treat it as fact. Don't let your personal opinion affect your answer. The keyword *most* in (A) and (E) should also call attention to those selections as possible wrong answers. According to Erik Erikson's stages of psychosocial development, older people develop a sense of ego integrity (versus despair) if they feel proud of their accomplishments.

40. (D)

President Nixon shook hands with the Chinese premier Chou En-Lai in what would become one of the most famous handshakes in diplomatic history. Nixon also met with Chairman Mao in what were the twilight days of China's Cultural Revolution. This trip was the first an American president had ever made to China and broke two decades of silence between the two nations.

41. (B)

William of Normandy brought the French language and French customs to Great Britain when he defeated the British at the Battle of Hastings and assumed the crown of England.

42. (A)

In a socialist country, the government makes all economic decisions. A capitalist system (B) is opposite a socialist system in that the means of production are privately owned and economic decisions are made by private individuals. All other answers are terms used to describe political rather than economic systems.

43. (B)

The U.S. government is a representative democracy, in which all citizens have the right to vote for people to represent them in the lawmaking process. In a dictatorship (E) or monarchy (A), the people have no voting rights and no control over how they are governed.

44. (E)

When Congress established the Federal Reserve System in 1913, politicians from the rest of the country feared that it would be a tool of the Northeastern economic and business establishment. The original Federal Reserve Act established 12 regional Federal Reserve banks that were overseen by a Federal Reserve Board appointed by the president and confirmed by the Senate.

45. (D)

The Federalist Papers, written by Alexander Hamilton, James Madison, and John Jay, were an attempt to convince citizens of the need to enact the proposed Constitution. Written under the pen name "Publius," they give insight into exactly what the framers of the Constitution were intending to accomplish and why they created the document as they did.

46. (C)

More than a half-century after the close of World War II, Russia and Japan have yet to sign a peace treaty to formally end the war. To this day, the two nations are unable to resolve their dispute over four islands located to the north of Japan. Answers (A), (D), and (E) can all be eliminated—in these cases the two countries named were allies.

47. (D)

Alexander Hamilton, the nation's first secretary of the treasury, was the principal designer of the American monetary system.

48. (D)

The Electoral College was formed in part to ensure that small states had a voice in national elections. Other reasons were that having Congress or state legislatures choose the president—both original ideas—could lead to a president being beholden to special interests. The Framers also feared that popular election would cause voters to vote for a "favorite son" from their own region. Answer (C) is the opposite of answer (D). Whenever opposites appear in the answer choices, it is likely that one of these choices is correct.

49. (E)

The first four statements are all true, illustrating that global warming is a more complex issue than it might first appear to be. Option (E) is just there to confuse you—it is about globalization, not global warming.

50. (D)

These wealthy "Gilded Age" Americans garnered their fortunes as a result of monopolies, so answer (A) is incorrect. In addition, all three men were self-made, so (B) is also incorrect.

51. (B)

The Ottoman empire rose from the ashes of the old Byzantine empire, which collapsed at the hands of the Ottoman Turks in the mid-fifteenth century. The Turkish ruler, Mehmed II, made Constantinople his capital, renaming it Istanbul. Constantinople had been the Byzantine capital.

52. (D)

The unemployment rate tends to be higher in the presence of generous unemployment benefits, as the need to return to work is lessened. Logic alone can help solve this question. Answers (A) and (E) can be rejected—there is an obvious correlation between the amount of time individuals can collect benefits and the speed with which they will look for a new job. Unemployment benefits *may* very well contribute to illegal immigration, but the question does not mention immigration trends, so (C) is also incorrect. Never read more into a question than the information provided.

53. (E)

Although the idea of keeping church and state separate appears in the First Amendment, which is in the Bill of Rights, the words "separation of church and state" do not appear anywhere in the Constitution.

54. (A)

Swiss psychologist Carl Jung was a longtime admirer of the eminent Dr. Freud, but though Freud saw Jung as his heir apparent, Jung had some different ideas. Jung, not Freud, applied the "collective unconscious" theory to dream analysis, so (B) is incorrect. Similarly, answer (E) can be eliminated. Freud or Jung appear in three of the five choices, indicating a high probability that they have to do with the correct answer.

55. (D)

Franklin Delano Roosevelt said this in his first inaugural address on March 4, 1933, in response to fears about the Great Depression.

56. (C)

The Republican Party has historically supported lower taxes and less government spending. Traditionally, the Democrats have endorsed higher taxes on the upper classes and increased entitlements for the poor, so (A) is incorrect.

57. (B)

This question is not as straightforward as some, but if you pay close attention to what the question is really asking—which answer is true—then you can avoid confusion. The 1950s are typically portrayed as repressive and the 1960s as turbulent and socially progressive, so (C) and (D) can be dismissed. Eisenhower, not Kennedy, was in office for most of the 1950s, so (A) is incorrect. As a Republican, Eisenhower held conservative fiscal views, so his policies wouldn't be misconstrued as socialist, which eliminates (E).

58. (B)

The desire to win back the Holy Land was an overriding concern among many European monarchs and nobles in the Middle Ages. Answer (D) can be ruled out because the Israeli-Palestinian clash is contemporary and the question is phrased in the past tense. Answer (E) can also be eliminated as most Christians have not inhabited their Holy Land in great numbers since well before the Crusades.

59. (D)

The native inhabitants of the Australian outback are typically referred to as "aborigines." Answer (B) is easy to rule out since it is highly unlikely that anyone lives *in* the vaguely defined "south seas."

60. (D)

It is tempting to assume that the United States is the biggest democracy because of its great land mass; however, India, with over 1 billion citizens, is the world's most populous democracy.

61. (A)

The Kurds are a stateless people: a recognizable, culturally homogenous group of people living within the borders of other nations because they have no nation of their own.

62. (E)

Interest in exploring Africa began as a means of finding a water route to India. Once Africa's riches came to the attention of the Europeans, mining, colonies, slaves, and Christianity became reasons to exploit it, but all those reasons came after the desire to reach India by sea. Overpopulation in Europe would not necessarily have led to the desire to explore new lands; therefore, answer (C) can be eliminated.

63. (B)

This anthropology question can be solved by thinking logically, even if the term *precontact* is unfamiliar. By reading the answer choices, you can see that the term has something to do with "society" and "outsiders." An industrialized nation probably wouldn't be in a stage of "pre-contact" since technology relies upon the sharing of ideas between nations, so (C) is incorrect. Since (E) contains the clichéd and vague phrase "global technological revolution," it's pretty safe to eliminate this choice as well.

64. (B)

Freud postulated that individuals progress through a series of stages in a predetermined sequence that ultimately lead to a healthy/unhealthy personality, the last of which is the genital stage. Freud also theorized the Electra complex (C), but it is not one of the stages.

65. (E)

The speaker of the House is second in succession to the presidency, behind the vice president. Only elected officials may succeed to the presidency, so the secretary of state (A) and the attorney general (D)—both presidential appointees—are ineligible.

66. (C)

Located in what is currently Iraq, this rich area between the Tigris and Euphrates Rivers saw the birth of many great civilizations, including the Sumerians, the Assyrians, and the Babylonians.

67. (D)

At the same time the Russians were fighting Germany in World War I, an internal political war raged at home: the Russian Revolution. The Great Potato Famine was an Irish, not a Russian, phenomenon, so (C) is wrong. Feudalism is a medieval construct, and since World War I took place in the twentieth century, answer (B) is also incorrect.

68. (C)

Sir Isaac Newton's three laws of physics make up the foundation of modern rocket science.

69. (B)

From 1812 to 1815, the United States and Great Britain fought the War of 1812. The raid at Harpers Ferry, an antislavery uprising led by abolitionist John Brown, took place in 1859, so answer (D) is incorrect. Answer (C) is also incorrect since the Battle of Midway was fought during World War II.

70. (A)

Diamonds are both rarer and harder to mine than salt—both factors that contribute to a commodity's overall value.

71. (B)

The Phillips curve graphically illustrates the relationship between inflation and unemployment. Typically, if one is low, the other is high. For example, during a period of rapid economic expansion when businesses must hire additional workers, the rate of unemployment will decline. At the same time, however, production costs will rise as business is forced to utilize less efficient means of production to increase output. This leads to higher inflation.

72. (C)

Interest rates and inflation move in the same direction because inflation is a component of interest rates. The nominal, or stated, interest rate is a function of inflation plus the perceived risk associated with the particular borrower. As the rate of inflation rises or falls, that component of the nominal interest rate will rise or fall as well.

73. (B)

In 1954, the Supreme Court ruled in the case of *Brown v. Topeka Board of Education* that the practice of "separate but equal" education for children of different races was

unconstitutional. Supreme Court rulings sometimes have the power to force social change, as this one did.

74. (D)

This question addresses the reader's understanding of the often confused and confusing terms *race* and *ethnicity*. *Race* is the social definition of people based on biological characteristics. *Ethnicity* is the social definition of people based on cultural characteristics (like style of dress, language, and norms).

75. (E)

The only other reasonable choice is answer (A). However, "peer pressure"—a pop-psychology term not likely to be part of a correct answer—means that changes in behavior result from external pressure, which is not implied by this question.

76. (C)

Monetary policy refers to the manipulation of the money supply by the Federal Reserve System. *Fiscal* policy refers to congressional spending of tax dollars. Clearly, the surgeon general (D) and the FBI (E) are not involved with any economic policy making.

77. (B)

The word *always* in answer (A) should indicate a potential wrong answer: ethnocentrism and cultural relativism are incompatible approaches. Similarly, answer (C) is incorrect since it is the *definition* of ethnocentrism.

78. (C)

The U.S. Mint—a division of the U.S. Treasury—prints all currency. Answers (A), (B), (D), and (E) fall under the umbrella of the Federal Reserve.

79. (C)

In the years following the Civil War, most of the newly freed slaves voted Republican, as the Democratic party was the favored party of white southerners. Furthermore, President Abraham Lincoln, the individual most closely associated with the freeing of the slaves, was a Republican. Today most African Americans vote Democratic.

80. (E)

In a 1946 speech, Winston Churchill said of Soviet domination of Eastern Europe that an "iron curtain has descended across the Continent." Some historians date the beginning of the Cold War to this pivotal speech by the former British prime minister.

81. (B)

Milton Friedman, who won the Nobel Prize for Economics in 1976, is one of the best-known economists of the monetarist school of thought. Answer (C) is incorrect: Keynesianism is an economic school of thought, but its primary proponent is more likely its founder John Maynard Keynes. Choice (E) is not even a school of thought.

82. (B)

Manifest Destiny is typically associated with a nineteenth-century ethos, a sense of duty to spread American ideals (as well as to expand settlement across the continent). It had nothing to do with slavery, so (E) is incorrect. Neither answer (D) nor answer (C) makes logical sense.

83. (C)

"Enfranchisement" and "suffrage" both refer to voting rights, but the suffrage movement focused on women, not former slaves, so (D) can be eliminated. Answer (E) may make you think of the Temperance Movement, which was responsible for the enactment (not the end) of Prohibition.

84. (A)

Crystallized intelligence is the store of knowledge or information that a given society has accumulated over time. It is based on learning and experience, not innate intelligence (E). It remains relatively stable over time, so (B) is incorrect. Since it refers to acquired knowledge, not how we use it, (C) also is incorrect.

85. (E)

Answer (A) can be ruled out since, although Teddy was a Roosevelt, his presidency was before the Great Depression. Answers (B) and (C) are both distracters. Similarly, answer choice (D) describes the modern free-trade alliance NAFTA.

86. (A)

McCarthy was a senator from Wisconsin in the 1940s and 1950s. He was not above relying upon rumor, slander, or innuendo in his personal campaign to root out the communists who supposedly had infiltrated American Society.

87. (E)

Answer (A) is illogical; the very essence of Cold War prevents a "thawing out." Similarly, the fear of "nuclear holocaust" was far greater during the Cold War than after, so answer (B) can also be eliminated.

88. (E)

Harriet Beecher Stowe's bestseller was published in 1852 and sold 300,000 copies in its first year, breaking all records at the time. Catherine Beecher, Harriet's sister, was also a writer; however, this isn't her book, so answer (B) is wrong. The book was heralded in the North and denounced in the slaveholding South (A).

89. (C)

The placebo effect is the measurable, observable, or felt improvement in health not attributable to treatment (for example, among participants in medical studies). Many psychiatrists believe that the placebo effect is due to a belief in the treatment or to a subjective feeling of improvement.

90. (C)

The Vikings were a group of people indigenous to Norway, Sweden, and Denmark. Valhalla is the mythical home of the gods in Norse mythology, so answer (D) can be ruled out. Nova Scotia, the Ottoman empire, and Denmark are too far removed geographically to have been the home of a common culture (B).

91. (E)

An indentured servant was a person who, in exchange for passage to the New World, agreed to work as a servant for a period of time to repay his or her debt. One-half to two-thirds of all immigrants to colonial America arrived as indentured servants. Even on the frontier, a small percentage of the population came under terms of indenture.

92. (E)

Cartels tend to be unstable over time because eventually one or more members will see an opportunity to undercut the prices charged by fellow members, increasing market share and profits at the other members' expense.

93. (B)

Answer choice (D) can be ruled out—Virginia planter Thomas Jefferson, not Byrd, had an affair with his slave Sally Hemings. And though Byrd had a sharp tongue, as a plantation owner, he would not likely have found himself at the mercy of a colonial governor. Therefore, (A) is also incorrect.

94. (D)

Switzerland was one of the few European countries not coveted by the French general and emperor. Italy, Russia, England, and Germany were all targets of Napoleon.

95. (D)

Turner, who felt he was directed by God, led this 1831 rebellion; it is one of the most famous slave insurrections in American history.

96. (E)

The so-called "Piltdown Man" was an elaborate hoax. All of the remaining choices were legitimate anthropological finds.

97. (E)

In 1820, Missouri was admitted to the Union as a slave state and Maine was admitted as a free state, which maintained the balance of slave states and free states in the Union. Slavery opponents resisted allowing new slave states to join the Union but agreed to accept Missouri with the stipulation that, except in Missouri, slavery would be banned north of the new state's southern boundary.

98. (D)

Archimedes' principle states that the weight of the water displaced by an object is equal to the weight of that object. This principle paved the way many hundreds of years later for the development of submarines. Archimedes lived in the third century B.C.E. in the city-state of Syracuse.

99. (E)

All of the other factors mentioned are reasons why a country such as Japan or Hong Kong is able to overcome significant obstacles to prosperity to become a major economic power.

100. (C)

Article II, Section 1 of the U.S. Constitution states that only native-born American citizens may be elected to the presidency.

101. (E)

This question addresses the classic nature versus nurture question. Several of the answer choices contain keywords indicating wrong answers. Absolute words like "entirely" in answer (B) and "never" in (D) are red flags.

102. (A)

St. Augustine, Florida, was the first European colony in North America.

103. (E)

Although considered an enlightened society by ancient standards, the Greeks did not consider all individuals to be equal. In particular, slavery was the norm, women had no political rights, and only native-born Greek men were eligible to vote.

104. (B)

In 1215 the British noble class rose up and demanded that King John sign the Magna Carta, a document that limited the power of the monarch. The Magna Carta was an effort to express the rights of the nobility but had little concern for average citizens.

105. (D)

The nation of Sri Lanka was known as Ceylon until 1972.

106. (A)

Abraham Lincoln was an early member of the Republican Party, formed in 1854 to oppose the expansion of slavery. The Republican Party evolved from the earlier Whig Party, so (D) is incorrect. In their time, the Whigs opposed the Federalists, another early American political party, so (B) is incorrect. The Democratic-Republican Party split in the 1820s into the Whig and Democratic Parties, so (E) is also incorrect.

107. (E)

Legend has it that twin brothers Romulus and Remus founded the city of Rome. Answers (A) and (B) can be eliminated since both Zeus and Aphrodite were Greek gods, not Roman gods.

108. (B)

In Articles I, II, and III of the U.S. Constitution, the government is divided into legislative, executive, and judicial branches. Answer (D) can be immediately ruled out since it lists political parties, not branches of the government. The president, vice president, and speaker of the House are officeholders, not governmental branches (E).

109. (A)

The Treaty of Versailles, signed at Versailles, France, on June 28, 1919, ended World War I, which had begun almost five years earlier.

110. (A)

Sensory memory only lasts a few seconds, when the senses send information immediately to the brain. This information is primarily unprocessed. Cognitive dissonance, the negative feeling one gets while holding contradictory thoughts at the same time, is an active way to process intellectual information (B). Sensory memory is even briefer than short-term memory (C). Answers (D) and (E) are nonsensical and just there to confuse you.

111. (A)

Some boys were hiking in the woods when they discovered the amazing cave at Lascaux. It features paintings of people and animals on the walls dating from c.15,000 B.C.E.

112. (A)

Virginia Dare was born in August 1587 in the lost colony of Roanoke, which was on the coast of present-day North Carolina. A close reading of the answer choices reveals the word *first* in answers (A), (D), and (E), indicating that one of those is probably correct. Betsy Ross designed the American flag, so (C) is incorrect.

113. (A)

Martin Luther's act of protest started the Protestant Reformation in 1517. The "Archbishop of Castlebury" (B) is a made-up name designed to confuse you. Similarly, the term "Reconstruction" in choice (C) sounds a bit like "Reformation" and is a distracter.

114. (C)

Passive personalities (B) do not speak out to protect their personal boundaries. Assertive people (D) differ from aggressive people in that they respect others while standing up for themselves. Answer (E) is a distractor.

115. (B)

The term *fraternal* refers to sibling relationships, and since siblings are rarely primary caregivers, (D) can be eliminated. *Pair-bonding* refers to a life mating and is often romantic in nature, so (A) is also incorrect.

116. (B)

Reconstruction clearly refers to a "rebuilding," but natural disasters are not the best answer to this question (A). Answer (D) mentions "reinforcement," but that is not the same as reconstruction.

117. (D)

A double-blind study is a research method in which both the subjects and the experimenter are unaware or "blind" to the anticipated results. It is a mechanism to counteract bias but is not based on randomness, so (A) is incorrect. Answers (B) and (C) are also incorrect, since they both describe situations in which only one party to the experiment is "blind."

118. (C)

The law of primogeniture allowed eldest sons to inherit the family property and titles. Younger sons were left to strike out on their own in search of fortune. Many joined the military in search of new opportunities or sought to explore new lands.

119. (C)

John Winthrop led the first mass emigration from England to the New World. The settlers established the Massachusetts Bay Colony in 1630. William Penn (A) founded Pennsylvania, and Roger Williams (B) founded Rhode Island.

120. (B)

Leif Erikson is believed to have sailed from Iceland to establish a colony in Vinland (present-day Newfoundland) around 1000, some 500 years earlier than either Columbus or Vespucci in the late fifteenth century. Cortes and de Leon arrived in the early sixteenth century.

Chapter Seventeen: **CLEP Social Sciences and History Review**

- The Big Picture: CLEP Social Sciences and History
- Nuts and Bolts
- History
- The Social Sciences
- Final Thoughts

You have embarked on a quest to test your knowledge of the social sciences by taking the CLEP Social Sciences and History exam. Congratulations! Since the exam covers a wide range of subjects within the social sciences, you need to pick up concepts from several subject areas in order to do well.

THE BIG PICTURE: CLEP SOCIAL SCIENCES AND HISTORY

The Social Sciences and History examination allows you 90 minutes to answer 120 questions. It covers a broad range of subjects from the social science and history fields. Emphasis is placed on Western cultural and intellectual history from ancient civilizations to the present; however, familiarity with world history also will help your score. Be particularly alert for questions that cross disciplines, movements, or periods. In addition, it's especially important for you to have a clear understanding of the key terminology for each subject area covered.

NUTS AND BOLTS

The approximate subject area breakdown of the CLEP Social Sciences and History exam is as follows.

    40% History

        17%   United States History

        15%   Western Civilization

        8%   World History

13% Government/Political Science

11% Geography

10% Economics

10% Psychology

10% Sociology

 6% Anthropology

Brace yourself: it is highly unlikely that you will achieve expert status in every section of the exam. The exam is designed so that you will *not* know the answer to every question. According to the test makers, the average college student completing a survey course in these subjects would get half the questions right. However, you can still rack up points within each subject area. While most students achieve a higher score in some sections than in others, it is a good strategy to keep in mind the percentage of the exam taken up by each topic.

The goal of this review is to help you solidify what you already know and increase your familiarity with other important topics on the exam. With that in mind, you will find a brief summary of the scope of the questions for each field covered on the exam. The history review section includes a master timeline of important people and places from all periods. The social sciences section contains a list of important terms for each discipline; you'll find the timeline a useful tool for these portions of the test as well. At the end of each subject review there are suggestions for further reading and study, as well as tips for better preparation in a shorter amount of time. Read on to begin compiling your knowledge database for the exam.

HISTORY

What You Need to Know

Since about 40 percent of the CLEP Social Sciences and History exam is devoted to history, it's essential that you brush up on different historical time periods and events. The history portion of the test will require a sound grasp of major chronological and geographical events in world history. You'll also need to understand the relationship between specific historical happenings and the development of ideas and major schools of thought—the big picture of human history. The questions will cover political, social, economic, intellectual, and cultural material from a range of periods and geographical locales.

Economics, politics, social issues, the history of ideas, and scientific progress all influence the development of any society. Even more importantly, they are all interrelated. The sort of interconnectivity, or globalization as we would call it today, of intellectual and cultural history has become more pronounced as technology and cultures have advanced. As international communications become more sophisticated, various world economies and cultures have found themselves increasingly interrelated. At the same time, the seeds of globalization were planted a very long time ago. As you study, keep up with current international events. Spend some time looking at an atlas or map. You can keep a notebook detailing current or past events, or make your own charts and timelines. Soon, the big picture of world history will start to make sense.

United States History

About 17 percent of the test questions will cover important events, people, and movements in
U.S. history—that translates to about 20 questions. The questions will cover the periods from
the European exploration of the New World at the close of the fifteenth century to the present.
As you prepare yourself for this exam, you will likely notice that many of the happenings on the
American scene dovetail with events in Europe and across the globe. While you will not become
an expert in the history of the United States just by reading this review, you will develop some
useful test-taking skills and improve your approach to studying history.

Western Civilization

About 15 percent of the test questions will deal with major figures, occurrences, and intellectual
movements of Western civilization from prehistory to modern times—approximately 18 questions.
The questions will address ancient Western Asia, Egypt, Greece, Rome, medieval and modern
Europe, as well as European colonization of other regions around the world.

World History

About 8 percent of the test questions will cover important people, places, and events in the
non-Western world from prehistory to the present. That means about 10 questions on the entire
exam will be derived from world history. But the smaller percentage of questions does not mean
you can gloss over world history. In fact, a sound grasp of this area of the test will probably result
in a much better overall performance; the knowledge will overlap with both Western civilization
and U.S. history. The questions often will be general and will address African, Asian, Australian,
European, North American (non-U.S.), and South American history.

Master Timeline

The following timeline represents a chronological progression of major periods and events in U.S.
history, Western civilization, and world history. The timeline is intended to be a general overview
and is by no means conclusive or absolute. It will give you a visual representation of the connections, or relationships, among the histories of various regions of the world. Use it to direct and
focus your studies. Make it your own: add images or graphs and charts, make a large version and
post it on the wall . . . use whatever method works for you. The operating principle of the timeline is that once you get the big picture, the details will begin to stand out.

From a strategic standpoint, if you're familiar with time periods and their general characteristics,
you'll quickly be able to rule out some of the multiple-choice answers on the test itself. Try to
remember at least one important fact about each era. You could create a mnemonic device for
each place or century. For example, *E* could stand for Enlightenment in England in the Eighteenth
century. The more personal the mnemonic, the easier it will be for you to remember it.

Timeline Key

The different areas of history are denoted as follows:

United States History (roman type)

Western Civilization (bold type)

World History (italics)

Since the CLEP emphasizes U.S. history, you will notice more events from U.S. history than from Western civilization or world history in the timeline. Keep in mind that these dates are approximate and the terms are fluid, with considerable overlap between periods and schools of thought.

Note: This exam uses the chronological designations B.C.E. (before common era) and C.E. (common era). These labels correspond to B.C. (before Christ) and A.D. (anno Domini), which are used in some other texts.

The Timeline

Ancient Civilization

The Fertile Crescent/Mesopotamia (pre-3500–32 B.C.E., ending with *conquest by Persian empire*)

Ascent of the Sumerians (c. 3500 B.C.E.)

Ascent of the Babylonians (c. 1800 B.C.E.)

Ascent of the Assyrians (c. 1350 B.C.E.)

Ancient Egypt (pre-3000 B.C.E–c. 30 B.C.E., ending with Roman invasion*)*

Ancient Greece (pre-500 B.C.E.–500 C.E.)

The Golden Age of Greece (c. 479 B.C.E., beginning with *defeat of the Persians*—429 B.C.E.**)**

The Peloponnesian War between Athens and Sparta (431–404 B.C.E.)

Ancient Rome and the Roman Empire (c. 509 B.C.E., beginning with birth of the Republic of Rome–c. 400 C.E.)

The Punic Wars (264–146 B.C.E.)

Africa and the Phoenicians

Other terms and names: *the Great Wall of China (at least 2,000 years old); India and the Himalayas*

Medieval and Early Modern Civilization

The Middle Ages (c. 500–1500)

The Crusades (the first c. 1095)

The Renaissance (c. 1400–c. 1700)

Other terms and names: *the Huns; the Kurds;* **the Vikings;** *the Turks;* **Giotto; Leonardo da Vinci; Michelangelo; Renaissance art**

The Seventeenth Century

Native American and Pre-Colonial Period (pre-1620)

Colonial Period (1620–1776)

> Other terms and names: **Spain; Italy and Age of Exploration; Martin Luther and the Protestant Reformation**

The Eighteenth Century

The Enlightenment (c. 1650–1800)

Galileo, Newton, and the Age of Discovery

The First Great Awakening (1730s–1740s)

Revolutionary Period (1775–1783, ending with the Peace of Paris)

Critical Period and Constitutional Convention (1780s)

Early Republic (pre-1763–1815)

French Revolution (1789–1799)

Federalist Period (1789–1801)

> Other terms and names: *Mexico and Central America*; **Spanish, French and Italian imperialism in the New World; colonial Africa; slavery**

The Nineteenth Century

Napoleonic Wars (1803–1815)

Jeffersonian Era and War of 1812 (1801–1814)

The Second Great Awakening (c. 1800–1861)

Nationalism and Sectionalism (1815–c. 1865)

Jacksonian Era (1820–c. 1845)

Revolutions of 1848

Expansion and Immigration

Antebellum America (1850–1861)

The Civil War (1861–1865)

Reconstruction (1865–1877)

The Frontier and Westward Expansion (1865–1900)

Early Industrial America (1865–1900)

Urban Culture (1865–1900)

> Other terms and names: *Australia and the aborigines*; *Japanese Meiji Restoration*; massive immigration to United States from Western and Eastern European nations; Triangular Trade

The Twentieth Century

The Gilded Age (1870s–1890s)

The Progressive Era (1879–1920)

World War I (1914–1918)

The "Roaring '20s"

The Stock Market Crash and the Great Depression (1929–1941)

The New Deal (1933–1940s)

World War II (1941–1945)

The 1950s and the Cold War (1950s–1980s)

The Civil Rights Era (1950s–1960s)

The 1960s and the Protest Era (1960s)

The Vietnam War (1960s–1970s)

Postmodern America (1990s–present)

> Other terms and names: Russia and communism; Hitler, Mussolini, and Fascism; *Vietnam and Southeast Asia; Chinese communism and the Cultural Revolution; conflict in the Middle East and international terrorism; American cultural imperialism; globalization and the Internet*

History Resources

To get yourself in an historical state of mind, watch the History Channel or *A & E Biographies*. Check out the Library of Congress and White House websites for American history references. You also can find useful glossaries of terms online. In addition, websites such as academicearth. org and the Massachusetts Institute of Technology's OpenCourseWare site (ocw.mit.edu) offer syllabi, exams, and even video lectures from thousands of college courses about every field of knowledge. The Public Broadcasting Service (pbs.org) is also a good resource for all sorts of fascinating information about historical happenings. If you can borrow history textbooks from your local library or school, they will help you prepare as well.

THE SOCIAL SCIENCES

What You Need to Know

Since about 60 percent of the CLEP Social Sciences and History exam is devoted to the social sciences, you'll need a plan of attack that can encompass a broad range of disciplines. The social sciences questions on the CLEP exam will cover the following fields: government/political science, geography, economics, psychology, sociology, and anthropology. You will be expected to have a general, broad-based understanding of each of these fields. Many of the questions will cross periods, geographical areas, and disciplines—meaning they will address more than one subject at a time. So you must prepare yourself well, and no one field can be entirely overlooked.

Just as with history, you should not expect to become an expert in each of the social sciences. The exam questions will give you the opportunity to demonstrate that you have a level of knowledge and general understanding expected of college students in an introductory survey course. Don't panic: this all may seem overwhelming at first, but as you begin preparing yourself for the exam by reviewing the individual subject areas, you will start to notice the connections between them. Many of the required skills, methodologies, and important terms are shared or similar.

As with history, paying close attention to connections between the areas of social science—the big picture—will help you score higher. Take note of these relationships in a journal or diary. Try out the methodologies of one field when you are studying another. Most importantly, make this knowledge your own; personalize it with mnemonics that work for you. Make your own color-coded flowcharts, tables, and graphs. If you have a friend who is taking the exam, you can do these things together. Tailor these study tools to your personal experiences, since the social sciences can be seen and experienced in everyday life. Train yourself to pay attention to how the social sciences are expressed around you on a daily basis. One way to start is by watching or reading the daily news.

Government/Political Science

About 13 percent of the exam will cover the fields of government and political science, which translates to approximately 16 questions. While we may think of political science as pertaining only to government, it also has to do with power dynamics in all social arenas; in other words, who gets what, when, and how. You participate in politics in some fashion all of the time, whether you know it or not—your goal now is to learn about the different aspects of politics. Specifically, the test focuses on comparative politics, international relations, and the institutions of American government, which you'll know a lot about already after studying U.S. history.

The questions on this portion of the exam will require a familiarity with political science terminology, facts, methodologies, and general principles and theories. You will be asked to apply these abstractions to particulars. You will have to combine a working knowledge of the big picture of political science (and its relationship to the other social sciences) with an ability to apply its principles to specific data. Always remember to keep in mind the important connections between political science and the other disciplines on the exam, currently and throughout history. This is where your customized study aids can help.

Political Science Terms to Learn

Anarchy	Elites
Aristocracy	Equality of Opportunity and Equal Rights
Checks and Balances	Fascism
Communism, Marxism, and Socialism	Federalism
Conservatism	Immigration and Emigration
Democracy: Direct, Parliamentary, and Representative	Liberalism
Despotism	Natural Law
Dictatorship	Republicanism
Electoral College	Tyranny

Political Science Resources

The previous list is just a sampling of the political science terms you should know for the exam. You can find their definitions easily by consulting political science textbooks or online resources. Two good sources for American political information are the online The Center on Congress at Indiana University (centeroncongress.com) and hippocampus.org, both of which offer easy-to-read summaries and videos. You can also tune in to NPR (National Public Radio) for lively discussions of the contemporary political scene in this country and around the globe. If you're feeling especially ambitious, why not flip over to CSPAN to watch our democratic process in action?

Geography

Eleven percent of the CLEP Social Sciences and History test questions will be drawn from the field of geography—that means 13 questions. When most people think of geography, they probably first think of maps, globes, or atlases. The practice of modern geography, however, involves much more than just memorizing the number of continents or the names of state capitals. Since World War II, the field has experienced an explosion of knowledge as a result of new technologies and the global communications revolution. Every time you get in a car or take a bus, train, or plane you are reaping the benefits of advances in geographical science.

The geography questions on the exam will require a familiarity with specific terms, tools, facts, and major principles. You will likely be asked to interpret data in the form of maps, charts, or tables. You will have to be able to apply a big-picture understanding of world geography to the particulars of a diagram or map. You can and do practice geographical methods all of the time—now you have to start paying attention to it. Look at a subway map with a fresh eye, and maybe check out the maps of your state capital or Washington, D.C. Think about looking at the world from a bird's-eye view or from the top of a mountain.

Geography Terms to Learn

Acid Rain

Aerial Photography

Biological Diversity and Functional Diversity

Continental Drift

Demography

Distance

Ecology

Fault Zones

Location

Overpopulation and Underpopulation

Physiography and Topography

Plate Tectonics

Quantitative and Qualitative Analysis

Regional Geography

Remote Sensors

Space Accessibility

Spatial Interaction

Urban, Suburban, and Exurban

Weather and Climate

Geography Resources

The previous list represents the kinds of terms and ideas you should investigate before you take the exam. You can learn these terms from a variety of sources from textbooks to websites, journals, and magazines. Flip on the Weather Channel, the Discovery Channel, and the Travel

Channel. You'll also find a world of up-to-the-minute data at nationmaster.com, ranging from the most populous country (China at 1.33 billion people) to the world's largest lake (the Caspian Sea at 143,000 square miles). Remember to refer to traditional globes, maps, and atlases as well.

Economics

Ten percent of the CLEP Social Sciences and History test questions will come from the field of economics, which translates into 12 questions. Economics can be loosely described as the study of how people allot scarce resources to produce needed commodities and how those commodities are distributed for consumption among the people in society; in other words, who makes, sells, and buys what; how commodities are produced, and at what cost. Some of the ways we participate in economics are obvious, but economics is at work in our lives all the time and in ways that you probably are not aware of. Today, economists are employed in almost every industry, from private corporations to the government and academia.

The questions on economics will require a knowledge of economics terms, methodologies, and principles. You will likely also be asked to interpret and analyze graphs or tables to test your ability to apply broad economic concepts to specific data. As you prepare for the exam, it will help if you start paying attention to how you participate in economics all of the time—from how you or your family manages the household economy to how your job allows you to participate in providing goods (i.e, commodities) and services. Keep in mind how the economy relates to the other social sciences, as well as to your personal life. You will begin to notice lots of connections with sociology and political science. Make sure to take note of these relationships, personalizing your study aids as you go along.

Economics Terms to Learn

Business Cycle

Capital and Capitalism

Commodities

Consumption

Depreciation and Appreciation

Distribution

Economies of Scale

Engel's Law

Free-Market Economy

Fiscalist and Monetarist View

Inflation and Deflation

Keynes Effect

Micro- and Macroeconomics

Obsolescence

Open and Closed Economies

Phillips Curve

Scarcity

Economics Resources

To learn more about these terms and others before the exam, go online. You can also check out magazines like the *Economist* and read newspapers like the *Wall Street Journal*. When you're channel-surfing, why not stop at CNBC or one of the other financial channels to further your knowledge of modern economics? For print resources, turn to your school or local library. A college-level economics textbook will be a help as well, and for an offbeat and entertaining introduction to the subject, pick up *The Cartoon Introduction to Economics: Vol. 1, Microeconomics,* by Grady Klein and Yoram Bauman, PhD (New York: Hill and Wang, 2010).

Psychology

Ten percent of the test questions will come from the field of psychology. That breaks down to 12 questions. We all use psychological principles every day without even thinking about it. Psychologists are interested in the study of human behavior or how people behave in certain situations, how our brains grow and why we think the way we do, as well as how emotions develop and what impact they have on our interactions with others. In preparing for the CLEP Social Sciences and History exam, a heightened awareness of these functions in your own life will help you. For example, when you experience anxiety about taking this exam, you are activating your autonomic nervous system. When you reward yourself with a treat for a job well done, you are also using a psychological principle.

The psychology questions on the exam will ask you about common terms, important figures, competing theories, and principles. The test will also ask you to apply certain research methodologies to specific data. As with all of the social sciences, psychology is intimately connected with the other disciplines—it is a good idea to keep a running tab of these connections. Pay attention to the behaviors of those around you. As you are learning a psychological theory, try to find an example of it in your daily life. Remember to personalize your study aids so that you remember terms more easily.

Psychology Terms to Learn

Aggression	Identity
Attachment	Intelligence
Behaviorism	Libido
Cognition	Lobes of the Human Brain
Collective Unconscious	Memory: (Types of) Retrieval and Storage
Conformity	Perception
Conscious and Subconscious	Performance
Egocentrism	Personality
Extroversion and Introversion	Placebo Effect
Experimental Method	Reasoning: Deductive and Inductive
Gestalt Theory	Socialization
Group Process	Stage Theory
Id, Ego, and Superego	Variables

Psychology Resources

The previous list represents a sampling of the types of terms you'll want to read about before the exam. You'll find a great web resource at allpsych.com—a virtual psychology classroom that has an extensive glossary of terms. Pick up a copy of *Psychology Today* magazine—it's available at most libraries and is an easy read. You can also look up the *Scientific American* at the library or borrow an introductory psychology textbook. In addition, the Discovery Channel and the Learning Channel both often feature programs about topics like the human brain, dreaming, and childhood development.

Sociology

Ten percent of the test questions will come from the field of sociology. That breaks down to 12 questions. Sociology is the scientific study of human social behavior in collective or group situations. As with political science, you participate in sociological concerns all the time. A sociologist studies everything from group dynamics (in the workplace or in high school cliques) to the sort of kinship (or family) relationships you experience from day to day.

The test questions will require a familiarity with sociological terminology, major thinkers and their theories, general principles, and methodologies. You will be asked to apply these abstract concepts to particular situations. You will need an overall knowledge of the big picture of sociology, as well as the connections among the other social sciences currently and throughout history, to do well on this portion of the exam. As you prepare for the exam, you will notice the cross-fertilization among sociology, political science, and anthropology. Remember to take note of the connections you observe in a journal or diary. Customizing your study aids to your personal experience is the best way to remember terms and concepts.

Sociology Terms to Learn

Behaviorism

Cultural Determinism

Cultural Lag

Cultural Relativism

Demography

Deviance

Ethnocentrism

Ethnography

Family: Matriarchy, Patriarchy, etc.

Gender and Gender Theory

Groups: Group Dynamics, Groupthink

Interaction and Interactionism

Marxism

Samples: Random, Representative, etc.

Social Conflict Theory

Social Organization

Social Stratification

Sociology Resources

The previous list gives examples of the sorts of terms and ideas that you'll likely encounter on the CLEP Social Sciences and History exam. For definitions of the terms, you can consult sociology textbooks; a good one is *Essentials of Sociology—A Down-to-Earth Approach, Eighth Edition* by James M. Henslin (New York: Allyn & Bacon, 2008); or online reference sites. Check out glossarist.com for thousands of glossaries and topical dictionaries with terms and definitions (particularly strong in the Humanities and Social Science fields). Visit your school or local library and read the *American Journal of Sociology*, which is also available online. Trinity University's website offers a rich clearinghouse of sociological links at trinity.edu/~mkearl/resource.html.

Anthropology

Only about 6 percent of the questions on the CLEP Social Sciences and History exam are drawn from anthropological subjects—that means approximately 7 questions. But that does not mean you can just skim over the subject. Nor will you want to once you start learning about this fascinating field. A general grasp of anthropology, the study of humankind in various regions of the world and over evolutionary time, will help you out in all of the other fields on the exam. You can hardly afford to overlook the study of human existence.

Anthropology Terms to Learn

Animism, Totemism, and Spiritualism

Archaeology

Artifact

Bipedalism

Biological Imperative

Bracchiation

Chronometric Dating and Absolute Dating

Cultural, Physical, and Social Anthropology

Ethnography

Evolutionary Theory

Hominid

Linguistics

Matrilineal and Patrilineal Societies

Paleontology

Primate

Anthropology Resources

For definitions of the previous terms you can go to the glossary of terms at the Leakey Foundation website at leakeyfoundation.org, where you can also learn about important figures and theories from the field. You should also check out the website of the American Anthropological Association at aaanet.org, where you'll get an excellent overview of the field and its many subfields. For a great interactive educational experience, visit the official website of the Cave at Lascaux: www.culture.fr/culture/arcnat/lascaux/en.; you'll feel like you're discovering prehistoric cave paintings for yourself. You also should look for anthropology textbooks and journals at your school or local library.

FINAL THOUGHTS

With all of these tools and resources, if you plan your study time well and follow through, you'll be well on your way to a great score on the CLEP Social Sciences and History exam.

Good luck!

Chapter Eighteen: **Practice Test 2**

Time—90 minutes
120 Questions

Directions: For each of the following questions or incomplete statements, select the best answer or completion from the five options given.

1. Which of the following statements best characterizes social stratification?

   (A) The process serves as a cultural leveler.

   (B) It is a hierarchical structure with a premise of the equal division of societies.

   (C) The practice is a persistent characteristic of all societies throughout the world.

   (D) It can be based on a broad range of factors including wealth, gender, and power.

   (E) Social stratification is always fixed or static.

2. With whom was Abraham Lincoln shaking hands when he famously remarked, "So you are the little woman who wrote the book that started this great war?"

   (A) Harriet Tubman

   (B) Rosa Parks

   (C) Harriet Beecher Stowe

   (D) Mary Todd

   (E) Harriet Jacobs

3. Which is TRUE about the growth of the human brain?

   (A) It continues to grow into early childhood but at a slower rate than in infancy.

   (B) It begins to grow exponentially after the age of three.

   (C) It reaches 75 percent of adult size by age five.

   (D) It reaches 90 percent of adult size by age three.

   (E) It continues to grow dramatically throughout the life span of the average person.

4. The economy of the United States can best be described as

   (A) a mixed economy.

   (B) a socialist economy.

   (C) a centrally planned economy.

   (D) a laissez-faire economy.

   (E) None of the above

GO ON TO THE NEXT PAGE

KAPLAN)

5. Which of the following is TRUE about the role of the Catholic Church in early and medieval Europe?

    I. It was the largest and most powerful patron of the arts.

    II. It settled disputes between emerging nations.

    III. Popes annointed kings, conferring a sort of divine authority.

  (A) I only

  (B) III only

  (C) II and III only

  (D) I and II only

  (E) I, II, and III

6. Charles Horton Cooley concluded that human development is socially created—that our sense of self develops from looking at others. To describe this process, he coined the term

  (A) mirroring.

  (B) mimesis.

  (C) looking-glass self.

  (D) social imprinting.

  (E) imitation impulse.

7. At the Battle at Bunker Hill, the American soldiers were ordered not to fire until they could see "the whites of their eyes" because

  (A) they had very little ammunition with which to attack the British soldiers.

  (B) the Native Americans often used captured colonial soldiers as human shields.

  (C) they knew the Native Americans were superstitious and would not fire back if they looked them directly in the eyes.

  (D) many American revolutionaries had Loyalist relatives fighting on the side of the British Crown.

  (E) French and British uniforms were easy to confuse from farther away.

8. A colony is

  (A) located in a previously unexplored area of the world.

  (B) often feared for its imperialistic tendencies.

  (C) always expensive for the mother country to maintain.

  (D) a settlement that is controlled by another country.

  (E) usually a poor source of natural resources.

9. Which of the following is NOT a component of the study of sociology?

  (A) Demography

  (B) Ethnography

  (C) Culture

  (D) Behaviorism

  (E) Fascism

10. Abraham Lincoln eventually promoted which military man to general and commander of all Union forces?

  (A) Stonewall Jackson

  (B) Ulysses S. Grant

  (C) Jefferson Davis

  (D) Dwight D. Eisenhower

  (E) Donald Custer

11. Julius Caesar was assassinated because

  (A) his ambitious son was eager to ascend to the throne.

  (B) he refused to return conquered lands to the Carthaginians.

  (C) his political enemies believed he was planning to declare himself king.

  (D) his wife was angry at his infidelities and lack of discretion.

  (E) of his Christian belief system.

GO ON TO THE NEXT PAGE

12. The theory of comparative advantage states that

    (A) countries that have no resources should invest in foreign economies.

    (B) countries should concentrate on producing the commodities and services that come naturally to them—therefore lowering their opportunity cost—and trade with countries specializing in the goods and services with which they are naturally endowed.

    (C) horizontally integrated monopolies are the most efficient economic systems.

    (D) money should flow from each according to his ability to each according to his needs.

    (E) tax cuts for the rich will spark investment, which will allow wealth to trickle down to the lower and middle classes.

13. Henry Kissinger served in foreign policy positions under several presidents, but historians generally agree his greatest influence came under Nixon and Ford. Which of the following statements is TRUE about Dr. Kissinger?

    (A) As Nixon's top security advisor, he guided Vietnam policy through the "Vietnamization" campaign.

    (B) As President Ford's chief of staff, he skillfully led the military invasions of Cambodia and Laos.

    (C) Under President Carter, he negotiated with South Vietnam, leading to the 1976 cease-fire.

    (D) He was the sole recipient of the Nobel Peace Prize in 1973.

    (E) He opposed a policy of détente with China and the Soviet Union.

14. Which of these is NOT a function of the United States government outlined in the preamble to the Constitution?

    (A) Provision for the common defense

    (B) The establishment of a system of justice

    (C) The preservation of domestic tranquility

    (D) Promotion of the general welfare of the body politic

    (E) The establishment of a uniform system of weights and measures

15. Who was the first secretary of the treasury in America?

    (A) Alexander Hamilton

    (B) Benjamin Franklin

    (C) John Jay

    (D) John Hancock

    (E) James Madison

16. When Jean Piaget studied children and IQ test results, he noted that young children consistently chose wrong answers while older children were able to give the expected answer. Piaget studied how children learn intellectually and how that ability matures—in other words, their

    (A) behavioral sociology.

    (B) cognitive development.

    (C) cognitive psychology.

    (D) sensorimotor socialization.

    (E) behavioral psychology.

17. The impairment of the ability to communicate either through oral or written discourse as a result of brain damage is usually

    (A) due to genetic mutation.

    (B) called amnesia.

    (C) termed aphasia.

    (D) totally reversible with therapy.

    (E) called apoplexy.

GO ON TO THE NEXT PAGE

KAPLAN)

18. What is animism?

    (A) The attribution of human characteristics to animals

    (B) A belief that the world is inhabited by impersonal supernatural powers

    (C) A belief in spirit beings that are associated with nature or natural objects

    (D) The belief in several gods and/or goddesses

    (E) The belief in one god or goddess

19. Famous for his frugality, homespun witticisms, and inventions, this patriot quipped, "Early to bed, early to rise, makes a man healthy, wealthy, and wise."

    (A) Daniel Boone

    (B) Henry David Thoreau

    (C) James Fenimore Cooper

    (D) Davy Crockett

    (E) Benjamin Franklin

20. The "lost" city of Machu Picchu was built by the Incas in what is now

    (A) Argentina.

    (B) Mexico.

    (C) Columbia.

    (D) Peru.

    (E) Guatemala.

21. One Frenchman was perhaps the most perceptive of all observers of American civilization; who is he?

    (A) Alexis de Tocqueville

    (B) William Dunlap

    (C) W. E. B. DuBois

    (D) Napoleon Bonaparte

    (E) Marquis de Sade

22. The African nations of Ethiopia and Eritrea have battled intermittently for many years over

    (A) illegal poaching of endangered species.

    (B) the annexation of Eritrea by Ethiopia in 1962.

    (C) trade arguments negotiated when Eritrea was an Italian territory.

    (D) ownership of ancient artifacts with significance for both nations.

    (E) rich mineral deposits along their shared border.

23. Which of the following describes Easter Island?

    (A) It can be found in the Pacific to the west of Chile.

    (B) It is known for its unusually large rabbit population.

    (C) It is named for its discoverer, the Earl of Easter.

    (D) It is the site of the observations Charles Darwin wrote about in *The Origin of Species*.

    (E) It resembles a cross in shape.

24. Sigmund Freud's "Pleasure Principle" is his theory

    (A) regarding the eternal struggle between the id and the ego for gratification.

    (B) that we remain in the oral stage of development in an effort to reenact the comfort we received from breast-feeding.

    (C) of the id's desire to maximize pleasure and minimize pain in order to achieve immediate gratification.

    (D) that all human pleasure is ultimately a result of parental approval.

    (E) regarding the id's desire to minimize pleasure and maximize pain in order to achieve immediate gratification.

GO ON TO THE NEXT PAGE

25. The field of geography includes all the following areas of research EXCEPT

    (A) cartography.

    (B) oceanography.

    (C) glaciology.

    (D) human geography.

    (E) All of the above

26. Functionalism, structuralism, symbolic interactionism, and gender theory are all examples of theoretical approaches to what field of study?

    (A) Sociology

    (B) Literature

    (C) Psychology

    (D) Social anthropology

    (E) Cultural anthropology

27. Rituals, often religious in nature, marking important stages in the lives of individuals such as marriage, birth, or death are known as

    (A) rites of intensification.

    (B) the sacraments, or holy unctions.

    (C) gender stratification rituals.

    (D) either incorporation or reincorporation rituals.

    (E) rites of passage.

28. Sparta was known for its

    (A) industry and commerce.

    (B) fierce warrior culture.

    (C) intellectual freedom.

    (D) scientific accomplishment.

    (E) epic poetry.

29. Which of the following is NOT an agent of socialization in the modern world?

    (A) The family unit

    (B) Social class

    (C) Sleep patterns

    (D) The mass media

    (E) Religion

30. In 1802, Napoleon Bonaparte arranged for the sale of

    (A) St. Augustine, Florida, and its environs to the Seminole Indians for use as a reservation.

    (B) the province of Louisiana to the Spanish Crown.

    (C) exclusive trading rights to Lewis and Clark along the Mississippi River in exchange for an elimination of Creole tariffs.

    (D) the Louisiana Territory to the United States.

    (E) one thousand Haitian slaves aboard the *Amistad* in return for the Canadian province of Acadia.

31. Psychology, like sociology, is often referred to as a social science or

    (A) absolute science.

    (B) soft science.

    (C) pseudoscience.

    (D) life science.

    (E) physical science.

32. The Monroe Doctrine was significant because

    (A) President Monroe declared that presidents should not run for office more than twice.

    (B) President Monroe was the first to receive a doctorate while in office.

    (C) it stated the U.S. policy against European expansion in the western hemisphere.

    (D) it officially declared the annexation of Texas by the United States.

    (E) it proposed isolationism as official U.S. policy.

GO ON TO THE NEXT PAGE

KAPLAN

33. When conducting a study using a random sample, the experimenter obtains the subjects

    (A) by chance from the larger population being studied.

    (B) using a specific set of demographic criteria.

    (C) from a representative sample of the population.

    (D) from groups that he or she has been observing over time.

    (E) with no regard to personal bias.

34. Which of these explorers was the first European to set foot in Florida?

    (A) Ferdinand Magellan

    (B) Robert de la Salle

    (C) John Cabot

    (D) Ponce de León

    (E) Christopher Columbus

35. A pattern in which a married couple may choose to live in the locality associated with either the husband's or the wife's relatives is known as

    (A) patrilocal residence.

    (B) matrilocal residence.

    (C) avunculocal residence.

    (D) ambilocal residence.

    (E) eneolocal residence.

36. Heinrich Schliemann is significant because he

    (A) found and translated the first known version of Homer's *Iliad*.

    (B) navigated the ship that charted the first trade route to China.

    (C) was the archaeologist who found the ancient city of Troy.

    (D) operated the first printing press famed for printing the Gutenberg Bible.

    (E) discovered the tomb of King Tuthankamen and its archaeological treasures.

37. The largest nonpolar desert in the world is the

    (A) Sahara.

    (B) Gobi.

    (C) Mohave.

    (D) Kalahari.

    (E) Arabian.

38. The phenomenon that occurs when a collection of people are in total agreement and uninterested in entertaining any opposing viewpoint is known as

    (A) group polarization.

    (B) social loafing.

    (C) peer pressure.

    (D) Stockholm syndrome.

    (E) groupthink.

39. As a result of mass immigration, by 1910, fully three-fourths of New York City's population

    (A) had been stricken with tropical viruses that traveled via steamer ships and locomotives.

    (B) were either recent émigrés or first-generation Americans.

    (C) were of Pacific Rim or Slavic ancestry.

    (D) left the bustling city center for the relative calm of the outer boroughs.

    (E) had displaced Native Americans, who were forced to move to the south or west.

40. Formerly an American ally, what Panamanian dictator was overthrown by his countrymen and then captured by the United States?

    (A) Daniel Ortega

    (B) Mario Vargas Llosa

    (C) Manuel Noriega

    (D) Juan Perón

    (E) Vicente Fox

GO ON TO THE NEXT PAGE ⟶

41. Émile Durkheim studied the social factors that underlie suicidal tendencies, concluding that

    (A) genetics is the sole determinant.

    (B) suicidal fantasies are much more common among females than males.

    (C) individual circumstance is a larger determinant of suicidal impulse than social factors.

    (D) the degree to which people are tied to a social structure is as important as individual circumstance.

    (E) individuals in urban environments are almost twice as likely to contemplate suicide as rural dwellers.

42. Which of the following people was an escaped slave who became a well-known spokesperson for abolitionism after the publication of his personal narrative?

    (A) Booker T. Washington

    (B) Washington Carver

    (C) Frederick Douglass

    (D) Frederick Jackson Turner

    (E) W. E. B. DuBois

43. Considered the upper house in the U.S. government, the Senate possesses what power that is NOT granted to the House of Representatives?

    (A) The power to levy and lower taxes

    (B) The ability to oversee and regulate the airline industry

    (C) The power to originate spending bills and propositions

    (D) The ability to override a presidential veto

    (E) The power to ratify treaties with foreign nations

44. When alone, people tend to be more relaxed and less concerned with their outward behavior. When two or more people are together, their behavior tends to change. What is the term for this phenomenon?

    (A) Social facilitation

    (B) Acquiescence

    (C) Behavior modification

    (D) Social morphism

    (E) Antisocial behavior

45. Which of the following statements is FALSE about the Puritans, the original settlers of the American colonies?

    (A) They were devoted to doctrinal purity in their methods of worship.

    (B) They were dissatisfied with the influence of Roman Catholicism on their Anglican faith.

    (C) They were suspicious of the ritual, dogma, and political influence of the Catholic Church.

    (D) They were a mainstream group motivated by radical religious idealism that was popular in eighteenth-century England.

    (E) They were convinced that the Reformation had not gone far enough and that Queen Elizabeth I was too tolerant.

46. Which of the following monarchs was honored by Pope Leo X for an eloquent and vigorous defense of the Church against Martin Luther's attacks?

    (A) Henry VIII

    (B) Mary I

    (C) Frederick the Great

    (D) Richard I

    (E) Louis XVI

GO ON TO THE NEXT PAGE ⟹

KAPLAN

47. Which of the following is TRUE of Transcendentalism?

    (A) It was practiced by Pennsylvania Quakers in an effort to communicate directly with the divine.

    (B) It was an intellectual, spiritual, and artistic movement that found its fullest expression at Brook Farm.

    (C) It represented the antithesis of the romantic ideals of Emerson and Thoreau.

    (D) It encouraged the practical and rational over the romantic and sublime.

    (E) It still thrives at Oneida, the utopian community in upstate New York.

48. The primary tools of fiscal policy are

    (A) restrictions on bank ownership.

    (B) restrictions on interest rates.

    (C) raising and lowering taxes and government spending.

    (D) increasing and decreasing the money supply.

    (E) raising and lowering the discount rate.

49. This thinker coined the term *sociology* and suggested the use of positivism—applying the scientific method to the social world—though he never used the approach himself. Who was he?

    (A) Herbert Spencer

    (B) Max Weber

    (C) Wright Mills

    (D) Erik Erikson

    (E) Auguste Comte

50. The "shot heard round the world" refers to

    (A) the assassination of Archduke Ferdinand in Sarajevo, which signaled the beginning of World War II.

    (B) the Japanese kamikaze-style attack at Pearl Harbor.

    (C) the execution-style death of a Chinese student at Tiananmen Square.

    (D) the unordered shot at Lexington that marked the beginning of the American Revolution.

    (E) a misfired cannon that led to the Battle of Troy.

51. Money, praise, intellectual stimulation—none of which are absolutely necessary for individual survival—are examples of

    (A) primary reinforcers.

    (B) independent variables.

    (C) secondary reinforcers.

    (D) socially reinforced variables.

    (E) situational attributes.

52. The remains of the Ottoman empire, which collapsed following World War I, are known today as

    (A) Turkey.

    (B) Mongolia.

    (C) Russia.

    (D) Iran.

    (E) Morocco.

GO ON TO THE NEXT PAGE

KAPLAN

53. The Temperance movement of the ninteenth century

    (A) essentially pioneered the platform for the anger-management programs that are widely practiced in the workplace today.

    (B) advocated the legalization and dispensation of birth control devices in overcrowded urban communities.

    (C) was initially more successful at the state and local levels but eventually found universal acceptance.

    (D) emphasized sexual abstinence until marriage with varying degrees of success.

    (E) blamed the consumption of alcohol for a wide range of social ills, from poverty to insanity.

54. Which of the following BEST explains the system of checks and balances?

    (A) The Federal Reserve System relies on people maintaining checking account balances in order to control the money supply.

    (B) The federal government checks into the background of individuals applying for sensitive government jobs.

    (C) Each of the three branches of the federal government has the ability to check the power of the other two.

    (D) The president and Congress work together to balance the federal budget.

    (E) Parties to a dispute can take their case all the way to the Supreme Court if they choose.

55. Polyandry is

    (A) the marriage custom of a woman having two or more husbands simultaneously.

    (B) the marriage custom of a man having two or more wives simultaneously.

    (C) a family consisting of related women, their offspring, and the women's brothers.

    (D) a form of marriage in which a man or a woman marries a series of partners in succession.

    (E) a family unit consisting of husband, wife, and more than one child.

56. Which of the following groups did NOT invade Rome during the final days of the empire?

    (A) Huns

    (B) Visigoths

    (C) Vandals

    (D) Tartars

    (E) Ostrogoths

57. Which of the following describes ethnocentrism?

    (A) It is an attitude in the study of society that always takes cultural uniqueness into consideration.

    (B) It is more common in urban than in rural communities.

    (C) It is an approach that views other cultures and societies from the point of view of one's own values and beliefs.

    (D) It is a variation of cultural relativism.

    (E) It is a very progressive attitude toward the study of preliterate societies.

GO ON TO THE NEXT PAGE

58. Which of the following statements is FALSE when drawing a comparison between the Enlightenment in America and the same period in Europe?

   (A) In Europe, as in America, engagement with ideas gradually became more public, moving from private spaces—drawing rooms and personal correspondence—into the public sphere of coffee houses, debating societies, and salons.

   (B) In America, where the king and the bishop were far away, the colonists were outspoken in their proclamation of new ideas.

   (C) Americans tended to be more abstract and less practical in the application of Enlightenment ideals than their European counterparts.

   (D) Europeans like Isaac Newton, Francis Bacon, and John Locke had done most of the technical thinking necessary for religious and political reform to flourish in America.

   (E) The abstract controversies of the European Enlightenment never made much of an impact on everyday life in America.

59. The story of human evolution has emerged slowly over the past two centuries. What was the effect of the discovery of the "Taung Child" in 1924?

   (A) It failed to prove the evolutionary link between humans and chimps.

   (B) It was a true missing link between humans and chimps, the significance of which was overlooked for many years.

   (C) It was later proven to be a hoax that set back evolutionary studies for forty years.

   (D) It helped Franz Boaz prove that fossilized skulls were not always indicators of brain capacity.

   (E) It affirmed the link between the Piltdown Man and early hominids.

60. Who famously said, "Religion is the opiate of the masses?"

   (A) Adolph Hitler

   (B) Jerry Falwell

   (C) Vladimir Lenin

   (D) Sigmund Freud

   (E) Karl Marx

61. In 1848, Elizabeth Cady Stanton and Lucretia Mott held a convention in Seneca Falls, New York that helped launch

   (A) the Women's Rights Movement.

   (B) child labor legislation.

   (C) the Temperance Movement.

   (D) women's colleges all over the Northeast, founding the Seven Sisters.

   (E) groundbreaking divorce and women's property rights legislation.

62. Cultural imperialism is the aggressive promotion of one's own (usually Western) culture, based on the assumption that its value system is superior to those of other cultures. Which of the following is NOT an example of cultural imperialism?

   (A) Permitting students to wear their religious symbols to school even if they are not the same as those of the dominant culture

   (B) Forcing capitalism on third-world countries before they are economically prepared for the change

   (C) Hollywood's exportation of American social mores in film, music videos, and television programming to the more conservative Middle East

   (D) McDonald's restaurants and Levi's stores opening in Red Square

   (E) The exportation of ideas like gender equality and democracy to non-Western nations

GO ON TO THE NEXT PAGE ⟶

63. The term *bicameral legislature* means

    (A) legislators are elected every two years.

    (B) two locations serve as the capital.

    (C) the legislature meets every two years.

    (D) both men and women may serve in the legislature.

    (E) there are two houses in the legislature.

64. From the 1950s on, this team conducted a series of expeditions to Olduvai Gorge, producing several important discoveries of early primate fossils.

    (A) Louis and Mary Leakey

    (B) Donald and Lucy Livingstone

    (C) Louis and Lucy Leakey

    (D) Boaz and Benedict

    (E) Margaret and Mary Mead

65. Which of the following is NOT a means by which islands are formed?

    (A) Erosion between two land masses causes land to break away, leaving an unattached portion surrounded by water.

    (B) Skeletal remains of coral build up over millions of years.

    (C) Underwater volcanic eruptions create mountains of lava, which eventually rise above the water.

    (D) A meteor crashes into the ocean.

    (E) Continental plates collide, creating undersea mountain ranges that break the surface of the water.

66. Peter the Great is credited with which of the following achievements?

    I. Opening new trade relationships between Russia and Western Europe
    II. Building the city of St. Petersburg
    III. Shaping Russia into a major European power

    (A) II only

    (B) I and II only

    (C) II and III only

    (D) III only

    (E) I, II, and III

67. Groups are the essence of life in society. Primary groups consist of

    (A) cooperative, intimate, face-to-face relationships.

    (B) the extended family network.

    (C) peer groups and superficial social networks.

    (D) coworkers and authority figures.

    (E) an individual's genus and species.

68. Assume that it is suddenly discovered that onions prevent hair loss and wrinkles. What will the impact be on the demand curve for onions?

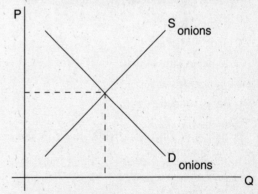

    (A) The price elasticity of onions will rise.

    (B) The demand curve will shift to the right.

    (C) The demand curve will shift to the left.

    (D) There will be no change.

    (E) The price elasticity of onions will fall.

GO ON TO THE NEXT PAGE ▷

69. What was the Donation of Pepin?

    (A) A gift of land that sealed the alliance between the Frankish dynasty and the papacy

    (B) The return to the Huns of their rightful lands

    (C) A deed to the Catholic Church of tax-free land for cathedrals

    (D) A bribe that helped Charlemagne ascend the throne

    (E) A grant to the Spanish of the right to explore freely throughout the New World

70. What is the significance of *Marbury v. Madison*?

    (A) It reiterated the official policy of separation of church and state.

    (B) It finally granted women the right to vote.

    (C) It extended the right to bear arms in the American West.

    (D) It established the tradition of judicial review.

    (E) It banned smoking in all government facilities.

71. Which Progressive-era reformist and social activist from Chicago founded Hull House?

    (A) James Hoffa

    (B) Jane Addams

    (C) William James

    (D) James Dewey

    (E) Jane Goodall

72. The nation of Tibet is currently under the control of what country?

    (A) Sri Lanka

    (B) The United Nations

    (C) India

    (D) Pakistan

    (E) China

73. Which of the following scientific accomplishments is NOT the result of Louis Pasteur's research?

    (A) The practice of heating milk to kill bacteria

    (B) Vaccinations for anthrax, rabies, and cholera

    (C) The insight that germs do not originate spontaneously

    (D) Saving France's silk industry by identifying the bacteria that attacked silkworms

    (E) The use of X-rays to view inside the body

74. George Herbert Mead is known for

    (A) first distinguishing between the "I" and the "me" in the development of the self.

    (B) his work with primates and tool usage in Nairobi.

    (C) his groundbreaking research on adolescent females in Samoa.

    (D) his first wife, Margaret, a famous anthropologist.

    (E) first distinguishing between the "ego" and the "superego."

75. Do rivers always flow from north to south?

    (A) Yes.

    (B) No, in the southern hemisphere they flow south to north.

    (C) No, they flow with gravity, from higher to lower elevations.

    (D) No, they flow toward the largest body of water.

    (E) No, some rivers do not flow at all.

76. Which famous wearer of a coonskin cap became a celebrity in his own time as tales of his exploits were told in popular books and produced for the stage?

    (A) John Quincy Adams

    (B) Benjamin Franklin

    (C) James Fenimore Cooper

    (D) Daniel Boone

    (E) Davy Crockett

GO ON TO THE NEXT PAGE

77. The term *centration*

    (A) refers to the bond a child forms with his or her primary caregiver.

    (B) describes a demographic shift toward urban or population centers.

    (C) denotes the tendency of a young child to focus only on his or her own perspective.

    (D) was conceptualized by Elizabeth Kübler-Ross as one of the stages of grief.

    (E) describes the tendency of parents to focus inordinately on their firstborn child.

78. After 395 C.E., the Roman empire was divided into the Eastern empire and the Western empire. What was the capital of the Eastern empire?

    (A) Cairo

    (B) Mesopotamia

    (C) Baghdad

    (D) Constantinople

    (E) Peking

79. Which statement is NOT true about Queen Elizabeth I of England?

    (A) Her reign was a time of peace and prosperity.

    (B) Arts and culture flourished while she was in power.

    (C) England enjoyed resounding military triumph under her stewardship.

    (D) She never married, and she left her throne to her nephew.

    (E) She restored the Catholic church as the official church of England.

80. Which of the following is TRUE about the Spanish Inquisition?

    (A) Only Muslims were targeted.

    (B) Only Jews were targeted.

    (C) It lasted 200 years.

    (D) Stung by the long occupation of Spain by the Moors, Pope Sixtus IV pressured Ferdinand and Isabella into starting it.

    (E) Accused heretics were entitled to a trial, but even so, they often endured torture and, if found guilty, they could be burned at the stake.

81. The precipitating causes of the French Revolution did NOT include

    (A) economic disarray brought on by bad weather and poor crop harvests.

    (B) dissatisfaction with an unwieldy and inefficient bureaucracy.

    (C) higher taxes to support an increasingly expensive government.

    (D) the inability or lack of desire of the king to address the need for real reform.

    (E) the desire of French women to be given the right to vote and hold office.

82. What leader emerged in the chaotic aftermath of World War II France to restore that nation to a position of European power?

    (A) Charles de Gaulle

    (B) Jean Monet

    (C) Georges Pompidou

    (D) François Mitterand

    (E) Pierre Mendès-France

GO ON TO THE NEXT PAGE ⇒

KAPLAN

83. Which of the following is NOT a condition for nationhood?

    (A) A sustained native population

    (B) An organized government

    (C) Boundaries defined by a river or other natural landmarks

    (D) External recognition by other countries

    (E) An official currency

84. Memories for facts, life events, and information

    (A) are a product of the somatic memory response system.

    (B) are most often stored in short-term memory.

    (C) are rapidly displaced when traumatic events occur.

    (D) are stored in declarative memory.

    (E) are stored in sensory memory.

85. Niccoló Machiavelli was

    (A) the first man to circumnavigate the globe commanding the Spanish Armada.

    (B) a sixteenth-century Italian writer who originated the idea of political pragmatism.

    (C) a foreign policy advisor to King Ferdinand and Queen Isabella of Spain.

    (D) the first scientist to determine that the earth revolves around the sun.

    (E) a Renaissance sculptor from Naples.

86. What drawback is common to all countercyclical economic policy?

    (A) There are time lags involved in implementing the policy.

    (B) It is subject to political interference.

    (C) It may be hindered by congressional recess.

    (D) The Supreme Court may declare it to be unconstitutional.

    (E) The Federal Reserve may choose not to act at all.

87. When a society adds a new cultural element—an invention or discovery—it takes some time for the culture to adjust; an example of this is the introduction of the automobile. What did William Ogburn call this tendency?

    (A) Technological lag

    (B) Symbiosis

    (C) Cultural lag

    (D) The placebo effect

    (E) A cultural anomaly

88. The Hindu religion as we know it today was first practiced in

    (A) Malaysia.

    (B) India.

    (C) Nepal.

    (D) Indonesia.

    (E) Its origins are unclear.

89. In the thirteenth century, the teenaged Marco Polo traveled to China with his father and uncle, where they were guests at the court of

    (A) Confucius.

    (B) Mao Tse-tung.

    (C) Liu Pang.

    (D) Chairman Mao.

    (E) Kublai Khan.

90. The "Roundheads" and the "Cavaliers" were nicknames given to opposing factions in which country's revolution?

    (A) France

    (B) United States

    (C) Russia

    (D) England

    (E) Chile

GO ON TO THE NEXT PAGE

91. The decision-making process in which ideas are processed from the general to the specific is called

    (A) deductive reasoning.
    (B) inductive reasoning.
    (C) circular logic.
    (D) reductive reasoning.
    (E) logical reductivism.

92. Which of the following is NOT attributed to the Mesopotamians?

    (A) Calculus
    (B) Metal coinage
    (C) Flood control and irrigation
    (D) Use of the arch and dome
    (E) A system of weights and measures

93. Which of the following is a reasonable possible reaction to a period of rising inflation?

    (A) The Federal Reserve could lower interest rates.
    (B) Congress could increase government spending.
    (C) The FDIC could close the banks for a period of time.
    (D) The Federal Reserve could decrease the money supply.
    (E) Congress could either raise or lower taxes.

94. Who were the "Reagan Democrats"?

    (A) Republicans who switched to the Democratic party because they disagreed with Ronald Reagan
    (B) Individuals who had traditionally been Democrats but who began to vote Republican with Reagan's first presidential election
    (C) Individuals who, like Ronald Reagan, switched from the Democratic party to the Republican party
    (D) Democrats who abstained from voting because they disliked both Ronald Reagan and his Democratic opponents
    (E) Republicans who became Democrats after Reagan's presidency because they disliked his successor

95. Which of the following does NOT contribute to acid rain?

    (A) Sulphur dioxide emissions from industrial plants
    (B) Nitrogen oxide emissions from automobiles
    (C) Volcanic eruptions
    (D) Lightning strikes
    (E) An unusually warm current in the Pacific Ocean

96. Karl Marx is considered the father of what philosophy of government?

    (A) Democracy
    (B) Nazism
    (C) Fascism
    (D) Communism
    (E) Oligarchy

GO ON TO THE NEXT PAGE

97. Which of these oil-producing countries is NOT a member of OPEC?

    (A) Mexico

    (B) Venezuela

    (C) Kuwait

    (D) Iraq

    (E) Iran

98. In his "Fourteen Points" speech before Congress in 1918, President Woodrow Wilson began explaining his strategy for peace following World War I. In his speech, he introduced his idea of a "peace without victory." Which of the following is NOT one of the main tenets of his plan?

    (A) The idea of an "open" world after the war

    (B) Freedom to navigate the seas

    (C) An affirmation of imperialism

    (D) Equal trading practices and elimination of protective tariffs

    (E) An association of nations to ensure political independence and territorial integrity

99. An example of a government that has a ceremonial monarchy and an elected governing body is

    (A) Korea.

    (B) Great Britain.

    (C) Saudi Arabia.

    (D) South Africa.

    (E) Mexico.

100. What is the name of the fault along which most of the major earthquakes in the United States have occurred?

    (A) San Jacinto

    (B) Balcones

    (C) New Madrid

    (D) Denali

    (E) San Andreas

101. Keynes argued that the level of economic activity is primarily determined by the level of

    (A) aggregate supply.

    (B) unemployment.

    (C) interest rates.

    (D) inflation.

    (E) aggregate demand.

102. What word best describes American policy toward the Soviet Union from 1947 until the early 1980s?

    (A) Containment

    (B) Glasnost

    (C) Appeasement

    (D) Alliance

    (E) Détente

103. Cartography is

    (A) a means of transporting goods over long distances.

    (B) the study of handwriting analysis.

    (C) the history of the automobile industry.

    (D) the science of mapmaking.

    (E) the charting of ancient trade routes.

104. In 1954 the Supreme Court unanimously agreed that segregation in public schools is unconstitutional. What is the name of this landmark decision?

    (A) *Plessy v. Ferguson*

    (B) *Brown v. the Board of Education of Topeka, Kansas*

    (C) *Loving v. Virginia*

    (D) *Brown v. Charlotte-Mecklenburg Board of Education*

    (E) *Plessy v. the Board of Education of Topeka, Kansas*

GO ON TO THE NEXT PAGE

105. Which of the following statements about political lobbying is TRUE?

 (A) The McCain-Feingold Campaign Reform Act makes it illegal.

 (B) The practice is limited to the national level.

 (C) The practice has far-reaching effects on all aspects of the political process.

 (D) Only certain government-sanctioned groups are permitted to have lobbyists.

 (E) The practice is most common at the local level.

106. Which is NOT a reason why some countries with tremendous natural wealth may remain relatively poor?

 (A) They lack technology to fully utilize their natural resources.

 (B) There is government corruption and personal greed.

 (C) The infrastructure—such as roads, electricity, and transportation—is inadequate.

 (D) The uneducated workforce is not trained to make full use of natural resources.

 (E) The dominant culture encourages asceticism.

107. Hurricane season in the United States is

 (A) June to November.

 (B) September to January.

 (C) March to August.

 (D) October to May.

 (E) Hurricanes occur year-round in the United States.

108. Say's law holds that

 (A) as inflation rises, interest rates will go up as well.

 (B) the income earned by people for producing goods allows them to purchase the goods produced by others.

 (C) people prefer tangible assets to paper currency during times of economic uncertainty.

 (D) people prefer to hold liquid assets during times of rapid interest rate fluctuation.

 (E) lower interest rates stimulate economic growth.

109. The compromise that settled the dispute over how to count slaves for the purpose of congressional representation was called the

 (A) Albany Compromise.

 (B) Great Compromise.

 (C) Connecticut Compromise.

 (D) Three-Fifths Compromise.

 (E) Forty Acres Compromise.

110. Which economist espoused the theory of "creative destruction"?

 (A) Ludwig von Mises

 (B) Joseph Schumpeter

 (C) John Maynard Keynes

 (D) Anna Schwartz

 (E) Alan Greenspan

111. The Bikini atoll gained significance becuase

 (A) it was the site of early nuclear research in the development of the atomic bomb.

 (B) the naval battle fought there led to the surrender of the Japanese Navy.

 (C) the Rosetta stone was uncovered there, allowing archaeologists to decipher early writing.

 (D) it was the site of a massive volcanic eruption.

 (E) Napoleon was exiled there in 1812 and lived there until his death.

GO ON TO THE NEXT PAGE

KAPLAN)

112. Which of the following methods of amending the Constitution has never been used?

    (A) An amendment is proposed by a two-thirds vote in Congress and ratified by three-fourths of the state legislatures.

    (B) An amendment is proposed by Congress and ratified by conventions called for that purpose by three-fourths of the states.

    (C) An amendment is proposed by a national convention and ratified by conventions in three-fourths of the states.

    (D) An amendment is proposed by a national convention called by Congress and ratified by three-fourths of the state legislatures.

    (E) All four methods have been used.

113. The Southern Cross is

    (A) the criss-cross pattern made by the stars on the Confederate flag.

    (B) a pattern of crosswinds in the southern Pacific ocean.

    (C) a constellation entirely visible in the southern hemisphere.

    (D) the labyrinthine approach to Mt. Everest originating in the southern part of Nepal.

    (E) a group of islands south of Australia where Franciscan monks trace their roots.

114. In economics, the term *equilibrium* means that

    (A) demand for a good exceeds the supply.

    (B) the government has enacted price controls.

    (C) prices of all similar goods are equal.

    (D) demand and supply are equal.

    (E) the number of sellers of a particular good is fixed.

115. Senator Joseph McCarthy first entered the public spotlight in 1950 by claiming

    (A) that communists had infiltrated the American military and the FBI.

    (B) that communists had "infested" the state department.

    (C) that the Jews were running Hollywood and controlling the media.

    (D) a vast conspiracy existed between the Soviets and traitorous American politicians.

    (E) that no one in the government could be trusted.

116. Supreme Court justices serve

    (A) for as long as the president keeps them.

    (B) for ten tears.

    (C) for life.

    (D) as long as the president's political party remains in power.

    (E) until the president who appointed them leaves office.

117. Which of the following statements about outsourcing is TRUE?

    (A) It typically leads to rising standards of living in developing countries.

    (B) It can lower a company's operational costs.

    (C) It exports technology around the world.

    (D) It may temporarily displace workers in developed countries.

    (E) All of the above statements are true.

GO ON TO THE NEXT PAGE →

118. What are the climatic consequences of the Andes Mountains on the surrounding regions?

    (A) The range blocks the sunlight from reaching the western slope of the mountains.

    (B) The snow in the mountains melts and provides water for the lower elevations.

    (C) The mountains prevent much of the moisture carried by the Atlantic trade winds from passing to the western side of the range.

    (D) The Andes shift the direction of Atlantic trade winds to the south.

    (E) The Andes shift the direction of the Atlantic trade winds to the north.

119. Which of the following is NOT a component of gross national product?

    (A) Consumer spending

    (B) Business investment

    (C) Government expenditures

    (D) Interest rates

    (E) Exports

120. What was the policy toward Hitler's Germany advocated by British prime minister Neville Chamberlain?

    (A) To go to war immediately before Hitler could gain more strength

    (B) To impose economic sanctions, forcing Germany to withdraw troops from occupied territory

    (C) To allow Hitler to continue to occupy the land he wanted and hope he would be satisfied

    (D) To have the United Nations send in troops in hopes of forcing the Germans to leave Czechoslovakia

    (E) To ask the United States for military aid in the event of war

END OF TEST. STOP

ANSWER KEY

1. D	21. A	41. D	61. A	81. E	101. E
2. C	22. B	42. C	62. A	82. A	102. A
3. A	23. A	43. E	63. E	83. C	103. D
4. A	24. C	44. A	64. A	84. D	104. B
5. E	25. E	45. D	65. D	85. B	105. C
6. C	26. A	46. A	66. E	86. A	106. E
7. A	27. E	47. B	67. A	87. C	107. A
8. D	28. B	48. C	68. B	88. B	108. B
9. E	29. C	49. E	69. A	89. E	109. D
10. B	30. D	50. D	70. D	90. D	110. B
11. C	31. B	51. C	71. B	91. A	111. A
12. B	32. C	52. A	72. E	92. A	112. D
13. A	33. A	53. E	73. E	93. D	113. C
14. E	34. D	54. C	74. A	94. B	114. D
15. A	35. D	55. A	75. C	95. E	115. B
16. B	36. C	56. D	76. E	96. D	116. C
17. C	37. A	57. C	77. C	97. A	117. E
18. C	38. E	58. C	78. D	98. C	118. C
19. E	39. B	59. B	79. E	99. B	119. D
20. D	40. C	60. E	80. E	100. E	120. C

PRACTICE TEST 2 QUICK REFERENCE TABLES

Use the following tables to determine which topics you still need to review.

Topic	Test Question
History	
United States History	2, 7, 10, 15, 19, 21, 32, 39, 42, 45, 47, 50, 53, 61, 70, 71, 76, 98, 104, 115
Western Civilization	5, 11, 28, 30, 34, 46, 52, 56, 58, 60, 78, 79, 80, 81, 82, 85, 90, 120
World History	20, 22, 40, 66, 69, 73, 88, 89, 92, 111
Social Sciences	
Government/Political Science	8, 13, 14, 43, 54, 63, 83, 94, 96, 99, 102, 105, 106, 109, 112, 116
Geography	23, 25, 37, 65, 72, 75, 95, 97, 100, 103, 107, 113, 118
Economics	4, 12, 48, 68, 86, 93, 101, 108, 110, 114, 117, 119
Psychology	3, 16, 17, 24, 31, 41, 44, 51, 77, 84, 91
Sociology	1, 6, 9, 18, 26, 29, 35, 38, 49, 67, 74, 87
Anthropology	33, 36, 55, 57, 59, 62, 64

Topic	Number of Questions on Test	Number Correct
History	48	
United States History	20	
Western Civilization	18	
World History	10	
Social Sciences	72	
Government/Political Science	16	
Geography	13	
Economics	12	
Psychology	12	
Sociology	12	
Anthropology	7	

Answers and Explanations

1. (D)

Though social stratification *is* a hierarchical structure, answer (B) is incorrect since stratification is not premised upon the *equal* division of societies but, rather, a broad range of factors. Stratification can be fixed, but it is more often a fluid process, so (E) is incorrect.

2. (C)

Harriet Beecher Stowe (1811–1896) was an abolitionist who wrote *Uncle Tom's Cabin* in 1852. This controversial antislavery novel focused public attention on the issue of slavery and the underground railroad. Stowe became a celebrity who spoke out against slavery in America and Europe.

3. (A)

In early childhood, the brain continues to grow but not as quickly as in infancy. By age three, the brain has reached 75 percent of adult size; by age five, 90 percent. Though recent research indicates the brain grows throughout a person's life (E), growth slows dramatically after childhood.

4. (A)

A mixed economy falls somewhere between a centrally planned economy (like socialism) and a laissez-faire economy. Since the United States regulates much of its economy—for example, raising and lowering interest rates—while also allowing much freedom for businesses and investors, it's a mixed economy. A socialist economy (B) *is* a centrally planned economy (C), so neither of those answers is correct.

5. (E)

The Catholic Church was the single unifying influence in early and medieval Europe for all of the reasons stated.

6. (C)

According to the sociologist, this process of identification has three steps. First, we imagine how we appear to others; second, we interpret how others evaluate us; and, third, we develop a sense of self through others' evaluations. A favorable reflection in the "social mirror" helps to engender a positive self-image.

7. (A)

This battle was the first major clash between the British and the American troops during the American Revolution. The Americans actually did run out of ammunition and were left with only bayonets and stones to defend themselves. Terms like *human shield* in answer (B) would not have been in common usage during the colonial period and should indicate an incorrect answer.

8. (D)

A colony is a settlement established and controlled by another nation. During the Age of Exploration, colonies were valued as a source of wealth for the controlling nation (C). Answer (B) is illogical since colonies are the *result* of the imperialistic tendencies of the mother country. In addition, colonies are not necessarily restricted to previously unexplored areas of the world (for example, India and Iraq were both British territories at one time). Therefore, answer (A) is also incorrect.

9. (E)

Fascism is a form of government and so is part of the study of political science. All the other options are aspects of the field of sociology.

10. (B)

After his appointment, Grant soon became well known for his aggressive drives through enemy territory. The general led the Union forces to defeat the Confederacy in 1864. Stonewall Jackson (A) and Jefferson Davis (C) were famous Confederate leaders.

11. (C)

As Caesar's power increased, his political enemies in the Roman senate feared that he was planning to declare himself king, therefore eliminating their own power and influence.

12. (B)

Answer (A) can't be correct because every country must have some resources, and (E) describes the trickle-down theory, which has nothing to do with the question. Answers (C) and (D) are fancy-sounding distracters.

13. (A)

Dr. Kissinger did serve under President Ford but was not his chief of staff (B). He was awarded the Nobel Peace Prize, but he shared the honor with Le Duc Tho (although the Vietnamese leader ultimately declined), so (D) is incorrect. He also advocated for, not opposed, détente (E) and did not serve under Carter (C).

14. (E)

The preamble to the Constitution outlined general goals of the new government, such as providing for the common defense. Specific powers and functions, such as establishing a uniform system of weights and measures, are listed in Article I, Section 8 of the Constitution.

15. (A)

When President George Washington chose a circle of advisors to help him create policy—establishing the precedent of a cabinet—he chose Alexander Hamilton as the first secretary of the treasury.

16. (B)

In this context, the term *cognitive* refers to the way the brains of children process information. Cognitive psychology and behavioral psychology are competing disciplines, so (C) and (E) are incorrect. Answer (A) is scientific-sounding but incorrect, as there is no such field.

17. (C)

Answer (B), amnesia, sounds like answer (C). In answer (D), the absolute term *totally* ought to suggest that the answer is incorrect.

18. (C)

Common among preliterate societies, this belief system attributes consciousness or a "soul" to nature or natural objects.

19. (E)

Franklin is the only option recognized both for patriotism and witticisms. While both Thoreau and Franklin are known for frugality, Thoreau is not famous for his patriotism. Boone (A) and Crockett (D) are both known more as frontiersmen than as wits. James Fenimore Cooper (C)

was a writer, not an inventor, and his historical novels such as *The Last of the Mohicans* were more serious than witty.

20. (D)

Machu Picchu is located in the mountains of Peru. The city was originally built by the Incas in the 1400s, and was unknown to the outside world until 1911. The means by which the city was constructed remains a mystery.

21. (A)

Alexis de Tocqueville was an aristocratic Frenchman who toured America in 1831. He later wrote *Democracy in America*, a two-volume study of the American people and their institutions. Covering everything from the press, race relations, money, and the judicial system, de Tocqueville's observations about American life are still widely studied.

22. (B)

Eritrea gained independence from Italy in 1952. Ten years later, Ethiopia annexed the new nation. The countries have been in conflict ever since, even after Eritrea gained independence in 1993. Although it is a poor country with relatively few natural resources, Eritrea does offer access to the Red Sea.

23. (A)

Easter Island, known for its great stone statues, is located off the coast of Chile in the Pacific Ocean.

24. (C)

Answer (E) is the exact opposite of answer (C), suggesting that one of these is the correct answer. Though answer (A) is close and employs Freudian terms, answer (C) is the most specific and the best choice.

25. (E)

A very broad field, geography is the study of the Earth, its physical characteristics, and the distribution of life on the planet, including human life.

26. (A)

Though gender theory and structuralism are theoretical approaches to literature and anthropology, only sociology employs all four methodologies.

27. (E)

Answers (A) and (C) are both ritualistic practices, but they do not answer the question asked. Answer (D) is also wrong. If you encounter a choice using the either/or format, it is likely to be wrong because most questions have only one correct answer.

28. (B)

The Spartans were so dedicated to creating the perfect warrior that they deliberately led lives of great harshness to make themselves better able to cope with the rigors of war. They had no time for or interest in music, art, literature (E), or science (D).

29. (C)

Answers to NOT questions should be deduced using the process of elimination. Socialization occurs throughout a person's lifetime; the family unit, social class, religion, and the mass media can all influence the way an individual learns to participate in modern society. Sleep patterns have nothing at all to do with the socialization process.

30. (D)

Louisiana was a territory, not a province, so (B) is incorrect. The other wrong answer choices use terms like *Creole* and *Haitian* that have some relationship to the French.

31. (B)

Soft science is another term for the social sciences—these disciplines are not intrinsically absolute or empirical, so (A) is incorrect. The hard sciences, like chemistry or physics, rely much more heavily on empirical methods of observation and experimentation. Life sciences (D) comprise any science field that concentrates on the study of living organisms but extends only to biological aspects, not behavioral aspects.

32. (C)

The Monroe Doctrine was named for the sixth president of the United States, James Monroe. In 1823, Monroe asserted that the Western hemisphere was no longer available to be colonized by European nations and that attempts to do so or to meddle in the affairs of sovereign nations would be considered "dangerous to the peace and safety" of the United States.

33. (A)

A random sample is selected by chance from the group being studied. By contrast, when conducting a study using a representative sample (C), the experimenter draws the subjects from a sample or subgroup of the population that possesses the same characteristics as the population.

34. (D)

Ponce de Leon, a Spanish explorer who had sailed with Columbus, arrived in Florida in 1513. Legend has it that he was seeking the "Fountain of Youth."

35. (D)

Even if you aren't familiar with these terms, you can eliminate many incorrect answers by looking at the prefixes of the answer choices. *Patri* is Latin for "father" (reflected in terms such as *patriarchy*), and *matri* is Latin for "mother," so both (A) and (B) can be ruled out. *Ambi*, used in the term *ambidextrous* for a person who can write with the left or right hand, implies an either/or meaning.

36. (C)

Heinrich Schleimann was a nineteenth-century German businessperson who had a lifelong dream of finding the lost city of Troy. He pioneered modern archaeological techniques, and in 1872 he unearthed significant remains in what is now Turkey.

37. (A)

The Sahara desert, located in northern Africa, is the largest desert in the world, at 3.5 million square miles. The second largest, the Arabian, in the Middle East, encompasses only 900,000 square miles, so answer (B) is incorrect.

38. (E)

Though similar in function, peer pressure (C) is typically imposed from without, while groupthink is conceived from within.

39. (B)

The correct answer is the most logical conclusion to the statement given. Answers (A), (C), (D), and (E) cannot be assumed with the information given in the introductory portion of the statement. Never read anything more into a question than what is actually supplied.

40. (C)

From the 1950s to the 1980s, Manuel Noriega worked with the U.S. Central Intelligence Agency until it was revealed he was a major drug trafficker who had used his connections and power to seize control of the Panamanian government. In 1989, the United States invaded Panama, captured him, and tried and sentenced him to prison for his crimes.

41. (D)

In answer (A) the word *sole* should be a red flag: absolutes usually indicate wrong answers. Durkheim did not study the relationship between urban/country dwellers and suicide, so answer (E) is also incorrect.

42. (C)

Abolitionist and orator Frederick Douglass was born into slavery, but in 1838 he escaped to freedom in New York. Though both Booker T. Washington (A) and W. E. B. DuBois (E) were famous proponents of African-American rights, they were of a younger generation than Douglass and are typically associated with the late nineteenth and early twentieth centuries.

43. (E)

The Senate is given the power to ratify treaties in Article II, Section 2 of the U.S. Constitution.

44. (A)

Social facilitation is the phenomenon that people perform tasks better in groups or in front of people than they do alone. Though scientific sounding, answers (B) and (D) are made-up terms. Answers (C) and (E) are actual psychology terms that do not refer to the concept in question.

45. (D)

This answer is written in a deliberately confusing manner, but when read carefully, its lack of logic is clear. It just doesn't make sense that a group could be "mainstream" and "radical" at the same time.

46. (A)

In 1521 Pope Leo X awarded King Henry VIII of England the title "Defender of the Faith." Ironically, in 1534 Henry would break away from the Church.

47. (B)

Transcendentalism was an important American movement in philosophy and literature that flourished during the early to middle years of the nineteenth century. To its practitioners, the soul of each individual was identical with the soul of the world and contained the world's essence. Emerson and Thoreau were two of the most well-known transcendental writers, so answer (C) is incorrect. This was a romantic movement, so (D) is also wrong.

48. (C)

The primary tools of fiscal policy are the raising and lowering of taxes and government spending. These decisions are made by Congress.

49. (E)

Auguste Comte (1798–1857) was a French philosopher and the originator of positivism. He sought to apply methods of observation and experimentation, which were beginning to be used in the hard sciences, to the field we now known as sociology.

50. (D)

The assassination of Archduke Franz Ferdinand ignited World War I, so answer (A) can't be correct. Answer (C) is also an unlikely choice since the Tiananmen Square events are too recent. Answer (E) doesn't make sense because the Trojan War occurred in antiquity, long before the invention of the cannon.

51. (C)

The key here is the phrase "none of which are absolutely necessary for individual survival." Answer (A) must be incorrect since it only stands to reason that "primary" reinforcers *are* necessary for survival. Though answers (D) and (E) are sociological terms, they do not match the introductory portion of the question.

52. (A)

The nation of Turkey makes up the core of the former Ottoman Empire, which held sway as a global power from the fourteenth century until the end of World War I.

53. (E)

The terms "essentially" and "widely practiced" in answer (A) and the phrase "with varying degrees of success" in answer (D) should alert you: such vague terms often indicate incorrect answers. While the Temperance Movement did gain success at the state levels and then nationally (C), it never gained universal acceptance; the Eighteenth Amendment, passed in 1919 to ban alcohol, was never strongly enforced, and it was finally repealed in 1933.

54. (C)

The U.S. government is structured so that each branch of government can check or restrain the power of the other two. The framers of the Constitution wrote in a system of checks and balances so that no one branch of government could become too powerful and subvert the will of the people.

55. (A)

Even if the you recognize that the prefix *poly* usually means "many," the correct answer is not obvious. Polygamy is when a man has two or more wives (B). Since polyandry and polygamy are similar words, (A) would be a good guess.

56. (D)

The Tartars, an Asian tribe, never invaded Rome, preferring to conduct their pillaging and plundering closer to home. The other four answer choices list Germanic tribes who were based nearer to Rome.

57. (C)

Ethnocentrism is the *opposite* of cultural relativism, so (D) is incorrect. Answer (A) contains the word *always*, and (E) uses the word *very*—both of which should suggest a probable wrong answer.

58. (C)

This question is not as difficult as it may appear. When looking for an answer that is false, you can usually learn quite a bit about the subject from reading the answer choices carefully. Four of the five choices are true, so the challenge is to find the answer that does not fit in. In this case, one need only think about the public protests leading up to the Declaration of Independence—the Stamp Act Congress, the Committees of Correspondence, etc.—to know that Americans were very practical (C) in their application of Enlightenment thought.

59. (B)

In questions like this one, it can sometimes help to tune out the first sentence, which contains extra information, and focus specifically on what's being asked. It took 20 years after the discovery of the Taung Child in Africa for scientists to recognize its importance as an early human biped. The Piltdown Man was the hoax that set back evolutionary studies, so both answers (C) and (E) are incorrect. Answer (A) is the opposite of the correct answer.

60. (E)

This is perhaps the best-known quotation by Karl Marx, originator of communism. What is less well known is that Marx actually viewed religion as the primary solace of the oppressed proletarian classes.

61. (A)

This is a straightforward history question, but a few answers can be eliminated using careful reasoning. The year 1848 is a little early for child labor legislation (B), which didn't become an issue until the Progressive Movement. Similarly, (E) is unlikely since women didn't even have voting rights until 1920.

62. (A)

Allowing students to express their religion freely even if it is not in line with the dominant culture would be an example of tolerance of difference rather than an imposition of dominant values.

63. (E)

A bicameral legislature is one with an upper and a lower house. In the formation of the U.S. government, this model served the purpose of allowing smaller states equal footing with larger states in the Senate, while giving the larger states greater representation based on their size in the House of Representatives.

64. (A)

The Leakeys were a husband-and-wife archaeologist-anthropologist team famous for their work in Africa, in particular at the Olduvai Gorge site.

65. (D)

There is no evidence that a meteor has ever crashed into the ocean and created an island. Common means of island origin are by erosion of a land bridge, by growth of coral islands, and by volcanic activity.

66. (E)

Peter the Great ruled Russia from 1682 until 1725, propelling his country from slumbering giant to a major factor in European politics.

67. (A)

The keyword in this sociology question is *primary*. Answer (B) is wrong since it uses terms like *extended* and *network*, which by definition cannot be primary in nature. Likewise, the word *superficial* in (C) should signal an incorrect answer.

68. (B)

This new use for onions will cause a shift to the right in the entire demand curve. More onions will be demanded at every price because of a change in perception about their value to consumers.

69. (A)

Pepin, king of the Franks, earned the gratitude of the pope in 756 when he restored lands that had been seized by the Lombards to papal control.

70. (D)

Marbury v. Madison, heard by the U.S. Supreme Court in 1803, established the tradition of judicial review. The Court curtailed its own power by declaring the Judicial Act of 1789 unconstitutional, but in doing so, it positioned itself as interpreter of the Constitution.

71. (B)

Jane Addams was an activist in the late 1800's who played a pivotal role in the development and promotion of social work. She founded Hull House in Chicago—a settlement home to provide support for the immigrants who were flocking to the city at the end of the nineteenth century.

72. (E)

Tibet, a holy place to millions of Buddhists all over the world, is under the control of China. Answer (B) can be ruled out since the UN is not a country.

73. (E)

Pasteur was responsible for discoveries that formed the foundation of many scientific advancements, but the X-ray is the result of pioneering work done by the German physicist Wilhelm Röntgen

74. (A)

George Herbert Mead was a sociologist who believed that the mind developed through one's interactions with the social environment. He called this idea "social behaviorism." Answers (B), (C), and (D) are all distracters as they refer to anthropologist Margaret Mead, who has no relationship to the sociologist.

75. (C)

To be a river, the body of water must flow (E), and since water is subject to the effect of gravity, rivers always flow from higher to lower elevations.

76. (E)

Davy Crockett was a frontiersman, congressman from Tennessee, and hero of the Alamo. The popular play *The Lion of the West* told his story. He died at the Alamo in 1836. Adams and Franklin were statesmen, and Cooper was a writer, so options (A), (B), and (C) are incorrect.

77. (C)

If you don't recognize a word, it can be useful to read all of the answer choices for clues about the question category. Answers (A), (C), (D), and (E) all involve psychology, so it is pretty safe to assume the term is a psychological one.

78. (D)

After the Western empire fell, the Eastern half survived for a thousand years as the Byzantine empire. Constantinople was its the capital.

79. (E)

As head of the Church of England, Queen Elizabeth was Protestant.

80. (E)

Not only Muslims (A) and Jews (B) but also Protestants and *Moriscos*—converts to Catholicism from Islam—were targeted. Beware of words like *only*; most likely those answers are incorrect. The Inquisition lasted more than 350 years (C).

Ferdinand and Isabella actually pressured a reluctant Pope Sixtus IV (D) into signing a papal bull to start the Inquisition.

81. (E)

In the late eighteenth century, when the French Revolution took place, almost no one championed the cause of women's suffrage. The other four answer choices are all true. Economic hardship brought on by bad harvests and dissatisfaction with the response by the king and royal bureaucracy brought down the throne in 1789.

82. (A)

Charles de Gaulle, who had served his country during World War II, was twice elected president of France.

83. (C)

Nations can draw their boundaries in whatever way they choose. They do not have to be defined by natural landmarks.

84. (D)

Answer (B) is easy to rule out, as it doesn't make sense that memories for "life events" would be stored in short-term memory. Sensory memory (E) would logically involve one of the five senses.

85. (B)

Machiavelli was an Italian political theorist who outlined strategies for achieving and maintaining power. The quote "The end justifies the means," is from Machiavelli's most famous work, *The Prince*.

86. (A)

Monetary policy is conducted by the Federal Reserve and has nothing to do with politics; therefore (B) and (C) are incorrect. Likewise, (D) is wrong since the Supreme Court has no role in any economic policy making.

87. (C)

William F. Ogburn was the American sociologist who coined the term *cultural lag*. Answer (A) is a made-up distracter. The placebo effect (D) and symbiosis (B) are completely unrelated constructs.

88. (B)

The roots of the Hindu faith can be traced back to the Indus Valley in northwest India.

89. (E)

The Mongol emperor Kublai Khan founded the Yuan dynasty of China in 1271. He became the first non-Chinese emperor to rule all of China when Yuan armies defeated the remaining Southern Song Dynasty in 1279. He was the grandson of Genghis Khan.

90. (D)

The "Roundheads" and the "Cavaliers" were opposing factions in the English Civil War. The names referred to the appearance of the two groups. The "Roundheads" were primarily Puritans who eschewed frivolity and wore their hair in a classic bowl cut. In contrast, the fashionable "Cavaliers" donned long-haired wigs and extravagant costumes.

91. (A)

Answer (B) is the opposite. All of the other choices are distracters that sound like the correct answer.

92. (A)

Calculus was developed by Sir Isaac Newton (1642–1727), a scientist of the British Enlightenment. (The German scientist Leibniz also developed calculus at this time.) This occurred 3,000 years after the Mesopotamian civilizations ended.

93. (D)

During a period of rising inflation, a decrease in the money supply can slow economic growth and ease inflationary pressures. Answer (E) contains the terms *either/or*, which should signal a possible wrong choice.

94. (B)

In the 1980s, a shift in voting patterns occurred as voters who had formerly been reliable Democrats began to vote Republican, especially in the South. This trend was first noted in the 1980 presidential election.

95. (E)

Answers (A), (B), (C), and (D) can all contribute to acid rain, demonstrating the complexity of the problem. Answer (E) describes El Niño, which contributes to unusual weather but not acid rain.

96. (D)

Karl Marx (1818–1883) was a German social and political theorist who, after a failed career in journalism, wrote *The Communist Manifesto* in 1848 with Friedrich Engels. His radical theories advocating the overthrow of existing economic and political systems were the model used by Lenin and the Bolshevik Party in the Russian Revolution.

97. (A)

Mexico, the world's sixth-largest oil-producing country, is not a member of OPEC.

98. (C)

A careful read of all of the answer choices reveals the only choice that does not fit in with the theme of the question. The term *imperialism* is out of place among the other choices, which emphasize ideas like freedom, equality, and openness.

99. (B)

The British monarchy has no role in the governing process. Mexico has not had a monarchy for many years, so (E) is incorrect. Saudi Arabia has no "elected" governing body, so (C) is also incorrect.

100. (E)

The San Andreas Fault runs north and south through the western United States.

101. (E)

In 1936, John Maynard Keynes, a British economist, was the first to develop the theory that aggregate demand determines the level of economic activity.

102. (A)

Containment refers to a policy of checking the expansion or influence of a hostile power or ideology such as communism. *Détente* (E) describes a relaxation of tensions between rivals. *Glasnost* (B) is a Russian term meaning "openness" and applies to the period following the containment policy when tensions between the United States and the Soviet Union began to gradually decline.

103. (D)

Cartography, the science of mapmaking, dates back as far as c. 2500 B.C.E., when Babylonians made maps on clay tablets.

104. (B)

Plessy v. Ferguson held that "separate but equal" railway cars were not an unconstitutional infringement of civil liberties. *Brown v. the Board of Education* overturned this decision and the "separate but equal" construct.

105. (C)

Lobbying of elected officials takes place at all levels of local, state, and national government.

106. (E)

Nations such as Zimbabwe and Tanzania, which are rich in mineral wealth, remain poor for a variety of reasons, including the first four listed. Though an ascetic culture (E) would consume less, such a culture would not necessarily remain poor.

107. (A)

According to the National Hurricane Center, most hurricane activity in the United States occurs between the months of June and November.

108. (B)

The eighteenth-century French economist Jean-Baptiste Say formed the theory that the level of aggregate in an economic supply will drive the level of overall economic activity. This theory was the foundation of supply-side economics theory almost 200 years later.

109. (D)

The Three-Fifths Compromise, reached by Northern and Southern states at the 1787 Constitutional Convention, called for each slave to be counted as three-fifths of a person for purposes of determining legislative apportionment.

110. (B)

Joseph Schumpeter, a twentieth-century economist, believed that economic progress was achieved through a continual process of technological advancement, in which old industries are replaced by new ones.

111. (A)

The Bikini atoll in the southwest Pacific Ocean was the site of extensive atomic and hydrogen bomb testing from 1946–1958. Before testing began, the indigenous population was relocated to neighboring islands.

112. (D)

Answers (A) through (C) are each methods that have been used to amend the Constitution. This question is an example of the importance of reading each answer choice thoroughly—Congress does not call national conventions. You may encounter questions with an "all of the above" option among the answer choices. Be sure to read all answer options thoroughly.

113. (C)

The Southern Cross, a kite-shaped constellation, is the signature constellation of the southern hemisphere. It was first seen by European explorers in the early sixteenth century and was the inspiration for the Australian flag.

114. (D)

When a market is at equilibrium, sellers are able to sell their product at just the price buyers wish to pay. There is no pressure for prices to rise or fall and no shortage or surplus of the product.

115. (B)

A special Senate committee investigated the charges and found them groundless. McCarthy was undaunted and continued to use his position to wage a relentless anti-communist crusade.

116. (C)

Article III, Section 1 states that Supreme Court judges "shall hold their offices during good behavior," which has since its inception been interpreted to mean that they serve life terms.

117. (E)

Be sure to read all answer choices carefully before making your selection. Outsourcing is a means of lowering costs by shifting production to areas where labor costs are lower. This has been a boon to countries such as India, where a well-educated, English-speaking workforce has enjoyed new prosperity and the availability of technology that might otherwise have been unavailable in that nation. Workers in higher-wage countries may find themselves displaced by these changes until job markets adjust to the changes in labor demand.

118. (C)

The Andes have a significant effect on the climate of the region. As air moves up over the eastern slope of the Andes, it cools, causing moisture to freeze and fall to the ground as snow. Once across the mountains, the air warms up as it descends and is able to hold on to its moisture as it passes west of the Andes. This part of South America, the Atacama desert, is one of the driest places on Earth.

119. (D)

The term *rate* is the keyword here. Interest rates have no set dollar value—they are always calculated in percentage form—as such, there is no definite dollar figure that can be assigned. The remaining answer choices can be assigned stable dollar values, and all contribute to the GNP.

120. (C)

In 1938, British prime minister Neville Chamberlain and other European leaders met with Adolf Hitler in Munich to plot a peaceful solution to a crisis brought on by Hitler's seizure of a portion of Czechoslovakia. Hitler promised that if he were allowed to keep it, he would be satisfied and not invade additional lands. Chamberlain was convinced that this appeasement of the German dictator had worked and promised his country "peace in our time." Months later, Hitler seized the rest of Czechoslovakia.

Chapter Nineteen: **Practice Test 3**

Time—90 minutes
120 Questions

Directions: For each of the following questions or incomplete statements, select the best answer or completion from the five options given.

1. Which of the following was NOT a shortcoming of the Articles of Confederation?

   (A) Measures approved by Congress had to be approved by nine of the thirteen states.

   (B) Congress could not collect taxes to pay its bills.

   (C) There was no authority to regulate foreign trade.

   (D) The Articles of Confederation were very difficult to amend when the need arose.

   (E) Congress had no power to declare war.

2. The gross domestic product (GDP) is the same as the gross national product (GNP) EXCEPT

   (A) the GDP does not include the value of goods and services produced in U.S. territories and protectorates.

   (B) the GDP includes only the value of the housing industry, and the GNP includes the value of everything produced nationally.

   (C) the GNP functions according to the Kondratieff long wave cycle.

   (D) the GDP excludes the values of foreign trade and investments and limits the value of goods and services within the borders of the country.

   (E) the GNP includes the income earned by foreign residents within the domestic economy.

3. Which two ancient city-states fought the Peloponnesian Wars?

   (A) Athens and Babylonia

   (B) Rome and Carthage

   (C) Athens and Sparta

   (D) Rome and Syracuse

   (E) Sumeria and Sparta

4. *Socialization* and *enculturation* are both terms describing the process by which an individual adopts/learns the behavior patterns of the surrounding culture. Which of the following is NOT a component of either process?

   (A) Values

   (B) Norms

   (C) Mores

   (D) Genetics

   (E) Conformity

GO ON TO THE NEXT PAGE

5. Bipedalism is the fundamental characteristic used to define hominids. To what does the term refer?

   (A) Two-legged upright gait

   (B) The ability to operate cognitively using both lobes of the brain

   (C) A stooped-over gait typically accompanied by knuckle-dragging

   (D) The propensity to pair-bond and typically mate for life

   (E) The use of tools

6. Carl Jung—a younger colleague of Sigmund Freud—took his mentor's idea of the unconscious and expanded upon it. Jung drew on religion, mythology, philosophy, and mysticism to develop what he called the

   (A) symbolic unconscious.

   (B) conscious unconscious.

   (C) collective unconscious.

   (D) unconscious dialectic.

   (E) seismic unconscious.

7. Which of these events caused a dramatic deterioration in Arab-Jewish relations?

   (A) The creation of the nation of Israel

   (B) The death of the shah of Iran

   (C) The founding of OPEC

   (D) The collapse of the Soviet Union

   (E) The attacks on the World Trade Center

8. Lt. Col. Custer, who titled his memoirs *My Life on the Plains,* commanded his infamous "last stand" at the Little Big Horn in June 1876. Toward whom was this surprise assault directed?

   (A) A Cree Indian reservation in Idaho

   (B) A coalition of renegade mountain men and fur traders

   (C) French-Canadian soldiers from Acadia

   (D) The British

   (E) A Sioux/Cheyenne encampment

9. Which continent is home to the most countries?

   (A) Asia

   (B) North America

   (C) Europe

   (D) Africa

   (E) South America

10. What role did Charles de Gaulle play in the liberation of France?

   (A) He served in the government set up by the Germans and tried to negotiate their withdrawal from France.

   (B) He escaped to England where he met with Churchill, then addressed the occupied French nation over the radio, urging the people to continue to fight.

   (C) He hid in Paris for the entire duration of the occupation, spying on the Nazis and secretly sending intelligence information to the Allies.

   (D) He helped smuggle weapons into France to be used when the time came to liberate the country.

   (E) He was imprisoned in Germany during the war and was not able to participate in the liberation of Paris.

11. The U.S. Constitution grants the House of Representatives, but NOT the Senate, the power to do which of the following?

   (A) Regulate TV and radio broadcasting

   (B) Originate spending bills

   (C) Declare war

   (D) Approve Supreme Court nominees

   (E) Override a presidential veto

GO ON TO THE NEXT PAGE

12. Known to his men as "Old Hickory," which Major General did the citizens of the Crescent City turn to for protection from the British in late 1814?

    (A) Andrew Johnson
    (B) Lafayette
    (C) Andrew Jackson
    (D) Washington Lee
    (E) John Laffitte

13. If the price of input I rises, the price of finished good G will rise if

    (A) there are ample acceptable substitutes for input I.
    (B) there is no other way to produce finished good G.
    (C) input I makes up a minor portion of finished good G.
    (D) consumers will purchase good G only when its price is low.
    (E) good G is an inferior product that consumers prefer in hard times.

14. William Graham Sumner coined the term *folkways* as a subset of *customs* to denote group habits that are common to a society or culture. Which of the following is NOT an example of *folkways*?

    (A) Accent
    (B) Clothing fashions
    (C) Modes of recreation
    (D) Traditional garb
    (E) Ceremonial headwear

15. Which of the following was NOT an objection to the Constitution raised by the Anti-Federalists?

    (A) The lack of a bill of rights
    (B) The failure to provide women the right to vote
    (C) Increased powers of the central government
    (D) The process by which it would be ratified
    (E) The absence of a mention of God

16. The psychological term for the stable set of individual characteristics that make an individual unique is

    (A) perception.
    (B) sense of self.
    (C) genetic makeup.
    (D) personality.
    (E) genotype.

17. Which of the following individuals did NOT leave written accounts of history?

    (A) Tacitus
    (B) Herodotus
    (C) Attila the Hun
    (D) Julius Caesar
    (E) Suetonius

18. South Dakota senator George McGovern ran for president in 1972 on the Democratic ticket, promising to bring home the remaining American troops from Vietnam. To whom did he lose?

    (A) Jimmy Carter
    (B) Lyndon Baines Johnson
    (C) Robert F. Kennedy
    (D) Gerald Ford
    (E) Richard Nixon

19. Which was the last Russian dynasty?

    (A) Romanov
    (B) Tolstoy
    (C) Federov
    (D) Kruschev
    (E) Godunov

GO ON TO THE NEXT PAGE

KAPLAN

20. Which of the following was NOT a contributing factor to the collapse of the Roman empire?

    (A) A papal edict freeing all slaves

    (B) Invading tribes from north of the empire

    (C) A costly bureaucracy increasingly unable to manage imperial affairs

    (D) Such a vast expanse of territory was difficult to control

    (E) A series of corrupt and inept emperors

21. The primary significance of El Niño is that it

    (A) causes an increase in electromagnetic activity, which can interfere with radio transmissions.

    (B) lowers average ocean surface water temperatures, causing less plankton growth.

    (C) affects the gravitational force exerted by the moon on the tides.

    (D) increases average ocean surface water temperature, causing climatic change around the world.

    (E) changes seismic activity on the ocean floor that can cause underwater volcanic eruptions.

22. The shrine at Delphi was dedicated to

    (A) Zeus.

    (B) Apollo.

    (C) Homer.

    (D) Aphrodite.

    (E) Poseidon.

23. Oligopoly is a market structure characterized by

    (A) few or no barriers to entry.

    (B) many sellers offering similar products.

    (C) aggressive price competition by sellers.

    (D) a single seller.

    (E) a few sellers offering similar products.

24. While Karl Marx stressed economic conflict as the guiding force in social evolution and Sigmund Freud emphasized psychosexual maturation, Émile Durkheim's vision was more peaceful and progressive. Durkheim was one of the creators of

    (A) positivism.

    (B) neo-positivism.

    (C) progressive evolution theory.

    (D) optimism.

    (E) causal positivism.

25. Which U.S. president said, "Go ahead, make my day," as a warning to Congress not to submit a tax increase?

    (A) Bill Clinton

    (B) Ronald Reagan

    (C) Gerald Ford

    (D) George H. W. Bush

    (E) Harry S. Truman

26. According to psychiatrists, a compulsive act is typically done in an attempt to alleviate the discomfort caused by

    (A) a fixation.

    (B) a manic episode.

    (C) bipolar disorder.

    (D) an obsession.

    (E) a repressed memory.

GO ON TO THE NEXT PAGE

27. What is meant by the phrase "dirty war" as it was carried out in Argentina?

    (A) The use of radioactive devices to terrorize the population

    (B) Secret forays into neighboring countries to assassinate political rivals

    (C) A secret campaign by the government against political dissenters

    (D) The dispute with Great Britain over the Falkland Islands

    (E) Deliberate pollution of a neighboring country's waterways

28. The Council of Nicea in 325 established all of the following EXCEPT

    (A) the writing of the first part of the Nicene Creed.

    (B) the divinity of Jesus Christ as being one with God and of the same substance as God.

    (C) the date when Easter should be celebrated.

    (D) various canonical laws, including the prohibition of self-castration.

    (E) electing Pope Martin V, thus ending the Great Schism.

29. What is a tsunami?

    (A) A giant wave caused by seismic activity in the ocean

    (B) A rainforest in central Asia

    (C) A large fish native to the South Pacific

    (D) A tornado that forms over water

    (E) A hurricane occurring in the Pacific Ocean

30. The patricians were noble families of Rome who, in 509 B.C.E., expelled the Etruscan king and decreed that Rome would become a republic. The other citizens of Rome, including farmers, merchants, and artisans, were known as

    (A) serfs.

    (B) plebeians.

    (C) drones.

    (D) proletariats.

    (E) vassals.

31. Which of the following did NOT contribute to the decline of feudalism in Europe?

    (A) Greater social mobility as a result of a more diversified field economy

    (B) The Black Plague, which reduced the labor force and resulted in higher wages

    (C) A papal edict declaring the feudal system to be in violation of Church law

    (D) Rising growth and influence of urban towns

    (E) The rise of humanistic philosophy with its emphasis on individual self-worth

32. The policy of executive privilege came into effect during the Nixon administration when members of the executive branch were being questioned by authorities. What does executive privilege provide for?

    (A) The right for the president to plead the Fifth Amendment

    (B) The residence of impeachment powers exclusively in the executive branch

    (C) The need for presidential approval before Congress can question any executive branch staff member

    (D) The right for the president to grant pardons without any recourse from the judicial branch

    (E) The right to choose cabinet members without congressional approval

33. One argument for using fiscal policy rather than monetary policy to influence the economy is that

    (A) it is easier to implement than monetary policy.

    (B) it takes effect more rapidly than monetary policy.

    (C) monetary policy is unfair to the middle class.

    (D) monetary policy is too extreme a measure.

    (E) fiscal policy has a more precise effect on the economy.

GO ON TO THE NEXT PAGE ⟹

KAPLAN)

34. Modern humans and apes share the same brachiating anatomy of the upper torso. The style of movement this enables

    (A) is only present in upright-walking primates with a hunter-gatherer social past.

    (B) has evolved over the last 25,000 years.

    (C) allows humans to swivel their hips.

    (D) is known as "arm-swinging," since the arms pull the body along while walking as apes use their arms when moving through trees.

    (E) traditional displays of physical strength (for example, chest-pounding among apes and muscle-flexing in modern humans).

35. *Theory* can be defined as "a general statement about how some parts of the world fit together and how they work." Which of the following concepts is primarily a sociological theory?

    (A) Marxism

    (B) Fascism

    (C) Monarchy

    (D) Monopoly

    (E) Anarchy

36. What is meant by the term *federalism*?

    (A) The Federalist Party is in control of the government.

    (B) Power is divided between a strong central government and several regional governments.

    (C) The Federal Reserve System uses monetary policy to manage the money supply.

    (D) It is a political-economic system where the federal government controls all industry.

    (E) It is a political system in which all federal officers are elected.

37. Which of the following thinkers is NOT associated with childhood developmental stages?

    (A) Jean Piaget

    (B) Sigmund Freud

    (C) Eric Erikson

    (D) Margaret Mead

    (E) Elizabeth Kübler-Ross

38. Which of the following was NOT a reason for the United States' entry into World War I?

    (A) The sinking of the *Lusitania* by the Germans

    (B) The discovery of a plot by Germany to get Mexico to enter the war against the United States

    (C) The bombing of Pearl Harbor by the Japanese

    (D) The disruption of Atlantic shipping lanes by unrestricted German submarine warfare

    (E) Germany's attempts to lure Japan into the war

39. With what traveling show did sharpshooter "Wild Bill" Hickock and his girlfriend "Calamity Jane" tour?

    (A) The Greatest Show on Earth

    (B) The Ringling Brothers Circus

    (C) P. T. Barnum's Side Show and Oddities

    (D) Buffalo Bill Cody's Wild West Show

    (E) The Columbia World's Exposition

40. Its defeat in World War II changed Japan in which of the following ways?

    (A) The emperor lost his complete control of the government and became a purely ceremonial figure.

    (B) A new constitution was written, and women were given the right to vote.

    (C) Western-style democracy was abolished.

    (D) Japan no longer strove to emulate the United States' economic success.

    (E) Japan reverted to its earlier reclusive ways.

GO ON TO THE NEXT PAGE →

41. According to Charles Horton Cooley (1864–1929), our sense of self develops from interaction with others. For Cooley, this process contains three steps. Which of the following choices lists them correctly?

   (A) We imagine how we look to others; we negatively compare ourselves to others; we develop a self-concept.

   (B) We develop a self-concept; we positively compare ourselves to others; we negatively compare ourselves to others.

   (C) We imagine how we look to others; we interpret how others react to us; we develop a self-concept.

   (D) We interpret how others react to us; we develop a self-concept; we perfect our self-concept with constant adjustments.

   (E) We negatively compare ourselves to others; we positively compare ourselves to others; we interpret how others react to us.

42. The low-pressure area of light variable winds near the equator is known to sailors as the

   (A) doldrums.
   (B) trade winds.
   (C) Bermuda Triangle.
   (D) Corolis effect.
   (E) Southern Cross.

43. On April 14, 1775, the colonial governor of Massachusetts, General Gage, was secretly ordered by the British to suppress rebellion by any means necessary. Four days later, Gage sent seven hunded British soldiers to destroy the colonists' weapons depot. What famous event happened later that night?

   (A) John Hancock placed his signature—the largest and the final—on the Declaration of Independence.

   (B) George Washington declared war against King George of England.

   (C) Paul Revere set out from Boston to Lexington to warn the colonial militiamen.

   (D) Plans for the Underground Railroad were finally put into action.

   (E) Vast stores of English tea were thrown into Boston Harbor.

44. What is the relationship between real and nominal interest rates?

   (A) Nominal interest rates take inflation into account, while real rates do not.

   (B) Real interest rates are paid to borrowers, and nominal interest rates are paid to lenders.

   (C) Real interest rates are paid on government bonds, and nominal interest rates are paid on bank deposits.

   (D) Real interest rates take inflation into account, while nominal interest rates do not.

   (E) Real and nominal rates are the same thing.

GO ON TO THE NEXT PAGE

KAPLAN

45. Great Britain's defeat of the Spanish Armada in 1588 is often considered a turning point in world history. Which of the following was NOT a result of this landmark victory?

    (A) English replaced Spanish as the most commonly spoken language in Europe.

    (B) Great Britain replaced Spain as the dominant world power.

    (C) Spain's influence in the New World gradually declined.

    (D) English imperial interests widened as the British gained superiority over the seas.

    (E) Spanish influence across Europe began to subside.

46. What is the meaning of the term *gerrymandering*?

    (A) Attempts by interest groups to influence politicians by contributing to their campaigns

    (B) Drawing of electoral districts to adjust the voting strength of a particular group

    (C) Levying of poll taxes to discourage voting by minority groups

    (D) The process of choosing a political party's slate of candidates

    (E) A method to delay a vote on a bill by talking for hours to keep the debate open

47. What controversy surrounds the Elgin Marbles?

    (A) The Nazis commandeered them prior to the outbreak of World War II.

    (B) They have been discovered to be forgeries.

    (C) The government of Greece wants them back.

    (D) Museum officials have done restoration work that has altered their historical value.

    (E) Money raised for the building of a new wing of their museum was misappropriated by employees.

48. In 1729, Benjamin Franklin began publishing *The Pennsylvania Gazette* and two years later founded the first American public library. While visiting the library, colonists could have read Franklin's annual almanac written under the pseudonym of

    (A) Little Richard.

    (B) Little Peter.

    (C) Poor Little Richard.

    (D) Poor Richard.

    (E) Peter Pilgrim.

49. The "Forbidden City" is located in

    (A) Beijing.

    (B) Riyadh.

    (C) Machu Picchu.

    (D) Moscow.

    (E) Tokyo.

50. Sociologists employ many research methods when they are studying a given population, including demography. Which of the following is NOT an example of a demographic study?

    (A) A study of divorce rates in the rural Midwest based on statistical analysis

    (B) A study of marital satisfaction of women who married later in life based on perceived quality of life

    (C) A statistical analysis of birth rates in urban populations compared to the same rates in rural populations

    (D) A study of infant mortality rates in the Pacific Northwest

    (E) A comparison of divorce rates in families with no children and families with at least one child

GO ON TO THE NEXT PAGE

KAPLAN

51. Which of the following was NOT a consequence of the 1991 Mt. Pinatubo eruption?

    (A) The height of the volcano was reduced by 800 feet.

    (B) Valleys were buried by as much as 650 feet of ash and pumice.

    (C) The Earth's temperature fell by one degree.

    (D) Ash covered the Earth's stratosphere within twelve months.

    (E) An ancient city was preserved as it was the day of the eruption.

52. In psychoanalytical theory, the part of our personality that contains our primitive impulses such as sex, anger, and hunger is called

    (A) the ego.
    (B) the id.
    (C) the superego .
    (D) the uber-ego.
    (E) the under-ego.

53. In 1857, the U.S. Supreme Court made a benchmark ruling; what did the Dred Scott decision determine?

    I. African Americans, free or not, could not be citizens.
    II. Slaves brought into free territory by their owners remained property.
    III. Any escaped slave who reached the North would be granted citizenship and all the rights that came accordingly.

    (A) I only
    (B) II only
    (C) III only
    (D) I and III only
    (E) I and II only

54. An increase in the money supply will generally cause the economy to

    (A) stagnate.
    (B) expand.
    (C) contract, then expand.
    (D) contract.
    (E) inflate.

55. Thermoluminescence is

    (A) a technique for determining the age of burnt flint or ceramics found at archaeological sites.

    (B) the amount of heat or energy remaining in a skeleton after decomposition begins.

    (C) a technique for determining the sex of primate remains by measuring light refracted through gender-specific cells.

    (D) a gradual heating and cooling of the Earth as a result of seismic activity.

    (E) a technique for determining the age of archaeological artifacts by using a gradual heating and cooling process.

56. Which of the following statements is TRUE about the relationship between the North and the South in the antebellum period?

    (A) The North, chiefly an agricultural region, was threatened by the South's economic strength.

    (B) The South was chiefly an agricultural region eager to expand into factory-based industries.

    (C) The North was chiefly a manufacturing region seeking justification to appropriate the natural resources in the South.

    (D) A flood of immigrants to Southern cities had Atlanta and Chattanooga vying with Boston and New York to be the seat of education and culture in the country.

    (E) As the United States became more established, the two regions found themselves increasingly at odds over their economic, social, and political beliefs.

GO ON TO THE NEXT PAGE

KAPLAN

57. Which political party would agree with the statement "The government that governs best governs least"?

   (A) Socialist
   (B) Green
   (C) Democratic
   (D) Libertarian
   (E) Communist

58. Kai Erikson is known for his work on the function of deviance in group situations. Which of the following statements would he most likely agree with?

   (A) Deviant behavior typically serves a disruptive function and should therefore be discouraged as counterproductive to the group's long-term survival.
   (B) Deviant behavior should be encouraged as a force for innovation.
   (C) A group will accept and sustain deviant behavior rather than eliminate it because it maintains the boundaries of acceptable and unacceptable behavior.
   (D) Deviance is never functional—it decreases group solidarity and encourages nonconformist group behavior.
   (E) As a group becomes more established, its standards of behavior become more rigid and codified.

59. Which of the following is TRUE of the Salic law?

   (A) It said that only male descendants of the king could inherit the throne.
   (B) It spelled out how the royal court of France should function.
   (C) It regulated the French winemaking industry.
   (D) It governed the French monetary system.
   (E) It made Paris the capital of France.

60. Which faith stresses the importance of meditation and the Middle Way?

   (A) Judaism
   (B) Hinduism
   (C) Buddhism
   (D) Islam
   (E) Jainism

61. According to psychologists, which of the following is an example of "inappropriate affect"?

   (A) Smiling when recounting a happy childhood memory
   (B) Crying when remembering a lost loved one
   (C) Laughing when talking about the death of a loved one
   (D) A racing pulse and sweaty palms in a panic situation
   (E) Inability to determine appropriate personal space

62. What happened in 1870 in Italy and in 1871 in Germany?

   (A) Unified nations were formed when smaller kingdoms agreed to join together.
   (B) Women were granted the right to vote, well before they were given that right in the United States.
   (C) The Catholic Church was made the official state religion, resulting in a consolidation of papal authority.
   (D) They both joined the League of Nations, a predecessor to today's United Nations.
   (E) Their monarchs were assassinated, and the tide of communism could no longer be contained.

GO ON TO THE NEXT PAGE

63. Although she did not live long enough to see women at voting booths, Susan B. Anthony fought tirelessly for women's suffrage in her lifetime. In 1872, she led a group of women to the polls in Rochester, New York, demanding that

    (A) African-American women and men be given the same voting rights as whites.

    (B) women be given the same civil and political rights that had already been extended to African-American males under the Fourteenth and Fifteenth Amendments.

    (C) landholding women—black or white—be given the same voting and civil rights given to African-American males under the Fourteenth and Fifteenth Amendments.

    (D) white women who held property should have some say over how their tax dollars were spent.

    (E) the ability to read and write, rather than one's gender, should be the test for voting rights.

64. Henry the Navigator played an important role in the Age of Exploration because he

    (A) was the first person to circumnavigate the globe.

    (B) encouraged Europeans to explore the African continent.

    (C) invented the sextant, which was vital to marine navigation and mapmaking.

    (D) discovered through scientific calculation that the world was not flat.

    (E) financed Columbus' voyage to the New World.

65. One definition of *sociology* is "the study of social order." The term was coined by a Frenchman, August Comte, but didn't come into usage until after the French Revolution. Which of the following conditions had to be in place before the study of social order could become established?

    I. The old absolutist monarchies were overthrown.
    II. New classes demanding citizens' rights appeared.
    III. Enlightenment philosophy emphasized humanism and the individual in relation to society.

    (A) I only

    (B) II only

    (C) III only

    (D) I and II only

    (E) I, II, and III

66. When there are many sellers and few buyers for a certain product, which of the following will NOT occur?

    (A) More buyers will enter the market.

    (B) Prices will tend to rise.

    (C) Sellers may attempt to differentiate their product from the other similar products.

    (D) Prices will tend to fall.

    (E) Prices will remain constant.

GO ON TO THE NEXT PAGE

KAPLAN

67. From June through September of 1692, nineteen men and women were hanged at Gallows Hill in Massachusetts, and many more languished in jails for months without trial. For what offense were teenagers Ann Putnam and Mercy Lewis eventually put on trial?

    (A) Treason—they were both Tories and loyal to the British crown.

    (B) Witchcraft—after they exhibited some unusual behavior, the local magistrates attributed their afflictions to the supernatural.

    (C) Vandalism—they were the first to be charged with this crime in the New World.

    (D) Suicide—the girls were unsuccessful, and since taking one's life went against Puritan doctrine, they were sentenced to life in prison.

    (E) Unlawful pregnancies—they were unwed mothers who would not reveal the fathers of their children.

68. What was the primary significance of the Strategic Defense Initiative?

    (A) This act of Congress founded the first U.S. space program, which eventually put a man on the moon.

    (B) This international agreement compelled non-oil-producing nations to stockpile oil in the event of a war in the Middle East.

    (C) This post–World War II committee ceded Israeli settlements in the West Bank, causing additional violence between Jews and Palestinians.

    (D) This policy motivated the Soviet Union to compete with the American arms program, spending much more than it could afford.

    (E) American surveillance satellites were launched to provide constant tracking of enemy movements.

69. The systematic picking through the hair of one individual by another to remove foreign matter and parasites is called "grooming behavior." Why is this practice so important for primates?

    (A) The activity reduces the spread of disease within particular communities.

    (B) Grooming behavior helps create and maintain social bonds.

    (C) As a mating ritual, this practice has its own well-defined and gender-specific roles.

    (D) This behavior helps establish desirable traits of physical attractiveness.

    (E) The practice helps regulate primate body temperature and metabolism.

70. The American Puritans only extended church membership to those they called "True Believers," people who made public professions of their faith. New members soon wanted their children to be baptized, creating a dilemma for the church elders. They advocated doctrinal purity but also sought to keep as many people as possible under the sway of the church. What was their solution?

    (A) The "Halfway" covenant

    (B) The Inner Light

    (C) The "One-Drop" rule

    (D) Adult baptism

    (E) The original sin construct

71. The ancient nation of Nubia is now contained within the borders of what two nations?

    (A) Algeria and Libya

    (B) Iran and Iraq

    (C) Egypt and Sudan

    (D) Columbia and Venezuela

    (E) Brazil and Peru

GO ON TO THE NEXT PAGE

KAPLAN

72. Which of two following sociological perspectives are in direct opposition to one another?

   (A) Marxism and socialism

   (B) Socialism and cultural relativism

   (C) Behaviorism and ethnocentrism

   (D) Cultural relativism and ethnocentrism

   (E) Behaviorism and Marxism

73. Which of the following is NOT one of the four major islands of Japan?

   (A) Nagasaki

   (B) Hokkaido

   (C) Honshu

   (D) Kyushu

   (E) Shikoku

74. The essay "The Crisis," written in 1776, was a call to arms for Americans. The essay opens with the following sentence: "These are the times that try men's souls." Who was its author?

   (A) Thomas Jefferson

   (B) James Madison

   (C) Benjamin Franklin

   (D) John Adams

   (E) Thomas Paine

75. The tendency of an individual to focus energy inward resulting in decreased social interaction, as opposed to focusing energy outward toward others and group activity, is known as

   (A) introspection.

   (B) internal orientation.

   (C) an internal locus of control.

   (D) introversion.

   (E) intrinsic motivation.

76. What archaeological breakthrough was made possible by the discovery of the Rosetta Stone?

   (A) The discovery of the lost city of Atlantis

   (B) The ability to decipher the meaning of hieroglyphics

   (C) Uncovering the secret of how the ancient Babylonians made fire

   (D) Understanding the meaning of the ring of giant stones at Stonehenge

   (E) Knowledge of the method the ancient Egyptians used to mummify their dead

77. Throughout the colonial period in America, one of the greatest sources of irritation between England and the colonies

   (A) was the religious dogma of the British colonial governors.

   (B) was the restrictions placed on religious freedoms in the colonies.

   (C) was the Navigation Acts, which protected British shipping while garnishing a profit for the king.

   (D) was the insistence by the throne that debtors and criminals be sent to the New World rather than to prison.

   (E) was King George's rampant profiteering of the abundant natural resources available in America.

78. What was the outcome of the Bretton Woods conference?

   (A) It signaled the end of World War II.

   (B) It established the Federal Reserve System.

   (C) It returned the United States to the gold standard.

   (D) It established a system of fixed exchange rates.

   (E) It returned lands seized by Hitler to the French.

GO ON TO THE NEXT PAGE ⟶

KAPLAN

79. Social anthropology seeks to understand cultural diversity, including relationships between culture and power. Social anthropologists identify specific social issues and compare them across societies. Which of the following subjects would NOT be addressed by the discipline?

    (A) Intelligence and its measurement
    (B) Kinship and colonialism
    (C) Class and caste
    (D) Politics and power
    (E) Myth and ritual

80. Which of these factors is contributing to deforestation of the Amazon rainforest?

    I. The land is needed for farming and ranching.
    II. The trees themselves are used for lumber.
    III. City dwellers seek land in the country for recreational use.

    (A) I only
    (B) II only
    (C) III only
    (D) I and II only
    (E) I, II, and III

81. The research method using random assignment of subjects and the manipulation of variables in order to determine cause and effect is known as

    (A) the experimental method.
    (B) the variation method.
    (C) deductive reasoning.
    (D) causal analysis.
    (E) longitudinal study.

82. What led to the establishment of the United Nations?

    (A) The world lacked an international standard of weights and measures.
    (B) Famine in Africa demonstrated the need for a humanitarian relief agency.
    (C) The charter of the League of Nations had expired.
    (D) The nations of the world wanted to fight terrorism.
    (E) The League of Nations had failed to keep the world at peace.

83. In the period from about 1900 through the 1920s, African-American literature, art, music, dance, and social commentary flourished. This movement was named for the community that was at its center. What is this cultural movement now known as?

    (A) The Jazz Age
    (B) The Village Revival
    (C) The Harlem Renaissance
    (D) The Delta Diaspora
    (E) The New Nubian Movement

84. The *Book of the Dead* is a remnant of what country's ancient culture and rituals?

    (A) China
    (B) Mexico
    (C) Egypt
    (D) Babylonia
    (E) Greece

GO ON TO THE NEXT PAGE

KAPLAN

85. Psychologists use the term *learned helplessness* to describe a condition that occurs

    (A) after a period of sustained negative consequences when individuals begin to believe they have no control over their environment.

    (B) when individuals are prevented from taking any proactive measures to improve their circumstances and subsequently believe they are powerless.

    (C) when a child is rendered helpless and ineffectual because of a domineering mother figure.

    (D) when either member of a pair-bond begins to rely too heavily on the other for primary reinforcers.

    (E) when invalids subconsciously prevent themselves from regaining physical health because they have become conditioned to expect constant care.

86. Who were the two anarchists arrested for robbery in 1920s New York, resulting in one of the most sensational trials of the early twentieth century?

    (A) Plessy and Ferguson

    (B) Sacco and Vanzetti

    (C) Capone and Capellini

    (D) Katzmann and Coletti

    (E) Julius and Ethel Rosenberg

87. Why is the Dead Sea given this name?

    (A) No aquatic life can survive there.

    (B) Many ferocious battles have been fought nearby.

    (C) It is slowly evaporating.

    (D) Many of the sailors who set sail from there never returned.

    (E) It has a large shark population.

88. Which economist first advocated the concept of countercyclical economic policy?

    (A) Adam Smith

    (B) Arthur Laffer

    (C) John Maynard Keynes

    (D) Joseph Schumpeter

    (E) Milton Friedman

89. Frictional unemployment occurs when

    (A) factories close, leaving workers without jobs.

    (B) individuals leave their jobs to seek other opportunities.

    (C) consumers stop buying certain products, causing entire industries to falter.

    (D) technology causes some products to become obsolete.

    (E) individuals leave the labor force.

90. Known for her unorthodox style, this proto-feminist declared herself the first woman candidate for president of the United States in 1870—she lost by a large margin. Who was she?

    (A) Susan B. Anthony

    (B) Charlotte Perkins Gilman

    (C) Victoria Woodhull

    (D) Dorothy Parker

    (E) Gloria Steinem

91. Charlemagne's reign was significant because he

    (A) was the first king of France to be crowned by the Pope.

    (B) led the first Crusade to the Holy Land.

    (C) defeated the British at the Battle of Hastings.

    (D) established a central government over western Europe.

    (E) built the Cathedral of Notre Dame in Paris.

GO ON TO THE NEXT PAGE

KAPLAN

92. The most recent amendment to the Constitution of the United States

    (A) limited the presidency to two terms.

    (B) abolished the poll tax.

    (C) lowered the voting age to eighteen.

    (D) provided for presidential disability.

    (E) prohibited immediate congressional pay raises.

93. Thorndike's "law of effect" states that

    (A) those responses that are followed by negative reinforcers will be repeated more often than those that are not.

    (B) those responses that are followed by a positive consequence will be repeated more frequently than those that are not.

    (C) there is no relationship between positive reinforcers and negative behavior.

    (D) those responses that are followed by negative reinforcers are repeated more frequently in some destructive personality types.

    (E) most individuals alter unacceptable responses when repeatedly subjected to negative consequences.

94. The only crime specifically mentioned in the U.S. Constitution is

    (A) tax evasion.

    (B) mail fraud.

    (C) perjury.

    (D) counterfeiting.

    (E) treason.

95. We know about the Peloponnesian War principally from the writings of

    (A) Herodotus.

    (B) Livy.

    (C) Tacitus.

    (D) Thucydides.

    (E) Aeschylus.

GO ON TO THE NEXT PAGE ▷

96. The darkly shaded country was once known as

    (A) Ceylon.

    (B) Rhodesia.

    (C) Persia.

    (D) Burma.

    (E) Siam.

97. What does it mean to say that archaeological remains—such as fossilized animals—are found *in situ*?

    (A) They are located in an area previously beneath sea level.

    (B) They are not found in their original ecosystem.

    (C) They have been removed and relocated, perhaps by scavenging animals.

    (D) They are found in their natural position— buried in the place where they died.

    (E) They are found perfectly preserved.

98. What is the difference between a continental island and an oceanic island?

    (A) A continental island has the same plant and animal life as the nearest continent, and an oceanic island has its own plant and animal life.

    (B) A continental island lies off the coast of a continent, and an oceanic island is located in the ocean away from major land masses.

    (C) A continental island is a large island, and oceanic islands are small islands.

    (D) A continental island has fresh water, and an oceanic island does not.

    (E) There is no difference.

GO ON TO THE NEXT PAGE

KAPLAN

99. Commonly used to describe the domination of one class, nation, or group of people over others, this notion was extended by Antonio Gramsci to denote dominance over people's political and cultural perceptions. Gramsci's idea was known as

(A) hierarchy.

(B) imperialism.

(C) hegemony.

(D) cultural imperialism.

(E) cultural persuasion.

100. What was Napoleon's primary motive in his desire to conquer Egypt?

(A) To win glory for himself

(B) To explore the tombs of the pharaohs

(C) To crown himself king of Egypt

(D) To cut off British access to India

(E) To follow in the footsteps of his hero, Alexander the Great

101. A dream in which an individual is aware that he or she is dreaming and sometimes even able to manipulate the dream is called

(A) R.E.M. state.

(B) an illusive dream.

(C) a waking dream.

(D) an out-of-body experience.

(E) a lucid dream.

102. In 1893, Frederick Jackson Turner presented his seminal paper, "The Significance of the Frontier in American History" at the World's Columbia Exposition in Chicago. Turner introduced his concept of American "exceptionalism" in his presentation. What is its central premise?

(A) It is a refutation of the previously widely accepted concept of "Manifest Destiny."

(B) The frontier experience explains the development of democracy in the United States and is key to understanding a uniquely American cultural identity.

(C) Although the literal American frontier essentially ended around 1865, the frontier experience imprinted itself on the American psyche.

(D) The frontier ideal and the notion of "Manifest Destiny" were popular mythologies to justify unbridled westward expansion.

(E) The American frontier took the place of the long-exploited European frontier in the imaginations of settlers.

103. The hypothesis, based on studies of modern human mitochondrial DNA, that all modern humans descended from one closely related population, or even one woman, who lived in Africa approximately 100,000 to 200,000 years ago is

(A) the Original Eden hypothesis.

(B) the Adam's Rib theory.

(C) the Hanging Gardens hypothesis.

(D) the African Eve hypothesis.

(E) the Hellenic Origins hypothesis.

GO ON TO THE NEXT PAGE ⟹

104. Which of the following statements about Alexander the Great is NOT true?

    (A) The great Greek philosopher Aristotle was his tutor.

    (B) He ordered the construction of the Great Pyramid of Egypt.

    (C) His empire included Greece, Macedonia, Persia, Egypt, and parts of India.

    (D) His mother plotted to have his father assassinated.

    (E) His horse, Bucephalus, was said to be a horse no other man could ride.

105. What is meant by the expression "There is no such thing as a free lunch"?

    (A) The government prohibits spoiled food from being given to charity.

    (B) There are costs associated with providing goods and services.

    (C) A restaurant will have to close if no one pays for the food.

    (D) In many cities it is illegal to serve meals to homeless people.

    (E) Regulation of the restaurant industry drives up the costs of doing business.

106. The exclusionary rule is derived from

    (A) Article I, Section 1 of the Constitution.

    (B) English common law.

    (C) the Fifth Amendment to the Constitution.

    (D) congressional mandate.

    (E) the Fourth Amendment to the Constitution.

107. Who were the Boers?

    (A) The ruling family of the Netherlands during World War II

    (B) A missionary order working to convert the Indians in South America

    (C) Dutch settlers in South Africa

    (D) A secret society of knights during the time of the Crusades

    (E) The family controlling most of the diamond trade in Africa

108. Which of the following works was written by Homer?

    (A) *The Iliad*

    (B) *Antigone*

    (C) *Medea*

    (D) *The Oresteia*

    (E) *The Frogs*

109. Who is considered to be the Father of the Constitution?

    (A) Thomas Jefferson

    (B) John Hancock

    (C) George Washington

    (D) John Adams

    (E) James Madison

110. A nation-state is one where the majority of citizens share a common culture, language, and ethnicity. Select the BEST example of a nation-state from the choices listed.

    (A) Switzerland

    (B) India

    (C) Australia

    (D) Iceland

    (E) United States

GO ON TO THE NEXT PAGE

111. As a result of the widespread bank failures that took place during the Great Depression, which of the following institutions was formed?

    (A) Federal Reserve System

    (B) Federal Deposit Insurance Corporation

    (C) Comptroller of the Currency

    (D) Federal Home Loan Bank Board

    (E) Office of Thrift Supervision

112. Lech Walesa was

    (A) the first Pole to be elected to the papacy.

    (B) the discoverer of the element polonium.

    (C) the leader of the Solidarity trade union movement.

    (D) a leader in the Polish resistance to the Nazis.

    (E) the composer of the Polish national anthem.

113. The Saffir-Simpson scale is used to measure

    (A) the strength of hurricanes.

    (B) relative annual rainfall.

    (C) the strength of tornadoes.

    (D) the magnitude of earthquakes.

    (E) the level of particulate matter in the atmosphere.

114. To which school of economic thought does the Laffer curve belong?

    (A) Monetarism

    (B) Supply-side economics

    (C) Capitalism

    (D) Keynesianism

    (E) Socialism

115. Why did the Founding Fathers create the Bill of Rights?

    (A) To ensure that the costs of the Revolutionary War would be repaid

    (B) To reassure the small states that their right to participate in the decision-making process would remain safe

    (C) Because the citizens had been accustomed to similar protection under British rule

    (D) To guarantee that individual liberties would be respected

    (E) To prevent the states from enacting their own individual bills

116. The strength of a research study is only as good as its ability to be replicated. What does this mean?

    (A) The scientific method requires duplicate studies before any results are accepted as fact.

    (B) If a study has significant results but cannot be done again with the same results, it is difficult to assess whether the results were due to error.

    (C) A good study is one that has predictable results.

    (D) If a study has significant results and is well documented throughout, it is not necessary to replicate the study.

    (E) If a study has insignificant results but it can be replicated, it is a good study.

GO ON TO THE NEXT PAGE ⇨

117. As the military and spiritual leader of the Sioux tribe, Sitting Bull

(A) advocated firm resistance to white encroachment and settlement.

(B) encouraged assimilation, even intermarriage, between the Sioux and the American settlers.

(C) never made peace with the U.S. Army, and as a result, the Sioux have no reservation today.

(D) was educated abroad and therefore unused to the nomadic lifestyle of his fellow tribespeople.

(E) sought conciliation with both the Cheyenne and Arapahoe tribes.

118. Frederick Law Olmsted was an American landscape architect prominent for designing many well-known urban parks. Which of the following is NOT one of his creations?

(A) Central Park

(B) Prospect Park

(C) Golden Gate Park

(D) Jackson Park at the World's Columbian Exposition

(E) Washington Park at the World's Columbian Exposition

119. What is the world's tallest waterfall?

(A) Victoria Falls

(B) Yellowstone Falls

(C) Niagara Falls

(D) Angel Falls

(E) Tugela Falls

120. The formation of OPEC led to

(A) lower domestic oil production.

(B) falling oil prices worldwide.

(C) a transfer of wealth from oil-consuming nations to oil-producing nations.

(D) less concentration in the domestic oil industry.

(E) government regulation of oil imports.

END OF TEST. STOP

ANSWER KEY

1. E	21. D	41. C	61. C	81. A	101. E
2. D	22. B	42. A	62. A	82. E	102. B
3. C	23. E	43. C	63. B	83. C	103. D
4. D	24. A	44. D	64. B	84. C	104. B
5. A	25. B	45. A	65. E	85. A	105. B
6. C	26. D	46. B	66. B	86. B	106. E
7. A	27. C	47. C	67. B	87. A	107. C
8. E	28. E	48. D	68. D	88. C	108. A
9. D	29. A	49. A	69. B	89. B	109. E
10. B	30. B	50. B	70. A	90. C	110. D
11. B	31. C	51. E	71. C	91. D	111. B
12. C	32. C	52. B	72. D	92. E	112. C
13. B	33. E	53. E	73. A	93. B	113. A
14. A	34. D	54. B	74. E	94. E	114. B
15. B	35. A	55. A	75. D	95. D	115. D
16. D	36. B	56. E	76. B	96. C	116. B
17. C	37. E	57. D	77. C	97. D	117. A
18. E	38. C	58. C	78. D	98. A	118. C
19. A	39. D	59. A	79. A	99. C	119. D
20. A	40. B	60. C	80. E	100. D	120. C

PRACTICE TEST 3 QUICK REFERENCE TABLES

Use the following tables to determine which topics you still need to review.

Topic	Test Question
History	
United States History	8, 12, 18, 25, 38, 39, 43, 48, 56, 63, 67, 68, 70, 74, 77, 83, 86, 90, 102, 117
Western Civilization	3, 10, 17, 20, 22, 28, 30, 31, 40, 45, 47, 62, 64, 91, 95, 100, 108, 112
World History	7, 19, 27, 51, 59, 60, 84, 104, 107, 120
Social Sciences	
Government/Political Science	1, 9, 11, 15, 32, 36, 46, 53, 57, 82, 92, 94, 106, 109, 111, 115
Geography	21, 29, 42, 49, 71, 73, 80, 87, 96, 98, 113, 118, 119
Economics	2, 13, 23, 33, 44, 54, 66, 78, 88, 89, 105, 114
Psychology	6, 16, 26, 37, 41, 52, 58, 61, 69, 85, 93, 101
Sociology	4, 14, 24, 35, 50, 65, 72, 75, 81, 99, 110, 116
Anthropology	5, 34, 55, 76, 79, 97, 103

Topic	Number of Questions on Test	Number Correct
History	48	
United States History	20	
Western Civilization	18	
World History	10	
Social Sciences	72	
Government/Political Science	16	
Geography	13	
Economics	12	
Psychology	12	
Sociology	12	
Anthropology	7	

Answers and Explanations

1. (E)

The Articles of Confederation were an attempt to craft an agreement by which the newly independent nation could function. There were many things the new federal government could not do, but it could declare war.

2. (D)

The GDP is the total market value of goods and services produced by a country's economy within the borders of that country. The GNP is the GDP plus foreign investment and foreign trade.

3. (C)

Athens and Sparta fought the Peloponnesian Wars over the time period 431–404 B.C.E. Eventually, Sparta emerged victorious, but the extended conflict weakened both city-states grievously.

4. (D)

Both socialization and enculturation refer to lifelong processes by which cultural and social identity are learned or passed down to an individual: values, norms, mores, and conformity are all learned. Answer (D) is correct since genetic makeup is determined at birth and cannot be taught.

5. (A)

The key to this question is breaking down the term *bipedalism*: *bi* means two, *ped* means foot. If you don't know this, you can see that two of the five choices have to do with gait, while four describe characteristics of modern humans. Answer (A) combines these ideas.

6. (C)

For Freud, the goal of psychotherapy was to make the unconscious conscious, so answer (B) is not Jung's idea. All of the other answer choices are sound-alike distracters.

7. (A)

Though answer (E) may have contributed to poor relations today, the best answer is (A). When the nation of Israel was created in 1948, already strained Arab-Jewish relations became dramatically worse.

8. (E)

Custer's Seventh Calvary was sent on a mission to help force roaming bands of Sioux and Cheyenne Indians back to their reservation, part of which had been repossessed by President Grant. Spying a large encampment, Custer tried to surprise them, but his troops were overwhelmed. Custer became a hero to some and a symbol of white oppression of the Indians to others.

9. (D)

Africa has the greatest number of countries. There are 53, of which 6 are islands.

10. (B)

Charles de Gaulle may have saved France when he addressed the nation from London in June 1940. He rallied his countrymen, assuring them they were not alone in their fight against the Nazis. De Gaulle formed the Free France movement and fought with the French and the British to liberate France. He was later elected president of France.

11. (B)

Article I, Section 7 of the Constitution states that all bills for raising revenue must originate in the House of Representatives. Answer (A) is incorrect, since neither house has absolute authority over the media, and both houses must approve Supreme Court nominees (D).

12. (C)

The "Crescent City" in question refers to New Orleans, and the question is asking about Andrew Jackson's victory in the Battle of New Orleans. Answers (B) and (E) are French names meant to confuse you.

13. (B)

The effect of an increase in the price of I on the price of G will depend upon the dependence of G on I. If there is a significant amount of I involved in the production of G, then the manufacturer will have to continue to use it, and the manufacturer pass the increase in price along to the customers. Answers (A) and (C) describe scenarios where G does not depend on I, so G probably can be produced without the more expensive input.

14. (A)

The term *folkways* is used to describe the cultural output (often material) of a particular group, such as woven baskets or headdresses, as well as traditional customs in dance and song. Only answer (A) is incorrect; accent is not a result of custom but rather of geography, class, or linguistics.

15. (B)

Neither the Federalists nor the Anti-Federalists addressed the right of women to vote, as it was not an issue at the time and would not become one for a century.

16. (D)

While personality may not seem to be a stable set of individual characteristics, psychologists believe that our patterns of thought, feelings, and behaviors are consistent throughout our lives. Genetic makeup (C) and genotype (E) are biological terms, not psychological terms.

17. (C)

Tacitus, Herodotus, Julius Caesar, and Suetonius were all avid writers who recorded ancient historical events. Attila could not read or write.

18. (E)

Lyndon Baines Johnson (B) was president during the Vietnam conflict, but he preceded Nixon. Robert F. Kennedy (C) was assassinated in 1968.

19. (A)

The Romanov dynasty ruled Russia from 1613 until 1917, when the royal family was executed by the Bolsheviks. Tolstoy (B) was the famous Russian author of *War and Peace*.

20. (A)

The Roman empire eventually collapsed under the weight of its own ineptitude and corruption; at the same time it was being battered from the outside by barbarian invasions. The papacy was not a factor.

21. (D)

El Niño is a regularly occurring climatic feature in which warm water moves back and forth across the Pacific ocean. The warmer water temperatures affect rainfall and temperature around the world.

22. (B)

Delphi was a shrine erected near a sacred stream and was considered to be the navel of the world. People traveled from all around Greece to hear the oracle Pythia, Apollo's priestess, tell prophecies about their future. Appropriately, Apollo was the god of light and truth, among other things.

23. (E)

Oligopoly exists when there are only a few sellers in a market. It typically occurs in industries where there are significant barriers to entry (such as high start-up costs).

24. (A)

Answers (B) and (E) should suggest that (A), (B), or (E), is the answer. Test writers often simply add a prefix (like *neo-*) or another word to the correct answer to create distracters. Positivism holds that adhering to the scientific method is the best way to conduct social research.

25. (B)

In 1985 Ronald Reagan quoted a Clint Eastwood movie when he spoke these words.

26. (D)

If you have heard of obsessive-compulsive disorder, the right answer will be clear. The incorrect answer choices employ other familiar-sounding terms from pop psychology.

27. (C)

From 1976 to 1983, thousands of political opponents of the Argentine government simply disappeared in the middle of the night. Many were tortured and eventually killed.

28. (E)

The Great Schism, which lasted from 1378 to 1417, was ended by the Council of Constance (1414–1418), more than a century after the Council of Nicea.

29. (A)

Tsunamis are huge waves caused by earthquakes on the ocean floor, sometimes powerful enough to cause damage hundreds of miles away. Since tornados never form over water, answer (D) can be eliminated.

30. (B)

Answers (A) and (E) both refer to feudalism, the medieval socioeconomic system. The proletariat is the working class in Marxist theory, so (D) is also wrong.

31. (C)

The Church did not take a position on feudalism. All of the other answer choices are logical contributing factors to the decline of feudalism.

32. (C)

Since every American can plead the Fifth Amendment in a court of law, answer (A) is incorrect. Impeachment powers (B) reside in Congress, not in the executive branch; in addition, the keyword *exclusively* should indicate a potential wrong answer.

33. (E)

Those economists favoring fiscal policy (changes in taxation and government spending) over monetary policy (enacted by the Federal Reserve) believe that it can be more precisely targeted at those sectors of the economy in need of intervention.

34. (D)

Answer choice (A) contains the absolute word *only*, and can probably be eliminated. Answer (E) is designed to confuse you—a "traditional display" has nothing to do with a "style of movement."

35. (A)

Marxism is a theory of social conflict, which is a subject for study by sociologists. Fascism (B), monarchy (C), and anarchy (E) are all political subjects. Monopoly (D) is an economic concern.

36. (B)

Federalism refers to the system of dividing power between a central government and regional governments. The division of powers is spelled out in a constitution or other document.

37. (E)

Elizabeth Kübler-Ross is a sociologist known for her pioneering work on death, dying, and the aging process. Margaret Mead is an anthropologist known for her research on adolescent girls (D), and Jean Piaget (A) is a famous developmental psychologist.

38. (C)

World War I lasted from 1914 to 1918. The Japanese did not bomb Pearl Harbor until 1941, and that attack led the United States to enter World War II.

39. (D)

Wild Bill Hickock represents one of the earliest commercial pop cultural icons in American history. Hickock starred as "Wild Bill" in the play *Scouts of the Prairies* and toured throughout America and Europe with Buffalo Bill Cody's Wild West Show in 1872–1873.

40. (B)

Japan was an imperial monarchy (A) before World War II, but the emperor did not play a fundamental role in governing Japan. Before the war, women did not have the right to vote. When the United States defeated Japan, it became a role model for that country, as the Japanese sought to achieve a similar level of economic prosperity.

41. (C)

Cooley's three steps are as follows: 1) we imagine how we look to others; 2) we interpret other's reactions; and 3) we develop a self-concept. Comparison and constant adjustment are not steps in this process, so all the other choices can be eliminated.

42. (A)

The doldrums, also known as equatorial belts of calm, are areas slightly north and south of the equator characterized by warm moist air as well as various forms of severe weather. The doldrums are also known for calms, periods when the winds die down altogether, leaving ships stranded.

43. (C)

Answer (A) can be eliminated because the Declaration of Independence was signed in 1776, and (E) is incorrect because the Boston Tea Party happened in 1773. The Underground Railroad (D) was not in place until the following century.

44. (D)

Real interest rates take into account the effect of inflation on the rate of return the investor will receive. The word *real* used in economics always indicates that the effect of inflation has been considered.

45. (A)

Answers (B) through (E) are all accurate characterizations of the balance of imperial power in Europe after 1588. Spanish was never the most commonly spoken language on the Continent.

46. (B)

Gerrymandering is the process of drawing legislative districts in such a way as to either minimize or maximize the voting strength of a particular group. It is done to benefit the political party that is drawing the districts. It gets its name from Eldridge Gerry, governor of Massachusetts from 1810 to 1812.

47. (C)

The Elgin Marbles, named for the Earl of Elgin who brought them from Greece to England in 1806, are a series of sculptures from the Parthenon in Athens. The Greek government contends that they were illegally sold to Lord Elgin and wants them back.

48. (D)

From 1732 to 1757, Benjamin Franklin published *Poor Richard's Almanac*—an encyclopedic text containing weather predictions, proverbs, and epigrams, which sold nearly 10,000 copies per year.

49. (A)

The "Forbidden City" is in Beijing. It was built between 1406 and 1420 during the Ming dynasty, and it was the home of emperors of China until the end of the Qing dynasty in 1924.

50. (B)

A demographic is a statistic characterizing human populations, or segments of populations broken down by things like age, gender, or income. Demographic studies are quantitative—they can be measured in numbers. In answer (B), the phrase "perceived quality of life" indicates a study of qualitative rather than quantitative factors.

51. (E)

The eruption of Mt. Pinatubo in the Philippines in 1991 was one of the twentieth century's most devastating volcanic events. The environmental consequences of the Mt. Pinatubo eruption were far reaching and long lasting. The city famously preserved by a volcanic eruption was Pompeii, which fell victim to the eruption of Mt. Vesuvius in 79 C.E.

52. (B)

Sigmund Freud created the concept of the id, the ego, and the superego as the driving structure of the personality, as well as ideas about ego defense mechanisms like denial and projection. Answers (D) and (E) are distracters that sound like Freudian terms.

53. (E)

The key to this question is the pre–Civil War date, 1857. The ruling probably did not go in favor of African Americans, so (C) can be immediately ruled out, as can (D).

54. (B)

An increase in the money supply typically causes lower interest rates, leading to additional investment by business, increased employment, and greater economic output.

55. (A)

Thermoluminescence is used on archaeological artifacts. The technique measures the amount of light emitted by electrons as heat forces them out of pockets in a crystal and converts that measurement into an age. The other answer choices all employ scientific-sounding language, but don't make sense upon closer reading.

56. (E)

This question is designed to test your understanding of the socioeconomic characteristics of the North and South. Often, drawing a chart can simplify this type of question: write "North" in one column and "South" in a second column and place the appropriate traits underneath. Answers (A), (B), (C), and (D) are all false statements.

57. (D)

The Libertarian Party advocates the least possible amount of interference by government. Environmentalism is the primary platform of the Green Party (B). Both the Communist (E) and Socialist (A) Parties advocate a strong central government.

58. (C)

Watch out for terms like *should be* in answers (A) and (B) that express opinion instead of fact. In answers (D) and (E), words like *never* and *rigid* are warning signs of potential wrong answers. The more ambiguous and nuanced statement, answer (C), is the right choice.

59. (A)

The Salic law required that only male descendants of the king inherit the throne. The desire for a male heir was one of many factors considered by the French monarchy when negotiating for a bride or when discarding a wife who had failed to produce the desired heir.

60. (C)

Buddhists seek to find the Middle Way in life, avoiding extremism in all forms. One way they seek to do this is through meditation.

61. (C)

This psychology question can be deciphered even if you've never heard the term *inappropriate affect*: expressing contradictory behavior when describing or experiencing an emotion. A careful reading of the answer choices reveals that answer (C) is out of place.

62. (A)

Prior to 1870, both Italy and Germany were made up of several smaller kingdoms sharing similar cultures. Both groups realized that to be taken seriously by the rest of Europe, they would need to unite into larger nations.

63. (B)

African-American men were granted the right to vote in 1868, well before women of any color, so (A) is incorrect.

64. (B)

Henry the Navigator, a prince of Portugal who lived 1394–1460, was among the first to see the value of exploring beyond the known world. He founded a center for cartography and sponsored ocean expeditions.

65. (E)

This question draws on sociology, political science, and Western civilization, among other topics. The key to the answer lies in the Enlightenment idea of individualism and free will; because of this new emphasis on the individual's capacity for reason, new disciplines like sociology were born.

66. (B)

If there are many sellers and few buyers for a product, a seller cannot raise prices without losing market share.

67. (B)

The hysteria surrounding the Salem witch trials that swept rapidly through Puritan Massachusetts ended almost as suddenly as it had begun.

68. (D)

First proposed in the 1980s, the Strategic Defense Initiative was a plan to shoot incoming missiles out of the sky while they were too far away to damage the United States. It would have made Soviet missiles useless. The plan forced the Soviet Union to spend huge amounts of money to find a way to neutralize the S.D.I. The aging Soviet economy could not support this expense, and the government was forced to cut subsidies to satellite nations. The communist governments in those nations were unable to hold on to power, and in 1991, the Soviet Union itself collapsed.

69. (B)

There is no evidence to suggest that disease is preventable as a result of grooming behaviors, so (A) is incorrect. Additionally, among primates this is not a gender-specific behavior, so answer (C) can also be eliminated.

70. (A)

The "One-Drop" construct (C) refers to a slavery-era idea about racial classification, so (C) is incorrect. Similarly, the notion of "original sin" (E) predates the Puritans by centuries.

71. (C)

The kingdom of Nubia now lies within the borders of Egypt and Sudan. Modern inhabitants of southern Egypt and northern Sudan still speak the Nubian language.

72. (D)

Cultural relativism is a critical perspective that takes the uniqueness of a subject into consideration, whereas an ethnocentric approach looks at a subject through one's own cultural lens. Marxism and socialism are closely related, so (A) can be immediately eliminated.

73. (A)

Japan is a nation of over 2,000 islands. The four major islands are Hokkaido, Honshu, Kyushu, and Shikoku. Nagasaki is the Japanese city where the second atomic bomb was dropped by the United States in World War II.

74. (E)

Essayist and pamphleteer Thomas Paine (1737–1809) also wrote *Common Sense* in 1776—a strong defense of American independence from England.

75. (D)

This psychology question addresses the concepts of introversion and extroversion. These are familiar concepts to most test takers—don't just choose an answer because it sounds more formal, as with (B), (C), and (E).

76. (B)

In 1799, a French soldier in Napoleon's army was working at a fort on the Rosetta branch of the Nile River. He discovered a stone slab with carved inscriptions that would unlock the mystery of hieroglyphics years later. French linguist Jean-François Champollion would use these inscriptions to translate the ancient writing.

77. (C)

Many colonists came to the New World for the express purpose of practicing their religion free from government interference. This makes it easy to rule out both answers (A) and (B).

78. (D)

In 1944, delegates from 45 nations met at Bretton Woods, New Hampshire, to discuss the postwar recovery in Europe, as well as other issues. Some of the outcomes were a system of fixed exchange rates and the establishment of the International Monetary Fund and the World Bank.

79. (A)

Answers (B) through (E) are all social anthropological concerns. Psychologists would be most likely to study intelligence and its measurement (A).

80. (E)

All of the factors listed contribute to the deforestation of the Amazon—the world's largest tropical rainforest, home to the greatest variety of plants and animals on Earth.

81. (A)

The experimental method uses observation and theory to prove or disprove a hypothesis.

82. (E)

The United Nations was established in 1945 to replace the League of Nations, which had been unable to maintain peace in the world. To do this, the United Nations is authorized to send troops into areas of instability. The League had no such authority.

83. (C)

The Jazz Age does encompass the Harlem Renaissance but refers to a much broader movement that crossed racial barriers, so (A) is incorrect.

84. (C)

The *Book of the Dead* is a collection of ancient Egyptian hieroglyphic texts that explain funeral customs and the proper spells to send the dead on a successful journey to the afterlife. The earliest collection dates from approximately 1500 B.C.E.

85. (A)

To reach the correct answer here, eliminate the choices that don't make sense. Each incorrect choice contains deliberately confusing language. Answer (C) can be ruled out, as the phrase "domineering mother figure" is really a matter of opinion, not fact. Terms like "pair-bond" and "primary reinforcer" in answer (D) refer to psychological concepts but have nothing to do with "learned helplessness."

86. (B)

Nicola Sacco and Bartolomeo Vanzetti were two poor Italian immigrants (who happened to be anarchists). They were found guilty of attempted robbery and attempted murder with very little evidence of either crime.

87. (A)

The Dead Sea has its name because no plants or animals can live in it due to high concentrations of minerals.

88. (C)

John Maynard Keynes (1883–1946) is one of the most important figures in the history of economics. He revolutionized the field with his classic book *The General Theory of Employment, Interest and Money* in 1936. Prior to Keynes, it was considered best to let the business cycle run its course—the length and severity of the Great Depression led him to question whether governments ought to step in and attempt to restore a nation to prosperity.

89. (B)

In a free economy, individuals may choose to leave a job in search of other opportunities. This is called frictional unemployment, and it may actually rise when the economy is prospering because job seekers perceive their chances of finding a better job than the one they have to be greater at that time.

90. (C)

Dorothy Parker (D) was an American writer of the 1920s, and Gloria Steinem (E) was part of the 1970s feminist movement.

91. (D)

Charlemagne established a central government over western Europe, restoring much of the unity of the old Roman empire and paving the way for the development of modern Europe.

92. (E)

In 1992, the Twenty-seventh Amendment to the Constitution was adopted. This law prohibits Congress from recklessly raising its own pay by requiring that no pay raises take effect until after the next election.

93. (B)

The phrases "destructive personality types" in answer (D) and "unacceptable responses" in (E) are both subjective terms, indicating that both choices probably are incorrect.

94. (E)

Article III, Section 3 of the Constitution defines treason as levying war against the United States or adhering to or giving aid and comfort to the enemy.

95. (D)

Herodotus wrote *The Histories* about the Greco-Persian Wars in the fifth century B.C.E. Livy (B) and Tacitus (C) were both Roman historians. Aeschylus (E) is famous for his tragedies.

96. (C)

Iran was known to Europeans as Persia until 1935, when the Persian ambassador to Nazi Germany suggested a name change to celebrate the country's Aryan heritage.

97. (D)

The Latin term *in situ* loosely means "on-site." It has nothing to do with "sea level" or "ecosystem."

98. (A)

It is likely that continental islands were once part of the continent with which they share plant and animal species.

99. (C)

Antonio Gramsci (1891–1937) was an Italian revolutionary, socialist, and political theorist. Gramsci developed the concept of hegemony in response to the rise of fascism in the late 1920s and 1930s and the failure of the socialist experiment—he was puzzled by the fact that the working class did not uniformly resist.

100. (D)

Although Napoleon was certainly motivated by dreams of personal glory, his primary goal was to cut off British access to their richest possession, India.

101. (E)

R.E.M. or rapid eye movement is the sleeping state in which all dreams occur, so (A) is incorrect. Answer (B) is a distracter that sounds like the real answer.

102. (B)

Answer (A) can be ruled out since the concept of "Manifest Destiny" has not been refuted. The phrases "popular mythologies" and "unbridled westward expansion" are subjective statements of opinion, so (D) is incorrect. Similarly, "long-exploited" in answer (E) is the sort of value judgment that typically indicates a wrong answer.

103. (D)

Although they are biblical references, Eden, Adam, and Eve all stand for ideas about human origins. The clues in this question are the location and the fact that the possibility of a common female ancestor is mentioned.

104. (B)

Alexander the Great (356–323 B.C.E.) led an extraordinary life, but the pyramids were built thousands of years before he was born.

105. (B)

This phrase was adopted by the well-known economist Milton Friedman to make the point that there is a cost to providing all goods and services. If the consumer of those goods does not pay, then the cost will be borne by others.

106. (E)

The exclusionary rule, which states that illegally obtained evidence may not be used against an individual, is derived from the Fourth Amendment, which protects against unreasonable search and seizure.

107. (C)

The Boers were a group of Dutch settlers in South Africa. They arrived between the years 1652 and 1795 during the course of trade by the Dutch East India Company. These people were repeatedly driven further inland by British settlers and finally defeated in the Boer War of 1899–1902. *Boer* is the Dutch word for "farmer."

108. (A)

Antigone was written by Sophocles, *Medea* by Euripides, *The Oresteia* by Aeschylus, and *The Frogs* by Aristophanes.

109. (E)

James Madison is considered to be the Father of the Constitution because he was the best-prepared delegate to the Constitutional Convention, took many notes on the proceedings, and wrote a number of the *Federalist Papers* in support of the Constitution.

110. (D)

The people of Iceland share an ethnicity and language. The United States and Australia are home to citizens of many different ethnicities, and in Switzerland and India, multiple languages are spoken.

111. (B)

The Federal Deposit Insurance Corporation was formed in 1933 to regulate the solvency of commercial banks and to insure consumers' deposits in the event that a bank failed.

112. (C)

Lech Walesa was a Polish shipyard worker who led the trade union movement that eventually led to the end of totalitarianism in Poland, a former member of the Soviet bloc. He won the 1983 Nobel Peace Prize and was elected president of Poland in 1990.

113. (A)

The Saffir-Simpson scale to measure hurricane strength was developed in 1969 by civil engineer Herbert Saffir and National Hurricane Center director Bob Simpson.

114. (B)

Economist Arthur Laffer theorized that at certain high levels of taxation, actual output would fall short of potential output because of the disincentives created by excessive rates of taxation. He postulated that as tax rates were lowered, revenues to the government would actually rise, because there would be less incentive to avoid paying taxes. The name comes from the emphasis on the supply side of the economy.

115. (D)

The Bill of Rights was included to reassure citizens that their individual liberties would be protected from the abuses they had suffered under colonial rule. These assurances were essential before delegates agreed to approve the new Constitution.

116. (B)

Replication is critical in determining the strength or weakness of a hypothesis.

117. (A)

Sitting Bull (1831–1890) was vehemently opposed to assimilation and would never have tolerated intermarriage, so (B) is incorrect. However, the Sioux chief did make peace with the U.S. Army in 1868 in exchange for a sizable reservation free of white settlers. Therefore, answer (C) is incorrect.

118. (C)

Frederick Law Olmsted was fascinated with nature from the time of his youth and was known for his designs in the accidental, naturalistic style of the British landscape garden. William Hammond Hall, the designer of the Golden Gate Park (C), spurned Olmsted's suggestion that San Francisco would be best served by a greenbelt plan instead of a central area like Central Park. Both parks were part of a social reform movement in America to encourage healthy, orderly communities through green space.

119. (D)

Angel Falls, in the Guayana highland region of Venezuela, plunges off the side of a flat-topped mountain, free-falling 2,421 feet. In total, Angel Falls is 2,937 feet high.

120. (C)

When OPEC was formed in 1973 (by Iran, Iraq, Kuwait, Saudi Arabia, and Venezuela), the days of low oil prices ended. Prior to 1973, oil was priced based on how much it cost to produce, which in OPEC countries was virtually nothing.

The CLEP Natural Sciences Exam

Chapter Twenty: **Practice Test 1: Diagnostic**

Time—90 minutes
120 Questions

Directions: Each question below has five lettered answer choices. For each question or phrase, choose the most closely related answer. For multiple questions that refer to the same group of lettered answer choices, each choice can be used more than once, once, or not at all.

Questions 1–3

    (A) DNA

    (B) Mitochondrion

    (C) Vacuole

    (D) Plasma membrane

    (E) Cell wall

1. Not found in a prokaryotic cell

2. Not found in an animal cell

3. Storage organelle

Questions 4–6

    (A) Apomorphy

    (B) Homologous

    (C) Analogous

    (D) Homoplasy

    (E) Adaptation

4. Similar features that share a common evolutionary origin such as the wings of a bat and the flippers of a whale

5. A novel feature that was derived over evolutionary time

6. A feature that provides a selective advantage to an organism

Questions 7–8

    (A) Active transport

    (B) Diffusion

    (C) Facilitated diffusion

    (D) Osmosis

    (E) Concentration gradient

7. Term for chemical substances passing through a membrane with the expenditure of energy

8. A special term for the simple diffusion of water across a selectively permeable membrane

GO ON TO THE NEXT PAGE →

Questions 9–10

Human Heart

9. Left ventricle

10. Right atrium

Questions 11–13

    (A) Phloem
    (B) Xylem
    (C) Roots
    (D) Stomata
    (E) Tracheids

11. Has its transport interrupted by cavitation.

12. Transports food from sources to sinks.

13. Regulate transpiration by opening or closing.

Questions 14–16

(A) $H-C\equiv C-H$

(B) $\left[\begin{array}{c} H \\ | \\ H-N-H \\ | \\ H \end{array}\right]^{+}$

(C) $H-\overset{\overset{\displaystyle H}{|}}{C}=\overset{\overset{\displaystyle H}{|}}{C}-H$

(D) $H-\overset{\overset{\displaystyle H}{|}}{\underset{\underset{\displaystyle H}{|}}{C}}-H$

(E) CH_3-CH_2-OH

14. Ethanol

15. Methane

16. An ion

GO ON TO THE NEXT PAGE

Directions: For each of the following questions or incomplete statements, select the best answer or completion from the five options given.

17. In natural selection, "fitness" is the ability of organisms to survive and reproduce successfully. At which of the following levels does natural selection act?

    (A) Species
    (B) Community
    (C) Ecosystem
    (D) Individual
    (E) Population

18. A number of populations of different species in a given habitat represent a(n)

    (A) biosphere.
    (B) biome.
    (C) ecosystem.
    (D) community.
    (E) population.

19. Many species are capable of exponential (ever-increasing) population growth rates. In reality, which of the following organisms exhibit this pattern?

    (A) Humans
    (B) Rabbits
    (C) Ants
    (D) Algae
    (E) Grasshoppers

20. The mass number of an atom is derived from which of the following?

    (A) The number of protons
    (B) The number of neutrons
    (C) The number of protons plus electrons
    (D) The number of neutrons plus electrons
    (E) The number of protons plus neutrons

21. Which of the following is TRUE of an atom having 12 protons and 12 electrons?

    (A) It has a net positive charge.
    (B) It has an atomic number of 24.
    (C) It has a neutral charge.
    (D) It has a mass number of 24.
    (E) It has a net negative charge.

5	6	7
B	**C**	**N**
10	12	14

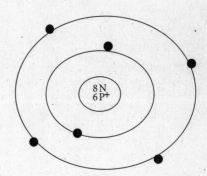

22. Based on the information from the periodic table entries, which of the following is TRUE of the atom shown?

    (A) It represents boron.
    (B) Since it has two more neutrons than the carbon shown in the box, it must be nitrogen N.
    (C) It cannot be carbon because the mass numbers are different.
    (D) It is carbon but must be synthesized in the lab.
    (E) It is a carbon isotope because the atomic numbers are identical.

GO ON TO THE NEXT PAGE ⟩

KAPLAN

Questions 23–25 refer to the following diagram, which represents equal volumes of water being heated in two beakers of differing shape on a laboratory hot plate.

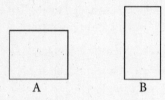

23. Which processes are involved in heating the water in these beakers?

    I.   Conduction
    II. Convection
    III. Radiation

    (A) I only
    (B) II only
    (C) III only
    (D) I and II only
    (E) I, II, and III

24. Between the contents of beakers A and B, which will increase in temperature faster and why?

    (A) A, because there is less water to heat.
    (B) B, because the container shape will make convection more efficient.
    (C) They will heat at the same rate.
    (D) A, because there is a greater surface area for conduction.
    (E) There is no way to tell for sure with the information provided.

25. Which hypothesis could beakers A and B potentially test?

    (A) The shape of the container holding water has an effect on its heating rate.
    (B) Laboratory hot plates differ in heat efficiency.
    (C) Water heats at a faster rate than milk.
    (D) Heating rates of water are affected by the volume of water.
    (E) None of these could be tested.

GO ON TO THE NEXT PAGE

26. According to the diagram shown here, which of the following stars would have the highest surface temperature but lowest luminosity?

    (A) Supergiants

    (B) Pulsars

    (C) White dwarfs

    (D) Giants

    (E) Main sequence stars

27. Which of the following is NOT true of a black hole?

    (A) It is formed by the collapse of a very massive star.

    (B) Its gravity can pull in light.

    (C) It requires a highly specialized form of telescope to view from Earth.

    (D) It can warp space-time.

    (E) It cannot be viewed directly.

28. What discovery did Edwin Hubble make that supports the big bang theory?

    (A) Background radiation from the big bang can still be detected.

    (B) The existence of quasars

    (C) Objects in the universe are moving away from each other.

    (D) The existence of the asteroid belt

    (E) The existence of black holes

GO ON TO THE NEXT PAGE

KAPLAN

29. The force that moves the plates that make up the Earth's crust arises from

    (A) volcanic activity in the crust.

    (B) convection currents in the mantle.

    (C) centripetal force from the rotation of the Earth.

    (D) tectonic activity in the crust.

    (E) the magnetic field generated by the rotating Earth.

30. Most earthquakes and volcanoes occur

    (A) near the center of the continental plates where the mantle temperatures are greater.

    (B) in young mountain ranges.

    (C) at the equator.

    (D) at the boundary of two moving continental plates.

    (E) at or near the poles.

31. The boundary between two plates shown here would most likely result in

    (A) mountains.

    (B) earthquakes.

    (C) volcanoes.

    (D) none of the above.

    (E) (A), (B), and (C).

GO ON TO THE NEXT PAGE

Illinois Glaciation: Before and After

32. The diagram shows the most recent glacial advance in Illinois. What is probably the main difference in soils between region A and region B today?

(A) A is a much poorer soil.

(B) B is a flat and poorly drained soil.

(C) A has shallower topsoil.

(D) A has a much younger and richer soil.

(E) B has much older soil with more organic matter and nutrients.

33. Which of the following scientists provided the foundation for our current method of classification of organisms using binomial nomenclature?

(A) Charles Lyell (1797–1875)

(B) Charles Darwin (1809–1882)

(C) Carolus Linnaeus (1707–1778)

(D) Aristotle (384–322 B.C.E.)

(E) Gregor Mendel (1822–1884)

34. All of the following contribute to variation in the genetic code EXCEPT

(A) mutation.

(B) cloning.

(C) recombination.

(D) crossover.

(E) sexual reproduction.

35. Darwin used evidence from all of the following sources to construct his theory of evolution due to natural selection EXCEPT

(A) embryology.

(B) comparative anatomy.

(C) genetics.

(D) selective breeding.

(E) population biology.

Questions 36–37 refer to the following figure of a theoretical cladogram.

36. Which of the following statements can be correctly inferred from the cladogram?

(A) Taxon A is an extinct animal.

(B) Taxon C is a mammal.

(C) Taxon D evolved from taxon C.

(D) Together, taxon E and *Homo sapiens* form a monophyletic group.

(E) *Homo sapiens* is the most advanced organism.

37. If taxon C is known to be a species of fish, which of the following statements must also be TRUE?

(A) Taxon D and taxon E must also be fish.

(B) Taxon A and taxon B must also be fish.

(C) Taxon B must be an amphibian.

(D) Taxon D and taxon E must be vertebrates.

(E) Taxon A and taxon B must be vertebrates.

GO ON TO THE NEXT PAGE

KAPLAN

38. Which of the following statements describes the "Cambrian Explosion"?

    (A) It is the point in time when the universe came into being.

    (B) It is the period in evolutionary history when most of the major groups of animals appeared on Earth.

    (C) It is the period in evolutionary history when human impact caused the first great artificial extinction event.

    (D) It is the point in scientific history when the discovery of DNA led to an understanding of how molecular genetics contributes to evolutionary theory.

    (E) Indicated by the iridium layer, it marks the time when the "Age of Dinosaurs" ended due to a natural mass extinction event.

39. Which of the following correctly lists the chronological order of the cell cycle?

    (A) Interphase-Prophase-Metaphase-Anaphase-Telophase-Cytokinesis

    (B) Interphase-Anaphase-Prophase-Metaphase-Telophase-Cytokinesis

    (C) Prophase-Anaphase-Metaphase-Telophase-Interphase-Cytokinesis

    (D) Prophase-Interphase-Metaphase-Telophase-Anaphase-Cytokinesis

    (E) Interphase-Telophase-Metaphase-Anaphase-Cytokinesis-Prophase

40. What is the net energy yield from a molecule of glucose that is metabolized in the presence of oxygen?

    (A) 34 ATP

    (B) 2 ATP

    (C) 40 ATP

    (D) 4 ATP

    (E) 36 ATP

41. Which of the following groups of organisms represents the greatest fraction of the Earth's biodiversity?

    (A) Insecta

    (B) Mammalia

    (C) Annelida

    (D) Aves

    (E) Reptilia

42. Assuming Mendel's laws of inheritance are met, the ratio of phenotypes in a standard dihybrid cross will be

    (A) 3:1

    (B) 5:3:2:1

    (C) 1:1

    (D) 2:1

    (E) 9:3:3:1

43. The self-replicating molecules that were the possible precursors to life on Earth include

    (A) glucose polymers.

    (B) adenosine triphosphate.

    (C) amino acids.

    (D) nucleotides.

    (E) proteins.

44. The primary form of energy storage in plants is

    (A) simple sugars.

    (B) complex carbohydrates.

    (C) amino acids.

    (D) proteins.

    (E) triglycerides.

GO ON TO THE NEXT PAGE ⇒

45. Ribosomes are important cellular organelles involved in the production of

    (A) RNA.
    (B) DNA.
    (C) cellulose.
    (D) protein.
    (E) plasma membranes.

46. Which of the following contributes significantly to the compact tertiary structure of DNA?

    (A) Histones
    (B) Nuclear membrane
    (C) Ribosomes
    (D) mRNA
    (E) tRNA

47. Gluconeogenesis describes the process of

    (A) synthesizing glycogen from glucose molecules.
    (B) metabolizing glycogen into glucose molecules.
    (C) synthesizing glucose from noncarbohydrate sources.
    (D) synthesizing lipids from glucose molecules.
    (E) metabolizing glucose to liberate energy for protein synthesis.

48. Meiosis is crucial for gametogenesis and sexual reproduction because it

    (A) produces very small gametes that are easily transported.
    (B) reduces the number of chromosomes from 2N to N.
    (C) creates the X and Y chromosomes that determine gender.
    (D) requires less energy than mitosis.
    (E) occurs in the early stages of development.

49. All of the following are parts of a flower EXCEPT

    (A) petal.
    (B) stamen.
    (C) sepal.
    (D) petiole.
    (E) anther.

50. The countercurrent exchange system is used to enhance the exchange of substrate between two oppositely directed flows of fluid. Which of the following systems employs a countercurrent exchange?

    (A) Human circulation
    (B) Bird gas exchange
    (C) Amoeba food uptake
    (D) Barnacle filtering
    (E) Spider web spinning

51. A sex-linked gene is one that has a locus

    (A) close to the promoter region of another gene.
    (B) on the same chromosome as another gene.
    (C) on the Y chromosome.
    (D) on the X chromosome.
    (E) on either the X or Y chromosome.

52. Which part of the human body produces insulin?

    (A) Liver
    (B) Spleen
    (C) Pancreas
    (D) Kidney
    (E) Brain

GO ON TO THE NEXT PAGE

KAPLAN

53. All of the following are true about protostome development EXCEPT

    (A) they have indeterminate cleavage.

    (B) they have holoblastic cleavage.

    (C) they have spiral cleavage.

    (D) they have holoblastic determinate cleavage.

    (E) the blastopore becomes the mouth.

54. Which of the following is a neurotransmitter eliciting a depolarization of skeletal muscle tissue, causing a contraction?

    (A) Serotonin

    (B) Dopamine

    (C) Acetylcholine

    (D) Calcium

    (E) Histamine

55. A scientific hypothesis advances to the status of a theory after it

    (A) has been published in a scientific journal.

    (B) has been approved by a scientific committee.

    (C) has been discussed among the scientific community for several years.

    (D) has been modified by a subsequent scientist.

    (E) has been supported by a significant amount of research.

56. All of the following are modes of pollination EXCEPT

    (A) wind.

    (B) water.

    (C) insects.

    (D) birds.

    (E) roots.

57. The main function of the small intestine is to absorb nutrients that are released during the digestion of ingested food. What is the main function of the large intestine?

    (A) Storage of waste material

    (B) Reclamation of water from the lumen

    (C) Storage of water

    (D) Concentration of urine

    (E) Production of digestive enzymes

58. Which of the following is NOT one of the lobes of the human brain?

    (A) Parietal

    (B) Temporal

    (C) Occipital

    (D) Corpus callosum

    (E) Frontal

59. Skeletal muscle provides the force for flexing and extending joints. How does smooth muscle function in animal bodies?

    (A) Smooth muscle provides regulatory functions such as peristalsis.

    (B) Smooth muscle has endurance for long-term flight.

    (C) Smooth muscle squeezes cells and aids in transport across cell membranes.

    (D) Smooth muscle keeps joints rigid during sleep.

    (E) Smooth muscle is located in jaw muscles for chewing tough fibers.

GO ON TO THE NEXT PAGE ⟹

60. Desert-dwelling animals have several adaptations that equip them for survival in arid environments. All of the following are some adaptations of desert plants and animals EXCEPT

    (A) waxy cuticle on leaves to prevent water loss.

    (B) structures with large surface area for dissipating heat.

    (C) moist, water-permeable skin to increase evaporative cooling.

    (D) extremely efficient kidneys that relieve the need to drink water.

    (E) the ability to produce water internally through metabolism.

61. Which of the following diseases is inherited genetically from one or both of the parents?

    (A) Tay-Sachs

    (B) Emphysema

    (C) AIDS

    (D) Cirrhosis

    (E) Hepatitis

62. Animals store calories in their bodies in the form of fat, but animals also will catabolize large amounts of glycogen during periods of low activity to make blood sugar available if needed in the future. Where is this glycogen stored?

    (A) Brain

    (B) Muscles and liver

    (C) Blood

    (D) Below the skin

    (E) Bone marrow

63. Holometabolous insects undergo complete metamorphosis. This means that they

    (A) emerge directly from eggs as adults.

    (B) have no periods of hibernation as they develop.

    (C) grow completely developed wings.

    (D) can reproduce asexually before reaching maturity.

    (E) have four different life stages: egg, larva, pupa, and adult.

64. Which of the following mammals has the longest gestation period?

    (A) Mouse

    (B) Bat

    (C) Rhinoceros

    (D) Elephant

    (E) Wolf

65. The endocrine system involves which of the following structures and products?

    (A) Digestive enzymes and the organs of digestion

    (B) Aqueous gases and the lungs and airway

    (C) Chemical messengers, the brain, and nerves

    (D) Hormones and the glands that secrete hormones

    (E) Antibodies and the lymph nodes

66. Every organism on Earth requires which of the following to be able to exchange gases with the external environment?

    (A) A steep diffusion gradient

    (B) Moist membranes

    (C) Gills

    (D) Lungs

    (E) Hemoglobin

GO ON TO THE NEXT PAGE

KAPLAN

67. A scientist has a flask of flies that exhibit the dominant trait of red eye color, but does not know the eye-color genotypes of the flies in the culture. In order to determine the unknown genotype, she breeds them with flies that are homozygous recessive. This is an example of a

    (A) recombination experiment.

    (B) mutation experiment.

    (C) sex-linkage experiment.

    (D) genetic depression.

    (E) testcross.

68. In a seminal ecological paper, a sea star species was removed from an intertidal zone and the population densities of other species changed drastically, upsetting the balance of the entire ecosystem. Which of the following statements is likely TRUE about the intertidal zone?

    (A) The intertidal ecosystem was under pollution stress.

    (B) The sea star was a keystone predator species.

    (C) The intertidal ecosystem was being affected by global warming.

    (D) The sea star monopolized the ecosystem.

    (E) The sea star was a primary producer.

69. Which of the following terms best describes a large, continuous ecological system like a desert?

    (A) Habitat

    (B) Community

    (C) Ecosystem

    (D) Biome

    (E) Niche

70. The logistic growth equation is a simple mathematical model to explain the growth of natural populations and is expressed as $\frac{\Delta N}{\Delta t} rN\left(\frac{K-N}{K}\right)$. Which term in the equation represents the carrying capacity of the environment?

    (A) $\frac{\Delta N}{\Delta t}$

    (B) r

    (C) K

    (D) N

    (E) $K - N$

71. A tree falls in the middle of a tropical rainforest, providing an open space for plants to colonize. This is an example of

    (A) exotic invasion.

    (B) primary succession.

    (C) secondary succession.

    (D) competition.

    (E) extinction.

72. All of the following factors will directly affect the number of individuals of a predatory species in a population EXCEPT

    (A) the predator's metabolic rate.

    (B) the predator's prey density.

    (C) the predator's home range.

    (D) the predator's reproductive rate.

    (E) the predator's natural enemies.

GO ON TO THE NEXT PAGE

73. An *r*-selected species has which one of the following reproductive strategies?

    (A) Producing one offspring when ecological conditions are most advantageous

    (B) A long gestation period and long-term adult care

    (C) Producing a higher ratio of females to males

    (D) A short life span and the ability to produce a large number of offspring quickly

    (E) A reproductive rate responsive to environmental conditions

74. Species richness is an ecological measure of a habitat's

    (A) stage of succession.

    (B) conservation status.

    (C) nutrient availability.

    (D) age.

    (E) biodiversity.

75. Which of the following organisms would be best suited for stage-dependent life table analysis?

    (A) Human

    (B) Housefly

    (C) Freshwater sponge

    (D) Bacterium

    (E) Earthworm

76. Mistletoe utilizes the nutrients, structural support, and protection of other trees while providing no resources to the trees. The relationship between the mistletoe and a tree can be classified as

    (A) predation.

    (B) mutualism.

    (C) commensalism.

    (D) parasitism.

    (E) herbivory.

77. The half-life of the element thorium is twenty-five days, whereupon it decays into protactinium. How much thorium will have decayed to protactinium in seventy-five days if there was 120 g of thorium to begin with?

    (A) 100 g

    (B) 40 g

    (C) 105 g

    (D) 15 g

    (E) 30 g

78. How many electrons does it take to fill the 3*d* subshell of an element with an atomic number over 30?

    (A) 2

    (B) 3

    (C) 6

    (D) 8

    (E) 10

79. Which of the following is the best possible definition of valence electrons?

    (A) The number of electrons an atom has in the outer shell

    (B) The number of electrons in surplus beyond the number of protons

    (C) The number of electrons an atom has in double bonds

    (D) The number of electrons an atom has in the 1*s* shell

    (E) The number of electrons an atom has in all of its shells

GO ON TO THE NEXT PAGE

80. What is the purpose of the cadmium rods in a nuclear reactor?

    (A) To dissipate heat so the reactor does not overheat
    (B) To absorb neutrons so the fission reaction occurs slowly
    (C) To donate neutrons to replenish the decaying uranium
    (D) To centralize electrons to harness electro-chemical energy
    (E) To create a magnetic field to contain electrons

81. Which of the following subatomic particles is the smallest?

    (A) Electron
    (B) Proton
    (C) Neutron
    (D) Up quark
    (E) Neutrino

82. How many electrons exist in the orbitals surrounding the nucleus of a neutral atom containing 10 protons?

    (A) 5
    (B) 6
    (C) 8
    (D) 10
    (E) 20

83. The atomic number of an element indicates

    (A) the molecular weight.
    (B) the order in which it was discovered.
    (C) the number of protons in the nucleus.
    (D) the number of elementary particles in the nucleus.
    (E) the energy state of the outer shell of electrons.

84. Heisenberg discovered that there was a certain level of uncertainty involved with electrons orbiting atomic nuclei. His uncertainty principle states that

    (A) it is impossible to know both the position and velocity of an electron.
    (B) it is impossible to know how many electron shells exist around the nucleus.
    (C) the probability of an atom ionizing in solution is not quantifiable.
    (D) charges of electron orbitals are unstable.
    (E) the speed of an electron varies disproportionately with the size of the nucleus.

85. How many neutrons are there in this isotope of uranium, $^{234}_{92}U$?

    (A) 92
    (B) 234
    (C) 117
    (D) 46
    (E) 142

86. Which of the following is the correct chemical formula for the compound silver chloride?

    (A) $FeCl_3$
    (B) $FeCl_2$
    (C) Ag_2Cl_3
    (D) $AgCl$
    (E) $CuCl_2$

87. Which of the following techniques involves quantifying the concentration of an unknown reagent by reacting the reagent until it is equivalent to a reagent with a known concentration?

    (A) Titration
    (B) Distillation
    (C) Condensation
    (D) Filtration
    (E) Amalgamation

GO ON TO THE NEXT PAGE

88. Which of the following choices illustrates the balanced equation for the reaction $NaOH + H_2SO_4 \rightarrow Na_2SO_4 + H_2O$?

    (A) $NaOH + 2H_2SO_4 \rightarrow 2Na_2SO_4 + H_2O$
    (B) $2NaOH + H_2SO_4 \rightarrow Na_2SO_4 + 2H_2O$
    (C) $NaOH + H_2SO_4 \rightarrow Na_2SO_4 + H_2O$
    (D) $2NaOH + 2H_2SO_4 \rightarrow Na_2SO_4 + H_2O$
    (E) $4NaOH + H_2SO_4 \rightarrow Na_2SO_4 + 3H_2O$

89. What is the percent by mass of carbon in the compound CO_2? (atomic weights: $C = 12.0$ g/mole, $O = 16$ g/mole)

    (A) 12.0 percent
    (B) 33.3 percent
    (C) 50 percent
    (D) 27.3 percent
    (E) 43.0 percent

90. Nonmetal elements adhere closely to the octet rule, which states that an atom

    (A) tends to lose or gain electrons so that there are eight electrons in the outer shell.
    (B) will form crystalline structures in a lattice of eight atoms.
    (C) releases energy to support the activation of eight electrons.
    (D) combines with another atom with eight valence electrons.
    (E) spins electrons eight revolutions before switching orbitals.

91. What volume of H_2O must be added to 100.0 ml of 10M HCl to obtain a 5M solution of HCl?

    (A) 100.0 ml of H_2O
    (B) 150.0 ml of H_2O
    (C) 250.0 ml of H_2O
    (D) 1,000.0 ml of H_2O
    (E) 1,500.0 ml of H_2O

92. A 70-kilogram man standing at rest on ice with a friction force of zero tries to push a resting mass of 70 kilograms forward by extending his arms. Which of the following is likely to occur?

    (A) The man pushes the mass away from him.
    (B) The man pushes himself away from the mass.
    (C) The man and the mass move away from each other at equal velocity.
    (D) Nothing moves because there is no friction.
    (E) An angular moment is created around the man's heels and he falls backward.

93. Water has physical properties that enable it to exist naturally in all three states of matter with only a limited amount of energy needed for it to transition between states and exist in liquid form at room temperature. What common metal exists in liquid form at room temperature?

    (A) Mercury
    (B) Gold
    (C) Silver
    (D) Potassium
    (E) Magnesium

GO ON TO THE NEXT PAGE

KAPLAN

94. Air temperatures in areas near large bodies of water (coastline) are much more moderate than inland areas at the same latitude and altitude. What is the probable explanation for this phenomenon?

    (A) Large bodies of water retain heat and warm the soil at the soil/water interface.

    (B) The temperature difference between the ocean and coast is minimal, so there is very little airflow (wind).

    (C) Water has a higher specific heat than soil, so air temperatures above large bodies of water are more stable, while the air above land cools as the soil cools.

    (D) The air above large bodies of water is denser, so it retains heat.

    (E) The ocean environment has greater primary productivity and therefore creates more ambient heat from metabolic activity.

95. Which of the following examples would demonstrate the greatest increase in entropy?

    (A) A dead battery is recharged from AC current.

    (B) A child tows a sled up a snow-covered hill.

    (C) A puddle of water evaporates off hot pavement.

    (D) An avalanche drops fifty acres of snow down a mountainside.

    (E) A smoker strikes a match and lights a cigarette.

96. A 1 kilogram mass slides down a ramp so that it accelerates from a velocity of zero at the top of the ramp to a velocity of 50 m/s at the bottom of the ramp, where it reaches its top speed. What was the potential energy stored in the 1 kilogram mass at the top of the ramp?

    (A)   9.8 N
    (B) 1,250 N
    (C) 2,500 N
    (D) 5,000 N
    (E) The mass had no potential energy while at rest.

97. A pressure cooker, a common kitchen appliance several decades ago, is used less often today. What was the purpose of using a container with an airtight lid to cook on a stove?

    (A) The sealed container loses less water, so the food does not dry out.

    (B) The pot loses less heat from heat dissipation into the air.

    (C) The lid creates a continuous connection of metal, spreading the heat more evenly.

    (D) The lid was a safety measure to protect the cook.

    (E) The boiling point of water increases with increased pressure, so it allows cooking at a higher temperature.

98. Which of the following items does NOT pertain to the theory of relativity?

    (A) The Twin Paradox

    (B) A moving clock ticks slower than one at rest.

    (C) The speed of light in free space has the same value for all observers.

    (D) Planetary motion is elliptical in nature.

    (E) Moving objects are shorter than when they are at rest.

99. What happens to the angular acceleration of a particle as its radius of circular motion decreases?

    (A) It increases.
    (B) It decreases.
    (C) It stays the same.
    (D) Its tangential acceleration decreases.
    (E) Its tangential acceleration increases.

GO ON TO THE NEXT PAGE

100. An object's weight is actually

    (A) the amount of matter it contains.
    (B) the force of gravity pulling it toward the Earth.
    (C) the resistance it exerts toward changes in motion.
    (D) the same quantity as its mass.
    (E) the weight of the volume of water displaced by the object.

101. The center of gravity of an object can be all of the following EXCEPT

    (A) the center of mass.
    (B) outside of the object.
    (C) the point where it can be suspended without rotating.
    (D) the average of the center of masses of the units that make up the object.
    (E) the point of minimum momentum of the moving object.

102. Which of the following substances requires the greatest amount of heat per kilogram for a given increase in temperature?

    (A) Water
    (B) Ice
    (C) Steam
    (D) Copper
    (E) Aluminum

103. When a pistol fires, it emits both a loud sound and a bright flash. An observer 100 m away is exposed to both effects of the firing of the gun. Which of the statements below is TRUE?

    (A) The observer hears the shot and sees the flash at the same time.
    (B) The observer sees the flash before he hears the shot.
    (C) The observer hears the shot before he sees the flash.
    (D) The observer sees the flash but does not hear the shot.
    (E) The observer hears the shot but does not see the flash.

104. The magnitude of charge between two parallel plates of equal and opposite charge is

    (A) zero.
    (B) greater near the positive plate.
    (C) greater near the negative plate.
    (D) the same throughout.
    (E) twice the charge of either plate individually.

105. How many colors are there in the spectrum of light visible to most humans?

    (A) Three
    (B) Five
    (C) Seven
    (D) Eight
    (E) Ten

GO ON TO THE NEXT PAGE

106. What is the effect of a magnetic field on a charged particle?

    (A) It changes its charge.

    (B) It changes its direction.

    (C) It changes its mass.

    (D) It changes its energy.

    (E) It changes its velocity.

107. The main properties of a wave are defined by all of the following EXCEPT

    (A) duration.

    (B) wavelength.

    (C) amplitude.

    (D) frequency.

    (E) speed.

108. When a star explodes and releases an incredible amount of energy and light, it is called a

    (A) supernova.

    (B) quasar.

    (C) pulsar.

    (D) black hole.

    (E) red giant.

109. The Doppler effect is important to the science of astronomy because it allows scientists to measure

    (A) the size of celestial bodies.

    (B) the distance between celestial bodies.

    (C) the cosmological age of celestial bodies.

    (D) the gravitational pull between celestial bodies.

    (E) the speed celestial bodies move away from or toward the Earth.

110. Which celestial body possesses a body and a tail; orbits the sun; and is composed of frozen gas, ice, and rocky debris?

    (A) Meteor

    (B) Comet

    (C) Asteroid

    (D) Planet

    (E) Moon

111. Which of the following planets has the longest year?

    (A) Mercury

    (B) Earth

    (C) Neptune

    (D) Mars

    (E) Venus

112. This scientist described three laws of planetary motion that mathematically predicted the shape of planets' orbits and their velocities.

    (A) Stephen Hawking (1942–)

    (B) Edmond Halley (1656–1742)

    (C) Nicolaus Copernicus (1473–1543)

    (D) Galileo Galilei (1564–1642)

    (E) Johannes Kepler (1571–1630)

113. A rainbow is a common atmospheric phenomenon created by the optical disturbance called

    (A) reflection.

    (B) illusion.

    (C) refraction.

    (D) flare.

    (E) diffusion.

GO ON TO THE NEXT PAGE

114. Which of the following describes the climatic condition that causes an arid area to form on the leeward side of a mountain range?

    (A) Rain shadow
    (B) Santa Ana
    (C) El Niño
    (D) La Niña
    (E) Zephyr

115. An earthquake with a magnitude of 4 on the Richter magnitude scale is _____ time(s) greater in amplitude than an earthquake with a magnitude of 3.

    (A) 1
    (B) 1.5
    (C) 10
    (D) 31
    (E) 100

116. Which of the following answers describes a subduction zone?

    (A) Two tectonic plates collide, forcing an elevated ridge to form.
    (B) A thin area in the Earth's crust occurs, and volcanoes are more probable there.
    (C) Two tectonic plates collide and grind past each other at oblique angles.
    (D) Two tectonic plates collide, and the older, denser plate bends under the younger, less dense plate.
    (E) An area has many quake faults.

117. Which of the following geologic periods is the oldest?

    (A) Cretaceous
    (B) Permian
    (C) Quaternary
    (D) Cambrian
    (E) Carboniferous

118. Which process from the following list is NOT part of the hydrologic cycle?

    (A) Fixation
    (B) Evaporation
    (C) Condensation
    (D) Transpiration
    (E) Interception

119. By far, the most common gas in the Earth's atmosphere is

    (A) oxygen.
    (B) nitrogen.
    (C) carbon dioxide.
    (D) hydrogen.
    (E) water vapor.

120. The changing seasons on the Earth are best explained by

    (A) the tilt in its rotational axis.
    (B) its proximity to the sun.
    (C) the gravitational pull from the moon.
    (D) its ellipsoidal revolution around the sun.
    (E) the large amount of water on its surface.

END OF TEST. STOP

KAPLAN

ANSWER KEY

1. B	19. A	37. D	55. E	73. D	91. A	109. E
2. E	20. E	38. B	56. E	74. E	92. C	110. B
3. C	21. C	39. A	57. B	75. B	93. A	111. C
4. B	22. E	40. E	58. D	76. D	94. C	112. E
5. A	23. D	41. A	59. A	77. C	95. D	113. C
6. E	24. D	42. E	60. C	78. E	96. B	114. A
7. A	25. A	43. D	61. A	79. A	97. E	115. C
8. D	26. C	44. B	62. B	80. B	98. D	116. D
9. D	27. C	45. D	63. E	81. E	99. A	117. D
10. B	28. C	46. A	64. D	82. D	100. B	118. A
11. B	29. B	47. C	65. D	83. C	101. E	119. B
12. A	30. D	48. B	66. B	84. A	102. A	120. A
13. D	31. E	49. D	67. E	85. E	103. B	
14. E	32. D	50. B	68. B	86. D	104. D	
15. D	33. C	51. E	69. D	87. A	105. C	
16. B	34. B	52. C	70. C	88. B	106. B	
17. E	35. C	53. A	71. C	89. D	107. A	
18. D	36. D	54. C	72. A	90. A	108. A	

DIAGNOSTIC TEST QUICK REFERENCE TABLES

Use the following tables to determine which topics you need to review most.

Topic	Test Question
Biological Science	
Evolution and Diversity of Life	4, 5, 6, 33, 35, 36, 37, 38, 41, 43, 53, 55
Cell Biology and Biochemistry	1, 2, 3, 7, 8, 39, 40, 45, 46, 47, 48, 51
Organisms and Heredity	9, 10, 11, 12, 13, 34, 42, 44, 49, 50, 52, 54, 56, 57, 58, 59, 60, 61, 62, 63, 64, 65, 66, 67
Ecology and Population Biology	17, 18, 19, 68, 69, 70, 71, 72, 73, 74, 75, 76
Physical Science	
Atoms and Subatomic Structures	20, 21, 22, 77, 80, 81, 82, 84, 85
Elements, Molecules, and Compounds	14, 15, 16, 78, 79, 83, 86, 87, 88, 89, 90, 91
Energy, Matter, and Mechanics	23, 24, 25, 92, 93, 94, 95, 96, 97, 98, 99, 100, 101, 102
Electricity, Magnetism, and Waves	103, 104, 105, 106, 107
The Universe	26, 27, 28, 108, 109, 110, 111, 112
Earth Science	29, 30, 31, 32, 113, 114, 115, 116, 117, 118, 119, 120

Topic	Number of Questions on Test	Number Correct
Biological Science	60	
Evolution and Diversity of Life	12	
Cell Biology and Biochemistry	12	
Organisms and Heredity	24	
Ecology and Population Biology	12	
Physical Science	60	
Atoms and Subatomic Structures	9	
Elements, Molecules, and Compounds	12	
Energy, Matter, and Mechanics	14	
Electricity, Magnetism, and Waves	5	
The Universe	8	
Earth Science	12	

KAPLAN

Answers and Explanations

1. (B)

Prokaryotes do not have mitochondria or chloroplasts, and it is surmised that these organelles in eukaryotic cells are descendants of prokaryotic organisms that took on a symbiotic relationship with eukaryotes.

2. (E)

Animal cells do not have cell walls. Cell walls are present in plant cells and some fungal and prokaryotic cells.

3. (C)

The sole purpose of a cell vacuole is for storage. Vacuoles may store products of cell synthesis, waste products, or water.

4. (B)

The wings of a bat and the flippers of a whale are homologous structures because they share all of the same bones and it is probable that these bones have a common evolutionary origin. The contrary example would be the wings of a bat and the wings of a butterfly. Although both provide flight, the wings of a butterfly are formed from an exoskeleton and from completely different developmental tissues.

5. (A)

Apomorphy is defined as a derived or specialized characteristic. It is a novel trait that was not present in an organism's ancestor.

6. (E)

When an organism obtains an apomorphy, it may be advantageous or deleterious. Most derived traits are harmful to an already successful organism, but some provide an advantage that makes the organism more successful and allows it to produce more offspring (higher fitness). Such a trait is adaptive and is naturally selected for within the population.

7. (A)

Active transport requires external energy. It involves the transport of a substance through the plasma membrane via a channel protein or membrane protein. Diffusion refers to movement of a substance across the membrane without the need for external energy.

8. (D)

Osmosis is the passive transport of water across a selectively permeable membrane.

Questions 9 (D), 10 (B)

Blood flow through the human heart is part of a continuous closed system, so a starting point is somewhat arbitrary (although conventionally we begin where the two vena cavae empty their blood into the right atrium). Blood returns to the heart through the vena cava and empties into the right atrium. The blood then passes to the right ventricle where it is pumped to the lungs through the pulmonary artery and oxygenated. Blood returning from the lungs enters the left atrium, then the left ventricle, and is then pumped to the rest of the body through the aorta.

11. (B)

Cavitation is the suspension of a continuous flow of liquid. This prevents the proper functioning of the rising water column in the xylem.

12. (A)

Leaves produce sugar (source), and the sugar travels to other parts of the plant (sink) with lower sugar concentrations through a continuous chain of lower osmotic pressure. The transport of sugar occurs in the phloem.

13. (D)

Stomatal opening and closing controls the rate of gas exchange in the plant cells and controls the amount of water that is lost.

14. (E)

This question requires a certain amount of recall. Ethanol is the combination of the two-carbon molecule ethane and an alcohol unit. An alcohol is signified by the attachment of a hydroxyl group (-OH) to a carbon atom.

15. (D)

Methane is the simplest organic molecule; it combines one carbon atom with four hydrogens.

16. (B)

An ion is an atom that has donated or borrowed an electron or a proton so that it is no longer neutral. Ammonium (NH_4^+) has an extra proton, so it has a charge of +1.

17. (E)

It is the reproductive success in a given population that determines fitness. A population with a greater number of individuals better suited to their environment will have a greater number that survive and reproduce. Fitness can vary widely from population to population within a species as well as among individuals in a population.

18. (D)

A community exists when several species utilize the same geographic area and resources but generally do so in a sustainable way.

19. (A)

While many organisms could exhibit this pattern of population growth, limited resources, disease, predation, or other factors generally prevent this. Humans, however, have developed extraordinary means of exploiting resources and have shown exponential population growth in modern times.

20. (E)

Since electrons have almost no mass, the mass number is derived from the number of protons and neutrons in the nucleus of the atom

21. (C)

Protons are positively charged particles, and electrons are negative. Since the atom described has an equal number of positive and negative particles, it is neutral.

22. (E)

Since the atomic numbers are identical, the element shown is in fact carbon, but it is called carbon-14 because it has two additional neutrons. Carbon-14 is a radioactive isotope of the common carbon-12.

23. (D)

Conduction will pass heat directly from the hot plate through the glass and to the water. However, as the temperature in the water rises, convection currents will form and the water will begin to circulate, thus speeding up the heating process.

24. (D)

Although the two containers have the same volume of water, A has a greater surface area contact with the hot plate. Thus, conduction will be greater.

25. (A)

Even though this experiment would be very simple, it could provide a basic test of the effect of container shape on the rate of heating. Keep in mind that a true test of this would require a control situation and many replications of the experiment.

26. (C)

White dwarfs are small, hot stars that have a very low luminosity.

27. (C)

Since light is not reflected but in fact pulled into a black hole, it is not possible to view black holes with any standard telescope. Evidence of their existence is sought by looking for the effects they have on surrounding space.

28. (C)

As a bright object moves farther away, the light energy it emits will gradually shift toward the red end of the spectrum (lower energy). This tendency is known as the Doppler effect. It was the observation that the light emitted from stars and galaxies was shifting toward the low-energy end of the spectrum (Doppler shift) that led Hubble to conclude the universe is expanding.

29. (B)

Because the mantle has molten areas, some of which are hotter than others, differential heating occurs and convection currents are formed. These are capable of moving the continental plates.

30. (D)

When two tectonic plates meet, pressure can build up because of opposing forces. Earthquakes and volcanoes are most common at these regions, though they can occur with any type of fault or crack in a plate.

31. (E)

Earthquakes can occur at any tectonic boundary or fault. However, when one of the Earth's plates is pushed under another as shown, tremendous pressure causes subducted plate to turn to molten rock. The pressure from this molten layer will cause some to push upward, which can cause uplift and form volcanic peaks. An example of this is the Cascade mountain range in the western United States.

32. (D)

Soils within the region impacted by glaciers are very young. In Illinois, these soils are rich in organic matter and constitute some of the best agricultural lands in the world.

33. (C)

Linnaeus is the father of modern nomenclature and his hierarchy is still in use today. The binomen consists of the genus and species names, such as *Homo sapiens*, and is always portrayed in italics with the genus name capitalized.

34. (B)

A clone of an individual, by definition, is an exact duplicate. There cannot be any variation in a clone except through mutation.

35. (C)

Darwin stood on the shoulder of previous scientists, particularly geologists and Malthus, who created important mathematical principles. Darwin also collected data himself. Although Gregor Mendel was Darwin's historic contemporary, Mendel's work was not recognized and the appreciation for genetics was not realized until after Darwin's death.

36. (D)

Cladograms must be interpreted according to the relationships evident in the tree. The nodes of each branch can represent either extinct or extant taxa. The branching pattern can show relative ages of divergence but not exact dates. Also, taxa more basal on the tree are not necessarily ancestral forms; they can be just as derived as the organisms at the tips of the top of the tree. A monophyletic group is one that is defined jointly by a derived characteristic (a synapomorphy) and is represented on the tree as sharing a branch.

37. (D)

If taxon C is a fish, then all of the taxa that are within the same monophyly must be part of an inclusive group that includes fish (i.e. fish, vertebrates, chordates, etc.), but are not necessarily fish. Taxa D and E do not have to be fish, but they must be vertebrates.

38. (B)

The Cambrian period occurred 500 million years ago and is noted for containing an incredible diversity of fauna. Up to this point in geological time the fauna was comparatively homogenous and static.

39. (A)

The cell cycle is composed of a long gap (called interphase) when cell growth and DNA replication take place, followed by the formation of two cells from one (called mitosis). A great way to remember this is by the acronym IPMAT. The order of mitosis is prophase, prometaphase, metaphase, anaphase, and telophase, followed by cell division or cytokinesis.

40. (E)

If metabolism occurs in the presence of oxygen, the cells can use aerobic pathways in the mitochondria to obtain energy from pyruvate in addition to the ATP liberated during glycolysis.

41. (A)

The most diverse group of organisms by far is the arthropods, which make up over 80 percent of Earth's biodiversity. The class Insecta is the largest and most diverse group within Arthropoda. There are over 1 million named species of insects and as many as 10 million still undescribed.

42. (E)

The standard dihybrid cross is between parents that are both heterozygous for two different traits (TtWw). If the parents' gametes assort independently, they will have offspring with the phenotype TW with a probability of 9 out of 16, offspring with the phenotype Tw with a probability of 3 out of 16, offspring with the phenotype tW with the probability of 3 out of 16, and offspring with the phenotype of tw with the probability of 1 out of 16.

43. (D)

The current prevailing hypothesis on the early origins of life is that nucleotides were synthesized in an organic soup with lightning as a possible source of energy. Nucleotides then formed long chains that could act as a template to replicate themselves on a regular basis. These nucleotides went on to form the DNA of simple organisms like viruses and ultimately prokaryotes.

44. (B)

Unlike animals that store body fat, plants store energy in the form of long sugar polymers. Plants like the potato have been cultivated for their energy storage qualities and incorporated into the human diet.

45. (D)

Ribosomes are the organelles that translate mRNA from the nucleus into proteins. They read down the length of the mRNA molecule, adding amino acids brought by tRNA according to the DNA code.

46. (A)

During most of the life of a cell, the cell's DNA is stretched out and invisible, even under a microscope. During cell division, the DNA condenses into thick chromosomes. The condensation is facilitated by specialized proteins called histones.

47. (C)

This process describes the synthesis of glucose rather than glycogen. The neo- prefix indicates that these are glucose rings that are formed from compounds other than sugar, such as fat or protein.

48. (B)

Gametes are not always small, especially in relation to the organism's body size. The key to carrying out sexual reproduction is that the gametes have to combine to result in a complete set of chromosomes. The chromosome number has to be halved first in meiosis; otherwise, the chromosome number would double after each generation.

49. (D)

Flowers are the reproductive part of a plant and are composed of structures that produce gametes and attract pollinators. *Petiole* is a descriptive term for a particular shape of a structure that is narrow at the base and widens toward the tip.

50. (B)

In a countercurrent exchange, a fluid with high osmolarity passes a fluid with low osmolarity, thus enhancing the exchange of substances across the cell membranes. These systems are used whenever extremely concentrated solutions are needed or when substrates need to be extracted from dilute solutions. Birds require hypoxic blood for both flight muscle and to dissipate heat.

51. (E)

Sex-linked genes are those on the sex chromosomes. They can occur either on the X or Y chromosome.

52. (C)

Insulin is produced by the pancreas. Insulin is released in response to elevated blood glucose and causes glucose to enter the cells of the body.

53. (A)

Protostomes have determinate cleavage. Cells have a predetermined fate early in development, so removal of a cell or region of cells causes abnormal development.

54. (C)

Skeletal muscle action potentials are elicited exclusively by acetylcholine. The signal for muscle contraction comes across the synapse of a motor neuron.

55. (E)

Despite common misconceptions, a theory is a well-supported hypothesis. Once a scientist proposes a hypothesis, she or he tests several sources of data to see if the hypothesis can be refuted. If the hypothesis stands up to these tests or is supported even more by the data, it eventually becomes a theory within the discipline.

56. (E)

Pollen must reach the female flower structures of a plant. Flowers are never located below the soil in roots, where pollen cannot gain access.

57. (B)

Waste is accumulated in the large intestine, but the body doesn't store waste material. The large intestine absorbs the majority of the remaining water from digested material.

58. (D)

The medial portion of the brain is composed of a corpus callosum, which joins the right and left sides of the brain. There is no medial lobe.

59. (A)

Smooth muscle tissue lines the walls of the arteries, digestive tract, and bladder. These muscles are controlled involuntarily through the autonomic nervous system.

60. (C)

Although evaporation would help in cooling an organism in a hot environment, moist tissues would allow too much water loss.

61. (A)

The only disease in the list that is not acquired from the environment is Tay-Sachs, which is caused by a lethal double recessive genetic inheritance. Although some children acquire HIV infections from their mothers, they do so through contaminated blood rather than genes.

62. (B)

Although technically not storage, large concentrations of glycogen are accumulated in liver and muscle tissue during periods of high blood glucose concentrations and low activity.

63. (E)

Holometabolous insects have four stages of development. They begin life as an egg and hatch as a larva. The larva is the feeding stage of the insect until it grows to maximum size. The larva then pupates and emerges as an adult.

64. (D)

Elephants have the longest gestation period of any mammal, roughly 22 months.

65. (D)

The endocrine system releases chemicals called hormones that affect bodily function. That is the purpose of the glands and their secretions.

66. (B)

Gases can only exchange across moist membranes, regardless of the possession of lungs or gills.

67. (E)

When an organism exhibits a dominant phenotype; the individual might be homozygous for the gene or it might be heterozygous dominant. The way to test this is to cross the individual with a recessive homozygote. This is called a test cross.

68. (B)

According to the hypothesis, a keystone predator species is so integral to the functioning of the ecosystem that the ecosystem will collapse if the species is removed.

69. (D)

A biome is the largest division of the Earth's differential landscape. A biome is typically defined by climate, soil, and vegetation type.

70. (C)

The logistic growth curve has three parameters. The value r is the intrinsic growth rate of the population, which is mainly affected by rates of birth and death. The parameter N is the initial value of the population. The carrying capacity is designated by K.

71. (C)

Secondary succession explains the colonization of open space by organisms that are in nearby areas or that had been in that area before, perhaps represented by a seed bank. Primary succession takes place on soil that has never contained these organisms before, such as a new volcanic island.

72. (A)

Factors that affect the population density directly affect birth rate, death rate, and competition for resources with other populations in the same niche. Other factors more inherent to the individual that have less of an effect on community interaction will have less effect on population density.

73. (D)

A species that is r-selected is opportunistic. Exotic species and species that take advantage of a disturbance in the ecosystem are typical examples of r-selected species. By contrast, K-selected species take better care of their young by either providing them with nourishment or parental care.

74. (E)

Species richness is the count of the number of species in a continuous ecological unit. This is one of the ways ecologists measure biodiversity.

75. (B)

A stage-dependent life table analysis portrays the distribution of individuals in a population based on discrete developmental stages such as egg, larva, adult, etc. Organisms that have more ambiguous development or only one life stage are more appropriate for age-dependent analysis.

76. (D)

Since the mistletoe is taking away resources and not providing resources in this symbiotic relationship, this is an example of parasitism. Other examples of symbiosis have organisms sharing resources to enhance the survival of both organisms (i.e., food for protection, protection for structural support, etc.).

77. (C)

In 75 days, thorium will go through three half-life decays, and on average half of the thorium will have decayed at each half-life. At day 25 the mass will have been reduced by half, to 60 g. By day 50 the mass will reduce to 30 g, and by day 75 the mass will only be 15 g. If only 15 g is left, then 105 g must have decayed.

78. (E)

All d subshells, no matter what their level, are full with 10 electrons.

79. (A)

Valence electrons are the electrons that are used by an atom to form electrochemical bonds with other atoms. These are the electrons in the outer shell, and only they can interact with the shells of other atoms.

80. (B)

The fission reaction in a nuclear reaction is only possible if the chain reaction is not allowed to take place too rapidly. Otherwise, the reactions would be like a nuclear bomb exploding. Rods of certain metals can act as neutron acceptors to limit the rate of the reaction.

81. (E)

It was once thought that atoms were the smallest particles, but even they are made up of parts. An atom has a nucleus composed of protons and neutrons (which contain mass) and electrons with no mass that circle the nucleus. Scientists have discovered that even these particles are made up of smaller units. For example, a proton contains two up quarks and one down quark. Neutrinos have almost no mass, so they are the smallest subatomic particle.

82. (D)

A neutral atom has no charge. The charges are balanced because the number of positively charged protons equals the number of negatively charged electrons.

83. (C)

The atomic number does not indicate chronology or mass. Each atom in the periodic table is numbered based on the quantity of protons in its nucleus. The mass of atoms can change in different isotopes with different quantities of neutrons.

84. (A)

Since we measure and observe electrons according to the activity of those electrons, we cannot know both the position of an electron and the direction in which it is traveling.

85. (E)

When an isotope is signified as in the question, the bottom number indicates the number of protons (as well as the number of electrons in neutral elements). The top number indicates the number of particles in the nucleus (the protons and neutrons combined). By subtracting the two numbers, the number of neutrons can be determined.

86. (D)

Every atom combines with others so that the number of electrons in its outer shell is full. Silver has one s electron in the fifth subshell (the s subshell is full with two electrons) that can contribute to a bond, and chloride has seven electrons ($3s^2 \ 3p^5$) in its third subshell. These atoms combine one-to-one to make both of their outer shells filled.

87. (A)

Titration usually involves investigating a solution with an unknown concentration. Using some form of visible indicator such as a color change or precipitate, a solution with a reacting reagent and known concentration is added to the unknown until all of the reagent in the unknown has reacted. The concentration of the original can then be determined by quantifying the amount of known reagent used.

88. (B)

A balanced equation has the quantity of each type of atom equal on both sides of the arrow. The arrow is equivalent to an equal sign in a mathematical equation. Coefficients are placed in front of each compound formula by process of elimination until the counts of atoms are equal.

89. (D)

The entire mass of CO_2 is 12.0 g/mole + 2(16 g/mole) = 44 g/mole. The fraction of the mass contributed by carbon is 12.0 g/mole ÷ 44 g/mole = 27.3 percent.

90. (A)

The nonmetal elements try to fill their outer shell with eight electrons to attain the noble gas configuration of s^2p^6. Other elements either share their electrons or donate them to the outer shell, so the nonmetal elements can have a full outer shell of eight electrons.

91. (A)

Dilution equations can be solved with the equation $M_iV_i = M_fV_f$ where the subscripts i = initial and f = final. The initial volume of solution is 100 ml, and the initial and final molarities are 10M and 5M respectively, so one simply needs to solve for the final volume of solution and find the difference. V_f = (10 M × 100.0 ml)/5 M = 200.0 ml, so the volume of water that was added was 100.0 ml.

92. (C)

Both bodies at rest have inertia that resists movement. The force exerted by the extended arms of the man must overcome either the inertia of the man's body or the inertia of the mass. Since the masses are equal and the ice is frictionless, if they move at all, they will both move equally. Assuming the man can generate enough force to move the mass, both the man and the mass will move away from each other at the same velocity.

93. (A)

The element mercury is also called quicksilver because it is liquid metal. Mercury was used in thermometers because of its sensitivity to temperature and rate of expansion. Today, thermometers made of mercury have been replaced with electric and water thermometers due to mercury's toxicity.

94. (C)

Water has a higher specific heat than soil, so it retains heat better. Although air temperatures change rapidly, climates near large bodies of water are more moderate because the water temperature remains stable.

95. (D)

Entropy is a measure of discord and chaos. Systems that increase in entropy lose energy by going from states of order to disorder, such as in the breaking of a glass. Systems that store energy lose entropy.

96. (B)

The potential energy at the beginning of the slide will equal the kinetic energy when the mass reaches its final velocity. Kinetic energy is equal to $\frac{1}{2}mv^2$, so the energy of the mass at final velocity is $\frac{1}{2}$ (1 kg)(50 m/s)^2 = 1,250 N.

97. (E)

Water boils at a higher temperature when the pressure increases. Pressure cookers were used to increase the amount of heat that could be delivered to food to either decrease the cooking time or increase the temperature. The opposite occurs at high altitudes where it takes much more heat to boil water.

98. (D)

Planetary motion only involves relativity in the sense that the moving bodies always move in relation to each other. The shape of the orbits is dictated by the combined gravitational pull of the objects with mass around the planets.

99. (A)

This can be observed in the spinning of an ice skater. The speed at which a skater spins is increased when the skater pulls the arms into the body. The skater's arms as they are pulled into the body decrease the radius of circular motion.

100. (B)

In physics, the object's weight is measured by how its mass is pulled by gravity. The larger the mass, the larger the force exerted, and the larger the weight.

101. (E)

The center of gravity is the point at which an object can be suspended and not rotate. It is the sum of the combined center of masses of all the atoms that make up the object. The center of gravity can be outside of the object, such as in the hole of a doughnut. An object's center of gravity is the point at which all calculations of linear motion are made, since the center of gravity typifies the entire object. The momentum of the center of gravity is the object's momentum.

102. (A)

This question asks about the stability of temperature of the given substances. The substance that is most resistant to changes in temperature is water.

103. (B)

This question explores the wave speeds of sound and light. Sound travels at only about 330 m/s, while light travels at almost 300,000,000 m/s. The light from the gun flash will reach the observer's eye long before the sound from the shot. The slow speed of sound is what causes the echo effect in large sports stadiums.

104. (D)

If two plates are arranged an equal distance from each other and have equal and opposite charge, the entire area between the plates will have a uniform charge. This is due to the electrons being able to leave from any place on the plate and pass to the other plate. The plates must be perfectly parallel in order for this to be true.

105. (C)

This question can be addressed by memorizing the mnemonic device ROYGBIV. The letters stand for red, orange, yellow, green, blue, indigo, and violet: the seven colors of the rainbow.

106. (B)

Since a magnetic field is a charged region with positive and negative poles, a charged particle will orient to these poles based on the charge of the particle. Electrons travel at right angles to the magnetic lines of an electromagnetic field, so they will usually change direction when entering the field.

107. (A)

A wave diagram shows the length, crests, frequency, and amplitude of a wave. The duration of a wave is dependent upon whether the source of the wave continues to emit the wave. The properties of the wave will be constant if the source of the wave does not change in frequency, amplitude, wavelength, etc.

108. (A)

Stars in the universe age and eventually collapse or explode. These explosions or supernovas are sometimes visible on Earth to astronomers using telescopes. Since the distance between Earth and these stars is vast, explosions often take place millions of years before we can see them.

109. (E)

The Doppler effect causes waves to be pushed together or spread apart directly in front of or behind a moving object that is emitting waves. This can be witnessed by listening to a car moving toward and away from you with its horn honking. The horn has a higher pitch when it is approaching and a lower pitch as it is moving away. Scientists can use this shift in the electromagnetic spectrum of objects transmitting light to measure their movement in relation to Earth.

110. (B)

Comets travel through the solar system in a large ellipse and begin to burn up as they approach the heat of the the sun. The gases released from the icy, rocky comet create a tail that can be many millions of miles long.

111. (C)

The planet that has the longest year is the planet that has the largest orbit. The planet with the largest orbit is the planet that is farthest away from the sun. This planet is Neptune.

112. (E)

Johannes Kepler was a mathematician who studied the motion of the planets. Kepler's laws are mathematical proofs that describe the conservation of periodicity of angular motion as the distance between a planet and the sun decreases.

113. (C)

When water or water vapor is present in the atmosphere, the droplets act as little prisms that break up white light into the seven colors of the rainbow. This phenomenon is called refraction or bending of light. The rainbow is caused by different wavelengths of light bending at different angles through the prism.

114. (A)

When warm, wet air climbs up the face of a mountain, the air experiences drops in temperature and pressure. The water trapped in the air condenses and falls as rain or snow. As the air travels over the mountain and down the other side, it warms up again but has lost most of its moisture. This effect is called a rain shadow because very little rain occurs on the back side of the mountain range.

115. (C)

The Richter scale is measured logarithmically. A change in one unit on the Richter scale is equal to ten times the magnitude of the previous value. A magnitude 4 quake is ten times greater than a magnitude 3 quake and 100 times greater than a magnitude 2 quake.

116. (D)

When the Earth's tectonic plates move, they run into each other at their borders. Some plates are more dense than others because of the varying consistency of the crust. The less dense plate floats above the more dense plate, while the more dense plate bends downward. This kind of meeting between plates is a subduction.

117. (D)

There are no defined periods older than the Cambrian. Although pre-Cambrian time accounts for about 90 percent of Earth's history, there are few markers to distinguish divisions over that time period.

118. (A)

The hydrologic cycle describes the fate of water as it changes states of matter from liquid to gas during its use by organisms on Earth and through evaporation and condensation. Fixation is a process that occurs in the nitrogen cycle.

119. (B)

Although living organisms rely mainly on the presence of CO_2 and O_2 gas, these are not the most common gases in the atmosphere. Nitrogen is the most common gas in the atmosphere, making up approximately 78 percent compared to the 21 percent made up by oxygen.

120. (A)

Earth's seasons occur over an annual cycle that takes the planet through an entire orbit around the sun. Although the Earth spins so that no one side is entirely away from the sun during the year, a tilt in the Earth's axis means that it doesn't spin perpendicular to the direction of the orbit. The portion of the Earth that faces away from the sun during the year is going through winter. The northern hemisphere faces away from the sun during the months of December through March.

Chapter Twenty-One: **CLEP Natural Sciences Review**

- The Big Picture: CLEP Natural Sciences
- Nuts and Bolts
- Biological Sciences
- Physical Sciences
- Natural Sciences Resources
- Final Thoughts

Congratulations on deciding to take the CLEP Natural Sciences exam! This review section and the accompanying practice tests will help ensure you test your best.

THE BIG PICTURE: CLEP NATURAL SCIENCES

The exam covers a wide range of science topics, so you will have to bring all of your knowledge of the sciences together. A full 50 percent of the test requires you to recall and apply knowledge of the biological sciences, while the remaining 50 percent of the exam requires you to tackle physical science topics. This may sound challenging, perhaps, but it is not insurmountable. After all, the exam includes information that you would learn in introductory college-level science courses usually taken by non–science majors. It's time to borrow or purchase some introductory biology, physics, and chemistry textbooks and get cracking!

The problems on the exam test your knowledge of factual information (approximately 40 percent of the test), as well as the ability to apply concepts to problems (another 40 percent of the test). Most of the problems that require you to apply concepts are based on reasoning ability, but some do include some math. The remaining 20 percent of the test involves the ability to understand and interpret information presented in paragraph form or as graphs, diagrams, tables, or equations.

NUTS AND BOLTS

The full CLEP Natural Sciences exam is composed of 120 multiple-choice questions, with 90 minutes to answer these questions. That means you need to answer more than one question per minute. The breakdown of topics on the exam is as follows:

Biological Sciences (50%)

Evolution and Diversity of Life	10%
Cell Biology and Biochemistry	10%
Organisms and Heredity	20%
Ecology and Population Biology	10%

Physical Sciences (50%)

Atoms and Subatomic Structures	7%
Elements, Molecules, and Compounds	10%
Energy, Matter, and Mechanics	12%
Electricity, Magnetism, and Waves	4%
The Universe	7%
Earth Science	10%

In the following review section, important terms to know for the exam appear in bold type. Be sure to look up any unfamiliar words or concepts in a college-level textbook.

BIOLOGICAL SCIENCES

Evolution and Diversity of Life

Although life on Earth shows extreme diversity, it also shows incredible unity. All living things share certain characteristics. All have one or more of the basic functional units called cells. All require energy to carry out life functions and to maintain **homeostasis**, the maintenance of stable internal conditions. All living things carry genetic information in the form of **DNA** and **RNA** (deoxyribonucleic acid and ribonucleic acid), and all pass on that information in the process of reproduction.

The earliest fossil evidence indicates that the first living things on Earth were single-celled, **prokaryotic** bacteria that appeared more than 3.5 billion years ago. Current theories on the origin of life focus on spontaneous formation of simple **amino acids** near thermal vents in the deep ocean or in subterranean caves, followed by incorporation of simple strands of nucleic acids, the building blocks of the genetic code. It is thought that all life on Earth today represents changes in the genetic code of those earliest bacteria through the process of evolution due to natural selection, genetic drift, gene flow, and mutation.

There are several kinds of evidence that support **evolutionary theory**. They include the fossil record, biogeographical evidence, **comparative anatomy** and physiology, and comparison of the genetic material itself. **Fossils** are the remains or traces of living things laid down in sediments that ultimately turned to rock. The fossil record is most complete for vertebrates—animals with backbones—and shows many transitional forms. **Biogeography** refers to the study of distribution of living things around the world. By comparing the structure and function of cells and organs, simple modifications can be seen in closely related organisms. Comparison of **genes** shared by many organisms is a powerful tool in understanding evolution.

Modern evolutionary theory originated when geologists began dating the age of rocks in which fossils were found. Charles **Lyell** wrote *Principles of Geology* (1830), which suggested that the Earth was much older than the few thousand years it was thought to be at the time. That, in conjunction with an essay on human populations written by Thomas **Malthus** in 1798, helped Charles Darwin develop his theory of evolution based on natural selection. Darwin calculated that two elephants could produce 19 million descendants in 750 years. Obviously, that was not happening, so it became clear that only some of the offspring survived. Darwin concluded that certain characteristics would favor survival for some individuals over others.

In 1809, Jean Baptiste **Lamarck** theorized that characteristics acquired by an organism during its lifetime could be passed on to its offspring. This theory was false, since organisms take tens of thousands of years to evolve and exhibit new traits that can be passed on to offspring. While Lamarck's theory was false, his acceptance of evolution as an explanation of biological diversity was important.

The theory of **natural selection** was written by Charles **Darwin** in his book *The Origin of Species* (1859). Darwin studied finches and tortoises on the Galapagos Islands, leading him to propose that organisms better adapted to their environment will survive (survival of the fittest) while their less well-adapted peers will not. **Adaptations** that organisms acquire that suit their environment are passed on to offspring through the process of natural selection.

Mutations are rare changes in the DNA that can be passed on to succeeding generations. Many mutations make the organism less likely to survive and procreate, but a few mutations may help an organism adapt to the environment or cope with environmental changes. Over billions of years, favorable mutations have led to development of more complex and diverse organisms adapted to almost every environment on Earth.

Mutation leads to **microevolution**—changes at the population level. **Macroevolution** is the formation of new species and mass extinction of existing ones. According to the Hardy-Weinberg theorem, the proportion of genes in a large, randomly breeding population will tend to stay the same over time. Changes in frequency of traits occur due to things like migration of a particular type of individual at a higher rate than other types of individuals or selection for favorable characteristics.

When organisms such as Darwin's finches produce many offspring, some tend to migrate and occupy new niches. New species are formed when populations of organisms adapted to specific conditions become reproductively isolated from other populations, unable to interbreed with them to produce fertile offspring.

To name and classify organisms, the system of taxonomy was developed. In taxonomy, organisms are categorized into increasingly closely related groups based on assumed evolutionary relationships and shared characteristics. Most systems currently recognize eight levels of classification according to the revised Linear taxonomy: **Domain**, **Kingdom**, **Phylum** (**Division** for plants), **Class**, **Order**, **Family**, **Genus**, and **Species**.

There are three **Domains** of organisms. The **Archaea** are a small group of prokaryotes well adapted to extreme environments such as very hot or salty conditions. They are thought to be the most evolutionarily ancient group of organisms. The **Bacteria** include all other prokaryotic organisms. All prokaryotes lack a true cell nucleus and cellular organelles. Bacteria can be differentiated from Archaea by the presence of peptidoglycans, which form a mesh like layer of sugars and amino acids in their cell walls. The third domain of organisms is comprised of all other living things, the **Eukaryota**. Eukaryotes have cells with a true cell nucleus and organelles. All plants and animals are members of the domain Eukaryota.

Most classification systems now recognize **six Kingdoms** of living things. They are **Archaea**, **Bacteria**, **Protista**, **Fungi**, **Plantae**, and **Animalia**. Archaea and Bacteria are single-celled prokaryotes. Protists are unicellular eukaryotes. Protists can be heterotrophic, mixtotrophic, or photoautotrophic. Most are found in aquatic environments or as parasites. (**Photoautotrophs** such as green plants produce their own food, while **heterotrophs** must obtain nutrition from outside sources.) Fungi are mostly multicellular, terrestrial, heterotrophic organisms with cell walls containing chitin. Plants are multicellular, terrestrial, autotrophic (photosynthetic) organisms with cell walls containing cellulose. Animals are multicellular aquatic and terrestrial heterotrophs whose cells lack a cell wall.

Viruses are agents that traditionally have not been considered to be living organisms. (Currently, scientists are debating this topic.) The defining characteristics of life include cellular structure and metabolic activity, and viruses lack both. Like living things, viruses are capable of reproduction and contain genetic information in the form of nucleic acids, but they cannot reproduce outside of a host cell.

The chart on the following page provides an overview of the origins of life and the classification system.

Diversity of Life Chart

Appeared (yrs before present)

Prokaryotes: The simplest and most ancient organisms
      Kingdom Archaea   Kingdom Bacteria   3.5 billion
Eukaryotes

      Kingdom Protista: unicellular eukaryotes and algae   1.7 billion
            Amoebas
            Flagellates
            Ciliates
            Sporozoans
            Algae (some are multicellular)   1 billion
            Slime molds
      Complex Multicellular Eukaryotes
      Kingdom Fungi: filamentous hyphae, heterotrophic, chitin cell wall   *500 million
            Ascomycota—sac fungi, yeasts, truffles, morels
            Imperfect fungi—penicillium, aspergillis
            Basidiomycota—mushrooms, toadstools
            Zygomycota—black molds
      Kingdom Plantae: photosynthetic, terrestrial, cellulose cell wall   *500 million
            Nonvascular plants: bryophytes, liverworts, mosses
            Seedless vascular plants: ferns, horsetails, club mosses   400 million
            Vascular seed plants
                  Gymnosperms: seeds born "naked" on cones   300 million
                        Conifers
                        Cycads
                        Ginkgoes
                        Gnetophytes
                  Angiosperms: flowering plants   65 million
                        Monocots
                        Dicots
      Kingdom Animalia: complex heterotrophs that lack cell walls
            Phylum Porifera: sponges   600 million
            Phylum Cnidaria: jellyfish, anemones
            Phylum Platyhelminthes: flatworms
            Phylum Nematoda: roundworms
            Phylum Annelida: segmented worms
            Phylum Mollusca:
                        gastropods—snails, slugs
                        bivalves—clams, oysters
                        cephalopods—squids, octopi
            Phylum Arthropoda: *450 million
                        crustaceans—crabs, barnacles
                        arachnids—spiders, scorpions
                        insects—the most abundant eukaryotes
            Phylum Echinodermata: sea stars, sand dollars
            Phylum Chordata: Tunicates, Lancelets, Vertebrates
                  Vertebrates
                        Fish   425 million
                        Amphibians   300 million
                        Reptiles
                        Birds   150 million
                        Mammals   50 million
                        Humans   100 thousand

*The first organisms to inhabit land were plants and fungi, which appeared together 500 million
years ago. The first animals to inhabit land were arthropods 450 million years ago.

Cell Biology and Biochemistry

All living things are composed of one or more cells. Cells are the functional unit of life and are composed of nucleic acids and other macromolecules surrounded by a **phospholipid plasma membrane**. All cells have ribosomes for protein synthesis in the **cytoplasm**. Cells move materials across the cell membrane by the processes of **active transport**, **osmosis**, and **diffusion**.

The DNA of prokaryotes (bacteria) is not separated from the rest of the cell in a membrane-bound nucleus but resides in a region called the nucleoid. Bacteria also lack membrane-bound structures called **organelles** and reproduce asexually through a process called **binary fission.**

Eukaryotic cells do have a membrane-bound nucleus, and their genetic material is carried by chromosomes in that nucleus. Eukaryotic organisms also have membrane-bound organelles that compartmentalize various cellular functions. The membrane-bound organelles of eukaryotic cells are as follows:

- **Chloroplasts (only in plant cells)**—Perform photosynthesis and contain chlorophyll; occur in leaves and stems of plants.

- **Golgi apparatus**—Lies adjacent to the nucleus of a cell; produces secretions of the cell.

- **Lysosomes**—Contain hydrolytic enzymes; important in intracellular digestion.

- **Mitochondria**—Contain genetic material and enzymes necessary for converting food to usable energy; are the site of cellular respiration.

- **Nucleus**—Contains nucleoli (involved in ribosome formation) and chromatin (DNA).

- **Rough endoplasmic reticulum**—Membrane network in the cytoplasm covered with ribosomes; is involved in the transport, synthesis, and modification of proteins.

- **Smooth endoplasmic reticulum**—Membrane network in the cytoplasm *not* covered with ribosomes; is involved in the transport, synthesis, and modification of proteins.

- **Vacuoles**—Found in the cytoplasm of plants and fungi; are vesicles containing water, metabolic waste, or food.

Cells and their organelles are composed of four basic kinds of complex **organic macromolecules: carbohydrates** (starches and sugars), **lipids** (fats), **proteins**, and **nucleic acids**. Carbohydrates and fats are primarily used as short- and long-term energy sources, respectively. Proteins support cellular structure and carry out many important functions by acting as organic catalysts in the form of **enzymes**. Nucleic acids carry the genetic information as DNA and RNA.

Many organic macromolecules are **polymers** made up of simple units called **monomers**. The monomers of carbohydrates are called **monosaccharides**. **Glucose** is a common monosaccharide, and **sucrose** (table sugar) is a common **disaccharide**. Complex carbohydrates **(polysaccharides)** include **starch** and **cellulose**. The monomers of proteins are called **amino acids**. Amino acids form **polypeptide chains**, which fold to form complex protein structures. Protein function is related to its structure. DNA and RNA are made up of nucleotide monomers, and the **nitrogenous base** of each monomer is what creates the genetic code.

All living things need to acquire energy. The usable form of energy for living things is in the high-energy bonds of a molecule called **ATP (adenosine triphosphate)**. ATP is often stored in the bonds of complex molecules such as glucose. Plants are **autotrophic**, meaning they can produce their own energy by using the sun's energy to fix carbon dioxide in the process of **photosynthesis**:

$$6\ CO_2\ +\ 6\ H_2O\ +\ \text{light energy}\ \rightarrow\ 6\ O_2\ +\ C_6H_{12}O_6$$

(translation: carbon dioxide + water + light energy → oxygen + glucose)

To release the energy in glucose and produce ATP, most organisms perform **cellular respiration**:

$$C_6H_{12}O_6\ +\ 6\ O_2\ \rightarrow\ 6\ CO_2\ +\ 6\ H_2O\ +\ ATP$$

(translation: glucose + oxygen → carbon dioxide + water + ATP)

If no oxygen is present, organisms can produce energy via **fermentation**:

$$C_6H_{12}O_6\ \rightarrow\ 2\ C_2H_5OH\ +\ 2\ CO_2\ +\ ATP$$

(translation: glucose → ethyl alcohol + carbon dioxide + ATP)

Organisms that can produce ATP without oxygen by using fermentation are called **anaerobic** organisms. Yeast is an example of an organism that uses fermentation to produce ATP.

Chemical energy that was originally produced through photosynthesis is used by eukaryotic organisms in the form of sugars. Heterotrophic organisms (organisms that cannot perform photosynthesis) obtain their energy for cellular respiration by consuming other organisms.

Organisms build complex proteins from instructions carried on DNA molecules called **chromosomes**, and those proteins facilitate and control all long growth, development, and function. The genetic "blueprint" of organisms is stored in DNA in the form of long chains of nucleotides.

DNA is found in the nucleus of eukaryotic organisms and is expressed through the process of **transcription** and **translation**. The structure of DNA is composed of two complementary strands of nucleotides, which wrap around each other to form a **double helix**. The two strands of nucleotides have a sugar-phosphate backbone. The bases are connected through hydrogen bonds. In each strand of DNA, **guanine** pairs with **cytosine** (G-C), and **adenine** pairs with **thymine** (A-T).

Sequences of DNA called **genes** code for the synthesis of a protein. Within each protein are amino acids that are coded by sequences of triplets of nucleotide bases in the DNA and mRNA. These triplets are called **codons** in mRNA. In the transcription of DNA to RNA for transport to the cytoplasm of the cell, DNA is copied to complementary RNA base pairs that form the other side of the DNA double-helix, with the exception of the base **uracil** (U). **Messenger RNA (mRNA)** contains uracil (U) instead of thymine (T), and uracil matches with adenine (A) in DNA. Copying

DNA to mRNA is called **transcription**. Once DNA has been copied to mRNA for transport to the cytoplasm for protein synthesis, the mRNA attaches to the ribosome, which contains **ribosomal RNA (rRNA)**. **Transfer RNA (tRNA)** strands contain codons that are complementary to codons on the strands of mRNA; these complementary codons are called **anticodons**. When an anticodon (of tRNA) binds to a codon (of mRNA), the tRNA knows to carry only a specific amino acid. The amino acid is packaged into a protein (series of amino acids) with the aid of a ribosome. The formation of the protein is called translation. Each amino acid that is formed is attached to the growing protein through a peptide bond.

In order for unicellular organisms to reproduce and for multicellular organisms to grow and develop, new cells must be produced. New cells can only arise from preexisting cells, so cells must divide to produce exact copies of themselves in order to transfer the genetic information necessary for protein synthesis.

The **cell cycle** is a repeating pattern of events during which cells grow, make copies of their DNA, and then divide to produce new cells. Most of the cell cycle alternates interphase, a period of growth and **DNA replication**, with **mitosis**, when the cell divides to form two new cells. There are several phases of the cell cycle:

Interphase—DNA replication creates **sister chromatids** joined at a **centromere**.

Prophase—DNA condenses into distinct chromosomes.

Prometaphase—Nuclear envelope disassembles.

Metaphase—Chromosomes line up along the **central metaphase plate**.

Anaphase—Sister chromatids split and are pulled to opposite ends of the cell.

Telophase—Nuclear envelopes begin to form; chromosomes uncoil and lengthen.

Cytokinesis—Division of the cytoplasm occurs, and two new cells form.

For organisms that reproduce sexually, meiosis reduces the number of **chromosomes** from the number found in somatic (body) cells to half the number of chromosomes, thereby forming **haploid gametes** (reproductive cells). **Diploid somatic cells** have twice the number of chromosomes as the haploid gametes. **Meiosis** involves one round of DNA replication followed by two rounds of cell division (meiosis I and meiosis II), which reduces the number of chromosomes by half.

During meiosis I, genetic variation can be introduced through the processes of **crossing over** and **independent assortment** of **homologous chromosomes**. Meiosis II is similar to mitosis. Four genetically unique haploid daughter cells are produced in meiosis, while two genetically identical daughter cells are produced by mitosis. The genetically unique haploid cells are called **gametes**. Gametes from male parents are called sperm and from females are called eggs. The gametes combine at fertilization to create a **zygote**. Since it has genetic information from both a mother and father, the zygote is **diploid**. **Genetic diversity** and **heredity** are two sides of the same diploid coin: different DNA combinations introduce new traits and create genetic diversity, while strong genetic characteristics that survive despite the introduction of new DNA are hereditary characteristics.

Organisms and Heredity

The study of the inheritance of traits can be termed **heredity**. Genes are the fundamental units of inheritance. They are comprised of sequences of DNA that code for proteins that ultimately control the structure and function of living things, including appearance and other traits.

Much of what we know about heredity was first described by Gregor **Mendel** based on experiments he performed through breeding pea plants. Mendel's theories include the idea that inherited traits are carried on the factors we now call genes, that an individual inherits one copy of a gene from each parent (an **allele**), and that the presence of one allele of a gene (**dominant**) can mask the presence of the other allele (**recessive**). By looking at how multiple traits were passed from generation to generation, Mendel also determined that genes from each parent are passed to offspring independently of each other.

An allele is one of two or more alternative forms of a gene. In sexually reproducing organisms, each individual has two copies of a gene, one inherited from the mother and one from the father. If both inherited alleles are the same, the individual is **homozygous** for that gene. If the inherited alleles differ, the individual is **heterozygous**. A dominant allele is one that controls how the gene will be expressed; a recessive allele is one that is masked by expression of a dominant allele in a heterozygous individual. The **genotype** is the actual set of alleles at the gene locus on homologous chromosomes. The **phenotype** is the observable expression of the trait based on the two alleles.

Uppercase letters are used to represent dominant alleles. The same letter in lower case represents the recessive version of the allele. For example, to represent the genotype of purple pea flowers (a dominant trait) and white pea flowers (a recessive trait), an uppercase letter is used to represent the dominant allele and the same lowercase letter is used to represent the recessive:

PP (homozygous dominant), Pp (heterozygous), and pp (homozygous recessive)

By using a simple diagram called a **Punnett square**, predictions about how traits will be passed to offspring can be made. Those predictions are based on the original observations Mendel made with traits in peas and were the basis for his theories. When a homozygous dominant individual is crossed with a homozygous recessive (the **P generation**), all of the offspring (the **F1 generation**) will be heterozygous and show the dominant phenotype. If members of the F1 generation are crossed (two heterozygotes), the ratio of offspring (the **F2 generation**) will be 1:2:1 homozygous dominant, heterozygous, and homozygous recessive, respectively, such that 1 in 4 will show the recessive trait.

Humans have 23 pairs of chromosomes: 22 pairs of **somatic chromosomes** and one pair of **sex chromosomes**. Female humans have two X chromosomes, and male humans have one X chromosome and one Y chromosome. Other species may have different chromosomes to determine gender.

Changes in the DNA sequence that can be inherited by offspring are termed **mutations**. Some mutations cause inheritable disease. Human diseases caused by detrimental genetic inheritance include sickle-cell anemia, hemophilia, Tay-Sachs disease, Huntington's disease, Parkinson's disease, and cystic fibrosis. If a condition is a recessive disorder, both parents must carry a copy of the defective allele to pass it on to offspring, and they will not show the trait unless they have homozygous alleles for the trait. If the allele for the condition is dominant, only one parent has to have the allele to pass it on, and that parent will be affected by the disorder. Other chromosomal disorders such as Down syndrome (trisomy: 3 copies of a chromosome instead of 2) are caused by changes in the number of chromosomes due to errors that occur during meiosis.

Some genetic conditions are **sex-linked**, most often carried on the X chromosome. Since males only have one X chromosome, they will be affected by a sex-linked recessive disorder, such as hemophilia. Since females have two X chromosomes, a dominant form of the allele will mask the disorder unless it is inherited from both parents, a relatively rare occurrence. Sometimes environmental factors affect the onset of a genetic disease. Other diseases may be characterized by late onset of symptoms. Huntington's disease, for example, typically isn't expressed until a person is at least in his or her thirties.

Organization of Systems

All living things are organized at varying levels of complexity. Organic macromolecules come together to form cells and their organelles. In multicellular organisms, similar cells make up **tissues**, and different tissues come together to make up **organs**. Organs are arranged in **organ systems** that work together to form a functioning organism.

The simplest unicellular organisms have only the cellular level of organization. Very simple fungi, plants, and animals may have only the cellular or tissue level of organization. The organs of plants include leaves (photosynthetic organs) and flowers (reproductive organs). Among animals, the simplest sponges and Cnidarians are the only groups that do not have organs and organ systems.

A **zygote** is a fertilized egg and starts out as a single cell containing all the genetic information for growth and development. As cell division occurs, more complex levels of organization are encoded to develop in multicellular organisms. A **morula** forms from the dividing zygote, a process called **cleavage**. By the time the morula has divided into about a hundred cells (a hollow ball of cells) it is called a **blastula**. **Gastrulation** is the process by which tissue differentiation begins. The outer layer of the gastrula, called the **ectoderm**, becomes epidermis (skin) and the nervous system. The middle layer or **mesoderm** becomes muscle, skeleton, and many internal organs. The inner layer, the **endoderm**, becomes the gut and associated organs. Very simple animals have no developmental germ layers or only two germ layers. Organisms with two germ layers can develop a tissue level of organization. Those with all three germ layers are more complex and form organs and organ systems.

Humans and other vertebrates have only four main types of tissue that make up all of their organs and organ systems. **Epithelial tissue** includes skin and linings of blood vessels and organs. **Connective tissue** includes bone and cartilage, ligaments and tendons, blood, and adipose (fat) tissues. Many organs contain structural connective tissue. **Muscle tissue** is contractile tissue and includes skeletal muscle, smooth muscle, and cardiac muscle. **Nervous tissue** is found in the brain, spinal cord, and peripheral nervous system.

Humans have many important organ systems that work together to maintain bodily function.

Cardiovascular System—The **heart**, blood vessels, and blood. The primary function of the cardiovascular system is transport of substances such as gases (oxygen and carbon dioxide). Organic nutrients like glucose and proteins, as well as wastes, are transported. The heart is composed of cardiac muscle tissue and pumps blood throughout the body. Blood vessels include **arteries** and arterioles, which carry blood away from the heart, and **veins** and venules, which carry blood to the heart. **Capillaries** are beds of tiny blood vessels embedded in tissue and are the site of exchange for gases and nutrients. Arteries have thicker walls because they carry blood at high pressure. Conversely, veins have thinner walls because they carry blood at a lower blood pressure. Blood flow rate is slowest in capillary beds to allow for exchange of materials. The human heart has four chambers, two upper atria and two lower ventricles. There are two circuits of circulation in the cardiovascular system. The **pulmonary circuit** takes blood from the right ventricle to the lungs via the pulmonary arteries. Blood is returned to the left atrium of the heart through the pulmonary veins. In the **systemic circuit**, blood is pumped from the left ventricle to all of the tissues of the body via the **aorta**, the largest artery in the body. The right ventricle pumps blood to the lungs. Blood is composed of about 55 percent liquid plasma, in which proteins, nutrients, and waste products are dissolved. The rest of the blood is made up of formed elements: the blood cells and platelets. Red blood cells (erythrocytes) contain the pigment hemoglobin, which carries oxygen. White blood cells (leukocytes) are associated with immunity, and platelets help blood to clot.

Digestive System—The digestive tract (mouth, esophagus, stomach, small intestine, large intestine, anus) and accessory organs (liver, gall bladder, pancreas). The main functions are ingestion and absorption of energy and nutrients and removal of wastes. Food enters the body through the mouth and passes down the **esophagus** and into the **stomach**. The stomach begins digestion with a mixture of hydrochloric acid and pepsin. The food passes into the **small intestine** where bile and **pancreatic enzymes** continue digestion. Most nutrient absorption takes place in the small intestine. The large intestine includes the **colon,** which reabsorbs water and some minerals, and the rectum, which stores feces until they are expelled through the anus. The **liver** produces bile to emulsify fats and processes everything absorbed in the small intestine. The liver is important in detoxification of drugs and other substances. The **gall bladder** stores bile. The pancreatic juices include **amylase** to digest carbohydrates, **lipase** to digest fats, and **trypsin** for digestion of proteins.

Endocrine System—A group of organs, **glands**, and tissues that secrete **hormones**. Hormones control many physiological processes by acting as chemical messengers. The pituitary gland secretes many hormones, some of which act directly and others that stimulate other endocrine organs. Some important hormones include the reproductive hormones (testosterone in males, estrogen and progesterone in females) and **pituitary** hormones such as growth hormone and thyroid stimulating hormone. Blood glucose levels are normally maintained by two hormones produced by the pancreas: insulin, which decreases glucose levels in the blood, and glucagon, which increases glucose levels in the blood. Adrenaline, the "fight or flight" hormone, is produced by the **adrenal gland**. Thyroid hormones affect normal tissue growth and increase metabolism.

Excretory System—kidneys, ureters, bladder, urethra. The **kidneys** filter blood to allow excretion of **nitrogenous wastes**, help maintain salt and water balance, and help regulate blood pH. The functional unit of the kidney is called the **nephron**, and each kidney has about a million nephrons. Blood under high pressure enters a dense bed of capillaries in each nephron called the glomerulus, where filtration occurs. The water portion of the blood and small molecules such as wastes, sugars, salts, and amino acids are pushed into tubules, while blood cells and large molecules remain in the blood vessels. In the tubules of the nephrons, selective reabsorption allows desirable molecules like glucose and amino acids to be reabsorbed and for salts to be retained or removed as needed, while wastes are passed on to collecting tubules and eventually to the ureters. **Ureters** take the wastes, now called urine, from the kidneys to be stored in the **bladder** until the urine is expelled from the body through the urethra.

Integumentary System—The skin and associated glands, hair, nails. Functions include protection from infection and dehydration, maintaining body temperature, allowing sensation, and synthesizing vitamin D.

Lymphatic/Immune System—Lymph tissues, vessels, and lymphoid organs. The lymphatic system is responsible for recycling body fluids and combating disease. Lymphatic vessels throughout the body return tissue fluids to the blood. Lymphoid tissues, such as the spleen and tonsils, help combat disease by trapping foreign matter, while structures such as the thymus and bone marrow produce white blood cells and cleanse pathogens from lymph tissue. Nonspecific defenses include the inflammatory reaction and involve production of white blood cells called phagocytes that ingest invading pathogens. Specific defenses involve white blood cells called lymphocytes and production of antibodies in response to a specific antigen—usually an invading pathogen. **Immunity** occurs when the body learns how to produce an antibody to a specific condition quickly because of previous exposure.

Musculoskeletal System—Bones, cartilage, tendons and ligaments, skeletal muscle. The contraction of muscle anchored to bone allows complex movement when muscles contract. Bones come together at flexible joints and are attached to one another by ligaments. Tendons bind muscle to bone. Muscles are made of proteins called **actin** and **myosin**, which slide past one another when signals that are received from the nervous system cause muscles to contract.

Nervous System—Brain and **spinal cord** (central nervous system) and **peripheral nerves** (peripheral nervous system). The nervous system is responsible for coordination and integration of sensory input and motor output. Nerve cells called **neurons** have branched dendrites, which receive signals, and long axons along which those signals are transmitted. The endings of axons are called **synaptic terminals**; the connections between the terminals and target cells are called **synapses**. **Neurotransmitters** are chemicals released at **synaptic terminals** to transfer signals from one neuron to another. Important structures of the brain include the cerebrum (higher learning, language, rational thought), cerebellum (motor coordination), thalamus (sensory processing), hypothalamus (basic drives like hunger, thirst, sex), and the brain stem (breathing and heartbeat). The brain and spinal cord are surrounded by membranes called meninges.
The spinal cord connects the brain and the peripheral nervous system. Reflexes are unconscious responses of the nervous system conveyed by the spinal cord and brain stem. **Sensory receptors** for touch, taste, smell, sound, and vision are part of the peripheral nervous system and are processed in the brain. Chemoreceptors in the tongue (taste buds) and nasal passages (olfactory receptors) react with chemical molecules that they come in contact with. Mechanoreceptors in the ear respond to physical movement in the form of sound waves or motion and allow us to hear and maintain our sense of balance. Photoreceptors in the eyes called cones and rods allow vision.

Reproductive Systems—Male: **testes**, seminiferous tubules, vas deferens, prostate gland, ejaculatory duct, penis. Female: **ovaries**, fallopian tubes, uterus, cervix, vagina, clitoris. Sperm is produced in the seminiferous tubules in males. Eggs are produced from oocytes in the female ovaries. Once each month, a mature egg is released from the ovaries, where it travels through the fallopian tubes to the uterus to be fertilized. If the egg is not fertilized, menstruation occurs, but if the egg is fertilized, a zygote implants in the endometrial lining of the uterus. Male sperm move from the scrotum through the vas deferens and the penis to fertilize an egg in the female fallopian tube. When an egg is fertilized, becomes a zygote, and grows into an embryo in the uterus, the embryo is provided nutrients and oxygen through the placenta. The embryo grows into a baby, which exits the uterus at the end of nine months via the cervix and vagina.

Respiratory System—Nasal passages, trachea, bronchi, and lungs. The primary function is to provide oxygen for cellular respiration and remove the carbon dioxide that is produced as a waste product by working in conjunction with the cardiovascular system to allow exchange of those gases in the lungs and body tissues. Oxygenated air enters the mouth or nose and is passed into the **trachea**, which branches into **bronchi** at the lungs. Each bronchus further branches into bronchioles, which terminate at capillary-rich **alveoli**, the site of gas exchange. Oxygen is absorbed and carbon dioxide is released by red blood cells in the capillary beds of the alveoli. Breathing involves muscular contraction of the diaphragm, which increases the volume of the chest cavity, causing a reduction in pressure and inflow of air during inhalation. Exhalation follows when signals for contraction of the diaphragm are stopped, the volume of the chest cavity decreases, and elastic recoil of the connective tissue of the lungs forces air to be expelled.

Plant Tissues

Plants have many tissues and organs that differ from those of animals. Plants have actively dividing cells called **meristems** in the regions of growth. Growth at the tips of shoots (the aboveground portion) and roots (the underground portion) occurs at apical meristems. Increase in girth in woody plants occurs at lateral meristems in the vascular cambium.

Many plants have vascular tissue for transport of water and nutrients. **Xylem** is vascular tissue that allows transport of water and minerals up from the soil through the roots to the plant leaves. **Phloem** is vascular tissue that allows transport of sugars, the products of photosynthesis, throughout the plant and to the roots. Nonvascular plants lack specialized structures for transport of water and depend on moisture in the surrounding habitat. They are often low growing and are generally found in moist environments.

Leaves are specialized photosynthetic organs. Pores in the leaf surface called **stomata** allow carbon dioxide to enter the leaf and enter the cell chloroplasts, the organelles where photosynthesis occurs. Chloroplasts contain the pigment **chlorophyll**, which harvests the sun's energy by absorbing light. When leaf stomata are open, water evaporates from the leaves in a process called **transpiration**. Plants can regulate water loss by closing stomata.

Like many animals, plants produce hormones that regulate growth and development. In addition, special receptors in plants allow detection of light and shade, change in seasons, and other signals important to dormancy and reproductive cycles. Many plants grow flowers to enable them to reproduce. The male part of a flower is the **stamen**, which includes the **pollen**-producing **anther**. The pollen must find its way to the **pistil**, the female part of the flower, which contains the ovary and the egg cells. **Seeds** are created when the pollen and eggs meet.

Ecology and Population Biology

The study of the interaction between organisms and their environment is termed **ecology.** Most living things ultimately depend on the process of photosynthesis, which harvests the sun's energy. Plants and other photosynthetic organisms are **primary producers** because they use the sun's energy to incorporate (fix) carbon dioxide into organic compounds. Plants also take up water and important nutrients like nitrogen from the soil. Plant bodies represent the first link in ecosystem **food chains** or **food webs**. All other organisms get their energy by being **consumers** of other organisms.

An **ecosystem** is a group of organisms and all of the nonliving **(abiotic)** environmental factors with which the organisms interact. The fish, algae, and snails in an aquarium, along with the water, food, and wastes of the organisms, constitute an ecosystem. The climate, soil, and organisms of a tropical rainforest constitute an ecosystem as well.

Energy and matter are cycled through ecosystems via both **abiotic factors**, things like climate and water flow, and **biotic factors**, living organisms. The movement of matter and energy through ecosystems is called **biogeochemical cycling**. Several biogeochemical cycles are important to ecologists. The **water cycle** involves the movement of water via precipitation, evaporation, transpiration, movement as surface and ground water, and its use by organisms. The **carbon cycle** involves the uptake of atmospheric carbon dioxide via photosynthesis and its return to the atmosphere via cellular respiration and decomposition of carbon compounds by bacteria and fungi. Combustion of fossil fuels has become a very important element of the carbon cycle. **Nitrogen**, one of the primary components of proteins, is also cycled through ecosystems. Although most of the atmosphere is composed of nitrogen, only certain bacteria are able to fix it into a form usable by living things. Bacteria are also very important in breaking nitrogen back down into its gaseous form. Many important organic and inorganic molecules cycle through living things by way of complex food webs.

The **trophic level** of an organism is determined by the position of the organism on a food chain or within a complex food web. Autotrophic plants are the primary producers, so they occupy the first trophic level. **Herbivores** occupy the second trophic level because they are animals that eat plants. **Carnivores** eat other animals and occupy the third trophic level, etc. Fungi and bacteria are important decomposers, breaking down plants and animals to return the organic elements they contain to the earth. Typically, the trophic structure of any ecosystem can be represented by a pyramid. The primary producers represent the greatest biomass and the top carnivores the least biomass. This is because as energy and nutrients move up the food chain, some energy is used by each trophic level, making less energy available for the next higher level.

Organisms interact with each other in many ways. **Predator-prey** relationships exist when one organism consumes another, such as a cow eating grass or a wolf eating a cow. **Competition** exists when two organisms must use a limited resource such as food or water. Plants sometimes compete for sunlight. **Symbiotic relationships** occur when two organisms interact closely. In **mutualism**, both organisms benefit from the relationship. In **commensalism**, only one organism benefits from a relationship but no harm is done to the other. **Parasitism** involves benefit to one organism at the expense of the other.

Organisms live as members of **populations**, groups of individuals of the same species that live together. The availability of food, competition, predation, and other factors will influence the number of individuals within a population. Populations of different species within an area represent a **community**, and community dynamics influence individual populations. Population growth without limits would be exponential and is called the population's **biotic potential**. Actual population growth is limited; some individuals die, and others move in or out. The **carrying capacity** of a system is the number of individuals a system can actually support given environmental factors such as space, light, water, or nutrients.

Succession is the process by which ecological communities change over time. Many of the changes associated with succession are due to factors such as competition and symbiosis. Examples of succession include occupation of a cleared vacant lot by weeds, insects, and small animals over time or the gradual filling of a small pond by sediment. When an existing community has been destroyed by some **disturbance event**, such as clearing a lot, it is called secondary succession. When organisms gradually inhabit an area previously barren, such as after a glacial retreat, it is called primary succession.

Biomes are areas characterized by patterns of climate and vegetation. Similar biomes can often be found at the same latitude around the world. In addition, biomes are related to altitude. Changes in biomes moving from low areas up to the top of mountains are similar to changes that occur as one moves north or south from the equator. The characteristics of various biomes determine what types of organisms will live there.

- **Tropical Rain Forest**—Warm and wet most of the year. They contain at least half of the Earth's terrestrial plant and animal species. Rain forests are found near the equator. Because most nutrients are contained in the vegetation, they have very poor soils.
- **Deciduous Forests**—Distinct seasons with warm summers, cool winters, and plenty of moisture. Many species of birds and mammals and hardwood trees such as oak and maple dominate these forests of North America and Eurasia.
- **Grasslands**—Distinct wet and dry seasons, few dispersed trees, rich soil, and low annual rainfall. They are found in temperate and tropical regions. Both the American prairie and African savannah are grassland biomes. Grasslands can support large populations of grazing mammals.
- **Taiga**—A coniferous forest that extends around the upper northern hemisphere with cold, dry winters and limited precipitation during a short summer. Moose, elk, and large carnivores such as bears and wolves live in a taiga. Marshes and lakes are common. Vegetation is dominated by cold-tolerant needle-bearing trees such as fir and spruce.
- **Tundra**—Arctic and alpine locations with permanently frozen soil layer (permafrost), low-growing plants and lichens, and many migratory species. The landscape is boggy (in the summer) and windy. Tundra regions are characterized by short growing seasons and long, cold winters. Tundra covers one-fifth of the Earth's land surface.
- **Deserts**—May be hot or cold, but are always very dry. Deserts tend to occur at around 30 degrees latitude north and south. Deserts are marked by low primary productivity and organisms adapted to conserve water.
- **Aquatic**—May be marine or freshwater. Freshwater has a low salt concentration and includes ponds, lakes, streams, rivers, and wetlands. Marine regions cover three-quarters

of the Earth's surface and include oceans, coral reefs, and estuaries. Aquatic ecosystems are very diverse and are divided into **pelagic** (open water), **benthic** (deep water), **abyssal** (deepest ocean), and **intertidal** habitats. The pelagic zone is far from land but reaches the surface, where ocean-going mammals like whales and dolphins can breathe. The benthic zone is below the pelagic and may include the ocean floor. The intertidal zone is where the ocean meets land and may feature rocky coasts and sandy beaches.

PHYSICAL SCIENCES

Many of the subjects in the physical sciences overlap and intertwine. For example, you need to have a basic understanding of chemistry in order to complete some physics and astronomy problems. The movement of planets in astronomy can be explained by physics. You can't have a basic understanding of one concept without considering how that subject interacts with and impacts other disciplines.

The Metric System

The metric system is used for measurement in everyday life, as well as in the biological and physical sciences. Units of measurement used in the metric system include the following:

Measurement	Units
length	meters
mass	grams
temperature	degrees Celsius
time	seconds
volume	liters

These units of measurement can be increased or decreased by powers of ten with the following prefixes:

Prefix	Amount Increased/Decreased by	Symbol
micro-	one millionth	μ
milli-	one thousandth	m
centi-	one hundredth	c
deci-	one tenth	d
kilo-	one thousand	k
mega-	one million	M

Atoms and Subatomic Structures

Matter has **mass** and occupies space. Air, rocks, water, and living organisms are all made of matter. **Elements** such as iron, carbon, and helium are matter. Elements are composed of **atoms**. Atoms are composed of three subatomic particles: protons, electrons, and neutrons. **Protons** and **neutrons** are found in the nucleus of each atom. **Electrons** occur in regions of probability called **orbitals**, centered around the nucleus. Each orbital contains **shells** designated by letters including s, p, d, and f.

An atom is composed primarily of empty space between the electrons and the nucleus, but the **nucleus** makes up nearly all of the mass of the atom. The nucleus houses positively charged protons and electrically neutral neutrons. The number of protons in the nucleus, Z, determines the **atomic number** and what chemical element the atom is. The number of neutrons in the nucleus is denoted by N. The **atomic mass** of the nucleus, A, is equal to $Z + N$.

Elements, such as carbon (C), cannot be broken down into simpler compounds by chemical means. The chemical behavior of an element is determined by the number of electrons in its outer shell. An ionic form of an element occurs when an element either loses or gains one or more electrons from its outer shell during ionic bonding. A neutral atom, with the same number of protons and electrons, is the form of an element that is placed in the **periodic table**. The elements of the periodic table are arranged according to increasing numbers of protons.

The electrons are placed in orbitals that are spherical (s orbitals), or are more complex in shape (p, d, and f orbitals). The electron configuration of an element describes how the atoms are arranged in the element. The electron configuration notation of an element can be figured out by noting how many electrons are found in each orbital of an element. According to the **octet rule**, the outer orbital, or shell, of each element must be filled in order for an element to not react with other elements. In order to fill an outer shell that is not completely full, an element will share, donate, or obtain enough electrons to fill its outer shell (usually eight electrons, except in elements that only have one s shell).

An isotope of an element has the same atomic number but a different atomic mass—the number of neutrons differs. An element can have several isotopes. Among all of the known elements are approximately 270 stable isotopes and more than 2,000 unstable isotopes.

Radioactivity is the phenomenon whereby some unstable atomic nuclei spontaneously emit particles in a process called radioactive decay. Radioactive decay can lead to formation of isotopes or new elements. **Alpha particles** emitted by nuclei can be stopped by a piece of paper. **Beta particles**, electrons or positrons, are much smaller and have less effect on the mass of the atom emitting them. Beta particles convert neutrons into protons, increasing the atomic number of the element. The isotope ^{14}C is unstable and emits a beta particle, becoming the stable isotope ^{14}N. **Neutrinos** are associated with beta decay. **Gamma rays** are a type of electromagnetic radiation that results from a redistribution of electric charge within a nucleus. There is no change in mass or atomic number.

Half-life is the time required for half of the atoms in any given quantity of a radioactive isotope to decay. Each particular isotope has its own half-life. The half-life of ^{14}C is 5,730 years, so that is the time it takes for half of some mass of the isotope to disappear. Nuclear half-lives range from fractions of a second to many times the age of the universe.

If atomic nuclei come close enough together, they can interact with one another through strong nuclear force, and reactions between them can occur. Such nuclear reactions can either be exothermic and release energy or endothermic, requiring the input of energy to occur.

Fusion is a nuclear process in which two light nuclei combine to form a single heavier nucleus. The fusion reaction used in some nuclear weapons is the reaction between two different hydrogen isotopes to form an isotope of helium (thus the term "hydrogen bomb" or "H-bomb"). The reaction releases a huge amount of energy—more than a million times greater than a typical chemical reaction. Fusion occurs when two light nuclei fuse such that the sum of the masses of the fused nuclei is less than the sum of the masses of the initial nuclei. The mass that is lost in the reaction is converted into energy. Fusion is the process that takes place in stars like our sun, providing all of the energy used by life on Earth.

Fission is a nuclear process in which a heavy nucleus, such as that in uranium, splits into two smaller nuclei. Fission reactions were used in the first atomic bombs and are still used in nuclear reactors and as triggers for fusion bombs. A great amount of energy is released in fission reactions because for heavy nuclei, the summed masses of the lighter product nuclei are less than the mass of the original heavy nucleus. Fission occurs because of the electrostatic repulsion created by the large number of positively charged protons contained in a heavy nucleus. The two smaller nuclei formed in the reaction have less internal electrostatic repulsion than one larger nucleus, allowing the larger nucleus to overcome the strong nuclear force that holds it together. Fission can be seen as a tug-of-war between the strong attractive nuclear force and the repulsive electrostatic force, which ultimately wins.

Elements, Molecules, and Compounds

The following types of elements can be found in the periodic table.

Type of Element	Features	Location in the Periodic Table
Metals	High densities, solid at room temperature, conduct electricity, shiny, malleable. Examples: sodium, magnesium, iron, and silver	Left side to center
Nonmetals	Many gaseous at room temperature; some react easily with other substances. Examples: carbon, nitrogen, oxygen, and hydrogen	Central-right, top to bottom
Halogens	Nonmetallic compounds that form gases (sometimes diatomic) at room temperature. Examples: fluorine, chlorine, bromine, and iodine	Second group (column # 17) from far right
Noble Gases	Filled outer electron shells; do not react easily with other atoms. Examples: helium, argon, krypton, neon, xenon, and radon	Far right group (column # 18)

Periodic Table of the Elements

Atomic Number — 6
Symbol — C
Atomic Mass — 12.01

* Numbers in parentheses are the *mass numbers* of the most stable isotope of the element.

1	2	3	4	5	6	7	8	9	10	11	12	13	14	15	16	17	18
1 H 1.008																	2 He 4.003
3 Li 6.941	4 Be 9.012											5 B 10.81	6 C 12.01	7 N 14.01	8 O 16.00	9 F 19.00	10 Ne 20.18
11 Na 22.99	12 Mg 24.31											13 Al 26.98	14 Si 28.09	15 P 30.97	16 S 32.07	17 Cl 35.45	18 Ar 39.95
19 K 39.10	20 Ca 40.08	21 Sc 44.96	22 Ti 47.88	23 V 50.94	24 Cr 52.00	25 Mn 54.94	26 Fe 55.85	27 Co 58.93	28 Ni 58.69	29 Cu 63.55	30 Zn 65.39	31 Ga 69.72	32 Ge 72.61	33 As 74.92	34 Se 78.96	35 Br 79.90	36 Kr 83.80
37 Rb 85.47	38 Sr 87.62	39 Y 88.91	40 Zr 91.22	41 Nb 92.91	42 Mo 95.94	43 Tc (98)	44 Ru 101.1	45 Rh 102.9	46 Pd 106.4	47 Ag 107.9	48 Cd 112.4	49 In 114.8	50 Sn 118.7	51 Sb 121.8	52 Te 127.6	53 I 126.9	54 Xe 131.3
55 Cs 132.9	56 Ba 137.3	57–70	72 Hf 178.5	73 Ta 181.0	74 W 183.8	75 Re 186.2	76 Os 190.2	77 Ir 192.2	78 Pt 195.1	79 Au 197.0	80 Hg 200.6	81 Tl 204.4	82 Pb 207.2	83 Bi 209.0	84 Po (209)	85 At (210)	86 Rn (222)
87 Fr (223)	88 Ra 226.0	89–102	104 Rf (261)	105 Db (262)	106 Sg (263)	107 Bh (262)	108 Hs (265)	109 Mt (268)	110 Uun (269)	111 Uuu (272)	112 Uub (277)	113 Uut	114 Uuq (289)	115 Uup	116 Uuh	117 Uus	118 Uuo

57 La 138.9	58 Ce 140.1	59 Or 140.9	60 Nd 144.2	61 Pm (145)	62 Sm 150.4	63 Eu 152.0	64 Gd 157.3	65 Tb 158.9	66 Dy 162.5	67 Ho 164.9	68 Er 167.3	69 Tm 168.9	70 Yb 173.0
89 Ac 227.0	90 Th 232.0	91 Pa 231.0	92 U 238.0	93 Np 237.0	94 Pu (244)	95 Am (243)	96 Cm (247)	97 Bk (247)	98 Cf (251)	99 Es (252)	100 Fm (257)	101 Md (258)	102 No (259)

Molecules contain two or more atoms that are bonded together. **Compounds** are molecules composed of more than one element. Compounds are named by the types of bonds that hold them together. **Ionic compounds** are formed from the attraction between charged particles called ions. Ions are formed when one atom gives up an electron to another so that both have filled outer orbitals. The atom giving up an electron gains a positive charge, while the atom receiving the electron gains a negative charge, causing an attraction that bonds the two elements. In **covalent compounds**, electrons are shared between two atoms. **Hydrogen bonds** form between polar molecules such as water. Water molecules are **polar** because the electrons from hydrogen spend more time orbiting the more positively charged nucleus of the oxygen atom, creating unequal charges at opposite ends of the molecule.

A **solution** is a uniform mixture of different substances. Air is a solution of various gases, and sea water is a solution of various solids dissolved in water, a **solvent**. A solution differs from a compound in that a solution can be separated into the elements or compounds it contains by boiling or freezing. A compound is not altered by a change in state and always has the same proportion of elements present.

Acids are substances that increase the concentration of hydrogen ions in water, decreasing the pH of the solution. They can be defined as proton donors (Bronsted-Lowry) or electron-pair acceptors (Lewis). Examples of acids include hydrochloric acid (HCl) and nitric acid (HNO_3). **Bases** are substances that produce hydroxide ions in water, increasing the pH of the solution. They can be defined as proton acceptors (Bronsted-Lowry) or electron-pair donors (Lewis). Examples of bases include sodium hydroxide (NaOH) and potassium hydroxide (KOH). The pH scale ranges from 1 to 14. It is a negative and logarithmic scale of the number of hydrogen ions, H^+, in a solution. A solution with more hydrogen ions is more acidic and will have a smaller pH number. A solution with a pH of 1 is ten times more acidic than a solution with a pH of 2, and a solution with a pH of 1 is 100 times more acidic than a solution with a pH of 3. A solution with a pH of 2 is 100 times more acidic than a solution with a pH of 4. A pH of 1 to 6 is acidic, a pH of 7 is neutral, and a pH of 8 to 14 is basic. A **buffer** absorbs or releases hydrogen ions to prevent changes in pH of a solution.

Through chemical **reactions**, compounds combine to form more complex products or break down into simpler components. Reactions occur when there is instability or when compounds can achieve a lower energy state by reacting. **Reactants** are the chemicals that combine or decompose to form **products**. Products are the end result of a chemical reaction. **Combustion** (burning) was the first extensively studied chemical reaction. Combustion always produces carbon dioxide and water. The mass relationships of reactants and products can be calculated for chemical reactions.

A **mole** of a substance is defined as its gram molecular or atomic weight, which always contains 6.022×10^{23} molecules (**Avogadro's number**) of that substance. The atomic mass of an atom has the same molecular weight as one mole of the atom. For example, the molecular weight of carbon is 12.0 grams per mole of carbon atoms. The **formula mass** of a substance is the sum of the atomic masses of the atomic elements it contains, each multiplied by the number of times it appears in the formula of the substance. A mole of carbon dioxide (CO_2) molecules has a mass of 44 grams: 12 grams of carbon and 32 (2×16) grams of oxygen.

When writing **chemical equations**, the atoms on each side of the reaction must balance. A chemical equation is used to express the changes that take place during a chemical reaction. The number of atoms of each element at the beginning of the reaction must be accounted for at the end of the reaction.

Chemical reactions such as combustion that release energy, often in the form of heat, are called **exothermic**, and the amount of energy released by the reaction can be predicted. Reactions that occur only when heat or other energy is added to the system are called **endothermic**. The law of conservation of energy shows that if a given reaction is exothermic, the reverse reaction will be endothermic and that the amount of heat absorbed or given off will be the same.

If a reaction is strongly endothermic, it means that the reactants are relatively stable; it takes a lot of energy to break the bonds of those compounds. Reactants in exothermic reactions are unstable. **Chemical energy** is the **potential energy** of electrons—the potential for electrons to be transferred in chemical reactions.

Endothermic reactions always require an input of energy, but many exothermic reactions also do not occur spontaneously. **Activation energy** is the minimum amount of energy required to start some exothermic reactions by loosening or breaking some bonds of the reactants. That is why combustion of fossil fuels in your automobile cannot proceed without a spark plug. The rate of chemical reactions depends on the nature of the reacting substances, temperature, the amount of each reactant present, and the presence or absence of an appropriate catalyst. A **catalyst** is a substance that alters the rate of a reaction without being changed chemically by the reaction, often by lowering the activation energy.

Organic chemistry focuses on carbon compounds, especially as related to living things. Carbon tends to form strong covalent bonds, including double and triple bonds (multiple shared electrons). In addition to being important to living things (see Cell Biology and Biochemistry on page 528), organic compounds are also important as synthetic fibers and plastics in the form of polymers.

Energy, Matter, and Mechanics

Energy is the ability to do work. The basic unit of work is the **joule**. Energy takes several forms. **Potential energy** is stored energy; a large rock on the edge of a steep hill has potential energy. **Kinetic energy** is the energy of motion; the rock rolling down the hill has kinetic energy and the ability to damage objects in its path. **Mass energy** is the energy of **relativity** ($E = mc^2$). Einstein's equation shows that mass and energy are just two forms of the same thing and that each has the capability to become the other. In his famous equation, E represents energy, m stands for mass, and c^2 is the speed of light, squared. It demonstrates the equality of matter and energy relative to velocity.

Electrical energy is associated with the number and kinds of charges on the atoms of a substance and with the movement of electrons. **Chemical energy** is energy stored in chemical bonds. **Thermal energy** is the total internal kinetic and potential energy of an object due to the random motion of its atoms and molecules.

The first law of thermodynamics is the law of conservation of energy and states that energy cannot be created nor destroyed; it can only change form (potential → kinetic energy).

The second law of thermodynamics states that in every energy transformation, some energy is always lost as heat, increasing entropy.

Heat is the thermal energy of random molecular motion. The heat of an object depends on temperature, mass, and the physical properties of the object, such as density. The unit of heat is the joule. Heat is always transferred from areas of high energy (fast motion) to areas of low energy (slow motion). A **calorie** is the amount of heat energy necessary to raise the temperature of one gram of water one degree Celsius. The term "calorie" that we use on food labels actually represents a kilocalorie of energy. If a banana has 110 calories, then it has 110 kilocalories.

Temperature is a measure of the average energy of random motion of the particles of a substance. Absolute temperature is measured in degrees **Kelvin**, with absolute zero representing no molecular motion. The **Celsius** scale is based on the freezing (0°C) and boiling (100°C) temperatures of water. Experimental evidence shows that absolute zero is –273.15°C, so the conversion formula is simply: °C = K – 273.15. **Fahrenheit** establishes 0°F as the stabilized temperature when equal amounts of ice, water, and salt are mixed and, rather arbitrarily, 96°F (originally) as the body temperature of a person in good health (the scale was recalibrated eventually, resulting in 98.6°F becoming the body temperature). The conversion formula is more complex: °F = (°C × 1.8) + 32

Matter exists in one of three states: **solid**, **liquid**, or **gas**. Solids have a fixed shape, with molecules held close together by strong bonds. Liquid molecules move around and trade places, while maintaining a strong attraction to each other. Gases have particles that are separated by large amounts of space and expand at high temperatures, due to rapidly moving and colliding molecules. A gas will fill the shape of a container enclosing it.

Most compounds can undergo **state changes** if temperatures are raised or lowered. An input of heat energy is required to change the state of a substance from solid to liquid form **(melting)** or from liquid to gas form **(evaporation)**. When gases are cooled they change to liquids **(condensation)** and then to solids **(crystallization)**, and energy is released.

Everything in the universe is in constant motion, from the atoms in our bodies to the galaxies of the universe. Understanding **mechanics**, the effects of physical forces acting upon bodies, is one of the cornerstones of understanding the physical universe.

Speed (velocity) of a moving object, such as a molecule, is the constant rate at which it covers a distance ($v = d/t$, speed = distance/time elapsed). The rate of change of speed, or **acceleration**, can be calculated as the difference in the beginning speed (v_o) and ending speed (v_f) over some period of time ($a = (v - v_o)/t$). The acceleration due to **gravity** (g) is a constant 9.8 meters per second^2, a calculation established in 1901 based on Galileo's research during the early seventeenth century. Isaac Newton developed the Second Law of Motion based on Galileo's discovery of the constant acceleration of falling bodies due to gravity. The Second Law states that the force of attraction between two objects is a function of the masses of the objects and the distance between them, described by the equation $F = g(m_1 m_2)/r^2$, where g is the gravitational constant, m_1 and m_2 are the masses of the two objects, and r is the distance between the two objects.

Classical mechanics is often referred to as "Newtonian mechanics" after Newton and his laws of motion. **Newton's first law of motion** states that an object will remain in its state of rest or its state of motion in a straight line at a constant speed if no net force acts upon it. A **force** is any influence that can change the speed or direction of motion of an object. An object will not begin to move by itself. A moving object in the vacuum of space continues to move at a constant speed. On Earth or in our atmosphere, forces such as friction and resistance slow and eventually stop moving objects. **Inertia** is defined as the resistance of an object at rest or an object in motion to change its state of rest or motion. Inertia offers a way to measure the amount of matter in an object. Mass is a measure of the inertia of a body.

Newton's second law of motion states that force on an object is equal to the product of its mass and acceleration. The greater the force applied to an object, the greater the acceleration. The greater the mass of the object, the smaller the acceleration. This relationship can be expressed in the equation $F = ma$ (force = mass × acceleration). The unit of force is the newton (N).

Newton's third law of motion states that when an object exerts force on another object, the second object exerts an equal force in the opposite direction. For instance, if you tried to push an object that has more mass than you do, you would find yourself being pushed backward. This occurs because while the force the object exerts on you is the same as the force you exert on it, your mass is smaller so your acceleration due to the force is greater. Newton's law restated says that for every action, there is an equal and opposite reaction. When a person walks, the action of walking causes the force of the Earth's surface to push her or him forward.

Classical mechanics is subdivided into statics, which concerns objects at rest; kinematics, which concerns objects in motion; and dynamics, which concerns objects subjected to various forces. Classical mechanics does not apply for systems moving at high velocities near the speed of light, where quantum mechanics and relativity come into play. **Quantum mechanics** is used to describe motion in atoms, while **relativity** describes motion in the vastness of space.

Einstein's theory of general relativity concerns gravity and inertia of massive objects in space and is a modification of Newtonian gravitational theory based on special relativity. The **theory of special relativity** put forth by Einstein is based on two ideas. First, it assumes that the laws of physics are constant from any frame of reference. This means that the laws of physics observed by a hypothetical observer traveling with a particle near the speed of light must be the same as those observed by an observer who is stationary in an observatory. The second is that the speed of light is constant regardless of the speed of the observer. This idea is important when one considers planetary motion and the point from which one is making observations. The Earth is moving relative to the objects being observed. Based on these two assumptions, Einstein showed that space and time are relative concepts rather than absolute concepts; that is, one is always a function of the other.

Electricity, Magnetism, and Waves

When you rub your stockinged feet across the carpet in a dry heated house, you get a little shock when you touch an object. This is an electrical phenomenon that can't be explained by chemical equations or gravitational theory. In fact, all matter, including our bodies, has an electrical nature, because electrical forces are what keep electrons in orbit around the nuclei of all of our atoms. All of the properties of matter except mass are related to **electrical forces.**

All electric **charges** are either positive or negative. Like charges (two positives for example) repel each other, and unlike charges (opposites) attract each other. Most objects normally contain equal amounts of positive and negative charges (protons and electrons). Sometimes when two objects are rubbed together, such as your socks and the carpet, the frictional motion is enough to break some of the electrons away. Depending upon the materials rubbed together, one object will pick up the electrons and become negatively charged, while the other object will lose electrons and become positively charged. While rubbing your feet, you've created a charge on your skin; when you touch an uncharged object, electrons fly over to equalize the charge difference.

The unit of electrical charge is the **coulomb (C).** The smallest unit of charge is abbreviated (e) and is based on the charge of single protons and electrons (+ or $- 1.6 \times 10^{-19}$ C).

Coulomb's law of electric force states that the force between two electric charges is directly proportional to both charges and inversely proportional to the square of the distance between them. The force is termed repulsion if the charges are the same and attraction if the charges are different.

Conductors such as metals allow free movement of electrons. An **insulator** such as glass or plastic tends to inhibit the flow of electrons. **Semiconductors** are intermediate. The **ampere** is the unit that measures electrical flow or **current.** An ampere is equal to movement of 1 coulomb per second. The **volt** is the unit of potential difference between negatively and positively charged surfaces, such as the poles of a battery, and is expressed as joules per coulomb. **Current** is the term used to describe the actual movement of electrons and is described by **Ohm's law** (current = voltage/resistance, or $I = V/R$). The **resistance** is a function of the medium of flow; that is, resistance is low for a good conductor like copper and high for a poor conductor (a good insulator) such as plastic. The amount of work that can be done by electricity is expressed as **watts** (W), and can be calculated as amperes $\times$ volts. This is derived from the idea that power = current $\times$ voltage.

Magnetism is the force that moving charges such as electric currents exert on each other. The magnetic force between charges is a function of both the charges and their relative motion. Magnetic forces always come in pairs, and they can occur without objects coming into physical contact. **Magnetic fields** are regions of space altered by an electric charge. Every electric current has a magnetic field around it. An electric motor uses magnetic fields to turn electrical energy into mechanical energy. A generator uses magnetic fields to turn mechanical energy into electrical energy. Electromagnetic waves are coupled electric and magnetic disturbances that originate from accelerated electrical charges. Examples of electromagnetic waves include gamma rays, X-rays, and light.

Some **waves**, such as those in water and sound waves, carry energy from one point to another via periodic motion of individual particles in a medium. There is no net transfer of matter in wave motion. In **transverse waves**, the particles of the medium move perpendicular to the wave, while in a **longitudinal wave**, they move parallel to the wave. **Sound waves** are longitudinal and are produced by vibration of an object, causing changes in the pressure and density of the surrounding medium, such as air or water.

Waves are described in terms of **frequency**, **wavelength**, and **amplitude**. The frequency of a wave describes how many wave peaks pass a given point per second. The wavelength describes the distance between crests. The amplitude is the vertical distance from trough to peak. Frequency and wavelength are related by the equation: $v = $ wavelength $(\lambda) \times$ frequency (f), where v is the wave speed. Amplitude is independent of frequency and wavelength.

Electromagnetic radiation with a very short wavelength, such as ultraviolet light, has high energy. Long-wavelength radiation, such as infrared radiation, is often associated with heat. Very long wave radiation, such as radio waves, has very low energy. Light has intermediate wavelengths and energy.

Light is a kind of electromagnetic radiation that exhibits properties of both waves and particles. Light generally travels in straight lines; to see this, just shine a flashlight into the nighttime sky. Light can also be reflected, refracted, and even transmitted through surfaces. Light is **reflected** when it bounces off a surface, such as a mirror. **Refraction** occurs when light is bent when passing through different media, such as the transition from air to water. Each frequency or wavelength of light produces a visual image of a different color, and the dispersion of light (as refracted through a prism) causes the appearance of a rainbow.

The Universe

The **big bang** theory is the most widely accepted theory among scientists about the origin of the universe. Based on recent calculations, scientists believe that the universe was created between 13 and 24 billion years ago. In 1930, Georges Lemaître was the first to visualize matter condensed into a "primeval atom" that exploded and created the universe. The idea gained support with astronomer Edwin Hubble's finding that distant galaxies in every direction are going away from us at speeds proportional to their distance. This phenomenon is known as the **red shift**, a displacement of the spectra of distant objects. It is due to the fact that light from an object moving away shifts toward the "red" region of the spectrum (red and infrared wavelengths).

Initially, a star is composed mostly of hydrogen and helium. The star continues to turn hydrogen to helium through the process of nuclear fusion. When hydrogen is exhausted, some stars burn into embers. If the star is large enough, it can suddenly expand and produce a huge explosion; this star is now called a **supernova**. Elements heavier than iron can be formed during the supernova phase, such as gold, lead, and silver.

The distance of planets from the sun, with a descending order of planet size, are as follows:

Planet	Diameter of planet (in approx. miles)	Distance from sun (miles x 104)
Jupiter	88,700	48,300
Saturn	74,900	88,600
Uranus	31,800	178,300
Neptune	30,700	279,300
Earth	8,000	9,300
Venus	7,600	6,700
Mars	4,200	14,200
Mercury	3,000	3,600

Comets are aggregates of frozen matter that follow regular orbits in the solar system. They appear to viewers on Earth as patches of light accompanied by long tails when they near the sun. An **asteroid** is a solid body that orbits around the sun. Many asteroids form a belt between Mars and Jupiter. **Meteoroids** are very small pieces of solid matter moving through space; when they enter the Earth's atmosphere, they produce flashes of light as **meteors**, and **meteorites** are the remains that reach the ground. It is thought that the mass extinction of dinosaurs 65 million years ago occurred when an asteroid or giant meteorite collided with the Earth, putting up a dense cloud of debris that disrupted the planetary climate. A thin layer of the element iridium, which is uncommon on Earth but common in meteorites, can be found around the world in geologic strata of that era.

The origin of the Earth's moon is still a mystery, but the most widely accepted theory today is that an object struck the Earth some 4.5 billion years ago, sending large fragments of the object into space. Some of those fragments are thought to have been held by the Earth's gravitational field and aggregated into the orbiting moon. The moon has no atmosphere or water and has been bombarded by meteorites over a long period, forming lunar craters.

Lunar eclipses occur when the Earth passes between the sun and moon, casting a shadow on the moon. **Solar eclipses** occur when the moon passes between the Earth and sun, casting a shadow on the sun.

Our sun is a member of an immense swirling group of stars called the Milky Way galaxy. The Milky Way is one of an estimated hundreds of billions of **galaxies** in the universe. The universe is continually expanding. In addition to galaxies and clusters of stars, clouds of gas and dust called **nebulae** are scattered throughout the universe. A **black hole** is an old star that has contracted so much that its gravitational field prevents the escape of light.

Earth Science

The Earth and surrounding sky can be thought of as comprising several spheres. The **atmosphere** is an envelope of gases surrounding the Earth. The **lithosphere** is Earth's rocky shell. The **hydrosphere** is the water in and on the Earth, including what lies below the surface. The **biosphere** includes all the living things on Earth.

The air we breathe consists of mostly nitrogen (78 percent) and oxygen (21 percent) with traces of argon (0.9 percent) and carbon dioxide (0.03 percent). Water vapor is also present in various amounts (up to 4 percent) depending upon climate and weather. The lower atmosphere also contains particulate matter such as dust and pollen.

The atmosphere is divided into four layers. Near the Earth's surface, within the **troposphere,** atmospheric pressure and temperature both decrease with altitude. Between 7 and 17 km above the Earth's surface, the atmosphere abruptly becomes less dense and colder, and most weather phenomena cease. This is the boundary of the **stratosphere**; it is slightly higher near the equator and lower at the poles. The stratosphere contains **ozone**, a form of oxygen that absorbs ultraviolet radiation and prevents it from damaging life on Earth. The layer lying between 50 and 80 km is called the **mesosphere**. At 80 km the atmosphere changes greatly. Ions become more abundant, and temperatures increase up to 2,000°C, earning this outer layer the name **thermosphere.**

The hydrosphere includes all of the water on the surface of the Earth (such as oceans, rivers, and ponds), groundwater, water stored in soil, and water in the atmosphere. Water is important to living things and is an important erosive force that has shaped the Earth. It is also important to climate and weather. The oceans and ocean currents serve as huge influences over climate, both by acting as temperature buffers and by transporting warm or cold waters.

The energy that powers climate and weather is **insolation**—incoming solar radiation balanced with radiation generated by the Earth. The uneven heating of the Earth's surface by the sun along with atmospheric moisture create the climates and weather of the Earth. **Weather** is the day-to-day conditions of temperature, precipitation, and wind in a given area. **Climate** is the long-term pattern of weather in an area. **Clouds** form as atmospheric moisture rises and condenses when cooler temperatures are encountered at higher altitudes. Rain falls when air becomes saturated with water. Since warm air is less dense than cool air, winds are generated by temperature differences.

The **lithosphere** includes the Earth's **crust** and the outermost part of the **mantle**. The crust includes the surface to 40 km deep and is composed chiefly of **silicates** (compounds with silicon and oxygen); **carbonates** such as limestone; metals and metal ores; and coal, oil, and natural gas. The mantle (40–2,900 km) is mostly silicates of magnesium and iron. The Earth's core is composed mostly of iron and nickel.

Common silicate minerals include quartz, feldspar, mica, ferrous (iron) and magnesium silicates, clays, and calcites. Rocks are aggregates of minerals formed by various processes. **Igneous rocks** are cooled from a molten state and are often associated with volcanoes. **Sedimentary rocks** are formed by the deposition of materials following processes including compaction. **Metamorphic rocks** are existing rocks that have been changed by heat and pressure. **Soil** is a combination of rock fragments, clay particles, and decomposed organic matter.

The surface of the Earth represents millions of years of changes, some very slow and others very fast. **Erosion** is a term that refers to all of the processes by which rocks are worn down and debris carried away, changing the physical character of the Earth's surface. **Weathering** can be chemical or mechanical. Water does both. The Grand Canyon is an example of chemical and mechanical weathering of rock by water. Glaciers also erode the Earth, as do groundwater and wind.

The Earth's crust is actually a group of plates moving against one another. The forces exerted by the movement of these plates are called **tectonic forces** and are responsible for **continental drift**, **earthquakes**, **volcanoes**, and the formation of great mountain ranges and deep trenches or rifts. A **fault** is a fracture in the Earth's crust along which movement of the tectonic plates has occurred. Sudden jerking movements of such faults cause earthquakes.

Faults can also cause formation of cliffs such as those found in the Rocky Mountains. **Folding** takes place as slow, continuous tectonic movement, producing hills and depressions that erode into parallel ridges and valleys, as in the Appalachians. Mountains form in several ways. They may result from accumulation of volcanic lava or be raised by faults. The largest and tallest mountain ranges in the world show sedimentation, faulting, folding, volcanic activity, **uplifts**, *and* erosion.

Movement of the Earth's crust is most dramatically demonstrated by continental drift and **sea floor spreading**. Looking at a modern map of the world, one can easily see that the land masses fit together like the pieces of a puzzle. At the edges of each continent, a **continental shelf** gradually slopes to a depth of around 130 m, where a dramatic drop occurs and the bottom slopes more steeply along the **continental slope** to the **abyssal plain**. When the margins of the land masses are extended to include their continental slopes, the fit of land masses is clearly evident. It is a near certainty based on geological and biogeographical evidence that the land masses were once a single land mass, which has been named **Pangaea**. In addition, the sea floor is continuously producing new crust via volcanic activity in **midocean ridges**, while other portions of crust are **subducted** back into the mantle in **deep ocean trenches**.

The Earth has been continuously changing since it was formed with the solar system some 4.5 billion years ago. The oldest surface rocks are around 3.8 billion years old and are igneous rocks embedded with sedimentary and metamorphic rocks, suggesting that shaping of the Earth's surface had already begun. The splitting of Pangaea into two and then several land masses began less than 200 million years ago, long after life appeared on the planet. The geologic and biological history of the Earth is divided into **eras**, **periods**, and **epochs**, each associated with climate conditions, landforms, and biota (living things).

The earliest era in the Earth's history is the **Precambrian Era**, which lasted from 4.5 billion to around 570 million years ago. During the early Precambrian period, simple bacteria and marine algae were the dominant life forms. By the late Precambrian, marine invertebrates had evolved.

The **Paleozoic** era lasted from the Cambrian period (550 million years ago) until the Permian period (around 250 million years ago). The main geological event influencing this era was the repeated advance and retreat of shallow sea over the continents. During this era, the first marine vertebrates (fish) and land plants evolved. During the Carboniferous period of the Paleozoic era, large forests of nonflowering plants lived and died, producing many of the fossil fuels we use today. By the end of the Paleozoic era 225 million years ago, the first reptiles had appeared, and insects were abundant.

The **Mesozoic** era occurred between 245 and 65 million years ago and coincided with the splitting of Pangaea. In addition, the great impact thought to have led to the extinction of the dinosaurs occurred during the late Mesozoic era. During the Triassic period, dinosaurs and mammals appeared. During the Jurassic, dinosaurs dominated the land. By the end of the Mesozoic era, during the Cretaceous period, dinosaurs became extinct and the first flowering plants appeared.

The past 65 million years, the **Cenozoic** era, consist of the Tertiary and Quaternary periods. One characteristic of Cenozoic times has been significant volcanic and tectonic activity, forming the Alps and Himalayas. The first primates appeared during the Paleocene epoch around 65 million years ago, as did many large mammals over the next millions of years. Flowering plants have dominated the Earth's flora during the Cenozoic era. Modern man has only appeared in recent history, around 0.01 million years ago, although early hominids arose during the Pliocene epoch, over 2 million years ago. During the Pleistocene epoch, the last ice age occurred, covering much of the northern hemisphere with glaciers. Although *ice age* is a term associated with the Pleistocene and is the major climatic change with which we are most familiar, many such climatic changes have occurred throughout the Earth's long history.

NATURAL SCIENCES RESOURCES

The CLEP Natural Sciences exam covers a broad range of topics. Many of these topics are discussed in the review you have just read. There is always room to study more about each subject, however. Keep in mind that the majority of the exam will require you to apply knowledge to problems or questions, so you must be able to synthesize your knowledge of all natural sciences topics into a plausible answer to each question. Practice taking the sample tests in this book and figure out what areas you need to work on.

Use textbooks, library materials, museum exhibits, television programs, and other sources to expand your knowledge of the natural sciences. You can increase your chances of getting a good score on the exam by broadening your base of natural sciences knowledge. Here are some books and websites you can look up when studying on your own.

Biology Resources

The Biology Project (biology.arizona.edu)

Ecology.com

Campbell, Neil A. and Jane B. Reece. *Biology*. 6 ed. Menlo Park, CA: Benjamin Cummings, 2001.

Chemistry Resources

WebElements Periodic Table (webelements.com)

Brown, Theodore L. et al. *Chemistry: The Central Science*. 9 ed. New York: Prentice Hall, 2002.

Houk, Clifford C. and Richard Post. *Chemistry: Concepts and Problems*. 2 ed. New York: Wiley, 1996).

Physics Resources

physics.org

Goldstein, Herbert et al. *Classical Mechanics*. 3 ed. New York: Addison Wesley, 2002.

Griffiths, David J. *Introduction to Electrodynamics*. 3 ed. New York: Prentice Hall, 1998.

Shankar, R. *Principles of Quantum Mechanics*. Boston: Kluwer Academic, 1994.

Earth Science Resources

United States Geological Survey (geology.usgs.gov)

Bennett, Jeffrey. *The Cosmic Perspective*. 3 ed. New York, Addison Wesley, 2003.

Denecke Jr., Edward J. *Let's Review Earth Science*. 2 ed. New York, Barron's, 2001.

FINAL THOUGHTS

With the information and resources listed here, you're on your way to a great CLEP Natural Sciences score.

Good luck on the exam!

Chapter Twenty-Two: **Practice Test 2**

Time—90 minutes
120 Questions

Directions: Each question below has five lettered answer choices. For each question or phrase, choose the most closely related answer. For multiple questions that refer to the same group of lettered answer choices, each choice can be used more than once, once, or not at all.

Questions 1–3

    (A) Lewis acid

    (B) Lewis base

    (C) Bronsted-Lowry acid

    (D) Bronsted-Lowry base

    (E) Buffer

1. A proton donor

2. Able to absorb small additions of either a strong acid or strong base with little change in pH

3. Electron pair donor during the formation of a coordinate covalent bond

Questions 4–6

    (A) Competitive exclusion

    (B) Niche breadth

    (C) Food web

    (D) Natural selection

    (E) Ecosystem

4. Two species utilize the same limited resource, causing the elimination of one of the species from the community.

5. A multidimensional hyperspace contains all of the biotic and abiotic factors that affect a species.

6. A homogenous ecological unit is comprised of a community and the abiotic factors that affect the species in that community.

GO ON TO THE NEXT PAGE

Questions 7–9

    (A) Convection

    (B) Conduction

    (C) Radiation

    (D) Specific heat capacity

    (E) Triple point

7. The temperature and pressure at which a substance can be at equilibrium in all three states of matter

8. The transfer of heat from one place to another by the motion of a volume of hot fluid

9. The transfer of energy from one place to another in the form of electromagnetic waves

Questions 10–12

    (A) Proxima Centauri

    (B) Sun

    (C) Jupiter

    (D) Saturn

    (E) Mercury

10. The second-closest star to the Earth

11. The ringed planet

12. The planet with the most moons

Questions 13–16 refer to the following diagram of a cross section of the Earth.

Cross Section of Earth

13. Mantle

14. Upper mantle

15. Crust

16. Outer core

GO ON TO THE NEXT PAGE

Directions: For each of the following questions or incomplete statements, select the best answer or completion from the five options given.

17. Had the Earth formed as a smaller planet with a lesser gravitational pull, what key event in the formation of life might not have been possible?

    (A) Living cells could not have evolved in a lower-gravity system.

    (B) The crust of the Earth might not have cooled enough for land masses and water to form.

    (C) The atmosphere would not have been able to produce enough oxygen for life.

    (D) The Earth could not have formed an atmosphere capable of retaining surface water.

    (E) The Earth might have become a moon of a larger planet.

18. A critical event in the development of living organisms was the formation of molecules that could

    (A) form complex cell organelles.

    (B) utilize oxygen.

    (C) self-replicate.

    (D) carry out photosynthesis.

    (E) carry out chemosynthesis.

19. The oldest fossils date to approximately 3.5 billion years ago and resemble what group of organisms found today?

    (A) Algae

    (B) Molds

    (C) Primitive plants

    (D) Protists

    (E) Bacteria

20. As photosynthetic organisms increased the oxygen in the atmosphere, which adaptation then made the evolution of advanced life forms possible?

    (A) Anaerobic respiration

    (B) Aerobic respiration

    (C) Photosynthesis

    (D) Transpiration

    (E) Osmosis and diffusion

21. Which of the following adaptations is NOT found in mammals?

    (A) Egg laying

    (B) Four-chambered hearts

    (C) Dry skin

    (D) Mammary glands

    (E) Cold-blooded

22. Which choice shows the outdated five kingdom system of classification?

    (A) Monera, Protista, Plantae, Fungi, Animalia

    (B) Plantae, Fungi, Chordata, Amelida, Animalia

    (C) Monera, Fungi, Animalia, Chordata, Plantae

    (D) Animalia, Monera, Protista, Fungi, Bacteria

GO ON TO THE NEXT PAGE

23. Embryonic development can provide clues to evolutionary development by noting structure and form through the various stages of development. Which of the following structures is NOT found in human embryos?

    (A) Gill slits

    (B) Three-chambered heart

    (C) A tail

    (D) Dorsal nerve cord

    (E) Notochord

24. Which are in the correct order from general to specific?

    (A) Kingdom, phylum, order, class, family, genus, species

    (B) Kingdom, phylum, class, order, genus, family, species

    (C) Kingdom, genus, family, order, class, phylum, species

    (D) Kingdom, order, phylum, class, genus, family, species

    (E) Kingdom, phylum, class, order, family, genus, species

25. Why has the status of viruses as living organisms been in doubt?

    (A) They can only reproduce inside of living cells.

    (B) They contain nucleic acids and can reproduce.

    (C) They lack major cell organelles.

    (D) They are found inside living organisms.

    (E) They cannot move independently.

26. What trait could be used to classify the following plants into two equal groups?

    Pine tree, maple tree, moss, fern, liverwort, carnation

    (A) Vascular versus nonvascular

    (B) Seeds versus spores

    (C) Land versus aquatic

    (D) Photosynthetic versus non photosynthetic

    (E) Naked seeds versus seeds contained in a fruit

27. You have found an unidentified species and need to place it into one of the five major kingdoms. Which characteristic below would prevent this organism from being placed into the animal kingdom?

    (A) Multicellular

    (B) Sessile (does not move freely)

    (C) No backbone

    (D) Cell walls

    (E) Lacks complex body organs

28. Which of the following is NOT a component of the process of natural selection?

    (A) Competition for limited resources occurs.

    (B) Surplus offspring are typically produced.

    (C) Traits acquired by parents are passed to offspring.

    (D) Some traits are more beneficial than others.

    (E) Traits must be genetic.

GO ON TO THE NEXT PAGE

29. Which of the following components are required even in the most primitive cells?

    A. Organelles
    B. Cell membrane
    C. Cytoplasm
    D. Nucleus

    (A) A and B
    (B) B and C
    (C) A and C
    (D) B and D
    (E) C and D

30. Which of the following processes would NOT require energy to move substances across the cell membrane?

    I. Active transport
    II. Facilitated diffusion
    III. Osmosis

    (A) I only
    (B) II only
    (C) III only
    (D) I and II only
    (E) II and III only

31. In a cell with 60 chromosomes, which of the following would be the sequence of chromosome numbers through the processes of mitosis and cell division?

    (A) 60-30-60
    (B) 30-60-120-60
    (C) 120-60
    (D) 60-120-60
    (E) 120-60-30

32. All of the following are a function of the plasma membrane of a cell EXCEPT

    (A) cell-to-cell recognition.
    (B) regulation of movement into and out of the cell.
    (C) providing a rigid support structure.
    (D) signal reception.
    (E) containing cytoplasm.

33. Which organelle is responsible for energy production in the cytoplasm?

    (A) Lysosomes
    (B) Nucleus
    (C) Ribosomes
    (D) Mitochondria
    (E) Endoplasmic reticulum

34. Which of the following is NOT a function of one of the specialized forms of RNA in a eukaryotic cell?

    (A) Duplicate the DNA molecule.
    (B) Carry transcripts of portions of DNA out of the nucleus.
    (C) Translate the code of DNA.
    (D) Protein manufacture.
    (E) All are RNA functions.

35. Which of the following do NOT represent human base-pairings?

    (A = Adenine, T = Thymine, C = Cytosine, G = Guanine, U = Uracil)

    I. A-T
    II. G-C
    III. A-U

    (A) I only
    (B) II only
    (C) III only
    (D) I, II, and III
    (E) None of the above

GO ON TO THE NEXT PAGE

36. In the process of DNA transcription and translation, several forms of RNA are used: transfer RNA
(tRNA), messenger RNA (mRNA), and ribosomal
RNA (rRNA). Which of the following has these
in the correct order of use from transcription
through translation?

(A) mRNA, rRNA, tRNA

(B) rRNA, tRNA, mRNA

(C) tRNA, rRNA, mRNA

(D) rRNA, mRNA, tRNA

(E) mRNA, tRNA, rRNA

37. During transcription, a specific code on the DNA
molecule will signal the start and the end of transcription. The region of the DNA between these
start and stop codes is called a

(A) codon.

(B) mRNA.

(C) gene.

(D) chromosome.

(E) mutation.

38. In photosynthesis, how does the light energy
actually interact with the plant pigments such as
chlorophyll to start the process?

(A) Chlorophyll uses light energy to produce
carbohydrates like glucose.

(B) The chlorophyll's temperature rises and
drives the remaining processes.

(C) Chlorophyll is split into smaller carbohydrates such as glucose and fructose.

(D) ATP in the chlorophyll molecule is
transported to the mitochondria in order
to produce carbohydrates.

(E) An electron in the pigments is boosted to a
higher energy level and releases energy as it
drops back to its original level.

39. In cellular respiration, it is the movement of electrons that makes the production of ATP molecules
possible. What acts as the final acceptor of electrons in this process?

(A) Hydrogen

(B) Carbon

(C) Phosphorous

(D) Water

(E) Oxygen

40. Which of the following events during meiosis
would result in a chromosome abnormality in the
offpsring?

(A) Spermatogenesis

(B) Oogenesis

(C) Cytokinesis

(D) Crossing over

(E) Nondisjunction

41. The wings in bats and the wings in birds are said
to be analogous structures because

(A) they have a similar function but different
structure.

(B) they have a similar structure but different
function.

(C) they reveal a common ancestry.

(D) they reveal a similar embryonic development
pattern.

(E) they have a similar function and structure.

GO ON TO THE NEXT PAGE ⇒

KAPLAN

Acoelomate, Pseudocoelomate, Coelomate.

42. Which of the cross sections shown here reveals an animal that would have the most complex body organs and systems?

   (A) I only

   (B) II only

   (C) III only

   (D) I and III only

   (E) I and II only

43. If a tree grows at 1.5 cm per year, how much higher would a nail hammered into the trunk of the tree be after 12 years?

   (A) 8 cm

   (B) 0 cm

   (C) 18 cm

   (D) 13.5 cm

   (E) 10.5 cm

44. What physiological feature helped early primitive plants move out of water onto land?

   (A) Flowers

   (B) Seeds

   (C) Leaves

   (D) Roots

   (E) Cuticle

45. All animals but the sponges have some form of

   (A) dorsal nerve cord.

   (B) brain.

   (C) reproduction.

   (D) symmetry.

   (E) segmentation.

46. Which is actually considered a form of connective tissue in animals?

   (A) Skin

   (B) Blood

   (C) Smooth muscle

   (D) Neuron

   (E) Skeletal muscle

47. When our body temperature approaches a certain point, the sweat glands are activated, and we begin to perspire. This is an example of

   (A) a circulatory response.

   (B) an immune response.

   (C) a conditioned response.

   (D) positive feedback.

   (E) negative feedback.

GO ON TO THE NEXT PAGE

48. Which of the following is/are NOT a part of the circulatory system?

    (A) Arteries

    (B) Veins

    (C) Lungs

    (D) Heart

    (E) Capillaries

49. Organisms that exhibit the greatest diversity and the most adaptations generally utilize

    (A) sexual reproduction.

    (B) asexual reproduction.

    (C) binary fission.

    (D) budding.

    (E) regeneration.

50. A single cell resulting from fertilization of an egg by sperm is called a(n)

    (A) embryo.

    (B) fetus.

    (C) zygote.

    (D) trimester.

    (E) blastocyst.

51. In egg-laying animals, the developing embryo is nourished and protected by structures in the egg, including a yolk sac and amnion. In mammals, the structure responsible for exchange of nutrients with the mother's bloodstream is/are the

    (A) placenta.

    (B) amnion.

    (C) uterine wall.

    (D) fallopian tubes.

    (E) ovaries.

52. The fruit in a flowering plant may function in any of the following EXCEPT

    (A) dispersal.

    (B) protection of the embryo.

    (C) pollination.

    (D) attraction of animals.

    (E) food storage.

53. An insect changing from a larva to an adult or a tadpole developing into a frog does so in a process called

    (A) embryonic development.

    (B) binary fission.

    (C) oogenesis.

    (D) external fertilization.

    (E) metamorphosis.

GO ON TO THE NEXT PAGE

Questions 54–56 are based on the following pedigree.

Pedigree

54. If the trait shown as shaded is an X-linked trait, what chance is there that the mother (number 2) is a carrier?

(A) 100 percent

(B) 75 percent

(C) 50 percent

(D) 25 percent

(E) 0 percent

55. Using the same pedigree for a recessive non-sex-linked trait, what chance do the daughters (7 and 8) have of being carriers of this trait?

(A) 100 percent

(B) 75 percent

(C) 50 percent

(D) 25 percent

(E) 0 percent

56. If the recessive allele of the trait in the pedigree is shown with a "t" and the dominant allele is shown with a "T," for which individual in the pedigree can a genotype NOT be determined?

(A) 5

(B) 6

(C) 7

(D) 8

(E) All genotypes can be determined.

Questions 57–59 are based on the following scenario.

In a certain plant, red flowers (R) are dominant over white (r), and smooth seeds (S) are dominant over rough seeds (s). Two plants are crossed and produced the following offspring:

Red/Smooth:	26
Red/Rough:	24
White/Smooth:	30
White/Rough:	20

57. Given this information, what must the parental genotypes have been?

(A) RRSS * rrss

(B) RrSs * RrSs

(C) rrSs * rrSs

(D) rrss * rrss

(E) RrSs * rrss

58. Which of the following processes could result in a pattern of inheritance different than expected based on the principle of independent assortment and probability?

(A) Gene linkage

(B) Crossing over in meiosis

(C) Mutation

(D) All of the above

(E) None of the above

GO ON TO THE NEXT PAGE

KAPLAN

59. In the example on the previous page, an Rr combination that produced a pink flower could be an example of

    (A) plietropy.
    (B) heterozygous traits.
    (C) codominance.
    (D) polygenic traits.
    (E) incomplete dominance.

60. Most genetic traits cannot be worked out with a Punnett square or pedigree because they are

    (A) not expressed.
    (B) monohybrid.
    (C) polygenic.
    (D) codominant.
    (E) too much affected by environment.

61. Inserting a gene into a bacterial strand of DNA to produce a specific compound would be an example of

    (A) DNA fingerprinting.
    (B) electrophoresis.
    (C) gene cloning.
    (D) karyotyping.
    (E) cross-breeding.

62. A mutagen that can affect a cell's DNA and cause cancer to form is called a

    (A) carcinogen.
    (B) antioxidant.
    (C) toxin.
    (D) oncogene.
    (E) codon.

63. Blood type is determined by three different alleles (A, B, and i). A person with type AB blood will have the A and B alleles. What genotype will account for type O blood?

    (A) Ai
    (B) Bi
    (C) ii
    (D) AB
    (E) None of the above

64. A gene that is more commonly expressed in one gender is said to be

    (A) sex-linked.
    (B) X-linked.
    (C) recessive.
    (D) sex-influenced.
    (E) dominant.

GO ON TO THE NEXT PAGE ▷

Carrying Capacity

Growth rate

Time (Months)

Pop. Size

Time

65. This graph shows the concept of habitat carrying capacity. As a population continues to increase, some factor generally limits the rate of growth until it levels off or even declines. Which of the following is NOT a likely factor limiting the growth rate of a population?

(A) Excessive food supply
(B) Competition
(C) Limited food supply
(D) Predation
(E) Limited space

66. This graph most likely shows which of the following interactions between species?

(A) Competitive exclusion
(B) Mutualism
(C) Predator-prey
(D) Overexploitation
(E) Mimicry

67. Which of the following involves direct harm or exploitation of one organism by another?

(A) Commensalism
(B) Biological invasions
(C) Competition
(D) Mutualism
(E) Parasitism

GO ON TO THE NEXT PAGE

68. The effects of predation, carrying capacity, competition, disease, and parasitism are frequently density dependent, which means

    (A) their impact is greater when populations are growing.

    (B) they tend to have a greater impact in more dense populations.

    (C) they have a greater impact when populations are low.

    (D) they have the same impact regardless of density.

    (E) they have no impact at low densities.

69. Which of the following would most likely act as a density-independent factor?

    (A) Predation

    (B) Parasitism

    (C) Seasonal food supply

    (D) Weather

    (E) Reproductive success

70. A scientist wanted to assess the reproductive success of a small mammal population and measured population size, number of births, and number of deaths over three years. He found that the number of births in the population slightly exceeded the number of deaths but that population size had remained roughly the same.

    Which of the following estimates would help determine the reproductive success of this population?

    (A) Immigration rate

    (B) Emigration rate

    (C) Survival rate

    (D) Both (A) and (B)

    (E) (A), (B), and (C)

71. What is the most direct effect of agricultural and technological advances on human population growth-rate increases in the past two hundred years?

    (A) They have decreased reliance on hunting.

    (B) They have increased carrying capacity.

    (C) They have increased the number of habitats we can utilize.

    (D) They have decreased competition for food.

    (E) They have increased life span.

72. The greatest threat to species diversity and survival today is

    (A) habitat loss.

    (B) predation.

    (C) disease.

    (D) exploitation/overhunting.

    (E) pollution.

73. The energy supplied by the sun is essential to life on Earth but is essentially unavailable to most living things. The organisms capable of converting this energy to a form usable by other organisms are called

    (A) herbivores.

    (B) primary consumers.

    (C) omnivores.

    (D) producers.

    (E) top consumers.

GO ON TO THE NEXT PAGE

74. If carbon-14 has a half-life of 5,730 years, how much of a 50-gram sample will remain after 17,190 years?

   (A) 16.7 grams

   (B) 6.25 grams

   (C) 12.5 grams

   (D) 25 grams

   (E) 3.5 grams

Questions 75–76 are based on the following equation.

$$^{235}_{92}\text{U} + ? \rightarrow {}^{142}_{56}\text{Ba} + {}^{91}_{36}\text{Kr} + 3{}^{1}_{0}\text{n}$$

75. In this fission reaction, what is missing from the left side of the equation?

   (A) The element barium (Ba)

   (B) The element krypton (Kr)

   (C) A single neutron

   (D) Both barium and krypton

   (E) Three protons

76. A high amount of energy is released in a very short period of time from this reaction. Which of the following contributes to the speed of this reaction?

   (A) Barium and krypton, which contain high amounts of chemical energy, are formed.

   (B) The three neutrons released will collide with other uranium atoms and start a chain reaction.

   (C) Over time much more krypton will be formed than barium, and krypton contains more kinetic energy.

   (D) Barium and krypton will combine with the released neutrons and will split again.

   (E) The by-products of fission reactions are radioactive and thus can be used as energy sources.

77. Given the ability of nuclear fission to accelerate so rapidly, what allows nuclear power plants to use these reactions to produce electricity?

   (A) They use other fuel sources such as plutonium.

   (B) The fission reaction is produced far underground.

   (C) Only trace amounts of radioactive materials are needed.

   (D) The reactions are controlled by using materials to slow down the flow of neutrons.

   (E) Fission by-products are encased in safe containers.

78. The electron configurations for two different atoms are shown. Based on these, which of the following is TRUE?

$$1s^2\,2s^2\,2p^6\,3s^2 \qquad 1s^2\,2s^2\,2p^6$$
$$\text{A} \qquad\qquad\qquad \text{B}$$

   (A) The atom shown in A has eight electrons in its outermost energy level.

   (B) To be neutrally charged, atom B will need to have eight protons in its nucleus.

   (C) Atom A is more likely to enter into a chemical bond.

   (D) Atom B could be an electron acceptor.

   (E) Atom A has a full outer electron shell.

79. The bond that forms sodium chloride (NaCl) is an ionic bond. Which of the following is TRUE of this type of chemical bond?

   (A) Can only be broken in water.

   (B) Is based on the attraction of positively and negatively charged ions.

   (C) Requires a minimal amount of energy to break.

   (D) Is common in organic compounds such as glucose.

   (E) Involves the sharing of electrons between two atoms.

GO ON TO THE NEXT PAGE

KAPLAN

Questions 80–83 refer to the periodic table.

Periodic Table of the Elements

1																	**18**
1 **H** 1.008																	2 **He** 4.003
	2											**13**	**14**	**15**	**16**	**17**	
3 **Li** 6.941	4 **Be** 9.012											5 **B** 10.81	6 **C** 12.01	7 **N** 14.01	8 **O** 16.00	9 **F** 19.00	10 **Ne** 20.18
11 **Na** 22.99	12 **Mg** 24.31	**3**	**4**	**5**	**6**	**7**	**8**	**9**	**10**	**11**	**12**	13 **Al** 26.98	14 **Si** 28.09	15 **P** 30.97	16 **S** 32.07	17 **Cl** 35.45	18 **Ar** 39.95
19 **K** 39.10	20 **Ca** 40.08	21 **Sc** 44.96	22 **Ti** 47.88	23 **V** 50.94	24 **Cr** 52.00	25 **Mn** 54.94	26 **Fe** 55.85	27 **Co** 58.93	28 **Ni** 58.69	29 **Cu** 63.55	30 **Zn** 65.39	31 **Ga** 69.72	32 **Ge** 72.61	33 **As** 74.92	34 **Se** 78.96	35 **Br** 79.90	36 **Kr** 83.80
37 **Rb** 85.47	38 **Sr** 87.62	39 **Y** 88.91	40 **Zr** 91.22	41 **Nb** 92.91	42 **Mo** 95.94	43 **Tc** (98)	44 **Ru** 101.1	45 **Rh** 102.9	46 **Pd** 106.4	47 **Ag** 107.9	48 **Cd** 112.4	49 **In** 114.8	50 **Sn** 118.7	51 **Sb** 121.8	52 **Te** 127.6	53 **I** 126.9	54 **Xe** 131.3
55 **Cs** 132.9	56 **Ba** 137.3	57–70	71 **Lu** 175.0	72 **Hf** 178.5	73 **Ta** 181.0	74 **W** 183.8	75 **Re** 186.2	76 **Os** 190.2	77 **Ir** 192.2	78 **Pt** 195.1	79 **Au** 197.0	80 **Hg** 200.6	81 **Tl** 204.4	82 **Pb** 207.2	83 **Bi** 209.0	84 **Po** (209)	85 **At** (210)	86 **Rn** (222)
87 **Fr** (223)	88 **Ra** 226.0	89–102	103 **Lr** (260)	104 **Rf** (261)	105 **Db** (262)	106 **Sg** (263)	107 **Bh** (262)	108 **Hs** (265)	109 **Mt** (268)	110 **Uun** (269)	111 **Uuu** (272)	112 **Uub** (277)	113 Uut	114 **Uuq** (289)	115 Uup	116 Uuh	117 Uus	118 Uuo

Atomic Number ——— 6
Symbol ——— C
Atomic Mass ——— 12.01

* Numbers in parentheses are the *mass numbers* of the most stable isotope of the element.

57 **La** 138.9	58 **Ce** 140.1	59 **Or** 140.9	60 **Nd** 144.2	61 **Pm** (145)	62 **Sm** 150.4	63 **Eu** 152.0	64 **Gd** 157.3	65 **Tb** 158.9	66 **Dy** 162.5	67 **Ho** 164.9	68 **Er** 167.3	69 **Tm** 168.9	70 **Yb** 173.0
89 **Ac** 227.0	90 **Th** 232.0	91 **Pa** 231.0	92 **U** 238.0	93 **Np** 237.0	94 **Pu** (244)	95 **Am** (243)	96 **Cm** (247)	97 **Bk** (247)	98 **Cf** (251)	99 **Es** (252)	100 **Fm** (257)	101 **Md** (258)	102 **No** (259)

80. The majority of elements seen on the periodic table are classified as

   (A) gases.

   (B) metals.

   (C) semi-metals.

   (D) radioactive.

   (E) synthetic.

GO ON TO THE NEXT PAGE

81. The last column on the periodic table has the group number 8 and represents the "noble gases," which are largely nonreactive with other elements. What does the group number refer to?

    (A) The number of electrons in the outer shell of elements in a group
    (B) The number of electron orbits or shells in elements from each group
    (C) The average mass number of elements in that group
    (D) The number of protons in the nucleus
    (E) The average atomic number of elements in a group

82. Which of the following is NOT true about elements when moving from the top to the bottom of the periodic table?

    (A) The number of electron orbitals or "shells" increases.
    (B) Elements generally become more metallic.
    (C) Elements become more stable and less reactive.
    (D) Mass numbers increase.
    (E) Atomic numbers increase.

83. The horizontal rows on the table are called "periods." Moving from left to right within one of these rows, which of the following is TRUE?

    (A) The number of electron shells increases.
    (B) The number of protons increases.
    (C) The mass number remains roughly the same, but the atomic number changes.
    (D) Elements become increasingly metallic.
    (E) An increasing number of synthetic elements occur.

84. Which of the following does NOT represent a compound?

    (A) H_2
    (B) H_2O
    (C) H_2O_2
    (D) CO
    (E) NaCl

85. A solution is a(n) _____ mixture in which one or more compounds are dissolved in a solute.

    (A) homogeneous
    (B) heterogeneous
    (C) suspension
    (D) colloidal
    (E) acidic

86. Metal alloys are examples of

    (A) pure forms of a given metal.
    (B) metals that are liquid at room temperature.
    (C) metals that can act as conductors.
    (D) homogeneous mixtures of two or more metals.
    (E) heterogeneous mixtures of two or more metals.

87. Two atoms that fill their outer electron energy levels by sharing electrons are forming

    (A) an ionic bond.
    (B) a mixture.
    (C) an alloy.
    (D) a covalent bond.
    (E) an electronic bond.

GO ON TO THE NEXT PAGE

88. Which is NOT a property of an acid solution?

    (A) Can conduct electricity.
    (B) Is corrosive to other materials.
    (C) Has an excess of H^+ ions.
    (D) Has an excess of OH^- ions.
    (E) Many are essential to living things.

89. The pH scale is based upon of which of the following?

    (A) The electrical conductivity of an acid
    (B) The corrosive strength of an acid
    (C) The concentration of hydroxide (OH^-) ions
    (D) The ability of a base to neutralize acid
    (E) The concentration of hydrogen ions

Questions 90–91 refer to the following equation.

$$CH_4 + O_2 \rightarrow CO_2 + 2H_2O$$

90. Which of the following changes is needed to balance this equation?

    (A) CH_4 should be $1CH_4$.
    (B) Add H_2O to the left side of the equation.
    (C) CO_2 should be $2CO_2$.
    (D) $2H_2O$ should be $4H_2O$.
    (E) O_2 should be $2O_2$.

91. Which "law" makes it important to balance chemical equations?

    (A) Law of conservation of matter
    (B) Law of conservation of energy
    (C) Law of gravity
    (D) Law of mechanics
    (E) Law of thermodynamics

92. Energy is defined as the ability to do work. Which formula below defines the physical concept of work?

    (A) force × distance
    (B) mass × acceleration
    (C) distance/time
    (D) $E = mc^2$
    (E) energy/time

93. Which of the following is NOT a form of kinetic energy?

    (A) A moving car
    (B) A car battery
    (C) Electrical current
    (D) Molecules moving in a heated liquid
    (E) A falling rock

94. A thermometer (alcohol, mercury, or metallic spring) works because matter

    (A) contracts when cooled.
    (B) expands when heated.
    (C) contracts when heated.
    (D) Both (A) and (B)
    (E) Both (B) and (C)

GO ON TO THE NEXT PAGE

KAPLAN

95. Specific heat of a substance is the amount of energy required to raise the temperature of 1 gram of that substance 1°C. The formula is shown here.

$$S = \frac{\text{Energy Transferred (joules)}}{\text{Mass (g)} \ * \ \text{Temperature Change}}$$

The resulting units for S are J/g °C

Given 100 g of the following substances, which would require the most energy to increase in temperature by 1 degree Celsius?

(A) Hydrogen ($S = 14.3$)

(B) Mercury ($S = 0.13$)

(C) Oxygen ($S = 0.92$)

(D) Lead ($S = 0.13$)

(E) Water ($S = 4.2$)

96. Two drills put the same amount of work into drilling a hole into a metal sheet. One drill is unable to make a hole as deep as the other, even though the input of work energy was the same. Based on this, which of the following is most likely TRUE of the less efficient drill?

(A) It will generate less heat during the drilling process.

(B) It has a smaller drill bit.

(C) Both drills generate the same amount of heat because they put in the same amount of work.

(D) The more efficient drill actually worked harder because it drilled a deeper hole.

(E) It will generate more heat during the drilling process.

97. Which of the following would decrease the entropy in a body of water?

(A) Heating

(B) Freezing

(C) Letting it stand

(D) Adding an acid or a base

(E) Stirring

98. When a piston is used to compress gas at constant temperature in a cylinder, which of the following will occur?

(A) Pressure will decrease.

(B) Mass will decrease.

(C) Volume will increase.

(D) Temperature will increase.

(E) Pressure will increase.

99. In rolling a ball down a ramp, which of the following measurements would have to be known to calculate velocity?

(A) Slope and distance

(B) Distance and mass

(C) Distance and time

(D) Slope and time

(E) Force and mass

100. An astronaut on the moon once dropped a brick and a feather from the same height. Since the moon has no air resistance and only a fraction of the Earth's gravity, which hit(s) the surface first?

(A) The brick hits first.

(B) The feather hits first.

(C) They hit simultaneously.

(D) Neither hits because of low gravity.

(E) None of the above

GO ON TO THE NEXT PAGE

101. The moon has one-sixth the gravitational pull of the Earth. An object that had a mass of 120 kg on Earth then would have a mass of _____ kg on the moon.

    (A) 100
    (B) 40
    (C) 60
    (D) 120
    (E) 20

102. A train car is moved along a track until it couples with another identical car, which is not moving. Both cars move away together at half the original speed. What has happened to the momentum of the original car?

    (A) It has decreased by 50 percent.
    (B) It has doubled because of the weight of the two cars together.
    (C) It has decreased by 75 percent because the first car was moving.
    (D) It has increased by 50 percent.
    (E) It is the same as before because mass has increased.

103. A ball on the end of a string is twirled in a circle. What type of force is the string exerting on the ball?

    (A) Centripetal
    (B) Centrifugal
    (C) Acceleration
    (D) Frictional
    (E) Gravitational

104. Which would NOT be true of a spaceship traveling very near light speed?

    (A) It would begin to lose mass and convert mass to energy.
    (B) The size and shape of the object would change.
    (C) Time would move more slowly for those on the spaceship.
    (D) The mass of the ship would approach infinity.
    (E) All of the above are true.

GO ON TO THE NEXT PAGE

Electromagnetic Spectrum Showing Wavelengths

Questions 105–106 are based on the diagram shown here.

105. Which region of the spectrum shown indicates the most high-energy form of radiation?

(A) Visible

(B) Ultraviolet

(C) Infrared

(D) Gamma rays

(E) X-rays

106. In the electromagnetic spectrum, higher energy is indicated by having a higher

(A) reflection.

(B) refraction.

(C) frequency.

(D) amplitude.

(E) wavelength.

107. Voltage is a measure of what type of energy?

(A) Magnetic

(B) Potential

(C) Atomic

(D) Kinetic

(E) Chemical

108. Resistors are placed into electrical circuits to

(A) increase current.

(B) decrease current.

(C) divert current.

(D) increase voltage.

(E) decrease voltage.

GO ON TO THE NEXT PAGE

109. The amount of electrical charge moving through a circuit is measured in

(A) volts.

(B) amperes.

(C) ohms.

(D) resistance.

(E) joules.

110. Positive and negative charges can be separated and stored such as in a battery. What happens to a permanent magnet when cut in half to separate the north and south poles?

(A) The cutting tool becomes magnetized.

(B) Two smaller magnets with a north and south pole are produced.

(C) The magnetic properties will be lost.

(D) The north pole will dominate.

(E) The south pole will dominate.

111. The four inner planets in our solar system are known as

(A) planetoids.

(B) terrestrial.

(C) gaseous.

(D) Jovian.

(E) solar.

112. What discovery by Galileo contradicted the idea that objects in space revolved around the Earth?

(A) Moons orbiting Jupiter

(B) Elliptical planet orbits

(C) Halley's Comet

(D) Saturn's rings

(E) The existence of the asteroid belt

113. If light travels nearly 6 trillion miles in a year, approximately how old is the light we see from Proxima Centauri, which is 24×10^9 miles from Earth?

(A) Four years

(B) Eight years

(C) Two years

(D) One year

(E) We still see the light instantaneously.

114. Rocks formed by materials deposited by water over many years are called

(A) depositional.

(B) metamorphic.

(C) stratified.

(D) sedimentary.

(E) igneous.

115. What percentage of the Earth's atmosphere is comprised of oxygen?

(A) 79

(B) 21

(C) 53

(D) 14

(E) 85

116. What percentage of water on Earth is NOT found in the oceans?

(A) 10

(B) 5

(C) 3

(D) 20

(E) 50

GO ON TO THE NEXT PAGE

117. The two most dominant processes in the water cycle are

    (A) evaporation and precipitation.

    (B) evaporation and transpiration.

    (C) transpiration and precipitation.

    (D) evaporation and runoff.

    (E) photosynthesis and respiration.

118. The vast majority of geologic history occurred during the

    (A) Jurassic era.

    (B) Precambrian era.

    (C) Paleozoic era.

    (D) Cenozoic era.

    (E) Mesozoic era.

119. Which of the following would be most useful for accurately estimating the age of a previously unidentified fossil?

    (A) The body form of the animal or plant

    (B) Radiometric dating

    (C) The position of the fossil in the rock strata

    (D) The composition of the rocks around the fossil

    (E) The geographic location of the fossil

120. The greenhouse effect stems from the fact that CO_2 and other gases

    (A) block ultraviolet radiation, thus causing the atmosphere to warm.

    (B) slow down evaporation and transpiration, thus altering precipitation patterns.

    (C) block infrared wavelengths that would have reradiated back to space.

    (D) transmit infrared wavelengths but trap ultra-violet wavelengths, thus decreasing ozone.

    (E) interfere with ozone creation, thus increasing the effect of ultraviolet rays.

END OF TEST. STOP

KAPLAN

ANSWER KEY

1. C	19. E	37. C	55. A	73. D	91. A	109. B
2. E	20. B	38. E	56. B	74. B	92. A	110. B
3. A	21. E	39. E	57. E	75. C	93. B	111. B
4. A	22. A	40. E	58. D	76. B	94. D	112. A
5. B	23. B	41. A	59. E	77. D	95. A	113. A
6. E	24. E	42. C	60. C	78. C	96. E	114. D
7. E	25. A	43. B	61. C	79. B	97. B	115. B
8. A	26. B	44. E	62. A	80. B	98. E	116. C
9. C	27. D	45. D	63. C	81. A	99. C	117. A
10. A	28. C	46. B	64. D	82. C	100. C	118. B
11. D	29. B	47. E	65. A	83. B	101. D	119. B
12. C	30. E	48. C	66. C	84. A	102. E	120. C
13. C	31. D	49. A	67. E	85. A	103. A	
14. D	32. C	50. C	68. B	86. D	104. A	
15. E	33. D	51. A	69. D	87. D	105. D	
16. B	34. A	52. C	70. E	88. D	106. C	
17. D	35. E	53. E	71. B	89. E	107. B	
18. C	36. A	54. A	72. A	90. E	108. E	

PRACTICE TEST 2 QUICK REFERENCE TABLES

Use the following tables to determine which topics you still need to review.

Topic	Test Question
Biological Science	
Evolution and Diversity of Life	17, 18, 19, 20, 21, 22, 23, 24, 25, 26, 27, 28
Cell Biology and Biochemistry	29, 30, 32, 33, 34, 35, 36, 37, 38, 39, 61, 62
Organisms and Heredity	31, 40, 41, 42, 43, 44, 45, 46, 47, 48, 49, 50, 51, 52, 53, 54, 55, 56, 57, 58, 59, 60, 63, 64
Ecology and Population Biology	4, 5, 6, 65, 66, 67, 68, 69, 70, 71, 72, 73
Physical Science	
Atoms and Subatomic Structures	74, 75, 76, 77, 78, 80, 81, 82, 83
Elements, Molecules, and Compounds	1, 2, 3, 79, 84, 85, 86, 87, 88, 89, 90, 91
Energy, Matter, and Mechanics	7, 8, 9, 92, 93, 94, 95, 96, 97, 98, 99, 102, 103, 104
Electricity, Magnetism, and Waves	105, 106, 107, 108, 109, 110
The Universe	10, 11, 12, 100, 101, 111, 112, 113
Earth Science	13, 14, 15, 16, 114, 115, 116, 117, 118, 119, 120

Topic	Number of Questions on Test	Number Correct
Biological Science	60	
Evolution and Diversity of Life	12	
Cell Biology and Biochemistry	12	
Organisms and Heredity	24	
Ecology and Population Biology	12	
Physical Science	60	
Atoms and Subatomic Structures	9	
Elements, Molecules, and Compounds	12	
Energy, Matter, and Mechanics	14	
Electricity, Magnetism, and Waves	6	
The Universe	8	
Earth Science	11	

Answers and Explanations

1. (C)

The Bronsted-Lowry system of acids and bases describes an acid as an element that can donate a proton (hydrogen ion) to another atom in solution. This system is more exclusionary than the Lewis system. The Lewis system only requires the liberation of electrons, which can be performed by any atom.

2. (E)

A buffer solution, such as human blood, has a mixture of both acid and base so that the addition of small quantities of other acids or bases does not greatly affect the pH. Buffers are necessary in biological systems because most reactions require or are at least maximized at specific pHs.

3. (A)

This is the definition of a Lewis acid. More kinds of molecules can be electron donors than proton donors.

4. (A)

Since these two species are utilizing the same resource, they are in competition. The competition causes the elimination (exclusion) of one of the species.

5. (B)

Niche breadth explains all the factors that contribute to the survival of a species and the fitness of the species. It is almost inconceivable to attempt to list all of the factors that make up one species niche.

6. (E)

A community is the collection of species that interact in a particular habitat. An ecosystem is the combination of the community and the environmental factors that affect the habitat.

7. (E)

The thermodynamic equilibrium of a substance occurs at a certain temperature and pressure that allow all three states of matter to exist simultaneously. The temperature and pressure for the triple point of water are 273.01 K and 611.73 pascals.

8. (A)

Heat can move in different ways. Convection is the movement of heat by the movement of heated liquids. Air is a less dense liquid than water, but air movements would be considered movement of liquid and considered convection.

9. (C)

Radio frequencies, heat from the sun, and X-rays are all different forms of electromagnetic radiation. These are forms of energy that transfer from one place to another with wavelike properties.

10. (A)

The star nearest the Earth itself is of course the sun. The next closest star to the Earth is Proxima Centauri, which is 4.2 light years away. It isn't the brightest star, which is Sirius (the dog star), but it is closer to Earth than Sirius.

11. (D)

All of the giant planets have rings, but only the rings of Saturn are significant enough to be almost visible from Earth with binoculars. Neptune's rings are curiously oriented at a right angle to the direction of its orbit.

12. (C)

The planet with the most moons is Jupiter with an estimated sixty moons. The next largest number of moons occurs with the planet Saturn, with thirty-one moons, and Uranus, with twenty-seven.

13. (C)

The Earth is a dynamic object that is not solid all the way through. It has a solid crust around the outside surface, but most of the interior is composed of liquid, molten rock. The interior is made up of the mantle and the core, which are subdivided further based on distance from the center and temperature.

14. (D)

See explanation to question 13.

15. (E)

See explanation to question 13.

16. (B)

See explanation to question 13.

17. (D)

Had the Earth been smaller, it is possible that gravity would not have been sufficient for an atmosphere to form that could have retained surface water and supported life.

18 (C)

All of these functions are critical to life, but the formation of compounds that could replicate themselves (along with the development of plasma membranes) was a critical first step toward forming living cells.

19. (E)

These early cells were prokaryotic and resembled the bacteria found in today's mud flats, bogs, and pond mud where oxygen is largely absent.

20. (B)

Aerobic respiration is more efficient than anaerobic (without oxygen) respiration. Thus organisms capable of using the increasing oxygen in the atmosphere had an evolutionary advantage over those that could not and were capable of developing more complex structures.

21. (E)

While mammals do share some characteristics with groups like reptiles and amphibians, only birds and mammals have a constant and internally regulated body temperature. The duck-billed platypus is a mammal that lays eggs (A).

22. (A)

The five-kingdom system (now outdated) consisted of Monera, Protista, Plantae, Fungi, and Animalia.

23. (B)

Like all other members of the phylum Chordata, humans possess at one time gill slits, a tail, a dorsal nerve cord, and a notochord.

24. (E)

These categories begin with all organisms in a group such as animals and end with an individual species, which is given a scientific name based on its genus and species. An example with the common housecat would be Animalia, Chordata, Mammalia, Carnivora, Felidae, *Felis domesticus.*

25. (A)

Viruses can carry out many of the processes of living organisms but must reproduce using the cell organelles of other organisms and cannot reproduce themselves.

26. (B)

The mosses, ferns, and liverworts are all seedless plants and instead use spores and must remain near water to reproduce.

27. (D)

The animal kingdom is highly diverse, and all of the listed characteristics can be found except for cells containing cell walls.

28. (C)

Acquired traits cannot be passed from parent to offspring, and only those traits that are hereditary can play a role in natural selection.

29. (B)

The cell membrane and cytoplasm are essential and found in all cells, whereas the nucleus and organelles are only found in eukaryotic cells.

30. (E)

Diffusion and osmosis move materials from higher to lower concentrations and require no external energy. Active transport can move materials against the concentration gradient when necessary and requires an input of energy.

31. (D)

Mitosis is the copying, duplication, and division of the nucleus. Cell division follows mitosis, and chromosome numbers through this process will double and then return to normal.

32. (C)

Unlike a cell wall, the cell membrane is not a rigid structure but a lipid bilayer that regulates movement of materials into and out of the cell.

33. (D)

The mitochondria are the organelles where ATP is formed during the Krebs cycle and used to operate the activities within the cell.

34. (A)

Duplication of DNA takes place in the nucleus but is controlled by enzymes and does not require a specialized form of RNA.

35. (E)

The base pairings in DNA and RNA are identical for all organisms. Adenine will bond with thymine and guanine with cytosine. In the RNA molecule, uracil replaces thymine.

36. (A)

mRNA copies the code from the DNA molecule in the nucleus and carries it to rRNA, which then attaches and allows the tRNA molecule containing the appropriate amino acid molecule to place that amino acid on the polypeptide chain.

37. (C)

The regions of the DNA molecule between the stop and start codes will have information necessary to build a specific protein molecule in the cytoplasm. These units are known as genes.

38. (E)

The energy released by this initial electron movement starts the electron transport chain that eventually drives the production of ATP.

39. (E)

Oxygen acting as an electron acceptor essentially pulls the electrons through the transport chain and makes aerobic respiration possible.

40. (E)

Nondisjunction involves two chromosomes that do not separate in meiosis I; hence, an extra chromosome is sent through meiosis II. An example of this is Down syndrome; an affected individual has an extra twenty-first chromosome.

41. (A)

Both structures are used for flying; hence, they are analogous. However, the structure of the two wings is markedly different. Analogous structures can develop when two organisms occupy a similar habitat (such as whales and fish) or when a similar function is needed.

42. (C)

The presence of a lined body cavity means that more complex organs can develop and are better protected as organisms become larger.

43. (B)

Trees, like other plants, grow from the tips of the roots and shoots. Thus, the only growth on the trunk of a tree will be outward as its diameter increases.

44. (E)

Early land plants had to develop a means of avoiding water loss, and the waxy outer cuticle is found in all land plants.

45. (D)

Only the sponges lack any sort of regular body plan. Most animals we are familiar with have a bilateral symmetry with a distinct front, back, right, and left side.

46. (B)

There are really four general tissue types in most animals: connective, epithelial, muscle, and nervous. Blood in general is considered a fluid connective tissue.

47. (E)

Many of the body's mechanisms for maintaining homeostasis rely on negative feedback, which will seek to return some condition such as temperature to a previous state. Other examples could be insulin responding to high blood sugar levels or water retention resulting from high salt intake.

48. (C)

Though the lungs work very closely with the circulatory system to deliver oxygen to cells and remove carbon dioxide, they are in the respiratory system.

49. (A)

Sexual reproduction results in greater genetic variety and hence is more advantageous in variable environments.

50. (C)

The first stage in development after fertilization is termed a zygote, which is a single $2n$ cell formed from the fertilization of the egg by the sperm.

51. (A)

The placenta is specialized tissue through which nutrients from the mother's bloodstream can pass and be carried through the umbilical cord to the developing fetus.

52. (C)

Fruits have a variety of functions but are formed after pollination and fertilization.

53. (E)

The cellular and physiological changes in changing from a larva to an adult can be dramatic and are termed metamorphosis.

54. (A)

Since X-linked traits are carried on the X chromosome, there is no way the son (number 5) could have inherited this trait from his father. The trait had to be carried on one of his mother's X chromosomes.

55. (A)

Since the trait in this case is recessive, the father (number 5) must have both recessive genes and would have to pass at least one of them to all of his offspring regardless of gender.

56. (B)

Until at least one child actually shows up with both recessive alleles, there is no way to know for sure based on a pedigree whether the mother (number 6) is TT or Tt. Since only one allele will be sent with each fertilized egg, the dominant allele could appear in every child even if the mother is a carrier.

57. (E)

The important thing to note here is the relative proportion of each trait in the offspring. The proportions are approximately equal for each trait. However, since there are completely recessive individuals in the offspring, answer (A) is eliminated. Since most had at least one dominant trait, answer (D) is eliminated. Of the remaining combinations the only one that would produce an approximately equal number of each trait would be answer (E). If you look at the possible gametes from each parent, you will see that the first parent has four possible combinations (RS, Rs, rS, rs) and that the second has only rs. This combination predicts an equal proportion of each trait in the offspring.

58. (D)

Punnett squares show the probability of a particular combination of genes, but factors such as mutation or gene linkage (genes carried on the same chromosome) as well as crossing over (exchanging pieces of chromosome during meiosis) can all result in patterns somewhat different than expected.

59. (E)

When two traits appear to blend, then neither is completely dominant over the other. This is called incomplete dominance. In codominance, both traits are expressed equally, and the offspring will express both traits. In the example in question, this could be a flower with a mix of red and white petals or a plant with red and white flowers.

60. (C)

Most genetic traits are the result of two or more genes and are called polygenic. Eye color is an example of a polygenic trait, with many factors affecting the actual eye color.

61. (C)

Since the new gene is now a part of the bacterial cell's DNA, it will be replicated and read each time the bacterial cell replicates and translates its own DNA. Hence the gene has been spliced and cloned.

62. (A)

Carcinogens are a specialized form of mutagens that are known to cause cancerous growth.

63. (C)

O is a recessive genotype where both the A and B factors are absent. A and B are codominant which is why a person can have type AB blood.

64. (D)

A sex-influenced trait is not one that is carried on the X chromosome. Rather, it is one in which gender plays a role in expression, and it will be found more in either males or females.

65. (A)

An excessive food supply will usually raise carrying capacity, whereas the other factors can act (alone or in combination) to hold a population near carrying capacity.

66. (C)

Since species B increases after A but then decreases again when A declines, this most likely represents a predator-prey cycle, which can persist over time. An example is the apparent cycles of the lynx and snowshoe hare, which seem to have a period of about ten years.

67. (E)

Although competition and invasive species can affect other species dramatically, parasites directly exploit their hosts in some way that can be harmful or, in rare cases, fatal to the host.

68. (B)

Though these factors can act at any population level, their impacts are frequently dependent on the density of individuals within a population (not population size). Highly dense populations can be more susceptible to predators, spread disease and parasites more easily, and place a great deal of stress on natural resources, increasing competition and even exacerbating the effects of the other factors.

69. (D)

Factors like weather and climate generally act independently of population density. A severe flood can have devastating effects, even in a healthy, stable population.

70. (E)

Since all of these factors can influence the size of a population, it is the combination of these plus the birth and death rates that would give a much more complete picture.

71. (B)

While these have had a number of impacts, they have greatly increased the number of people the planet can support because they have increased the overall food supply.

72. (A)

While any one of these factors does affect species survival, the loss of habitat that has occurred as human populations have grown is the most significant threat.

73. (D)

By converting the input of solar energy to carbohydrates, and by taking in carbon dioxide and releasing oxygen in the process, producers such as plants are critical to life on Earth.

74. (B)

A half-life is the time during which 50 percent of the mass of sample is lost. The term of 17,190 years is three "half-lives," which means that 6.25 grams will remain.

75. (C)

It is the bombarding of uranium with a neutron that causes the uranium atom to split. Thus, a single neutron should be shown as $_0^1n$ on the left side of the equation.

76. (B)

This reaction is started from the addition of one neutron in order to split uranium; however, three neutrons are released, which can then strike other uranium atoms, which will release even more neutrons. This allows the reaction to accelerate very rapidly.

77. (D)

By using water or other materials, the actual flow of neutrons is moderated or slowed so that rapid acceleration of the reaction and uncontrolled release of energy are prevented.

78. (C)

Because atom A has only two electrons in its outer shell, it will seek to share or release those electrons and would be more likely than B to form a chemical bond.

79. (B)

To form sodium chloride, the Na^+ cation, which is positively charged, will bond with the Cl^- anion, which is negative. These bonds are relatively strong, which is why most ionic compounds (such as sodium chloride, table salt) exist as solids at room temperature and pressure.

80. (B)

The molecules in the right quarter of the table are mostly gases, but the majority of the elements are classified as metallic.

81. (A)

The group number is based on the number of electrons found in the outermost electron shell for an element. The noble gases each have eight electrons in their outer shell and thus do not need to fill this shell and are not commonly found reacting with other elements.

82. (C)

In general, the elements in the lower portion of the table have more metallic properties than those at the top. There are exceptions to this (groups 7 and 8 are nonmetals), but it is a useful guideline when trying to interpret the overall patterns in the table.

83. (B)

Within each period or row, elements are arranged by the atomic number, which is the number of protons in the nucleus and which increases from left to right. In addition, as one moves from left to right within a period, the atomic radii decrease due to increasing nuclear charge.

84. (A)

A compound is a substance whose molecules consist of more than one element. Even though H_2 is a molecule with two atoms, it is still only one element and thus not a compound.

85. (A)

A solution is a mixture of compounds in which molecules cannot easily be separated; thus, the mixture appears homogeneous throughout. Solutions can be solid, liquid, or gaseous.

86. (D)

Alloys are examples of solutions that are solids. Examples include bronze (copper and tin) and brass (copper and zinc).

87. (D)

The outer-shell electrons are called the "valence" electrons. Thus, "co-valent" refers to the sharing of these electrons.

88. (D)

For most acid solutions, the solvent is water. In a neutral water solution there are equal concentrations of each of these ions. When placed into water, an acid will release H^+ ions, and an acid solution will have a greater concentration of H^+ than OH^-. Bases, on the other hand, will have more OH^-.

89. (E)

The pH scale is based upon the negative logarithm of the hydrogen ion concentration. Hence, the lower the value, the greater the concentration of hydrogen ions.

90. (E)

There are four oxygen atoms on the right side of the equation, so to balance this, there must be four in the reactants on the left side as well.

91. (A)

The law of conservation of matter states that matter cannot be created or destroyed. A balanced equation is one that accounts for all atoms throughout the reaction.

92. (A)

If we push an object such as a car and make that object move, we have done work by applying a force to move an object. Work is calculated by multiplying the force we apply times the distance over which we apply it.

93. (B)

A car battery is a means of storing potential electrical energy. Until this energy is moving, however, it remains potential.

94. (D)

As the liquid, such as mercury, absorbs or loses heat energy, it will expand or contract accordingly. Different measurement scales (Celsius, Fahrenheit) are used to note points along the scale where water will freeze or boil.

95. (A)

To determine the amount of energy required you need to rearrange the equation to get the following:

$$\text{Energy} = S \times \text{Mass} \times \text{Temperature Change}$$

The mass in each case is 100 g, and the temperature change in each case is 1°C. Thus, the sample with the largest specific heat is hydrogen, and it will require 1,430 joules of energy to raise the sample 1 degree. Hydrogen is much less dense than any of the other substances, and thus energy conduction in a 100 g sample is much less efficient and more energy is required to heat the sample.

96. (E)

Since energy cannot be created or destroyed, the input of work into both drills has to be accounted for as either mechanical work or as heat. Because the same energy was put into both machines, the one that drilled a deeper hole made more efficient use of the work energy. The less efficient drill will convert more of its energy to heat due to friction than the more efficient drill.

97. (B)

Since entropy is a measure of the disorder or randomness in a system, and freezing water slows down the molecules in motion, freezing increases the structure and order and decreases entropy.

98. (E)

As a gas is compressed and the rate of collisions between molecules increases, pressure will increase. Unless controlled in some way (as in this scenario), temperature will generally increase as well.

99. (C)

Velocity is the distance divided by the time, so no matter what other measures are made, these must be available.

100. (C)

Because the pull of gravity is proportional to mass, acceleration due to gravity is constant for all objects regardless of mass. Without air resistance to slow the feather, the brick and feather fell at the same rate.

101. (D)

Mass remains constant no matter what the gravitational pull. Weight is a measure of the force of gravity on an object. The greater the mass, the greater the weight.

102. (E)

Momentum is proportional to mass and velocity, and since the mass has doubled, the velocity will change but the momentum will be conserved.

103. (A)

The force that pulls an object into a circular motion is called centripetal. In this case the ball's momentum wants to travel in a straight line, but the string pulls inward and the path is circular.

104. (A)

Because energy and mass are equivalent, but the speed of light is constant, $E = mc^2$ means that as more energy is put into making an object accelerate, mass must go up. This is true even of objects moving at everyday speeds here on Earth. However, when the speed of the object begins to approach that of light speed, mass increases more and more rapidly, and eventually the energy required to move the object would become infinite. As the object became more massive, it would become harder to accelerate, and some of the energy used to move it would not be converted to kinetic energy but instead would be converted to matter thus increasing the mass.

The increase in mass from moving objects in our everyday life is negligible, but near light speed the increase is much greater. Physicists have proven this by accelerating particles to 99 percent of light speed.

105. (D)

The gamma rays are very high-energy waves. They are used in medicine but can be dangerous to humans because of the impact their energy has on living tissue.

106. (C)

All of the waves have the same amplitude, and as energy increases, wavelength decreases. Thus, frequency must increase in higher-energy waves.

107. (B)

Voltage is the measure of the potential energy from the positive to the negative side of a circuit. This is essentially a measure of the amount of work possible with the amount of energy contained at one point of a circuit such as a battery.

108. (E)

Any component of a circuit has some level of resistance to electron flow, but resistors are used specifically to reduce the voltage by a predetermined level.

109. (B)

Amperes measure the unit of charge moving per second. This is a velocity measurement, but it is also similar to the amount of water coming out of a hose in a given time.

110. (B)

The result will be two smaller magnets, each with a distinct north and south pole.

111. (B)

Unlike the gas giants Jupiter, Saturn, Uranus, and Neptune, the inner planets all have a solid surface and are called terrestrial planets.

112. (A)

Using a telescope of his own construction, Galileo was able to see that Jupiter had moons that were in orbit around it, casting doubt on the Earth-centered view of the universe.

113. (A)

At that distance, images will take light four years to reach the Earth. Thus the closest star to our planet (apart from the sun) will appear to us as it existed four years ago.

114. (D)

Sediments dissolved in water or another medium that are deposited over thousands of years form sedimentary rocks. Sandstone, limestone, and shale are common examples.

115. (B)

Around 78 percent of our atmosphere is nitrogen, with only about 21 percent being oxygen. The nitrogen in the atmosphere is largely inert, and species needing oxygen have adapted to the 21 percent present.

116. (C)

Humans depend on fresh water, and it is a very limited resource on our planet. Ninety-seven percent of the Earth's water is found in the oceans.

117. (A)

The vast majority of the water cycle is driven by the processes of precipitation and evaporation. Water from the oceans and other bodies of water will evaporate, cool, and fall back to earth as precipitation. Some of this precipitation will find its way to the underground aquifers or be taken up by plants, while some will end up in ponds, rivers, lakes, or the ocean to be evaporated again.

118. (B)

The Precambrian era lasted approximately 4 billion years and comprises over 88 percent of the time of Earth's history.

119. (B)

A variety of methods exist for placing a fossil in "relative time," where the general sequence of events can be determined and age may even be estimated. However, to estimate an accurate age of a fossil, more precise measures such as radioactive dating are needed.

120. (C)

A greenhouse works on the principle that the sun's rays can pass through the glass but much of the infrared radiation radiated back from the ground does not. Hence, it is trapped by the greenhouse, which raises the temperature. This is the same reason that a car heats up on a hot day. Higher-energy radiation can pass through the glass and heat the surfaces of the car, but the heat energy in the form of infrared radiation cannot pass back through the glass windows and is trapped.

Chapter Twenty-Three: **Practice Test 3**

Time—90 minutes
120 Questions

Directions: Each question below has five lettered answer choices. For each question or phrase, choose the most closely related answer. For multiple questions that refer to the same group of lettered answer choices, each choice can be used more than once, once, or not at all.

Questions 1–2

    (A) Chordata
    (B) Cnidaria
    (C) Porifera
    (D) Platyhelminthes
    (E) Echinodermata

1. The animal phylum that includes jellyfish and anemones

2. Simple multicellular organisms lacking tissues and organs

Questions 3–5

    (A) NAD
    (B) ATP
    (C) RNA
    (D) DNA
    (E) AUG

3. A codon for amino acid production

4. The energy currency of the cell

5. The nucleic acid associated with translation

Questions 6–7

    (A) Sex-linked
    (B) Genotype
    (C) Dominant
    (D) Phenotype
    (E) Heterozygous

6. The set of alleles at a gene locus of homologous chromosomes

7. A gene carried on the X or Y chromosome

Questions 8–10

    (A) Nephron
    (B) Neuron
    (C) Myosin
    (D) Cellulose
    (E) Glucagon

8. A protein found in muscle

9. The functional unit of the kidney

10. A pancreatic hormone

GO ON TO THE NEXT PAGE

Questions 11–13

    (A) Cystic fibrosis

    (B) Hemophilia

    (C) Sickle-cell anemia

    (D) Huntington's disease

    (E) Down syndrome

11. A sex-linked recessive disorder

12. A defect affecting production of normal hemoglobin

13. A condition caused by nondisjunction of chromosomes during meiosis

Questions 14–15

    (A) Producers

    (B) Herbivores

    (C) Top consumers

    (D) Omnivores

    (E) Decomposers

14. Autotrophic organisms

15. Fungi and bacteria

Questions 16–18

    (A) Tundra

    (B) Taiga

    (C) Savannah

    (D) Desert

    (E) Tropical rain forest

16. A biome characterized by grasslands and large grazers

17. Alpine peak ecosystems

18. The biome with the greatest biodiversity

GO ON TO THE NEXT PAGE

Directions: For each of the following questions or incomplete statements, select the best answer or completion from the five options given.

19. Which of the following is NOT a kind of evidence that supports evolutionary theory?

    (A) Distribution of organisms on Earth

    (B) Fossils

    (C) Homologous structures

    (D) DNA comparison

    (E) Inheritance of acquired traits

Questions 20–21 are based on the following passage.

   Microevolution occurs when changes in allele frequency for a particular trait lead to changes within populations. Macroevolution occurs when separate populations of a species become reproductively isolated from one another.

20. Which of the following is an example of micro-evolution?

    (A) Industrial melanism in moths

    (B) Sterile hybrids like mules

    (C) Geographic isolation

    (D) Formation of a new species

    (E) Species extinction

21. Which of the following is an example of behavioral reproductive isolation?

    (A) Reptiles unable to tolerate disparate environmental conditions

    (B) Arthropods with incompatible reproductive structures

    (C) Birds with different mating rituals

    (D) Trees separated by a mountain range

    (E) Incompatible gametes preventing zygote formation

22. While walking in the forest, you come across a plant that has frondlike leaves and bears seeds naked on a reproductive structure called a strobilus. What type of plant is it?

    (A) Moss

    (B) Fern

    (C) Palm tree

    (D) Gymnosperm

    (E) Angiosperm

23. What is the most abundant group of terrestrial eukaryotes?

    (A) Bacteria

    (B) Protozoans

    (C) Humans

    (D) Birds

    (E) Insects

24. Which of the following characteristics is NOT shared by all living things?

    (A) Plasma membrane

    (B) Cell wall

    (C) DNA

    (D) Reproduction

    (E) Metabolism

25. Which characteristic is common to all viruses?

    (A) Plasma membrane

    (B) Cell wall

    (C) DNA

    (D) Reproduction

    (E) Metabolism

GO ON TO THE NEXT PAGE

KAPLAN

Questions 26–28 are based on the following passage.

Reptiles and land plants such as conifers evolved during the Paleozoic era over 225 million years ago. During the Mesozoic era between 225 and 65 million years ago, the phenomenon of continental drift began and progressed. Near the end of the Mesozoic, mass extinction of the dinosaurs and many coniferous plants was followed by the rise of mammals and flowering plants.

26. Based on the passage, what might you infer to be TRUE?

    (A) Mammals should be similar all over the world.

    (B) Flowering plants should be similar all over the world.

    (C) Conifers should be similar all over the world.

    (D) The rise of mammals likely led to dinosaur extinction.

    (E) The rise of flowering plants likely led to extinction of many conifers.

27. What type of evidence best supports the idea that a large asteroid impacted the Earth and led to extinction of dinosaurs and many coniferous plants?

    (A) A layer of iridium in the geologic strata of the era

    (B) The distribution of conifers in the world today

    (C) The distribution of dinosaur fossils

    (D) The distribution of mammals in the world today

    (E) The absence of mammals and flowering plants during the Paleozoic

28. Why might an asteroid impact have been more devastating to conifers than flowering plants?

    (A) Flowering plants have tougher leaves.

    (B) Herbivorous dinosaurs fed more on conifers.

    (C) Conifers have more resistant seeds.

    (D) Flowering plants reproduce more quickly.

    (E) Mammals feed more on angiosperm seeds.

29. Which of the following organelles contains the cell's genetic information?

    (A) Mitochondria

    (B) Chloroplasts

    (C) Nucleus

    (D) Endoplasmic reticulum

    (E) Ribosomes

Questions 30–31 are based on the following passage.

During interphase of the somatic cell cycle of an organism with a diploid chromosome number of 26, DNA replication produces sister chromatids that will divide during anaphase of mitosis. A germ cell from the same organism will undergo meiosis to produce haploid gametes via one round of DNA replication and two rounds of cell division.

30. What will mitosis of one of the organism's somatic cells produce?

    (A) Two identical daughter cells with 26 chromosomes each

    (B) Two unique daughter cells with 13 chromosomes each

    (C) Four identical daughter cells with 26 chromosomes each

    (D) Four unique daughter cells with 13 chromosomes each

    (E) Four identical daughter cells with 13 chromosomes each

GO ON TO THE NEXT PAGE

31. During the first round of meiosis in the germ cell, genetic material is exchanged between homologous chromosomes. This phenomenon is called

    (A) nondisjunction.
    (B) crossing over.
    (C) independent assortment.
    (D) point mutation.
    (E) frame-shift mutation.

32. A template strand of DNA that codes for production of a series of amino acids has the following sequence of nucleotides: 3'-TACACAGAAGGA-5'. What would the complementary strand of mRNA produced be?

    (A) 5'-UACACAGAAGGA-3'
    (B) 3-AGGAAGACACAT-5'
    (C) 3'-AUGCUGUCUUCC-5'
    (D) 5'-ATGTGTCTTCCT-3'
    (E) 5'-AUGUGUCUUCCU-3'

33. Which is NOT a way materials enter cells?

    (A) Osmosis
    (B) Facilitated diffusion
    (C) Endocytosis
    (D) Exocytosis
    (E) Active transport

Questions 34–36 are based on the following passage.

A laboratory experiment is set up to study the processes of photosynthesis and respiration. Four test tubes are filled with a pH indicator called phenol red. Under neutral conditions, the indicator is orange, under alkaline conditions it turns red, and under acidic conditions it turns yellow. Addition of carbon dioxide to the solution will produce carbonic acid, while removal of carbon dioxide will make the solution more alkaline. The following experimental design is applied:

Tube 1—*Elodea* plants are added and placed in light.
Tube 2—Brine shrimp are added and placed in light.
Tube 3—*Elodea* plants are added and placed in the dark.
Tube 4—Brine shrimp are added and placed in the dark.

34. Which tube(s) would you expect to turn red over time?

    (A) Tube 1 only
    (B) Tubes 1 and 3
    (C) Tube 2 only
    (D) Tubes 2, 3, and 4
    (E) Tubes 2 and 4

35. Which of the tubes would you expect to turn yellow?

    (A) Tube 1 only
    (B) Tubes 1 and 3
    (C) Tube 2 only
    (D) Tubes 2, 3, and 4
    (E) Tubes 2 and 4

GO ON TO THE NEXT PAGE

KAPLAN

36. In which tubes is cellular respiration occurring?

    (A) Tubes 2 and 4

    (B) Tubes 1 and 3

    (C) Tube 2 only

    (D) Tubes 2, 3, and 4

    (E) All tubes

37. Which of the following is NOT an organic compound?

    (A) Glucose

    (B) Water

    (C) Amino acid

    (D) Lipid

    (E) Nucleic acid

38. What is the primary function of the endocrine system?

    (A) Transport of gases and nutrients

    (B) Excretion of metabolic wastes

    (C) Production of hormones

    (D) Immunity and fluid balance

    (E) Production of enzymes for digestion

39. What phase of embryonic development is associated with development of three distinct germ layers?

    (A) Zygote

    (B) Cleavage

    (C) Morula

    (D) Blastula

    (E) Gastrula

40. Plant growth occurs in specific regions called

    (A) collenchyma.

    (B) phloem.

    (C) meristems.

    (D) tracheids.

    (E) stomata.

Questions 41–43 are based on the following passage.

In an experiment studying heredity, a P generation of true-breeding pea plants that produced purple flowers (a dominant characteristic) were cross-pollinated with those that produced white flowers (a recessive characteristic), and 500 offspring were produced in the F1 generation. A member of the F1 generation was allowed to self-pollinate, and 400 F2 offspring were produced.

41. Which of the following represents the parental cross?

    (A) $Pp \times Pp$

    (B) $PP \times WW$

    (C) $Pw \times Pw$

    (D) $PP \times pp$

    (E) $PP \times ww$

42. How many white-flowered offspring would you expect in the F1 and F2 generations, respectively?

    (A) 0 and 100

    (B) 250 and 200

    (C) 125 and 300

    (D) 0 and 0

    (E) 250 and 0

GO ON TO THE NEXT PAGE

43. What percentage of the F2 generation would you expect to be heterozygous for the trait?

    (A) 100 percent
    (B) 75 percent
    (C) 50 percent
    (D) 25 percent
    (E) 0 percent

44. Which of the following occurs in the sacs of the alveoli?

    (A) Filtration of metabolic wastes
    (B) Exchange of gases
    (C) Absorption of nutrients
    (D) Production of antibodies
    (E) Filtration of lymph

45. What accessory organ is responsible for detoxifying materials in the blood that have been absorbed through the intestines before they enter general circulation?

    (A) Pancreas
    (B) Kidney
    (C) Spleen
    (D) Gall bladder
    (E) Liver

46. A person with type O blood

    (A) has both the A and B antigens on the surface of red blood cells.
    (B) can safely receive transfusions of any blood type.
    (C) does not have any blood type antibodies.
    (D) has both anti-A and anti-B antibodies.
    (E) has only anti-O antibodies.

47. Tay-Sachs disease is a recessive genetic disorder that affects production of an enzyme necessary for fat metabolism in the brain and usually causes death by age 5 for those homozygous for the mutation. Which of the following statements must be TRUE?

    (A) The allele should disappear from the gene pool quickly.
    (B) Both parents must pass the defective allele to the affected offspring.
    (C) At least one parent must show symptoms of the disorder.
    (D) The mutated gene codes for many different proteins.
    (E) Mutation must involve a frame shift to be so serious.

GO ON TO THE NEXT PAGE

KAPLAN

Questions 48–49 are based on the following figure.

The figure here shows air temperature and the rate of net photosynthesis in plants during the course of single day. For the day shown, the sun rose at 6:00 A.M. and set at 6:00 P.M.

48. Which of the following statements is FALSE?

   (A) Photosynthesis was inhibited before sunrise and after sunset.

   (B) Temperature was highest at 4:00 P.M.

   (C) Photosynthesis rate was highest between noon and 2:00 P.M.

   (D) Photosynthesis rate increased consistently with temperature.

   (E) Both temperature and photosynthesis rate decreased after 4:00 P.M.

49. Which of the following is NOT a possible explanation for the decreased rate of net photosynthesis from 2:00 P.M. until sunset?

   (A) Less sunlight to provide energy for photosynthesis

   (B) Inhibition of photosynthesis by low temperatures

   (C) Increase in photorespiration due to high temperature

   (D) Stomatal closure due to water stress

   (E) Reduction in RUBISCO activity due to high temperature

50. Which of the following characteristics is NOT associated with human embryonic development?

   (A) Pharyngeal slits

   (B) Post-anal tail

   (C) Cartilaginous skeleton

   (D) Notochord

   (E) Oviparity

51. Which of the following is NOT a type of connective tissue?

   (A) Blood

   (B) Bone

   (C) Nerves

   (D) Tendons

   (E) Adipose (fat)

52. How are nerve impulses transmitted along axons?

   (A) Release of neurotransmitters at nodes of Ranvier on the myelin sheath

   (B) Interaction between glial cells and dendrites

   (C) Electrical signals transmitted at synapses

   (D) Depolarization of the axon cell membrane

   (E) Interaction of Schwann cells on sensory neurons

53. Peas can be either yellow or green and have smooth or wrinkled surfaces. There is no relationship between the way pea color and pea surface are passed from one generation to the next. This is an example of which phenomenon?

   (A) Independent assortment

   (B) Codominant alleles

   (C) Incomplete dominance

   (D) Pleiotrophic effects

   (E) Continuous variation

GO ON TO THE NEXT PAGE ⟶

KAPLAN

54. Which is NOT part of the water cycle?

    (A) Transpiration
    (B) Evaporation
    (C) Precipitation
    (D) Condensation
    (E) Denitrification

55. Which of the following is NOT an example of a predator-prey relationship?

    (A) Mycorrhizal fungi infecting plant roots
    (B) A cow grazing grass
    (C) A spider eating a fly
    (D) A caterpillar eating leaves
    (E) A bobcat eating a rabbit

56. If a population grows exponentially as the human population has done in the past 200 years, what will be the shape of the growth curve?

    (A) A straight diagonal line
    (B) A straight horizontal line
    (C) J-shaped
    (D) S-shaped
    (E) A bell-shaped curve

57. As energy flows from one trophic level to the next higher trophic level in an ecosystem, the amount of available energy

    (A) stays the same.
    (B) increases due to concentration of organic elements.
    (C) increases due to accumulation of biomass.
    (D) decreases due to loss as heat.
    (E) varies depending on the trophic structure of the community.

58. The gradual repopulation of an area by a sequence of plant and animal communities after a disturbance event such as a fire is called

    (A) primary succession.
    (B) secondary succession.
    (C) spontaneous generation.
    (D) restoration ecology.
    (E) primary productivity.

Questions 59–60 are based on the following figure.

The figure here shows the number of hares and bobcats populating an area from 1970 to 1980.

59. Which of the following is probably NOT occurring in these populations?

    (A) The number of bobcats depends on the number of hares available as prey.
    (B) Competition occurs between the hares and bobcats for limited food resources.
    (C) The number of hares depends on the number of bobcat predators.
    (D) Competition occurs between bobcats for limited food resources.
    (E) Resource limitation occurs for hares at high population density.

GO ON TO THE NEXT PAGE

KAPLAN

60. What might you expect to happen if wolves, which also preyed upon hares, were introduced to the system?

    (A) The number of bobcats would increase.

    (B) The number of hares would increase.

    (C) No change would be expected.

    (D) Both hare and bobcat numbers would decrease.

    (E) The amount of food available at all trophic levels would decrease.

61. An isotope of an element

    (A) has the same atomic number but a different atomic mass.

    (B) has the same atomic mass but a different atomic number.

    (C) has the same number of neutrons.

    (D) is always unstable.

    (E) is always radioactive.

62. An element that contains more electrons than protons is

    (A) neutral.

    (B) a cation.

    (C) an anion.

    (D) positively charged.

    (E) an isotope.

63. Which of the following are examples of electrons and positrons?

    (A) Photon strings

    (B) Omega waves

    (C) Alpha particles

    (D) Beta particles

    (E) Gamma rays

64. Splitting a heavy atomic nucleus into two smaller nuclei results in

    (A) a fusion reacton.

    (B) a fission reaction.

    (C) alpha particles.

    (D) beta particles.

    (E) gamma rays.

65. Which of the following are high-energy photons?

    (A) Photon strings

    (B) Omega waves

    (C) Alpha particles

    (D) Beta particles

    (E) Gamma rays

66. If the half-life of radioactive carbon-14 is 5,730 years, that means that

    (A) it takes 5,730 years for it to be half as radioactive.

    (B) in 11,460 years a sample will completely disappear.

    (C) the mass of C-14 present will be reduced by half in 5,730 years.

    (D) the radioactivity of C-14 will double in 5,730 years.

    (E) the rate of decay will decrease by half in 5,730 years.

67. The electron configuration notation $1s^2 \, 2s^2 \, 2p^6 \, 3s^2 \, 3p^4$ indicates

    (A) there is one s electron in the first energy shell.

    (B) there are two p electrons in the second energy shell.

    (C) the element has six valence electrons.

    (D) the element has eleven total electrons.

    (E) there are three s electrons in the third energy shell.

GO ON TO THE NEXT PAGE

68. Indicate the number of each type of subatomic particle in a neutral atom of the radioactive isotope $^{60}_{27}Co$ and its atomic mass.

	Protons	Neutrons	Electrons	Mass
(A)	33	27	33	60
(B)	27	60	27	87
(C)	27	27	60	54
(D)	60	27	60	87
(E)	27	33	27	60

69. Which of the following form diatomic gases at room temperature?

   (A) Halogens
   (B) Metals
   (C) Nonmetals
   (D) Noble gases
   (E) Heavy metals

70. Which of the following are very nonreactive elements?

   (A) Halogens
   (B) Metals
   (C) Nonmetals
   (D) Noble gases
   (E) Heavy metals

71. Which of the following are solid, malleable, and conductive at room temperature?

   (A) Halogens
   (B) Metals
   (C) Nonmetals
   (D) Noble gases
   (E) Heavy metals

Questions 72–73 are based on the following equation.

$$C_3H_8 + 5O_2 \rightarrow 3CO_2 + ?\ H_2O + heat$$

72. How many molecules of H_2O will be produced by the reaction shown?

   (A) 1
   (B) 2
   (C) 4
   (D) 6
   (E) 8

73. Which of the following statements about the reaction is FALSE?

   (A) It requires activation energy.
   (B) It is endothermic.
   (C) Carbon dioxide is one of the products.
   (D) Oxygen is one of the reactants.
   (E) It is a combustion reaction.

74. If you added a strong base such as KOH to a solution, what change would you expect in the solution?

   (A) The pH would increase.
   (B) The hydrogen ion concentration would increase.
   (C) The solution would become more acidic.
   (D) The pH would not be affected.
   (E) The KOH would act as a buffer, reducing pH.

75. Which type of compound is most likely to dissociate in water?

   (A) A phospholipid
   (B) A protein
   (C) A covalent compound
   (D) An organic compound
   (E) An ionic compound

GO ON TO THE NEXT PAGE

KAPLAN

76. If the atomic mass of carbon is 12.0 grams per mole, hydrogen is 1.0 grams per mole, and oxygen is 16, what percentage by mass of glucose ($C_6H_{12}O_6$) is carbon?

    (A) 10 percent
    (B) 20 percent
    (C) 30 percent
    (D) 40 percent
    (E) 50 percent

77. How do catalysts work?

    (A) By giving up electrons to reactants
    (B) By participating in oxidation reactions
    (C) By participating in reduction reactions
    (D) By being used up to form products
    (E) By lowering activation energy of reactions

78. Which of the following molecules is most abundant in the atmosphere?

    (A) $N \equiv N$
    (B) $O = O$
    (C) Cl–Cl
    (D) $O = C = O$
    (E) H–O–H

79. Which of the molecules shown is polar?

    (A) $N \equiv N$
    (B) $O = O$
    (C) Cl–Cl
    (D) $O = C = O$
    (E) H–O–H

80. The energy stored in the bonds of molecules is known as

    (A) kinetic energy.
    (B) chemical energy.
    (C) heat.
    (D) mass energy.
    (E) electrical energy.

81. Which is the energy of relativity?

    (A) Kinetic energy
    (B) Chemical energy
    (C) Heat
    (D) Mass energy
    (E) Electrical energy

82. The energy of random molecular motion is called

    (A) kinetic energy.
    (B) chemical energy.
    (C) heat.
    (D) mass energy.
    (E) electrical energy.

GO ON TO THE NEXT PAGE

Questions 83–85 are based on the following figure.

The figure shown here represents two watermelons of equal mass (1 kg) being dropped from rest (not thrown up or down) from the tops of two buildings. The distance to the ground is 10 meters from the top of the building on the left and 5 meters from the top of the building on the right. The acceleration of gravity is 9.8 m/s^2. The velocity of each watermelon when it reaches the ground can be calculated as $v = v_0 + at$, where v is the final velocity, v_0 is the initial velocity, a is acceleration, and t is time.

83. If the final velocity of the watermelon on the left was 50 m/s, how long did it take to reach the ground (to the nearest second)?

 (A) 1 second
 (B) 3 seconds
 (C) 5 seconds
 (D) 10 seconds
 (E) 15 seconds

84. Assume that the watermelon dropped from the building on the right took 3 seconds to reach the ground. What was its approximate final velocity?

 (A) 30 meters per second
 (B) 20 meters per second
 (C) 10 meters per second
 (D) 5 meters per second
 (E) 1 meter per second

85. How would these calculations be affected if the mass of the watermelons were doubled?

 (A) The final velocities of both would double.
 (B) The final velocities of both would be reduced by half.
 (C) The time to reach the ground would change, but the final velocity would remain constant.
 (D) Both time to reach the ground and final velocity would be affected, depending on height of building.
 (E) Changing the mass of the watermelons would not change the calculations.

86. The second law of thermodynamics states that in every energy transformation, some usable energy is lost as heat. Because of this,

 (A) the amount of energy in the universe is steadily decreasing.
 (B) the disorder (entropy) of the universe is steadily increasing.
 (C) heat is generated in every chemical reaction.
 (D) the amount of heat in the universe is steadily decreasing.
 (E) the entropy of the universe is the only constant.

GO ON TO THE NEXT PAGE

Questions 87–88 are based on the following passage.

A glass of liquid water left outside freezes during a cold night. The following morning, a film of moisture can be seen on the outside of the glass. By late afternoon, some of the water from the glass has evaporated.

87. What process caused the film of moisture on the outside of the glass?

   (A) Condensation
   (B) Melting
   (C) Sublimation
   (D) Evaporation
   (E) Crystallization

88. Which of the following shows the correct order of energy transformations that have occurred?

   (A) energy released → energy absorbed → energy released
   (B) energy absorbed → energy absorbed → energy released
   (C) energy released → energy released → energy released
   (D) energy released → energy released → energy absorbed
   (E) energy absorbed → energy absorbed → energy absorbed

89. What does Newton's first law of motion state?

   (A) The greater the force applied to an object, the greater the acceleration.
   (B) The greater the mass of the object, the smaller the acceleration.
   (C) An object will remain in its state of rest if no net force acts upon it.
   (D) The force on an object is equal to the product of its mass and acceleration.
   (E) For every force exerted, there is an equal and opposite force at work.

Questions 90–91 are based on the following passage.

The universal gas law is written $PV = nRT$, where P is pressure, V is volume, n is the number of moles of the gas present, R is the gas constant, and T is temperature. Assume that a sealed balloon with a maximum volume of 5 liters contains 0.25 moles of some gas at a pressure of 1 atm at a temperature of 25°C.

90. What might happen if temperature is raised to 30°C?

   (A) The pressure in the balloon would decrease.
   (B) The volume of the balloon would increase.
   (C) The number of moles of gas in the balloon would increase.
   (D) The pressure and volume of the balloon would decrease.
   (E) The pressure would increase and the volume decrease.

91. Assuming that volume and temperature were held constant, what effect would adding another 0.25 moles of gas to the balloon have?

   (A) It would double the pressure.
   (B) It would reduce the pressure by half.
   (C) It would increase the pressure by 25 percent.
   (D) It would decrease the pressure by 25 percent.
   (D) It would quadruple the pressure.

92. The resistance of a moving object to change its state of motion is called

   (A) entropy.
   (B) inertia.
   (C) force.
   (D) mechanics.
   (E) gravity.

GO ON TO THE NEXT PAGE

93. If the gravity of Mars is 0.4 times the gravity of Earth, what would be the mass of an object on Mars that has a mass of 1,000 kg on Earth?

    (A) 4,000 kg
    (B)   400 kg
    (C) 2,500 kg
    (D)   250 kg
    (E) 1,000 kg

94. What scientist first put forth the idea that all objects fall to Earth with the same acceleration?

    (A) Aristotle
    (B) Newton
    (C) Galileo
    (D) Einstein
    (E) Copernicus

95. What is the unit of electrical charge?

    (A) Coulomb
    (B) Ohm
    (C) Volt
    (D) Ampere
    (E) Watt

96. The electromagnetic radiation with the longest wavelength is

    (A) ultraviolet.
    (B) radio waves.
    (C) microwaves.
    (D) infrared.
    (E) visible light.

97. The electromagnetic radiation with the highest energy is

    (A) ultraviolet.
    (B) radio waves.
    (C) microwaves.
    (D) infrared.
    (E) visible light.

98. How does sound travel?

    (A) As transverse waves
    (B) As magnetic fields
    (C) As longitudinal waves
    (D) As particles
    (E) As gamma rays

99. When light bends as when passed through water or a prism, it is termed

    (A) reflection.
    (B) transmission.
    (C) absorption.
    (D) refraction.
    (E) magnetism.

100. Evidence supporting the big bang theory includes

    (A) the asteroid belt.
    (B) supernovas.
    (C) red dwarfs.
    (D) the red shift.
    (E) black holes.

101. An old very massive star contracted on itself is called

    (A) the asteroid belt.
    (B) a supernova.
    (C) a red dwarf.
    (D) a white dwarf.
    (E) a black hole.

GO ON TO THE NEXT PAGE

Questions 102–104 are based on the following figure.

102. Which of the planets labeled above represents the Earth?

(A) 1

(B) 3

(C) 4

(D) 5

(E) 6

103. Which planet has a highly visible ring?

(A) 1

(B) 3

(C) 4

(D) 5

(E) 6

104. Between which two planets does the asteroid belt occur?

(A) 1 and 2

(B) 3 and 4

(C) 4 and 5

(D) 5 and 6

(E) 6 and 7

105. Aggregates of frozen material in regular elliptical solar orbits that appear as patches of light with long tails are known as

(A) asteroids.

(B) comets.

(C) sun showers.

(D) meteorites.

(E) meteors.

106. The remains of objects from space that have passed through the Earth's atmosphere and hit the ground are called

(A) asteroids.

(B) comets.

(C) sun showers.

(D) meteorites.

(E) meteors.

107. What is a nebula?

(A) A diffuse mass of interstellar gas and dust

(B) A large group of distant galaxies

(C) An old star contracted upon itself

(D) The last remnants of the big bang

(E) The remains of an ancient galaxy

108. What is the main composition of the planet Jupiter?

(A) Lead and zinc

(B) Hydrogen and helium

(C) Liquid iron

(D) Ice

(E) Frozen methane

GO ON TO THE NEXT PAGE

109. Which is the atmospheric layer rich in ozone?

    (A) Thermosphere
    (B) Troposphere
    (C) Lithosphere
    (D) Stratosphere
    (E) Hydrosphere

110. Which is the Earth's crust and outermost mantle?

    (A) Thermosphere
    (B) Troposphere
    (C) Lithosphere
    (D) Stratosphere
    (E) Hydrosphere

111. Which is the atmospheric layer closest to the ground?

    (A) Thermosphere
    (B) Troposphere
    (C) Biosphere
    (D) Stratosphere
    (E) Hydrosphere

112. In general, as altitude increases, temperature and pressure decrease. As temperature decreases, air can hold less water. When water condenses, energy is released, and the surrounding air is slightly warmed. On hot, humid days, warm, moist air masses tend to rise into the atmosphere. What happens when a warm, moist air mass rises in the atmosphere?

    (A) Clouds form when water condenses at higher altitudes.
    (B) The relative humidity of the air decreases as it rises.
    (C) The temperature of the air mass increases as it rises.
    (D) High pressure builds in the rising air mass.
    (E) There is no change in the air mass as it rises.

113. What causes rain?

    (A) Sudden warming of a cloud causes ice crystals to melt.
    (B) Rapid vaporization of water from clouds.
    (C) Sudden cooling of clouds causes rapid condensation.
    (D) Sudden pressure changes in a cloud literally squeeze water out.
    (E) Rapid loss of condensation nuclei due to pressure changes.

114. Movement of magma from the interior of the Earth is known as

    (A) subduction.
    (B) folding.
    (C) tectonics.
    (D) vulcanism.
    (E) a fault.

115. A fracture of the Earth's crust that displaces rock is called

    (A) subduction.
    (B) folding.
    (C) tectonics.
    (D) vulcanism.
    (E) a fault.

116. Descent of the edge of one crustal plate under the edge of an adjoining plate is known as

    (A) subduction.
    (B) folding.
    (C) tectonics.
    (D) vulcanism.
    (E) a fault.

GO ON TO THE NEXT PAGE

KAPLAN

117. Global warming is caused by

(A) loss of long-wave radiation to the atmosphere due to increased albedo.

(B) increased ultraviolet radiation due to loss of the ozone layer.

(C) increased cloud cover due to the greenhouse effect.

(D) retention of infrared radiation by gases such as methane.

(E) decreased atmospheric moisture due to the greenhouse effect.

118. What is the depositional feature laid down from a stream issuing from a mountain canyon?

(A) Karst

(B) Alluvial Fan

(C) Bluff

(D) Cirque

(E) Delta

119. Which is a relatively steep slope at the outer edge of a flood plain?

(A) Karst

(B) Alluvial fan

(C) Bluff

(D) Cirque

(E) Delta

120. Slowing of a stream's velocity leads to deposition of materials at the mouth of a river in a formation bearing what name?

(A) Karst

(B) Alluvial fan

(C) Bluff

(D) Cirque

(E) Delta

END OF TEST. STOP

THE ANSWER KEY APPEARS ON THE FOLLOWING PAGE.

ANSWER KEY

1. B	19. E	37. B	55. A	73. B	91. A	109. D
2. C	20. A	38. C	56. C	74. A	92. B	110. C
3. E	21. C	39. E	57. D	75. E	93. E	111. B
4. B	22. D	40. C	58. B	76. D	94. C	112. A
5. C	23. E	41. D	59. B	77. E	95. A	113. C
6. B	24. B	42. A	60. D	78. A	96. B	114. D
7. A	25. D	43. C	61. A	79. E	97. A	115. E
8. C	26. C	44. B	62. C	80. B	98. C	116. A
9. A	27. A	45. E	63. D	81. D	99. D	117. D
10. E	28. D	46. D	64. B	82. C	100. D	118. B
11. B	29. C	47. B	65. E	83. C	101. E	119. C
12. C	30. A	48. D	66. C	84. A	102. B	120. E
13. E	31. B	49. B	67. C	85. E	103. E	
14. A	32. E	50. E	68. E	86. B	104. C	
15. E	33. D	51. C	69. A	87. A	105. B	
16. C	34. B	52. D	70. D	88. D	106. D	
17. A	35. E	53. A	71. B	89. C	107. A	
18. E	36. E	54. E	72. C	90. B	108. B	

PRACTICE TEST 3 QUICK REFERENCE TABLES

Use the following tables to determine which topics you still need to review.

Topic	Test Question
Biological Science	
Evolution and Diversity of Life	1, 2, 19, 20, 21, 23, 24, 25, 26, 27, 28
Cell Biology and Biochemistry	3, 4, 5, 13, 29, 30, 31, 32, 33, 34, 35, 36
Organisms and Heredity	6, 7, 8, 9, 10, 11, 12, 22, 38, 39, 40, 41, 42, 43, 44, 45, 46, 47, 48, 49, 50, 51, 52, 53
Ecology and Population Biology	14, 15, 16, 17, 18, 54, 55, 56, 57, 58, 59, 60, 78
Physical Science	
Atoms and Subatomic Structures	61, 62, 63, 64, 65, 66, 67, 68
Elements, Molecules, and Compounds	37, 69, 70, 71, 72, 73, 74, 75, 76, 77, 79, 80
Energy, Matter, and Mechanics	81, 82, 83, 84, 85, 86, 87, 88, 89, 90, 91, 92, 93, 94
Electricity, Magnetism, and Waves	95, 96, 97, 98, 99
The Universe	100, 101, 102, 103, 104, 105, 106, 107, 108
Earth Science	109, 110, 111, 112, 113, 114, 115, 116, 117, 118, 119, 120

Topic	Number of Questions on Test	Number Correct
Biological Science	60	
Evolution and Diversity of Life	11	
Cell Biology and Biochemistry	12	
Organisms and Heredity	24	
Ecology and Population Biology	13	
Physical Science	60	
Atoms and Subatomic Structures	8	
Elements, Molecules, and Compounds	12	
Energy, Matter, and Mechanics	14	
Electricity, Magnetism, and Waves	5	
The Universe	9	
Earth Science	12	

Answers and Explanations

1. (B)

The animal phylum Cnidaria includes jellyfish and anemones. Cnidarians have radial symmetry with tentacles arranged around a simple gut opening. They are almost all aquatic animals and represent one of the earliest phyla of animals, with only two cell layers making up the body wall. Their tentacles contain stinging cells called nematocysts.

2. (C)

The sponges are the simplest animals; they are multicellular but lack more complex organization into specialized tissues or organs.

3. (E)

AUG is a three-base sequence of RNA that codes to initiate protein production with the amino acid methionine.

4. (B)

The high-energy bonds of adenosine triphosphate (ATP) provide the usable form of energy for all living things.

5. (C)

Translation is the production of proteins at the ribosomes using the code transcribed by mRNA from DNA in the nucleus and the amino acids shuttled by tRNA to the ribosomes. DNA only actively participates in the transcription process; translation is carried out by RNA.

6. (B)

Although the set of alleles at a locus might be heterozygous, it might also be homozygous, so (E) is not the best answer.

7. (A)

Sex-linked characteristics are carried on the sex chromosomes, X and Y. Most sex-linked characteristics are carried on the X chromosome, which is much larger than the Y.

8. (C)

Myo- is a word root always associated with muscle.

9. (A)

Nephr- is a word root always associated with the kidney and its functional filtering unit, the nephron.

10. (E)

The pancreas produces two hormones that regulate blood glucose levels, insulin and glucagon. Insulin lowers blood glucose levels by getting the body's cells to take glucose out of the blood; glucagon raises blood glucose levels by stimulating the liver to convert glycogen to glucose and release it into the blood.

11. (B)

Hemophilia is a recessive disorder linked to the X chromosome.

12. (C)

Sickle-cell anemia is a recessive hereditary disorder associated with a point mutation on the gene that codes for production of hemoglobin, the protein that carries oxygen in red blood cells.

13. (E)

Nondisjunction leads to aneuploidy, an abnormal number of chromosomes. Down syndrome, a developmental disability, is caused by triploidy (three copies) of chromosome 21.

14. (A)

Autotrophic organisms are capable of producing their own food energy, usually via the process of photosynthesis. They are the first link in ecosystem food chains, the producers. All of the other kinds of organisms listed are heterotrophic and must get their energy from other organisms.

15. (E)

The fungi and bacteria are the decomposers of the biosphere, converting complex organic molecules into simpler inorganic compounds, often in the form of gases such as N_2 and CO_2.

16. (C)

The savannah in Africa and prairie of North America are both grassland biomes that support large grazing animals such as zebras and bison.

17. (A)

Biomes at high altitudes are similar to those at high latitudes, and there is a progression as one moves down a mountain similar to that seen as one moves more toward the equator. The tops of mountains, like the polar regions of Earth, are marked by the long, cold winters and small vegetation that characterize the tundra biome.

18. (E)

Because of consistently warm temperatures and heavy precipitation, tropical rain forests are home to more kinds of organisms than any other biome.

19. (E)

Evidence to support evolutionary theory includes biogeographical evidence; the fossil record; and comparative anatomy, physiology, and genetics of organisms. Inheritance of acquired traits was an idea put forth by Lamarck, later proven to be false.

20. (A)

The phenomenon of industrial melanism, an increase in the number of dark moths in areas with trees darkened by pollution, is an example of changes in allele frequency in a population due to adaptive advantages conferred by the trait. Answers (B) and (C) are examples of reproductive isolation, and answers (D) and (E) are examples of macroevolution.

21. (C)

Answer (A) represents adaptive isolation, answer (B) morphological isolation, and answer (D) geographic isolation. Incompatible gametes (E) represent a form of reproductive isolation unassociated with behavior. The disparate mating rituals are a form of behavioral reproductive isolation.

22. (D)

Mosses and ferns do not produce seeds, and palms are angiosperms, plants that produce seeds enclosed in a vessel. Gymnosperms are naked seeded plants.

23. (E)

Although bacteria outnumber insects, they are prokaryotic organisms. Most protozoans are aquatic, and insects far outnumber both birds and humans.

24. (B)

All living things are cellular and are bound by a cell membrane, all contain DNA or RNA, all are capable of reproduction, and all use energy via metabolism. Not all living things have cell walls; animals do not, for example.

25. (D)

Often not considered living things, viruses do not have cells or cellular structures or carry out metabolism. Some viruses have DNA, while others have RNA. All viruses are capable of reproduction (replication) within a host cell.

26. (C)

Given that conifers evolved before the land mass of Pangaea split, one would expect for examples around the world to share characteristics with a relatively recent common ancestor. Since the flowering plants and mammals arose after the split of the continents, they would be less likely to show similarities around the world. Although competition is one possible hypothesis for why dinosaurs became extinct and conifers reduced in number, it is not well supported, and in no way can it be inferred from the limited information given.

27. (A)

Only answer (A) can be related to an asteroid as the cause of the mass extinctions during the late Mesozoic era. Answers (B) and (C) might provide evidence for other events that occurred during or after the extinction, but they do not point to its cause. Answer (E) provides evidence for when mammals and flowering plants arose.

28. (D)

Answer (A) is incorrect because conifers tend to have tougher, needle-like leaves. (The fact that they are permanent and not deciduous would be a long-term disadvantage under stressful conditions.) All of the other choices except (D) would tend to favor conifers over angiosperms. It is thought that because angiosperms have tough seeds and reach reproductive maturity quickly, they were able to better withstand the stressful post impact environment and then multiply quickly when conditions became more favorable.

29. (C)

The nucleus contains the cell's genetic code in the form of DNA. The chloroplast (B) is associated with photosynthesis in autotrophic organisms, the endoplasmic reticulum (D) produces complex macromolecules, and the ribosomes (E) are the site of protein synthesis. Mitochondria (A) metabolize glucose to produce energy in the form of ATP via cellular respiration.

30. (A)

Mitosis is the process whereby a single cell divides to produce two genetically identical daughter cells with the same number of chromosomes as the parent cell. The somatic cells contain the diploid number of chromosomes, 26 in this example.

31. (B)

Crossing over occurs during synapsis, an event during prophase I when homologous chromosomes intertwine and sometimes exchange genetic material. Nondisjunction (A) is an error in cell division in which chromosomes don't separate properly, and independent assortment (C) is movement of homologous chromosomes to opposite sides of the metaphase plate. Mutations [(D) and (E)] are changes in the DNA sequences on chromosomes that result in formation of abnormal genes.

32. (E)

When mRNA transcribes the code from a template strand of DNA, it is transcribing the "antisense" strand (3' to 5'). The complementary bases are laid down such that uracil corresponds to adenine and cytosine to guanine.

33. (D)

All of the choices listed describe movement of materials across the cell membrane; however, exocytosis by definition is movement of materials out of the cell.

34. (B)

Photosynthesis will reduce the amount of carbon dioxide in solution, turning the indicator red. The Calvin cycle, carried out by plants independent of light, also uses carbon dioxide, so tube 3 will turn red as well.

35. (E)

In every tube, cellular respiration would lead to production of carbon dioxide, which would tend to acidify the solution and turn the indicator yellow. However, in tube 1, photosynthesis is using more carbon dioxide than is being produced, making the solution more alkaline. In tube 3, the Calvin "dark" cycle also uses more carbon dioxide than is produced in cellular respiration.

36. (E)

All of the organisms are respiring.

37. (B)

Organic compounds are those that contain carbon bound to hydrogen and other elements such as oxygen and nitrogen. Water does not contain carbon.

38. (C)

Answer (A) describes the function of the cardiovascular system, answer (B) refers to the urinary system, answer (D) is the function of the lymphatic system, and answer (E) is a subfunction of the digestive system.

39. (E)

Gastrulation is the point at which differentiation of the germ layers occurs. A zygote is a fertilized egg, which undergoes cleavage to form a solid ball of cells called the morula. A blastula is a hollow ball of cells, which will indent, ultimately developing into a gastrula.

40. (C)

Collenchyma (A) is a type of thickened plant tissue that supports the plants, while phloem (B) is vascular tissue used for transport of sugars. Tracheids (D) are xylem cells, and stomata (E) are pores formed by guard cells on leaves. Apical and lateral meristems are the areas of active growth in a plant body.

41. (D)

Dominant alleles for a trait are represented by an upper-case letter; the recessive form is indicated by a lowercase version of the same letter. True-breeding parental generation individuals are homozygous for their trait, dominant or recessive.

42. (A)

In a cross of true-breeding dominant and recessive individuals, all of the F1 offspring would be expected to be heterozygous for the trait and show the dominant phenotype. In the F2 generation, about 1 in 4 would be expected to be homozygous recessive and show the recessive phenotype.

43. (C)

The F2 generation is expected to show a ratio of 1:2:1 homozygous dominant, heterozygous, and homozygous recessive. Although 75 percent of the F2 generation shows the dominant trait, only half are heterozygotes.

44. (B)

The alveoli are the sites of exchange for oxygen and carbon dioxide in the lungs.

45. (E)

Materials absorbed into the bloodstream from the intestine are shunted to the liver via the hepatic portal vein. One of the primary functions of the liver is detoxification.

46. (D)

ABO blood type is a function of antigenic glycoproteins on the surface of the erythrocytes. People with type A have the A antigen and type B the B antigen. Type ABs have both, and type Os have neither. Naturally occurring antibodies to the blood type antigens we lack are the cause of blood transfusion reactions. Type O individuals have anti-A and anti-B and can only safely receive type O blood. There is no anti-O.

47. (B)

Allele frequency would not necessarily change if only homozygotes do not reach reproductive age, particularly if mating is nonrandom. Both parents must be heterozygous to produce a homozygous recessive offspring, and a homozygous recessive individual is not expected to live to reproductive maturity. Neither parent would show symptoms if the enzyme is produced sufficiently in heterozygotes. Tay-Sachs does in fact involve a point mutation, affecting production of a single amino acid, proving answers (D) and (E) to be false.

48. (D)

Although both photosynthesis and temperature increased for most of the day, after 4:00 P.M. temperature continued to rise while photosynthesis rate decreased.

49. (B)

Although photosynthesis can be inhibited by low temperature, clearly that is not the case in this data figure, since temperature is at its highest during the period in question when the photosynthesis rate is dropping. All of the other explanations are feasible. Reductions in radiant energy might be due to a setting sun or cloud cover, both of which induce stomatal closure. At high temperatures, photorespiration can increase, reducing *net* photosynthesis; in addition, the activity of RUBISCO, an important photosynthetic enzyme, is reduced at temperatures over 40ºC. Loss of water during a hot afternoon might also lead to stomatal closure and reduced photosynthesis.

50. (E)

All of the characteristics listed in answers (A)–(D) are associated with human embryos. Oviparity, which occurs in some fish, amphibians, birds, and a few mammals, involves laying eggs outside the mother's body for complete development.

51. (C)

There are four types of human tissue: epithelial, connective, muscle, and nervous. Since nerves are composed of nervous tissue, one can easily rule it out as a type of connective tissue, which all of the other choices are.

52. (D)

Nerve impulses are transmitted along axons when excitation causes sodium channels to open, allowing rapid depolarization of the membrane as sodium floods into the cell. Adjacent channels are then stimulated to open, sending the impulse down the long axon in a wave.

53. (A)

Mendel found in his work with peas that many genes are passed independently of each other; one has no effect on the other. This is because of independent assortment of homologous chromosomes during the first meiotic division of genes on different chromosomes. Each of the other choices describes interaction of alleles or genes to affect expression of some trait.

54. (E)

Water enters the atmosphere through transpiration and evaporation and comes to earth via precipitation and condensation. Denitrification is part of the nitrogen cycle.

55. (A)

Mycorrhizae are plant-symbiotic mutualists that benefit the plant by helping it get water and nutrients from the soil. Each of the other relationships described involves one organism consuming another, the defining characteristic of a predator-prey relationship.

56. (C)

Until resources become limiting, exponential population growth shows a J-shaped curve. Once carrying capacity is reached, death rate increases and an S-curve develops.

57. (D)

According to the laws of thermodynamics, all energy transformations increase entropy, a decrease in the amount of usable energy due to loss as heat. Since every link in a food chain represents an energy transformation, there is always a loss of available energy at higher trophic levels.

58. (B)

Succession is the population of an area by various communities of organisms over time; primary succession occurs where no organisms previously existed, such as on a new island or after glacial retreat. Secondary succession is associated with disturbance events and repopulation.

59. (B)

Hares are herbivores and bobcats carnivores, so they would not compete for food resources. All of the other choices might directly or indirectly influence the population of the primary consumers (the hares) and their predators (the bobcats).

60. (D)

Increased predation on hares would be expected to reduce the hare population, and increased competition for prey would be expected to reduce the bobcat population. The amount of vegetation available as a food source might actually increase due to reduced consumption by hares.

61. (A)

An isotope of an element has a different number of neutrons but the same number of protons; this affects the mass but not the atomic number of the element. An isotope may be radioactive, but this is not always the case.

62. (C)

An element with more electrons than protons is a negatively charged ion called an anion. A cation (B) is a positively charged ion, and an isotope (E) is an alternative form of an element with a different number of neutral neutrons in the nucleus, which does not affect charge.

63. (D)

Beta particles are tiny radioactive particles that have little effect on the mass of the atom emitting them.

64. (B)

Fission splits heavy nuclei into smaller ones; fusion is the creation of a heavy nucleus from smaller ones, as occurs in stars like the sun. Both processes release energy.

65. (E)

Gamma rays are a form of electromagnetic radiation that results from the redistribution of electric charge within the nucleus of an atom.

66. (C)

Half-life refers to the amount of time it takes for half of the mass of a radioactive isotope to decay.

67. (C)

The configuration shows two *s* electrons in the first shell ($1s^2$), two *s* electrons and six *p* electrons in the second shell ($2s^2$ and $2p^6$), and two *s* electrons and four *p* electrons in the third shell ($3s^2$ and $3p^4$) for a total of sixteen electrons, six of them valence electrons as they exist in the outermost shell.

68. (E)

The bottom number in front of the abbreviation for the element represents the number of protons in the nucleus (the atomic number). In a neutral atom the number of protons is equal to the number of electrons. The mass number is 60, and protons and neutrons each have a mass of 1 amu. Therefore, this isotope has 33 neutrons.

69. (A)

Halogens have seven valence electrons, so two atoms often share one electron to fill their outer shells, such as fluorine F_2 and chlorine Cl_2.

70. (D)

The noble or inert gases have full outer electron shells and so tend not to react with other elements.

71. (B)

The metals tend to be dense and solid at ambient temperatures and are good conductors.

72. (C)

To balance the equation, eight atoms of hydrogen and ten of oxygen are needed on the right side of the equation. Four water molecules will satisfy both.

73. (B)

The reaction shown is combustion of propane in the presence of oxygen, an exothermic reaction that produces three molecules of carbon dioxide and four molecules of water for every molecule of propane combusted. The reaction requires activation energy, often a spark.

74. (A)

Potassium hydroxide (KOH) is a strong base and in solution will decrease the concentration of free hydrogen ions, thus raising pH, making the solution more alkaline.

75. (E)

Ionic bonds are loose bonds, and ions tend to go into solution in water. The other types of compounds listed have stronger bonds and do not dissociate as easily.

76. (D)

The total molecular mass of a mole of glucose is 180 grams [$(6 \times 12) + (12 \times 1) + (6 \times 16)$]. The contribution to the total by carbon is 72 grams (6×12), which is 40 percent of the total.

77. (E)

Catalysts alter the rate of chemical reactions without being changed by the reaction, all of which would occur in choices (A)–(D). Most often, catalysts lower the activation energy for chemical reactions.

78. (A)

Nitrogen makes up about 78 percent of the Earth's atmosphere, oxygen (B) around 21 percent. Carbon dioxide (D) and water (E) are also present in much smaller quantities. Chlorine (C) is rare.

79. (E)

Because of the disproportionate charges in the hydrogen and oxygen atoms in water, the shared electrons spend most of their time orbiting the oxygen atom, producing a more negative charge on that side of the molecule.

80. (B)

Chemical energy is the kind of energy released by exergonic (exothermic) reactions, such as combustion reactions or respiration, when the bonds of organic molecules such as fossil fuels (or glucose) are broken.

81. (D)

Einstein's theory of special relativity describes the equality of mass and energy at velocities greater than the speed of light ($E = mc^2$).

82. (C)

Heat is the thermal energy associated with molecular motion; the greater the rate of motion, the more heat energy an object has.

83. (C)

To solve this equation, use t from the equation as the unknown. Since $v_0 = 0$ (the watermelons have zero initial velocity, since they were at rest), the equation simply becomes $t = v/a$. Since final velocity $v = 50$ m/s and $a = 9.8$ m/s^2, solving for t becomes 50 m/sec ÷ 9.8 m/sec^2 = 5.1 seconds.

84. (A)

This time one simply multiplies t (3 seconds) $\times a$ (9.8 m/s^2), since v_0 is still 0, to get a final v of 29.4 m/s.

85. (E)

Mass is not part of the equation, so it would not affect the calculated results. In practice, increased resistance due to more surface area of the watermelons might affect the outcome, but the mass could also effectively be increased without increasing resistance.

86. (B)

Entropy is a measure of the amount of disorder in a system, and with each energy transformation, when energy is "lost," entropy increases. Answer (A) is incorrect because energy is not destroyed; it is merely changing form to heat energy, which is a less available form of energy. Answer (C) is incorrect because some chemical reactions require input of energy. Answers (D) and (E) are both incorrect; the amount of heat in the universe is thought to be increasing along with entropy.

87. (A)

Condensation is a state change from gas to liquid. Water will condense on a surface when that surface is sufficiently cooled compared with the air. Warm air can hold more water than can cool air, so when air is rapidly cooled on the outside of the cold glass, water often condenses from it.

88. (D)

When the water's state changed from liquid to solid, molecular motion slowed, and energy was released. When atmospheric moisture condensed on the glass, another energy-releasing transformation took place. Evaporation required the input of energy (heat from the sun) to make the state change from liquid to gas.

89. (C)

Answers (A) and (B) are restatements of Newton's second law of motion, given in choice (D). Answer (E) is Newton's third law. Answer (C) puts forth half of Newton's first law, which also states that an object in motion will remain in motion unless some force acts upon it.

90. (B)

All one needs to know here is that if the right side of the equation gets bigger, so must the left side. So as T goes up, so must P and/or V, ruling out answers (A) and (D). Answer (C) is false because more moles of gas cannot spontaneously appear in the sealed balloon. Answer (E) is incorrect because a gas will always occupy as much volume as possible at the lowest pressure possible for a given temperature.

91. (A)

If both volume (V) and temperature (T) are held constant, then since R is always constant, doubling the number of moles of gas (n), as is the case in this example, will also double pressure (P).

92. (B)

By definition, inertia is the resistance of an object at rest or in motion to change its state of rest or motion unless some force acts upon it, as described by Newton's first law of motion.

93. (E)

The mass of an object is not influenced by gravity; only its weight is. Mass is an inherent characteristic of an object. Weight is the mass of an object times the acceleration of gravity, so the weight of the object would be reduced on Mars.

94. (C)

Galileo's ideas contradicted those of Aristotle, which were based on the idea of objects moving toward their natural places. Galileo conducted experiments with balls rolling down inclined planes. Ideas about gravity and motion put forth by Newton and Einstein came much later. Copernicus mainly concerned himself with planetary motion and the relative position of the Earth, planets, and stars.

95. (A)

An ohm (B) is a measure of resistance, a volt (C) is the potential difference between oppositely charged poles, an ampere (D) is a measure of electrical current, and a watt (E) is a measure of work that can be done (amperes × volts). The coulomb is based on the charge of a single proton or electron.

96. (B)

Radio waves have the longest wavelength.

97. (A)

The order of short wavelength (high energy) → long wavelength (low energy) for the types of electromagnetic radiation shown is ultraviolet → visible light → infrared → microwaves → radio waves.

98. (C)

As sound travels, particles in the medium that sound is traveling through vibrate parallel to the direction of energy, thereby producing longitudinal waves.

99. (D)

Refraction is the term for the bending of light waves.

100. (D)

The idea of the big bang gained support when astronomers found that distant galaxies in every direction are going away from us at speeds proportional to their distance. This displacement of the spectra of distant objects is known as the red shift.

101. (E)

When a star ages and contracts, its gravitational field becomes so great that even light cannot escape, creating a so-called "black hole" in space.

102. (B)

Earth is the third planet from the sun.

103. (E)

While other planets have rings, Saturn's are the most visible. It is the sixth planet from the sun.

104. (C)

The asteroid belt consists of thousands of small objects less than 1,000 km in diameter that follow separate orbits around the sun in the region between Mars and Jupiter, the fourth and fifth planets from the sun.

105. (B)

The appearance of a comet is due to the fact that as it nears the sun, heating of the frozen material within it produces a trail of gas and dust. The solar wind pushes the debris away to form the comet's tail.

106. (D)

A meteoroid is an object moving through space; when it enters the earth's atmosphere and produces a flash, it is termed a meteor, and what's left after it hits the ground is a meteorite.

107. (A)

The word *nebula* in Latin means "cloud." Nebulae come in different forms: planetary nebulae, supernova remnants, and diffuse nebulae. When stars form, they form as a result of a nebula condensing.

108. (B)

Jupiter, the largest of the gas giants, is similar in composition to the sun and is comprised mainly of hydrogen and helium.

109. (D)

The stratosphere is the atmospheric layer immediately above the troposphere and contains ozone, which is responsible for absorbing ultraviolet radiation, protecting life on Earth from its damaging effects.

110. (C)

The lithosphere is part of the geosphere (the Earth itself) and not part of the atmosphere.

111. (B)

The lowest layer of the atmosphere is the troposphere.

112. (A)

In the lower atmosphere, as air rises, it cools about 1°C for each 100 m increase in altitude. The amount of water it can hold is reduced as it cools. When dew point temperature is reached, water condenses, forming clouds. As the mass rises and is cooled, relative humidity increases (B). Since there is no volume limitation on an air mass in the atmosphere, warm air expands freely, decreasing pressure (D) and lowering temperature (C).

113. (C)

Answer (D) could be a correct alternative, although an apparatus or entity large enough to grasp and firmly squeeze a cloud would have to be found.

114. (D)

Vulcanism is most often associated with volcanoes but by definition refers to any movement of magma near the Earth's surface.

115. (E)

Faults form when fractures in the earth forcefully move the crust either horizontally or vertically. Folding (B) is the bending of crustal rocks by compression and uplift.

116. (A)

The plates of the Earth's crust are in constant slow motion. When two plates come together, one will be forced down and presumably melt into the Earth's magma.

117. (D)

Global warming is a result of the greenhouse effect. The greenhouse effect occurs when heat energy, mostly long-wave infrared radiation, is trapped by gases such as methane and carbon dioxide in the Earth's atmosphere.

118. (B)

Alluvium is any stream-deposited sedimentary material. When such material is deposited from mountain canyons, a characteristic fan shape occurs.

119. (C)

The outer edge of a river's flood plain is usually marked by a clear change in slope that marks the outer limit of erosion and undercutting. There is an abrupt rise to the flat terrain above, forming a ring of bluffs.

120. (E)

Deltas are formed when a relatively fast-moving stream is suddenly slowed, usually when it moves into a lake or ocean. Most of the stream load is dumped in a characteristic deltoid (triangular) pattern.

Computing Your Practice Test Score

Chapter Twenty-Four: **Scoring Your Test**

Now for the exciting part of the exam—computing your score! The score you obtain on each sample test in this book is an approximate score of what you would get on the actual test. The questions on the actual test are not exactly the same questions offered in this book, but they are as close as possible.

Let's recap some of the scoring information from chapter 1. The number of questions you get correct (designated by one point each) is called your *raw score*. Each *correct* multiple-choice answer receives one point, while each *wrong* or *skipped* answer does not receive any points. No points are subtracted for wrong or skipped answers.

The raw score is adjusted according to a formula specified by the College Board, and the result is your scaled score. Total *scaled scores* on the CLEP exams can range from 20 to 80. The American Council on Education's minimum recommended score for CLEP credit is 50.

The College Board has not released the exact scoring guidelines for each test, but you can estimate whether or not you have achieved a passing grade on the sample tests in this book. This does not determine what you will get on the actual test, but it is a good approximation.

To obtain your score for each test, add up the number of questions you got right and place that number over the total number of questions on each test. Complete the following formula to obtain your approximate score:

$$\frac{\text{\# of questions right}}{\text{Total \# of questions on test}} = \text{decimal} \times 100 = \text{percent of the exam you got correct}$$

The percent of the exam that you got correct should be over 70 percent (a grade of C) for you to expect to get a passing grade on the CLEP exam. Again, this is approximate. Remember that practice test conditions are not the same as real test conditions, so don't take your score too literally. But your score should give you a ballpark estimate of how comfortable you are with the material and how well prepared you are for the exam.

Good luck!

KAPLAN

| SECTION EIGHT |

CLEP Resources

Word Roots

Knowing roots of words can help you in two ways. First, instead of learning one word at a time, you can learn a whole group of words that contain a certain root. They'll be related in meaning, so if you remember one, it will be easier for you to remember others. Second, roots can often help you decode an unknown word. If you recognize a familiar root, you can get a good enough idea of the word to answer the question.

A, AN—not, without
amoral, atrophy, asymmetrical, anarchy, anesthetic

AB, A—from, away, apart
abnormal, abdicate, ablution, abnegate, absolve, abstemious, abstruse, annul, avert

AC, ACR—sour, sharp
acid, acerbic, exacerbate, acute, acrimony

AD, A—to, toward
adhere, adjacent, adjunct, admonish, adroit, adumbrate, accretion, accertion, alleviate, aspire, assail, assonance, attest

ALI, ALTR—another
alias, alienate, inalienable, altruism

AM, AMI—love
amorous, amicable, amiable, amity

AMBI, AMPHI—both
ambiguous, ambivalent, ambidextrous, amphibious

AMBL, AMBUL—walk
amble, ambulatory, perambulator, somnambulist

ANIM—mind, spirit, breath
animal, animosity, unanimous, magnanimous

ANN, ENN—year
annual, annuity, biennial, perennial

ANTE, ANT—before
antecedent, antediluvian, antiquated, anticipate

ANTHROP—human
anthropology, philanthropy

ANTI, ANT—against, opposite
antidote, antithesis, antacid, antagonist, antonym

AUD—hear
audio, audience, audition

AUTO—self
autobiography, autocrat, autonomous

BELLI, BELL—war
belligerent, bellicose, antebellum, rebellion

BENE, BEN—good
benevolent, benefactor, beneficent, benign

BI—two
bicycle, bisect, bilateral, bilingual, biped

BIBLIO—book
bibliography, bibliophile

BIO—life
biography, biology, amphibious, symbiotic, macrobiotics

BURS—money, purse
reimburse, disburse, bursar

CAD, CAS, CID—happen, fall
accident, cadence, cascade, deciduous

CAP, CIP—head
captain, decapitate, precipitate, recapitulate, accident

CARN—flesh
carnal, carnage, incarnate

CAP, CAPT, CEPT, CIP—take, hold, seize
capable, capacious, captivate, deception, intercept, inception, anticipate, emancipation

CED, CESS—yield, go
cede, precede, accede, cease, cessation, incessant

CHROM—color
chrome, chromatic, monochrome

CHRON—time
chronology, chronic, anachronism

CIDE—murder
suicide, homicide, regicide, patricide

CIRCUM—around
circumference, circumlocution, circumspect, circumvent

CLIN, CLIV—slope
incline, declivity, proclivity

CLUD, CLUS, CLAUS, CLOIS—shut, close
conclude, reclusive, claustrophobia, cloister, preclude, occlude

CO, COM, CON—with, together
coeducation, coagulate, coalesce, coerce, collateral, commodious, complaint, concord, congenial, congenital

COGN, GNO—know
recognize, cognition, diagnosis, agnostic, prognosis

CONTRA—against
controversy, incontrovertible, contravene

CORP—body
corpse, corporeal, corpulence

COSMO, COSM—world
cosmopolitan, cosmos, microcosm, macrocosm

CRAC, CRAT—rule, power
democracy, bureaucracy, autocrat, aristocrat

CRED—trust, believe
incredible, credulous, credence

CRESC, CRET—grow
crescent, crescendo, accretion

CULP—blame, fault
culprit, culpable, inculpate, exculpate

CURR, CURS—run
current, concur, cursory, precursor, incursion

DE—down, out, apart
depart, debase, debilitate, defamatory, demur

DEC—ten, tenth
decade, decimal, decathlon, decimate

DEMO, DEM—people
democrat, demographics, demagogue, epidemic

DI, DIURN—day
diary, quotidian, diurnal

DIA—across
diagonal, diatribe, diaphanous

DIC, DICT—speak
abdicate, diction, indict, verdict

DIS, DIF, DI—not, apart, away
disaffected, disband, disbar, distend, differentiate, diffidence, diffuse, digress, divert

DOC, DOCT—teach
docile, doctrine, doctrinaire

DOL—pain
condolence, doleful, dolorous, indolent

DUC, DUCT—lead
seduce, induce, conduct, viaduct, induct

EGO—self
ego, egoist, egocentric

EN, EM—in, into
enter, entice, encumber, embroil, empathy

ERR—wander
erratic, aberration, errant

EU—well, good
eulogy, euphemism, eurythmics, euthanasia

EX, E—out, out of
exit, exacerbate, excerpt, excommunicate, elicit, egress, egregious

FAC, FIC, FECT, FY, FEA—make, do
factory, facility, benefactor, malefactor, fiction, fictive, rectify, vilify, feasible

FAL, FALS—deceive
infallible, fallacious, false

FERV—boil
fervent, fervid, effervescent

FID—faith, trust
confident, diffidence, perfidious, fidelity

FLU, FLUX—flow
fluent, affluent, superfluous, flux

FORE—before
forecast, foreboding, forestall

FRAG, FRAC—break
fragment, fracture, refract

FUS—pour
profuse, infusion, effusive, diffuse

GEN—birth, class, kin
generation, congenital, homogeneous, ingenious, engender

GRAD, GRESS—step
graduate, gradual, retrograde, ingress, egress

GRAPH, GRAM—writing
biography, bibliography, epigram

GRAT—pleasing
grateful, gratitude, gratuitous, gratuity

GRAV, GRIEV—heavy
grave, gravity, aggrieve, grievous

GREG—crowd, flock
segregate, gregarious, aggregate

HABIT, HIBIT—have, hold
habit, cohabit, habitat, inhibit

HAP—by chance
happen, haphazard, hapless, mishap

HELIO, HELI—sun
heliocentric, heliotrope, aphelion, perihelion, helium

HETERO—other
heterosexual, heterogeneous, heterodox

HOL—whole
holocaust, catholic, holistic

HOMO—same
homogenize, homogeneous, homonym

HOMO—man
homo sapiens, homicide, bonhomie

HYDR—water
hydrant, hydrate, dehydration

HYPER—too much, excess
hyperactive, hyperbole, hyperventilate

HYPO—too little, under
hypodermic, hypothermia, hypochondria

IN, IG, IL, IM, IR—not
incorrigible, insomnia, interminable, incessant, ignorant, ignominious, ignoble, illicit, illimitable, immaculate, immutable, impertinent, improvident, irregular

IN, IL, IM, IR—in, on, into
invade, inaugurate, incandescent, illustrate, imbue, immerse, implicate, irrigate, irritate

INTER—between, among
intercede, intercept, interdiction, interject

INTRA, INTR—within
intrastate, intravenous, intramural, intrinsic

IT, ITER—between, among
transit, itinerant, transitory, reiterate

JECT, JET—throw
eject, interject, abject, trajectory, jettison

JOUR—day
journal, adjourn, sojourn

JUD—judge
judge, judicious, prejudice, adjudicate

JUNCT, JUG—join
junction, adjunct, injunction

JUR—swear, law
jury, abjure, perjure, jurisprudence

LAT—side
lateral, collateral, unilateral

LAV, LAU, LU—wash
lavatory, laundry, ablution, antediluvian

LEG, LEC, LEX—read, speak
legible, lecture, lexicon

LEV—light
elevate, levitate, levity, alleviate

LIBER—free
liberty, liberal, libertarian, libertine

LIG, LECT—choose, gather
eligible, elect, select

LIG, LI, LY—bind
ligament, oblige, religion, liable, liaison, lien, ally

LING, LANG—tongue
lingo, linguistics, bilingual, language

LITER—letter
literate, alliteration, literal

LITH—stone
monolith, lithograph, megalith

LOQU, LOC, LOG—speech, thought
eloquent, loqucaious, colloquial, circumlocution,
monologue, dialogue

LUC, LUM—light
lucid, elucidate, pellucid, translucent, illuminate

LUD, LUS—play
ludicrous, allude, delusion

MACRO—great
macrocosm, macrobiotics

MAG, MAJ, MAS, MAX—great
magnify, magnanimous, magnate, magnitude, majesty,
master, maximum

MAL—bad
malady, maladroit, malevolent, malodorous

MAN—hand
manual, manuscript, manifest

MAR—sea
submarine, marine, maritime

MATER, MATR—mother
maternal, matron, matrilineal

MEDI—middle
intermediary, medieval, mediate

MEGA—great
megaphone, megalomania, megaton, megalith

MEM, MEN—remember
memory, memento, memorabilia, reminisce

METER, METR, MENS—measure
meter, thermometer, commensurate

MICRO—small
microscope, microorganism, microcosm, microbe

MIS—wrong, bad, hate
misunderstand, misapprehension, misconstrue, mishap

MIT, MISS—send
transmit, emit, missive

MOLL—soft
mollify, emollient, mollusk

MON, MONIT—warn
admonish, monitor, premonition

MONO—one
monologue, monotonous, monogamy

MOR—custom, manner
moral, mores, morose

MOR, MORT—dead
morbid, moribund, mortal, amortize

MORPH—shape
amorphous, anthropomorphic, morphology

MOV, MOT, MOB, MOM—move
remove, motion, mobile, momentum, momentous

MUT—change
mutate, mutability, immutable, commute

NAT, NASC—born
native, nativity, cognate, nascent, renascent, renaissance

NAU, NAV—ship, sailor
nautical, nauseous, navy, circumnavigate

NEG—not, deny
negative, abnegate, renege

NEO—new
neoclassical, neophyte, neologism, neonate

NIHIL—none, nothing
annihilation, nihilism

NOM, NYM—name
nominate, nomenclature, nominal, synonym, anonymity

NOX, NIC, NEC, NOC—harm
obnoxious, internecine, innocuous

NOV—new
novelty, innovation, novitiate

NUMER—number
numeral, numerous, innumerable, enumerate

OB—against
obstruct, obdurate, obsequious, obtrusive

OMNI—all
omnipresent, omnipotent, omniscient, omnivorous

ONER—burden
onerous, exonerate

OPER—work
operate, cooperate, inoperable

PAC—peace
pacify, pacifist, pacific

PALP—feel
palpable, palpitation

PAN—all
panorama, panacea, pandemic, panoply

PATER, PATR—father
paternal, paternity, patriot, compatriot, expatriate

PATH, PASS—feel, suffer
sympathy, antipathy, pathos, impassioned

PEC—money
pecuniary, impecunious, peculation

PED, POD—foot
pedestrian, pediment, quadruped, tripod

PEL, PULS—drive
compel, compelling, expel, propel, compulsion

PEN—almost
peninsula, penultimate, penumbra

PEND, PENS—hang
pendant, pendulous, suspense, propensity

PER—through, by, for, throughout
perambulator, percipient, perfunctory, pertinacious

PER—against, destruction
perfidious, pernicious, perjure

PERI—around
perimeter, periphery, perihelion, peripatetic

PET—seek, go toward
petition, impetus, impetuous, petulant, centripetal

PHIL—love
philosopher, philanderer, philanthropy, philology

PHOB—fear
phobia, claustrophobia, xenophobia

PHON—sound
phonograph, megaphone, phonics

PLAC—calm, please
placate, implacable, placid, complacent

PON, POS—put, place
postpone, proponent, juxtaposition, depose

PORT—carry
portable, deportment, rapport

POT—drink
potion, potable

POT—power
potential, potent, impotent, potentate, omnipotence

PRE—before
precede, precipitate, premonition, preposition

PRIM, PRI—first
prime, primary, primordial, pristine

PRO—ahead, forth
proceed, proclivity, protestation, provoke

PROTO—first
prototype, protagonist, protocol

PROX, PROP—near
approximate, propinquity, proximity

PSEUDO—false
pseudoscientific, pseudonym

PYR—fire
pyre, pyrotechnics, pyromania

QUAD, QUAR, QUAT—four
quadrilateral, quadrant, quarter, quarantine

QUES, QUER, QUIS, QUIR—question
quest, inquest, query, querulous, inquisitive, inquiry

QUIE—quiet
disquiet, acquiesce, quiescent, requiem

QUINT, QUIN—five
quintuplets, quintessence

RADI, RAMI—branch
radiate, radiant, eradicate, ramification

RECT, REG—straight, rule
rectangle, rectitude, rectify, regular

REG—king, rule
regal, regent, interregnum

RETRO—backward
retrospective, retroactive, retrograde

RID, RIS—laugh
ridiculous, deride, derision

ROG—ask
interrogate, derogatory, arrogant

RUD—rough, crude
rude, erudite, rudimentary

RUPT—break
disrupt, interrupt, rupture

SACR, SANCT—holy
sacred, sacrilege, sanction, sacrosanct

SCRIB, SCRIPT, SCRIV—write
scribe, ascribe, script, manuscript, scrivener

SE—apart, away
separate, segregate, secede, sedition

SEC, SECT, SEG—cut
secant, sector, dissect, bisect, intersect, segment

SED, SID—sit
sedate, sedentary, supersede, reside, residence

SEM—seed, sow
seminar, seminal, disseminate

SEN—old
senior, senile, senescent

SENT, SENS—feel, think
sentiment, nonsense, consensus, sensual

SEQU, SECU—follow
sequence, sequel, subsequent, consecutive

SIM, SEM—similar, same
similar, verisimilitude, semblance, dissemble

SIGN—mark, sign
signal, designation, assignation

SIN—curve
sinuous, insinuate

SOL—sun
solar, parasol, solarium, solstice

SOL—alone
solo, solitude, soliloquy, solipsism

SOMN—sleep
insomnia, somnolent, somnambulist

SON—sound
sonic, consonance, sonorous, resonate

SOPH—wisdom
philosopher, sophistry, sophisticated, sophomoric

SPEC, SPIC—see, look
spectator, retrospective, perspective, perspicacious

SPER—hope
prosper, prosperous, despair, desperate

SPERS, SPAR—scatter
disperse, aspersion, sparse, disparate

SPIR—breathe
respire, inspire, spiritual, aspire, transpire

STRICT, STRING—bind
stricture, constrict, stringent, astringent

STRUCT, STRU—build
structure, obstruct, construe

SUB—under
subconscious, subjugate, subliminal, subpoena

SUMM—highest
summit, summary, consummate

SUPER, SUR—above
supervise, supercilious, superfluous, insurmountable, surfeit

SURGE, SURRECT—rise
surge, resurgent, insurgent, insurrection

SYN, SYM—together
synthesis, sympathy, symposium, symbiosis

TACIT, TIC—silent
tacit, taciturn, reticent

TACT, TAG, TANG—touch
tact, tactile, contagious, tangent, tangential, tangible

TEN, TIN, TAIN—hold, twist
detention, tenable, pertinacious, retinue, retain

TEND, TENS, TENT—stretch
intend, distend, tension, tensile, ostensible, contentious

TERM—end
terminal, terminus, terminate, interminable

TERR—earth, land
terrain, terrestrial, extraterrestrial, subterranean

TEST—witness
testify, attest, testimonial, protestation

THE—god
atheist, theology, apotheosis, theocracy

THERM—heat
thermometer, thermal, thermonuclear, hypothermia

TIM—fear, frightened
timid, intimidate, timorous

TOP—place
topic, topography, utopia

TORT—twist
distort, extort, tortuous

TORP—stiff, numb
torpedo, torpid, torpor

TOX—poison
toxic, toxin, intoxication

TRACT—draw
tractor, intractable, protract

TRANS—across, over, through, beyond
transport, transgress, transient, transitory, translucent

TREM, TREP—shake
tremble, tremor, trepidation, intrepid

TURB—shake
disturb, turbulent, perturbation

UMBR—shadow
umbrella, umbrage, adumbrate, penumbra

UNI, UN—one
unify, unilateral, unanimous

URB—city
urban, suburban, urbane

VAC—empty
vacant, evacuate, vacuous

VAL, VAIL—value, strength
valid, valor, ambivalent, convalescence, avail

VEN, VENT—come
convene, intervene, venue, convention, adventitious

VER—true
verify, verity, verisimilitude, verdict

VERB—word
verbal, verbose, verbiage, verbatim

VERT, VERS—turn
avert, convert, revert, incontrovertible, divert, aversion

VICT, VINC—conquer
victory, conviction, evict, evince, invincible

VID, VIS—see
evident, vision, visage, supervise

VIL—base, mean
vile, vilify, revile

VIV, VIT—life
vivid, convivial, vivacious, vital

VOC, VOK, VOW—call, voice
vocal, equivocate, invoke, avow

VOL—wish
voluntary, malevolent, benevolent, volition

VOLV, VOLUT—turn, roll
revolve, evolve, convoluted

VOR—eat
devour, carnivore, omnivorous, voracious

Vocabulary Word List

In general, the very best way to improve your vocabulary is to read. Choose challenging, college-level material. If you encounter an unknown word, put it on a flashcard or in a vocabulary notebook. Memorizing the words on the following list can help. Here are some techniques for memorizing words.

1. Learn words in groups. You can group words by a common root they contain (see the Root List for some examples), or you can group words together if they are related in meaning (i.e., word families). Memorizing words this way may help you to remember them.

2. Use flashcards. Write down new words or word groups and run through them when you have a few minutes to spare. Put one new word or word group on one side of a 3 × 5 card and put a short definition or definitions on the back.

3. Make a vocabulary notebook. List words in one column and their definitions in another. Test yourself. Cover up the meanings and see which words you can define from memory. Make a sample sentence using each word in context.

4. Think of hooks that lodge a new word in your mind—create visual images of words.

5. Use rhymes, pictures, songs, and any other devices that help you remember words.

To get the most out of your remaining study time, use the techniques that work for you and stick with them.

ABANDON

noun (uh <u>baan</u> duhn)

total lack of inhibition

The flamenco dancer performed with complete *abandon.*

ABATE

verb (uh <u>bayt</u>)

to decrease, to reduce

My hunger *abated* when I saw how filthy the chef's hands were.

ABET

verb (uh <u>beht</u>)

to aid; to act as an accomplice

While Derwin robbed the bank, Marvin *abetted* his friend by pulling up the getaway car.

ABJURE

verb (aab <u>joor</u>)

to renounce under oath; to abandon forever; to abstain from

After having been devout for most of his life, he suddenly *abjured* his beliefs, much to his family's disappointment.

ABNEGATE

verb (<u>aab</u> nih gayt)

to give up; to deny to oneself

After his retirement, the former police commissioner found it difficult to *abnegate* authority.

ABORTIVE

adj (uh <u>bohr</u> tihv)

ending without results

Mai's *abortive* attempt to swim the full five miles left her frustrated.

ABROGATE

verb (<u>aab</u> ruh gayt)

to annul; to abolish by authoritative action

The president's job is to *abrogate* any law that fosters inequality among citizens.

ABSCOND

verb (aab <u>skahnd</u>)

to leave quickly in secret

The criminal *absconded* during the night with all of his mother's money.

ABSTEMIOUS

adj (aab <u>stee</u> mee uhs)

done sparingly; consuming in moderation

The spa served no sugar or wheat, but the clients found the retreat so calm that they didn't mind the *abstemious* rules.

ACCEDE

verb (aak <u>seed</u>)

to express approval, to agree to

Once the mayor heard the reasonable request, she happily *acceded* to the proposal.

ACCLIVITY

noun (uh <u>klihv</u> ih tee)

an incline or upward slope, the ascending side of a hill

We were so tired from hiking that by the time we reached the *acclivity*, it looked more like a mountain than a hill.

ACCRETION

noun (uh <u>kree</u> shuhn)

a growth in size, an increase in amount

The committee's strong fund-raising efforts resulted in an *accretion* in scholarship money.

ACME

noun (<u>aak</u> mee)

the highest level or degree attainable

Just when he reached the *acme* of his power, the dictator was overthrown.

ACTUATE

verb (<u>aak</u> choo ayt)

to put into motion, to activate; to motivate or influence to activity

The leaders rousing speech *actuated* the crowd into a peaceful protest.

ACUITY

noun (uh <u>kyoo</u> ih tee)

sharp vision or perception characterized by the ability to resolve fine detail

With unusual *acuity*, she was able to determine that the masterpiece was a fake.

ACUMEN

noun (<u>aak</u> yuh muhn) (uh <u>kyoo</u> muhn)

sharpness of insight, mind, and understanding; shrewd judgment

The investor's financial *acumen* helped him to select high-yield stocks.

ADAMANT

adj (<u>aad</u> uh muhnt) (<u>aad</u> uh mihnt)

stubbornly unyielding

She was *adamant* about leaving the restaurant after the waiter was rude.

ADEPT

adj (uh <u>dehpt</u>)

extremely skilled

She is *adept* at computing math problems in her head.

ADJUDICATE

verb (uh <u>jood</u> ih kayt)

to hear and settle a matter; to act as a judge

The principal *adjudicated* the disagreement between two students.

ADJURE

verb (uh <u>joor</u>)

to appeal to

The criminal *adjured* to the court for mercy.

ADMONISH

verb (aad <u>mahn</u> ihsh)

to caution or warn gently in order to correct something

My mother *admonished* me about my poor grades.

ADROIT

adj (uh <u>droyt</u>)

skillful; accomplished; highly competent

The *adroit* athlete completed even the most difficult obstacle course with ease.

ADULATION

noun (<u>aaj</u> juh lay shuhn)

excessive flattery or admiration

The *adulation* she showed her professor seemed insincere; I suspected she really wanted a better grade.

ADUMBRATE

verb (<u>aad</u> uhm brayt) (uh <u>duhm</u> brayt)

to give a hint or indication of something to come

Her constant complaining about the job *adumbrated* her intent to leave.

AERIE

noun (<u>ayr</u> ee) (<u>eer</u> ee)

a nest built high in the air; an elevated, often secluded, dwelling

Perched high among the trees, the eagle's *aerie* was filled with eggs.

AFFECTED

adj (uh <u>fehk</u> tihd)

phony, artificial

The *affected* hairdresser spouted French phrases, though she had never been to France.

AGGREGATE

noun (<u>aa</u> grih giht)

a collective mass, the sum total

An *aggregate* of panic-stricken customers mobbed the bank, demanding their life savings.

ALGORITHM

noun (<u>aal</u> guh rith uhm)

an established procedure for solving a problem or equation

The accountant uses a series of *algorithms* to determine the appropriate tax bracket.

ALIMENTARY

adj (aal uh <u>mehn</u> tuh ree) (aal uh <u>mehn</u> tree)

pertaining to food, nutrition, or digestion

After a particularly good meal, Sherlock turned to his companion and exclaimed, "I feel quite good, very well fed. It was *alimentary* my dear Watson."

ALLAY

verb (uh <u>lay</u>)

to lessen, ease, reduce in intensity

Trying to *allay* their fears, the nurse sat with them all night.

AMITY

noun (<u>aa</u> mih tee)

friendship, good will

Correspondence over the years contributed to a lasting *amity* between the women.

AMORPHOUS

adj (<u>ay</u> <u>mohr</u> fuhs)

having no definite form

The Blob featured an *amorphous* creature that was constantly changing shape.

ANIMUS

noun (<u>aan</u> uh muhs)

a feeling of animosity or ill will

Though her teacher had failed her, she displayed no *animus* toward him.

ANODYNE

noun (<u>aan</u> uh dyen)

a source of comfort; a medicine that relieves pain

The sound of classical music is usually just the *anodyne* I need after a tough day at work.

ANOMALY

noun (uh <u>nahm</u> uh lee)

a deviation from the common rule, something that is difficult to classify

Among the top-ten albums of the year was one *anomaly*—a compilation of polka classics.

ANTHROPOMORPHIC

adj (<u>aan</u> thruh poh <u>mohr</u> fihk)

suggesting human characteristics for animals and inanimate things

Many children's stories feature *anthropomorphic* animals such as talking wolves and pigs.

ANTIQUATED

adj (<u>aan</u> tih kway tihd)

too old to be fashionable or useful

Next to her coworker's brand-new model, Marisa's computer looked *antiquated*.

APHORISM

noun (<u>aa</u> fuhr ihz uhm)

a short statement of a principle

The country doctor often spoke such *aphorisms* as "Still waters run deep."

APLOMB

noun (uh <u>plahm</u>) (uh <u>pluhm</u>)

self-confident assurance; poise

For such a young dancer, she had great *aplomb*, making her perfect to play the young princess.

APOSTATE

noun (uh <u>pahs</u> tayt)

one who renounces a religious faith

So that he could divorce his wife, the king scoffed at the church doctrines and declared himself an *apostate*.

APPOSITE

adj (<u>aap</u> puh ziht)

strikingly appropriate or well adapted

The lawyer presented an *apposite* argument upon cross-examining the star witness.

APPRISE

verb (uh <u>priez</u>)

to give notice to, inform

"Thanks for *apprising* me that the test time has been changed," said Emanuel.

APPROPRIATE

verb (uh <u>proh</u> pree ayt)

to assign to a particular purpose, allocate

The fund's manager *appropriated* funds for the clean-up effort.

ARABLE

adj (<u>aa</u> ruh buhl)

suitable for cultivation

The overpopulated country desperately needed more *arable* land.

ARCANE

adj (ahr <u>kayn</u>)

secret, obscure; known only to a few

The *arcane* rituals of the sect were passed down through many generations.

ARCHIPELAGO

noun (ahr kuh <u>pehl</u> uh goh)

a large group of islands

Between villages in the Stockholm *archipelago*, boat taxis are the only form of transportation.

ARREARS

noun (uh <u>reerz</u>)

unpaid, overdue debts or bills; neglected obligations

After the expensive lawsuit, Dominic's accounts were in *arrears*.

ARROGATE

verb (<u>aa</u> ruh gayt)

to claim without justification; to claim for oneself without right

Zeita watched in astonishment as her boss *arrogated* the credit for her brilliant work on the project.

ASKANCE
adv (uh skaans)

with disapproval; with a skeptical sideways glance

She looked *askance* at her son's failing report card as he mumbled that he had done all the schoolwork.

ASSENT
verb (uh sehnt)

to agree, as to a proposal

After careful deliberation, the CEO *assented* to the proposed merger.

ATAVISTIC
adj (aat uh vihs tik)

characteristic of a former era, ancient

After spending three weeks on a desert island, Jakome became a survivalist with *atavistic* skills that helped him endure.

AUTOCRAT
noun (aw toh kraat)

a dictator

Mussolini has been described as an *autocrat* who tolerated no opposition.

AVER
verb (uh vuhr)

to declare to be true, to affirm

"Yes, he was wearing a mask," the witness *averred*.

AVUNCULAR
adj (ah vuhng kyuh luhr)

like an uncle in behavior, especially in kindness and warmth

The coach's *avuncular* style made him well-liked.

AWRY
adv (uh rie)

crooked, askew, amiss

Something must have gone *awry* in the computer system because some of my files are missing.

BALK
verb (bawk)

to stop short and refuse to go on

When the horse *balked* at jumping over the high fence, the rider was thrown off.

BALLAST

noun (<u>baal</u> uhst)

a structure that helps to stabilize or steady

Communication and honesty are the true *ballasts* of a good relationship.

BEATIFIC

adj (bee uh <u>tihf</u> ihk)

displaying calmness and joy, relating to a state of celestial happiness

After spending three months in India, she had a *beatific* peace about her.

BECALM

verb (bih <u>kahm</u>)

to stop the progress of, to soothe

The warm air *becalmed* the choppy waves.

BECLOUD

verb (bih <u>klowd</u>)

to make less visible, to obscure, or blur

Her ambivalence about the long commute *beclouded* her enthusiasm about the job.

BEDRAGGLE

adj (bih <u>draag</u> uhl)

soiled, wet and limp; dilapidated

The child's *bedraggled* blanket needed a good cleaning.

BEGET

verb (bih <u>geht</u>)

to produce, especially as an effect or outgrowth; to bring about

The mayor believed that finding petty offenders would help reduce serious crime because, he argued, small crimes *beget* big crimes.

BEHEMOTH

noun (buh <u>hee</u> muhth)

something of monstrous size or power; huge creature

The budget became such a *behemoth* that observers believed the film would never make a profit.

BENEFICENT

adj (buh <u>nehf</u> ih sent)

pertaining to an act of kindness

The *beneficent* man donated the money anonymously.

BERATE

verb (bih <u>rayt</u>)

to scold harshly

When my manager found out I had handled the situation so insensitively, he *berated* me.

BILIOUS

adj (<u>bihl</u> yuhs)

ill-tempered, sickly, ailing

The party ended early when the *bilious* 5-year-old tried to run off with the birthday girl's presents.

BLASPHEMOUS

adj (<u>blaas</u> fuh muhs)

cursing, profane; extremely irreverent

The politician's offhanded comments seemed *blasphemous*, given the context of the orderly meeting.

BLATANT

adj (<u>blay</u> tnt)

completely obvious and conspicuous, especially in an offensive, crass manner

Such *blatant* advertising within the bounds of the school drew protest from parents.

BLITHELY

adv (<u>blieth</u> lee)

merrily, lightheartedly cheerful; without appropriate thought

Wanting to redecorate the office, she *blithely* assumed her co-workers wouldn't mind and moved the furniture in the space.

BOMBASTIC

adj (bahm <u>baast</u> ihk)

high-sounding but meaningless; ostentatiously lofty in style

The lawyer's speeches were mostly *bombastic*; his outrageous claims had no basis in fact.

BOVINE

adj (<u>boh</u> vien)

relating to cows; having qualities characteristic of a cow, such as sluggishness or dullness

His *bovine* demeanor did nothing to engage me.

BRAGGART

noun (<u>braag</u> uhrt)

a person who brags or boasts in a loud and empty manner

Usually the biggest *braggart* at the company party, Ayasha's boss was unusually quiet at this year's event.

BROACH

verb (brohch)

to mention or suggest for the first time

Dzhuan wanted to go to college away from home, but he didn't know how to *broach* the topic with his parents.

BUCOLIC

adj (byoo <u>kah</u> lihk)

pastoral, rural

My aunt likes the hustle and bustle of the city, but my uncle prefers a more *bucolic* setting.

BURNISH

verb (<u>buhr</u> nihsh)

to polish; to make smooth and bright

Mr. Frumpkin loved to stand in the sun and *burnish* his luxury car.

BURSAR

noun (<u>buhr</u> suhr) (<u>buhr</u> sahr)

a treasurer or keeper of funds

The *bursar* of the school was in charge of allocating all scholarship funds.

CACHE

noun (caash)

a hiding place; stockpile

It's good to have a *cache* where you can stash your cash.

CACOPHONY

noun (kuh <u>kah</u> fuh nee)

a jarring, unpleasant noise

As I walked into the open-air market after my nap, a *cacophony* of sounds surrounded me.

CALUMNY

noun (<u>kaa</u> luhm nee)

a false and malicious accusation; misrepresentation

The unscrupulous politician used *calumny* to bring down his opponent in the senatorial race.

CANTANKEROUS

adj (kaan <u>taang</u> kuhr uhs)

having a difficult, uncooperative, or stubborn disposition

The most outwardly *cantankerous* man in the nursing home was surprisingly sweet and loving with his grandchildren.

CAPTIOUS

adj (<u>kaap</u> shuhs)

marked by the tendency to point out trivial faults; intended to confuse in an argument

I resent the way he asked that *captious* question.

CATACLYSMIC

adj (kaat uh <u>klihz</u> mihk)

severely destructive

By all appearances, the storm seemed *cataclysmic*, though it lasted only a short while.

CATALYST

noun (<u>kaat</u> uhl ihst)

something that provokes or speeds up significant change, especially without being affected by the consequences

Technology has been a *catalyst* for the expansion of alternative education, such as home schooling and online courses.

CAUCUS

noun (<u>kaw</u> kuhs)

a closed committee within a political party; a private committee meeting

The president met with the delegated *caucus* to discuss the national crisis.

CAUSTIC

adj (<u>kah</u> stihk)

biting, sarcastic

Writer Dorothy Parker gained her reputation for *caustic* wit, and her tombstone is inscribed with a fittingly clever "Excuse my dust."

CEDE

verb (seed)

to surrender possession of something

Argentina *ceded* the Falkland Islands to Britain after a brief war.

CELERITY

noun (seh <u>leh</u> rih tee)

speed, haste

The celebrity ran past his fans with great *celerity*.

CENSORIOUS

adj (sehn <u>sohr</u> ee uhs)

critical; tending to blame and condemn

Closed-minded people tend to be *censorious* of others.

CERTITUDE

noun (<u>suhr</u> tih tood)

assurance, freedom from doubt

The witness's *certitude* about the night in question had a big impact on the jury.

CESSATION

noun (seh <u>say</u> shuhn)

a temporary or complete halt

The cessation of hostilities ensured that soldiers were able to spend the holidays with their families.

CHARY

adj (<u>chahr</u> ee)

watchful, cautious; extremely shy

Mindful of the fate of the Titanic, the captain was *chary* of navigating the iceberg-filled sea.

CHIMERICAL

adj (kie <u>mehr</u> ih kuhl) (kie <u>meer</u> ih kuhl)

fanciful; imaginary, impossible

The inventor's plans seemed *chimerical* to the conservative businessman from whom he was asking for financial support.

CIRCUITOUS

adj (suhr <u>kyoo</u> ih tuhs)

indirect, roundabout

The venue was only a short walk from the train station, but a roadblock meant I had to take a *circuitous* route.

CIRCUMVENT

verb (suhr kuhm <u>vehnt</u>)

to go around; avoid

Berta was able to *circumvent* the hospital's regulations, slipping into her mother's room long after visiting hours were over.

CLOYING

adj (<u>kloy</u> ing)

sickly sweet; excessive

When Dave and Liz were together, their *cloying* affection toward one another often made their friends ill.

COAGULATE

verb (koh <u>aag</u> yuh layt)

to clot; to cause to thicken

Hemophiliacs can bleed to death from a minor cut because their blood does not *coagulate*.

COGENT

adj (<u>koh</u> juhnt)

logically forceful; compelling, convincing

Swayed by the *cogent* argument of the defense, the jury had no choice but to acquit the defendant.

COLLOQUIAL

adj (kuh <u>loh</u> kwee uhl)

characteristic of informal speech

The book was written in a *colloquial* style so it would be more user-friendly.

COMMUTE

verb (kuh <u>myoot</u>)

to change a penalty to a less severe one

In exchange for cooperating with detectives on another case, the criminal had his charges *commuted*.

COMPLACENT

adj (kuhm <u>play</u> sihnt)

self-satisfied, smug

Vladimar always shows a *complacent* smile whenever he wins the spelling bee.

COMPLIANT

adj (kuhm <u>plie</u> uhnt)

submissive, yielding

The boss was unused to an assistant who spoke her mind, but he grew to respect the fact that she wasn't *compliant*.

CONCOMITANT

adj (kuh <u>kahm</u> ih tuhnt)

existing concurrently

A double-major was going to be difficult to pull off, especially since Lucy would have to juggle two papers and two exams *concomitantly*.

CONCORD

noun (<u>kahn</u> kohrd)

agreement

The sisters are now in *concord* about the car they had to share.

CONDOLE

verb (kuhn <u>dohl</u>)

to grieve; to express sympathy

My hamster died when I was in third grade, and my friends *condoled* with me and helped bury him in the yard.

CONFLAGRATION

noun (kahn fluh <u>gray</u> shuhn)

big, destructive fire

After the *conflagration* had finally died down, the city center was nothing but a mass of blackened embers.

CONFLUENCE

noun (<u>kahn</u> floo uhns)

the act of two things flowing together; the junction or meeting place where two things meet

At the political meeting, while planning a demonstration, there was a moving *confluence* of ideas between members.

CONSANGUINEOUS

adj (kahn saang <u>gwihn</u> ee uhs)

having the same lineage or ancestry; related by blood

After having a strange feeling about our relationship for years, I found out that my best friend and I are *consanguineous*.

CONSTERNATION

noun (kahn stuhr <u>nay</u> shuhn)

an intense state of fear or dismay

One would never think that a seasoned hunter would display such *consternation* when a grizzly bear lumbered too close to camp.

CONSTITUENT

noun (kuhn <u>stih</u> choo uhnt)

component, part; citizen, voter

A machine will not function properly if one of its *constituents* is defective.

CONSTRAINT

noun (kuhn <u>straynt</u>)

something that restricts or confines within prescribed bounds

Given the *constraints* of the budget, it was impossible to accomplish my goals.

CONTEMPTUOUS

adj (kuhn <u>tehmp</u> choo uhs)

scornful; expressing contempt

The diners were intimidated by the waiter's *contemptuous* manner.

CONTENTIOUS

adj (kuhn <u>tehn</u> shuhs)

quarrelsome, disagreeable, belligerent

The *contentious* gentleman ridiculed anything anyone said.

CONTIGUOUS

adj (kuhn <u>tihg</u> yoo uhs)

sharing a boundary; neighboring

The two houses had *contiguous* yards so the families shared the landscaping expenses.

CONTINENCE

noun (<u>kahn</u> tih nihns)

self-control, self-restraint

Elario exhibited impressive *continence* in steering clear of fattening foods.

CONVALESCE

verb (kahn vuhl <u>ehs</u>)

to recover gradually from an illness

After her bout with malaria, Tatiana needed to *convalesce* for a whole month.

CONVERGENCE

noun (kuhn <u>vehr</u> juhns)

the state of separate elements joining or coming together

A *convergence* of factors led to the tragic unfolding of World War I.

COQUETTE

noun (koh <u>keht</u>)

a flirtatious woman

The normally serious librarian could turn into a *coquette* just by letting her hair down.

COTERIE

noun (<u>koh</u> tuh ree)

an intimate group of persons with a similar purpose

Judith invited a *coterie* of fellow stamp enthusiasts to a stamp-trading party.

COUNTERVAIL

verb (kown tuhr <u>vayl</u>)

to act or react with equal force

In order to *countervail* the financial loss the school suffered after the embezzlement, the treasurer raised the price of room and board.

COVERT

adj (koh <u>vuhrt</u>)

secretive, not openly shown

The *covert* military operation wasn't disclosed until after it was determined to be a success.

CULL

verb (kuhl)

to select, weed out

You should *cull* the words you need to study from all the flash cards.

CUMULATIVE

adj (<u>kyoom</u> yuh luh tihv)

increasing, collective

The new employee didn't mind her job at first, but the daily, petty indignities had a *cumulative* demoralizing effect.

CURT

adj (kuhrt)

abrupt, short with words

The grouchy shop assistant was *curt* with one of her customers, which resulted in a reprimand from her manager.

DEARTH

noun (duhrth)

a lack, scarcity, insufficiency

The *dearth* of supplies in our city made it difficult to survive the blizzard.

DEBACLE

noun (dih <u>baa</u> kuhl)

a sudden, disastrous collapse or defeat; a total, ridiculous failure

It was hard for her to show her face in the office after the *debacle* of spilling coffee on her supervisor—three times.

DECLAIM

verb (dih <u>klaym</u>)

to speak loudly and vehemently

At Thanksgiving dinner, our grandfather always *declaims* his right, as the eldest, to sit at the head of the table.

DEFAMATORY

adj (dih <u>faam</u> uh tohr ee)

injurious to the reputation

The tabloid was sued for making *defamatory* statements about the celebrity.

DEMAGOGUE

noun (<u>deh</u> muh gahg) (<u>deh</u> muh gawg)

a leader, rabble-rouser, usually appealing to emotion or prejudice

The dictator began his political career as a *demagogue*, giving fiery speeches in town halls.

DENIZEN

noun (<u>dehn</u> ih zihn)

an inhabitant, a resident

The *denizens* of the state understandably wanted to select their own leaders.

DERIDE

verb (dih ried)

to laugh at contemptuously, to make fun of

As soon as Jorge heard the others *deriding* Anthony, he came to his defense.

DIFFUSE

verb (dih fyooz)

to spread out widely, to scatter freely, to disseminate

They turned on the fan, but all that did was *diffuse* the cigarette smoke throughout the room.

DIGRESS

verb (die grehs)

to turn aside, especially from the main point; to stray from the subject

The professor repeatedly *digressed* from the topic, boring his students.

DILAPIDATED

adj (dih laap ih dayt ihd)

in disrepair, run down

Rather than get discouraged, the architect saw great potential in the *dilapidated* house.

DILUVIAL

adj (dih loo vee uhl)

pertaining to a flood

After she left the water running in the house all day, it looked simply *diluvial*.

DISCOMFIT

verb (dihs kuhm fiht)

to disconcert, to make one lose one's composure

The class clown enjoyed *discomfiting* her classmates whenever possible.

DISCRETE

adj (dih skreet)

individually distinct, separate

What's nice about the CD is that each song functions as a *discrete* work and also as part of the whole compilation.

DISINGENUOUS

adj (dihs ihn jehn yoo uhs)

giving a false appearance of simple frankness; misleading

It was *disingenuous* of him to suggest that he had no idea of the requests made by his campaign contributors.

DISINTERESTED

adj (dihs <u>ihn</u> trih stihd) (dihs <u>ihn</u> tuh reh stihd)

fair-minded, unbiased

A fair trial is made possible by the selection of *disinterested* jurors.

DISPASSIONATE

adj (dihs <u>paash</u> ih niht)

unaffected by bias or strong emotions; not personally or emotionally involved in something

Ideally, photographers should be *dispassionate* observers of what goes on in the world.

DISSIDENT

adj (<u>dihs</u> ih duhnt)

disagreeing with an established religious or political system

The *dissident* had been living abroad and writing his criticism of the government from an undisclosed location.

DOCTRINAIRE

adj (dahk truh <u>nayr</u>)

rigidly devoted to theories without regard for practicality; dogmatic

The professor's manner of teaching was considered *doctrinaire* for such a liberal school.

DOGGED

adj (<u>daw</u> guhd)

stubbornly persevering

The police inspector's *dogged* determination helped him catch the thief.

DOLEFUL

adj (<u>dohl</u> fuhl)

sad, mournful

Looking into the *doleful* eyes of the lonely pony, the girl yearned to take him home.

DOUR

adj (<u>doo</u> uhr) (<u>dow</u> uhr)

sullen and gloomy; stern and severe

The *dour* hotel concierge demanded payment for the room in advance.

EFFLUVIA

noun (ih <u>floo</u> vee uh)

waste; odorous fumes given off by waste

He took out the garbage at 3 A.M. because the *effluvia* had begun wafting into the bedroom.

ELEGY

noun (<u>eh</u> luh jee)

a mournful poem, usually about the dead

A memorable *elegy* was read aloud for the spiritual leader.

ELUDE

verb (ee <u>lood</u>)

to avoid cleverly, to escape the perception of

Somehow, the runaway *eluded* detection for weeks.

EMOLLIENT

adj (ih <u>mohl</u> yuhnt)

soothing, especially to the skin

After being out in the sun for so long, the *emollient* cream was a welcome relief on my skin.

EMULATE

verb (<u>ehm</u> yuh layt)

to strive to equal or excel, to imitate

Children often *emulate* their parents.

ENCUMBER

verb (ehn <u>kuhm</u> buhr)

to weigh down, to burden

The distractions of the city *encumbered* her attempts at writing.

ENJOIN

verb (ehn <u>joyn</u>)

to direct or impose with urgent appeal, to order with emphasis; to forbid

Patel is *enjoined* by his culture from eating beef.

EPOCHAL

adj (<u>ehp</u> uh kuhl) (ehp <u>ahk</u> uhl)

momentous, highly significant

The Supreme Court's *epochal* decision will no doubt affect generations to come.

EPONYMOUS

adj (ih <u>pahn</u> uh muhs)

giving one's name to a place, book, restaurant

Macbeth was the *eponymous* protagonist of Shakespeare's play.

EQUIVOCATE

verb (ih kwihv uh kayt)

to avoid committing oneself in what one says, to be deliberately unclear

Not wanting to implicate himself in the crime, the suspect *equivocated* for hours.

ERSATZ

adj (uhr sahtz)

being an artificial and inferior substitute or imitation

The *ersatz* strawberry shortcake tasted more like plastic than like real cake.

ESCHEW

verb (ehs choo)

to shun; to avoid (as something wrong or distasteful)

The filmmaker *eschewed* artifical light for her actors, resulting in a stark movie style.

ESPOUSE

verb (ih spowz)

to take up and support as a cause; to marry

Because of his beliefs, he could not *espouse* the use of capital punishment.

ESPY

verb (ehs peye)

to catch sight of, glimpse

Amidst a crowd in black clothing, she *espied* the colorful dress that her friend was wearing.

EUPHEMISM

noun (yoo fuh mihz uhm)

an inoffensive and agreeable expression that is substituted for one that is considered offensive

The funeral director preferred to use the *euphemism* "passed away" instead of the word "dead."

EXCORIATE

verb (ehk skohr ee ayt)

to censure scathingly; to express strong disapproval of

The three-page letter to the editor *excoriated* the publication for printing the rumor without verifying the source.

EXPONENT

noun (ehk spoh nuhnt)

one who champions or advocates

The vice president was an enthusiastic *exponent* of computer technology.

EXPOUND

verb (ihk <u>spownd</u>)

to explain or describe in detail

The teacher *expounded* on the theory of relativity for hours.

EXPUNGE

verb (ihk <u>spuhnj</u>)

to erase, eliminate completely

The parents' association *expunged* the questionable texts from the children's reading list.

EXTIRPATE

verb (<u>ehk</u> stuhr payt)

to root out, eradicate, literally or figuratively; to destroy wholly

The criminals were *extirpated* after many years of investigation.

EXTRAPOLATION

noun (ihk <u>strap</u> uh lay shuhn)

using known data and information to determine what will happen in the future, prediction

Through the process of *extrapolation*, we were able to determine which mutual funds to invest in.

EXTRINSIC

adj (ihk <u>strihn</u> sihk) (ihk <u>strihn</u> zihk)

external, unessential; originating from the outside

"Though they are interesting to note," the meeting manager claimed, "those facts are *extrinsic* to the matter under discussion."

EXTRUDE

verb (ihk <u>strood</u>)

to form or shape something by pushing it out, to force out, especially through a small opening

We watched in awe as the volcano *extruded* molten lava.

FACETIOUS

adj (fuh <u>see</u> shuhs)

witty, humorous

Her *facetious* remarks made the uninteresting meeting more lively.

FACILE

adj (<u>faa</u> suhl)

easily accomplished; seeming to lack sincerity or depth; arrived at without due effort

Given the complexity of the problem, it seemed a rather *facile* solution.

FALLACIOUS

adj (fuh <u>lay</u> shuhs)

tending to deceive or mislead; based on a fallacy

The *fallacious* statement "the Earth is flat" misled people for many years.

FEBRILE

adj (<u>fehb</u> ruhl) (<u>fee</u> bruhl)

feverish, marked by intense emotion or activity

Awaiting the mysterious announcement, there was a *febrile* excitement in the crowd.

FECKLESS

adj (<u>fehk</u> lihs)

ineffective, worthless

Anja took on the responsibility of caring for her aged mother, realizing that her *feckless* sister was not up to the task.

FEIGN

verb (fayn)

to pretend, to give a false appearance of

Though she had discovered they were planning a party, she *feigned* surprise so as not to spoil the festivities.

FERAL

adj (<u>fehr</u> uhl)

suggestive of a wild beast, not domesticated

Though the animal-rights activists did not want to see the *feral* dogs harmed, they offered no solution to the problem.

FICTIVE

adj (<u>fihk</u> tihv)

fictional, relating to imaginative creation

She found she was more productive when writing *fictive* stories rather than autobiographical stories.

FILIBUSTER

verb (<u>fihl</u> ih buhs tuhr)

to use obstructionist tactics, especially prolonged speech making, in order to delay something

The congressman read names from the phonebook in an attempt to *filibuster* a pending bill.

FITFUL

adj (fiht fuhl)

intermittent, lacking steadiness; characterized by irregular bursts of activity

Her *fitful* breathing became cause for concern, and eventually, she phoned the doctor.

FLIPPANT

adj (flihp uhnt)

marked by disrespectful lightheartedness or casualness

Her *flippant* response was unacceptable and she was asked again to explain herself.

FLOUT

verb (flowt)

to scorn, to disregard with contempt

The protestors *flouted* the committee's decision and hoped to sway public opinion.

FODDER

noun (fohd uhr)

raw material, as for artistic creation, readily abundant ideas or images

The governor's hilarious blunder was good *fodder* for the comedian.

FOREGO

verb (fohr goh)

to precede, to go ahead of

Because of the risks of the expedition, the team leader made sure to *forego* the climbers.

FORGO

verb (fohr goh)

to do without, to abstain from

As much as I wanted to *forgo* statistics, I knew it would serve me well in my field of study.

FORMIDABLE

adj (fohr mih duh buhl) (fohr mih duh buhl)

fearsome, daunting; tending to inspire awe or wonder

The wrestler was not very big, but his skill and speed made him a *formidable* opponent.

FORTITUDE

noun (fohr tih tood)

strength of mind that allows one to encounter adversity with courage

Months in the trenches exacted great *fortitude* of the soldiers.

FORTUITOUS

adj (fohr <u>too</u> ih tuhs)

by chance, especially by favorable chance

After a *fortuitous* run-in with an agent, Roxy won a recording contract.

FRENETIC

adj (freh <u>neht</u> ihk)

frantic, frenzied

The employee's *frenetic* schedule left him little time to socialize.

FULSOME

adj (<u>fool</u> suhm)

abundant; flattering in an insincere way

The king's servant showered him with *fulsome* compliments in hopes of currying favor.

FURLOUGH

noun (<u>fuhr</u> loh)

a leave of absence, especially granted to soldier or a prisoner

After seeing months of combat, the soldier received a much-deserved *furlough*.

FURTIVE

adj (<u>fuhr</u> tihv)

sly, with hidden motives

The *furtive* glances they exchanged made me suspect they were up to something.

GALVANIZE

verb (<u>gaal</u> vuh niez)

to shock; to arouse awareness

The closing down of another homeless shelter *galvanized* the activist group into taking political action.

GAMELY

adj (<u>gaym</u> lee)

spiritedly, bravely

The park ranger *gamely* navigated the trail up the steepest face of the mountain.

GAUCHE

adv (gohsh)

lacking social refinement

Snapping one's fingers to get a waiter's attention is considered *gauche*.

GRANDILOQUENCE

noun (graan dihl uh kwuhns)

pompous talk; fancy but meaningless language

The headmistress was notorious for her *grandiloquence* at the lectern and her ostentatious clothes.

GREGARIOUS

adj (greh gaar ee uhs)

outgoing, sociable

Unlike her introverted friends, Susan was very *gregarious*.

GROTTO

noun (grah toh)

a small cave

Alone on the island, Philoctetes sought shelter in a *grotto*.

HARANGUE

verb (huh raang)

to give a long speech

Maria's parents *harangued* her when she told them she'd spent her money on magic beans.

HEDONIST

noun (hee duhn ihst)

one who pursues pleasure as a goal

Michelle, an admitted *hedonist*, lays on the couch eating cookies every Saturday.

HEGEMONY

noun (hih jeh muh nee)

the domination of one state or group over its allies

When Germany claimed *hegemony* over Russia, Stalin was outraged.

HERETICAL

adj (huh reh tih kuhl)

departing from accepted beliefs or standards, oppositional

Considering the conservative audience, her comments seemed *heretical*.

HIATUS

noun (hie ay tuhs)

a gap or interruption in space, time, or continuity

After a long *hiatus* in Greece, the philosophy professor returned to the university.

HISTRIONICS

noun (hihs tree <u>ahn</u> ihks)

deliberate display of emotion for effect; exaggerated behavior calculated for effect

With such *histrionics*, she should really consider becoming an actress.

HUBRIS

noun (<u>hyoo</u> brihs)

excessive pride or self-confidence

Nathan's *hubris* spurred him to do things that many considered insensitive.

HUSBAND

verb (<u>huhz</u> buhnd)

to manage economically; to use sparingly

The cyclist paced herself at the start of the race, knowing that if she *husbanded* her resources she'd have the strength to break out of the pack later on.

HYPOCRITE

noun (<u>hih</u> puh kriht)

one who puts on a false appearance of virtue; one who criticizes a flaw he in fact possesses

What a *hypocrite*: He criticizes those who wear fur, but then he buys a leather shearling coat.

IGNOBLE

adj (ihg <u>noh</u> buhl)

having low moral standards, not noble in character; mean

The photographer was paid a princely sum for the picture of the self-proclaimed ethicist in the *ignoble* act of pick-pocketing.

ILLUSORY

adj (ih <u>loo</u> suhr ee) (ih <u>loos</u> ree)

producing illusion, deceptive

The desert explorer was devastated to discover that the lake he thought he had seen was in fact *illusory*.

IMBIBE

verb (ihm <u>bieb</u>)

to receive into the mind and take in, absorb

If I always attend class, I can *imbibe* as much knowledge as possible.

IMPASSIVE

adj (ihm <u>pahs</u> sihv)

absent of any external sign of emotion, expressionless

Given his *impassive* expression, it was hard to tell whether he approved of my plan.

IMPERIOUS

adj (ihm <u>pihr</u> ee uhs)

commanding, domineering; urgent

Though the king had been a kind leader, his daughter was *imperious* and demanding during her rule.

IMPERTURBABLE

adj (<u>ihm</u> puhr <u>tuhr</u> buh buhl)

unshakably calm and steady

No matter how disruptive the children became, the babysitter remained *imperturbable*.

IMPLACABLE

adj (ihm <u>play</u> kuh buhl) (ihm <u>plaa</u> kuh buhl)

inflexible; not capable of being changed or pacified

The *implacable* teasing was hard for the child to take.

IMPORTUNATE

adj (ihm <u>pohr</u> chuh niht)

troublesomely urgent; extremely persistent in request or demand

Her *importunate* appeal for a job caused me to grant her an interview.

IMPRECATION

noun (ihm prih <u>kay</u> shuhn)

a curse

Spouting violent *imprecations*, Hank searched for the person who had vandalized his truck.

IMPUDENT

adj (<u>ihm</u> pyuh duhnt)

marked by cocky boldness or disregard for others

Considering the judge had been lenient in her sentence, it was *impudent* of the defendant to refer to her by her first name.

IMPUGN

verb (ihm <u>pyoon</u>)

to call into question; to attack verbally

"How dare you *impugn* my motives?" protested the lawyer, on being accused of ambulance chasing.

IMPUTE

verb (ihm <u>pyoot</u>)

to lay the responsibility or blame for, often unjustly

It seemed unfair to *impute* the accident on me, especially since they were the ones who ran the red light.

INCANDESCENT

adj (ihn kahn <u>dehs</u> uhnt)

shining brightly

The *incandescent* glow of the moon made it a night I'll never forget.

INCARNADINE

adj (ihn <u>kaar</u> nuh dien) (ihn <u>kaar</u> nuh dihn)

red, especially blood red

The *incarnadine* lipstick she wore made her look much older than she was.

INCHOATE

adj (ihn <u>koh</u> iht)

being only partly in existence; imperfectly formed

For every page of the crisp writing that made it into the final book, Akiko has 10 pages of *inchoate* rambling that made up the first draft.

INCIPIENT

adj (ihn <u>sihp</u> ee uhnt)

beginning to exist or appear; in an initial stage

The *incipient* idea seemed brilliant, but they knew it needed much more development.

INCORRIGIBLE

adj (ihn <u>kohr</u> ih juh buhl)

incapable of being corrected or amended; difficult to control or manage

"You're *incorrigible*," yelled the frustrated mother to her son, in the middle of his third tantrum of the day.

INCREDULOUS

adj (ihn <u>krehj</u> uh luhs)

unwilling to accept what is true, skeptical

The Lasky children were *incredulous* when their parents told them they were moving to Alaska.

INDOMITABLE

adj (ihn <u>dahm</u> ih tuuh buhl)

incapable of being conquered

Climbing Mount Everest would seem an *indomitable* task, but it has been done many times.

INGRATIATE

verb (ihn <u>gray</u> shee ayt)

to gain favor with another by deliberate effort, to seek to please somebody so as to gain an advantage

The new intern tried to *ingratiate* herself with the managers so that they might consider her for a future job.

INHERENT

adj (ihn <u>hehr</u> ehnt)

involving the essential character of something, built-in, inborn

The class was dazzled by the experiment and as a result more likely to remember the *inherent* scientific principle.

INQUEST

noun (<u>ihn</u> kwehst)

an investigation, an inquiry

The police chief ordered an *inquest* to determine what went wrong.

INSENSATE

adj (ihn <u>sehn</u> sayt) (ihn <u>sehn</u> siht)

lacking sensibility and understanding, foolish

The shock of the accident left him *insensate*, but after some time, the numbness subsided and he was able to tell the officer what had happened.

INSOLENT

adj (<u>ihn</u> suh luhnt)

insultingly arrogant, overbearing

After having spoken with three *insolent* customer service representatives, Shelly was relieved when the fourth one sympathized with her complaint.

INSULAR

adj (<u>ihn</u> suh luhr) (<u>ihn</u> syuh luhr)

characteristic of an isolated people, especially having a narrow viewpoint

It was a shock for Kendra to go from her small high school, with her *insular* group of friends, to a huge college with students from all over the country.

INSUPERABLE

adj (ihn <u>soo</u> puhr uh buhl)

incapable of being surmounted or overcome

Insuperable as our problems may seem, I'm confident we'll come out ahead.

INTER

verb (ihn <u>tuhr</u>)

to bury

After giving the masses one last chance to pay their respects, the leader's body was *interred*.

INTERLOCUTOR

noun (ihn tuhr <u>lahk</u> yuh tuhr)

ones who takes part in conversation

Though always the *interlocutor*, the professor actually preferred that his students guide the class discussion.

INTERNECINE

adj (ihn tuhr <u>nehs</u> een)

mutually destructive; equally devastating to both sides

Though it looked as though there was a victor, the *internecine* battle benefited no one.

INTERREGNUM

noun (ihn tuhr <u>rehg</u> nuhm)

a temporary halting of the usual operations of government or control

The new king began his reign by restoring order that the lawless *interregnum* had destroyed.

INTIMATION

noun (ihn tuh <u>may</u> shuhn)

a subtle and indirect hint

Abby chose to ignore Babu's *intimation* that she wasn't as good a swimmer as she claimed.

INTRACTABLE

adj (ihn <u>traak</u> tuh buhl)

not easily managed or manipulated

Intractable for hours, the wild horse eventually allowed the rider to mount.

INTRANSIGENT

adj (ihn <u>traan</u> suh juhnt) (ihn <u>traan</u> zuh juhnt)

uncompromising, refusing to abandon an extreme position

His *intransigent* positions on social issues cost him the election.

INTREPID

adj (ihn <u>trehp</u> ihd)

fearless, resolutely courageous

Despite freezing winds, the *intrepid* hiker completed his ascent.

INUNDATE

verb (<u>ihn</u> uhn dayt)

to cover with a flood; to overwhelm as if with a flood

Fans *inundated* the box office with requests for tickets to the award-winning play.

INVETERATE

adj (ihn <u>veht</u> uhr iht)

firmly established, especially with respect to a habit or attitude

An *inveterate* risk taker, Aarthi tried her luck at bungee-jumping.

IRASCIBLE

adj (ih <u>raas</u> uh buhl)

easily angered, hot-tempered

One of the most *irascible* warriors of all time, Attila the Hun ravaged much of Europe during his time.

IRONIC

adj (ie <u>rahn</u> ihk)

poignantly contrary or incongruous to what was expected

It was *ironic* to learn that shy Hieu from high school had grown up to be the host of a talk show.

IRREVERENT

adj (ih <u>rehv</u> uhr uhnt)

disrespectful in a gentle or humorous way

Kevin's *irreverent* attitude toward the principal annoyed the teacher but amused the other children.

ITINERANT

adj (ie <u>tihn</u> uhr uhnt)

wandering from place to place; unsettled

The *itinerant* tomcat came back to the Johansson homestead every two months.

JETTISON

verb (jeht ih zuhn) (jeht ih suhn)

to discard, to get rid of as unnecessary or encumbering

The sinking ship *jettisoned* its cargo in a desperate attempt to reduce its weight.

JOCULAR

adj (jahk yuh luhr)

playful, humorous

The *jocular* old man entertained his grandchildren for hours.

JUNTA

noun (hoon tuh) (juhn tuh)

a small governing body, especially after a revolutionary seizure of power

Only one member of the *junta* was satisfactory enough to be elected once the new government was established.

KISMET

noun (kihz meht) (kihz miht)

destiny, fate

When Eve found out that Garret also played the harmonica, she knew their meeting was *kismet*.

LAMPOON

verb (laam poon)

to ridicule with satire

The mayor hated being *lampooned* by the press for his efforts to improve people's politeness.

LARGESS

noun (laar jehs)

generous giving (as of money) to others who may seem inferior

She'd always relied on her parent's *largess*, but after graduation, she had to get a job.

LAUDABLE

adj (law duh buhl)

deserving of praise

Rosita's dedication is *laudable*, but she doesn't have the necessary skills to be a good paralegal.

LAX

adj (laaks)

not rigid, loose; negligent

Because our delivery boy is *lax*, the newspaper often arrives sopping wet.

LEVITY

noun (<u>leh</u> vih tee)

an inappropriate lack of seriousness, overly casual

The joke added needed *levity* to the otherwise serious meeting.

LEXICON

noun (<u>lehk</u> sih kahn)

a dictionary; a stock of terms pertaining to a particular subject or vocabulary

The author coined the term Gen-X, which has since entered the *lexicon*.

LIBERTARIAN

noun (lih buhr <u>tehr</u> ee uhn)

one who advocates individual rights and free will

The *libertarian* was always at odds with the conservatives.

LIBERTINE

noun (<u>lihb</u> uhr teen)

a free thinker, usually used disparagingly; one without moral restraint

The *libertine* took pleasure in gambling away his family's money.

LICENTIOUS

adj (lih <u>sehn</u> shuhs)

immoral; unrestrained by society

Conservative citizens were outraged by the *licentious* exploits of the free-spirited artists living in town.

LILLIPUTIAN

adj (lihl ee <u>pyoo</u> shun)

very small

Next to her very tall roommate, the girl seemed *lilliputian*.

LIMBER

adj (<u>lihm</u> buhr)

flexible, capable of being shaped

After years of doing yoga, the elderly man was remarkably *limber*.

LITHE

adj (lieth)

moving and bending with ease; marked by effortless grace

The dancer's *lithe* movements proved her to be a rising star in the ballet corps.

LOQUACIOUS

adj (loh <u>kway</u> shuhs)

talkative

She was naturally *loquacious*, which was always a challenge when she was in a library or movie theater.

MACABRE

adj (muh <u>kaa</u> bruh) (muh <u>kaa</u> buhr)

having death as a subject; dwelling on the gruesome

Martin enjoyed *macabre* tales about werewolves and vampires.

MACROCOSM

noun (<u>maak</u> roh cahz uhm)

the whole universe; a large-scale reflection of a part of the greater world

Some scientists focus on a particular aspect of space, while others study the entire *macrocosm* and how its parts relate to one another.

MALAISE

noun (maa <u>layz</u>)

a feeling of unease or depression

During his presidency, Jimmy Carter spoke of a "national *malaise*" and was subsequently criticized for being too negative.

MALAPROPISM

noun (<u>maal</u> uh prahp ihz uhm)

the accidental, often comical, use of a word which resembles the one intended, but has a different, often contradictory meaning

Everybody laughed at the *malapropism* when instead of saying "public broadcasting" the announcer said "public boredcasting."

MALEDICTION

noun (maal ih <u>dihk</u> shun)

a curse, a wish of evil upon another

The frog prince looked for a princess to kiss him and put an end to the witch's *malediction*.

MALEVOLENT

adj (muh <u>lehv</u> uh luhnt)

exhibiting ill will; wishing harm to others

The *malevolent* gossiper spread false rumors with frequency.

MALFEASANCE

noun (maal <u>fee</u> zuhns)

wrongdoing or misconduct, especially by a public official

Not only was the deputy's *malfeasance* humiliating, it also spelled the end of his career.

MALLEABLE

adj (<u>maal</u> ee uh buhl)

easily influenced or shaped, capable of being altered by outside forces

The welder heated the metal before shaping it because the heat made it *malleable*.

MANNERED

adj (<u>maan</u> uhrd)

artificial or stilted in character

The portrait is an example of the *mannered* style that was favored in that era.

MAVERICK

noun (<u>maav</u> rihk) (<u>maav</u> uh rihk)

an independent individual who does not go along with a group

The senator was a *maverick* who was willing to vote against his own party's position.

MAWKISH

adj (<u>maw</u> kihsh)

sickeningly sentimental

The poet hoped to charm his girlfriend with his flowery poem, but its *mawkish* tone sickened her instead.

MEGALOMANIA

noun (<u>mehg</u> uh loh <u>may</u> nee uh)

obsession with great or grandiose performance

Many of the Roman emperors suffered from severe *megalomania*.

MELLIFLUOUS

adj (muh <u>lihf</u> loo uhs)

having a smooth, rich flow

She was so talented that her *mellifluous* flute playing transported me to another world.

MICROCOSM

noun (<u>mie</u> kruh kahz uhm)

a small scale representation of a larger system

This department is in fact a *microcosm* of the entire corporation.

MILIEU

noun (mihl yoo)

the physical or social setting in which something occurs or develops, environment

The *milieu* at the club wasn't one I was comfortable with, so I left right away.

MISANTHROPE

noun (mihs ahn throhp)

a person who hates or distrusts mankind

Scrooge was such a *misanthrope* that even the sight of children singing made him angry.

MISNOMER

noun (mihs noh muhr)

an error in naming a person or place

Iceland is a *misnomer* since it isn't really icy; the name means "island."

MISSIVE

noun (mihs ihv)

a written note or letter

Priscilla spent hours composing a romantic *missive* for Elvis.

MITIGATE

verb (miht ih gayt)

to make less severe, make milder

A judge may *mitigate* a sentence if it's decided that the crime was committed out of necessity.

MODICUM

noun (mahd ih kuhm)

a small portion, limited quantity

I expect at least a *modicum* of assistance from you on the day of the party.

MOLLIFY

verb (mahl uh fie)

to soothe in temper or disposition

A small raise and increased break time *mollified* the unhappy staff, at least for the moment.

MORDANT

adj (mohr dnt)

biting and caustic in manner and style

Roald Dahl's stories are *mordant* alternatives to bland stories intended for kids.

MORES

noun (<u>mawr</u> ayz)

fixed customs or manners; moral attitudes

In keeping with the *mores* of ancient Roman society, Nero held a celebration every weekend.

MOROSE

adj (muh <u>rohs</u>) (maw <u>rohs</u>)

gloomy, sullen

After hearing that the internship had been given to someone else, Lenny was *morose* for days.

MOTE

noun (moht)

a small particle, speck

Monica's eye watered, irritated by a *mote* of dust.

MUTABILITY

noun (myoo tuh <u>bihl</u> uh tee)

the quality of being capable of change, in form or character; susceptibility of change

The actress lacked the *mutability* needed to perform in the improvisational play.

MYOPIC

adj (mie <u>ahp</u> ihk) (mie <u>oh</u> pihk)

lacking foresight, having a narrow view or long-range perspective

Not wanting to spend a lot of money up front, the *myopic* business owner would likely suffer the consequences later.

NEBULOUS

adj (<u>neh</u> byoo luhs)

vague, undefined

The candidate's *nebulous* plans to fight crime made many voters skeptical.

NEFARIOUS

adj (nih <u>fahr</u> ee uhs)

intensely wicked or vicous

Nefarious deeds are never far from an evil-doer's mind.

NEONATE

noun (<u>nee</u> uh nayt)

a newborn child

The *neonate* was born prematurely so she's still in the hospital.

NIHILISM

noun (<u>nie</u> hihl iz uhm)

the belief that traditional values and beliefs are unfounded and that existence is useless; the belief that conditions in the social organization are so bad as to make destruction desirable

Robert's *nihilism* expressed itself in his lack of concern with the norms of moral society.

NOMENCLATURE

noun (<u>noh</u> muhn klay chuhr)

a system of scientific names

In botany class, we learned the *nomenclature* used to identify different species of roses.

NON SEQUITUR

noun (nahn <u>sehk</u> wih tuhr)

a statement that does not follow logically from anything previously said

After the heated political debate, her comment about cake was a real *non sequitur*.

NOVEL

adj (<u>nah</u> vuhl)

new and not resembling anything formerly known

Piercing any part of the body other than the earlobes was *novel* in the 1950s, but now it is quite common.

OBDURATE

adj (<u>ahb</u> duhr uht)

stubbornly persistent, resistant to persuasion

The president was *obdurate* on the matter, and no amount of public protest could change his mind.

OBFUSCATE

verb (<u>ahb</u> fyoo skayt)

to confuse, make obscure

Catarina always *obfuscates* the discussion by bringing in irrelevant facts.

OBSTINATE

adj (<u>ahb</u> stih nuht)

unreasonably persistent

The *obstinate* journalist would not reveal his source, and thus, was jailed for 30 days.

OLFACTORY

adj (ohl <u>faak</u> tuh ree)

relating to the sense of smell

Whenever she entered a candle store, her *olfactory* sense was awakened.

OLIGARCHY

noun (<u>oh</u> lih gaar kee)

a government in which a small group exercises supreme control

In an *oligarchy*, the few who rule are generally wealthier and have more status than the others.

ONUS

noun (<u>oh</u> nuhs)

a burden, an obligation

Antonia was beginning to feel the *onus* of having to feed her friend's cat for the month.

OPINE

verb (oh <u>pien</u>)

to express an opinion

On the *Let's Chat Talk Show*, the audience member *opined* that the guest was in the wrong.

OPPORTUNIST

noun (aap ore <u>too</u> nist)

one who takes advantage of any opportunity to achieve an end, with little regard for principles

The *opportunist* wasted no time in stealing the idea and presenting it as his own.

OPPROBRIOUS

adj (uh <u>proh</u> bree uhs)

disgraceful, shameful

She wrote an *opprobrious* editorial in the newspaper about the critic who had torn her new play to shreds.

ORNERY

adj (<u>ohr</u> nuh ree)

having an irritable disposition, cantankerous

My first impression of the taxi driver was that he was *ornery*, but then he explained that he'd just had a bad day.

OSCILLATE

verb (<u>ah</u> sihl ayt)

to vary between opposing beliefs or feelings; to swing back and forth like a pendulum

The move meant a new house in a lovely neighborhood, but she missed her friends, so she *oscillated* between joy and sadness.

OSSIFY

verb (<u>ah</u> sih fie)

to change into bone; to become hardened or set in a rigidly conventional pattern

The forensics expert ascertained the body's age based on the degree to which the facial structure had *ossified*.

OSTRACIZE

verb (<u>ahs</u> truh size)

to exclude from a group by common consent

Despite the fact that Azilde had done nothing wrong, her friends *ostracized* her.

OUST

verb (owst)

to remove from position by force; eject

After President Nixon so offensively lied to the country during Watergate, he was *ousted* from office.

PAEAN

noun (<u>pee</u> uhn)

a tribute, a song or expression of praise

He considered his newest painting a *paean* to his late wife.

PALATIAL

adj (puh <u>lay</u> shuhl)

relating to a palace; magnificent

After living in a cramped studio apartment for years, Alicia thought the modest one bedroom looked downright *palatial*.

PALIMPSEST

noun (<u>pahl</u> ihmp sehst)

an object or place having diverse layers or aspects beneath the surface

Years ago, paper was very expensive, so the practice was to write over previous words, creating a *palimpsest* of writing.

PALPABLE

adj (<u>pahlp</u> uh buhl)

capable of being touched or felt; easily perceived

The tension was *palpable* as I walked into the room.

PALTRY

adj (<u>pawl</u> tree)

pitifully small or worthless

Bernardo paid the ragged boy the *paltry* sum of 25 cents to carry his luggage all the way to the hotel.

PANACHE

noun (puh <u>nahsh</u>)

flamboyance or dash in style and action

Miguel has such *panache* when planning parties, even when they're last-minute affairs.

PANDEMIC

adj (paan <u>deh</u> mihk)

occurring over a wide geographic area and affecting a large portion of the population

Pandemic alarm spread throughout Colombia after the devastating earthquake.

PANEGYRIC

noun (paan uh <u>geer</u> ihk)

elaborate praise; formal hymn of praise

The director's *panegyric* for the donor who kept his charity going was heart-warming.

PARADIGM

noun (<u>paar</u> uh diem)

an outstandingly clear or typical example

The new restaurant owner used the fast-food giant as a *paradigm* for expansion into new locales.

PARAGON

noun (<u>paar</u> uh gon)

a model of excellence or perfection

She's the *paragon* of what a judge should be: honest, intelligent, and just.

PARAMOUNT

adj (<u>paar</u> uh mownt)

supreme, of chief importance

It's of *paramount* importance that we make it back to camp before the storm hits.

PARE

verb (payr)

to trim off excess, reduce

The cook's hands were sore after she *pared* hundreds of potatoes for the banquet.

PARIAH

noun (puh <u>rie</u> ah)

an outcast

Once he betrayed those in his community, he was banished and lived the life of a *pariah*.

PATENT

adj (<u>paa</u> tehnt)

obvious, evident

Moe could no longer stand Frank's *patent* fawning over the boss and so confronted him.

PATHOGENIC

adj (paa thoh <u>jehn</u> ihk)

causing disease

Bina's research on the origins of *pathogenic* microorganisms should help stop the spread of disease.

PATRICIAN

adj (puh <u>trih</u> shuhn)

aristocratic

Though he really couldn't afford an expensive lifestyle, Claudius had *patrician* tastes.

PATRONIZE

verb (<u>pay</u> troh niez)

to act as patron of, to adopt an air of condescension toward; to buy from

LuAnn *patronized* the students, treating them like simpletons, which they deeply resented.

PECULATE

verb (<u>pehk</u> yuh layt)

to embezzle

These days in the news, we read more and more about workers *peculating* the system.

PECUNIARY

adj (pih <u>kyoon</u> nee <u>ehr</u> ee)

relating to money

Phuong's official title was office manager, but she ended up taking on a lot of *pecuniary* responsibilities such as payroll duties.

PELLUCID

adj (peh <u>loo</u> sihd)

transparently clear in style or meaning, easy to understand

Though she thought she could hide her ulterior motives, they were *pellucid* to everyone else.

PENCHANT

noun (<u>pehn</u> chehnt)

an inclination, a definite liking

After Sadiki visited the Grand Canyon, he developed a *penchant* for travel.

PENITENT

adj (<u>peh</u> nih tehnt)

expressing sorrow for sins or offenses, repentant

Claiming the criminal did not feel *penitent*, the victim's family felt his pardon should be denied.

PENURY

noun (<u>pehn</u> yuh ree)

an oppressive lack of resources (as money), severe poverty

Once a famous actor, he eventually died in *penury* and anonymity.

PEREGRINATE

verb (<u>pehr</u> ih gruh nayt)

to travel on foot

It has always been a dream of mine to *peregrinate* from one side of Europe to the other with nothing but a backpack.

PHALANX

noun (<u>fay</u> laanks)

a compact or close-knit body of people, animals, or things

A *phalanx* of guards stood outside the prime minister's home day and night.

PHILISTINE

noun (<u>fihl</u> uh steen)

a person who is guided by materialism and is disdainful of intellectual or artistic values

The *philistine* never even glanced at the rare violin in his collection but instead kept an eye on its value and sold it at a profit.

PHILOLOGY

noun (fih <u>lahl</u> uh jee)

the study of ancient texts and languages

Philology was the predecessor to modern-day linguistics.

PHLEGMATIC

adj (flehg <u>maa</u> tihk)

having a sluggish, unemotional temperament

His writing was energetic but his *phlegmatic* personality wasn't suited for television, so he turned down the interview.

PIQUE

verb (peek)

to arouse anger or resentment in; provoke

His continual insensitivity *piqued* my anger.

PLAINTIVE

adj (<u>playn</u> tihv)

expressive of suffering or woe, melancholy

The *plaintive* cries from the girl trapped in the tree were heard by all.

PLATITUDE

noun (<u>plaa</u> tuh tood)

overused and trite remark

Instead of the usual *platitudes*, the comedian gave a memorable and inspiring speech to the graduating class.

PLEBEIAN

adj (plee <u>bee</u> uhn)

crude or coarse; characteristic of commoners

After five weeks of rigorous studying, the graduate settled in for a weekend of *plebeian* socializing and television watching.

PLUCKY

adj (<u>pluh</u> kee)

courageous; spunky

The *plucky* young nurse dove into the foxhole, determined to help the wounded soldier.

POLITIC

adj (<u>pah</u> luh tihk)

shrewd and crafty in managing or dealing with things

She was wise to curb her tongue and was able to explain her problem to the judge in a respectful and *politic* manner.

POLYGLOT

noun (<u>pah</u> lee glaht)

a speaker of many languages

Ling's extensive travels have helped her to become a true *polyglot*.

PORE

verb (pohr)

to read studiously or attentively

I've *pored* over this text, yet I still can't understand it.

PORTENTOUS

adj (pohr <u>tehn</u> tuhs)

foreshadowing, ominous; eliciting amazement and wonder

Everyone thought the rays of light were *portentous* until they realized a nine-year-old was playing a joke on them.

POSIT

verb (<u>pohz</u> iht)

to assume as real or conceded; propose as an explanation

Before proving the math formula, we needed to *posit* that x and y were real numbers.

POTABLE

adj (<u>poh</u> tuh buhl)

suitable for drinking

Though the water was *potable*, it tasted terrible.

POTENTATE

noun (<u>poh</u> tehn tayt)

a ruler; one who wields great power

Alex was much kinder before he assumed the role of *potentate*.

PRECARIOUS

adj (prih <u>caa</u> ree uhs)

lacking in security or stability; dependent on chance or uncertain conditions

Given the *precarious* circumstances, I chose to opt out of the deal completely.

PRECIPITOUS

adj (pree <u>sih</u> puh tuhs)

steep

The *precipitous* cave was daunting for the first-time climber.

PRESAGE

noun (<u>preh</u> sihj)

something that foreshadows; a feeling of what will happen in the future

The demolition of the Berlin Wall was a *presage* to the fall of the Soviet Union.

PRESTIDIGITATION

noun (<u>prehs</u> tih <u>dihj</u> ih <u>tay</u> shuhn)

a cleverly executed trick or deception; sleight of hand

My hunch was that he won the contest not so much as a result of real talent, but rather through *prestidigitation*.

PRETERNATURAL

adj (pree tuhr <u>naach</u> uhr uhl)

existing outside of nature; extraordinary; supernatural

We were all amazed at her *preternatural* ability to recall smells from her early childhood.

PRIMEVAL

adj (priem <u>ee</u> vuhl)

ancient, primitive

The archaeologist claimed that the skeleton was of *primeval* origin, though in fact it was the remains of a modern-day monkey.

PRODIGAL

adj (<u>prah</u> dih guhl)

recklessly extravagant, wasteful

The *prodigal* expenditures on the military budget during a time of peace created a stir in the cabinet.

PROFFER

verb (<u>prahf</u> uhr)

to offer for acceptance

The deal *proffered* by the committee satisfied all those at the meeting, ending a month-long discussion.

PROGENITOR

noun (proh <u>jehn</u> uh tuhr)

an ancestor in the direct line, forefather; founder

Though he had been born here, his *progenitors* were from India.

PROLIFERATE

verb (proh lih fuhr ayt)

to grow by rapid production of new parts; increase in number

The bacteria *proliferated* so quickly that even the doctor was surprised.

PROMULGATE

verb (prah muhl gayt)

to make known by open declaration, proclaim

The publicist *promulgated* the idea that the celebrity had indeed gotten married.

PROPENSITY

noun (proh pehn suh tee)

a natural inclination or preference

She has a *propensity* for lashing out at others when stressed, so we leave her alone when she's had a rough day.

PROSAIC

adj (proh say ihk)

relating to prose (as opposed to poetry); dull, ordinary

Simon's *prosaic* style bored his writing teacher to tears, though he thought he had an artistic flair.

PROSCRIBE

verb (proh skribe)

to condemn or forbid as harmful or unlawful

Consumption of alcohol was *proscribed* in the country's constitution, but the ban was eventually lifted.

PROSTRATE

adj (prah strayt)

lying face downward in adoration or submission

My friends teased me for lying *prostrate* when I met my favorite musician.

PROVINCIAL

adj (pruh vihn shuhl)

limited in outlook, narrow, unsophisticated

Having grown up in the city, Anita sneered at the *provincial* attitudes of her country cousins.

PROXY

noun (prahk see)

a person authorized to act for someone else

In the event the shareholder can't attend the meeting, he'll send a *proxy*.

PSEUDONYM

noun (<u>soo</u> duh nihm)

a fictitious name, used particularly by writers to conceal identity

Though George Eliot sounds as though it's a male name, it was the *pseudonym* that Marian Evans used when she published her classic novel *Middlemarch*.

PUGILISM

noun (<u>pyoo</u> juhl ih suhm)

boxing

Pugilism has been defended as a positive outlet for aggressive impulses.

PUISSANT

adj (<u>pwih</u> sihnt) (<u>pyoo</u> sihnt)

powerful

His memoir was full of descriptions of *puissant* military heroics, but most were exaggerations or outright lies.

PUNCTILIOUS

adj (puhngk <u>tihl</u> ee uhs)

concerned with precise details about codes or conventions

The *punctilious* student never made spelling errors on her essays.

PUNDIT

noun (<u>puhn</u> diht)

one who gives opinions in an authoritative manner

The *pundits* on television are often more entertaining than the sitcoms.

PURLOIN

verb (puhr <u>loyn</u>)

to steal

His goal was to *purloin* the documents he felt belonged to him.

PURPORT

verb (puhr <u>pohrt</u>)

to profess, suppose, claim

Demarcus *purported* to be an opera lover, but he fell asleep at every performance he attended.

RANCOR

noun (<u>raan</u> kuhr)

bitter hatred

Having been teased mercilessly for years, Umberto became filled with *rancor* toward those who had humiliated him.

RANKLE

verb (<u>raang</u> kuhl)

to cause anger and irritation

At first the kid's singing was adorable, but after 40 minutes it began to *rankle*.

RAPACIOUS

adj (ruh <u>pay</u> shuhs)

taking by force; driven by greed

Sea otters are so *rapacious* that they consume 10 times their body weight in food every day.

RAPT

adj (raapt)

deeply absorbed

The story was so well performed that the usually rowdy children were *rapt* until the final word.

RAREFY

verb (<u>rayr</u> uh fie)

to make rare, thin, or less dense

The atmosphere *rarefies* as altitude increases, so the air atop a mountain is too thin to breathe.

RAZE

verb (rayz)

to tear down, demolish

The house had been *razed*; where it once stood, there was nothing but splinters and bricks.

REACTIONARY

adj (ree <u>aak</u> shuhn ayr ee)

marked by extreme conservatism, especially in politics

Her *reactionary* beliefs were misunderstood by her friends.

RECAPITULATE

verb (ree kuh <u>pihch</u> yoo layt)

to review by a brief summary

After the long-winded president had finished his speech, his assistant *recapitulated* for the press the points he had made.

RECIDIVISM

noun (rih <u>sihd</u> uh vih zihm)

a tendency to relapse into a previous behavior, especially criminal behavior

According to statistics, the *recidivism* rate for criminals is quite high.

REFRACT

verb (rih <u>fraakt</u>)

to deflect sound or light

The crystal *refracted* the rays of sunlight so they formed a beautiful pattern on the wall.

REFUTE

verb (rih <u>fyoot</u>)

to contradict, discredit

She made such a persuasive argument that nobody could *refute* it.

RELEGATE

verb (<u>reh</u> luh gayt)

to send into exile, banish; assign

Because he hadn't scored any goals during the season, Abe was *relegated* to the bench for the championship game.

REMISSION

noun (rih <u>mih</u> shuhn)

a lessening of intensity or degree

The doctor told me that the disease had gone into *remission*.

REMUNERATION

noun (rih <u>myoo</u> nuh <u>ray</u> shuhn)

payment for goods or services or to recompense for losses

You can't expect people to do this kind of boring work without some form of *remuneration*.

REPLETE

adj (rih <u>pleet</u>)

abundantly supplied, complete

The gigantic supermarket was *replete* with consumer products of every kind.

REPOSE

noun (rih <u>pohz</u>)

relaxation, leisure

After working hard every day in the busy city, Idros finds his *repose* on weekends playing golf with friends.

REPREHENSIBLE

adj (rehp ree <u>hehn</u> suh buhl)

blameworthy, disreputable

Lowell was thrown out of the restaurant because of his *reprehensible* behavior toward the other patrons.

REPROVE

verb (rih <u>proov</u>)

to criticize or correct, usually in a gentle manner

Mrs. Hernandez *reproved* her daughter for staying out late and not calling.

REQUITE

verb (rih <u>kwiet</u>)

to return or repay

Thanks for offering to lend me $1,000, but I know I'll never be able to *requite* your generosity.

RESCIND

verb (rih <u>sihnd</u>)

to repeal, cancel

After the celebrity was involved in a scandal, the car company *rescinded* its offer of an endorsement contract.

RESILIENT

adj (rih <u>sihl</u> yuhnt)

able to recover quickly after illness or bad luck; able to bounce back to shape

Psychologists say that being *resilient* in life is one of the keys to success and happiness.

RESOLUTE

adj (reh suh <u>loot</u>)

marked by firm determination

Jelena was *resolute*: She would get into medical school no matter what.

RESPLENDENT

adj (rih <u>splehn</u> dihnt)

splendid, brilliant

The bride looked *resplendent* in her gown and sparkling tiara.

REVILE

verb (rih <u>veye</u> uhl)

to criticize with harsh language, verbally abuse

The artist's new installation was *reviled* by critics who weren't used to the departure from his usual work.

RHETORIC

noun (<u>reh</u> tuhr ihk)

the art of speaking or writing effectively; skill in the effective use of speech

Lincoln's talent for *rhetoric* was evident in his beautifully expressed Gettysburg Address.

RIFE

adj (rief)

abundant prevalent especially to an increasing degree; filled with

The essay was so *rife* with grammatical errors that it had to be rewritten.

ROSTRUM

noun (<u>rahs</u> truhm)

an elevated platform for public speaking

Though she was terrified, the new member of the debate club approached the *rostrum* with poise.

SACCHARINE

adj (<u>saa</u> kuh ruhn)

excessively sweet or sentimental

Geoffrey's *saccharine* poems nauseated Lin, and she wished he'd stop sending them.

SACRILEGIOUS

adj (saak rih <u>lihj</u> uhs)

impious, irreverent toward what is held to be sacred or holy

It's considered *sacrilegious* for one to enter a mosque wearing shoes.

SALIENT

adj (<u>say</u> lee uhnt)

prominent, of notable significance

His most *salient* characteristic is his tendency to dominate every conversation.

SANCTIMONIOUS

adj (saangk tih <u>moh</u> nee uhs)

hypocritically devout; acting morally superior to another

The *sanctimonious* columnist turned out to have been hiding a gambling problem that cost his family everything.

SATIATE

verb (<u>say</u> shee ayt)

to satisfy (as a need or desire) fully or to excess

After years of journeying around the world with nothing but backpacks, the friends had finally *satiated* their desire to travel.

SATURNINE

adj (saat uhr nien)

cold and steady in mood, gloomy; slow to act

Her *saturnine* expression made her depressing to be around.

SAVANT

noun (suh vahnt)

a person of learning; especially one with knowledge in a special field

The *savant* so impressed us with his knowledge that we asked him to come speak at our school.

SCRUPULOUS

adj (skroop yuh luhs)

acting in strict regard for what is considered proper; punctiliously exact

After the storm had destroyed their antique lamp, the Millers worked to repair it with *scrupulous* care.

SEAMY

adj (see mee)

morally degraded, unpleasant

The tour guide avoided the *seamy* parts of town.

SECULAR

adj (seh kyoo luhr)

not specifically pertaining to religion, relating to the world

Although his favorite books were religious, Ben also read *secular* works such as mysteries.

SEDITION

noun (seh dih shuhn)

behavior that promotes rebellion or civil disorder against the state

Li was arrested for *sedition* after he gave a fiery speech in the main square.

SEMINAL

adj (seh muhn uhl)

influential in an original way, providing a basis for further development; creative

The scientist's discovery proved to be *seminal* in the area of quantum physics.

SEQUESTER

verb (suh kweh stuhr)

to set apart, seclude

When juries are *sequestered*, it can take days, even weeks, to come up with a verdict.

SERAPHIC

adj (seh <u>rah</u> fihk)

angelic, sweet

Selena's *seraphic* appearance belied her nasty, bitter personality.

SIMIAN

adj (<u>sih</u> mee uhn)

apelike; relating to apes

Early man was more *simian* in appearance than is modern man.

SINECURE

noun (<u>sien</u> ih kyoor)

a well-paying job or office that requires little or no work

The corrupt mayor made sure to set up all his relatives in *sinecures* within the administration.

SOBRIQUET

noun (<u>soh</u> brih <u>kay</u>) (<u>soh</u> brih <u>keht</u>)

a nickname

One of former president Ronald Reagan's *sobriquets* was "The Gipper."

SOJOURN

noun (<u>soh</u> juhrn)

a temporary stay, visit

After graduating from college, Iliani embarked on a *sojourn* to China.

SOLICITOUS

adj (suh <u>lih</u> sih tuhs)

anxious, concerned; full of desire, eager

Overjoyed to see the pop idol in her presence, the *solicitous* store owner stood ready to serve.

SOPHOMORIC

adj (sahf <u>mohr</u> ihk)

exhibiting great immaturity and lack of judgment

After Sean's *sophomoric* behavior, he was grounded for weeks.

SPARTAN

adj (<u>spahr</u> tihn)

highly self-disciplined; frugal, austere

When he was in training, the athlete preferred to live in a *spartan* room so he could shut out all distractions.

SPECIOUS

adj (<u>spee</u> shuhs)

having the ring of truth but actually being untrue; deceptively attractive

After I followed up with some research on the matter, I realized that the charismatic politician's argument had been *specious*.

SPORTIVE

adj (<u>spohr</u> tihv)

frolicsome, playful

The lakeside vacation meant more *sportive* opportunities for the kids than the culinary tour through France.

SQUALID

adj (<u>skwa</u> lihd)

filthy and degraded as the result of neglect or poverty

The *squalid* living conditions in the building outraged the new tenants.

STALWART

adj (<u>stahl</u> wuhrt)

marked by outstanding strength and vigor of body, mind, or spirit

The 85-year old went to the market every day, impressing her neighbors with her *stalwart* routine.

STASIS

noun (<u>stay</u> sihs)

a state of static balance or equilibrium; stagnation

The rusty, ivy-covered World War II tank had obviously been in *stasis* for years.

STINT

verb (stihnt)

to be sparing or frugal; to restrict with respect to a share or allowance

Don't *stint* on the mayonnaise, because I don't like my sandwich too dry.

STIPULATE

verb (<u>stihp</u> yuh layt)

to specify as a condition or requirement of an agreement or offer

The contract *stipulated* that if the movie was never filmed, the actress got paid anyway.

STRATIFY

verb (<u>straa</u> tuh fie)

to arrange or divide into layers

Schliemann *stratified* the numerous layers of Troy, an archeological dig that remains legendary.

STRIDENT

adj (<u>strie</u> dehnt)

loud, harsh, unpleasantly noisy

The traveler's *strident* manner annoyed the flight attendant, but she managed to keep her cool.

STRINGENT

adj (<u>strihn</u> juhnt)

imposing severe, rigorous standards

Many employees found it difficult to live up to the *stringent* standards imposed by the company.

STYMIE

verb (<u>stie</u> mee)

to block or thwart

The police effort to capture the bank robber was *stymied* when he escaped through a rear window.

SUBTERRANEAN

adj (<u>suhb</u> tuh <u>ray</u> nee uhn)

hidden, secret; underground

Subterranean tracks were created for the trains after it was decided they had run out of room above ground.

SULLY

verb (<u>suh</u> lee)

to tarnish, taint

His outrageous gaffe *sullied* his public image.

SUPERFLUOUS

adj (soo <u>puhr</u> floo uhs)

extra, more than necessary

The extra recommendations Pavel included in his application were *superfluous*, as only one was required.

SUPERSEDE

verb (soo puhr <u>seed</u>)

to cause to be set aside; to force out of use as inferior, replace

Her computer was still running version 2.0 of the software, which had been *superseded* by at least three more versions.

SUPPLANT

verb (suh <u>plaant</u>)

to replace (another) by force, to take the place of

The overthrow of the government meant a new leader would *supplant* the former one.

SURMOUNT

verb (suhr <u>mownt</u>)

to conquer, overcome

The blind woman *surmounted* great obstacles to become a well-known trial lawyer.

SYBARITE

noun (<u>sih</u> buh riet)

a person devoted to pleasure and luxury

A confirmed *sybarite*, the nobleman fainted at the thought of having to leave his palace and live in a small cottage.

TACTILE

adj (<u>taak</u> tihl)

producing a sensation of touch

The Museum of Natural History displays objects for people to touch so that they have a *tactile* understanding of how different peoples and animals lived.

TANTAMOUNT

adj (<u>taan</u> tuh mownt)

equal in value or effect

If she didn't get concert tickets to see her favorite band, it would be *tantamount* to a tragedy.

TAUTOLOGICAL

adj (tawt uh <u>lah</u> jih kuhl)

having to do with needless repetition, redundancy

I know he was only trying to clarify things, but his *tautological* statements confused me even more.

TAWDRY

adj (<u>taw</u> dree)

gaudy, cheap, showy

The performer changed into her *tawdry* costume and stepped onto the stage.

TEMERITY

noun (teh <u>mehr</u> ih tee)

unreasonable or foolhardy disregard for danger, recklessness

I offered her a ride since it was late at night, but she had the *temerity* to say she'd rather walk.

TEMPESTUOUS

adj (tehm <u>pehs</u> choo uhs)

stormy, turbulent

Our camping trip was cut short when the mild shower we were expecting turned into a *tempestuous* downpour.

TEMPORAL

adj (<u>tehmp</u> ore uhl)

having to do with time

The story lacked a *temporal* sense, so we couldn't figure out if the events took place in one evening or over the course of a year.

TENACIOUS

adj (teh <u>nay</u> shuhs)

tending to persist or cling; persistent in adhering to something valued or habitual

Securing women's right to vote required a *tenacious* fight.

TENET

noun (<u>teh</u> niht)

a principle, belief, or doctrine accepted by members of a group

One of the *tenets* of the school is that it is not acceptable to cheat.

TENUOUS

adj (<u>tehn</u> yoo uhs)

having little substance or strength; flimsy, weak

Francine's already *tenuous* connection to her cousins was broken when they moved away and left no forwarding address.

TERSE

adj (tuhrs)

concise, brief, free of extra words

Her *terse* style of writing was widely praised by the editors, who had been used to seeing long-winded material.

THWART

verb (thwahrt)

to block or prevent from happening; frustrate, defeat the hopes or aspirations of

The heavy lock *thwarted* his attempt to enter the building.

TITULAR

adj (<u>tihch</u> yoo luhr)

existing in title only; having a title without the functions or responsibilities

Carla was thrilled to be voted Homecoming Queen until somebody explained that the *titular* honor didn't mean she could boss anybody around.

TOADY

noun (<u>toh</u> dee)

one who flatters in the hope of gaining favors

The king was surrounded by *toadies* who rushed to agree with whatever outrageous thing he said.

TORTUOUS

adj (<u>tohr</u> choo uhs)

having many twists and turns; highly complex

To reach the remote inn, the travelers had to negotiate a *tortuous* path.

TOUT

verb (towt)

to praise or publicize loudly or extravagantly

She *touted* her skills as superior to ours, though in fact, we were all at the same level.

TRAJECTORY

noun (truh <u>jehk</u> tuh ree)

the path followed by a moving object, whether through space or otherwise; flight

The *trajectory* of the pitched ball was interrupted by an unexpected bird.

TRANSIENT

adj (<u>traan</u> see uhnt)

passing with time, temporary, short-lived

The reporter lived a *transient* life, staying in one place only long enough to cover the current story.

TRANSITORY

adj (<u>traan</u> sih tohr ee)

short-lived, existing only briefly

The actress' popularity proved *transitory* when her play folded within the month.

TREMULOUS

adj (<u>treh</u> myoo luhs)

trembling, timid; easily shaken

The *tremulous* kitten had been separated from her mother.

TROUNCE

verb (trowns)

to beat severely, defeat

The inexperienced young boxer was *trounced* in a matter of minutes.

TRUCULENT

adj (truhk yuh lehnt)

disposed to fight, belligerent

The bully was initially *truculent,* but eventually stopped picking fights at the least provocation.

TURGID

adj (tuhr jihd)

swollen as from a fluid, bloated

In the process of osmosis, water passes through the walls of *turgid* cells, ensuring that they never contain too much water.

TUTELAGE

noun (toot uh lihj)

guardianship, guidance

Under the *tutelage* of her older sister, the young orphan was able to persevere.

UNCANNY

adj (uhn kaa nee)

so keen and perceptive as to seem supernatural, peculiarly unsettling

Though they weren't related, their resemblance was *uncanny.*

UNCONSCIONABLE

adj (uhn kahn shuhn uh buhl)

unscrupulous; shockingly unfair or unjust

After she promised me the project, the fact that she gave it to someone else is *unconscionable.*

UNTOWARD

adj (uhn tō rd)

difficult to handle or work with

Charli's negative comments at work were a bit untoward.

USURY

noun (<u>yoo</u> zuh ree)

the practice of lending money at exorbitant rates

The moneylender was convicted of *usury* when it was discovered that he charged 50 percent interest on all his loans.

VARIEGATED

adj (<u>vaar</u> ee uh gayt ehd)

varied; marked with different colors

The *variegated* foliage of the jungle allows it to support thousands of animal species.

VEHEMENTLY

adv (<u>vee</u> ih mehnt lee)

marked by extreme intensity of emotions or convictions

She *vehemently* opposed the closing of the neighborhood garden, and was even arrested for protesting when the bulldozers came.

VERACITY

noun (vuhr <u>aa</u> sih tee)

accuracy, truth

She had a reputation for *veracity*, so everyone believed her version of the story.

VERBOSE

adj (vuhr <u>bohs</u>)

wordy

The DNA analyst's answer was so *verbose* that the jury had trouble grasping his point.

VERITABLE

adj (<u>vehr</u> iht uh buhl)

being without question, often used figuratively

My neighbor was a *veritable* goldmine of information when I was writing my term paper on the Civil Rights era because she had been a student organizer and protester.

VERNACULAR

noun (vuhr <u>naa</u> kyoo luhr)

everyday language used by ordinary people; specialized language of a profession

Preeti could not understand the *vernacular* of the South, where she had recently moved.

VERNAL

adj (<u>vuhr</u> nuhl)

related to spring; fresh

Anton basked in the balmy *vernal* breezes, happy that winter was coming to an end.

VICARIOUSLY

adv (vie <u>kaar</u> ee uhs lee)

felt or undergone as if one were taking part in the experience or feelings of another

She lived *vicariously* through the characters in the adventure books she was always reading.

VILIFY

verb (<u>vih</u> lih fie)

to slander, defame

Because gossip columnists often *vilify* celebrities, they're usually held in low regard.

VIM

noun (vihm)

vitality and energy

The *vim* with which she worked so early in the day explained why she was so productive.

VINDICATE

verb (<u>vihn</u> dih kayt)

to clear of blame; support a claim

Tess was *vindicated* when her prediction about the impending tornado came true.

VIRULENT

adj (<u>veer</u> yuh luhnt)

extremely poisonous; malignant; hateful

Alarmed at the *virulent* press he was receiving, the militant activist decided to go underground.

VISCERAL

adj (<u>vihs</u> uhr uhl)

instinctive, not intellectual; deep, emotional

When my twin was wounded many miles away, I had a *visceral* reaction.

VITUPERATE

verb (vih <u>too</u> puhr ayt)

to abuse verbally, berate

Vituperating someone is never a constructive way to effect change.

VOCIFEROUS

adj (voh <u>sih</u> fuhr uhs)

loud, noisy

Amid the *vociferous* protests of the members of parliament, the prime minister continued his speech.

VOLLEY

noun (<u>vah</u> lee)

a flight of missiles; round of gunshots

The troops fired a *volley* of bullets at the enemy, but they couldn't be sure how many hit their target.

VOLUBLE

adj (<u>vahl</u> yuh buhl)

talkative, speaking easily, glib

The *voluble* man and his reserved wife proved the old saying that opposites attract.

WAN

adj (wahn)

sickly pale

The sick child had a *wan* face, in contrast to her rosy-cheeked sister.

WANTON

adj (<u>wahn</u> tuhn)

undisciplined, unrestrained; reckless

The townspeople were outraged by the *wanton* display of disrespect when they discovered the statue of the town founder covered in graffiti.

WAX

verb (waaks)

to increase gradually; to begin to be

The moon was *waxing*, and would soon be full.

WIELD

verb (weeld)

to exercise authority or influence effectively

For such a young member of congress, he *wielded* a lot of power.

WILY

adj (<u>wie</u> lee)

clever; deceptive

Yet again, the *wily* coyote managed to elude the ranchers who wanted it dead.

WINSOME

adj (<u>wihn</u> suhm)

charming, happily engaging

Dawn gave the clerk a *winsome* smile, and he apologized for making her wait.

WORST

verb (wuhrst)

to gain the advantage over; to defeat

The North *worsted* the South in America's Civil War.

WRY

adj (rie)

bent or twisted in shape or condition; dryly humorous

Every time she teased him, she shot her friends a *wry* smile.

YEN

noun (yehn)

a strong desire, craving

Pregnant women commonly have a *yen* for pickles.

ZENITH

noun (<u>zee</u> nihth)

the point of culmination; peak

The diva considered her appearance at the Metropolitan Opera to be the *zenith* of her career.

ZEPHYR

noun (<u>zeh</u> fuhr)

a gentle breeze; something airy or unsubstantial

The *zephyr* from the ocean made the intense heat on the beach bearable for the sunbathers.

Math in a Nutshell

This list covers basic math topics including arithmetic, algebra, geometry, and probability. Be sure to brush up on other topics on your own.

Use this list to remind yourself of the key areas you'll need to know. Do four concepts a day, and you'll be ready within a month. If a concept continually causes you trouble, circle it and refer to it as you try to do the questions.

You've probably been taught most of these concepts in school already, so this list is a great way to refresh your memory.

NUMBER PROPERTIES

1. Number Categories

Integers are **whole numbers;** they include negative whole numbers and zero.

A **rational number** can be expressed as a **ratio of two integers. Irrational numbers** are real numbers—they have locations on the number line—but they **can't be expressed precisely as a fraction or decimal.** The most important **irrational numbers** are $\sqrt{2}$, $\sqrt{3}$, and π.

2. Adding/Subtracting Signed Numbers

To **add a positive and a negative,** first ignore the signs and find the positive difference between the number parts. Then attach the sign of the original number with the larger number part. For example, to add 23 and −34, first ignore the minus sign and find the positive difference between 23 and 34—that's 11. Then attach the sign of the number with the larger number part—in this case it's the minus sign from the −34. So, 23 + (−34) = −11.

Make **subtraction** situations simpler by turning them into addition. For example, you can think of −17 − (−21) as −17 + (+21).

To **add or subtract a string of positives and negatives,** first turn everything into addition. Then combine the positives and negatives so that the string is reduced to the sum of a single positive number and a single negative number.

3. Multiplying/Dividing Signed Numbers

To multiply and/or divide positives and negatives, treat the number parts as usual and **attach a minus sign if there was originally an odd number of negatives**. For example, to multiply −2, −3, and −5, first multiply the number parts: $2 \times 3 \times 5 = 30$. Then go back and note that there were *three*—an *odd* number—negatives, so the product is negative: $(−2) \times (−3) \times (−5) = −30$.

4. PEMDAS

When performing multiple operations, remember to perform them in the right order: **PEMDAS,** which means **Parentheses** first; then **Exponents;** then **Multiplication** and **Division** (left to right); and lastly **Addition** and **Subtraction** (left to right). In the expression $9 − 2 \times (5 − 3)^2 + 6 \div 3$, begin with the parentheses: $(5 − 3) = 2$. Then do the exponent: $2^2 = 4$. Now the expression is $9 − 2 \times 4 + 6 \div 3$. Next do the multiplication and division to get $9 − 8 + 2$, which equals 3. If you have difficulty remembering PEMDAS, use this sentence to recall it: **P**lease **E**xcuse **M**y **D**ear **A**unt **S**ally.

5. Counting Consecutive Integers

To count consecutive integers, **subtract the smallest from the largest and add 1.** To count the number of integers from 13 through 31, subtract: $31 − 13 = 18$. Then add 1: $18 + 1 = 19$.

NUMBER OPERATIONS AND CONCEPTS

6. Exponential Growth

If r is the ratio between consecutive terms, a_1 is the first term, a_n is the nth term, and S_n is the sum of the first n terms, then $a_n = a_1 r^{n-1}$ and $S_n = \dfrac{a_1 - a_1 r^n}{1 - r}$.

7. Union and Intersection of Sets

The things in a set are called elements or members. The union of Set A and Set B, sometimes expressed as $A \cup B$, is the set of elements that are in either or both of Set A and Set B. If Set $A = \{1, 2\}$ and Set $B = \{3, 4\}$, then $A \cup B = \{1, 2, 3, 4\}$. The intersection of Set A and Set B, sometimes expressed as $A \cap B$, is the set of elements common to both Set A and Set B. If Set $A = \{1, 2, 3\}$ and Set $B = \{3, 4, 5\}$, then $A \cap B = \{3\}$.

DIVISIBILITY

8. Factor/Multiple

The **factors** of integer n are the positive integers that divide into n with no remainder. The **multiples** of n are the integers that n divides into with no remainder. For example, 6 is a factor of 12, and 24 is a multiple of 12. 12 is both a factor and a multiple of itself, since $12 \times 1 = 12$ and $12 \div 1 = 12$.

9. Prime Factorization

To find the prime factorization of an integer, just keep breaking it up into factors until **all the factors are prime.** To find the prime factorization of 36, for example, you could begin by breaking it into 4×9: $36 = 4 \times 9 = 2 \times 2 \times 3 \times 3$.

10. Relative Primes

Relative primes are integers that have no common factor other than 1. To determine whether two integers are relative primes, break them both down to their prime factorizations. For example: $35 = 5 \times 7$, and $54 = 2 \times 3 \times 3 \times 3$. They have **no prime factors in common,** so 35 and 54 are relative primes.

11. Common Multiple

A common multiple is a number that is a multiple of two or more integers. You can always get a common multiple of two integers by **multiplying** them, but unless the two numbers are relative primes, the product will not be the *least* common multiple. For example, to find a common multiple of 12 and 15, you could just multiply: $12 \times 15 = 180$.

To find the **least common multiple (LCM),** check out the **multiples of the larger integer** until you find one that's **also a multiple of the smaller.** To find the LCM of 12 and 15, begin by taking the multiples of 15: 15 is not divisible by 12; 30 is not; nor is 45. But the next multiple of 15, 60, *is* divisible by 12, so it's the LCM.

12. Greatest Common Factor (GCF)

To find the greatest common factor, break down both integers into their prime factorizations and multiply **all the prime factors they have in common.** For example, $36 = 2 \times 2 \times 3 \times 3$, and $48 = 2 \times 2 \times 2 \times 2 \times 3$. What they have in common is two 2s and one 3, so the GCF is $2 \times 2 \times 3 = 12$.

13. Even/Odd

To predict whether a sum, difference, or product will be even or odd, just **take simple numbers like 1 and 2 and see what happens.** There are rules—"odd times even is even," for example—but there's no need to memorize them. What happens with one set of numbers generally happens with all similar sets.

14. Multiples of 2 and 4

An integer is divisible by 2 (even) if the **last digit is even.** An integer is divisible by 4 if the **last two digits form a multiple of 4.** The last digit of 562 is 2, which is even, so 562 is a multiple of 2. The last two digits form 62, which is *not* divisible by 4, so 562 is not a multiple of 4. The integer 512, however is divisible by four because the last two digits form 12, which is a multiple of 4.

15. Multiples of 3 and 9

An integer is divisible by 3 if the **sum of its digits is divisible by 3.** An integer is divisible by 9 if the **sum of its digits is divisible by 9.** The sum of the digits in 957 is 21, which is divisible by 3 but not by 9, so 957 is divisible by 3 but not by 9.

16. Multiples of 5 and 10

An integer is divisible by 5 if the **last digit is 5 or 0.** An integer is divisible by 10 if the **last digit is 0.** The last digit of 665 is 5, so 665 is a multiple of 5 but *not* a multiple of 10.

17. Remainders

The remainder is the **whole number left over after division.** For example, 487 is 2 more than 485, which is a multiple of 5, so when 487 is divided by 5, the remainder is 2.

FRACTIONS AND DECIMALS

18. Reducing Fractions

To reduce a fraction to lowest terms, **factor out and cancel** all factors the numerator and denominator have in common.

$$\frac{28}{36} = \frac{4 \times 7}{4 \times 9} = \frac{7}{9}$$

19. Adding/Subtracting Fractions

To add or subtract fractions, first find a **common denominator,** then add or subtract the numerators.

$$\frac{2}{15} + \frac{3}{10} = \frac{4}{30} + \frac{9}{30} = \frac{4 + 9}{30} = \frac{13}{30}$$

20. Multiplying Fractions

To multiply fractions, **multiply** the numerators and **multiply** the denominators.

$$\frac{5}{7} \times \frac{3}{4} = \frac{5 \times 3}{7 \times 4} = \frac{15}{28}$$

21. Dividing Fractions

To divide fractions, **invert** the second one and **multiply**.

$$\frac{1}{2} \div \frac{3}{5} = \frac{1}{2} \times \frac{5}{3} = \frac{1 \times 5}{2 \times 3} = \frac{5}{6}$$

22. Mixed Numbers and Improper Fractions

To convert a mixed number to an improper fraction, **multiply** the whole number part by the denominator, then **add** the numerator. The result is the new numerator (over the same denominator). To convert $7\frac{1}{3}$, first multiply 7 by 3 and then add 1 to get the new numerator of 22. Put that over the same denominator, 3, to get $\frac{22}{3}$.

To convert an improper fraction to a mixed number, divide the denominator into the numerator to get a **whole number quotient with a remainder.** The quotient becomes the whole number part of the mixed number, and the remainder becomes the new numerator—with the same denominator. For example, to convert $\frac{108}{5}$, first divide 5 into 108, which yields 21 with a remainder of 3. Therefore, $\frac{108}{5} = 21\frac{3}{5}$.

23. Reciprocal

To find the reciprocal of a fraction, **switch the numerator and the denominator.** The reciprocal of $\frac{3}{7}$ is $\frac{7}{3}$. The reciprocal of 5 is $\frac{1}{5}$. The product of reciprocals is 1.

24. Comparing Fractions

One way to compare fractions is to **re-express them with a common denominator.** For example, $\frac{3}{4} = \frac{21}{28}$ and $\frac{5}{7} = \frac{20}{28}$. Because $\frac{21}{28}$ is greater than $\frac{20}{28}$, $\frac{3}{4}$ is greater than $\frac{5}{7}$. Another method is to **convert them both to decimals.** In this example, $\frac{3}{4}$ converts to 0.75, and $\frac{5}{7}$ converts to approximately 0.714.

25. Converting Fractions and Decimals

To convert a fraction to a decimal, **divide the bottom into the top.** To convert $\frac{5}{8}$, divide 8 into 5, yielding 0.625.

To convert a decimal to a fraction, set the decimal over 1 and **multiply the numerator and denominator by 10** raised to the number of digits that are to the right of the decimal point.

To convert 0.625 to a fraction, you would multiply $\frac{0.625}{1}$ by $\frac{10^3}{10^3}$ or $\frac{1,000}{1,000}$. Then simplify: $\frac{625}{1,000} = \frac{5 \times 125}{8 \times 125} = \frac{5}{8}$.

26. Repeating Decimal

To find a particular digit in a repeating decimal, note the **number of digits in the cluster that repeats.** If there are 2 digits in that cluster, then every second digit is the same. If there are 3 digits in that cluster, then every third digit is the same. And so on. For example, the decimal equivalent of $\frac{1}{27}$ is 0.037037037…, which is best written $0.\overline{037}$. There are 3 digits in the repeating cluster, so every third digit is the same: 7. To find the 50th digit, look for the multiple of 3 just less than 50—that's 48. The 48th digit is 7, and with the 49th digit the pattern repeats with 0. The 50th digit is 3.

27. Identifying the Parts and the Whole

The key to solving most fraction and percent word problems is to identify the part and the whole. Usually you'll find the **part** associated with the verb *is/are* and the **whole** associated with the word *of.* In the sentence "Half of the boys are blonds," the whole is the boys ("*of the* boys"), and the part is the blonds ("*are* blonds").

PERCENTS

28. Percent Formula

Whether you need to find the part, the whole, or the percent, use the same formula:

$$\text{Part} = \text{Percent} \times \text{Whole}$$

Example: What is 12 percent of 25?
Setup: Part = 0.12 × 25

Example: 15 is 3 percent of what number?
Setup: 15 = 0.03 × Whole

Example: 45 is what percent of 9?
Setup: 45 = Percent × 9

29. Percent Increase and Decrease

To increase a number by a percent, **add the percent to 100 percent,** convert to a decimal, and multiply. To increase 40 by 25 percent, add 25 percent to 100 percent, convert 125 percent to 1.25, and multiply by 40: 1.25 × 40 = 50.

30. Finding the Original Whole

To find the **original whole before a percent increase or decrease,** set up an equation. Think of the result of a 15 percent increase over x as $1.15x$.

Example: After a 5 percent increase, the population was 59,346. What was the population before the increase?
Setup: $1.05x = 59,346$

31. Combined Percent Increase and Decrease

To determine the combined effect of multiple percent increases and/or decreases, **start with 100 and see what happens.**

Example: A price went up 10 percent one year, and the new price went up 20 percent the next year. What was the combined percent increase?
Setup: First year: 100 + (10 percent of 100) = 110. Second year: 110 + (20 percent of 110) = 132. That's a combined 32 percent increase.

RATIOS, PROPORTIONS, AND RATES

32. Setting up a Ratio

To find a ratio, put the number associated with the word *of* **on top** and the quantity associated with the word *to* **on the bottom** and reduce. The ratio of 20 oranges to 12 apples is $\frac{20}{12}$, which reduces to $\frac{5}{3}$.

33. Part-to-Part Ratios and Part-to-Whole Ratios

If the parts add up to the whole, a part-to-part ratio can be turned into two part-to-whole ratios by putting **each number in the original ratio over the sum of the numbers.**

If the ratio of males to females is 1 to 2, then the males-to-people ratio is $\frac{1}{1+2} = \frac{1}{3}$ and the females-to-people ratio is $\frac{2}{1+2} = \frac{2}{3}$. In other words, $\frac{2}{3}$ of all the people are female.

34. Solving a Proportion

To solve a proportion, **cross multiply:**

$$\frac{x}{5} = \frac{3}{4}$$

$$4x = 3 \times 5$$

$$x = \frac{15}{4} = 3.75$$

35. Rate

To solve a rate problem, **use the units** to keep things straight.

Example: If snow is falling at the rate of one foot every four hours, how many inches of snow will fall in seven hours?

Setup:

$$\frac{1 \text{ foot}}{4 \text{ hours}} = \frac{x \text{ inches}}{7 \text{ hours}}$$

$$\frac{12 \text{ inches}}{4 \text{ hours}} = \frac{x \text{ inches}}{7 \text{ hours}}$$

$$4x = 12 \times 7$$

$$x = 21$$

36. Average Rate

Average rate is *not* simply the average of the rates.

$$\text{Average } A \text{ per } B = \frac{\text{Total } A}{\text{Total } B}$$

$$\text{Average Speed} = \frac{\text{Total distance}}{\text{Total time}}$$

To find the average speed for 120 miles at 40 mph and 120 miles at 60 mph, **don't just average the two speeds.** First, figure out the total distance and the total time. The total distance is 120 + 120 = 240 miles. The times are 3 hours for the first leg and 2 hours for the second leg, or 5 hours total. The average speed, then, is $\frac{240}{5} = 48$ miles per hour.

AVERAGES

37. Average Formula

To find the average of a set of numbers, **add them up and divide by the number of numbers.**

$$\text{Average} = \frac{\text{Sum of the terms}}{\text{Number of terms}}$$

To find the average of the 5 numbers 12, 15, 23, 40, and 40, first add them: 12 + 15 + 23 + 40 + 40 = 130. Then, divide the sum by 5: 130 ÷ 5 = 26.

38. Average of Evenly Spaced Numbers

To find the average of evenly spaced numbers, just **average the smallest and the largest.** The average of all the integers from 13 through 77 is the same as the average of 13 and 77:

$$\frac{13 + 77}{2} = \frac{90}{2} = 45$$

39. Using the Average to Find the Sum

$$\text{Sum} = (\text{Average}) \times (\text{Number of terms})$$

If the average of 10 numbers is 50, then they add up to 10 × 50, or 500.

40. Finding the Missing Number

To find a missing number when you're given the average, **use the sum.** If the average of 4 numbers is 7, then the sum of those 4 numbers is 4 × 7, or 28. Suppose that 3 of the numbers are 3, 5, and 8. These 3 numbers add up to 16 of that 28, which leaves 12 for the fourth number.

41. Median and Mode

The median of a set of numbers is the **value that falls in the middle of the set.** If you have 5 test scores, and they are 88, 86, 57, 94, and 73, you must first list the scores in increasing or decreasing order: 57, 73, 86, 88, 94.

The median is the middle number, or 86. If there is an even number of values in a set (6 test scores, for instance), simply take the average of the two middle numbers.

The mode of a set of numbers is the **value that appears most often.** If your test scores were 88, 57, 68, 85, 99, 93, 93, 84, and 81, the mode of the scores would be 93 because it appears more often than any other score. If there is a tie for the most common value in a set, the set has more than one mode.

POSSIBILITIES AND PROBABILITY

42. Counting the Possibilities

The fundamental counting principle: If there are *m* **ways** one event can happen and *n* **ways** a second event can happen, then there are *m* × *n* **ways** for the two events to happen. For example, with 5 shirts and 7 pairs of pants to choose from, you can have 5 × 7 = 35 different outfits.

43. Probability

$$\text{Probability} = \frac{\text{Favorable Outcomes}}{\text{Total Possible Outcomes}}$$

If you have 12 shirts in a drawer and 9 of them are white, the probability of picking a white shirt at random is $\frac{9}{12} = \frac{3}{4}$. This probability can also be expressed as 0.75 or 75%.

POWERS AND ROOTS

44. Multiplying and Dividing Powers

To multiply powers with the same base, **add the exponents and keep the same base:**

$$x^3 \times x^4 = x^{3+4} = x^7$$

To divide powers with the same base, **subtract the exponents and keep the same base:**

$$y^{13} \div y^8 = y^{13-8} = y^5$$

45. Raising Powers to Powers

To raise a power to a power, **multiply the exponents:**

$$(x^3)^4 = x^{3 \times 4} = x^{12}$$

46. Simplifying Square Roots

To simplify a square root, **factor out the perfect squares** under the radical, unsquare them, and put the result in front.

$$\sqrt{12} = \sqrt{4 \times 3} = \sqrt{4} \times \sqrt{3} = 2\sqrt{3}$$

47. Adding and Subtracting Roots

You can add or subtract radical expressions **when the part under the radicals is the same:**

$$2\sqrt{3} + 3\sqrt{3} = 5\sqrt{3}$$

Don't try to add or subtract when the radical parts are different. There's not much you can do with an expression like this:

$$3\sqrt{5} + 3\sqrt{7}$$

48. Multiplying and Dividing Roots

The product of square roots is equal to the **square root of the product:**

$$\sqrt{3} \times \sqrt{5} = \sqrt{3 \times 5} = \sqrt{15}$$

The quotient of square roots is equal to the **square root of the quotient:**

$$\frac{\sqrt{6}}{\sqrt{3}} = \sqrt{\frac{6}{3}} = \sqrt{2}$$

49. Negative Exponent and Rational Exponent

To find the value of a number raised to a negative exponent, simply rewrite the number, without the negative sign, as the bottom of a fraction with 1 as the numerator of the fraction: $3^{-2} = \frac{1}{3^2} = \frac{1}{9}$. If x is a positive number and a is a nonzero number, then $x^{\frac{1}{a}} = \sqrt[a]{x}$. So $4^{\frac{1}{2}} = \sqrt[2]{4} = 2$. If p and q are integers, then $x^{\frac{p}{q}} = \sqrt[q]{x^p}$. So $4^{\frac{3}{2}} = \sqrt[2]{4^3} = \sqrt{64} = 8$.

ABSOLUTE VALUE

50. Determining Absolute Value

The absolute value of a number is the distance of the number from zero on the number line. Because absolute value is a distance, it is always positive. The absolute value of 7 is 7; this is expressed $|7| = 7$. Similarly, the absolute value of −7 is 7: $|-7| = 7$. Every positive number is the absolute value of two numbers: itself and its negative.

ALGEBRAIC EXPRESSIONS

51. Evaluating an Expression

To evaluate an algebraic expression, **plug in** the given values for the unknowns and calculate according to **PEMDAS**. To find the value of $x^2 + 5x − 6$ when $x = −2$, plug in −2 for x: $(−2)^2 + 5(−2) − 6 = −12$.

52. Adding and Subtracting Monomials

To combine like terms, **keep the variable part unchanged while adding or subtracting the coefficients:**

$$2a + 3a = (2 + 3)a = 5a$$

53. Adding and Subtracting Polynomials

To add or subtract polynomials, **combine like terms:**

$$(3x^2 + 5x - 7) - (x^2 + 12) =$$
$$(3x^2 - x^2) + 5x + (-7 - 12) =$$
$$2x^2 + 5x - 19$$

54. Multiplying Monomials

To multiply monomials, **multiply the coefficients and the variables separately:**

$$2a \times 3a = (2 \times 3)(a \times a) = 6a^2$$

55. Multiplying Binomials—FOIL

To multiply binomials, use **FOIL**. To multiply $(x + 3)$ by $(x + 4)$, first multiply the First terms: $x \times x = x^2$. Next the Outer terms: $x \times 4 = 4x$. Then the Inner terms: $3 \times x = 3x$. And finally the Last terms: $3 \times 4 = 12$. Then add and combine like terms:

$$x^2 + 4x + 3x + 12 = x^2 + 7x + 12$$

56. Multiplying Other Polynomials

FOIL works only when you want to multiply two binomials. If you want to multiply polynomials with more than two terms, make sure you **multiply each term in the first polynomial by each term in the second.**

$$(x^2 + 3x + 4)(x + 5) =$$
$$x^2(x + 5) + 3x(x + 5) + 4(x + 5) =$$
$$x^3 + 5x^2 + 3x^2 + 15x + 4x + 20 =$$
$$x^3 + 8x^2 + 19x + 20$$

After multiplying two polynomials together, the number of terms in your expression before simplifying should equal the number of terms in one polynomial multiplied by the number of terms in the second. In the example, you should have $3 \times 2 = 6$ terms in the product before you simplify like terms.

FACTORING ALGEBRAIC EXPRESSIONS

57. Factoring out a Common Divisor

A factor common to all terms of a polynomial can be **factored out.** All three terms in the polynomial $3x^3 + 12x^2 - 6x$ contain a factor of $3x$. Pulling out the common factor yields $3x(x^2 + 4x - 2)$.

58. Factoring the Difference of Squares

One of the test maker's favorite factorables is the **difference of squares.**

$$a^2 - b^2 = (a - b)(a + b)$$

$x^2 - 9$, for example, factors to $(x - 3)(x + 3)$.

59. Factoring the Square of a Binomial

Recognize polynomials that are squares of binomials:

$$a^2 + 2ab + b^2 = (a + b)^2$$
$$a^2 - 2ab + b^2 = (a - b)^2$$

For example, $4x^2 + 12x + 9$ factors to $(2x + 3)^2$, and $n^2 - 10n + 25$ factors to $(n - 5)^2$.

60. Factoring Other Polynomials—FOIL in Reverse

To factor a quadratic expression, **think about what binomials you could use FOIL on to get that quadratic expression.** To factor $x^2 - 5x + 6$, think about what First terms will produce x^2, what Last terms will produce $+6$, and what Outer and Inner terms will produce $-5x$. Some common sense—and a little trial and error—lead you to $(x - 2)(x - 3)$.

KAPLAN

61. Simplifying an Algebraic Fraction

Simplifying an algebraic fraction is a lot like simplifying a numerical fraction. The general idea is to **find factors common to the numerator and denominator and cancel them.** Thus, simplifying an algebraic fraction begins with factoring.

For example, to simplify $\frac{x^2 - x - 12}{x^2 - 9}$, first factor the numerator and denominator:

$$\frac{x^2 - x - 12}{x^2 - 9} = \frac{(x - 4)(x + 3)}{(x - 3)(x + 3)}$$

Canceling $x + 3$ from the numerator and denominator leaves you with $\frac{x - 4}{x - 3}$.

SOLVING EQUATIONS

62. Solving a Linear Equation

To solve an equation, do whatever is necessary to both sides to **isolate the variable.** To solve the equation $5x - 12 = -2x + 9$, first get all the x's on one side by adding $2x$ to both sides: $7x - 12 = 9$. Then add 12 to both sides: $7x = 21$. Then divide both sides by 7: $x = 3$.

63. Solving "In Terms Of"

To solve an equation for one variable **in terms of** another means to **isolate the one variable on one side of the equation,** leaving an expression containing the other variable on the other side of the equation. To solve the equation $3x - 10y = -5x + 6y$ for x in terms of y, isolate x:

$$3x - 10y = -5x + 6y$$

$$3x + 5x = 6y + 10y$$

$$8x = 16y$$

$$x = 2y$$

64. Translating from English into Algebra

To translate from English into algebra, look for the key words and systematically turn phrases into algebraic expressions and sentences into equations. Be careful about order, especially when subtraction is called for.

Example: Celine and Remi play tennis. Last year, Celine won 3 more than twice the number of matches that Remi won. If Celine won 11 more matches than Remi, how many matches did Celine win?

Setup: You are given two sets of information. One way to solve this is to write a system of equations—one equation for each set of information. Use variables that relate well with what they represent. For example, use r to represent Remi's winning matches. Use c to represent Celine's winning matches. The phrase "Celine won 3 more than twice Remi" can be written as $c = 2r + 3$. The phrase "Celine won 11 more matches than Remi" can be written as $c = r + 11$.

65. Solving a Quadratic Equation

To solve a quadratic equation, put it in the "$ax^2 + bx + c = 0$" form, **factor** the left side (if you can), and set each factor equal to 0 separately to get the two solutions. To solve $x^2 + 12 = 7x$, first rewrite it as $x^2 - 7x + 12 = 0$. Then factor the left side:

$$(x - 3)(x - 4) = 0$$

$$x - 3 = 0 \text{ or } x - 4 = 0$$

$$x = 3 \text{ or } 4$$

66. Solving a System of Equations

You can solve for two variables only if you have two distinct equations. Two forms of the same equation will not be adequate. **Combine the equations** in such a way that **one of the variables cancels out.** To solve the two equations $4x + 3y = 8$ and $x + y = 3$, multiply both sides of the second equation by -3 to get $-3x - 3y = -9$. Now add the two equations; the $3y$ and the $-3y$ cancel out, leaving $x = -1$. Plug that back into either one of the original equations, and you'll find that $y = 4$.

67. Solving an Inequality

To solve an inequality, do whatever is necessary to both sides to **isolate the variable.** Just remember that when you **multiply or divide both sides by a negative number,** you must **reverse the sign.** To solve $-5x + 7 < -3$, subtract 7 from both sides to get $-5x < -10$. Now divide both sides by -5, remembering to reverse the sign: $x > 2$.

68. Radical Equations

A radical equation contains at least one radical expression. Solve radical equations by using standard rules of algebra. If $5\sqrt{x} - 2 = 13$, then $5\sqrt{x} = 15$ and $\sqrt{x} = 3$, so $x = 9$.

FUNCTIONS

69. Function Notation and Evaluation

Standard function notation is written $f(x)$ and read "f of 4." To evaluate the function $f(x) = 2x + 3$ for $f(4)$, replace x with 4 and simplify: $f(4) = 2(4) + 3 = 11$.

70. Direct and Inverse Variation

In direct variation, $y = kx$, where k is a nonzero constant. In direct variation, the variable y changes directly as x does. If a unit of Currency A is worth 2 units of Currency B, then $A = 2B$. If the number of units of B were to double, the number of units of A would double, and so on for halving, tripling, etc. In inverse variation, $xy = k$, where x and y are variables and k is a constant. A famous inverse relationship is $rate \times time = distance$, where distance is constant. Imagine having to cover a distance of 24 miles. If you were to travel at 12 miles per hour, you'd need 2 hours. But if you were to halve your rate, you would have to double your time. This is just another way of saying that rate and time vary inversely.

71. Domain and Range of a Function

The domain of a function is the set of values for which the function is defined. For example, the domain of $f(x) = \dfrac{1}{1 - x^2}$ is all values of x except 1 and -1, because for those values the denominator has a value of 0 and is therefore undefined. The range of a function is the set of outputs or results of the function. For example, the range of $f(x) = x^2$ is all numbers greater than or equal to zero, because x^2 cannot be negative.

COORDINATE GEOMETRY

72. Finding the Distance Between Two Points

To find the distance between points, **use the Pythagorean theorem** or **special right triangles.** The difference between the x's is one leg and the difference between the y's is the other.

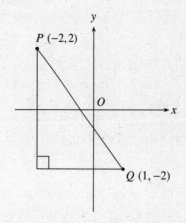

In the figure above, PQ is the hypotenuse of a 3-4-5 triangle, so $PQ = 5$.

You can also use the **distance formula:**

$$d = \sqrt{(x_1 - x_2)^2 + (y_1 - y_2)^2}$$

Find the distance between $R(3, 6)$ and $S(5, -2)$:

$$d = \sqrt{(3 - 5)^2 + [6 - (-2)^2]}$$

$$= \sqrt{(-2)^2 + (8)^2}$$

$$= \sqrt{68} = 2\sqrt{17}$$

73. Using Two Points to Find the Slope

$$\text{Slope} = \frac{\text{Change in } y}{\text{Change in } x} = \frac{\text{Rise}}{\text{Run}}$$

The slope of the line that contains the points $A(2, 3)$ and $B(0, -1)$ is

$$\frac{y_A - y_B}{x_A - x_B} = \frac{3 - (-1)}{2 - 0} = \frac{4}{2} = 2$$

74. Using an Equation to Find the Slope

To find the slope of a line from an equation, put the equation into the **slope-intercept** form:

$$y = mx + b$$

The **slope is m**. To find the slope of the equation $3x + 2y = 4$, rearrange it:

$$3x + 2y = 4$$

$$2y = -3x + 4$$

$$y = -\frac{3}{2}x + 2$$

The slope is $-\frac{3}{2}$.

75. Using an Equation to Find an Intercept

To find the y-intercept, you can either put the equation into $y = mx + b$ (**slope-intercept**) form—in which case **b is the y-intercept**—or you can just **plug $x = 0$** into the equation and **solve for y**. To find the x-intercept, **plug $y = 0$** into the equation and **solve for x**.

76. Finding the Midpoint

The midpoint of two points on a line segment is the average of the x-coordinates of the endpoints and the average of the y-coordinates of the endpoints. If the endpoints are (x_1, y_1) and (x_2, y_2), the midpoint is $\left(\frac{x_1 + x_2}{2}, \frac{y_1 + y_2}{2}\right)$. The midpoint of $(3, 5)$ and $(9, 1)$ is $\left(\frac{3 + 9}{2}, \frac{5 + 1}{2}\right)$.

LINES AND ANGLES

77. Intersecting Lines

When two lines intersect, **adjacent angles are supplementary and vertical angles are equal.**

In the figure above, the angles marked $a°$ and $b°$ are adjacent and supplementary, so $a + b = 180$. Furthermore, the angles marked $a°$ and $60°$ are vertical and equal, so $a = 60$.

78. Parallel Lines and Transversals

A transversal across parallel lines forms **four equal acute angles and four equal obtuse angles.** If the transversal meets the lines at a right angle, then all eight angles are right angles.

In the figure above, line 1 is parallel to line 2. Angles a, c, e, and g are obtuse, so they are all equal. Angles b, d, f, and h are acute, so they are all equal.

Furthermore, **any of the acute angles is supplementary to any of the obtuse angles.** Angles a and h are supplementary, as are b and e, c and f, and so on.

TRIANGLES—GENERAL

79. Interior and Exterior Angles of a Triangle

The three angles of any triangle **add up to 180 degrees.**

In the figure above, $x + 50 + 100 = 180$, so $x = 30$.

An exterior angle of a triangle is equal to the **sum of the remote interior angles.**

In the figure above, the exterior angle labeled $x°$ is equal to the sum of the remote angles: $x = 50 + 100 = 150$.

The three exterior angles of a triangle add up to 360 degrees.

In the figure above, $a + b + c = 360$.

80. Similar Triangles

Similar triangles have the same shape: **corresponding angles are equal, and corresponding sides are proportional.**

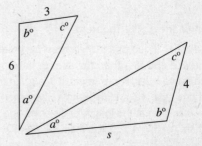

The triangles above are similar because they have the same angles. The 3 corresponds to the 4, and the 6 corresponds to the s.

$$\frac{3}{4} = \frac{6}{s}$$

$$3s = 24$$

$$s = 8$$

81. Area of a Triangle

$$\text{Area of Triangle} = \frac{1}{2}(\text{base})(\text{height})$$

The height is the perpendicular distance between the side that's chosen as the base and the opposite vertex.

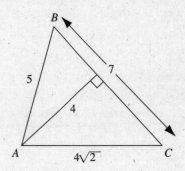

In the triangle above, 4 is the height when the 7 is chosen as the base.

$$\text{Area} = \frac{1}{2}bh = \frac{1}{2}(7)(4) = 14$$

82. Triangle Inequality Theorem

The length of one side of a triangle must be **greater than the difference and less than the sum** of the lengths of the other two sides. For example, if it is given that the length of one side is 3 and the length of another side is 7, then you know that the length of the third side must be greater than $7 - 3 = 4$ and less than $7 + 3 = 10$.

83. Isosceles and Equilateral Triangles

An isosceles triangle is a triangle that has **two equal sides.** Not only are two sides equal, but the angles opposite the equal sides, called **base angles**, are also equal.

Equilateral triangles are triangles in which **all three sides are equal.** Since all the sides are equal, all the angles are also equal. All three angles in an equilateral triangle measure 60 degrees, regardless of the lengths of sides.

RIGHT TRIANGLES

84. Pythagorean Theorem

For all right triangles,

$$(\text{leg1})^2 + (\text{leg2})^2 = (\text{hypotenuse})^2$$

If one leg is 2 and the other leg is 3, then

$$2^2 + 3^2 = c^2$$
$$c^2 = 4 + 9$$
$$c = \sqrt{13}$$

85. The 3-4-5 Triangle

If a right triangle's leg-to-leg ratio is 3:4, or if the leg-to-hypotenuse ratio is 3:5 or 4:5, it's a 3-4-5 triangle and you don't need to use the Pythagorean theorem to find the third side. Just figure out what multiple of 3-4-5 it is.

In the right triangle shown, one leg is 30 and the hypotenuse is 50. This is 10 times 3-4-5. The other leg is 40.

86. The 5-12-13 Triangle

If a right triangle's leg-to-leg ratio is 5:12, or if the leg-to-hypotenuse ratio is 5:13 or 12:13, then it's a 5-12-13 triangle and you don't need to use the Pythagorean theorem to find the third side. Just figure out what multiple of 5-12-13 it is.

Here one leg is 36 and the hypotenuse is 39. This is 3 times 5-12-13. The other leg is 15.

87. The 30-60-90 Triangle

The sides of a 30-60-90 triangle are in a ratio of
$x : x\sqrt{3} : 2x$. You don't need the Pythagorean theorem.

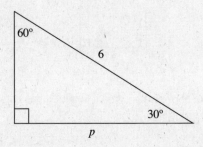

If the hypotenuse is 6, then the shorter leg is half that, or
3, and then the longer leg is equal to the short leg times
$\sqrt{3}$, or $3\sqrt{3}$.

88. The 45-45-90 Triangle

The sides of a 45-45-90 triangle are in a ratio of
$x : x : x\sqrt{2}$.

If one leg is 3, then the other leg is also 3, and the hypotenuse is equal to a leg times $\sqrt{2}$, or $3\sqrt{2}$.

OTHER POLYGONS

89. Characteristics of a Rectangle

A rectangle is a **four-sided figure with four right angles.**
Opposite sides are equal. Diagonals are equal.

Quadrilateral *ABCD* above is shown to have three right angles. The fourth angle therefore also measures 90 degrees, and *ABCD* is a rectangle. The perimeter of a rectangle is equal to the sum of the lengths of the four sides, which is equivalent to 2(length + width).

Area of Rectangle = length × width

The area of a 7-by-3 rectangle is $7 \times 3 = 21$.

90. Characteristics of a Parallelogram

A parallelogram has **two pairs of parallel sides.** Opposite sides are equal. Opposite angles are equal. Consecutive angles add up to 180 degrees.

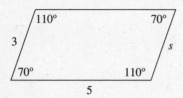

In the figure above, s is the length of the side opposite the 3, so $s = 3$.

Area of Parallelogram = base × height

In parallelogram *KLMN* above, 4 is the height when *LM* or *KN* is used as the base. Base × height = $6 × 4 = 24$.

91. Characteristics of a Square

A square is a **rectangle with four equal sides.**

If *PQRS* is a square, all sides are the same length as *QR*. The perimeter of a square is equal to four times the length of one side. Square *PQRS*, with sides of length 2, has a perimeter of $4 × 2 = 8$.

Area of Square = (side)²

The square above, with sides of length 5, has an area of $5^2 = 25$.

92. Interior Angles of a Polygon

The **sum of the measures of the interior angles of a polygon = $(n - 2) × 180$,** where n is the number of sides.

Sum of the Angles = $(n - 2) × 180$

The eight angles of an octagon, for example, add up to $(8 - 2) × 180 = 1,080$.

CIRCLES

93. Circumference of a Circle

Circumference = $2\pi r$

In the circle above, the radius is 3, so the circumference is $2\pi(3) = 6\pi$.

94. Length of an Arc

An **arc** is a piece of the circumference. If n is the degree measure of the arc's central angle, then the formula is

$$\text{Length of an Arc} = \left(\frac{n}{360}\right)(2\pi r)$$

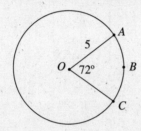

In the figure above, the radius is 5, and the measure of the central angle is 72 degrees. The arc length is $\frac{72}{360}$ or $\frac{1}{5}$ of the circumference:

$$\left(\frac{72}{360}\right)(2\pi)(5) = \left(\frac{1}{5}\right)(10\pi) = 2\pi$$

95. Area of a Circle

$$\text{Area of a Circle} = \pi r^2$$

The area of the circle is $\pi(4)^2 = 16\pi$.

96. Area of a Sector

A **sector** is a piece of the area of a circle. If n is the degree measure of the sector's central angle, then the formula is

$$\text{Area of a Sector} = \left(\frac{n}{360}\right)(\pi r^2)$$

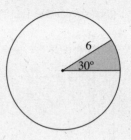

In the figure above, the radius is 6, and the measure of the sector's central angle is 30 degrees. The sector has $\frac{30}{360}$ or $\frac{1}{12}$ of the area of the circle:

$$\left(\frac{30}{360}\right)(\pi)(6^2) = \left(\frac{1}{12}\right)(36\pi) = 3\pi$$

97. Tangency

When a line is tangent to a circle, the radius of the circle is perpendicular to the line at the point of contact.

SOLIDS

98. Surface Area of a Rectangular Solid

The surface of a rectangular solid consists of three pairs of identical faces. To find the surface area, find the area of each face and add them up. If the length is l, the width is w, and the height is h, the formula is

$$\text{Surface Area} = 2lw + 2wh + 2lh$$

The surface area of the box above is
$(2 \times 7 \times 3) + (2 \times 3 \times 4) + (2 \times 7 \times 4) = 42 + 24 + 56 = 122$.

99. Volume of a Rectangular Solid

Volume of a Rectangular Solid = *lwh*

The volume of a 4-by-5-by-6 box is

$4 \times 5 \times 6 = 120$

A cube is a rectangular solid with length, width, and height all equal. If e is the length of an edge of a cube, the volume formula is

Volume of a Cube = e^3

The volume of this cube is $2^3 = 8$.

100. Volume of a Cylinder

Volume of a Cylinder = $\pi r^2 h$

In the cylinder above, $r = 2$, $h = 5$, so

Volume = $\pi(2^2)(5) = 20\pi$

Math Glossary

ABSOLUTE VALUE—the magnitude of a number, irrespective of its sign. Written as a number inside vertical lines: $|3| = 3$ and $|-3| = 3$.

ACUTE ANGLE—an angle measuring less than 90°. *A triangle with three acute angles is called an acute triangle.*

ADJACENT ANGLES—two angles having a common side and a common vertex.

In the figure shown here, angles x and y are adjacent. (They are also supplementary.)

ALGEBRAIC EXPRESSION—one or more algebraic terms connected with plus and minus signs. *An algebraic expression is not an equation because it has no equal sign.*

ALTITUDE—a perpendicular segment whose length can be used in calculating the area of a triangle or other polygon.

In the figure shown here, $\overline{BD}$ is an altitude of △ABC, and $\overline{GJ}$ is an altitude of parallelogram EFGH.

ANGLE—two line segments coming together at a point called the vertex.

The angle above could be called ∠ABC, ∠B, or ∠x.

ARC—a portion of the circumference of a circle.

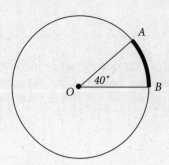

Because ∠O is $\frac{1}{9}$ of a full circle's 360°, the length of minor arc AB is $\frac{1}{9}$ the circumference.

AREA—a measure, in square units, of the size of a region in a plane. *Finding the area of a figure invariably involves multiplying two dimensions, such as length and width, or base and height.*

AVERAGE—the sum of a group of numbers divided by the number of numbers in the group. *To find the average of 2, 7, and 15, divide the sum (2 + 7 + 15 = 24) by the number of numbers (3): 24 ÷ 3 = 8.*

AVERAGE RATE—Average A per $B = \frac{\text{Total } A}{\text{Total } B}$. Average speed = $\frac{\text{Total distance}}{\text{Total time}}$. *To get the average speed, don't just average the speeds.*

AXES—the perpendicular "number lines" in the coordinate plane.

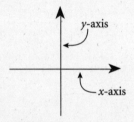

BASE—a side of a polygon that will be used with an altitude in calculating the area; a face of a solid, the area of which will be used with an altitude in calculating the volume.

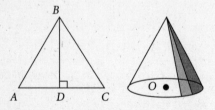

In the figure shown here, $\overline{AC}$ is the base of the triangle, and circle O is the base of the cone.

BINOMIAL—an algebraic expression with two terms. *The FOIL method of multiplying works only for a pair of binomials.*

BISECTOR—a line or line segment that divides an angle in half. *The bisector of a 90° angle divides it into two 45° angles.*

CENTRAL ANGLE—an angle formed by two radii of a circle.

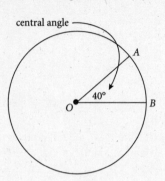

In the figure shown here, ∠AOB is a central angle.

CHORD—a line segment connecting two points on a circle.

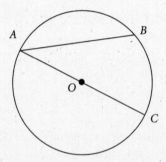

In the figure shown here, $\overline{AB}$ and $\overline{AC}$ are chords of circle O. Because it passes through the center, $\overline{AC}$ is also a diameter.

CIRCLE—the set of points in a plane at a particular distance from a central point. *A circle is not a polygon because it is not made up of straight sides.*

CIRCUMFERENCE—the distance around a circle. *The circumference of a circle is analogous to the perimeter of a polygon.*

CIRCUMSCRIBED—drawn outside another figure with as many points touching as possible.

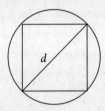

In the figure shown here, the circle is circumscribed about the square; d is both a diagonal of the square and a diameter of the circle.

COEFFICIENT—the numerical or "constant" part of an algebraic term. *In the monomial $-4x^2y$, the coefficient is -4. In the expression $ax^2 + bx + c$, a, b, and c are the coefficients.*

COMMON DENOMINATOR—a number that can be used as the denominator for two or more fractions so that they can be added or subtracted. *Before you can add the fractions $\frac{5}{6}$ and $\frac{5}{8}$, you first re-express them with a common denominator, such as 24: $\frac{5}{6} = \frac{20}{24}$ and $\frac{5}{8} = \frac{15}{24}$.*

COMMON FACTOR—a number that divides evenly into two integers. *Any two integers will have at least 1 for a common factor.*

COMMON MULTIPLE—a multiple shared by two integers. *You can always get a common multiple for two integers by multiplying them, though that will not necessarily be the least common multiple.*

COMPLEMENTARY ANGLES—two angles whose measures add up to 90°. *A 30° angle and a 60° angle are complementary.*

CONE—a solid with a circle at one end and a single point at the other.

CONGRUENT—identical; of the same size and shape. *Congruent polygons have the same angles and side lengths.*

CONSECUTIVE—one after another, in order, without skipping any. *The numbers 6, 9, 12, 15, 18, and 21 are consecutive multiples of 3.*

COORDINATES—the pair of numbers, written inside parentheses, that specifies the location of a point in the coordinate plane. *The first number is the x-coordinate and the second number is the y-coordinate.*

COSECANT—the ratio of the hypotenuse to the opposite leg. *The cosecant of ∠A in the following figure is $\frac{\text{hypotenuse}}{\text{opposite}} = \frac{13}{5}$.*

COSINE—the ratio of the adjacent leg to the hypotenuse. *The cosine of ∠A in the previous figure is $\frac{\text{adjacent}}{\text{hypotenuse}} = \frac{12}{13}$.*

COTANGENT—the ratio of the adjacent leg to the opposite leg. *The cotangent of* ∠A *in the previous figure is* $\frac{\text{adjacent}}{\text{opposite}} = \frac{12}{5}$.

CUBE—a rectangular solid whose faces are all squares.

CUBE (of a number)—the third power. *The cube of a negative number is negative.*

CYLINDER—a solid with two circular ends connected by "straight" sides.

DECIMAL—a noninteger written with digits and a decimal point. *A decimal is equivalent to a common fraction whose denominator is 10, 100, or 1,000, etc.*

DEGREE—one 360th of a full rotation. *A right angle measures 90 degrees—often written 90°.*

DEGREE OF AN EQUATION—the greatest exponent in a single-variable equation. *The equation* $x^3 - 9x = 0$ *is a third-degree equation because the biggest exponent is 3.*

DENOMINATOR—the number below the fraction bar. *When you increase the denominator of a positive fraction and keep the numerator the same, you decrease the value of the fraction:* $\frac{7}{11}$ *is less than* $\frac{7}{10}$.

DIAGONAL—a line segment connecting two nonadjacent vertices of a polygon. *A diagonal divides a rectangle into two right triangles.*

DIAMETER—(the length of) a line segment connecting two points on a circle and passing through the center. *A diameter is a chord of maximum length.*

DIFFERENCE—the result of subtraction. *The positive difference between 3 and 7 is 4.*

DIGIT—one of the numbers from 0 through 9. *In the 3-digit number 355, the hundreds digit is 3, the tens digit is 5, and the ones digit is 5.*

DISTINCT—different, distinguishable. *The number 355 has 2 distinct digits: 3 and 5.*

EDGE—a line segment formed by the intersection of two faces.

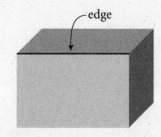

A rectangular solid has 12 edges.

ELLIPSE—a set of points in a plane for which the sum of the distances from two points (called *foci*) is constant.

The exterior angles of a regular pentagon each measure 72°.

EQUATION—a statement of equality between two quantities. *It's an equation if it includes an equal sign.*

EQUATION OF A LINE—an equation that describes the relationship between the *x*- and *y*-coordinates of every point on a line in the coordinate plane. *The equation of the x-axis is y = 0, and the equation of the y-axis is x = 0.*

EQUILATERAL TRIANGLE—a triangle with three equal sides.

All equilateral triangles are similar—they all have three 60° angles.

EVEN NUMBER—a multiple of 2. *The set of even numbers includes not only 2, 4, 6, etc, but also 0, –2, –4, –6, etc.*

EXPONENT—the small, raised number written to the right of a variable or number, indicating the number of times that variable or number is to be used as a factor. *In the expression $-4x^3$, the exponent is 3, so $-4x^3 = -4 \cdot x \cdot x \cdot x$.*

EXTERIOR ANGLE—the angle created outside a polygon when one side is extended. *The exterior angles of any polygon add up to 360°.*

FACE—a polygon formed by edges of a solid.

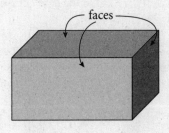

A rectangular solid has 6 faces.

FACTOR (of *n*)—a positive integer that divides into *n* with no remainder. *The complete list of factors of 18 is: 1, 2, 3, 6, 9, and 18.*

FACTORING (a polynomial)—re-expressing a polynomial as the product of simpler expressions. *The complete factorization of $2x^2 + 7x + 3$ is $(2x + 1)(x + 3)$.*

FRACTION—a number expressed as a ratio. *In everyday speech, the word* fraction *implies something less than 1, but to a mathematician, any number written in the form $\frac{A}{B}$ is a fraction.*

GRAPH OF AN EQUATION—a line or curve in the coordinate plane that represents all the ordered pair solutions of an equation.

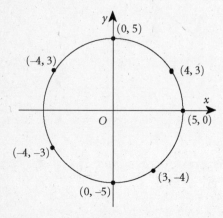

The figure shown here shows the graph of the equation $x^2 + y^2 = 25$.

GREATEST COMMON FACTOR—the greatest integer that is a factor of both numbers under consideration. *The greatest common factor (GCF) of relative primes is 1.*

HEXAGON—a six-sided polygon.

The six angles of a regular hexagon each measure 120°.

HYPOTENUSE—the side of a right triangle opposite the right angle.

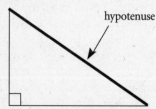

The hypotenuse is always the longest side.

IMAGINARY—not real, usually because of the square root of a negative number. *The square root of –4 is an imaginary number.*

IMPROPER FRACTION—a fraction with a numerator that's greater than the denominator. $\frac{35}{8}$ is an improper fraction and is therefore greater than 1.

INEQUALITY—a statement that compares the size of two quantities. *There are four inequality symbols: < ("less than"), ≤ "(less than or equal to"), > ("greater than"), and ≥ ("greater than or equal to").*

INSCRIBED—drawn inside another figure with as many points touching as possible.

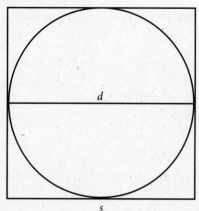

When a circle is inscribed within a square, the diameter d of the circle is the same as a length of a side s of the square.

INTEGER—one of the set of numbers {. . ., –3, –2, –1, 0, 1, 2, 3, . . .}. The set of integers combines the positive whole numbers, their opposites, and 0; *325, 7, and –29 are all integers.*

INTERCEPT—the point where a given line crosses the x-axis or y-axis.

Isosceles triangles

The angles opposite the equal sides of an isosceles triangle are also equal.

The y-intercept is the b in the slope-intercept form y = mx + b.

INTERIOR ANGLE—an angle inside a polygon formed by two adjacent sides. *Every polygon has the same number of interior angles as sides.*

LEAST COMMON MULTIPLE—the smallest number that is a multiple of both given numbers. *The least common multiple of relative primes is their product.*

LEGS (of a right triangle)—the sides that make up the right angle.

The interior angles of a regular pentagon each measure 108°.

IRRATIONAL—real, but not capable of being expressed as a ratio of integers. $\sqrt{2}$, $\sqrt{3}$, *and π are irrational numbers.*

ISOSCELES TRIANGLE—a triangle with two sides of equal length.

You can use the legs as the base and altitude to find the area of a right triangle.

LIKE TERMS—algebraic terms in which the elements other than the coefficients are alike. *2ab and 3ab are like terms, so they can be added: 2ab + 3ab = 5ab.*

LINE—a straight row of points extending infinitely in both directions. *A line has only one dimension.*

LINE SEGMENT—a straight row of points connecting two endpoints. *Each side of a polygon is a line segment.*

LINEAR EQUATION—a single-variable equation with no exponent greater than 1. *A linear equation is also called a first-degree equation.*

MIDPOINT—the point that divides a line segment in half.

In the figure shown here, B is the midpoint of $\overline{AC}$, so AB = BC.

MIXED NUMBER—a noninteger greater than 1 written with a whole number part and a fractional part. *The mixed number $4\frac{2}{3}$ can also be expressed as the improper fraction $\frac{14}{3}$.*

MONOMIAL—an algebraic expression consisting of exactly one term.

MULTIPLE (of n)—a number that *n* will divide into with no remainder. *Some of the multiples of 18 are: 0, 18, and 90.*

NEGATIVE—less than zero. *The greatest negative integer is –1.*

NUMERATOR—the number above the fraction bar. *When you increase the numerator of a positive fraction while keeping the denominator the same, you increase the value of the fraction: $\frac{13}{17}$ is greater than $\frac{12}{17}$.*

OBTUSE ANGLE—an angle measuring more than 90° and less than 180°. *An obtuse triangle is one that has one obtuse angle.*

OCTAGON—an eight-sided polygon.

Each of the interior angles of a regular octagon measures 135°.

ODD NUMBER—an integer that is not a multiple of 2. *Any integer that's not even is odd.*

ORIGIN—the point where the *x*- and *y*-axes intersect. *The origin represents the point (0, 0).*

PARABOLA—the set of points in a plane that are the same distance from a point called the *focus* and a line called the *directrix*.

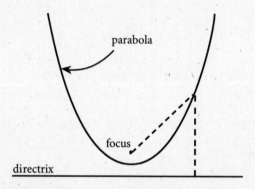

PARALLEL LINES—coplanar lines that never intersect. *Parallel lines are the same distance apart at all points.*

PARALLELOGRAM—a quadrilateral with two pairs of parallel sides.

Opposite sides of a parallelogram are equal; opposite angles of a parallelogram are also equal.

PENTAGON—a five-sided polygon.

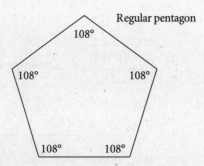

Regular pentagon

The interior angles of any pentagon add up to 540°. Each of the interior angles of a regular pentagon measures 108°.

PERCENT—one hundredth. *20% means 20 hundredths, or $\frac{20}{100} = \frac{1}{5}$.*

PERCENT INCREASE/DECREASE—amount of increase or decrease expressed as a percent of the original amount. *A decrease from 100 to 83 is a 17% decrease.*

PERIMETER—the sum of the lengths of the sides of a polygon. *Two polygons with the same area do not necessarily have the same perimeter.*

PERPENDICULAR—intersecting at a right angle. *The altitude and base of a triangle are perpendicular.*

PI—an irrational number, approximately 3.14, which is equal to the ratio of the circumference of any circle to its diameter. *The symbol for pi is π. Pi appears in the formulas for the circumference and area of a circle, as well for the volumes of a sphere, a cylinder, and a cone.*

POINT—a precise position in space. *A point has no length, width, or height.*

POLYGON—a closed figure composed of any number of straight sides.

Polygons

Triangles, squares, trapezoids, and pentagons are all polygons, but circles and ellipses are not.

POLYNOMIAL—an algebraic expression that is the sum of two or more terms. *Binomials and trinomials are just two types of polynomials.*

POSITIVE—greater than zero. *Zero is not a positive number.*

POWER—a product obtained by multiplying a quantity by itself one or more times. *The fifth power of 2 is 32.*

PRIME FACTORIZATION—an integer expressed as the product of prime numbers. *The prime factorization of 60 is $2 \times 2 \times 3 \times 5$.*

PRIME NUMBER—an integer greater than 1 that has no factors other than 1 and itself. *The first 10 prime numbers are 2, 3, 5, 7, 11, 13, 17, 19, 23, and 29. Notice that 2 is the only even prime number.*

PROBABILITY—the likelihood of a particular event, expressed as the ratio of the number of "favorable" outcomes to the total number of possible outcomes. *Probability is a part-to-whole ratio and can therefore never be greater than 1.*

PRODUCT—the result of multiplication. *The product of 3 and 4 is 12.*

PROPORTION—an expression of the equality of ratios. *Corresponding sides of similar figures are proportional.*

PYTHAGOREAN THEOREM—the rule that states, "for any right triangle, the sum of the squares of the legs is equal to the square of the hypotenuse."

If you call the lengths of the legs a *and* b *and the length of the hypotenuse* c, *you can write "*$a^2 + b^2 = c^2$*."*

QUADRANT—one of the four regions into which the axes divide the coordinate plane.

When you know the signs of the coordinates, you know which quadrant contains that point. For any point in quadrant IV, for example, the x-coordinate is positive and the y-coordinate is negative.

QUADRATIC EQUATION—a second-degree equation. *Quadratic equations with one unknown often have two solutions.*

QUADRILATERAL—a four-sided polygon. *Squares, rectangles, parallelograms, and trapezoids are all quadrilaterals.*

Quadrilaterals

QUOTIENT—the result of division. *When 12 is divided by 3, the quotient is 4.*

RADIAN—a unit for expressing the measure of an angle.

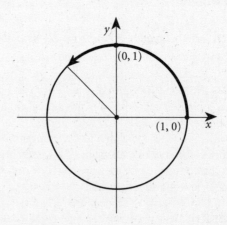

The angle in the figure shown here measures $\frac{3\pi}{4}$ radians, which is the same as 135°. It's no coincidence that $\frac{3\pi}{4}$ is also the length of the arc shown.

RADICAL—the symbol $\sqrt{}$, which by itself represents the positive square root, with a little number written in—as in $\sqrt[3]{32}$ —represents a higher root. *By convention, $\sqrt{}$ represents the positive square root only.*

RADIUS—(the length of) a line segment connecting the center and a point on a circle. *The radius is half the diameter.*

RATE—a ratio of quantities measured in different units. *The most familiar rates have units of time after the word per, such as: meters per second, pages per hour, inches per year.*

RATIO—a fraction that expresses the relative sizes of two quantities. *A ratio is generally expressed with the words "of" and "to": as in "the ratio of girls to boys."*

RATIONAL—capable of being expressed as a ratio of integers. *The repeating decimal .074074074074 . . . is a rational number because it can be written as $\frac{2}{27}$.*

REAL—having a place on the number line. *π is a real number because it has a location—somewhere just to the right of 3.14—on the number line.*

RECIPROCALS—a pair of numbers whose product is 1. *To get the reciprocal of a fraction, switch the numerator and denominator: the reciprocal of $\frac{2}{7}$ is $\frac{7}{2}$.*

RECTANGLE—a quadrilateral with four right angles. *All rectangles are parallelograms, but not all parallelograms are rectangles.*

RECTANGULAR SOLID—a solid whose faces are all rectangles.

rectangular solids

REDUCING A FRACTION—expressing a fraction in lowest terms by factoring out and canceling common factors. *$\frac{6}{8}$ reduces to $\frac{3}{4}$.*

REGULAR POLYGON—a polygon with all equal sides and all equal angles. *Equilateral triangles and squares are regular polygons.*

Regular polygons

RELATIVE PRIMES—positive integers that have no factors in common. *35 and 54 are relative primes because their prime factorizations (35 = 5 × 7, and 54 = 2 × 3 × 3 × 3) have nothing in common.*

REPEATING DECIMAL—a decimal with a digit or cluster of digits that repeats indefinitely. *The fraction $\frac{1}{7}$ is equivalent to the repeating decimal 0.142857142857142857. . . , which can be written $0.\overline{142857}$.*

RHOMBUS—a quadrilateral with four equal sides.

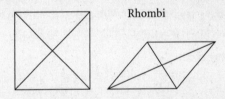
Rhombi

The diagonals of a rhombus are perpendicular.

RIGHT ANGLE—an angle measuring 90°. *A rectangle is a polygon with four right angles.*

RIGHT TRIANGLE—a triangle with a right angle. *Every right triangle has exactly two acute angles.*

ROOT—a number that when multiplied by itself a certain number of times will yield the given quantity. *The cube root of 8 is 2.*

SCALENE TRIANGLE—a triangle with sides of different lengths. *A 3-4-5 triangle is a scalene triangle.*

SECANT—the ratio of the hypotenuse to the adjacent leg. *The secant is the reciprocal of the cosine.*

In the figure shown here, the secant of $\angle A$ is $\frac{13}{12}$.

SECTOR—a region bounded by two radii and an arc.

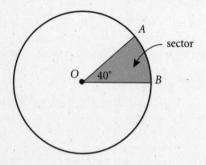

Because the central angle of 40° is $\frac{1}{9}$ of the full circle's 360°, the area of the shaded sector is $\frac{1}{9}$ of the area of the whole circle.

SIMILAR—proportional; of the same shape. *Similar polygons have the same angles.*

Similar triangles

SINE—the ratio of the opposite leg to the hypotenuse.

In the figure shown here, the sine of $\angle A$ is $\frac{5}{13}$.

SLOPE—a description of the "steepness" of a line in the coordinate plane, defined as $\frac{\text{Change in } y}{\text{Change in } x}$. *Lines that go "uphill" (left to right) have positive slopes, and lines that go "downhill" have negative slopes. A horizontal line— that is, a line parallel to the x-axis—is "flat" and has a slope of 0. A vertical line has an undefined slope.*

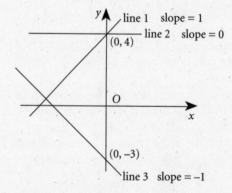

SLOPE-INTERCEPT FORM—an equation in the form $y = mx + b$. In this form, m is the slope and b is the y-intercept. *Line 1 in the figure shown here has a slope of 1 and a y-intercept of 4, so its equation is $y = x + 4$. Line 2's equation is $y = 4$. Line 3's equation is $y = -x - 3$.*

SOLID—a three-dimensional figure.

Cubes, cylinders, cones, and spheres are all solids.

SOLVING—isolating the given variable.

SPHERE—the set of all points in space that are a particular distance from a central point. *Visualize a sphere as a ball.*

SQUARE—a quadrilateral with four equal sides and four right angles. *A square can be thought of as a rectangular rhombus.*

SQUARE ROOT—a number that when squared yields the given quantity. *Positive numbers each have two square roots, but negative numbers have no real square roots.*

SUM—the result of addition. *The sum of 3 and 4 is 7.*

SUPPLEMENTARY ANGLES—two angles whose measures add up to 180°.

SURFACE AREA—the sum of the areas of the surfaces of a solid. *Surface area is measured in square units.*

SYSTEM OF EQUATIONS—two or more equations in which each variable represents the same quantity in one equation as in another.

TANGENT—the ratio of the opposite leg of a right triangle to the adjacent leg.

TANGENT (of a circle)—a line that intersects a circle at exactly one point. *Visualize a tangent as a line that just barely "touches" the circle.*

TERM—a part of an algebraic expression that either stands by itself or is connected to other terms with plus and minus signs. *A term has three parts: the coefficient, the variable(s), and the exponent(s).*

TRANSVERSAL—a line that intersects two parallel lines.

A transversal across parallel lines creates two sets of four equal angles.

TRAPEZOID—a quadrilateral with one pair of parallel sides.

TRIANGLE—a three-sided polygon. *The three angles of a triangle add up to 180°.*

UNDEFINED—not covered by the rules. *Division by 0 is undefined.*

VARIABLE—a letter representing an unknown or unspecified quantity. *The letter most commonly used for a variable is* x.

VERTEX—a point of intersection, such as a corner of a rectangular solid or a polygon.

vertices

VERTICAL ANGLES—angles across the vertex of intersecting lines. *Vertical angles are equal.*

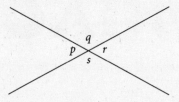

In the figure shown here, ∠q and ∠s are vertical angles, as are ∠p and ∠r.

VOLUME—a measure of the amount of "space" contained within a solid. *Computing volume invariably involves multiplying three dimensions, such as length, width, and height.*